Old English Literature

Blackwell Guides to Criticism

Editor Michael O'Neill

Blackwell's *Guides to Criticism* series offers students privileged access to and careful guidance through those writings that have most conditioned the historic current of discussion and debate as it now informs contemporary scholarship.

Early historic responses are represented by appropriate excerpts and described in an introductory narrative chapter. Thereafter, materials are represented thematically in extracts from important books or journal articles according to their continuing critical value and relevance in the classroom. Critical approaches are treated as tools to advance the pursuit of reading and study and each volume seeks to enhance the enjoyment of literature and to widen the reader's critical repertoire.

Published volumes

Old English Literature

A Guide to Criticism with Selected Readings

John D. Niles

WILEY Blackwell

This edition first published 2016
© 2016 John D. Niles

Registered Office
John Wiley & Sons, Ltd, The Atrium, Southern Gate, Chichester, West Sussex, PO19 8SQ, UK

Editorial Offices
350 Main Street, Malden, MA 02148-5020, USA
9600 Garsington Road, Oxford, OX4 2DQ, UK
The Atrium, Southern Gate, Chichester, West Sussex, PO19 8SQ, UK

For details of our global editorial offices, for customer services, and for information about how to apply for permission to reuse the copyright material in this book please see our website at www.wiley.com/wiley-blackwell.

Library of Congress Cataloging-in-Publication Data

Names: Niles, John D., author. | Niles, John D.
Title: Old English literature : a guide to criticism with selected readings / John D. Niles.
Description: 1 | West Sussex ; Malden, MA : Wiley-Blackwell, 2016. | Series: Blackwell guides to criticism | Includes bibliographical references and index.
Identifiers: LCCN 2015040684 (print) | LCCN 2015051344 (ebook) | ISBN 9780631220565 (hardback) | ISBN 9780631220572 (paper) | ISBN 9781118598832 (pdf) | ISBN 9781118598849 (epub)
Subjects: LCSH: English literature–Old English, ca. 450-1100–History and criticism–Theory, etc. | Criticism–History–20th century. | BISAC: LITERARY CRITICISM / European / English, Irish, Scottish, Welsh.
Classification: LCC PR173 .N65 2016 (print) | LCC PR173 (ebook) | DDC 829/.09–dc23
LC record available at http://lccn.loc.gov/2015040684

A catalogue record for this book is available from the British Library.

Cover image: Black and white of Alfred's Jewel, 9th Century Liszt Collection/Alamy

Set in 10/12.5pt Adobe CaslonPro by SPi Global, Pondicherry, India
Printed and bound in Malaysia by Vivar Printing Sdn Bhd

1   2016

Contents

Preface and Acknowledgements

In a broad sense of the term, the criticism of Old English literature (from Greek *kritikē* 'the critical art') began when certain pioneering English scholars of the sixteenth century published the first printed editions of works dating from the Anglo-Saxon period, accompanying those editions with remarks of their own so as to facilitate the reader's understanding. If those scholars gave a spin to the texts they edited, something similar can be said of the transmission of knowledge in general since the beginnings of time.

In the more narrow sense in which the term is used today, the criticism of Old English literature can be said to have begun in the first half of the nineteenth century, when men of letters including the English scholar William Conybeare, the Danish poet, scholar, and clergyman N.F.S. Grundtvig, and the American poet Henry Wadsworth Longfellow wrote appreciative commentaries on Old English poetic texts, calling attention to the aesthetic merits of those texts or, at times, noting what they believed to be their formal or stylistic defects. These writers, together with others of this general period, also translated Old English poems or passages into one or another of the modern languages, another form of homage and critique.

Not until the mid-twentieth century did the criticism of Old English literature come into its own. What is perhaps most striking about the criticism that had been undertaken up to that time is its invisibility, when compared with the criticism of literature of more recent date. When René Wellek brought out his multi-volume *History of Modern Criticism* in the years 1955–1992, for example, the fifth and sixth volumes of that work, published in 1986 and titled respectively *English Criticism 1900–1950* and *American Criticism 1900–1950*, included not a single notice of the criticism of Old English literature. It is as if this literature did not exist as a subject of critical inquiry.[1] Perhaps this conspicuous blank in what is otherwise a commendable set of volumes resulted from spot-blindness on the part

---

[1] Not much had changed in this regard even as late as the year 2000, when volume 7, titled *Modernism and the New Criticism*, of the collective edition *The Cambridge History of Literary Criticism* came out, covering literary criticism published during the period from 1900 to 1950. The only notice of Old English literature taken there (at p. 88) is a one-line allusion to Ezra Pound's translation of *The Seafarer*.

of its author, who could not be expected to have covered all topics; but perhaps it also tells us something about the place of Old English in the field of literary studies up to the mid-twentieth century.

This place was clearly a marginal one. While study of the Old English language had long been valued as a branch of philology and historical linguistics, and while Anglo-Saxon historical studies were being pursued with vigour (particularly in the United Kingdom), the criticism of Old English literature tended to be viewed as something like a contradiction in terms. The great tradition of English literature was widely – and, in a sense, correctly – thought to have begun with Chaucer, Malory, and other writers of the late medieval era, not with the Anglo-Saxons, for the relation of Old English literature to the poetry and prose of later periods was hard to discern. Twentieth-century literary critics therefore tended to direct their gaze to the period extending from Chaucer onwards while leaving Anglo-Saxon studies to the philologists and historians.

Such prejudices began early and have died hard. To cite just one example, the first incumbent of the Chair of English Language and Literature at the University of London, appointed in 1828, was the Reverend Thomas Dale, an evangelical clergyman. Dale's view of Old English literature was coloured by his desire to inculcate high moral character among his students. In 1845 he wrote:[2]

> The most complete poetical production extant in this language is the romance of *Beowulf*, a kind of Saxon *Iliad*, which has recently been edited by an accomplished Saxon scholar [by John Mitchell Kemble, in 1833 and 1835–37], and is further remarkable as being the earliest composition of an heroic kind in any vernacular language of Europe. It is characterized by the usual strain of Saxon sentiment, representing the drunken carousal as the chief of joys, and courage in the field as the first of duties, and with scarcely a recognition of the existence of a second sex. If to be poetical is to be imaginative, man is never likely to become so till he has learned to write on woman. The Saxons never learnt this […]. The reason of this may be sought in nature; they who delight in bloodshed will ever be the few, and they who degrade intelligence by intoxication will rarely be the many […]. And where is love without woman, and what is poetry without love?

What the Reverend Dale refers to in this address as 'the few' – those who 'delight in bloodshed' – are those who attribute much value to works like *Beowulf*. 'The many' are those who, like himself and his right-minded students, appreciate the beauties, subtleties, and moral qualities of the literature of later eras. While 'the few' will degrade their intelligence through scenes of carousal and carnage, 'the many' will admire writings that feature love and romance.

A binary opposition is thus confirmed that has been influential ever since, though rarely voiced so bluntly as here. One of its implications is that no texts dating from the Anglo-Saxon period can qualify as poetry worthy of that name, since poetry by its nature consists

---

[2]   T. Dale, introduction to H. Blair, *Lectures on Rhetoric and Belles Lettres* (1845), p. xxii, as cited by D.J. Palmer, *The Rise of English Studies* (London: Oxford University Press), 24, with typography slightly modernized.

of writings that have to do with complex ideas and refined sentiments. Subsequent studies in departments of English, once such departments gained a secure place in modern universities, were thus long defined by a split between the many scholars and teachers who cultivated the English literary tradition from Chaucer on, and those who dealt with the language and literature of the Anglo-Saxons. Scholars on one side of this divide tended to emphasize the courtly dimension of their subjects; on the other side, the heroic.

One of the aims of the present book is to undermine this false binary opposition. This is not difficult to do given the actual sophistication of a good deal of Anglo-Saxon literature, as well as the high quality of recent research into that sector of the past. A complementary aim is to call attention to the critical controversies that have emerged as the literature of that early period has been made subject to exacting scrutiny.

The critical selections that are featured at the end of Chapters 2–11 focus not just on individual literary texts, but also on such related topics as early medieval literacy, textuality, and orality, as well as questions of style, genre, gender, and theme. Efforts have been made, as well, to acknowledge the ways that the criticism of Old English literature is implicated in historical studies, religious studies, anthropology, and art history, among other disciplines. All the same, some lines had to be drawn if only for reasons of space. The full interdisciplinary scope of Anglo-Saxon studies is thus only partly made clear, even though I would be the first to argue that an openness to the perspectives offered by a wide range of disciplines is a prerequisite to sound research in this field. It is my hope that readers whose interest is sparked by anything in these pages will undertake more sustained research on their own, using the present book as a point of departure.

One selection, the essay by Joshua Byron Smith on Borges in Chapter 11, was commissioned for the present volume some few years ago, and I am grateful to the author for his patience in awaiting its eventual appearance in print. Another essay, a classic one by the Swiss scholar Ernst Leisi on the semantics of material wealth in *Beowulf*, appears here in Chapter 5 in English translation for the first time. These essays, as well as certain others, are presented in their entirety. If certain other essays featured in the volume are republished only in part, this is solely because of constraints of space.

Quotations of Old English poetic texts cited in the main body of the book are drawn from the collective edition The Anglo-Saxon Poetic Records (ASPR) with the exception of *Beowulf*, which is quoted from *Klaeber's Beowulf*. When the authors of the reprinted critical selections observe a different practice, then those passages are left as is. The same is generally true of the bibliographical apparatus used by those authors, though minor adjustments have been made for the sake of clarity or consistency. Likewise, for the sake of greater clarity, a comma has been added to the title of the excerpted essay by M.B. Parkes.

In the reprinted readings, the authors' original notes are printed as footnotes. Where I have added explanatory notes, they too are supplied at the foot of the page, cued to the main text by superscript letters rather than numbers. Editorial comments are set off by paired square brackets. Deletions are marked by an ellipsis of three periods, normally set between square brackets.

A number of libraries have provided invaluable assistance while I have researched this book. I wish to express my particular gratitude to the staff at the research libraries of the University of Cambridge, the University of Wisconsin – Madison, the University of California, Berkeley, and the University of Colorado, Boulder. In addition, an appointment as Senior Fellow at the Institute for Research in the Humanities at the University of Wisconsin – Madison (2004–9) enabled me to research the book among colleagues who stimulated my thinking about the place of Anglo-Saxon studies within a wider world of thought and letters. Ancillary funding was provided by the Wisconsin Alumni Research Fund (WARF) through the Graduate School of the University of Wisconsin – Madison.

My editors at Wiley Blackwell have been unfailingly helpful from start to finish, and their patience and sound advice have meant much to me. I am also grateful to a number of anonymous specialist readers, including those persons who evaluated the original book proposal as well as two reviewers of its penultimate draft. I regret that constraints of space have prevented me from adopting all of their constructive suggestions, though most have been incorporated into the book. As for the infelicities, errors, and shortcomings that remain, they are my own responsibility. I shall be happy to receive emailed notice of any corrections that should be made (email: jdniles@wisc.edu).

Thanks are due to the following presses and journals for permission to reprint copyrighted material.

- Brepols Publishers, Belgium, for an excerpt from Joyce Hill, 'Learning Latin in Anglo-Saxon England: Traditions, Texts and Techniques', which appeared in *Learning and Literacy in Medieval England and Abroad*, ed. Sarah Rees Jones (Turnhout, 2003), 7–29.
- Cambridge University Press, for an excerpt from M.B. Parkes, 'The Palaeography of the Parker Manuscript of the *Chronicle*, Laws, and Sedulius, and Historiography at Winchester in the Late Ninth and Tenth Centuries', *ASE* 5 (1976): 149–71.
- De Gruyter Press (Berlin), publishers of the journal *Anglia*, for permission to publish an English translation of Ernst Leisi's essay 'Gold und Manneswert im *Beowulf*', which first appeared in *Anglia* 71 (1952): 259–73.
- The editors and publishers of *English Studies*, for an excerpt from Hugh Magennis, 'Images of Laughter in Old English Poetry, with Particular Reference to the *Hleahtor Wera* of *The Seafarer*', *ES* 73 (1992): 193–204.
- The editors and publishers of *Neophilologus*, for J.R. Hall, 'Perspective and Wordplay in the Old English *Rune Poem*', *Neoph* 61 (1977): 453–60.
- Oxford University Press, for an excerpt from Malcolm Godden, 'Apocalypse and Invasion in Late Anglo-Saxon England', which appeared in *From Anglo-Saxon to Early Middle English: Studies Presented to E.G. Stanley*, ed. Malcolm Godden, Douglas Gray, and Terry Hoad (Oxford, 1994), 130–62.
- Slavica Publishers, Inc., for Donald K. Fry, 'The Memory of Cædmon', which appeared in *Oral Traditional Literature: A Festschrift for Albert Bates Lord*, ed. John Miles Foley (Columbus, OH, 1981), 282–93.
- The University of Chicago Press, for L.M.C. Weston, 'Women's Medicine, Women's Magic: The Old English Metrical Childbirth Charms', *MPh* 92 (1995): 279–93.
- The University of Toronto Press, for Edward B. Irving, Jr, 'Crucifixion Witnessed, or Dramatic Interaction in *The Dream of the Rood*', which appeared in *Modes of Interpretation in Old English Literature*, ed. Phyllis R. Brown et al. (Toronto, 1986), 101–13.

Abbreviations

ACMRS	Arizona Center for Medieval and Renaissance Studies
Aertsen & Bremmer	*Companion to Old English Poetry*, ed. Henk Aertsen and Rolf H. Bremmer, Jr (Amsterdam: VU University Press, 1994)
Anglo-Saxon Styles	*Anglo-Saxon Styles*, ed. Catherine E. Karkov and George Hardin Brown (Albany: State University of New York Press, 2003)
ASE	*Anglo-Saxon England*
ASPR	The Anglo-Saxon Poetic Records, ed. George Philip Krapp and Elliott Van Kirk Dobbie, 6 vols (New York: Columbia University Press, 1931–53)
Beowulf Handbook	*A Beowulf Handbook*, ed. Robert E. Bjork and John D. Niles (Lincoln: University of Nebraska Press, 1997)
Bessinger Studies	*Heroic Poetry in the Anglo-Saxon Period: Studies in Honor of Jess B. Bessinger, Jr*, ed. Helen Damico and John Leyerle (Kalamazoo: Medieval Institute Publications, 1993)
BJRL	*Bulletin of the John Rylands University Library of Manchester*
Blackwell Encyclopaedia	*The Blackwell Encyclopaedia of Anglo-Saxon England*, ed. Michael Lapidge et al. (Oxford: Blackwell, 1999)
Bosworth-Toller	James Bosworth and T. Northcote Toller, *An Anglo-Saxon Dictionary* (Oxford, 1898), with *Supplement* by T. N. Toller (1921) and *Revised and Enlarged Addenda* by A. Campbell (1972)
Brodeur Studies	*Studies in Old English Literature in Honor of Arthur G. Brodeur*, ed. Stanley B. Greenfield (Eugene: University of Oregon Books, 1963)
Cambridge History	*The Cambridge History of Early Medieval English Literature*, ed. Clare A. Lees (Cambridge: Cambridge University Press, 2013)
Cavill	*The Christian Tradition in Anglo-Saxon England: Approaches to Current Scholarship and Teaching*, ed. Paul Cavill (Woodbridge: D.S. Brewer, 2004)
CCSL	Corpus Christianorum Series Latina
CSEL	Corpus Scriptorum Ecclesiasticorum Latinorum

Crick & Van Houts	*A Social History of England 900–1200*, ed. Julia Crick and Elizabeth Van Houts (Cambridge: Cambridge University Press, 2011)
Damico & Olsen	*New Readings on Women in Old English Literature*, ed. Helen Damico and Alexandra Hennessey Olsen (Bloomington: Indiana University Press, 1990)
DOE	*Dictionary of Old English*, ed. Antonette diPaolo Healey et al. (Toronto: University of Toronto Press, 1986 to the present); as of the end of 2015, letters A–G have been published
Donoghue	*Beowulf: A Verse Translation*, trans. by Seamus Heaney, ed. Daniel Donoghue (New York: Norton, 2002)
EEMF	Early English Manuscripts in Facsimile
EETS	Early English Text Society
EHR	*English Historical Review*
ES	*English Studies*
Essential Articles	*Essential Articles for the Study of Old English Poetry*, ed. Jess B. Bessinger and Stanley J. Kahrl (Hamden, CT: Archon Books, 1968)
Fry	*The Beowulf Poet: A Collection of Critical Essays*, ed. Donald K. Fry (Englewood Cliffs, NJ: Prentice-Hall, 1968)
Fulk	*Interpretations of Beowulf: A Critical Anthology*, ed. R.D. Fulk (Bloomington: Indiana University Press, 1991)
Godden & Lapidge	*The Cambridge Companion to Old English Literature*, ed. Malcolm Godden and Michael Lapidge, 2nd edn (Cambridge: Cambridge University Press, 2013)
Greenfield & Calder	Stanley B. Greenfield and Daniel G. Calder, *A New Critical History of Old English Literature* (New York: New York University Press, 1986)
Greenfield Studies	*Modes of Interpretation in Old English Literature: Essays in Honour of Stanley B. Greenfield*, ed. Phyllis Rugg Brown, Georgia Ronan Crampton, and Fred C. Robinson (Toronto: University of Toronto Press, 1986)
Holy Men & Women	*Holy Men and Holy Women: Old English Prose Saints' Lives and Their Contexts*, ed. Paul E. Szarmach (Albany: State University of New York Press, 1996)
Howe	*Beowulf: A Prose Translation*, trans. by E. Talbot Donaldson, ed. Nicholas Howe (New York: Norton, 2002)
JEGP	*Journal of English and Germanic Philology*
Johnson & Treharne	*Readings in Medieval Texts: Interpreting Old and Middle English Literature*, ed. David F. Johnson and Elaine Treharne (Oxford: Oxford University Press, 2005)
Joy & Ramsey	*The Postmodern Beowulf*, ed. Eileen A. Joy and Mary K. Ramsey (Morgantown: West Virginia University Press, 2006)
Klaeber's Beowulf	*Klaeber's Beowulf and the Fight at Finnsburg*, ed. R.D. Fulk, Robert E. Bjork, and John D. Niles, 4th edn (Toronto: University of Toronto Press, 2008)

Klinck	Anne L. Klinck, *The Old English Elegies: A Critical Edition and Genre Study* (Montreal: McGill–Queens University Press, 1992; paperback edition with a supplementary bibliography, 2001)
Liuzza	*Old English Literature: Critical Essays*, ed. R.M. Liuzza (New Haven: Yale University Press, 2002)
LSE	*Leeds Studies in English*
MÆ	*Medium Ævum*
Magennis & Swan	*A Companion to Ælfric*, ed. Hugh Magennis and Mary Swan (Leiden: Brill, 2009)
MGH	Monumenta Germaniae Historica
Mitchell & Robinson	*A Guide to Old English*, 8th edn, ed. Bruce Mitchell and Fred C. Robinson (Oxford: Wiley-Blackwell, 2012)
MPh	*Modern Philology*
Muir	*The Exeter Anthology of Old English Poetry*, ed. Bernard J. Muir, 2 vols, 2nd edn (Exeter: University of Exeter Press, 2000); first published 1994
Neoph	*Neophilologus*
Nicholson	*An Anthology of Beowulf Criticism*, ed. Lewis E. Nicholson (Notre Dame: University of Notre Dame Press, 1963)
Niles	*Old English Literature in Context*, ed. John D. Niles (Cambridge: D.S. Brewer, 1980)
NM	*Neuphilologische Mitteilungen*
n.s.	new series
O'Brien O'Keeffe	*Reading Old English Texts*, ed. Katherine O'Brien O'Keeffe (Cambridge: Cambridge University Press, 1997)
OE	Old English
OEN	*Old English Newsletter*
o.s.	original series
PBA	*Proceedings of the British Academy*
PL	Patrologia Latina
PMLA	*Publications of the Modern Language Association of North America*
PQ	*Philological Quarterly*
Pulsiano & Treharne	*A Companion to Anglo-Saxon Literature*, ed. Phillip Pulsiano and Elaine Treharne (Oxford: Blackwell, 2001)
Readings: Beowulf	*Beowulf: Basic Readings*, ed. Peter S. Baker (New York: Garland, 1995). Also published as *The Beowulf Reader*, ed. Baker (New York: Garland, 2000)
Readings: Cynewulf	*Cynewulf: Basic Readings*, ed. Robert E. Bjork (New York: Garland, 1996)
Readings: Junius MS	*The Poems of MS Junius 11: Basic Readings*, ed. R.M. Liuzza (New York: Routledge, 2002)
Readings: MSS	*Anglo-Saxon Manuscripts: Basic Readings*, ed. Mary P. Richards (New York: Garland, 1994)
Readings: OE Prose	*Old English Prose: Basic Readings*, ed. Paul E. Szarmach (New York: Garland, 2000)

Readings: Shorter Poems	*Old English Shorter Poems: Basic Readings,* ed. Katherine O'Brien O'Keeffe (New York: Garland, 1993)
RES	*Review of English Studies*
Robinson	Fred C. Robinson, *The Tomb of Beowulf and Other Essays on Old English* (Oxford: Blackwell, 1993)
Saunders	*A Companion to Medieval Poetry,* ed. Corinne Saunders (Chichester: Wiley-Blackwell, 2010)
Speaking Two Languages	*Speaking Two Languages: Traditional Disciplines and Contemporary Theory in Medieval Studies,* ed. Allen J. Frantzen (Albany: State University of New York Press, 1991)
SPh	*Studies in Philology*
s.s.	supplementary series
Stevens & Mandel	*Old English Literature: Twenty-Two Analytical Essays,* ed. Martin Stevens and Jerome Mandel (Lincoln: University of Nebraska Press, 1968)
Stodnick & Trilling	*A Handbook of Anglo-Saxon Studies,* ed. Jacqueline Stodnick and Renée R. Trilling (Oxford: Wiley-Blackwell, 2012)
Toller Lectures	*Textual and Material Culture in Anglo-Saxon England: Thomas Northcote Toller and the Toller Memorial Lectures,* ed. Donald Scragg (Cambridge: D.S. Brewer, 2003)

Part I

Main Currents in Twentieth-Century Criticism

1

Old English Studies 1901–1975

Literary criticism is scarcely an autonomous enterprise; rather, it is intimately connected with the intellectual currents of the era when it is produced. About these currents several things can be said. One is that they are usually in a state of flux and turbulence. Another is that they are a bit obscure to most persons until they have become passé. At that point they will become increasingly subject to stereotyping by the thinkers of subsequent generations, who will often find it comforting to gaze back at those ideas with a mixture of condescension and contempt. This state of affairs is likely to continue until such time as the ideas in question have been dead and buried so long as to merit an act of archaeological recovery, at which point someone will rediscover them, with mild fanfare, as noteworthy contributions to intellectual history.

Regardless of the truth-value of these propositions, the criticism of Old English literature can be most meaningfully understood when it is seen as a development of – or, sometimes, a reaction against – trends that were influential at an earlier moment in history. The same comment applies to those prior trends. The present guide to criticism will therefore approach its subject by adopting a motto that is ignored at one's peril in literary studies: namely, 'Always historicize.'

Before considering some aspects of the criticism of Old English literature published during the last forty years or so, then, I will first review some leading work dating from the first three quarters of the twentieth century. The writings of the scholars of that period are of interest in their own right. If their work is ignored these days, then that may be owing less to its intrinsic merits (though it cannot all be said to be equally brilliant or meritorious) than to the fact that neither the students of today nor, far less, their teachers, can be expected to have read everything about everything.

Old English Literature: A Guide to Criticism with Selected Readings, First Edition. John D. Niles.

The Earlier Twentieth Century

In all respects but one, Anglo-Saxon scholarship was on a fairly sound footing by the beginning of the twentieth century.[1] By that time, the Old English language could be studied under trained professionals at more than four dozen universities located on at least two continents.[2] By the 1930s and 1940s, moreover, the foundations of the field were beginning to look rock solid. Philological scholarship undertaken on both sides of the Atlantic had gone far to establish the basis for understanding Old English texts at least as far as their linguistic and formal features were concerned. The close relationship of Old English religious literature to the much larger body of Latin Christian literature of the early Middle Ages had been fairly well charted as well, though more nuanced work of this kind remained to be done. Also well charted, as much as could be done given the scattered nature of the evidence, was the deep well, or whirlpool, of stories from the Northern past to which the allusions to legendary history in *Beowulf*, *Widsith*, *The Fight at Finnsburg*, *Deor*, and *Waldere* pertain.

By this time, the great majority of Old English texts that had survived into the modern period had been made available in reliable scholarly editions, thanks in part to two comprehensive series of editions of verse and prose undertaken in Germany, where the Anglo-Saxon period was approached as a branch of Germanic philology. These were C.M.W. Grein's *Bibliothek der angelsächsische Prosa* and his and Richard P. Wülker's *Bibliothek der angelsächsische Poesie*.[3] Moreover, certain of the freestanding scholarly editions that date from approximately this same period exemplify editorial practices that have stood the test of time. An example is Felix Liebermann's parallel-text edition of Anglo-Saxon laws, *Die Gesetze der Angelsachsen*.[4] This magisterial three-volume resource has remained in standard use for over a century, though a consortium of scholars associated with the Early English Laws project currently plans to replace it.[5] Likewise, the scholars Albert S. Cook, Frederick Tupper, and R.W. Chambers produced outstanding editions of poems from the Exeter Book of Old English poetry, thus setting high standards for the editing of verse. These editions covered respectively the first three items in the Exeter Book (known today as the Advent Lyrics, Cynewulf's signed poem *The Ascension*, and *Christ in Judgement*);

---

[1]   The history of Old English scholarship up to 1901 is treated in my companion volume *The Idea of Anglo-Saxon England 1066–1901: Remembering, Forgetting, Deciphering, and Renewing the Past* (Oxford: Wiley Blackwell, 2015).

[2]   J.R. Hall, 'Anglo-Saxon Studies in the Nineteenth Century: England, Denmark, America', in Pulsiano & Treharne, 434–54 (at 449).

[3]   *Bibliothek der angelsächsische Prosa*, ed. Christian W.M. Grein et al., 13 vols (Cassel, 1872–1933); *Bibliothek der angelsächsische Poesie*, ed. Richard P. Wülker, 3 vols (Cassel, 1881–98). This latter publication represented a revision of the two-volume edition with the same title that Grein had produced in 1857–58.

[4]   Felix Liebermann, *Die Gesetze der Angelsachsen*, 3 vols in 4 (Halle: Niemeyer, 1903–16). The centennial of the publication of this work has recently been the occasion of a celebratory volume, *English Law before Magna Carta: Felix Liebermann and 'Die Gesetze der Angelsachsen'*, ed. Stefan Jurasinski, Lisi Oliver, and Andrew Rabin (Leiden: Brill, 2010). In the first of these chapters Rabin provides a brief biographical tribute to Liebermann.

[5]   For information on the current laws project see www.earlyenglishlaws.ac.uk.

the complete set of riddles; and *Widsith*.[6] Each of these editions remains a treasure-trove of information sifted by a scholarly mind of great distinction. When one takes into account as well that Eduard Sievers's authoritative German-language grammar of the Old English language, his *Angelsächsische Grammatik*, had been in existence since 1882;[7] that a complete and, for that time, an authoritative dictionary of the Old English language was at last completed in the year 1921, when T. Northcote Toller brought out the second volume of his and Joseph Bosworth's *An Anglo-Saxon Dictionary*;[8] and that in 1934 Ferdinand Holthausen brought out a reliable etymological dictionary of Old English, one that has since been supplemented though never replaced,[9] then it is clear that Old English philological research was solidly anchored by the end of the first third of the century.

The quality of historical scholarship, too, reached a high level during roughly this same period. This is true both of research focusing on textual sources (chronicles, charters, wills, and other documents) and work in such ancillary fields as archaeology, art history, material culture, and place-name studies. Exemplary research in all these areas was conducted in Germany and Scandinavia.[10] The most influential continental scholar to be writing on *Germanistik* during this period – that is, on Germanic antiquities studied along the capacious philological lines established by Jacob Grimm by the mid-nineteenth century – was Andreas Heusler, a philologist and literary historian of the first rank.[11] Indispensable guides to research in this area were provided by the entries in Johannes Hoops's *Reallexikon*

---

6   Albert S. Cook, *The Christ of Cynewulf: A Poem in Three Parts* (Boston: Ginn & Co., 1909); Frederick Tupper, Jr, *The Riddles of the Exeter Book* (Boston: Ginn & Co, 1910); and R.W. Chambers, *Widsith: A Study in Old English Heroic Legend* (Cambridge: Cambridge University Press, 1912). Cook and his scholarly milieu are the subject of a discerning study by Michael D.C. Drout, 'The Cynewulf of Albert S. Cook: Philology and English Studies in America', *English Studies* 92 (2011): 237–58.

7   Eduard Sievers, *Angelsächsische Grammatik* (Halle: Niemeyer, 1882 and subsequent editions). This was translated into English by Albert S. Cook as *An Old English Grammar* (Boston: Ginn & Co, 1885); 3rd edn, 1903. The German edition is now superseded by *Altenglische Grammatik, nach der angelsächsische Grammatik der Eduard Sievers*, 3rd edn, ed. Karl Brunner (Tübingen: Niemeyer, 1965).

8   T. Northcote Toller, *An Anglo-Saxon Dictionary: Supplement* (Oxford: Clarendon Press, 1921). This volume represents an indispensable complement to the earlier one, titled *An Anglo-Saxon Dictionary Based on the Manuscript Collections of Joseph Bosworth*, ed. T. Northcote Toller (Oxford: Oxford University Press, 1898).

9   Ferdinand Holthausen, *Altenglisches etymologisches Wörterbuch* (Heidelberg: C. Winter, 1934); 2nd edn with a bibliographical supplement, 1963.

10 A helpful review of nineteenth-century European scholarship is provided by Hans Sauer, 'Anglo-Saxon Studies in the Nineteenth Century: Germany, Austria, Switzerland', in Pulsiano & Treharne, 455–71. Sauer takes note of landmark publications of the earlier twentieth century as well, demonstrating their connections with this earlier period.

11 See especially Andreas Heusler, *Die altgermanische Dichtung* (Potsdam: Athenaion, 1926), 2nd edn, 1941; this treats Old English poetry alongside Old German and Old Norse literature. For a biographical tribute see Heinrich Beck, 'Andreas Heusler (1865–1940)', in *Medieval Scholarship: Biographical Studies on the Formation of a Discipline*, vol. 2, ed. Helen B. Damico (New York: Garland, 1998), 283–96.

der germanischen Altertumskunde, a four-volume encyclopedia featuring articles on all aspects of *Germanistik*. This publication has now been replaced by a magnificent collaborative second edition published in no fewer than thirty-five volumes.[12] Another major contribution to Anglo-Saxon studies in this wider sense was Vilhelm Grønbech's three-volume study *Vor folkeæt i oldtiden* (*The Culture of the Teutons*), published in Danish in 1909–12 and translated into English somewhat later.[13] This wide-ranging inquiry into ancient social institutions such as the feud, marriage, and gift-giving has retained much of its value despite being based on an obsolete concept of the essentially unitary culture of the early 'Teutonic' (or 'Germanic') peoples. Of additional importance was a study of *Beowulf* by the Swedish scholar Knut Stjerna, published posthumously in 1912, that correlated that poem's references to material culture to finds in prehistoric Swedish Iron Age archaeology, thus filling out our knowledge of 'the world of *Beowulf*' while at the same time confirming the credibility of the poet's descriptions of weapons and other material objects.[14] Recent discoveries have extended such archaeological connections as these well beyond Swedish soil.

In England, steady advances in historical scholarship pertaining to the Anglo-Saxons reached a high water mark with Frank Stenton's 1943 landmark study *Anglo-Saxon England*.[15] Stenton (1880–1967) was educated at Keble College, Oxford, and was later appointed professor of history at Reading University (1926–46), where he also served as Vice-Chancellor. His detailed account of the period from late Roman Britain up to the establishment of the Norman state was then – and remains today – a remarkable work of synthesis, based as it is on the author's competence in political and constitutional history, social and economic history, the history of Christianity in early Britain, and such other sources as numismatics and place-name studies. One can scarcely conceive of an historian living today who could write a book of similar scope without being dependent on Stenton at many points. Complementing Stenton's historical research was that of Dorothy Whitelock (1901–82), whose year of birth happened to coincide with major celebrations held in Winchester in 1901 to commemorate the

---

12   *Reallexikon der germanischen Altertumskunde*, ed. Johannes Hoops, 4 vols (Strassburg: Trübner, 1911–19); 2nd edn 1968–2008 (Berlin: de Gruyter). The second edition includes a certain number of articles written in English.

13   Vilhelm Grønbech, *The Culture of the Teutons*, 3 vols in 2 (London: Oxford University Press, 1931), translated by W. Worster from *Vor folkeæt i oldtiden* (Copenhagen, 1909–12).

14   Knut Stjerna, *Essays on Questions Connected with the Old English Poem of Beowulf*, trans. and ed. John R. Clark Hall (Coventry: Viking Society for Northern Research, 1912). This English publication was based on independent articles published originally in Swedish.

15   Frank Stenton, *Anglo-Saxon England* (Oxford: Oxford University Press, 1943; 3rd edn, 1968). For an assessment of Stenton and his commanding place among British historians of his era, see Henry Loyn, 'Anglo-Saxon England', in *A Century of British Medieval Studies*, ed. Alan Deyermond (Oxford: Oxford University Press, 2007), 7–26. Another tribute, co-authored by Michael Lapidge and Stenton's wife Doris M. Stenton, is included in *Interpreters of Early Medieval Britain*, ed. Michael Lapidge (Oxford: Oxford University Press, 2002), 247–83.

millennium of the death of King Alfred the Great. The edition of Anglo-Saxon wills that Whitelock completed in 1930 demonstrated her mastery of early medieval documentary sources.[16] Equally at home in both literary and historical scholarship, Whitelock was appointed Elrington and Bosworth Professor of Anglo-Saxon at the University of Cambridge in 1957, holding that post until her retirement in 1969. Leaving aside her other significant publications, her book *The Beginnings of English Society* is admired by many as the best short social history of the Anglo-Saxon period.[17] A third English scholar of this period to make invaluable contributions to Anglo-Saxon studies was N.R. Ker (1908–1982), who has been characterized as 'the greatest scholar that Britain has ever produced' in the field of manuscript studies.[18] Born in London though of Scottish family background, Ker graduated from Magdalen College, Oxford, in 1931, and in succeeding years he was appointed successively Lecturer in Palaeography (in 1941) and then Reader in Palaeography (in 1946) at Oxford. His 1941 study *Medieval Libraries of Great Britain* sought to reconstruct the holdings of medieval libraries whose contents had since been dispersed or lost. His greatest contribution to Old English scholarship was to come a decade and a half later in the form of his 1957 book *Catalogue of Manuscripts Containing Anglo-Saxon*.[19] This supplanted, after an interim of 250 years, the catalogue of manuscripts containing Old English that the antiquarian scholar Humfrey Wanley had completed in 1705. Folded into the Introduction to Ker's book is a succinct guide to Anglo-Saxon palaeography.

The contributions to Anglo-Saxon studies made by other scholars based in the UK have been celebrated elsewhere.[20] Work done by several of them will be noted here in due course.

---

[16] *Anglo-Saxon Wills*, ed. and trans. Dorothy Whitelock (Cambridge: Cambridge University Press, 1930). Whitelock's career is reviewed by Henry Loyn in his study 'Dorothy Whitelock, 1901–1982', in *Medieval Scholarship: Biographical Studies on the Formation of a Discipline*, vol. 1, ed. Helen B. Damico and Joseph B. Zavadil, (New York: Garland, 1995), 289–311; by Loyn in Lapidge, *Interpreters of Early Medieval Britain*, 427–37; and by Jana K. Schulman, 'An Anglo-Saxonist at Oxford and Cambridge: Dorothy Whitelock (1901–1982)', in *Women Medievalists and the Academy*, ed. Jane Chance (Madison: University of Wisconsin Press, 2005), 552–63.

[17] Dorothy Whitelock, *The Beginnings of English Society* (Harmondsworth: Penguin, 1956; 2nd edn, 1968).

[18] A.I. Doyle, 'Neil Ripley Ker, 1908–1982', in Lapidge, *Interpreters of Early Medieval Britain*, 473–82 (at 482), quoting from an obituary published in the *Bodleian Library Review* in 1983.

[19] N.R. Ker, *Medieval Libraries of Great Britain: A List of Surviving Books* (London: Royal Historical Society, 1941; 2nd edn, 1964); *Catalogue of Manuscripts Containing Anglo-Saxon* (Oxford: Clarendon Press, 1957). Supplements to Ker's *Catalogue* are listed in the Select Bibliography at the end of the present book. Ker is the subject of a biographical tribute by Kevin Kiernan, 'N.R. Ker (1908–1982)', in *Medieval Scholarship*, vol. 2, ed. Damico (New York: Garland, 1998), 425–37. See also Richard W. Pfaff, 'N.R. Ker and the Study of English Medieval Manuscripts', in *Readings: MSS*, 55–77.

[20] Particularly in Lapidge, *Interpreters of Early Medieval Britain*. This book consists for the most part of obituaries, reprinted from *Proceedings of the British Academy*, of medievalists active during the late nineteenth and twentieth centuries, especially during the period 1900–1950.

Literary Criticism: A Slow Start

One area of Old English scholarship in which only intermittent progress was made during the first half of the twentieth century was literary criticism. To a large extent, persons who wrote about Old English literature were doing so in a belletrist manner, praising the poetry, in particular, for its real or imagined virtues and castigating its real or imagined vices. Approaches of this kind tended to shed their appeal as the century progressed. In addition, early twentieth-century criticism tended to be rooted in attitudes that were rapidly losing their persuasive power. Since many critics were subject to late Romantic influences as embodied in such a book as Francis T. Palgrave's *Landscape in Poetry*,[21] what especially captivated their attention were depictions of nature in its wilder forms. Criticism tended to focus on images of heroic men battling either the elements or each other, when they were not carousing. Moreover, some of this criticism was still anchored in nineteenth-century solar mythology, which tended to allegorize works of imaginative literature as representing the conflict of summer versus winter or of the sea versus the land. Interpretations along such lines began to look increasingly passé in an era when earlier modes of perception were being assaulted by Fauvism, Cubism, Vorticism, Surrealism, and other radical movements in the arts.

Another factor slowing the emergence of literary criticism in the current sense of that term was the connection, among some writers though not all, of Anglo-Saxon studies with racialist modes of thought. At least until the outbreak of the First World War, certain writers were frank in their promotion of the idea that practially all good things that pertained to the English, from their language to their moral character and their free democratic institutions, could be attributed to their German heritage. A noteworthy study along such lines was Frances B. Gummere's book *Germanic Origins*, published in 1892 and, tellingly, reissued in 1930 under the less polemical title *Founders of England*.[22] Gummere (1855–1919) was for many years professor of English at Haverford College, Pennsylvania, having previously undertaken postgraduate studies at Harvard University and at the University of Freiburg-im-Breisgau, where he earned the doctorate in 1881. In *Germanic Origins*, which was his major contribution to the field apart from his translations of Old English heroic poetry into a vigorous alliterative metre,[23] he argues that the English race, or 'our race' as he more inclusively calls it, is German to its core. In his view the Germanic-speaking ancestors of the English were of pure race, large physique, and passionate disposition, much as the Roman historian Tacitus had described them at the end of the first century AD. The free German was a warrior, 'and in the hour of rage or battle, his blue eyes flashed an uncanny fire' (p. 58). His bleak northern environs had an effect on his character: 'These swamps, these vast and sullen forests' made him 'of fitful and passionate temper, savage, inclined to

---

[21] Francis T. Palgrave, *Landscape in Poetry from Homer to Tennyson, with Many Illustrative Examples* (London: Macmillan, 1897).

[22] Frances B. Gummere, *Germanic Origins: A Study in Primitive Culture* (New York: Scribner, 1892), reissued as *Founders of England*, with supplementary notes by Francis Peabody Magoun, Jr (New York: Stechert, 1930). My quotations are drawn from the 1930 edition, which is unchanged from the earlier one except for its title and some notes added by Magoun.

[23] Frances B. Gummere, *The Oldest English Epic: Beowulf, Finnsburg, Waldere, Deor, Widsith, and the German Hildebrand* (New York: MacMillan, 1909).

gloom or to unchecked revelry' (ibid.). At the same time, the free German honoured 'the sanctity of the household, and in consequence the inviolable character of marriage' (p. 137). He had a natural 'passion of bravery', and as a chief virtue he cultivated fearlessness in the face of death. At one point Gummere comments as follows about the alliterative metre in which virtually all Old Germanic verse was composed: 'The very meter of their poetry is the clash of battle, and knows scarcely any other note' (p. 232). Thanks in part to such praise as this, Anglo-Saxon studies took on a retrograde appearance in the eyes of scholars who, cultivating a cosmopolitan outlook, turned their critical attention elsewhere.

One factor that contributed to a growing division between Anglo-Saxon studies and later English literary studies was the split that occurred in the liberal arts curriculum at the University of Cambridge when Hector Munro Chadwick (1870–1947), who from 1912 to 1941 held the post of Elrington and Bosworth Professor of Anglo-Saxon, founded a new academic department focused on the integrative study of Old English language and literature alongside Celtic studies, Old Norse studies, and other kindred subjects including history, prehistoric archaeology, and social anthropology.[24] Chadwick is perhaps best known today for his book *The Heroic Age* (1912), which developed the thesis that every early civilization went through a process of evolution that resulted, at an early stage, in a tradition of heroic oral poetry. According to this view, *Beowulf* and other Old English heroic verse could best be studied alongside the Homeric epics, the Old Irish sagas, and similar works grounded in archaic social institutions.[25] Regardless of that debatable claim, Chadwick and other like-minded scholars were persuaded that the ancient literatures of the British Isles were best studied in an integrative fashion, and the influence of that idea remains strong today.

The academic unit founded by Chadwick at the University of Cambridge, which continues in existence as the Department of Anglo-Saxon, Norse, and Celtic (ASNC), has had a major role in advancing Anglo-Saxon studies within a broad interdisciplinary framework, launching the career of many a distinguished medievalist.[26] Its influence on the development of Old English literary criticism is another matter. Under Chadwick's arrangement of the disciplines, Anglo-Saxon studies fell outside the curriculum for students concentrating in English. Correspondingly, the study of Old English literature at Cambridge tended to remain untouched by the kinds of questions being asked by leading literary critics, including such a figure as F.R. Leavis (1895–1978), who served for some decades as Director of Studies in English at Downing College, Cambridge. It was Leavis more than any other British intellectual who was responsible for establishing literary criticism as a key element of mid-twentieth-century academic discourse. Although Leavis is associated with no one school of criticism, his writings staunchly proclaimed the value of the study of literature in

---

[24] On Chadwick and his career see the tribute by J.M. de Navarro in Lapidge, *Interpreters of Early Medieval Britain*, 195–218.

[25] H. Munro Chadwick, *The Heroic Age* (Cambridge: Cambridge University Press, 1912). A similar evolutionary theory underlies the wide-ranging work of comparative literary scholarship that H.M. Chadwick subsequently wrote in conjunction with his wife Nora Kershaw Chadwick, *The Growth of Literature*, 3 vols (Cambridge: Cambridge University Press, 1932–40).

[26] Some very distinguished ASNC graduates (including Bruce Dickins, Dorothy Whitelock, and Peter Hunter Blair) are enumerated by Michael Lapidge in his chapter on 'Old English' in Deyermond, *A Century of British Medieval Studies*, 363–81 (at 372–73).

its connection to modern life.[27] But Leavis and his followers had little to say about English authors prior to Shakespeare, while Chadwick's concept of Anglo-Saxon scholarship left little room for post-medieval studies. This division became less pronounced when Whitelock in the 1960s brought the Anglo-Saxon tripos back into the School of English, thereby opening up closer communication between Anglo-Saxonists and modern critics.

While the situation at Cambridge was a unique one, it was symptomatic of a larger phenomenon. There existed – and, to some extent, there still exists – an opinion, held by persons situating themselves on either side of an intellectual divide, that the critical methods appropriate to the study of modern literature and those applicable to Old English literature have little to do with one another, given the different character of these two historical periods. Such an attitude persists in certain circles even though some distinguished poets and fiction-writers of the current era have been deeply affected by their reading of Old English literature.[28]

Two Scholars Representative of their Eras

In order to trace how attitudes towards Old English literature shifted over the first fifty years of the twentieth century – and to trace how in some ways they remained the same – it will be helpful to compare two books published close to the years 1900 and 1950, respectively. Each of these studies shaped the reception of that literature in a manner that must once have seemed definitive. One is by the London-based clergyman Stopford A. Brooke (1832–1916), the other by the American university professor George K. Anderson (1901–1980). These two authors are worth singling out for attention in part because, for the most part, they gave voice to the received views of their respective eras, as opposed to striving for originality. In addition, each of these books was widely read by specialists and non-specialists alike, thereby influencing the tenor of subsequent criticism.

Stopford A. Brooke's survey *English Literature from the Beginning to the Norman Conquest*, first published in 1898, was often reprinted during subsequent decades on both sides of the Atlantic.[29] A native of County Donegal, Ireland, Brooke attended University College, Dublin, before being ordained to the ministry in London, where he lived until his death in 1916. His success as a professional writer can be judged from the fact that sales of a primer that he wrote titled *English Literature* (first published in 1877) topped half a million copies during his lifetime. Significantly, Brooke withdrew from the Church of England in 1880, citing his inability to accept the Church's teachings on the incarnation. To the extent that he continued to preach the faith after that date, he maintained Unitarian sympathies.

Brooke's survey of pre-Conquest literature favours the secular and heroic elements of Old English literature at the expense of its religious ones. In its introductory chapter,

---

[27] Various assessments have been made of Leavis's career and influence; see for example Michael Bell, 'F.R. Leavis', in *The Cambridge History of Literary Criticism*, vol. 7: *Modernism and the New Criticism*, ed. A. Walton Litz et al. (Cambridge: Cambridge University Press, 2000), 389–422.

[28] See Chapter 11, 'Translating, Editing, and Making It New', where twentieth- and twenty-first-century authors are discussed whose careers were transformed by their study of Old English.

[29] Stopford A. Brooke, *English Literature from the Beginning to the Norman Conquest* (London: Macmillan, 1898), repr. 1899, 1903, 1908, 1912, etc.

Brooke writes in a well-informed manner about the isle of Britain and its ancient inhabitants, from the peoples of the ancient Stone Age to the respective arrivals of Celts, Anglo-Saxons, and Christian missionaries from Rome. Significantly, he speaks of the Anglo-Saxon settlers of Britain as simply 'the English', thus emphasizing the continuity of that people up to the present day rather than their continental Germanic origins. Like Gummere, however, he sees those incomers as having formed the nucleus of English national identity well before the arrival of Roman Christianity to Britain's shores. 'By that time', he writes, referring to the arrival of St Augustine's missionaries in the year 597, 'the special language, character, customs, ways of thought and feeling of the English people had so established themselves, that they remained [...] the foundation power, the most enduring note in our literature from the poems of Cædmon to the poems of Tennyson, from the prose of Ælfred to the prose of today' (pp. 19–20). Brooke thus sees no need to credit the Christian church with having had a transformative impact on either the character or the literature of the English.

With a confidence that may now seem excessive, Brooke characterizes the English as having been in their origins 'a singing folk' (p. 39). Moreover, he asserts that the earliest English-speaking inhabitants of Britain had worshipped 'the Heaven and the Earth, the Father and Mother of all things, and their son, the glorious Summer, who fought with the Winter and the Frost Giants' (p. 41). Brooke thus views certain Old English healing charms as pagan survivals that bear no more than a thin veneer of Christianity. His manner of reading *Beowulf* is along similar lines. He postulates that even though in its present form this work reflects the shaping presence of an eighth-century poet as well as some Christian editing, the main body of the poem arose on the Continent in the form of heathen sagas and lays. Following the German scholars Karl Müllenhof and Ludwig Ettmüller, Brooke identifies the hero of *Beowulf* as, in origin, the ancient god Beowa, 'the god of the sun and of the summer'. The hero's battles against Grendel and Grendel's mother, correspondingly, represent in their core meaning the ancient struggle of summer versus winter. The dragon episode is annexed to the same supposed struggle, 'the oldest myth in the world' (p. 59). Brooke associates Grendel and his mother with indigenous inhabitants of the northern regions who, fleeing from invaders, took up their abodes 'in the dark woods and moors, among the cliffs and caves, beyond the strip of cultivated land along the sea-shore' (p. 66). There they nursed their grievances, and venturing out from there they made horror-inspiring raids on the newer settlers. Brooke is indifferent to the fact that the *Beowulf* poet twice gives a different account of the origin of the Grendel creatures, ascribing them to the seed of Cain in a manner consistent with a large body of medieval learned writings.[30] As for Beowulf the hero, he represents for Brooke 'the English ideal of a prince and warrior of the seventh century' (p. 64). The hero's admirable moral qualities are encapsulated in his unbreakable courage in spite of Wyrd, whom Brooke identifies as 'the Fate Goddess of the North' (p. 64).

Literature on Christian themes receives little praise in these pages. Brooke speaks of the 'dull monotony' of the biblical verse paraphrase known as *Daniel*, for example (p. 148). In the poems of Cynewulf, likewise, 'we miss, with some regret, the bold, unconscious heathen

---

[30] Medieval traditions about the descent of monsters from the seed of Cain were discussed in detail as early as 1906 by Oliver F. Emerson, 'Legends of Cain, Especially in Old and Middle English', *PMLA* 21 (1906): 831–929.

note, the rude heroic strain' of earlier Germanic verse (p. 150). One poem of a religious character that Brooke singles out for praise is *Judith*, though what he finds uplifting in it is not its devotional spirit but rather its joyous treatment of the themes of liberty and patriotism. The ancient Jewish heroine Judith, to him, has a martial character 'like Joan of Arc'; and he adds, as a courteous tip of his hat to the imagined women of Anglo-Saxon England, that 'I do not doubt that there were many Englishwomen of the time capable of her warlike passion, and endowed with her lofty character' (p. 147). Another Christian poem that Brooke praises is *The Dream of the Rood*, which he admires for its blending of Christian doctrine with 'heathen war poetry and myth' (p. 101). His allusion here is to the use of heroic diction in a poem that, in his view, is indebted to the Old Norse myth of the death of Baldr. Ignoring this poem's manifest theological content, Brooke admires the way that Christ is imagined as a hero who meets his death unflinchingly, just as Beowulf does. 'It is the death and burial of an English hero' that the reader can identify with here (p. 101). As for the elegiac poems of the Exeter Book, in his view they have 'few if any connections with Christianity' (p. 152). Likewise, the Exeter Book riddles are 'heathen in heart' (p. 159), including certain ones that are 'of such primæval grossness' that, he infers, they must have been composed by a layman who lived a 'Bohemian' life, singing his riddles from hall to hall (p. 158). What Brooke must be alluding to here are the 'sex riddles', which, despite earlier thinking to the contrary, have recently been shown to have analogues in the medieval learned tradition.[31]

Old English prose has little interest for Brooke. What he most admires about the literature of this period is its poetic depictions of man plunged into the midst of a harsh natural world: 'What is most remarkable in the Elegies, as in many of the *Riddles*, is their pleasure in the aspects of wild nature' (p. 154). He cites for special admiration 'the fierce doings of the tempest and of the frost on the German ocean' in *The Seafarer* (whose Christian elements he views as an accretion), or 'the driving sleet and the snow sifted through with hail' of *The Wanderer* (pp. 154–55).[32] In keeping with a trend in early twentieth-century criticism, he sees in these scenes not just a fascination with untamed nature, but also a psychological correlative to the inner state of the poet. In his view, Old English literature deserves to be studied precisely for its parallels with a modern sensibility. This attitude exemplifies a common tendency in belletrist criticism; namely, to be quick to praise those features of a past or foreign literature that are thought to coincide with the sentiments of one's own time and place, while either ignoring or disparaging those elements that resist this kind of assimilation.

Offering a sharp contrast to Brooke's impressionistic style of criticism is George K. Anderson's survey *The Literature of the Anglo-Saxons*, published in 1949.[33] Born in 1901, Anderson spent his early childhood in China, Brazil, and Hong Kong before attending

---

[31] Note Mercedes Salvador-Bello, 'The Sexual Riddle Type in Aldhelm's Enigmata, the Exeter Book, and Early Medieval Latin', *PQ* 90 (2011): 357–85.

[32] Rather than exploring images of untamed nature in Old English literature, Jennifer Neville, *Representations of the Natural World in Old English Poetry* (Cambridge: Cambridge University Press, 1999), directs attention to how poets depict nature in such a way as to define the leading traits of human society, as well as to highlight the workings of God in the creation.

[33] George K. Anderson, *The Literature of the Anglo-Saxons* (Princeton: Princeton University Press, 1949), repr. in 1962 by Russell & Russell, New York.

Phillips Exeter Academy and then Harvard University, where he earned the PhD in 1925. From 1927 to 1972 he held the position of professor of English at Brown University in Rhode Island. Anderson can be caustic when assessing the merits of Old English literature, almost as if he wished to demonstrate that the evaluation of Old English literature by a learned North American critic writing at mid-century could be hard and objective, free from parochialism, aesthetic effusions, or racialist or patriotic biases. Backward-looking in some ways, forward-looking in others, often discerning in the quality of his judgements though not always so, Anderson too expresses the *Zeitgeist* of his book's time and place of origin.

In keeping with accepted views of the early Middle Ages, Anderson regards the Anglo-Saxons as invaders and conquerors who went on to become founders of England. He shares the long-standing conviction that 'it is from these fierce, virile bands of Germanic marauders that the Englishman has derived many of his habits of thought, much of his law and his social usage, the larger portion of his ethnic stock, and the entire framework of his language.' In his view, moreover, 'the Englishman has changed surprisingly little in temperament and in philosophical outlook from his ancestors of a thousand years ago' (p. 3). Since he regards Anglo-Saxon England as firmly separated from the Roman world (p. 10), he tends to minimize the role of Latinate education in the making of Old English literature. Instead, he cites as basic strands in the Anglo-Saxons' outlook on life 'the loyalty to king and state, the love of action and adventure, the moral earnestness implicit in the conservative adherence to an established code of conduct'. Unlike Gummere and Brooke, however, he presents an unflattering picture of certain Anglo-Saxon character traits, speaking of 'the grimness at need, the persevering and unimaginative plodding and muddling, the near-fatalistic acceptance of life as a sombre fight that must be endured to the setting of the sun'. These humourless traits, states Anderson – who, we should remember, was writing in pre-Monty-Python days – are 'all part and parcel of the English approach to living' (p. 4).

While asserting that 'the Anglo-Saxon [...] was not entirely an unseeing clod of barbarism', Anderson suggests that 'there was a grim vigor and vitality to his crudeness which can still assert themselves when we read his literature' (p. 16). This is apparently meant as a kind of praise. But the horizons of the Anglo-Saxon were constricted, according to Anderson: 'he possessed also an abysmal ignorance of the world outside his little community, and this ignorance continued among his people as a whole until long after the Norman Conquest' (pp. 20–21). As for the impact of Christianity on early England, Anderson has little to say about it apart from some glowing praise of Bede's Northumbria. While he views the period before the Conquest as scarcely admitting of evolutionary change – 'The social history of the Old English period seems to have been remarkably static' (p. 17) – the coming of the Normans introduced a clean break with the past: 'The Norman Conquest of 1066 is in the nature of a national upheaval and marks the beginning of a new era in English history, the Middle English period. With that period we have here nothing to do' (p. 27). Anderson's acceptance of a binary divide between two periods of history and literature, the Old English and the Middle English, is likely to strike present-day researchers as one of the least helpful of his premises.

In a manner that may seem surprising today but that is in keeping with views held widely during his lifetime, Anderson draws upon environmental determinism as a way of accounting for the character of the Anglo-Saxons and their literature. Climate and geography strongly affected the authors of that time, in his view (pp. 42–43):

> [Theirs] is precisely the sort of literature that one could expect from a people who lived in a damp climate, in raw sea-driving winds, with more than a happy share of foggy, overcast days in which sunlight too often shone feebly or was lost altogether. This literature, in all its forms, is inclined to speak but little of the all too brief northern summer; instead, it is cast in the mood of autumn and winter, to which spring comes but slowly if at all.

Anderson thus relates the more sombre aspects of Old English literature not to medieval Christian pessimism about the things of this world, but rather to the dreariness of the weather. It remains a mystery how these same British Isles also came to produce such authors as Shakespeare, Fielding, and Dickens, among other writers unencumbered by an unrelievedly soggy disposition.

In his concept of Anglo-Saxon poetry as being essentially primitive in spirit, Anderson reveals himself to be a man of his time. 'To the modern reader', he writes, 'it is inevitably the pagan elements in Old English literature which make it most attractive.' An example he cites is the 'tumultuous carnage' of *The Battle of Brunanburh*, a poem that he associates with the pagan past even though it was composed in mid-tenth-century England. Moreover, he sees in this poem an ancient Darwinian pattern, 'the spectacle of the ruthless survival of the fittest' (p. 45). Correspondingly, rather like Brooke, he sees *Beowulf* as 'the characteristic expression of a people in the hero-worshipping stage of their tribal civilization'. Old English poetry in general strikes Anderson as childlike in character: 'it exhibits [...] the childlike love of sound, rhythm, and fancy that is habitually associated with an untutored people' (p. 45). Correspondingly, he finds the alliterative verse form used by the Anglo-Saxons to be in essence a clumsy and ineffective medium, rather than its being the generative force producing the poetry's more flamboyant stylistic effects, as some might think today (p. 49):

> As is the case with all such formalistic poetry, the devices frequently get in the way of the poetic spirit, and technique often supplants essential poetry. The exigencies of alliteration, much more formidable than those of simple end-rime, require that the poet use words which alliterate, whether or not the alliterating words are the best that could be used. The repetitiousness clogs the syntax, to say nothing of the metrical movement, of the verses and gives a curious cloudiness or muddiness to many lines of the poetry [...] The general effect rendered is frequently that of great poetic naïveté.

Anderson's negative characterization of the Old English poetic style is understandable, seeing that mid-twentieth-century critics tended to admire poetry marked by terseness, economy, irony, and the use of verse-forms that broke with the requirements of traditional metre. Old English verse could readily be thought to be form-ridden if judged by such standards as these.

The large problem point in Old English poetry, in Anderson's view, is its incongruous mixture of pre-Christian and Christian elements. Assuming that Old Germanic legends, sagas, and lays had been transmitted from the Continent to Britain via oral tradition, Anderson supposes that it was in that insular context, with the advent of a literate clergy, that such poems were 'finally reduced to writing, subject to the philosophical comment or religious editing natural to their eventual redactor' (p. 58). Accretions, digressions, and modifications had thus come to mar the original narratives. *Beowulf*, in particular, is seen to contain an abundance of 'platitude and of Christian admonition' resulting from this process of redaction (p. 67). Moreover, this process resulted in odd contradictions, as in those passages where 'Fate (*Wyrd*) and her warriors, both the doomed and the undoomed, wrestle with the Christian God for supremacy' (p. 68). Anderson follows a well-established tendency in the modern critical literature to identify *Weird* or *Wyrd*, capitalized so as to personify that entity, as an autonomous pagan power acting independently of God.[34] In like manner, the Exeter Book elegies are seen to be essentially pagan in spirit. *The Wanderer* is 'stoical in tone', and only the last few lines of that poem, which are 'weak and intrusive' in Anderson's view, are of Christian inspiration. 'This is one case where pagan negation is artistically triumphant', he writes (p. 159), disregarding the possibility that certain modes of stoicism were valued within the framework of Christian spirituality. *The Seafarer* too, in Anderson's view, is to be read in naturalistic and psychological terms rather than religious ones. The speaker of this poem is 'a man who loves the sea and hates it, who has had cause to remember the sufferings it had wrought on him and so must return to its bosom'. The second half of *The Seafarer* – the overtly Christian half – has little interest for Anderson: 'it is static and pious and has no intimate relation to the earlier portion, although it does not necessarily form any illogical disunity' (p. 161). In sum, in his view, 'for all its pagan vitality', this poem 'did not escape the almost inevitable Christian adulteration' (p. 161). I quote this passage at a certain length because it is so expressive of the dominant critical thinking of its day.

Anderson's book was thus an important publication that will now seem a dated one. At its end, playing devil's advocate perhaps, Anderson remarks that the Anglo-Saxon period was 'Church-ridden', while the literature of that time 'lacks sensuousness and brilliance' and so might be thought to have 'little esthetic appeal' (p. 411). It is not clear if he himself subscribes to these negative assessments or not. The virtue of his book is that he presents a straightforward, learned, and carefully documented overview of a large body of Anglo-Saxon poetry and prose. Moreover, in a marked departure from previous studies of this literature, he devotes no fewer than six chapters to Old English prose, in addition to one on Anglo-Latin literature. Perhaps the main value of Anderson's book lies in these chapters, however cursory some of them are, since Old English prose had been so broadly neglected prior to this time. Indeed, in the closing section of his book, Anderson claims with some confidence that 'the immediate future of scholarly investigations' in Old English literary studies will be devoted to 'the widening of our knowledge of [...] hitherto neglected areas of the field', including 'the nearly forgotten prose', prose homilies in particular. To judge from this reflection, Anderson was something of a prophet.

During the quarter-century following the publication of Anderson's book, from roughly 1950 to 1975, a small revolution occurred in the critical reception of Old English literature.

---

[34] Excerpts from the modern criticism that are expressive of changing attitudes to *wyrd*, fate, and fatalism are gathered together with a running commentary by E.G. Stanley, *Imagining the Anglo-Saxon Past: The Search for Anglo-Saxon Paganism and Anglo-Saxon Trial by Jury* (Cambridge: D.S. Brewer, 2000), 85–109. The first half of this two-part book, *The Search for Anglo-Saxon Paganism*, was published on its own in book form in 1975. Stanley exposes the fallacies involved in interpreting *wyrd* as Anderson suggests.

Changes in the tenor of Old English scholarship are perhaps more noticeable during those years than during any other period of comparable length in the history of the field. Later in this chapter I will discuss three or four books dating from 1971–72 that exemplify these many-faceted changes. Before that, however, notice should be taken of certain publications that prepared the way for these developments. This will entail, as well, taking account of the critical reception of *Beowulf* during the middle decades of the twentieth century. Accordingly, the section that immediately follows will deal with some new directions in literary criticism during the years after 1950. This will be followed by a section on *Beowulf* criticism from the earlier twentieth century to the 1970s, with special attention to J.R.R. Tolkien.

New Directions after the Second World War

What is remarkable about Old English literary criticism during the period from about 1950 to 1975 is not just its quality and its diverse nature, but also its plenitude when compared with what was produced during earlier eras. While this phenomenon can be traced on both sides of the Atlantic, it is particularly evident in North America.

To some extent, the explosion in the criticism of Old English literature that occurred after the end of the Second World War can be attributed to social factors affecting North American society at large. One of these was the growth of departments of English, together with the establishment of academic programs in Medieval Studies, as part of an across-the-board expansion of colleges and universities during the late 1940s and 1950s.[35] Another factor was a boom in North American scholarly publishing, partly as a result of the founding of a number of new journals specializing in English literature or medieval studies. The post-war absorption of many former members of the Armed Forces into higher education thanks to the enlightened provisions of the GI Bill (the Servicemen's Readjustment Act of 1944) had a transformative impact on the university culture of this time, as well. So did the emigration from Europe into North America of numerous persons of intellectual distinction, including (but not limited to) Jews fleeing Nazi persecution. At certain universities, the influence was felt of outstanding scholar-teachers who promoted the study of Old English poetry with attention to its aesthetic qualities, as revealed through close philological analysis. Harvard University, where Francis P. Magoun, Jr, William Alfred, and Morton Bloomfield were influential teacher-scholars, and Yale University, where the beneficent influence of John Collins Pope was felt, offer examples of the importance of this kind of personal contact for young scholars setting out in their careers.

Things were somewhat different in Great Britain. Although such factors as the ones just mentioned can be traced in post-war Britain to some extent, both the depressed economy of the UK during the post-war era and the traditions of scholarship there differed markedly from their counterparts in North America. If a corresponding increase in the volume of Old English literary criticism can be traced in the British Isles at this time, it was less pronounced. Traditional philological and historical scholarship, however, continued to be

---

[35]   Gerald Graff, *Professing Literature: An Institutional History* (Chicago: University of Chicago Press, 1987), provides an overview of academic literary studies in the USA from their beginnings through the 1960s, including discussion of the 'great explosion in graduate programs' (p. 155) that began in the 1940s and reached its height in the 1950s and 1960s.

undertaken at a very high level in the UK, while fresh developments in archaeology, including the spectacular discoveries made at Sutton Hoo, East Anglia, in 1939, though published only later, stimulated research in that field while contributing to the public visibility of Anglo-Saxon studies.

One prerequisite for advanced literary criticism at this time was the publication of expert English-language scholarly editions of the surviving corpus of Old English texts. Setting a standard in this regard was the series The Anglo-Saxon Poetic Records (ASPR), edited by George Philip Krapp and Elliott Van Kirk Dobbie in six volumes from 1931 to 1953.[36] This is so even though the decision to limit the scope of ASPR to verse texts – a necessary decision, from a pragmatic perspective – leads to certain oddities. The metrical charms published in volume six of ASPR, for example, are abstracted from their manuscript context and hence dissociated from the prose healing texts that surround them. What may be the most important context for their interpretation is therefore missing from this volume. Moreover, the production of critical editions of certain whole manuscripts of the Anglo-Saxon period – cover to cover, including both verse and prose and including both Latin and Old English texts where the two languages are used side by side – would provide a valuable complement to the ASPR series and other modern editions. Still, approximately three generations of scholars have by now been well served by these editions. The fact that they are standardized in format and hence amenable to the production of concordances and lexical databases has likewise been a great aid to research. Another major publication series, one that began in the early 1950s and has continued for more than half a century, is Early English Manuscripts in Facsimile (EEMF). Produced with the aim of preserving a permanent record of manuscripts that were subject to destruction by chance or war, and made at a time before the production of digital facsimiles came within the realm of possibility, these volumes have served as an invaluable resource for specialists and have served to direct scholarly attention to the material text as artefact, a topic of sharp interest in recent years.[37]

Among freestanding scholarly editions produced during the 1950s and 1960s, two editions of homilies stand out for their importance. These are Dorothy Bethurum's 1957 edition *The Homilies of Wulfstan* and John Collins Pope's two-volume edition *Homilies of Ælfric: A Supplementary Collection*, published in 1967–68.[38] Exemplary as a student edition is John Collins Pope's *Seven Old English Poems*. Now updated by R.D. Fulk and retitled *Eight Old English Poems*, this book is widely admired for its detailed glossary, commentary, and notes.[39]

While historical research per se falls outside the scope of the present book, literary scholars have reason to be indebted to several mid-century publications for promoting the

---

[36] The six ASPR volumes are listed individually in the Select Bibliography at the end of this book.

[37] Individual volumes in the EEMF series, too, are listed in the Select Bibliography.

[38] Dorothy Bethurum, *The Homilies of Wulfstan* (Oxford: Clarendon Press, 1957); *Homilies of Ælfric: A Supplementary Collection*, ed. John Collins Pope, 2 vols, EETS 259–60 (London: Oxford University Press, 1967–68).

[39] *Seven Old English Poems*, ed. John C. Pope (Indianapolis: Bobbs-Merrill, 1966); 2nd edn, 1981; subsequently reissued as *Eight Old English Poems*, ed. John C. Pope, 3rd edn, prepared by R.D. Fulk (New York: Norton, 2001). The additional poem in the augmented edition is *The Wife's Lament*. The inclusion of this item is in keeping with self-conscious efforts being made at that time to widen the Old English curriculum so as to include more readings pertaining to women.

understanding of Old English literature within a broad cultural context. One of these, *An Introduction to Anglo-Saxon England* by the Cambridge historian Peter Hunter Blair, has long been esteemed for its judicious review of Anglo-Saxon history, social institutions, economy, literature, and learning.[40] Another volume, the anthology *English Historical Documents c. 500–1042*, edited by Dorothy Whitelock, remains an invaluable compendium of a wide range of both Latin and Old English writings presented in modern English translation, with a substantial introduction.[41] Another outstanding publication dating from slightly later is R.I. Page's *An Introduction to English Runes*.[42] Page (1924–2012), a native of Yorkshire and a leading expert on Old Norse antiquities, was Elrington and Bosworth Professor of Anglo-Saxon at the University of Cambridge from 1984 to 1991, serving also for many years as librarian of the Parker Library of Corpus Christi College, Cambridge. By cutting through much cant relating to runes and their use, Page's exemplary book has put English runology on a sound footing ever since. In the field of archaeology, the magnificent multi-volume publication *The Sutton Hoo Ship Burial* throws a spotlight on the real-world basis of the descriptions of precious material objects that are featured in *Beowulf* and other Old English poems (weapons, jewellery, the harp, the ship, and so forth).[43] These volumes were published during 1975–83 under the supervision of Rupert Bruce-Mitchell, the keeper of medieval and later antiquities in the British Museum.

Consciousness of the constructed nature of Anglo-Saxon studies as an academic discipline began to come into focus at roughly this same time. Influential in this regard was a series of articles published by E.G. Stanley in 1964 and 1965 in the pages of *Notes and Queries*. These articles were later gathered together in Stanley's freestanding volume *The Search for Anglo-Saxon Paganism* (1975), which has since been re-issued in conjunction with a second study by Stanley on a related subject, Anglo-Saxon trial by jury.[44] Stanley (b. 1923) was Rawlinson and Bosworth Professor of Anglo-Saxon at the University of Oxford from 1977 to 1991. His research had a major impact on the critical reception of Old English literature by showing how deeply the prior reception of *Beowulf* and other heroic and elegiac poems had been entrenched in late Romantic fallacies having to do with heathenism, fatalism, folk poetry, and 'monkish meddling' (as we have seen with reference to both Stopford Brooke and G.S. Anderson). Stanley thus pointed the way to an understanding of Anglo-Saxon literature as largely a creation of the Christian civilization of early medieval Europe with some special insular features of its own, as opposed to representing an imperfect set of survivals from an imagined northern past. In subsequent decades, Stanley's book has stimulated

---

[40] Peter Hunter Blair, *Introduction to Anglo-Saxon England* (Cambridge: Cambridge University Press, 1956); 2nd edn, 1977; 3rd edn with an introduction by Simon Keynes, 2003.

[41] *English Historical Documents*, gen. ed. David C. Douglas, vol. 1: *c. 500–1042*, ed. Dorothy Whitelock (London: Eyre Methuen, 1955); 2nd edn, 1979. Of related interest to Anglo-Saxonists is vol. 2 of this same series, ed. David C. Douglas and George W. Greenaway, covering the period 1042–1189.

[42] R.I. Page, *An Introduction to English Runes* (London: Methuen, 1973; 2nd edn, Boydell Press, 1999).

[43] Rupert Bruce-Mitford, *The Sutton Hoo Ship Burial*, 3 vols in 4 (London: British Museum Publications, 1975–83). Bruce-Mitchell also authored a well-illustrated single-volume guide to the subject: *The Sutton Hoo Ship Burial: A Handbook* (London: British Museum, 1968); 2nd edn, 1972.

[44] See n. 34 above for publishing information.

other scholars to try to recover – and to critique, from a contemporary standpoint – the history of Anglo-Saxon studies as a discipline, going back well beyond Romanticism to as early as the sixteenth century.

Anglo-Saxon studies during the period from about 1950 to 1975 were deeply affected as well by scholarship that cast light into medieval intellectual history, the medieval educational system, and the institution of monasticism. One foundational contribution to medieval studies as a twentieth-century discipline was M.L.W. Laistner's *Thought and Letters in Western Europe,* AD *500 to 900,* first published in 1931 and later revised.[45] Laistner sets the study of the literature of the Anglo-Saxons within the context of an educational tradition that reached England from ancient Rome via the Carolingian Empire. Also important for Anglo-Saxon studies were the publications of the English church historian David Knowles (1896–1974), including his influential history *The Monastic Order in England* (1940).[46] As a result of such publications as these, it soon became virtually impossible for Anglo-Saxonists to talk about the heroic literature of early England as if its Christian elements were somehow intrusive, the results either of 'scribal meddling' or of a thin veneer of religious sentiments applied to a pagan core. *Beowulf,* in particular, began to be examined anew as a product of the scriptorium rather than of a court culture, or as some combination of the two. Moreover, specialists in Old English literature were affected – some pro, some con – by the provocative claims of Princeton scholar D.W. Robertson, Jr, as expressed particularly in his 1962 book *A Preface to Chaucer,* to the effect that virtually all medieval literature should be construed as the expression of a Christian worldview that differed profoundly from modern secularist philosophies, particularly as regards its reliance on Augustinian doctrines of *caritas* versus *cupiditas.*[47] While Robertson advanced this sweeping claim chiefly with regard to the later Middle Ages, his arguments had a galvanizing effect among medievalists across the board. Moreover, his work encouraged Anglo-Saxonists to seek out connections between Old English literature and the contemporary visual arts, including religious manuscript illustration, as Robertson had done with regard to Chaucer and the fourteenth century.

One other area of literary studies had a transformative effect on the critical reception of Old English literature at this time: the study of oral poetry and poetics. The main stimulus to research in this area was provided by Harvard professor Milman Parry, a leading Homerist, and his assistant and collaborator Albert B. Lord, whose expertise spanned early Greek studies, Slavic studies, and the comparative study of medieval European epic poetry, including *Beowulf.* Lord's book *The Singer of Tales* (Cambridge, MA: Harvard University Press, 1960), based on fieldwork undertaken with skilled epic singers in the Balkans, soon became a classic of modern criticism, influencing scholarship in more fields than can be numbered. The oral-formulaic theory and its reception by Anglo-Saxonists will be discussed in a later

---

[45] M.L.W. Laistner, *Thought and Letters in Western Europe,* AD *500 to 900* (London: Methuen, 1931), revised edn 1957.

[46] David Knowles, *The Monastic Order in England: A History of its Development from the Times of St. Dunstan to the Fourth Lateran Council, 940–1216* (Cambridge: Cambridge University Press, 1940; 2nd edn, 1963). Knowles's complementary study *The Religious Orders in England,* 3 vols (Cambridge: Cambridge University Press, 1948–59), deals with the period after 1216.

[47] D.W. Robertson, Jr, *A Preface to Chaucer: Studies in Medieval Perspectives* (Princeton, Princeton University Press, 1962).

chapter. The point I wish to make here is that, in a manner analogous to Robertson's thesis, Lord's research energized the field of Old English studies by encouraging Anglo-Saxonists to examine at least the heroic literature of that time as a product of a mentality and a poetics radically unlike those often taken for granted today. The Parry/Lord model of oral-formulaic composition entailed very close attention to the linguistic texture of Old English poetry, especially its stylized diction, and this in itself had a stimulating effect on research. In addition, research into oral poetics encouraged Anglo-Saxonists to look more closely at the interface between literacy and orality, taking account of the functions of oral tradition as a chief vehicle of what is now called 'social memory'.

Changing Currents in *Beowulf* Studies

For understandable reasons, *Beowulf* has often served as the focal point of twentieth-century discussions of the character of Anglo-Saxon poetry. Indeed, this poem has been prominent in discussions of Old English literature ever since 1833–37, when it was edited and translated into modern English by John Mitchell Kemble, for its exceptional literary quality was recognized from the start. So as to highlight important directions taken in *Beowulf* criticism up to about the year 1975, I will single out for discussion four landmark publications that date from the earlier part of the twentieth century.

The first of these studies was R.W. Chambers's *Beowulf: An Introduction to the Study of the Poem* (Cambridge, Cambridge University Press, 1921), a book that presents a mine of information about the poem and its historical context. Chambers (1874–1942) taught for many years at University College, London, where he also served as librarian.[48] Different sections of his book address the poem's historical and legendary elements, its folkloric and mythological affinities, its Old Norse and medieval Latin parallels, and theories as to the poem's origin, date, and structure. Rather than attempting to settle questions relating to the poem's interpretation, Chambers wished to make available to scholars the full range of documentary information upon which critical judgements could be based. Updated editions of his book came out in 1932 and 1959. By the time the third edition appeared, the main body of the book had been augmented by a first supplement (added for the 1932 edition) and a second supplement (written by Oxford professor C.L. Wrenn for the 1959 edition) in addition to the somewhat miscellaneous appendix that concludes the original publication. *Beowulf: An Introduction* has therefore come to resemble an encyclopedia whose constituent parts are joined in an unwieldy fashion. Still it remains an indispensable resource for specialists.

A greater impact on the poem's critical reception was made by Friedrich Klaeber's magisterial edition *Beowulf and the Fight at Finnsburg*, first published in 1922, with updated versions appearing in 1928, 1936, 1941, and 1950.[49] In 2008, a trio of scholars brought out

---

[48]   Chambers was responsible for the revisions made to *Beowulf with the Finnsburg Fragment*, ed. A.J. Wyatt, new edn (Cambridge: Cambridge University Press, 1914). A biographical portrait of Chambers by C.J. Sissom is included in Lapidge, *Interpreters of Early Medieval Britain*, 221–33.

[49]   *Beowulf and the Fight at Finnsburg*, ed. Fr. Klaeber (Boston: Heath, 1922); 2nd edn 1928, issued with a supplement in 1936 and a second supplement in 1941; 3rd edn 1950. The author is known as either 'Friedrich' or 'Frederick' (the Americanized version of his name).

a thoroughly revised and updated version of the book under the title *Klaeber's Beowulf.*[50] In its successive incarnations, 'Klaeber' (as it tends to be known for short) has proven to be the most influential edition of *Beowulf* ever to see print. Meant especially for the use of postgraduate students, it has at the same time served scholars as a definitive tool for advanced research; and even in those instances where Klaeber's editorial judgements have been challenged, it is his reading of the text that is generally assumed to be the point of departure.

It is worth reflecting that Klaeber (1863–1954) was born in what was then the kingdom of Prussia in the same year, 1863, that marked the death, also in Prussia, of Jacob Grimm (1785–1863), the chief founder of the science of comparative Germanic philology. It is arresting to think that the lives of these two men, taken together, thus span the period from the French Revolution to the thermonuclear age. Something of the spirit of the master can be discerned in the man of later birth. After receiving the PhD at the University of Berlin in 1892, Klaeber accepted an appointment in the Department of English at the University of Minnesota, where he taught for the next thirty-nine years (1893–1931). For most of that period he held the position of Professor of English and Comparative Philology. Always attached to his homeland, after his retirement from teaching in Minnesota he and his wife returned to Germany, where he eventually died in impoverished circumstances after having suffered through both the devastation of the Second World War and the deprivations that attended the Soviet occupation of eastern Germany.[51]

The esteem in which Klaeber's edition of *Beowulf* is held rests on his command of comparative Germanic philology as that science had developed by the turn of the century. In addition, Klaeber prided himself on keeping abreast of virtually everything being written on *Beowulf*, and his critical judgements are invariably based on a scrupulous sifting of the evidence. The views he expresses as regards such questions as the poem's mythical or historical content, its structure and unity, its Christian versus pagan character, and its possible date and place of origin therefore called for respect from the time of the book's initial publication. Moreover, his critical judgements have retained their value over the years despite advances that have since been made in ancillary areas of research, including Iron Age archaeology and the comparative study of orality and literacy.

Klaeber viewed with scepticism his predecessors' theories about the poem's relations to a body of ancient Germanic mythology. Moreover, rejecting the idea that the poem had attained its existing shape as a result of the accretion of postulated shorter 'lays' that had once had independent existence, he viewed it as a unity as it stood in the single manuscript in which it is preserved. He thus saw no need for theories of 'monkish interpolation'. Correspondingly, he was able to demonstrate that Christian sentiments, doctrine, and phrasing permeate the text, so that there is no way to excise them so as to reveal a more primitive document.[52] Moreover, he viewed the

---

[50] *Klaeber's Beowulf and the Fight at Finnsburg*, 4th edn, ed. R.D. Fulk, Robert E. Bjork, and John D. Niles (Toronto: University of Toronto Press), abbreviated in the present book as '*Klaeber's Beowulf*'.

[51] There is a biographical tribute by Helen Damico, '"My Professor of Anglo-Saxon Was Frederick Klaeber": Minnesota and Beyond', in *The Preservation and Transmission of Anglo-Saxon Culture*, ed. Paul E. Szarmach and Joel T. Rosenthal (Kalamazoo: Medieval Institute Publications, 1997), 73–98.

poem as having been written, most likely in the first half of the eighth century, by a single poet. In his view this poet knew the Bible well, was learned enough to draw on Virgil's *Aeneid* as a source of inspiration, and was conversant with other works of classical or medieval antiquity.[53]

Klaeber's concept of the poem's authorship is expressed most directly in the following passage:[54]

> We may, then, picture to ourselves the author of *Beowulf* as a man connected in some way with an Anglian court, a royal chaplain or abbot of noble birth or, it may be, a monk friend of his, who possessed an actual knowledge of court life and addressed himself to an aristocratic, in fact a royal audience. A man well versed in Germanic and Scandinavian heroic lore, familiar with secular Anglo-Saxon poems of the type exemplified by *Widsið, Finnsburg, Deor*, and *Waldere*, and a student of biblical poems of the Cædmonian cycle, a man of notable taste and culture and informed with a spirit of broad-minded Christianity.

The image of the *Beowulf* poet presented here stands out as distinctive when we recall how that same poet had been imagined in the prior critical literature. In place of the Germanic *scop* or 'singer' of prior scholars, we are asked to contemplate an Anglo-Saxon court poet – 'a man of notable taste and culture' – writing (not singing) an epic poem along Virgilian lines for a cultivated Christian audience. A revolution in the scholarly reception of *Beowulf* was underway, even though not all experts have embraced all aspects of it.

The third of the books singled out for attention here was published six years later. This was William Witherle Lawrence's *Beowulf and Epic Tradition* (Cambridge, MA: Harvard University Press, 1928). Its author, a professor of English at Columbia University, drew on his expert knowledge of the complex world of Germanic legendary history to which the *Beowulf* poet alludes. Distinguishing his own contribution to *Beowulf* studies from that of Chambers, Lawrence makes clear that his aim is to provide a unified and coherent account, accessible to all readers, of how the poet formed his epic by drawing on a variety of constituent elements, whether these elements were originally folkloric, historical, or legendary in character and whether they originally pertained to the Germanic peoples of the Continent or to the cousin peoples of Scandinavia. Rejecting both mythological interpretations of the poem and the theory that the poem had been assembled out of a set of pre-existent heroic lays, Lawrence, following Klaeber, ascribed the composition of the poem to a court poet of the age of Bede living somewhere in the north of England. He attributes the *writing* of it, specifically, to that milieu, for (taking issue with H.M. Chadwick and others) he expresses confidence that the poem can be attributed to a single lettered author, whatever the origin of

---

[52] Much of this demonstration of the poem's Christian character was made in Klaeber's articles 'Die Christlichen elemente in *Beowulf*', *Anglia* 35 (1935): 111–36, 249–70, and 453–82, and *Anglia* 36 (1936): 169–99. These studies have been translated into modern English by Paul Battles under the title *The Christian Elements in Beowulf*, Old English Newsletter Subsidia 24 (Kalamazoo: Medieval Institute Publications, 1996).

[53] Klaeber's views on the *Beowulf* poet's debt to Virgil found expression in his study 'Aeneis und Beowulf', *Archiv für das Studium der neueren Sprachen und Literaturen* 126 (1911): 40–48, 339–59. The extent of classical influence on *Beowulf*, however, remains a vexed point.

[54] Quotation from Klaeber's 1922 edition of the poem, p. cxxii; the passage stands unaltered in his 1950 edition, p. cxix.

its constituent parts may have been (pp. 287–89). Although an analysis of the poem's Christian elements is far from his purpose, Lawrence views the poem as a unity and its author as a Christian: 'The older idea, that the Christian elements in *Beowulf* are interpolations in an originally heathen poem', he writes, 'is now [...] generally abandoned' (p. 282). While developing his own theory as to how the poem had evolved into its final form, Lawrence thus lends his authority to Klaeber's unitarian views.

One chapter of Lawrence's book that remains of lasting value is the one on 'Grendel and his Dam' (pp. 161–203). Here, drawing on the German scholar Friedrich Panzer's previous study of *Beowulf* in the light of analogous European *Märchen* (folktales) of the 'Bear's Son' type,[55] Lawrence argues persuasively that the first two parts of the poem – the episodes dealing with Grendel and Grendel's mother, respectively – are a unified conception, for what they represent is an epic elaboration upon a twofold pattern of adventures that is well attested in this folktale type. He was thus able to attribute noteworthy parallels between *Beowulf* and certain narratives from late medieval Scandinavian tradition, including the Icelandic *Grettir's Saga* and the *Saga of King Hrolf Kraki*, not to the direct influence of one tradition upon the other, but rather to their common indebtedness to this underlying pattern. Correspondingly, Lawrence recognized that the third episode of *Beowulf*, the dragon fight, must have separate origins, for nothing like it occurs in the analogous 'Bear's Son' folktales. He thus showed that the structure of *Beowulf* results from the merging of these two elements, the paired Grendel episodes and the dragon fight. As for the plot of the first two-thirds of the poem, it must be regarded as an epic elaboration of what was once a simpler tale localized at the court of the Danish Scylding (Skjølding) line of kings. These observations still stand as steady points in the flux of the poem's higher criticism. While not all the details of his analysis have stood the test of time, including his concept of the poem's Norwegian-style physical scenery, his book helped to establish a consensus upon which later scholars could build.

The most eloquent of the scholar-critics of the next generation was J.R.R. Tolkien (1892–1973). Since his career is well known in its essentials, it need only be sketched in here.[56] After spending his early childhood in South Africa, Tolkien was educated at King Edward's School, Birmingham, and thereafter at Exeter College, Oxford, from which he graduated in 1915. Although his academic career was interrupted by military service during the First World War, he afterwards took up university positions first at the University of Leeds and then at Oxford University, where in 1925 he was appointed Rawlinson and Bosworth Professor of Anglo-Saxon. He held that post for twenty years, thereupon being named the Merton Professor of English Language and Literature, a position that he held until his retirement in 1959. His most famous work of original fiction, his epic trilogy *The Lord of the Rings*, was published in 1954–55 after a long period of gestation.

---

[55] F. Panzer, *Studien zur germanischen Sagengeschichte, I: Beowulf* (Munich, 1910). No second volume of this work was published, although Panzer's title anticipates one.

[56] The bibliography on Tolkien is too large to enter into here. A helpful compendium is the *J.R.R. Tolkien Encyclopedia*, ed. Michael D.C. Drout (New York: Routledge, 2007); this includes a number of entries with a bearing on Tolkien's lifelong engagement with Old English language and literature.

While Tolkien never published extensively on *Beowulf,* his love for the poem is evident from his interweaving of echoes from it into *The Lord of the Rings* and other creative works. Moreover, among his papers at the time of his death was a complete translation of *Beowulf,* together with a detailed commentary on that poem. These were only published in 2014, after an interval of over forty years, as edited by his son Christopher Tolkien.[57] His landmark essay '*Beowulf*: The Monsters and the Critics' can be regarded as a definitive statement of his views about a poem that he deeply admired and that he regularly taught during his Oxford career.[58] The essay was delivered to the British Academy in 1936 as the annual Sir Israel Gollancz Lecture. A polished, annotated version of it was subsequently published in volume 22 of *Proceedings of the British Academy*, and this text has often been reprinted.[59]

It matters that Tolkien's essay was originally written for oral delivery, for the key to its subsequent popularity is its masterful rhetoric. The author's deployment of rhetorical tropes starts with the talk's paradoxical title, which plays on the droll conceit that critics and monsters inhabit a single plane. It continues with a lecturer's typical note of self-deprecation, as Tolkien, who had long occupied the Oxford chair in Anglo-Saxon, quotes a squib that a prior scholar once made with reference to a giant of nineteenth-century Anglo-Saxon scholarship: 'He may do very well for a professor' (p. 3). The use of medieval-style figures of rhetoric then begins in earnest as Tolkien twice draws on the device of allegory. He does so first with reference to 'lady Historia', who, rather than 'lady Poesia', had served as the poem's fairy godmother ever since the poem's 'christening' at the start of the eighteenth century. Then comes a more elaborate allegory about a man who constructs a tower built up of ancient stones, only to see it pushed over by a bevy of 'friends' who – having no concept of the tower's uplifting purpose – then busy themselves quarrying the rubble for trivial ends (pp. 6–7). The allusion to the lofty poem and its busybody critics is a transparent one.[60]

While there is no need to call attention to all the rhetorical flourishes by which Tolkien's lecture was enlivened for oral delivery, those who have read it with care will recall the author's use of literary allusion and metaphor when he speaks of 'the jabberwocks of historical and antiquarian research' who 'burble in the tulgy wood of conjecture, flitting from one tum-tum tree to another' (p. 8); or his plays on proverbial language (e.g. 'one dragon, however hot, does not makes a summer', p. 10); or the whimsical allusions he makes to Shakespeare's Shylock, or to the Book of St Albans, or to the juxtaposed figures of John Milton and Jack and the Beanstalk (p. 12). These are the gestures of a learned speaker

---

[57] J.R.R. Tolkien, *Beowulf: A Complete Translation and Commentary*, ed. Christopher Tolkien (New York: Houghton Mifflin Harcourt, 2014).

[58] Drafts of Tolkien's lecture survive, ones that are longer than the lecture in its published form. These have been edited by Michael D.C. Drout under the title *Beowulf and the Critics, by J.R.R. Tolkien* (Tempe, AZ: ACMRS, 2002).

[59] J.R.R. Tolkien, 'Beowulf: The Monsters and the Critics', *PBA 22* (1936): 245–95. The essay was subsequently reprinted by Oxford University Press on behalf of the British Academy as a free-standing publication. The page numbers given in my text refer to that reprint. Other reprinted versions are available in Nicholson, 51–103; Fry, 8–56; Fulk, 14–44; and Donoghue, 103–30 (here without Tolkien's appendices).

[60] The details of the allegory are neatly explicated by T.A. Shippey, *J.R.R. Tolkien: Author of the Century* (London: HarperCollins, 2000), 161–63.

addressing an audience made up of equally learned persons who will get the jokes and who will thereby, one hopes, be made receptive to the speaker's serious points. The original medium of these stratagems was the speaking voice, which one continues to hear through the printed version when attentive to its style.

The essay as published in the Academy's *Proceedings* is far more, though, than the record of an urbane talk. It is a well-documented piece of research that engages closely with the experts. While preparing his talk for print, Tolkien added thirty-nine footnotes, some of them substantial, in which he makes specific reference to the prior critical literature. Moreover, accompanying the main text is an eleven-page appendix divided into three parts (pp. 36–47). Analysing the specific language by which the poet describes Grendel, Tolkien first confirms that Grendel is conceived of as a devilish ogre rather than a devil revealing himself in ogre-form. Tolkien then offers a philological analysis of certain terms from *Beowulf* that appear to have Christian significance, including *lof* and *dom*, *hell* and *heofon*, showing that the poet uses these words in a discriminating manner so as to maintain verisimilitude in his depiction of the pagan past. He also offers the suggestion that lines 175–88 of the poem, which tell of the Danes' futile offering of sacrifices to idols, represent some kind of editorial or scribal alteration of the poet's original words. Tolkien's essay can thus be seen to represent not just a personal reading of the poem, but also a closely argued engagement with *Beowulf* studies such as they were by the time of his writing. While gently satirizing 'the critics' of his title, who turn out to be a mostly undifferentiated crowd of pedants, Tolkien also participates closely and passionately in the critical discourse of his day, naming esteemed *Beowulf* scholars by name and expressing judgements that often differ from theirs. As is to be expected of an Oxford don addressing his peers, he chiefly strives to distinguish his own views from those of highly regarded English scholars of the prior generation. It would have been out of place for him to display his wit and learning at the expense of an American scholar such as Lawrence, whom he does not mention, or a German-American scholar like Klaeber, whose work he acknowledges only briefly, chiefly by way of a gracious footnote. Two English scholars whom Tolkien singles out for praise, even while disagreeing with certain of their views, are W.P. Ker (1855–1923), the author of *The Dark Ages* (Edinburgh: Blackwood, 1904) and other authoritative studies of early medieval literature, and R.W. Chambers.[61] Through these acknowledgements, Tolkien achieves one of his chief aims, which is to justify the close study of *Beowulf* not just for antiquarian or philological purposes, but as a work of literary art worthy of the attention of the leading English intellectuals of his day.

In many regards though not all, Tolkien's view of the poem is consistent with Klaeber's. Both experts subscribe to a unitarian view of the poem: that is to say, each of them views it as a structural unity that is the creation of a single author looking back to the legendary past. As Tolkien puts the matter, the poem was obviously composed by 'an Englishman using afresh ancient and largely traditional material' (p. 8). Like Klaeber, Tolkien ascribes that act of composition to somewhere in the north of Britain during roughly the age of Bede. If there is a difference between Klaeber and Tolkien in regard to their concept of the poem's authorship, it is that Tolkien emphasizes that the poet, writing in the British Isles

---

[61] Tolkien makes complimentary reference to an essay by Chambers that served as the preface to *Beowulf Translated into Modern English Rhyming Verse*, trans. Archibald Strong (London: Constable, 1925).

long after the Heroic Age had come to an end, had 'an antiquarian curiosity' about that more ancient historical period (p. 22). Moreover, Tolkien characterizes the *Beowulf* poet as having been emotionally attached to the old heroic way of life even while knowing that 'the wages of heroism is death' (p. 27). Views of this kind are never expressed by Klaeber, who regards the hero as essentially selfless and noble, even to the point of being inclined to recognize in him 'features of the Christian Savior'.[62] While Klaeber thus sees the poet as projecting Christian ideals back into the Germanic past as if in a kind of secular saint's life, Tolkien sees the poet as nostalgically attached to a vanished past even while recognizing that it has rightly been superseded. One might see a parallel here to Tolkien's attachment to his own fantasy world in *The Lord of the Rings*.

Tolkien agrees with Klaeber, then, in accepting that the author of *Beowulf* was a literate Christian. All the same, the relatively few references that Tolkien makes to the poet's Christianity are overshadowed by his allusions to Old Norse literature and mythology. Tolkien seems to assume that the poet was familiar with old Northern myths of Thor and Fenrir and Ragnarǫk, something that Klaeber never takes for granted. Memorably, he treats with utter seriousness the poem's monsters, whom he sees as having once been identical with savage creatures of the old northern faith. Correspondingly, what Tolkien sees at the heart of *Beowulf* is 'the creed of unyielding will' (p. 20). By this phrase he refers to an archaic Northern ideal such as finds expression in the myth of Ragnarǫk, as recounted in the Old Norse eddic poem *Vǫluspá*. An almost Nietzschean or Wagnerian quality thus hovers about Tolkien's response to *Beowulf*, aligning his approach in some ways more closely with nineteenth-century mythological interpretations of the poem than with Klaeber's Christian perspective. In Tolkien's view, what the poem is most clearly about is 'man at war with the hostile world, and his inevitable overthrow in Time'. His capitalization of that last word, in the essay as published, contributes to one's sense that what he most values in this poem is its mythic dimension, its echoes of *Götterdämmerung* – the imagined time when the gods and their human allies wage war against their monstrous enemies until all are destroyed. The hero of the poem, in his view, is the unyielding protagonist of a struggle that is emblematic of the human condition in general: '*he is a man, and that for him and many is sufficient tragedy*' (p. 18, Tolkien's italics). How this essentially worldly view of the poem and its hero can be reconciled with one's knowledge that the poet speaks so frequently and directly of God and God's powers is a problem that Tolkien seeks to finesse in terms like the following (p. 23):

> [The poet] is still concerned primarily with *man on earth*, rehandling in a new perspective an ancient theme: that man, each man and all men, and all their works shall die. A theme no Christian need despise. Yet this theme plainly would not be so treated, but for the nearness of a pagan time.

Tolkien thus comes very close to embracing the notion of the poem's 'Christian colouring' that is often voiced in the earlier criticism. Indeed, the appeal of that idea has remained

---

[62] Klaeber, *Beowulf and the Fight at Finnsburg*, 3rd edn, p. li. Interestingly, Klaeber toned down his wording of this point over time. While in his Introduction to the 1922 and 1928 editions, he states that 'we need not hesitate to recognize' features of the Christian saviour in the hero of *Beowulf*, in the 1950 edition he declares at this point that 'we might even feel inclined to recognize' them.

strong among those who desire a *Beowulf* that is largely expressive of either modern existentialist philosophy or the imputed ideals of a pagan past.

Tolkien's account of the poem's structure and genre has been particularly influential and is worth the close attention it has received among later critics (p. 29):

> The general structure of the poem [...] is not really difficult to perceive, if we look to the main points, the strategy, and neglect the many points of minor tactics. We must dismiss, of course, from mind the notion that *Beowulf* is a 'narrative poem', that it tells a tale or intends to tell a tale sequentially. The poem 'lacks steady advance': so Klaeber heads a critical section in his edition. But the poem was not meant to advance, steadily or unsteadily. It is essentially a balance, an opposition of ends and beginnings. In its simplest terms it is a contrasted description of two moments in a great life, rising and setting; an elaboration of the ancient and intensely moving contrast between youth and age, first achievement and final death. It is divided in consequence into two opposed portions, different in matter, manner, and length: A from 1 to 2199 (including an exordium of 52 lines); B from 2200 to 3182 (the end).

Use of the rhetorical phrase 'of course' near the start of this passage is a deft means of deflecting a reader's common-sense notion that – of course – the *Beowulf* poet does have a sequential tale to tell, so that the poem is indeed a 'narrative'. This is true even though the narrative's progression is often interrupted so that the audience can savour a given moment in the action, or so that the poet can allude to different layers of the past or to future events. Regardless of this point, by focusing on the poem's binary structure, its 'two opposed portions', Tolkien arrives at an original concept of the poem's genre. Rather than being an epic in anything like the usual sense of that term, *Beowulf* is 'a heroic-elegiac poem'. This phrase is chosen with care. More acutely than other readers of the poem, Tolkien had a sense of its tragic dimension, to which he alludes again and again. He found in *Beowulf* an intensely moving awareness of loss and sorrow, something akin to what one encounters not just in *The Wanderer* but also in Sophoclean tragedy or in Shakespeare's late play *King Lear*. The effect of this reading of the poem as 'an elaboration of the ancient and intensely moving contrast between youth and age, first achievement and final death' is to project *Beowulf* into the company of some of the loftiest expressions of the human spirit.

Much is gained through Tolkien's emphasis on the poem's binary structure, including an enhanced appreciation of the part played by the dragon, whose role as 'a potent creation of men's imagination' (p. 16) seemed to Tolkien to need no defence. Still we may ask: Is anything essential to the poem lost by being projected into this bipartite scheme?

As has since been pointed out, quite a good deal is lost through an analysis along such lines. The poem's central episode, in particular, is largely effaced.[63] Tolkien's decision not to engage with the hero's fight against Grendel's mother must have been a self-conscious one, for greater attention to this episode would have weakened the binary opposition of 'two

---

[63] H.L. Rogers, 'Beowulf's Three Great Fights', *RES* n.s. 6 (1955): 339–55, repr. in Nicholson, 233–56, points out that Tolkien's nearly exclusive focus on Grendel and the dragon scarcely does justice to the poem's second main episode. George Clark, too, in his book *Beowulf* (Boston: Twayne, 1990), calls attention to Tolkien's effacement of that episode while offering an incisive critique of additional aspects of Tolkien's essay (at 7–15).

moments in a great life'. Tolkien's concept of *Beowulf* as a 'heroic-elegiac' poem would then have lost much of its authority, for it is in the hero's second great fight that his fortunes reach their apogee: Beowulf achieves the greatest personal victory of his life, purges an otherworldly realm of its monstrous inhabitants, definitively settles a twenty-year feud, cements the good relations of his people with the Danes, is properly rewarded, and proceeds back home with his surviving men unscathed and in triumph. As we all know, this does not mean the end of the poem (though the poem's folkloric analogues do end at this point), for events of a more sombre inflection are to follow. To efface this episode from critical consciousness, however, is to dwell on the poem's dark notes at the expense of its triumphant ones.

Moreover, it is in the hero's second great fight, the one against Grendel's mother, that the poem's Christian elements come especially to the fore. At the moment of the hero's most desperate need, when his uncanny enemy has him down and drives her knife right at his chest (at lines 1545–56), the poet declares that God, who is named three times in this passage, determined his victory. The hero's byrnie holds firm, and he comes to his feet again. Correspondingly, the hero's ensuing victory is accompanied by three miracles. These are the shining of a light like that of the sun (1570–72a); the melting of the blade of the hero's giant-wrought sword like ice in springtime (1605b–11); and the miraculous purging of the waters of Grendel's mere (1620–22). I call attention to these details so as to make clear that Tolkien's analysis downplays the poem's unmistakable Christian elements, which in the passage just alluded to are associated with life, light, warmth, springtime, purity, and joy.

Just as importantly, perhaps, Tolkien's concept of the binary structure of *Beowulf* effaces the poem's connections to the realm of the feminine, just as it downplays those elements of the poem that have to do with courtly decorum rather than the male heroic ethos.[64] Not only is the remarkable fact obscured that one of the hero's three great antagonists is a she-demon. In addition, Tolkien takes very little notice of the roles played by the leading women in the poem, namely the Danish queen Wealhtheow, the Danish princess Freawaru, and the Geatish queen Hygd. Since his strategy is to emphasize two moments in a male hero's life, Tolkien likewise skirts a topic that was of apparent interest to the poet: namely, court etiquette, or the right conduct of men and women of the ruling class in their everyday dealings with one another. These civic relations include gift-giving, inheritance, the etiquette of speech (including verbal combat), social outlawry (and the redemption of criminals from exile), and the complex tensions attendant upon marital unions involving rival groups. Such matters as these would scarcely make for a compelling poem in the absence of a strong plot, but the poet obviously cared enough about them to speak of them again and again. This is particularly true in the Danish episodes, where women are granted a role that perhaps mirrors their actual role in the upper ranks of Anglo-Saxon society.

While Tolkien's essay deserves admiration for its eloquence and depth of insight, then, it scarcely represents the final word on many issues of importance relating to *Beowulf*. The aspect of his essay that is arguably the most arresting is his praise of the poem as an example of what today would be called 'fantasy literature'. No one writing prior to this time had

---

[64]   Clare A. Lees, 'Men and *Beowulf*', in *Medieval Masculinities: Regarding Men in the Middle Ages*, ed. Lees (Minneapolis: University of Minnesota Press, 1994), 130–35, repr. in Joy & Ramsey, 417–38, identifies Tolkien's silence concerning female characters as an aspect of his masculinism.

granted nearly so much respect to 'the monsters' or had been so keenly appreciative of their role. 'I would suggest', he writes, 'that the monsters are not an inexplicable blunder of taste; they are essential, fundamentally allied to the underlying ideas of the poem, which give it its lofty tone and high seriousness' (p. 19). No one in later years would venture the opinion that a poem recounting a hero's struggle to the death against otherworldly adversaries should be regarded as a cheap tale unworthy of serious attention.

Reading Tolkien's essay with hindsight, one can see that the break it makes with the earlier critical reception of that poem stops short of being a decisive one. In particular, Tolkien never seems quite comfortable accepting the poem's Christian intellectual content at its face value. In the appendix to his essay, he argues that several passages that are couched in overtly Christian terms (lines 181–88 and 1740–60) may have been the result of scribal interpolation. What he seems most eager to celebrate is an '*ur-Beowulf*' of the imagination; that is to say, a poem that historically preceded the extant scribal text. That earlier poem, in his apparent view, can only be recovered through acts of restorative criticism such as the ones he offers in this essay. Favouring a quasi-mythic approach to that imagined earlier *Beowulf*, he sees in it traces of old Northern pessimism and fatalism, much as prior critics had seen in it the workings of Wyrd. This backward-looking quality to his essay, when coupled with its wit, learning, and passion, has doubtless contributed to its appeal in the years since 1936. Just as the public has always preferred the monsters to the critics – for who would not? – many non-specialist readers have remained attached to an essentially pagan and heroic *Beowulf*, while it is only certain specialists who have been content with a *Beowulf* that is just as expressive of the early medieval Christian worldview as is most other Anglo-Saxon verse that has survived, even given that poem's setting in the Germanic Heroic Age.

Tolkien's essay is often spoken of as the point of origin for modern critical appreciations of Old English literature. It can more aptly be characterized as a brilliant moment in a scholarly discourse that began well before 1936 and that has continued up to the present day. In any event, mid-twentieth-century writers on *Beowulf* soon adopted the gesture of complimenting Tolkien's essay before venturing their own individual analyses of the poem.

This is true of a perceptive study that appeared in print just two years after Tolkien's, namely Joan Blomfield's 1938 essay 'The Style and Structure of *Beowulf*'. While acknowledging Tolkien's influence and speaking of the poem's structure as being based on balanced contrasts – 'the ever-present identity of seed in fruit and fruit in seed' – Blomfield also emphasizes the 'high degree of abstraction and formalism' shown in the poem as a whole. The poem, she argues, has an 'underlying structural unity' thanks to its thematic patterning, regardless of what Klaeber called its 'lack of steady advance'.[65] In her view the poem's so-called digressions, including moralizing passages, participate in its overall unity by contributing to complex thematic pairings. A more systematic argument along similar lines was advanced by the Swiss scholar Adrien Bonjour in his 1950 book *The Digressions in Beowulf*,[66] which was based in part on articles he had published previously. Bonjour gives credit not

---

[65]   Joan Blomfield, 'The Style and Structure of *Beowulf*', *RES* 14 (1938): 396–403. Blomfield's married name was Joan Turville-Petre; under that name she later edited *The Old English Exodus* from the papers of J.R.R. Tolkien (Oxford: Clarendon Press, 1981).

[66]   Adrien Bonjour, *The Digressions in Beowulf* (Oxford: Blackwell, 1950). Bonjour had previously studied at Harvard University under the direction of Francis Peabody Magoun, Jr.

just to Tolkien but also to Klaeber, Lawrence, Blomfield, and the learned and influential German scholar Levin L. Schücking for having explicated many aspects of the poem's art.[67] Bonjour's thesis in brief, for which he argues convincingly, is that 'each digression brings its distinct contribution to the organic structure and the artistic value of the poem' (p. 75).

Such critical terms as these ('organic structure', 'artistic value') are central to Arthur Gilchrist Brodeur's purposes in his 1959 book *The Art of Beowulf*, one of the most perceptive studies of the poem's style and aesthetics that has yet been written.[68] After receiving the PhD from Harvard University in 1916, Brodeur (1888–1971) taught for most of his career at the University of California, Berkeley, where he held appointments in both the Department of English and the Department of Scandinavian Studies, a unit that he helped to found and that is now of international distinction. His book's succinct title underscores the point that *Beowulf* is indeed a work of art whose language, style, and structure repay the closest attention. While Brodeur covers a wide range of topics – the poem's structure and unity, its setting and action, its episodes and digressions, its Christian and pagan elements, its Tolkienesque 'design for terror' in the three monster fights – of particular value are his discussions of poetic diction, including kennings and the use of compound diction, and of the syntactic device of variation, also known as grammatical apposition, by which the same essential idea is repeated two, three, or more times with alternative phrasing. Brodeur clarifies the role of variation as the chief stylistic device by which the poet puts on display his unparalleled store of poetic diction. While Brodeur's book represents a triumph of older philological modes of inquiry, it also contributed to the New Critical modes of analysis that were gaining popularity in the 1940s and 1950s and that Tolkien's essay anticipated to some extent. Brodeur's closing chapter, for example, features the poet's use of anticipation, contrast, and irony – three poetic stratagems that New Critics showcased as aspects of complex literary art.

The methods of the New Criticism are clearly on display in the innovative study *A Reading of Beowulf* by Edward B. Irving, Jr (1923–98), which appeared in 1968.[69] While New Criticism is a label that has meant many things to many people, what tended to unite the writers, almost all of them North Americans, who were closely linked to this movement was a common distaste for doctrinaire modes of literary scholarship, whether these took the form of aestheticism, Marxism, or old-school philological or historical analysis. Joined with this predilection was a belief that 'literature matters' in modern life, as well as a conviction that the value and meaning of literature can best be ascertained through alertness to the precise verbal features of texts. It is not true that New Critics favoured a revival of 'art for art's sake', or were simply 'formalists', or were opposed to historicism in literary studies, or favoured *explication de texte* merely as a pedagogical device, although statements of these

---

[67]   Schücking's major contributions to the study of Old English literature include his book *Heldenstoltz und Würde im Angelsächsischen, mit einem Anhang: Zur Charakterisierungstechnik im Beowulfepos* (Leipzig: Abhandlungen der Sächsischen Akademie der Wissenschaften, 1933), and his article 'Das Königsideal im *Beowulf*', *Bulletin of the Modern Humanities Research Association* 3 (1929): 143–54, trans. in Nicholson, 35–49, as 'The Ideal of Kingship in *Beowulf*'.

[68]   Arthur Gilchrist Brodeur, *The Art of Beowulf* (Berkeley: University of California Press, 1959).

[69]   Edward B. Irving, Jr, *A Reading of Beowulf* (New Haven: Yale University Press, 1968).

kinds are sometimes heard.[70] By offering what he calls a 'reading' of *Beowulf*, Irving positioned himself to glide past such venerable topics as the poem's place and date of origin, its mode of composition, its legendary allusions, and its Christian dimension. While acknowledging the work of predecessors at many points, Irving makes no systematic effort to situate his study within the prior discourse of *Beowulf* criticism. As he states in his preface, 'My intention here was to lighten ship as much as possible in order to move unimpeded toward examining *Beowulf* closely, in its own terms as nearly as I could conceive them, and from several different angles of approach' (p. vii).

Irving's starting point is the poem's hero and the means by which the hero is characterized. Often, Irving shows, this is through the rhetorical device of negation, as in such a statement as 'Never was he the one to strike comrades over drinks by the hearth' (2179b–80a). The demonic creature Grendel, too, is shown to be characterized through negation, often with an admixture of irony, as when that creature is described as a mock-thane who 'wished no peace-settlement with any man of the Danish force' (154b–55): on the contrary, he ate them whole. In many other ways as well, Irving shows that key elements of the poem's meaning and art-istry are revealed through attention to rhetorical idioms specific to this poem, or to shifts in narrative point of view, or to instances of dramatic irony, or to the kinds of thematic layering and contrast that Joan Blomfield had earlier identified. Never before this time, it is safe to say, had a book-length study of Old English poetry approached its subject in the same close and discriminating manner in which modern works were analysed. In other ways as well, Irving's book went far to establish a way of reading *Beowulf* that has remained attractive up to the present time. Writing in the Cold War era in a manner that reminds one of Tolkien's prior meditation on the poem's tragic dimension, Irving sees in the more violent legendary episodes of *Beowulf* 'a vision of the perpetual violence which is man's lot' (p. 190). If there is a measure of relief from the mood of desolation that pervades the poem's close, Irving suggests, it is provided by the example of the man Beowulf himself, whom Irving celebrates as 'the incarna-tion of the heroic spirit and the radiant centre of the poem' (p. 246). As for the role of Christianity in shaping the poem's values, Irving seems to take it for granted but has little to say about it, as is in keeping with late twentieth-century secularist and existentialist philosophies.

Taken together, despite their many differences of detail and emphasis, the views expressed in the books and essays discussed in the present section of this chapter reveal certain common elements. Thanks to the influence of Klaeber and Tolkien in particular, a mid-century consen-sus had emerged that the poem as we have it is a great work of art that had come into being as a result of the merging of two cultures, one of them 'Germanic' and the other one 'Christian' (with whatever precise meaning these terms were thought to bear). *Beowulf* was thought to express a synthesis of these perspectives in a traditional verse medium that was epic in scale, dignified in manner, stylistically brilliant, and largely elegiac in tone. A similar revolution in popular conceptions of the poem has never taken place, to judge from journalistic accounts and cinematic versions that project an image of the *Beowulf* story as a crude and violent expression of some Dark Age of the imagination.

---

[70] For discussion see René Wellek, *A History of Modern Criticism: 1750–1950*, vol. 6: *American Criticism, 1900–1950* (New Haven: Yale University Press, 1986), esp. 144–58, and A. Walton Litz et al., *The Cambridge History of Literary Criticism*, vol. 7: *Modernism and the New Criticism*, esp. 181–218.

Key Works from the Early Seventies

The years 1971 and 1972 were unusually fertile ones for Old English literary studies. At least four books published in those two years had a distinct impact in that field, among a wide range of other studies contributing to the advancement of knowledge. Moreover, as we will see, steps were taken in these same two years to establish Anglo-Saxon studies as a recognized academic discipline, with Old English literature assumed to be a key component of that field.

One of these four books was pedagogical in aim. This was a fully refashioned version of *Bright's Old English Grammar and Reader* edited jointly by Frederic G. Cassidy and Richard N. Ringler.[71] Cassidy (1907–2000), a native of Jamaica, served for many years as the founding editor of the *Dictionary of American Regional English* while holding the position of Professor of English at the University of Wisconsin, Madison. Ringler, who was then Cassidy's junior colleague at Madison, has since distinguished himself as the author of translations from both modern Icelandic verse and Old English poetry that brilliantly match the technical artistry of the original texts. In 'Cassidy and Ringler's Bright', as it is known for short, a generous selection of Old English prose and verse texts is preceded by a grammar presented in lessons of increasing difficulty. The grammar of Old English is presented within the framework of comparative Germanic grammar, with corresponding attention paid to the phonological changes that distinguish Old English from its closest relatives. This linguistic material is presented in a clear and uncluttered manner, and each chapter is accompanied by 'user-friendly' exercises designed to confirm the philological principles involved. Enhancing the book's value are photographic facsimiles of the manuscript pages on which a number of the reading selections are based. All in all, the book is arguably the finest one-volume introduction to Old English language and literature ever produced; it attests to the high level in Anglo-Saxon scholarship that was taken for granted in North American universities at this time.

Another outstanding book dating from 1971–72 is *The Interpretation of Old English Poems*, by Stanley B. Greenfield.[72] Greenfield (1922–87) enjoyed a long and distinguished career as Professor of English at the University of Oregon. He was a tireless promoter of the study of Old English literature within critical frameworks that had gained a firm presence in English departments by the 1950s and 1960s, including the New Criticism among other schools and approaches. In *The Interpretation of Old English Poems* he relies on methods of close reading so as to probe not just what a problematic passage from the poetry is likely to mean, but what the criteria are for validity in interpretation. His book stands out for the variety of critical methods it puts on display, including historicist, New Critical, linguistic, and oral-formulaic approaches. In his preface Greenfield warns that an indiscriminate attachment to just one stream or type of criticism will 'tend to detract from the

---

[71] *Bright's Old English Grammar and Reader*, 3rd edn, ed. Frederic G. Cassidy and Richard N. Ringler (New York: Holt, 1971). The second corrected printing of this book eliminates certain misprints that found their way into the initial print run.

[72] Stanley B. Greenfield, *The Interpretation of Old English Poems* (London: Routledge & Kegan Paul, 1972). Parts of this book were based on articles Greenfield had placed in leading journals from 1954 to 1967.

special nature, the unique identity, of particular poems' (p. ix). Instead, what he attempts to illustrate is 'the convergence of various kinds of poetic and extra-poetic elements in the immediate text', so that the text, when judiciously explicated, will 'speak to us across the years with the dignity and self-assurance of its individuality' (ibid.).

The six chapters of Greenfield's book examine a number of specimen texts with this factor of 'convergence' in mind. Rather than adopting a set view as to the value of any one critical method, Greenfield shows how a reader's alertness to such factors as generic expectations, syntactic patterns, or modes of medieval allegory may help to confirm, cast doubt on, or complicate one's understanding of a given poem. The passages discussed by Greenfield range from the genre of heroic poetry (*Beowulf, The Battle of Maldon, The Fight at Finnsburg*), to that of elegy (*The Wanderer, The Seafarer, The Husband's Message*), to biblical paraphrases (*Genesis A* and *Genesis B*), to poems of a symbolic or allegorical character (*The Dream of the Road, The Phoenix*). Problems specific to language and style remain in the foreground, sometimes leading the author to what he believes to be a secure interpretation but at other times to the conclusion that 'the interpretation of poems is at best a precarious business' (p. 159). Greenfield's imagined dialogue with critics whom he names by name, and whose views he treats with respect even when attempting to refute them, makes this book an apt complement to his 1965 study *A Critical History of Old English Literature*.[73] The title of that book alerts readers that the author's subject is both Old English literature itself, in its different types and historical periods, and the critical currents that have shaped the modern reception of that literature.

A third landmark book published in 1971–72 is *Loyalties and Traditions*, an elegant study written by the medievalist Milton McC. Gatch (b. 1932).[74] After receiving the PhD at Yale University in 1963, Gatch taught for many years as Professor of English at Union Theological Seminary, New York City, where in the course of time he also served as Academic Dean and Provost and as Director of The Burke Library. While his book has the stated purpose of elucidating the early medieval background of Old English literature, it also explicates certain individual texts by projecting the understanding of those works into the realm of Christian monasticism. Rather than dwelling on the Germanic origins of the English, Gatch emphasizes that there were continuities in the transmission of culture from ancient Rome to Anglo-Saxon England. Like many other scholar-critics, he expresses admiration for the aesthetic qualities of Old English literature, *Beowulf* in particular. Reacting against the modern appreciation of these writings chiefly on aesthetic grounds, however, Gatch emphasizes their value for cultural historians, for 'the Anglo-Saxons [...] left the largest, most varied, and oldest body of non-Latin European literature which has survived' (p. 17). The literature that Gatch finds most important in this regard is the corpus of texts written down from the end of the reign of King Alfred to the early eleventh century (ca. AD 900–1020). This emphasis on the late Anglo-Saxon period, the era when most of the extant prose was produced, marks a shift away from earlier scholars' concentration on

---

[73] Stanley B. Greenfield, *A Critical History of Old English Literature* (New York: New York University Press, 1965). As will be discussed in due time, a second edition of this book appeared in 1986 (the one abbreviated here as 'Greenfield & Calder').

[74] Milton McC. Gatch, *Loyalties and Traditions: Man and His World in Old English Literature* (New York: Bobbs-Merrill, 1971).

the 'early' (hence 'heathen' or 'semi-heathen') poetry of the Anglo-Saxons. In this later historical period, as Gatch makes clear, 'Anglo-Saxon culture was a Christian culture' (p. 25); and order to understand it, he argues, the modern reader should try to enter into the thinking of that time. Much of the task of understanding Old English literature is thus seen to be a problem in the history of mentalities. The modern reader may respond sympathetically, for example, to the images of man 'alone and cruelly buffeted by fate and nature' to be found in the elegies, but may find it more difficult to relate to the conclusion, embraced by these poets, that 'the way out of that alienation is through a relationship with the Christian God' (p. 22).

In the first main chapter of his book, Gatch draws upon contemporary theorists to account for the importance of oral heroic poetry as 'the medium of memory' in a traditional society. In his view, the formulaic style of Old English poetry may be an inherent aspect of works 'written deliberately in the manner of the oral poetic tradition' (p. 43). Viewing the Anglo-Saxons as 'Christians of fairly remote German ethnic origins' (p. 60), Gatch discounts the value of Tacitus's *Germania* as a means of understanding their culture. Instead, he sees *Beowulf* and other Old English heroic poetry as possible evidence for myth-making on the part of Anglo-Saxons looking back to a former legendary age. The banqueting scene in Heorot, for example, may be more 'the creation of a fertile imagination working on traditional themes' than it is 'a product either of disciplined historical investigation or of the folk memory' (p. 58). Gatch likewise draws on archaeological and art historical sources to suggest that there was a 'continued interest in Germanic legend' among the Anglo-Saxons 'at a very late period' (p. 33).

In a chapter on 'Early Medieval Christianity', Gatch first gives an account of early medieval monasticism and the system of monastic education, then discusses the system of exegesis that was used to expound the levels of meaning and the spiritual sense of Scripture. The exegetical method 'was literary criticism' for the Middle Ages, Gatch argues: it 'was designed both to expound the profundity of the passages under consideration and to move the audience' (p. 93). Moreover, he shows, this same system of typological or figural interpretation influenced the composition of original texts. Gatch's main exhibit in this connection is Advent Lyric 5 from the opening pages of the Exeter Book. After identifying this poem as a meditation on a Latin antiphon that was sung before and after the Magnificat at the office of Vespers during Advent, Gatch shows that the image of the rising sun that is featured in this lyric has Christological significance, in accord with a medieval tradition of exegesis whereby the rising sun is equated with the acquisition of spiritual knowledge as well as with the figure of Christ. This set of equations, in turn, would have been recognized by early medieval readers as an example of *enigma*, a subtype of the figure or trope of allegory in which 'the meaning of a statement is hidden by the use of obscure analogies' (p. 98, quoting from Bede's treatise *De figuris et tropis*, a common early medieval school text). This trope is just one among many rhetorical figures and schemata that can be identified either in the Advent Lyrics or elsewhere in the Exeter Book. Gatch concludes that though Advent Lyric 5 'appears to be a simple and moving hymn of thanksgiving for the coming of Christ, the Light, into the world', it is also a poem with complex intellectual presuppositions (p. 100). Through this kind of analysis, he argues, the modern reader can be led into an understanding of Old English Christian literature in the terms in which it was produced.

In the concluding chapter of his book, Gatch explores more fully the topic of 'man and his world' in Old English literature, drawing on a variety of source-texts in an effort to clarify the Anglo-Saxons' basic ideas pertaining to Providence, law, justice, the structure of the cosmos, and the bonds of loyalty – bonds thought to be equally essential to human society and the divine order. The texts he singles out for discussion include not just familiar ones like *The Wanderer*, *The Dream of the Rood*, and *The Battle of Maldon*, but also little-known works such as the preface to King Alfred's translation of Boethius's *De Consolatio philosophiae*. Another neglected text to which Gatch directs attention is archbishop Wulfstan's eleventh-century prose treatise *The Institutes of Polity*, a compendium of reflections on secular and canon law. The effect of these choices is to open up a wide perspective as to what constitutes 'Old English literature'. Moreover, through an Appendix that features 'some notes on Anglo-Saxon art and architecture' (pp. 151–67), Gatch reinforces the arguments presented elsewhere in his book through reference to elaborate late tenth-century manuscript illuminations of the Winchester school, as well as to archaeological investigations at Canterbury and Winchester that had revealed the remains of impressive stone churches, as opposed to the wooden buildings that had formerly been associated with the Anglo-Saxons. In sum, Gatch makes such a clean break with prior assumptions having to do with the criticism of Old English literature that a person comparing *Loyalties and Traditions* to Stopford Brooke's *English Literature from the Beginning to the Norman Conquest*, published seventy-five years before, would scarcely recognize that the same subject is being discussed.

The last book published in 1971–72 that calls for attention here is T.A. Shippey's radically innovative study *Old English Verse*.[75] At the time when this book came out, its author was a relatively unknown scholar in his late twenties. Born in Calcutta (present-day Kolkatta) in 1943, Shippey was educated, like J.R.R. Tolkien, at King Edward's School in Birmingham. After earning the MA degree at the University of Cambridge in 1968, he taught for a while at Oxford University and at the University of Birmingham before being appointed Chair of English Language and Medieval Literature at the University of Leeds. He later held the Walter J. Ong Chair of Humanities at St. Louis University, Missouri, a post from which he retired in 2008. He is widely known for his writings on J.R.R. Tolkien and fantasy literature as well as on Old English literature. Rather than, like Gatch, pursuing the interpretation of Old English verse through an understanding of its Latinate intellectual background, Shippey engages with the corpus of that verse as a meaningful and largely self-sufficient body of writings. Probing that verse for meanings that are not necessarily self-evident, interrogating it at point after point with questions that are either rhetorical or real, he asks how we as modern readers can respond to it in a manner consistent with how it was originally received. As New Critics had long maintained, any such search for meaning requires an alertness to paradox, verbal ambiguity, irony, narrative pacing, and authorial point of view, among other aspects of a work's verbal texture. Moreover, Shippey argues, the analysis of Old English verse requires a sensitivity to the poetics of composition in a social setting dramatically unlike what is taken for granted in the individualistic societies of today, for poetry then was largely a public,

---

[75] T.A. Shippey, *Old English Verse* (London: Hutchinson University Library, 1972). Six years later Shippey published a short book titled simply *Beowulf* (London: Edward Arnold, 1978). This is the most vigorous compact study of *Beowulf* of which I know. It provides a valuable complement to Shippey's discussion of Old English heroic poetry in chap. 2, 'The Argument of Courage: *Beowulf* and Other Heroic Poetry', of his *Old English Verse*.

anonymous, formulaic medium whereby a society defined the bedrock attitudes that allowed it to function with a minimum of friction and a maximum of communal assent.

Shippey's starting point is the seemingly unpromising observation that Old English verse is essentially dead, as far as modern readers are concerned. That is to say, there is no unbroken tradition linking that poetry to the English-language verse that most readers can identify with today. As moderns, therefore, we must approach that literature as if it were the product of an alien time and place, painstakingly reconstructing both its inner poetics and its intellectual content when neither one is self-evident. This could be called the opposite of belletrist appreciations of archaic literature on the grounds that it expresses a spirit 'like our own'.

The first comparison that Shippey makes linking the poetry of the Anglo-Saxons to that of other peoples of the world is arresting, for it has nothing directly to do with ancient Germania or the Latinate Middle Ages. Instead, he asks us to contemplate the performance of oral heroic poetry in Turkmenistan, as witnessed by a nineteenth-century Hungarian traveller who was struck by 'the ardour of the singer and the enthusiasm of his youthful listeners'. These men, 'uttering deep groans, hurled their caps to the ground and dashed their hands in a passion through the curls of their hair'.[76] Shippey's aim in citing this passage is to bring home the point that the poetry of the Anglo-Saxons too, once had living audiences, even if those people are next to unknown to us today.

The subsequent thrust of Shippey's argument is to read Old English poems not as the discrete and self-contained products of an authorial elite, but rather as parts of 'one body' of verse, one that sometimes defies analysis in the vocabulary of modern criticism. The people who made up the audiences for that verse would have been familiar with its conventions, unlike readers of today, who can easily be misled by inappropriate expectations. As Shippey states at the end of his introductory chapter (p. 16):

> What I hope to avoid is the urge to make the unfamiliar conform to the accepted, to label genres and mark transitions. It is worth remembering that no Old English poem has a title in the manuscripts, and that many have only slight indications of where they begin and end. Nor are they arranged as we see them printed, half-line by half-line, but are written out simply as rhythmic prose. Indeed the terms 'prose' and 'poetry' are not Old English ones at all and in this case may not represent the most important distinction; 'song' and 'speech' might be better. It is one more reminder that since so many modern assumptions are wrong it will be as well, so far as one can, to do without them – to seek comparison as well as pursue analysis, and so to see not many individual parts but one body.

It is in this spirit of 'lightening ship', to recall Irving's characterization of his stripped-down method of approaching *Beowulf*, that Shippey then proceeds to analyse the whole body of Old English verse, starting from *Beowulf* and other heroic poetry and moving on to the so-called elegies, to considerations of language and style, to anonymous saints' lives and the saints' lives of Cynewulf, and to the biblical paraphrases of the Junius manuscript (Oxford, Bodleian Library MS Junius 11). The book concludes with discussion of certain verse productions of

---

[76] Shippey, *Old English Verse*, 10, with reference to Nora K. Chadwick and Victor Zhirmunsky, *Oral Epics of Central Asia* (Cambridge: Cambridge University Press, 1969). The main part of this latter book drew on volume 3 of the Chadwicks' major study *The Growth of Literature*.

the late Old English period, including the *Meters of Boethius*, the historical poems inset into the Anglo-Saxon Chronicle, and *The Battle of Maldon*.

A keyword in Shippey's analysis of these poems is 'traditional'. In his view, for example, the poems from the Exeter Book that are customarily discussed under the generic term 'elegy' all depend on an 'alternation of involvement and detachment, and share as a basic theme the ability of the mind to control itself and resist its surroundings'. It is for such a reason as this that we can speak of them as a group, Shippey argues, not on account of their conformity to some autonomous concept of genre. 'The group as a whole exemplifies the great strength of a traditional literature', he writes: namely, 'the ability to use common thoughts and images as a springboard, so that poets need only small additions to create great effects without baffling their audiences' (pp. 78–79). As for the 'one body' of Old English poetry, Shippey argues that its many constituent groups are linked to one another through a common formulaic language. 'Any piece of Old English verse', he argues, regardless of how we imagine it to have been composed, 'is liable to resemble others, those others themselves contain echoes from further away, and so on' (p. 95). Here he draws on research into living traditions of oral poetry so as to suggest that in such traditions, a basic conservative impulse coexists with a state of 'permanent flux': that is to say, all the poems in the tradition share certain verbal resemblances, and yet each song is an original, for 'no song is older than the day it is sung' (p. 89). He then asks to what extent such a model of composition as this is relevant to the Anglo-Saxon context. In the end, like Gatch, he is inclined to see the formulaic language of Old English verse as an inherent aspect of the tradition regardless of how a particular work might have been composed. As he writes at the end of the chapter titled 'Language and Style':

> Old English verse is strangely homogeneous over a long period; this inner consistency is the result of a mode of composition not present in the modern world, nor understood till recently. That mode is formulaic, expressing itself through pattern rather than through single examples, and it needs to be appraised in the same way. Central to all these points is the conviction that Old English poetry has an individual voice distinct from all others, ancient or modern, though, like the voice of any human being, it is capable of great variation while remaining recognisably 'the same'.

The chief payoff of this approach is that Shippey is able to show the existence of parallels knitting together poems that modern critics have often separated out from one another as belonging either in different historical periods or in distinct generic categories. His discussion of verbal and thematic connections between the 'elegies' of the Exeter Book and the 'wisdom poems' of that same compendium is a fruitful example of this approach (pp. 53–69).

Anyone who studies side by side the three books that have just been discussed – Greenfield's *Interpretation of Old English Poems*, Gatch's *Loyalties and Traditions*, and Shippey's *Old English Verse* – will gain much insight into the state of the art of Old English literary criticism at about the end of the third quarter of the twentieth century. None of these three books, in my opinion, could have been written before approximately this moment in the history of Old English scholarship. Although each study is unique in character and emphasis, the three authors share certain attitudes in common. Each author is deeply persuaded that Old English literature can 'speak' with eloquence – and sometimes, indeed, with wisdom – to readers of the present day, and so it matters greatly that this literature exists. Each of the three authors, likewise, is committed to analysing Old English literature in terms historically consistent with the culture that produced it. In addition, each is committed to the close reading of the actual words of that literature as a prerequisite to its valid interpretation, regardless of what other guides to its meaning may exist.

Each of these three books established a pattern for other critics to follow. Greenfield's study prepared the way for the rational explication of Old English verse with reference – though never with slavish obeisance – to emergent schools of criticism and theory. Gatch's study nourished what soon became a steady stream of criticism locating works of Old English literature, especially ones of relatively late date, within the world of medieval Christian education and learning. Shippey's book provided a model for critics striving to read Old English poems in period-specific, traditionary terms while liberating the criticism of that literature from the tyranny of false preconceptions as to its 'proper' style or generic characteristics. Taken together, these three studies indicate how thorough a transformation the criticism of Old English literature had undergone since the time of G.K. Anderson, let alone that of Stopford Brooke.

The year 1972 thus serves as an apt cut-off date for the present discussion of changing currents in the criticism of Old English literature during the main part of the twentieth century. The choice of that date is not arbitrary, for it was in the year 1972 that the annual interdisciplinary journal *Anglo-Saxon England* was founded, edited initially by Peter Clemoes (1920–96), who by then had succeeded Dorothy Whitelock as Elrington and Bosworth Professor of Anglo-Saxon at the University of Cambridge. To quote from the front matter of its inaugural issue, *Anglo-Saxon England* was designed to express 'the growing sense of community among scholars working in the various branches of Anglo-Saxon studies in many parts of the world'. This same inaugural notice registered the co-editors' conviction that the different disciplines subsumed in Anglo-Saxon studies 'aid each other and are but aspects of a common interest'.[77]

Since one of the tasks undertaken by the editors of the new journal was to include an annual bibliography of Anglo-Saxon studies at the back of each volume, the standard freestanding bibliography of Old English literary studies, namely the 1980 *Bibliography of Publications on Old English Literature* that was jointly prepared by Stanley B. Greenfield and Fred C. Robinson, extends to the year 1972 and not farther.[78] Moreover, the growing professionalism of Anglo-Saxon studies that is reflected in the founding of *Anglo-Saxon England* and the publication of the Greenfield–Robinson *Bibliography* can be observed in the concurrent efforts that were made by a consortium of scholars to organize an international society whose purpose would be to promote and coordinate research in all aspects of this field. This organization, the International Society of Anglo-Saxonists (ISAS), held its inaugural

---

[77] Quotation from the preface to the journal's initial volume (1972), p. ix. At the time of its founding, the journal had twelve co-editors drawn from six different countries of the world, each man an acknowledged expert in at least one branch of Anglo-Saxon studies. It will not do to dwell on the apostolic overtones of this arrangement, as these were probably unconscious. The fact that all thirteen of the original editors were men is more likely to be noticed today than in 1972, when women played a less prominent role in academia across the board.

[78] Stanley B. Greenfield and Fred C. Robinson, *A Bibliography of Publications on Old English Literature to the End of 1972* (Toronto: University of Toronto Press, 1980). The authors interpret 'literature' in a broad sense so as to include a number of studies in related fields.

conference in Belgium in 1983. Since then ISAS has sponsored a conference every other year in one or another part of the world. Each has featured a certain number of presentations relating to the interpretation of Old English literature, and some of these papers have subsequently been published in *Anglo-Saxon England*. In addition, each conference held since 2001 has been the basis of a volume of critical essays sponsored by ISAS and published by ACMRS in the series 'Essays in Anglo-Saxon Studies'.

Where, then, did the criticism of Old English literature stand by the end of the third quarter of the twentieth century?

'Well situated at last', a dispassionate observer might have said. 'In a creative ferment', an optimist might have ventured. 'In a fix', I hear someone else saying. Certainly it is true that many useless assumptions had by then been discarded. It was seldom now that one heard any one speak of the essential paganism of *The Seafarer*, or of Grendel as an embodiment of the wintry North Sea, or of the goddess Wyrd in her struggles against the Christian God. But it is also true that this was a time of polemical differences among the experts. To one side, committed oral-formulaicists were ignoring practically all that the Robertsonians had to say, while in the next room, hard-core Robertsonians were discounting practically anything anyone else might have to say. While scholars of a New Critical persuasion were looking at the text, the whole text, and nothing but the text, source hunters were tracking down Latinate models for Old English texts with such assiduity as to leave no time for anything else. Meanwhile many good scholars continued to go about their business, oblivious to these divisions and generally grateful to be so; while hulking over the horizon, peering with a jaundiced eye over fiefs that it knew it would soon possess, was the postmodern giant named Theory.

Some people might think of a situation as confused as this as disconcerting. As for myself, I found it invigorating, back then; and I think of myself as having been fortunate, speaking now with over forty years' hindsight, to have been able to launch the coracle of my own professional career onto the deeps of English studies in a year – the same year 1972, by happenstance – when all these storms were blowing up in the Old English sector. It has made for a serious learning experience over the years, as many other persons of my generation will affirm.

The subsequent chapters of this book will suggest some ways in which others can participate in a similar learning experience by studying select examples of criticism published during recent decades. The point of this review, it should be understood, is not to encourage readers to reiterate the same discoveries and repeat the same mistakes of the scholars of an earlier generation. Rather, it is to help them to be well situated to make valuable original contributions to Old English literary studies in the years ahead, wherever the path may lead.

For Further Reading

Calder, Daniel G. 1982. 'Histories and Surveys of Old English Literature: A Chronological Review'. *ASE* 10: 201–44.

Jones, Chris. 2011. '"Birthplace for the Poetry of the Sea-Ruling Nation": Stopford Brooke and Old English'. In *The Sea and Englishness in the Middle Ages: Maritime Narratives, Identity and Culture*, ed. Sebastian I. Sobecki, 179–94. Cambridge: D.S. Brewer.

Liuzza, Roy Michael. 1994. 'The Return of the Repressed: Old and New Theories in Old English Literary Criticism'. In *Readings: Shorter Poems*, 103–47.

Shippey, T.A., and Andreas Haarder, eds. *Beowulf: The Critical Heritage*. London: Routledge, 1998.

Part II
Anglo-Saxon Lore and Learning

2

Literacy and Latinity

Responses to the question of how the Anglo-Latin literature that dates from the pre-Conquest period relates to the vernacular literature of that same era have changed during the past half-century or so, doing so in a manner that involves a significant shift of perspective. The result of that process of evolution is that rather than taking up a separate place on the periphery of the field, Anglo-Latin studies now occupy a position near to its centre, often pursued in conjunction with the study of Old English texts.

During this same time, critics of Old English literature have largely turned away from preoccupations with the Germanic origins of the poetry so as to concentrate on both prose and verse texts as products of the monastic culture of their time. This is so not just with respect to the labours and the material productions of scribes, but also, to a significant extent, as regards the intellectual purposes of these works. Certain scholarly research has been directed to ascertaining the core curriculum in monastic schools, where formal learning took place; other research has explored the reciprocal influences of oral and literate modes of thought among members of the Anglo-Saxon communities where texts were produced and preserved. Questions as to the holdings of Anglo-Saxon libraries, the circulation of books as part of a system of social and intellectual exchange, the relation of written texts to liturgical practices, and related matters, including the role of high-ranking members of the laity in textual production, are asked with greater frequency and urgency than in the past, and the answers to these questions are having an impact on critical approaches to the literature.

While it was commonplace fifty years ago for critics to approach at least some Old English literary works (those composed in verse, in particular) as if they were products of a milieu only superficially influenced by Christianity – or, alternatively, to view them as autonomous expressions of one or another creative impulse – today those same works are likely to be seen as implicated in a system of literacy and learning whose dominant elements were Latin letters and orthodox Christian belief. Needless to say, not everyone adopts such a point of view with the same assumptions or conviction,

Old English Literature: A Guide to Criticism with Selected Readings, First Edition. John D. Niles.
© 2016 John D. Niles. Published 2016 by John Wiley & Sons, Ltd.

while open-minded critics have always accepted that each and every literary work asks to be approached in its own terms, independent of totalizing generalizations.

These matters, together with some related achievements and controversies, will be taken up in the present chapter. A concern with literacy and learning will extend into the following chapter, as well, which deals with the status of texts as such and with the transformations that occurred when elements of the Latinate culture of early England were introduced into the vernacular.

Anglo-Latin Literature: Background or Mainstream?

A change of attitude towards the place of Anglo-Latin literature in Old English literary studies can be discerned when one compares Stanley B. Greenfield's 1965 book *A Critical History of Old English Literature* with the revised version of that book that came out in 1986 under the title *A New Critical History of Old English Literature*, co-authored by Stanley B. Greenfield and Daniel G. Calder.[1] The original version of the book includes an initial chapter by Greenfield on Anglo-Latin prose. This sets the stage for the rest of the book, in which Greenfield approaches Old English literature for the most part as a self-contained subject for research and criticism. In the thoroughly revised, co-authored 1986 version of the book, this initial chapter is replaced by a longer and more wide-ranging one, written for the occasion by Michael Lapidge, titled 'The Anglo-Latin Background'. While acknowledging this new chapter's condensed nature, Greenfield and Calder speak of it as 'the only complete history of Anglo-Latin literature' then in existence.[2] As for Lapidge himself, he gives the following justification for his chapter (pp. 5–6):

> Any literate person in the Anglo-Saxon period would have been trained by the Church, either in a monastery, cathedral, lesser canonry, or small minster. If we are properly to understand Old English literature, we must know something of the circumstances and context in which it was composed; in short, we must study the Anglo-Saxon church. In Anglo-Saxon times, the language of Christianity was Latin. [...] Learning to read and write necessarily implied the study of Latin, and a critical examination of Old English literature should best begin with some reflections on the workings of the Anglo-Saxon school.

Writing in 1965, Greenfield had addressed Anglo-Latin prose alone, confining that discussion to a separate intellectual compartment, as it were. By way of contrast, writing about two decades later, Lapidge (encouraged by Greenfield and Calder) folds the study of all Anglo-Latin writings, whether poetry or prose, into a consideration of the Anglo-Saxon church and its

---

[1]   Stanley B. Greenfield, *A Critical History of Old English Literature* (New York: New York University Press, 1965); Greenfield and Daniel G. Calder, *A New Critical History of Old English Literature* (New York: New York University Press, 1986). I refer to this latter book as 'Greenfield & Calder'.

[2]   Greenfield & Calder, p. 4 n. 3. Although Whitney F. Bolton had previously published *A History of Anglo-Latin Literature*, vol. 1: *597–740* (Princeton: Princeton University Press, 1967), the projected second volume of this work never appeared.

system of education, arguing that an understanding of these subjects is a prerequisite for the critical understanding of the whole body of literature produced during this period.

This is a claim that Lapidge has since supported through a battery of publications that surely represents the most significant body of scholarship produced by an Anglo-Saxonist of his generation. Born in 1942, Lapidge studied at the University of Calgary and the University of Alberta before receiving the PhD in 1971 from the Centre for Medieval Studies at the University of Toronto. He subsequently held the positions of Lecturer and then Reader in the Department of Anglo-Saxon, Norse and Celtic at the University of Cambridge, and in 1991 he was appointed the Elrington and Bosworth Professor of Anglo-Saxon at Cambridge. He held this chair until 1998, thereafter serving on the faculty at the University of Notre Dame until his retirement in 2004. As the author or editor of more than forty books on medieval Latin literature, medieval palaeography, textual criticism, and Anglo-Saxon literature composed in either Latin or the vernacular, the value of his contributions to the study of the literary culture of the early Middle Ages can scarcely be exaggerated.

In the chapter he wrote for *A New Critical History of Old English Literature*, Lapidge first offers a succinct account of the system of monastic education with attention to the early medieval school curriculum. He then summarizes the achievements of a number of authors who were products of this system and whose chief language of literacy was therefore Latin, although they were native speakers of English. Most are known by name. A selective list of the most important of these authors is suggestive of the size of this literature at a glance:[3]

- Aldhelm (d. 709 or 710), a prodigious man of letters who became successively abbot of Malmesbury and then bishop of Sherbourne, in the kingdom of Wessex;
- Bede (ca. 623–735), a member of the linked monastic communities of Wearmouth and Jarrow in Northumbria, a towering figure in early Anglo-Saxon letters about whom more will be said in due course;
- Boniface (ca. 675–754), best known for his missionary work on the Continent, who authored a Latin grammar, a number of letters that survive, and a collection of metrical *enigmata*;
- Alcuin (ca. 735–804), a native of York who in 781 or 782 left Britain so as to become master of Charlemagne's palace school at Aachen and who authored a large body of writings including some distinguished verse;
- Asser (d. 908–9), a Welsh-speaking priest active at the court of King Alfred the Great and the author of a noteworthy biography of that king;[4]
- Æthelwold (d. 984), the leading scholar and teacher of his day, who together with Dunstan was a key sponsor of the Benedictine Revival of the later tenth century;

---

[3] For a more complete inventory of the Anglo-Latin literature of the Anglo-Saxon period see Joseph P. McGowan, 'An Introduction to the Corpus of Anglo-Latin Literature', in Pulsiano & Treharne, 11–49. Since Lapidge omits mention of Asser (doubtless because discussion of Asser is folded into chap. 2 of Greenfield & Calder, 'The Alfredian Translations and Related Ninth-Century Texts'), I have added Asser's name to the list.

[4] Note the helpful compendium *Alfred the Great: Asser's Life of King Alfred and Other Contemporary Sources*, trans. with an introduction and notes by Simon Keynes and Michael Lapidge (Harmondsworth: Penguin, 1983).

- Æthelweard (d. ca. 998), an Anglo-Saxon ealdorman (a layman, remarkably), who was Ælfric's chief patron and whose *Chronicon*, though scarcely a model of good Latinity, merits attention as a Latin paraphrase of a now-lost version of the Anglo-Saxon Chronicle;
- Ælfric (ca. 950–ca. 1010), monk at Cerne Abbas in Wessex and later abbot of Eynsham, a prolific homilist, hagiographer, and pedagogue and another towering figure about whom more will be said later; and
- Byrhtferth (ca. 970–ca. 1020), a monk at Ramsey in East Anglia, who wrote two saints' lives and is best known for the ambitious scientific compendium known as his *Enchiridion*, or Handbook.

After discussing these authors plus a number of additional authors and works, Lapidge remarks that certain of them were among 'the most articulate and learned men of Europe' in their day. These men 'and the scholarly tradition which trained them', he remarks, deserve attention 'not only as background for Old English literature, but also for the interest they have in their own right' (p. 32).

Significantly, although the authors just enumerated may be remembered today chiefly for their writings in prose, a number of them composed verse as well. Aldhelm, Bede, and Alcuin stand out in this regard. In addition, certain of these authors appear to have been equally at ease whether writing in Latin or the vernacular. Ælfric, Æthelwold, and Byrhtferth are examples. Indeed, Ælfric was not only a superb Latinist; he was also the most productive writer of Old English texts of whom we know, and an estimated ten per cent of all extant Old English writings can be attributed to him alone. By ignoring the boundary separating verse from prose, as well as by taking note of the range of writings produced by bilingual authors,[5] Lapidge lays the foundations of an integrated history of Anglo-Saxon literature.

The term 'background' that figures in the title of Lapidge's contribution to Greenfield and Calder's *New Critical History* seems to have sat uneasily with that author, for when he included a revised and updated version of this chapter in a volume of his collected essays that appeared in 1996, he changed its title from 'The Anglo-Latin Background' to 'Anglo-Latin Literature'.[6] The change signposts an ongoing shift in how Anglo-Latin studies have been perceived in relation to the vernacular literature of the period. In a different study included in that same essay collection, 'Schools, Learning and Literature in Tenth-Century England', Lapidge makes explicit a mode of thought that had perhaps been implicit in his career from the start. 'We should always remember that works in Latin and the vernacular were copied together in Anglo-Saxon scriptoria, and were arguably composed together in Anglo-Saxon schools', he writes. '*What is needed, therefore, is an integrated literary history which treats Latin and vernacular productions together as two facets of the one culture, not as isolated phenomena*' (my emphasis).[7]

---

5 Since Ælfric's accomplishments as a writer of English prose are reviewed in a different chapter of Greenfield & Calder (chap. 3, on 'Ælfric, Wulfstan, and Other Late Prose'), Lapidge omits discussion of them here.

6 Michael Lapidge, *Anglo-Latin Literature 600–899* (London: Hambledon Press, 1996), 1–36.

7 Michael Lapidge, 'Schools, Learning and Literature in Tenth-Century England', in *Il secolo di ferro: mito e realta del secolo X*, Settimane de studio del centro italiano di studi sull'alto medioevo 38 (Spoleto, 1991), 951–1005, repr. in his *Anglo-Latin Literature 900–1066*, 1: 1–48 (quotation from p. 2, n. 2 of the reprinted essay).

This is a revolutionary call, even if it is only presented via a footnote in an article that has had only limited circulation. Whether such an integrated literary history of the Anglo-Saxon period as Lapidge foresees should in fact be attempted, however, remains an open question. One obstacle to such a programme is the difficulty of ascribing the extant records of Old English verse to particular authors, dates, and places of origin, given the anonymous nature of that verse as well as its highly traditional language and metre. A literary history of Old English poetry, at least, seems almost out of the question, for opinions are divided about even the century in which certain anonymous works (including *Beowulf*) were composed, if indeed it is meaningful to ascribe such works to individual authorship. Another factor to take into account is the critical consensus that the Old English verse tradition was a product of two cultures, one of which, perhaps somewhat simplistically, is usually characterized as Germanic, ancestral, and oral-traditional and the other as Latinate and Mediterranean. Not every critic would be content to locate a reading context for each and every Old English poem in an educated milieu alone, even if its manuscript record is obviously a scribal production. These are perhaps the main reasons why no such integrative literary history has yet been written. There is also the wrinkle that not all Anglo-Latin authors would have thought of themselves as being part of a distinctively 'Anglo-Saxon' tradition. This is true of the greatest of them, Bede, who, though an Englishman writing with Northumbrian regional sympathies, still doubtless thought of himself as addressing his works, all of which are composed in Latin, to a pan-European audience consisting of educated members of the clergy.

Perhaps more to the point is the practical and human question of whether such an integrated history as Lapidge envisions ever *can* be produced. The structure of present-day academic disciplines works against that prospect, seeing that most departments of English are divided off from departments of Classics and make little provision for Anglo-Latin studies in their curriculum. As for classicists, it is hard to find more than a few who have a lively interest in Anglo-Latin literature, while fewer still are competent in Old English. The result of these entrenched divisions – ones that are widespread though not universal, since a handful of integrated programmes of medieval studies exist – is that very few scholars are sufficiently capable in both languages, as well as being adept enough in the literary analysis of texts, to be in a position to communicate a detailed and penetrating understanding of the whole body of literature produced in England before the Conquest. Still, the ideal of an integrated history of the literature of Anglo-Saxon England remains an enticing one, especially as regards the later period (ca. 900–1066), when bilingual literacy in English and Latin became the norm and a number of translations and bilingual manuscripts were produced.

One prerequisite for the eventual achievement of such an integrated literary history is the publication of high-quality scholarly editions of the whole body of major writings of the Anglo-Saxon period, whether composed in Latin or the vernacular. Another desideratum is the publication of reliable translations of those works into current English, particularly for the benefit of non-specialists who deserve ready access to these texts. In an ideal world, each and every scholarly edition would include a translation of the edited text as part of the same volume, presented in a facing-page format for the sake of immediate comparisons. Since the world of publishing is governed by practicalities as well as principles, however, this format is only sometimes used.

While high-quality English-language editions of certain major works of both Anglo-Latin and Old English literature had been made available by the mid-twentieth century, much work of this kind still remained to be done. On the Old English side, as has been mentioned, the six-volume collective edition The Anglo-Saxon Poetic Records (ASPR) was completed by the year 1953. Many outstanding stand-alone editions of individual Old English poems or related groups of poems have since appeared in print. To cite just a few (limiting the examples to books published during the past forty-five years), these include Michael Swanton's 1970 edition of *The Dream of the Rood*, from the Vercelli Book of Old English prose and verse; Robert Farrell's 1974 edition of the poems *Daniel* and *Azarias*, from the Junius manuscript and the Exeter Book, respectively; Peter J. Lucas's 1977 edition of the Old English poetic paraphrase of the book of Exodus, from the Junius manuscript; Craig Williamson's 1977 edition of the Exeter Book riddles; A.N. Doane's 1978 edition of the poem *Genesis A*, from the Junius manuscript; Jane Roberts's 1979 edition of the Exeter Book poems *Guthlac A* and *Guthlac B*; Donald Scragg's 1981 edition of *The Battle of Maldon*, together with a major anthology that Scragg edited on the occasion of the 1991 millennium of that battle; Anne L. Klinck's 1992 edition *The Old English Elegies*, featuring generically related poems from the Exeter Book; Bernard J. Muir's two-volume 1994 edition of the whole contents of the Exeter Book; Mark Griffith's 1997 edition of the fragmentary poem *Judith*, from the *Beowulf* manuscript; and *Klaeber's Beowulf*, brought out by R.D. Fulk, Robert E. Bjork, and the present writer in 2008.[8]

Old English prose is another matter. The need for superior editions of vernacular prose works of the Anglo-Saxon period has not yet been addressed in a systematic fashion, even though individual exemplary editions have appeared. Among scriptural texts, these include R.M. Liuzza's two-volume edition of the Gospels in Old English (1994–2000) and volume 1 of Richard Marsden's projected two-volume edition of the Old English Heptateuch.[9] Two exemplary editions of Old English homilies have been produced in recent decades, namely Malcolm Godden and Peter Clemoes's edition of Ælfric's two series of Catholic Homilies – a monumental contribution to the field – and D.G. Scragg's edition of the anonymous Vercelli homilies.[10] Among the texts loosely called Alfredian, Janet Bately's

---

[8] See respectively *The Dream of the Rood*, ed. Michael Swanton (Manchester: Manchester University Press, 1970), 2nd edn, 1987; *Daniel and Azarius*, ed. R.T. Farrell (London: Methuen, 1974); *Exodus*, ed. Peter J. Lucas (London: Methuen, 1977), 2nd edn 1994; *The Old English Riddles of the Exeter Book*, ed. Craig Williamson (Chapel Hill: University of North Carolina Press, 1977); *Genesis A: A New Edition*, ed. A.N. Doane (Madison: University of Wisconsin Press, 1978, 2nd edn 2013); *The Guthlac Poems of the Exeter Book*, ed. Jane Roberts (Oxford: Clarendon Press, 1979); *The Battle of Maldon*, ed. D.G. Scragg (Manchester: Manchester University Press, 1981), together with *The Battle of Maldon* AD *991*, ed. Donald Scragg (Oxford: Blackwell, 1991); Klinck; Muir; *Judith*, ed. Mark Griffith (Exeter: University of Exeter Press, 1997); and *Klaeber's Beowulf*.

[9] *The Old English Version of the Gospels*, ed. R.M. Liuzza, 2 vols, EETS o.s. 304 and 314 (Oxford: Oxford University Press, 1994–2000); Richard Marsden, *The Old English Heptateuch and Ælfric's Libellus de Veteri Testamento et Novo*, vol. 1, EETS o.s. 330 (Oxford: Oxford University Press, 2008).

[10] *Ælfric's Catholic Homilies: The Second Series, Text*, ed. Malcolm Godden, EETS s.s. 5 (London: Oxford University Press, 1979); *Ælfric's Catholic Homilies: The First Series, Text*, ed. Peter Clemoes, EETS s.s. 17 (Oxford: Oxford University Press, 1997); Malcolm Godden, *Ælfric's Catholic Homilies: Introduction, Commentary and Glossary*, EETS s.s. 18 (Oxford: Oxford University Press, 2000); *The Vercelli Homilies and Related Texts*, ed. D.G. Scragg, EETS o.s. 300 (Oxford: Oxford University Press, 1992).

1980 edition of the Old English translation of Orosius's history of the ancient world stands out as exemplary, as does Malcolm Godden and Susan Irvine's 2009 edition of the Old English translation of Boethius's *De consolatione philosophiae* (including both prose and verse versions).[11] Importantly, a major collective multi-volume edition of the numerous versions of the Anglo-Saxon Chronicle, under the general direction of David Dumville and Simon Keynes, has been under way since 1983; this will include some seventeen volumes when complete.[12] Among other important editions, Edward Pettit has prepared an invaluable (though hard to obtain) two-volume edition and translation of the 'Lacnunga' manuscript, a major collection of healing texts; while Andy Orchard's 1995 book *Pride and Prodigies: Studies in the Monsters of the Beowulf Manuscript* presents, with an informed commentary, texts and modern English translations of three prose works, two of which are written in the vernacular and are included, probably not just by chance, in the same manuscript in which *Beowulf* is preserved.[13] This too is just a partial list.

Much remains to be done before the whole corpus of Old English prose is made available in reliable, up-to-date scholarly editions accompanied by readable translations into modern English. To cite just one example, what are still today the standard editions of Ælfric's grammar-and-glossary, saints' lives, and pastoral letters – three important bodies of work by the greatest man of letters writing in England between Bede and the twelfth century – date from the years 1880, 1881–1900, and 1914, respectively.[14] Two of these are German-language editions produced at a time when virtually all medievalists were capable in that language, a situation that scarcely prevails today.

---

[11]   *The Old English Orosius*, ed. Janet M. Bately, EETS s.s. 6 (Oxford: Oxford University Press, 1980); *The Old English Boethius: An Edition of the Old English Versions of Boethius's De Consolatione Philosophiae*, ed. Malcolm Godden and Susan Irvine, 2 vols (Oxford: Oxford University Press, 2009). A streamlined version of this latter edition, with translation, is included in the Dumbarton Oaks Medieval Library series: *The Old English Boethius, with Verse Prologues and Epilogues associated with King Alfred*, ed. and trans. Susan Irvine and Malcolm Godden (Cambridge, MA: Harvard University Press, 2012).

[12]   *The Anglo-Saxon Chronicle: A Collaborative Edition*, gen. ed. David Dumville and Simon Keynes (Cambridge: D.S. Brewer, 1983–), 8 vols in print as of 2014. Those wishing to consult a modern English translation of the Chronicle have several options. One of these is *The Anglo-Saxon Chronicle*, trans. and ed. Michael Swanton (London: Dent, 1996), not transparent in its organization but with a helpful introduction, maps, genealogies, a bibliography, and an index of proper names. Another is *The Anglo-Saxon Chronicle*, trans. and ed. Dorothy Whitelock (London: Eyre & Spottiswoode, 1961), with introduction, genealogies, an index of proper names, and a clear parallel-text presentation. Much of this latter translation is incorporated into Whitelock's volume *English Historical Documents*, vol. 1: *c. 500–1042*, 2nd edn (London: Eyre Methuen, 1979).

[13]   *Anglo-Saxon Remedies, Charms, and Prayers from British Library MS Harley 585: The Lacnunga*, ed. Edward Pettit, 2 vols (Lewiston: E. Mellen Press, 2001); Andy Orchard, *Pride and Prodigies: Studies in the Monsters of the Beowulf Manuscript* (Cambridge: D.S. Brewer, 1995).

[14]   These are *Ælfrics Grammatik und Glossar*, ed. Julius Zupitza (Berlin: Weidmannsche Buchhandlung, 1880), an edition without introduction, notes, or glossary; *Ælfric's Lives of Saints*, ed. Walter W. Skeat, 2 vols, EETS o.s. 76, 82, 94, and 114 (London: Oxford University Press, 1881–1900); and *Die Hirtenbriefe Ælfrics in altenglischer und lateinischer Fassung*, ed. Bernhard Fehr (Hamburg: H. Grand, 1914).

One problematic aspect of the present somewhat disorderly array of scholarly editions of Old English prose is that there exists no agreement among the respective editors as to what standards to observe regarding the orthography, capitalization, and punctuation of Old English texts, as well as the use or avoidance of abbreviations. While the Old English texts that are featured in one edition may be presented in a semi-diplomatic fashion so as to retain a likeness of their appearance in the original manuscripts, the texts in another edition may be fully modernized except for retention of the special characters þ, ð, and æ. For experts in Old English philology, these matters may be inessential, since specialists will know how to read either diplomatic or modernized texts. For other readers, however, an edition that makes few gestures towards modernizing Old English texts may be the source of frustration as well as admiration. This is apt to be true, for example, of the Godden/Clemoes edition of Ælfric's Catholic Homilies, or (even more so) of the volumes included in the ongoing collective edition of the Anglo-Saxon Chronicle. Despite their manifest value for specialists, these volumes include no translations and make few concessions to non-specialists in their typographical setting of the texts.

As for Anglo-Latin literary texts, one of the great achievements of the past fifty years or so is that increasing numbers of excellent editions have been produced, including many that are amenable to use by specialists and non-specialists alike. An admired edition of Bede's *Historia ecclesiastica*, for example, was brought out by Bertram Colgrave and R.A.B. Mynors in 1969, with facing-page modern English translation. The inclusion of only minimal annotations in that single-volume publication is more than made up for by the abundance of other scholarly publications on Bede's masterwork, including an historical commentary by J.M. Wallace-Hadrill.[15] Previous to that time, Colgrave had produced a scholarly edition and translation of Felix of Croyland's Latin life of St Guthlac.[16] Anglo-Saxonists are indebted to Michael Lapidge for a series of volumes of Anglo-Latin texts that he has co-edited over the past thirty-five years. These include an edition of Aldhelm's prose works, co-edited by Michael W. Herren in 1979; a complementary edition of Aldhelm's poetry, co-edited by James L. Rosier in 1985; an edition of the life of Æthelwold by Wulfstan Cantor, co-edited by Michael Winterbottom in 1991; and, in 2012, an edition of the early lives of Dunstan, also co-edited by Winterbottom. Worth special note because of the linguistic difficulties of its bilingual text is an edition of Byrhtferth's *Enchiridion* that Peter S. Baker and Michael Lapidge brought out in 1995.[17] All these editions include facing-page modern English translations.

---

[15] *Bede's Ecclesiastical History of the English People*, ed. Bertram Colgrave and R.A.B. Mynors (Oxford: Clarendon Press, 1969); J.M. Wallace-Hadrill, *Bede's Ecclesiastical History of the English People: A Historical Commentary* (Oxford: Clarendon Press, 1988).

[16] *Felix's Life of Saint Guthlac*, ed. Bertram Colgrave (Cambridge: Cambridge University Press, 1956).

[17] *Aldhelm: The Prose Works*, ed. Michael Lapidge and Michael Herren (Cambridge: D.S. Brewer, 1979); *Aldhelm: The Poetic Works*, ed. Michael Lapidge and James L. Rosier (Cambridge: D.S. Brewer, 1985); *The Life of St Æthelwold*, ed. Michael Lapidge and Michael Winterbottom (Oxford: Clarendon Press, 1991); *The Early Lives of St Dunstan*, ed. Michael Winterbottom and Michael Lapidge (Oxford: Clarendon Press, 2012); *Byrhtferth's Enchiridion*, ed. Peter S. Baker and Michael Lapidge, EETS o.s. 177 (Oxford: Oxford University Press, 1995).

Leaving aside the task and challenge of editing, there is a place for criticism that approaches the literature of the Anglo-Saxons in an integrated fashion. Andy Orchard's book *Pride and Prodigies* sets a standard in this regard, for Orchard presents on an equal footing a pair of Old English texts telling of the exotic East, namely *The Wonders of the East* and *The Letter of Alexander to Aristotle*, and the text of a third work of a comparable kind that is composed in Latin, the *Liber monstrorum*. Orchard's book goes far to break down the binary divisions that have traditionally governed the field of Old English studies. In another study, 'Enigma Variations: The Anglo-Saxon Riddle-Tradition', Orchard showcases the value of reading the riddles of the Exeter Book in conjunction with Latin *enigmata* of the early Middle Ages, including Aldhelm's century of riddles. Orchard thus demonstrates what he terms 'the longevity and vigour of an Anglo-Saxon riddle-tradition that can be traced at home and abroad, in prose and in verse, in Latin and Old English, in written and oral forms, on secular and religious topics, in the classroom and the mead-hall, from the seventh century to the eleventh, which is to say throughout the entire period of Anglo-Saxon literature'.[18] Such an approach to the riddle collections of the early Middle Ages might profitably be extended to other genres as well, such as hagiography; for there is good reason to read insular saints' lives, too, in an integrated manner regardless of the language in which a particular example is composed.

Likewise exemplary for its integrated approach to Anglo-Saxon literary studies is Seth Lerer's 1991 book *Literacy and Power in Anglo-Saxon Literature*.[19] Lerer takes his reader on an adventurous journey that proceeds from Bede's *Historia ecclesastica*, to King Alfred's biographer the Welsh priest Asser, to three examples of anonymous Old English verse that were recorded close to the year 1000 (namely, certain riddles of the Exeter Book, the paraphrase of the book of Daniel from the Junius manuscript, and *Beowulf*). The common element in his discussion of these works is their allusion to some kind of strange or arresting script, whether this is runes (as in the riddles or in the stories from Bede or *Beowulf*), or the letters of a Latin book written out in beautiful characters (as in Asser's account of the young prince Alfred), or the mysterious 'writing on the wall' in the Old English poem *Daniel*. Drawing on the anthropological writings of Claude Lévi-Strauss and other specialists in the social functions of writing, as well as on a well-known critique of Lévi-Strauss by the French philosopher Jacques Derrida, Lerer draws attention to a 'cultural mythology of literacy' that permeates the Anglo-Saxon literary imagination. By treating these works as aspects of a single tradition, Lerer comes to terms with the collective mentality that underlies them, one that has to do with the authority that is often ascribed to script itself. Lerer could not well have developed his theme of 'the making of a literate imagination' (p. 195) without engaging with works composed both in Latin – the language of the 'fathers' – and English, the mother tongue.

---

[18] Andy Orchard, 'Enigma Variations: The Anglo-Saxon Riddle-Tradition', in *Latin Learning and English Lore: Studies in Anglo-Saxon Literature for Michael Lapidge*, ed. Katherine O'Brien O'Keeffe and Andy Orchard, 2 vols (Toronto: University of Toronto Press, 2005), vol. 1: 284–304 (at 299).

[19] Seth Lerer, *Literacy and Power in Anglo-Saxon Literature* (Lincoln: University of Nebraska Press, 1991).

Education in Two Languages

One topic of recent critical interest in Anglo-Saxon studies is the acquisition of literacy in the early medieval context; another is the relationship between Latin and Old English in the classrooms of the Anglo-Saxon period. Concentrating on the Latin tradition though with attention to the use of the vernacular, the medievalist Nicholas Orme provides an overview of Anglo-Saxon schooling in Chapter 2 of his 2006 book *Medieval Schools*. Tellingly, in the precursor of this book, his 1973 study *English Schools in the Middle Ages*, Orme offered virtually no discussion of England before the Conquest, though other scholars had previously touched at least lightly on this topic.[20] In *Medieval Schools*, Orme first reviews the process by which schools based on Roman models were established in Britain in conjunction with the establishment of monasteries with ties to Rome. He then traces the impact on English schooling of the disruptions of the first Viking Age, when monasticism in Britain was put under such strain as to come close to disappearing. Addressing the period from AD 800 to 1100, Orme traces a surge in the number of monastic and cathedral schools established during the second half of the tenth century, chiefly in the south of England, all of them organized along Benedictine lines. Only at this time, during the period of the Benedictine Reform and its aftermath, does literacy in English seem to have become at all common. Only starting at this time, as well, did substantial numbers of insular manuscripts composed in either English or Latin come to be written down.

The chief classroom texts by which Anglo-Saxon students learned the rudiments of *grammatica* included the *Ars minor* of Donatus and the two parts of Priscian's *Institutiones grammaticae*, in addition to treatises on grammar, metre, and rhetoric written by Isidore of Seville and, in the course of time, by the insular authors Bede, Aldhelm, and Ælfric, among others.[21] In a chapter on 'The World of Anglo-Saxon Learning' included in the second (2013) edition of *The Cambridge Companion to Old English Literature*, Patrizia Lendinara offers a concise overview of Anglo-Saxon schools and their curriculum.[22] The first (1991) edition of this anthology included no such chapter; and this change in the contents of the book reflects the editors' heightened sense of the bearing of the topic of education on the understanding of Anglo-Saxon literature. It seems that by 2013, the whole of this literature, whether composed in English or Latin, was understood to be indebted in one way or another to the large body of early medieval literature produced in Latin, even if the extent of this debt varies from work to work.

The effects of King Alfred's educational programme, which led the way to the tenth-century Benedictine Reform, receive close attention in Michael Lapidge's study 'Schools, Learning and Literature in Tenth-Century England' (cited near the start of this chapter). Lapidge emphasizes that the number of high-level schools in England was always few, while those that did exist were generally dependent on foreign-born scholars. Moreover, he notes that members of the laity, not just ecclesiastics, were involved in English schooling,

---

[20] Nicholas Orme, *Medieval Schools* (New Haven: Yale University Press, 2006); Orme, *English Schools in the Middle Ages* (London: Methuen, 1973).

[21] See on this topic Vivien Law, *Grammar and Grammarians in the Early Middle Ages* (London: Longman, 1997), a study on which Orme relies.

[22] Patrizia Lendinara, 'The World of Anglo-Saxon Learning', in Godden & Lapidge, 295–312.

whether as patrons of learning or as pupils themselves. Both here and elsewhere in his voluminous writings, Lapidge draws attention to the crucial role of verse, especially medieval Latin verse paraphrases of Scripture, in the training of students in *grammatica*. In Anglo-Saxon schools, this was a subject that encompassed much of what today would be called rhetoric.

Lapidge gives forthright credit to King Alfred the Great (r. 865–99) for his vision and energy in undertaking the restoration of learning in England after the ravages of the first Viking wars. He likewise calls attention to the role of King Athelstan (r. 924–39), King Alfred's grandson, as a collector and donor of books and as a patron of scholars from abroad. He sees both these kings as responsible for an unprecedented turn towards the use of English side by side with Latin in tenth-century schools. Of exceptional importance in this regard is the letter that King Alfred sent to the bishops of his realm to accompany copies of his vernacular translation of Gregory the Great's *Cura pastoralis* (or *Pastoral Care*).[23] In this epistle, which exemplifies a layman's use of the vernacular for important communications, the king first recalls a prior golden age of Latin learning in the realm. He then refers to the devastation caused by the Vikings as the reason for the decline of learning in the realm, and to conclude the letter he sets out a new programme for the restitution of literacy and learning. Famously, this programme was to feature the translation of a number of key works of Latin learning into English. Alfred also promoted the founding of schools where the leading young men of the realm would be taught the arts of literacy in English, with instruction in Latin to follow for those who chose to pursue a career in the church.

While many scholars have accepted at face value King Alfred's account of the decayed state of learning in England before he succeeded to the throne, the king's letter has also been subject to critique as an expression of propagandist tendencies on the part of the king and his immediate successors.[24] In a study published in 1986, Jennifer Morrish suggests that the reason why Alfred presented such an unrealistically bleak view of the state of Latin learning before the start of his reign was to underscore the need for reform while at the same time casting the king's personal leadership in a favourable light.[25] Morrish points out that, rather than being rhetorically naive, the king's letter draws on a number of commonplace rhetorical *topoi* such as the notion of a lost blessed age. As 'a mosaic of borrowings from written sources' (p. 91), the letter is prone to exaggeration in its account of the past.

While discussing the tenth-century revival of monasticism and schooling, Lapidge singles out the monastic community at Glastonbury, under the leadership of the remarkable spiritual leader Dunstan, as having laid the 'intellectual foundations of the Benedictine Reform' (p. 24). Mechthild Gretsch adapted that same phrase for use as the title of her 1999 book *The Intellectual Foundations of the English Benedictine Reform*, which focuses on the

---

[23] *King Alfred's West-Saxon Version of Gregory's Pastoral Care*, ed. Henry Sweet, EETS 45, 50 (London: Trübner, 1871). The text of the letter has often been reproduced, for example in Mitchell & Robinson, 212–15. For recent discussion see Nicole Discenza, 'The Persuasive Power of Alfredian Prose', in Johnson & Treharne, 122–35.

[24] See R.H.C. Davis, 'Alfred the Great: Propaganda and Truth', *History* 56 (1971): 169–82.

[25] Jennifer Morrish, 'King Alfred's Letter as a Source on Learning in England in the Ninth Century', in *Studies in Earlier Old English Prose*, ed. Paul E. Szarmach (Albany: State University of New York Press, 1986), 87–107.

community of scholars centred at the Old Minster at Winchester, the capital city of Wessex and of England.[26] Winchester was where both Dunstan and Æthelwold were chiefly educated and where Æthelwold subsequently served as bishop for over twenty years (963–84). Æthelwold founded a school at the Old Minster that became the leading one in the realm. By this time many aspects of life in a newly united England had taken a new turn, in keeping with an economic uplift that stimulated the building of towns, churches, monasteries, and cathedrals. It was at Winchester that the form of insular script known as insular square minuscule was developed, and this soon took on the status of a standard for vernacular writings. Use of this script, or variants of it, can sometimes be correlated with an author's use of the 'Winchester vocabulary', a set of lexical items favoured by writers who were either trained by Æthelwold or influenced by his writings.

The increasing use of English side by side with Latin in English schools of the late tenth century is the subject of D.A. Bullough's study 'The Educational Tradition in England from Alfred to Ælfric'.[27] Recent criticism, indebted to Bullough's research, has approached certain manuscripts dating from the second half of the tenth century as products of the bilingual textual communities that were flourishing in England at this time. One such manuscript is the Vercelli Book (also known as the Codex Vercellensis, now in northern Italy), which consists of a mix of Old English devotional prose and verse. Another is the Exeter Book (Exeter, Cathedral Library MS 3501), which consists almost wholly of Old English verse. While in former years the tendency was to read the Exeter Book as a compilation of poems, some of which were of early date, that happened to be preserved in a relatively late manuscript copy (one that can be dated on palaeographic grounds to ca. AD 975), critics are now less likely to speak with assurance about the dating of these poems, some of which may be contemporary with the manuscript itself.

Patrick Conner's 1993 study 'Source Studies, the Old English *Guthlac A* and the English Benedictine Reformation' is of interest for showing that at least one poem of the Exeter Book, *Guthlac A*, could not have been composed more than a very few years before the Exeter Book itself was written out.[28] Writing along comparable lines in her 2006 essay 'Architectural Metaphors and Christological Imagery in the Advent Lyrics', Mercedes Salvador sees the Advent Lyrics of the Exeter Book as expressly designed to further the

---

[26] Mechthild Gretsch, *The Intellectual Foundations of the English Benedictine Reform* (Cambridge: Cambridge University Press, 1999).

[27] D.A. Bullough, 'The Educational Tradition in England from Alfred to Ælfric: Teaching *utriusque linguae*', in *La scuola nell' occidente latino dell' alto medioevo*, Settimane di studio del centro italiano di studi sull' alto medioevo 19 (Spoleto, 1972), 453–94. Bullough's essay is reprinted in a slightly revised version, with updated references, in his essay collection *Carolingian Renewal: Sources and Heritage* (Manchester: Manchester University Press, 1991), 297–334. The phrase '*utriusque linguae*' used in the title of his article refers to pedagogy 'in either of two languages'. With reference to the classical world the phrase is used of Latin and Greek; here it refers to Latin and English.

[28] P.W. Conner, 'Source Studies, the Old English *Guthlac A* and the English Benedictine Reformation', *Revue Bénédictine* 103 (1993): 380–413. In his book *Anglo-Saxon Exeter: A Tenth-Century Cultural History* (Woodbridge: Boydell, 1993), Conner provides a wealth of information with a bearing on the historical and cultural context of the place where the Exeter Book is still preserved. No consensus, however, has emerged around his argument that the book itself originated at Exeter, since other points of origin are thought to be at least as likely.

intellectual programme of the Reform.[29] Likewise Brian O'Camb, in his 2009 essay 'Bishop Æthelwold and the Shaping of the Old English *Exeter Maxims*', detects instances of the 'Winchester vocabulary' in the *Exeter Maxims* while also relating certain themes of that work, ones that have to do with the proper training of the young, to the pedagogy of the Reform.[30] The possibility that the Exeter Book as a whole was meant for pedagogical use in the schools of the Reform has been raised by Seth Lerer, as well.[31]

Schooling of a different kind was available to persons who never walked in a cloister and never partook of a meal in a refectory. As the historian Patrick Wormald emphasized in his 1977 study 'The Uses of Literacy in Anglo-Saxon England and its Neighbours', 'a consistently powerful alternative educational tradition' to that of the church existed throughout the early Middle Ages.[32] This was the system of face-to-face interaction whereby respected members of society passed on their knowledge, skills, and wisdom to younger persons through personal tutoring or mentoring, or simply by affirming socially approved codes and standards through their spoken words and the force of personal example. Poetry composed on secular themes, like *Beowulf* or *The Battle of Maldon* – or hypothetical precursors of such poems as these in the Anglo-Saxon oral tradition – may have had a role in this process of instruction by exhibiting models of conduct to be emulated or shunned. The prevalence of education of this alternative kind goes far to account for the 'indifference or even hostility to literacy' that Wormald traces 'within classes of society which cherished other values' (p. 97). What we study when we study the system of formal schooling in early England is therefore only part of the story of Anglo-Saxon education in the full sense of that term.

The Student in the Classroom

The only solid evidence that comes down to us concerning the relations of teachers (*magistri*) and pupils (*pueri*) during the Anglo-Saxon period comes from texts, authored by members of the clergy, that were themselves intended for use in monastic or cathedral schools. The content of those works is thus subject to a certain ideological inflection.

The leading example of such a work is Ælfric's Latin *Colloquy*, which apparently dates from the time when Ælfric was a monk and schoolmaster at Cerne Abbas in Wessex (ca. 987–1005).[33]

---

[29] Mercedes Salvador, 'Architectural Metaphors and Christological Imagery in the Advent Lyrics: Benedictine Propaganda in the Exeter Book?', in *Conversion and Colonization in Anglo-Saxon England*, ed. Catherine E. Karkov and Nicholas Howe (Tempe, AZ: ACMRS, 2006), 169–211.

[30] Brian O'Camb, 'Bishop Æthelwold and the Shaping of the Old English *Exeter Maxims*', *ES* 90 (2009): 253–73.

[31] Lerer develops this argument in chap. 3, 'The Riddle and the Book', of his book *Literacy and Power*.

[32] C.P. Wormald, 'The Uses of Literacy in Anglo-Saxon England and its Neighbours', *Transactions of the Royal Historical Society*, 5th series, 27 (1977): 95–114 (at 98).

[33] *Ælfric's Colloquy*, ed. G.N. Garmonsway, 2nd edn (Exeter: University of Exeter Press, 1978); first published 1939. An Old English version of the Colloquy, somewhat factitious in nature but still a good teaching tool for the modern student, is included in Mitchell & Robinson, 190–97. Ælfric's range of pedagogical writings is surveyed by Thomas N. Hall, 'Ælfric as Pedagogue', in Magennis & Swan, 193–216.

The point of the *Colloquy* is to provide the students of his day with practice in speaking Latin while also introducing them, semantic field by semantic field, to Latinate vocabulary that would anchor the world of Latin letters to the real world in which they lived. Featuring imagined speakers from many walks of life, Ælfric's *Colloquy* has attracted attention for its evocations of the lifeways and sentiments of ordinary people – a fisherman, a hunter, a blacksmith, a ploughman, and so forth – something rarely encountered in the literature of the early Middle Ages.

The high quality of the *Colloquy* as a literary production has led to its being praised for its 'fine organization and structure' and its animated use of the dialogue form.[34] An additional point of interest, as Earl R. Anderson has argued in his 1974 article 'Social Idealism in Ælfric's *Colloquy*',[35] is that the *Colloquy* has a consistent ideological content, one that Anderson situates squarely within the framework of Benedictine monasticism, an institution for which Ælfric was the leading English spokesman in his time. The theme of the 'gifts of men' that Anderson traces in the *Colloquy* is a primary element of medieval social thought, as is the concept of the 'three estates' of workers, clergymen, and the warrior aristocracy (the *laboratores*, *oratores*, and *bellatores*, respectively), each with its own contribution to make to the workings of a stable and harmonious society. It comes as no surprise that, while presenting this system of thought, Ælfric prioritizes the contribution made to society by monks, whose prayers had the great function of imploring the deity for mercy for all the brutish deeds of humankind. This is a task, some might say, for which the need has not diminished over time, though the number of persons engaged in it has. In Anderson's view, all the crafts and trades to which Ælfric refers would have been practised on a monastic estate, for like a Roman villa, a Benedictine monastery functioned largely like a self-contained society in miniature. The model of social harmony that Ælfric holds out as an ideal – that of mutual support among members of a Christian fraternity – would have been valued within the microcosm of the monastery while also applying to society at large.

A more cynical view of what Anderson calls the 'social idealism' of Ælfric's *Colloquy* is taken by John Ruffing in his 1994 study 'The Labor Structure of Ælfric's *Colloquy*'.[36] Ruffing sees the roles of the labourers who figure in the *Colloquy* as 'negotiated in a prisonhouse of language overseen by the monastic master' (p. 68). This master is presumably either the novice monk, learning the language by which in future he will be able to control the lay workers whose labour was essential to the running of the estate, or the abbot himself. Either of these figures would benefit from the monastic interpretation of Scripture ('of which the monks are conveniently sole proprietors', p. 66), so as to keep under control 'the entire condition of food production, especially the crucial surplus that feeds non-producers like kings and monks' (p. 67). Although Ruffing does not use the terms 'Marxist' or 'post-Marxist' when characterizing his approach, what he offers is a decidedly late-twentieth-century, secularist, class-conscious perspective on the literature of the Benedictine Reform.

---

[34]   Greenfield & Calder, 86.

[35]   Earl R. Anderson, 'Social Idealism in Ælfric's *Colloquy*', *ASE* 3 (1974): 153–62, repr. in Liuzza, ·204–14.

[36]   John Ruffing, 'The Labor Structure of *Ælfric's Colloquy*', in *The Work of Work: Servitude, Slavery, and Labor in Medieval England,* ed. Allen J. Frantzen and Douglas Moffat (Glasgow: Cruithne Press, 1994), 55–70.

Of related interest is the set of Latin colloquies subsequently written by Ælfric Bata, a monk who at one point identifies himself as having been a student of Ælfric of Eynsham. Whether or not this claim can be taken at its face value, Ælfric Bata's ambitions in this genre exceeded those of his predecessor, for he wrote no fewer than four dozen colloquies in addition to spending much energy augmenting the one colloquy written by Ælfric himself.[37] Orme identifies this set of colloquies as 'most helpful [...] for reconstructing the work of a late Anglo-Saxon school' (*Medieval Schools*, 44), for Bata provides information that is otherwise unavailable about such matters as students' age, church duties, meals, bathing, discipline, and hours of prayer or study or sleep. Moreover, the author enters into the spirit of schoolboy culture, as Orme notes (p. 46), for his fictive boys 'quarrel and hurl scatological insults – "Goat shit!" "Cow dung!" "Pig turd!"' These colloquies thus promote mastery of a semantic field suitable for use when the abbot is out of hearing. This style of comic verbal aggression is guaranteed to capture the interest of readers – whether medieval or modern – sooner than the serious scriptural and moral lessons that these same dialogues express. Unlike Ælfric of Eynsham, who was a pillar of both orthodoxy and sobriety, Ælfric Bata knew how to get to the heart of the student's worldview: 'Bonam ceruisam habemus, Deo gratias!' ('Thank God we have good beer!').[38]

The theme of pain and corporal punishment that is a recurrent element in the dialogues of Ælfric Bata is of lively interest to contemporary critics of Old English literature. It receives attention in Irina Dumitrescu's 2009 article 'The Grammar of Pain in Ælfric Bata's Colloquies',[39] a study that centres on 'the repeated staging of conflict and violence' in these dialogues, particularly as regards the representation of boys being beaten or whipped, sometimes to a hyperbolic extreme. An instance is the following exchange from colloquy no. 28, in which a *magister* is imagined to be punishing a *puer* for the near-capital offence of having stolen some apples. The master speaks first to two different boys who have been given the task of beating the culprit's rear:[40]

'Percute, tu stulte, melius! Deridet uerbera uestra, et ea non sentit omnino.'
'Amodo, pater, cessare ab hac fraude uolo, pro qua hęc patior. Satis sum modo flagellatus et punitus hac uice. Fac in me aliquam benignitatem et indulgentiam! Iam moriturus sum.'
'Non es mortuus adhuc, sed uiuis.'

Translated into modern English, what this means is:

'Hit harder, you fool! He's making fun of your blows. He doesn't feel them at all.'
'Father, from this moment on I'll stop the cheating I'm suffering for. I've been beaten and punished enough this time. Show me some kindness and forbearance! I'm about to die!'
'But you're not dead yet – you're still breathing.'

---

[37] On Ælfric's augmentation of this earlier work see David W. Porter, 'Ælfric's *Colloquy* and Ælfric Bata', *Neoph* 80 (1996): 639–60.

[38] *Anglo-Saxon Conversations: The Colloquies of Ælfric Bata*, ed. Scott Gwara and trans. David W. Porter (Woodbridge: Boydell Press, 1997), 180–81.

[39] Irina Dumitrescu, 'The Grammar of Pain in Ælfric Bata's Colloquies', *Forum for Modern Language Studies* 45 (2009): 239–53.

[40] Gwara and Porter, *Anglo-Saxon Conversations*, 166–67, with both the translation and the typography slightly adapted.

Whether a scene like this is intended to be comic or not (and personally I think it was, like much else in these dialogues), it reminds us that the *virga* or 'rod' was yet another element in the ideology of the Benedictine Rule. So too were the fear and pain that were associated with that slender pedagogical instrument, with both these emotions seen as aspects of the order of the world.

When viewing such a passage as the foregoing one from a current moral perspective, it is worth keeping in mind that not all the oblates who experienced the rigours of the medieval schoolroom were necessarily scarred for the rest of their lives as a result. Alcuin, for example, while residing at Charlemagne's royal court in Francia, wrote in a tone of love and longing of his simpler life in former years as a member of the monastic community at York, where he was trained as a boy and where he probably continued to live until he was over fifty:[41]

> O mea cella, mihi habitatio dulcis, amata,
>   Semper in aeternum, o mea cella, vale. [...]
> In te personuit quondam vox alma magistri,
>   Quae sacro sophiae tradidit ore libros.

(O my cell, a dwelling sweet to me, beloved, / Always and forever, O my cell, hail and farewell. / [...] In you once echoed a teacher's kindly voice / Which with sacred lips taught books of wisdom.)

Unforgettable, as well, are the terms in which Alcuin's predecessor the Venerable Bede looked back on his long life within his monastic precinct at Jarrow as he wrote the last pages of his great work the *Historia ecclesiastica*, at a time when his life was drawing towards its close:[42]

> I was born on the lands of this monastery, and on reaching seven years of age, I was entrusted by my family first to the most reverend Abbot Benedict and later to Abbot Ceolfrith for my education. I have spent all the remainder of my life in this monastery and devoted myself entirely to the study of the Scriptures. And while I have observed the regular discipline and sung the choir offices daily in church, my chief delight has always been in study, teaching, and writing.

Bede speaks without a trace of regret about his way of life after he became an oblate. Of course, Alcuin and Bede were two of the success stories of the medieval system of English schooling; we do not hear from the others.

The Venerable Bede

A chapter on Anglo-Saxon literacy and learning would not be complete without attention to Bede and his writings, given the very large body of scholarship devoted both to him and to the period of early Anglo-Saxon history that, in recognition of his eminence, is commonly

---

[41] Alcuin's poem *O mea cella*, lines 1–2 and 13–14, as quoted and translated by Carole E. Newlands, 'Alcuin's Poem of Exile: *O Mea Cella*', *Mediaevalia* 11 (1989 for 1985): 19–45 (at 21–22). Newlands argues persuasively that, although meant to have universal significance, this poem does indeed look retrospectively back to its author's former home at York.

[42] Bede, autobiographical note appended to *Historia ecclesiastica* 5: 24; translation from *Bede: Ecclesiastical History of the English People*, trans. Leo Sherley-Price, revised by R.E. Latham, revised edn (London: Penguin, 1990), 329.

known as 'the age of Bede'. Along with his later counterpart Ælfric of Eynsham, Bede was one of the most productive authors of the English Middle Ages. Unlike Ælfric, who wrote with equal facility in either Latin or English at a time when literacy in general (including bilingual literacy) was increasingly widespread, Bede is the leading representative of that phase of Christianity when intense missionary work was followed by the consolidation of Latin Christian learning among a relatively small elite living in those special sites, including Bede's Jarrow, where Roman-style monasticism was established. Bede penned all that he wrote in Latin, at least as far as can be known from those works of his that survive.[43]

One reason for Bede's pre-eminent status in the modern critical literature is that he wrote eloquently and authoritatively on such a number of topics. Another is that he wrote in a plurality of literary modes, from prose treatises to verse hymns. Although best known as 'Bede the historian', he has been celebrated by one modern admirer as 'Bede the scholar', by another as 'Bede the educator', and by another as 'Bede the poet'; while I have myself called attention to his exceptional abilities as 'Bede the storyteller', in which capacity he could be thought to eclipse any other figure from the Anglo-Saxon period with the sole exception of the *Beowulf* poet.[44] Other scholars as well, too many to mention, have elucidated Bede's work as a poet, as a hagiographer, as a metrist, as a guide to the schemes and tropes of rhetoric, and as a scientist with special competence in temporal reckoning. And then there is 'Bede the exegete', the most prolific author of them all.[45]

To take in the full scope of Bede's writings, together with the modern critical commentary on them, is a daunting task for anyone to undertake. Fortunately two books have recently appeared in print, each of which provides an entry point to relevant scholarship. One of these, George Hardin Brown's *A Companion to Bede*, reviews Bede's corpus of writings from

---

[43] Bede's authorship of the short poem known as 'Bede's Death Song' is open to question, as is the story from the same source – a letter by a monk named Cuthbert that went into circulation soon after Bede's death – that in the last days and hours of his life Bede was occupied translating into English the first part of the Gospel of John (for which story see *Bede: Ecclesiastical History*, trans. Sherley-Price, 355–60). Both the poem and the story can be suspected of pertaining to the apocryphal Bede rather than to the historical one, though many critics have accepted both sources as evidence of Bede's facility in written English. Howell D. Chickering, Jr, 'Some Contexts for Bede's *Death-Song*', *PMLA* 91 (1976): 91–100, considers the attribution of this poem to Bede himself 'questionable' but still finds Cuthbert's letter worth attention as 'a remarkable human document' (p. 91).

[44] Note respectively Paul Meyvaert, 'Bede the Scholar', in *Famulus Christi: Essays in Commemoration of the Thirteenth Centenary of the Birth of the Venerable Bede*, ed. Gerald Bonner (London: SPCK, 1976), 40–69; George Hardin Brown, 'Bede the Educator', Jarrow Lecture 1996 (Jarrow: St Paul's Church, 1997); Michael Lapidge, 'Bede the Poet', Jarrow Lecture 1993 (Jarrow: St Paul's Church, 1994), repr. in his essay collection *Anglo-Latin Literature 600–899* (London: Hambledon Press, 1996), 313–38; and my own essay 'Bede's Cædmon, 'The Man Who Had No Story' (Irish Tale-Type 2412B)', *Folklore* (London) 117 (2006): 141–55.

[45] Helpful for study of Bede's methods of exegesis is the recent publication *Bede: On Genesis*, trans. with an introduction, notes, and bibliography by Calvin Kendall (Liverpool: Liverpool University Press, 2008). On Bede's use of rhetorical figures as a component of his devotional purposes, see Kendall, 'Bede's *Historia ecclesiastica*: The Rhetoric of Faith', in *Medieval Eloquence: Studies in the Theory and Practice of Medieval Rhetoric*, ed. James J. Murphy (Berkeley: University of California Press, 1978), 145–72.

a single scholar's vantage point.[46] Different sections of the book treat Bede's life and times, his historical writings including the *Historia ecclesiastica*, his educational works, his biblical commentaries, and his homilies, saints' lives, poems, and miscellaneous works. Rounding off the book is a brief account of the afterlife of Bede's works in later eras. The other book, *The Cambridge Companion to Bede*, edited by Scott DeGregorio, embodies a multitude of critical perspectives. It includes sixteen chapters, each written by a different specialist, covering such topics as 'Church and Monastery in Bede's Northumbria', 'Bede and Preaching', and 'The Cult of Bede', to cite just three.[47] This last-named chapter explores how Bede the man became an object of veneration not long after his death. As is clear from these two volumes alone, one tendency in the recent criticism is to approach Bede's whole body of writings as the expression of a single well-educated mind, rather than singling out the *Historia ecclesiastica* as a self-contained accomplishment. Bede is thus seen as an exceptional individual who gave full and supple expression to a system of collective thinking, that of Western Christendom, as that system had developed by the late seventh or early eighth century, particularly in monastic communities.

The shift of perspective just mentioned is not without implications for one's reading of the *Historia ecclesiastica* – the most English of Bede's works and the one that remains most essential for students of Anglo-Saxon England to know. Certain aspects of the *Historia* that might otherwise seem puzzling, such as Bede's evident interest and belief in miracles, visions, and out-of-body experiences, are then readily seen as consistent with a worldview that Bede shared with numberless other people of faith at the time when he lived.[48] Far from being a rationalist who happened to be stranded in the monkish Dark Ages, as he was sometimes characterized in former years, Bede is now more often approached as a writer who aligned himself with the point of view of the Church Fathers, perhaps even to the point of daring to think of himself as one of them, as the historian Roger Ray has suggested in his 2006 essay 'Who Did Bede Think He Was?'.[49] As for the supposed problem of Bede's miracles – one that once troubled critics – it can be said no longer to exist. Those of Bede's embedded narratives that tell of the miraculous

---

[46] George Hardin Brown, *A Companion to Bede* (Woodbridge: Boydell Press, 2009). Brown earlier authored a succinct introduction to Bede that suits the needs of students and more advanced scholars alike: *Bede the Venerable* (Boston: Twayne, 1987).

[47] *The Cambridge Companion to Bede*, ed. Scott DeGregorio (Cambridge: Cambridge University Press, 2010).

[48] See Joel T. Rosenthal, 'Bede's Use of Miracles in the *Ecclesiastical History*', *Traditio* 31 (1975): 328–35; Meyvaert, 'Bede the Scholar', 51–55; Benedicta Ward, 'Miracles and History: A Reconsideration of the Miracle Stories Used by Bede', in Bonner, *Famulus Christi*, 70–76; and Karl Lutterkort, 'Beda Hagiographicus: Meaning and Function of Miracle Stories in the *Vita Cuthberti* and the *Historia Ecclesiastica*', in *Beda Venerabilis: Historian, Monk and Northumbrian*, ed. L.A.J.R. Houwen and A.A. MacDonald (Groningen: Egbert Forsten, 1996), 81–106. Moreover, stories of native saints and their miracles are scarcely downplayed in the Alfredian-era translation of Bede's history into Old English, as is pointed out by Antonina Harbus, 'The Presentation of Native Saints and their Miracles in the Old English Translation of Bede's *Historia Ecclesiastica*', in *Miracles and the Miraculous in Medieval Germanic and Latin Literature*, ed. K.E. Olsen and A. Harbus (Leuven: Peeters, 2004), 155–74; rather, such stories tend to be highlighted or embellished (173–74).

[49] Roger Ray, 'Who Did Bede Think He Was?', in *Innovation and Tradition in the Writings of The Venerable Bede*, ed. Scott DeGregorio (Morgantown: West Virginia University Press, 2006), 11–35.

workings of divine power on earth serve to confirm the point that the same God who revealed himself to Old Testament prophets, and who worked miracles through the hands of Jesus of Nazareth, also graced human society with manifestations of divine power even in the England of St Alban, St Aidan, St Cuthbert, and other holy men and women whose lives are celebrated in the chapters of the *Historia ecclesiastica*. Bede's gaze on the human condition can thus be imagined to radiate out from his monastic home of Jarrow in concentric circles. These centre on (1) Northumbrian local history; (2) English history as seen from a European perspective, especially with regard to the insular church's connections to St Gregory the Great and Rome; and (3) the drama of human existence in its eschatological dimension, with all three of these fields of vision linked through correspondences that were visible to the Northumbrian author's eye.

If a second trend in the recent criticism on Bede can be discerned, it is one that cuts transversely across the path of the one just mentioned. This is to view certain aspects of the *Historia ecclesiastica* with considerable scepticism while remaining alert to the author's ideological biases. Walter Goffart, in particular, characterizes Bede's history as 'a deliberate, conscious creation', emphasizing the implications of that author's Northumbrian regional attachments as well as his Romanist commitment.[50] In like manner, Nicholas Brooks has seen reason to question the historical value of much of what Bede has to say about the coming of Christianity to Britain, emphasizing instead the limits of Bede's actual knowledge about matters other than the Roman missionary effort.[51] With regard to the Anglo-Saxon conquest of Britain, too (1: 15 in particular), Bede is now seen as an influential mythmaker rather than as someone whose story of the Anglo-Saxon advent can be taken at its face value. Thus when Nicholas Howe, in his 1989 book *Migration and Mythmaking*, set out to trace the influence of Bede's 'myth of migration' on the Anglo-Saxons' sense of their national or ethnic identity, he did so without any presuppositions as to the historical validity of Bede's account.[52] Similarly, as Audrey L. Meaney has pointed out in her 1985 article 'Bede and Anglo-Saxon Paganism', Bede is no longer taken as a privileged witness to pre-Christian religion, for it is far from clear that he had reliable knowledge of ancient Germanic mythology or of the heathen religious practices of the early English.[53] Nor, in particular, is Bede considered a trustworthy authority as to the contributions of native Britons or of the Irish church to the establishment of Christianity in Britain. On the contrary, Nicholas J. Higham and others have called pointed attention to the pro-Roman bias by which Bede denigrates the British church and veils the

---

[50] See Walter Goffart, 'The *Historia Ecclesiastica*: Bede's Agenda and Ours', *Haskins Society Journal* 2 (1990): 29–45 (at 31), as well as chap. 4 (pp. 235–328) of that same author's book *The Narrators of Barbarian History (A.D. 550–800): Jordanes, Gregory of Tours, Bede, and Paul the Deacon* (Princeton: Princeton University Press, 1988). Cf. the sometimes opposed views of N.J. Higham, *(Re)Reading Bede: The Ecclesiastical History in Context* (London: Routledge, 2006).

[51] Nicholas Brooks, 'From British to English Christianity: Deconstructing Bede's Interpretation of the Conversion', in *Conversion and Colonization in Anglo-Saxon England*, ed. Catherine E. Karkov and Nicholas Howe (Tempe, AZ: ACMRS, 2006), 1–30.

[52] Nicholas Howe, *Migration and Mythmaking in Anglo-Saxon England* (Notre Dame: University of Notre Dame Press, 1989; repr. 2001 with a new introduction).

[53] Note Audrey L. Meaney, 'Bede and Anglo-Saxon Paganism', *Parergon* n.s. 3 (1985): 1–29, as well as S.D. Church, 'Paganism in Conversion-Age Anglo-Saxon England: The Evidence of Bede's *Ecclesiastical History* Reconsidered', *History* 93 (2008): 162–80.

significance of Irish missionary efforts emanating from St Columba's island monastery of Iona, in the Gaelic-speaking Inner Hebrides.[54]

These are just a few of the revisionist impulses that can be traced in recent scholarship on Bede. In no way do they detract from the value of Bede's *Historia ecclesiastica* as a kind of 'mythistory' – that is to say, a priceless record of the mental world that he and his Northumbrian fellow-monks inhabited, especially as regards their historical consciousness.

A Selection from the Criticism

Regretfully, given his stature and importance, Bede will not be the subject of the critical selection that follows, nor will any other Anglo-Latin author, including Aldhelm, a writer of prodigious output whom Andy Orchard, in his 1994 study and edition *The Poetic Art of Aldhelm*, has characterized as 'not merely the first but the finest of the Anglo-Latin poets'.[55] Instead, the excerpt chosen for attention here features the theme of literacy itself. In an essay dating from 2003, the distinguished Anglo-Saxonist Joyce Hill discusses the means by which oblates gained competence in Latin, which remained the primary language of literacy in England as in all of Western Christendom throughout the Middle Ages even if English letters had a relatively brief period of florescence during the late Anglo-Saxon period. Hill's essay treats three classroom texts written by Ælfric of Eynsham so as to ease the path of Latin language acquisition for students. These are Ælfric's *Grammar*, his English–Latin *Glossary*, and his *Colloquy*. The first of these is composed in English as an aid to students' acquisition of Latin. It exemplifies a general movement during Ælfric's lifetime to make the elements of Latin Christian learning accessible to native speakers of English. Hill's study casts light on the process by which Anglo-Saxon students learned Latin through intellectual concentration, memorization, vocabulary lists, and occasional staged dialogues or recitations, just as twenty-first-century students do, with the difference that a pedagogy suitable for that purpose can now be taken for granted whereas in Ælfric's England it had to be devised.

Joyce Hill retired in 2008 from her position as Professor of Old and Middle English Language and Literature at the University of Leeds, where she also served as Director of the Centre (now Institute) for Medieval Studies, Head of the School of English, and Pro-Vice-Chancellor. She has written extensively on both Old English poetry and prose and is well known for her contributions to the study of Ælfric, Wulfstan, insular manuscript culture, source studies, preaching, and the Benedictine Reform. Related to the theme of her present

---

[54] Brooks, 'From British to English Christianity'; W. Trent Foley and Nicholas J. Higham, 'Bede on the Britons', *Early Medieval Europe* 17 (2009): 154–85. This topic and others pertaining to early English history and historiography come in for discussion in Nicholas J. Higham and Martin J. Ryan's *The Anglo-Saxon World* (New Haven: Yale University Press, 2013), a book that cannot be commended too warmly for its up-to-date synthesis of information drawn from a wide range of sources.

[55] Andy Orchard, *The Poetic Art of Aldhelm* (Cambridge: Cambridge University Press, 1994), 2.

essay is the authoritative chapter on 'Ælfric: His Life and Works' that she contributed to the 2009 *Companion to Ælfric*.[56]

While Hill's essay illuminates how Anglo-Saxon students learned Latin, much less is known about how they gained competence in English letters. This was not an intuitive matter, since the ability to speak a language does not necessarily entail the ability to read it, much less to write it in a manner considered to be correct. That latter task, in whatever era, requires knowing how to handle the physical materials of writing, shaping each letter aright, spelling each word in an accepted manner, observing the standards of written grammar, and mastering a literate vocabulary that does not necessarily correspond to one's natural speech. Perhaps this was not a major issue for either Anglo-Saxon students or their teachers, however, seeing that the same tools that they used for the study and writing of Latin were easily adapted to the vernacular context. Ælfric's *Grammar*, in particular, was capable of doing double duty as a grammar of Latin that by its nature also offered entry to the grammar of English. The major transition experienced by Anglo-Saxon students, as recent scholarship suggests, was not from literacy in one language to literacy in another. Rather, it was from the dominantly oral, face-to-face interchanges of society at large to the exquisitely – and sometimes painfully – lettered environment of the schoolroom.

For Further Reading

Brown, George Hardin. 1993. 'Latin Writing and the Old English Vernacular'. In *Schriftlichkeit im frühen Mittelalter*, 36–57. Tübingen: Gunter Narr.

Brown, George Hardin. 1995. 'The Dynamics of Literacy in Anglo-Saxon England'. *BJRL* 77: 109–42. Repr. with additional notes in *Toller Lectures*, 183–212.

Brown, George Hardin. 1999. 'The Psalms as the Foundation of Anglo-Saxon Learning'. In *The Place of the Psalms in the Intellectual Culture of the Middle Ages*, ed. Nancy van Deusen, 1–24. Albany: State University of New York Press.

Crick, Julia. 2011. 'Learning and Training'. In Crick & Van Houts, 352–72.

Gretsch, Mechthild. 2013. 'Literacy and the Uses of the Vernacular'. In Godden & Lapidge, 273–94.

Lapidge, Michael. 1999. 'Schools'. In *Blackwell Encyclopaedia*, 407–09.

Liuzza, R.M. 2012. 'Literacy'. In Stodnick & Trilling, 99–114.

Love, Rosalind. 2013. 'Insular Latin Literature to 900'. In the *Cambridge History*, 120–57.

Orchard, Andy. 2010. 'Old English and Latin Poetic Traditions'. In Saunders, 65–82.

Treharne, Elaine. 2011. 'Textual Communities (Vernacular)'. In Crick & Van Houts, 341–51.

Webber, Teresa. 2011. 'Textual Communities (Latin)'. In Crick & Van Houts, 330–40.

---

[56] Joyce Hill, 'Ælfric: His Life and Works', in Magennis & Swan, 35–65.

Joyce Hill, 'Learning Latin in Anglo-Saxon England: Traditions, Texts and Techniques' (2003)[1]

In the Old English preface to his Latin *Grammar*, the homilist Ælfric, monk and mass priest at the Benedictine foundation of Cerne Abbas, rightly equated the learning of Latin with the acquisition of literacy.[2] Recognising the practical realities of the situation in Anglo-Saxon England, however, he had written a *Grammar* in which Latin would be taught through the medium of English, by means of which, as he explains, literacy in both languages would be acquired. Acknowledging by implication that the ability to read English would naturally come first, he describes the art of letters, Old English "*stæf-cræft*", Latin "*grammatica*", as the key for unlocking the sense of his own *Catholic Homilies*, that compendium of orthodox, patristically-based biblical exegesis and doctrinal exposition which he had adapted (his own term is "translated") from Latin authorities not long before, and through which he hoped to raise the standards of pastoral teaching and transmit some of the scholarship of the monastic reform to the secular church, where, as we know from Ælfric's *Pastoral Letters*, there were priests who knew no Latin.[3] For Ælfric, learning meant Christian learning and for him personally, the key to it was knowledge of Latin; the transmission of such learning through the vernacular was a decided second best and a contingency which repeatedly gave him a great deal of anxiety.[4] The use of the

---

[1]   Excerpted from Joyce Hill, 'Learning Latin in Anglo-Saxon England: Traditions, Texts and Techniques', in *Learning and Literacy in Medieval England and Abroad*, ed. Sarah Rees Jones, Utrecht Studies in Medieval Literacy 3 (Turnhout: Brepols, 2003), 7–29. Used with permission from Brepols Publishers NV.

[2]   *Ælfrics Grammatik und Glossar*, ed. J. Zupitza (Berlin, 1880), repr. with a preface by H. Gneuss (Berlin, 1966), pp. 2–3.

[3]   For a discussion of what Ælfric meant by "translation" in connection with the *Catholic Homilies*, see: J. Hill, "Translating the tradition: manuscripts, models and methodologies in the composition of Ælfric's *Catholic Homilies*", *BJRL* 79 (1997), pp. 43–65. (Also published separately as the Toller Memorial Lecture for 1996.) On the standards of learning assumed within the *Pastoral Letters*, see: J. Hill, "Monastic reform and the secular church: Ælfric's pastoral letters in context", in: *England in the Eleventh Century: Proceedings of the 1990 Harlaxton Symposium*, ed. C. Hickes (Stamford, 1992), pp. 103–17. The standard editions of the texts referred to are: *Ælfric's Catholic Homilies: The First Series. Text*, ed. P. Clemoes (Oxford, 1997: EETS s.s. 17); *Ælfric's Catholic Homilies: The Second Series. Text*, ed. M. Godden (London, 1979: EETS s.s. 5); *Die Hirtenbriefe Ælfrics*, ed. B. Fehr (Hamburg, 1914: *Bibliothek der angelsächsischen Prosa* 9), repr. with a supplementary introduction by P.A.M. Clemoes (Darmstadt, 1964).

[4]   Ælfric's anxieties were most fully expressed in his: *Preface to Genesis: The Old English Version of the Heptateuch, Ælfric's Treatise on the Old and New Testament and his Preface to Genesis*, ed. S.J. Crawford (London, 1922: EETS o.s. 160), pp. 76–80. But see also: *Ælfric's Catholic Homilies: The Second Series*, p. 345, for the various places throughout the homilies where he declines to provide certain material in English, and *Ælfric's Lives of Saints*, ed. W.W. Skeat (Oxford, 1881–1900; repr. as 2 volumes, Oxford, 1966: EETS o.s. 76, 82, 94, 114), I, pp. 2–4. Notker of St Gall expressed a similar anxiety when writing to Bishop Hugo von Sitten (*c.* 1015): R. Copeland, *Rhetoric, Hermeneutics and Translation in the Middle Ages: Academic Traditions and Vernacular Texts* (Cambridge, 1991), pp. 97–99. See Copeland's chaps 1, 2 and 4 for comments on the problem of translation in the classical and patristic and early medieval periods.

vernacular *was* a legitimate option in some circumstances, and Ælfric had a model in his revered teacher Æthelwold,[5] but Latin could not be avoided: it was the indispensable foundation subject, the language of learning and 'real' literacy, and the language of the church, which was the guardian of scholarship in early medieval Europe. My purpose here is to examine some of the traditions, texts and techniques by which the Anglo-Saxons struggled to master this language of literacy and learning, the language which unites and characterises medieval Europe. It is, of course, a huge topic, even within the confines of the Anglo-Saxon period. My focus will be on the response by Anglo-Saxons to local needs, and in particular on Ælfric's grammatical works and their varying reception by his fellow Anglo-Saxons, and by modern scholars.

We have first to understand that, in England, there was a particular pedagogical problem to be addressed, for which a measure of innovation was essential, since Latin was so far removed from the Germanic vernacular that it had to be learnt and maintained in a situation of linguistic disjunction, always as a hard-won, bookish second language. In this respect the linguistic conditions in England were significantly different from the conditions prevailing in those areas of the old Roman Empire where the evolving vernacular was a development of vulgar Latin, for in these areas the formal Latin that was learnt in the process of acquiring literacy existed on a continuous spectrum with the native language.[6] Thus, in Francia, for example, perhaps up until the tenth century, and in parts of southern Europe for rather longer still, the difficulty of language learning in the context of learning literacy was nowhere near as great as it was in Anglo-Saxon England. In these regions, the tried and tested texts and pedagogical practices which had developed in classical and late-antique times remained accessible and thus usable. There were established grammars, of varying levels of difficulty, and glossaries and practice dialogues or colloquies, many of which had been developed for Latin language-teaching in the Graeco-Latin bilingual context of the late imperial and early Christian period.[7]

---

[5]   See the discussion 6–7 pages below.

[6]   For more detailed discussion of the situation summarised in the remainder of this paragraph, see: *Latin and the Romance Languages in the Early Middle Ages*, ed. R. Wright (University Park, 1991); M. Banniard, *Viva voce; communication écrite et communication orale du IVe au IXe siècle en occident latin* (Paris, 1992); idem, "Language and communication in Carolingian Europe", in: *The New Cambridge Medieval History: II. c. 700 – c. 900*, ed. R. McKitterick (Cambridge, 1995), pp. 695–708; B. Bischoff, *Manuscripts and Libraries in the Age of Charlemagne*, trans. M.M. Gorman (Cambridge, 1994), especially chap. 5: "Libraries and schools in the Carolingian revival of learning", pp. 93–114; V. Law, "The study of grammar", in: *Carolingian Culture: Emulation and Innovation*, ed. R. McKitterick (Cambridge, 1994), pp. 88–110; idem, *Grammar and Grammarians in the Early Middle Ages* (London and New York, 1997).

[7]   Bilingual materials in Greek and Latin continued to be copied in continental Europe and Anglo-Saxon England, where, from the Carolingian period onwards, they were useful in fostering the hermeneutic style of Latin [...]. For an example in London, British Library, MS Harley 3826, written in the late tenth or early eleventh century, possibly at Abingdon, and a list of the continental manuscripts of this text, see H. Gneuss, "A grammarian's Greek-Latin glossary in Anglo-Saxon England", in: *From Anglo-Saxon to Early Middle English: Studies presented to E.G. Stanley*, ed. M. Godden, D. Gray and T. Hoad (Oxford, 1994), pp. 60–86.

In what was to be the Romance-language area, these well-tested texts remained useful, even though, in the Carolingian period, there is some sense of a rearguard action being mounted as the formally educated become increasingly aware of a growing linguistic disjunction within their own culture, between their learned Latin and the rustic Latin of the laity. Their response to that situation is part of the immediate context for the work of Ælfric, and I shall return to it later.

For the moment, however, I want to stay in the earlier part of the period and focus on the Insular (Celtic as well as Anglo-Saxon) early response to the language problem which was brought about by the conversion to Christianity. The traditional language-teaching texts were, of course, introduced to England along with the introduction of Latin itself, some of them already responsive to Christian needs. But they were less serviceable in England than in continental Europe because of the nature of the native language. The innovative response, within the space of three or four generations, was to develop grammars expressly designed for those whose native language was not Latin or an evolved form of Latin.[8] They still had the disadvantage of being written in Latin, but at least in the elementary ones the paradigms and examples were systematically set out with a minimum of commentary, features which are not characteristic of the major grammars of the antique world. For the more advanced student there were exegetical grammars which explained the grammatical phenomena they had already encountered – also developments from classical traditions, but of that branch concerned more with rhetoric, metrics and theoretical linguistics: Donatus's *Ars Maior*, we might say, rather than his elementary *Ars Minor*, which dealt only with the parts of speech. These early grammatical works are not the subject of the present study, but I draw attention to them in order to establish two fundamental points: that the Anglo-Saxons had particular difficulties in teaching and learning Latin which, at this date, were not experienced to the same extent by most of the old Western Roman Empire; and that there was a tradition of pedagogical innovation in responding to that need, even as early as the eighth century, when the first of the 'new' elementary grammars made their appearance.

The next innovation in initial language learning texts by an Anglo-Saxon writer was not to come until after the Viking invasions when, prompted by the Benedictine Reform with its renewed commitment to the study of Latin, testified by the importation of texts and the survival of classbooks of various

---

[8]   V. Law, *The Insular Latin Grammarians* (Woodbridge, 1982). See also: idem, *Grammar and Grammarians*.

kinds,[9] Ælfric produced a *Grammar, Glossary* and *Colloquy*,[10] probably between 992 and 1002, when he was monk and mass priest at Cerne Abbas.[11] Only the *Grammar* has contextualising prefatory material by Ælfric and it concludes with the words "*Sy þeos boc ðus her geendod*" ("Let this book thus here be ended").[12] There is no comment in any manuscript of the *Glossary* or *Colloquy* which indicates a formal relationship to any other text. But all seven of the extant copies of the *Glossary* nonetheless appear with the *Grammar*, which suggests that a formal, manuscript relationship was recognised as pedagogically useful. The *Colloquy*, which is attributed to Ælfric by his pupil Ælfric Bata,[13] is somewhat different in kind. Unlike the *Grammar* and *Glossary*, which present grammatical and lexical elements of Latin in a systematic way, the *Colloquy* is an example of the next stage in language learning, when the systematically acquired linguistic phenomena are put into practice and fluency is tested. We may see the trio of texts as a graded set of instructional tools which perhaps represent Ælfric's own

[9]   H. Gneuss, "Anglo-Saxon libraries from the conversion to the Benedictine reform", *Angli e Sassoni al di qua e al di là del mare* (Spoleto, 1986: *Settimane di studio del Centro Italiano di Studi sull'Alto Medioevo* 32), pp. 643–699; and: M. Lapidge, "Schools, learning and literature in tenth-century England", *Il secolo di ferro: mito e realtà del secolo X* (Spoleto, 1991: *Settimane di studio del Centro Italiano di Studi sull'Alto Medioevo* 38), pp. 951–1005, provide complementary overviews. For imported manuscripts, see: F.A. Rella, "Continental manuscripts acquired for English centers in the tenth and early eleventh centuries: a preliminary checklist", *Anglia* 98 (1980), pp. 107–16. There is also some information in: H. Gneuss, "A preliminary list of manuscripts written or owned in England up to 1100", *ASE* 9 (1981), pp. 1–60, but there are manuscripts listed here with a note of their Anglo-Saxon provenance without reference to their continental origin, so that the extent of the importation is understated. For classbooks, see: A.G. Rigg and G.R. Wieland, "A Canterbury classbook of the mid-eleventh century", *ASE* 4 (1975), pp. 113–30; *Latin and the Vernacular Languages in Early Medieval Britain*, ed. N. Brooks (Leicester, 1982), in particular the articles by: M. Lapidge, "The study of latin texts in late Anglo-Saxon England (1): the evidence of Latin glosses", pp. 99–140; and R.I. Page, "The study of Latin texts in late Anglo-Saxon England (2): the evidence of English glosses", pp. 141–65; G. Wieland, "The glossed manuscript: classbook or library book?", *ASE* 14 (1985), pp. 153–73.

[10] Ælfric, *Colloquy*, ed. G.N. Garmonsway (London, 1939; 2nd edn, 1947). For the edition of the *Grammar* and *Glossary*, see n. 2 above.

[11] P.A.M. Clemoes, "The chronology of Ælfric's works", in: *The Anglo-Saxons: Studies in some Aspects of their History and Culture presented to Bruce Dickins*, ed. P.A.M. Clemoes (London, 1959), pp. 212–47, at p. 244.

[12] *Ælfrics Grammatik und Glossar*, p. 296.

[13] The attribution, in the form of a Latin note, is at the head of Ælfric Bata's augmented version of Ælfric's *Colloquy* in Oxford, St John's College, MS 154. Ælfric Bata identifies Ælfric as having been "*meus magister*", "my teacher".

pedagogy, and we can recognise in them a degree of interconnectedness of language and pedagogical intent which suggests that, in Ælfric's hands at least, they could be exploited as a linguistically self-referential instructional sequence. As such, they stand within a tradition going back to the days of imperial bi-lingualism, when glossary and colloquy supplemented formal grammatical instruction by extending vocabulary and providing a model dialogue in which could be exercised the grammatical rules and the student's lexical store in a practical and idiomatic mode.[14]

The obvious novelty of the *Grammar* is that it is written in English, the first ever, and the only one for centuries to come.[15] We should not, however, deduce from this that it is a book for absolute beginners, despite Ælfric's apologetic remarks in the Latin preface about its elementary nature,[16] because he assumes that the "*pueruli tenelli*" ("tender little boys") who will use it have already gone through the eight parts of speech in Donatus's *Ars Minor*, a standard elementary text of the mid-fourth-century which sets out in question and answer form a summary of the most important features of each part of speech in the traditional order of noun, pronoun, verb, adverb, participle, conjunction, preposition, and interjection. In fact Ælfric claims that he has produced a modified translation of what was used in the school of his teacher Æthelwold, who was one of the leading Benedictine reformers and Bishop of Winchester (963–84). This work is identified in the Latin preface as "*has excerptiones de Prisciano minore uel maiore*"

---

[14] For examples of classical colloquies, see: *Anthologia latina sive poesis latinae supplementum. I. Carmina in codicibus scripta*, ed. A. Riese, fasc. 1 (Leipzig, 1868). *Carmen 199*, pp. 140–44, provides a telling contrast with the *Colloquy* of Ælfric: although there is a sequence of speeches, which are clearly vocabulary exercises, followed by an adjudication by Vulcan (lines 95–99), the exchange lacks the variety and allusion to daily life which is characteristic of Ælfric's, and there is further formality in that it is in verse, whilst Ælfric's is in prose. The scholarship on Greek-Latin bilingual instructional manuals is extensive. A sense of the traditions and their transmission to medieval Europe may be had from: A. Bataille, "Les glossaires gréco-latins sur papyrus", *Recherches de Papyrologie* 4 (Paris, 1967: Travaux de l'institut de papyrologie de Paris 5), pp. 161–69; A.C. Dionisotti, "Greek grammars and dictionaries in Carolingian Europe", in: *The Sacred Nectar of the Greeks: The Study of Greek in the West in the Early Middle Ages*, ed. M.W. Herren (London, 1988: King's College London Medieval Studies 2), pp. 1–56; G.N. Garmonsway, "The development of the colloquy", in: *The Anglo-Saxons* [ed. P.A.M. Clemoes], pp. 248–61.

[15] H. Gneuss, "The study of language in Anglo-Saxon England", *BJRL* 72 (1990), pp. 3–32 (also separately published as "The 1989 Toller Memorial Lecture"), provides a context for Ælfric's *Grammar*. See also: D.A. Bullough, "The educational tradition in England from Alfred to Ælfric: teaching *utriusque linguae*", in: idem, *Carolingian Renewal: Sources and Heritage* (Manchester 1991), pp. 297–334 (a revised version of an article originally published in 1972).

[16] For the Latin preface, see: *Ælfrics Grammatik und Glossar*, pp. 1–2. It is also edited by: J. Wilcox, *Ælfric's Prefaces* (Durham, 1994), pp. 114–15, and provided with explanatory notes on pp. 151–52 and an English translation on p. 130.

("these excerpts from the greater and lesser Priscian") but this is a statement which needs careful interpretation. Priscian was active in Constantinople in the reign of Anastasius (491–518) and produced a monumental grammatical treatise in eighteen books, the *Institutiones grammaticae*, and a number of other grammatical works, but the *Excerptiones de Prisciano* to which Ælfric alludes is not an *ad hoc* compilation of extracts from these. It is, rather, an intermediate-level grammar which fuses together material from Priscian's various treatises, Donatus's *Ars minor*, and at least one other unidentified medieval source.[17] The title, which appears with some variation in medieval booklists and eleventh century manuscripts as well as in Ælfric's preface,[18] has an element of truth in it from a modern point of view because Priscian's work is by far the most extensively exploited. Furthermore, since there are manuscripts of it in which the source-authority for various extracts is indicated in the margin, Priscian's contribution would be plain to see, even for a medieval user. But the title must also be understood as one which lends authority to the work, an authority which, in Ælfric's case, is given local reinforcement by the reference to Æthelwold.

What we actually have here, as Ælfric's immediate source, is a text which should be regarded as a work in its own right. It is of uncertain date and origin, but the manuscript tradition suggests that it is continental[19] and, if this is so, we are dealing with a

---

[17] V. Law, "Anglo-Saxon England: Ælfric's *Excerptiones de arte grammatica anglice*", *Histoire Épistémologie Langage* 9 (1987), pp. 47–71. On the different pedagogical needs met by the various works of Donatus and Priscian, see: idem, "Late Latin grammars in the early Middle Ages: a typological history", *Historiographia Linguistica* 13 (1986), pp. 365–80. Both articles are reprinted in: idem, *Grammar and Grammarians*. Priscian's *Institutiones* was 'rediscovered' by the Carolingians and Alcuin, among others, made extracts from it. It is in this context of new grammatical compilations drawing upon the *Institutiones* that we should probably see the origins of the *Excerptiones de Prisciano* as a discrete work. On Priscian and the Carolingians, see: idem, "The study of grammar", pp. 95–96 (*Grammar and Grammarians*, pp. 136–37, where the article is reprinted under the title: "The study of grammar under the Carolingians", pp. 129–53).

[18] M.R. James, *The Ancient Libraries of Canterbury and Dover* (Cambridge, 1903) provides three instances from booklists: "*Exceptiones* [*sic*] *de Prisciano*" (item 17, discussed p. xxvii); "*Expositiones de Prisciano exposite Anglice*" (item 297, p. 50); "*Excepciones de Prisciano, a*" (item 302, p. 51). James also notes (pp. xxvii–xxviii) that the copy of Ælfric's *Grammar* now preserved as Cambridge University Library, MS Hh. 1.10 has a note "*Excerpta ex Prisc*" on the back. This is in an eighteenth century hand and was done when the fly-leaves were destroyed in rebinding. It may therefore reflect an earlier, possibly medieval, title or designation of contents. James observes that this is not the natural title for Ælfric's *Grammar*, but we know now that it is indeed an apt designation, given Ælfric's own identification of his text in the *Grammar*'s Latin preface, our modern understanding of his immediate source, and the fact that some of the other expositions or excerpts of Priscian listed later by James and identified as being in English ("*anglice*" or "*a*") are more than likely to be copies of Ælfric's work. There is also an eleventh century copy of the *Excerptiones*, probably made in Abingdon, which begins "*Incipiunt excerptiones de Prisciano*". One of the copies of Ælfric's *Colloquy* (the Antwerp-London manuscript) survives in the margin of this text.

[19] Law, "Ælfric's *Excerptiones*", p. 52 (*Grammar and Grammarians*, p. 204).

text which, like so much else, must have come to England with the Benedictine Reform.[a]
As a modification of late antique instructional texts, which had previously met the needs
of the vulgar Latin language area, it could well be a response to that growing disjunction
between rustic Latin and the Latin of the "*eruditi*" which is famously commented upon
in canon 17 of the Council of Tours held in 813,[20] and which is a cause of continuing
concern in successive continental councils of the ninth century.[21] As a *compilatio* both in
practice and presentation (through title and marginalia) the *Excerptiones de Prisciano* is
entirely in harmony with other products of the Carolingian reform, such as the exegetical
compilationes, similarly constructed and presented, which also came to England with the
Benedictine Reform, and which Ælfric used extensively.[22] The Carolingian Reform certainly provided a powerful impetus for grammatical compilations and practice texts,
because grammar was recognised, as it had been since late antique Christianity, as the
necessary means of penetrating the mysteries of sacred literature and the first step
towards "*divina sapientia*". Improved knowledge of Latin grammar, straightforwardly

---

[a] [In a short postscript to her article (not reproduced here), Hill calls attention to the publication of *Excerptiones de Prisciano: The Source for Ælfric's Latin-Old English Grammar*, ed.
David W. Porter (Woodbridge: D.S. Brewer, 2002), featuring the text of the *Excerptiones*
together with a modern English translation and a discussion of the textual traditions. Porter
makes the suggestion (not embraced by Hill) that Ælfric himself may have been the author
of this work, either alone or in cooperation with others.]

[20] *Concilium Turonense a. 813*, ed. in: *Concilia aevi Karolini*, ed. A. Werminghoff, 2 parts, 1
(Hannover, 1908: MGH, Concilia II), pp. 286–93, at p. 288. The Council specified that
preachers should "openly endeavour to translate sermons into the rustic Roman language"
("*aperte transferre studeat in rusticam romanam linguam*") so that "all might the more easily understand" ("*quo facilius cuncti possint intelligere*"). It is in such a context that those who were attempting to attain a respectable level of literate Latinity would need instructional material which was
no longer quite what the classical world had devised. The value for Anglo-Saxon England of
such modified materials would be all the more evident, given the complete linguistic disjunction
between Latin and the Germanic vernacular. For a discussion of the significance of canon 17,
see: Banniard, *Viva voce*, pp. 405–13; idem, "Language and communication", pp. 699–701.

[21] John Contreni draws attention to the Council of Mainz in 847: "The Carolingian
Renaissance: education and literary culture", in: *New Cambridge Medieval History: II*,
pp. 709–57, at pp. 725–26.

[22] For Ælfric, see: C.L. Smetana, "Ælfric and the early medieval homiliary", *Traditio* 15 (1959), pp.
163–204; and a number of my own articles, in particular: "Ælfric and Smaragdus", *ASE* 21
(1992), pp. 203–37; "Ælfric's sources reconsidered: some case studies from the *Catholic Homilies*",
in: *Studies in English Language and Literature. "Doubt Wisely": Papers in honour of E.G. Stanley*, ed.
M.J. Toswell and E.M. Tyler (London and New York, 1996), pp. 362–86; and "Translating the
tradition". On *compilatio* and *catena* more generally, see: J. Contreni, "Carolingian biblical studies",
in: *Carolingian Essays: Andrew W. Mellon Lectures in Early Christian Studies* (Washington, 1983),
pp. 71–98; Bischoff, *Manuscripts and Libraries*, pp. 109–13; G. Brown, "Introduction: the
Carolingian Renaissance", in: *Carolingian Culture*, pp. 1–51, at pp. 39–42; M. Irvine, *The Making
of Textual Culture: "Grammatica" and Literary Theory, 350–1100* (Cambridge, 1994); idem,
"Medieval textuality and the archaeology of textual culture", in: *Speaking Two Languages*,
pp. 181–210; J. Hill, *Bede and the Benedictine Reform* (Jarrow, 1998: Jarrow Lecture).

equated with improved literacy since Latin was the only language under consideration, was a major item on Charlemagne's agenda, as set out in his *Admonitio generalis* of 789 and the *Epistola de litteris colendis*, which he sent to Abbot Baugulf of Fulda (780–802) and other ecclesiastics. Those who had any aptitude for learning or teaching were to be set to the task, in order to overcome the fear that

> sicut minor erat in scribendo prudentia, ita quoque et multo esset quam recte esset debuisset in sanctarum scripturarum ad intelligendum sapientia.

> as skill in writing was less, wisdom to understand the sacred scriptures might be far less than it ought rightly to be.[23]

In seeing *grammatica* as the key to scriptural understanding, in urging those who could to teach and to learn, and in providing instruction on the basis of what is probably a Carolingian grammatical text, Ælfric shows himself, as he does in almost all his work, to be inspired by the Carolingian reform and up-to-date in his choice of immediate sources, although characteristically the Old English version which Ælfric gives us is far from being a translation as we would understand it. Vernacular grammatical terms had to be developed, examples were introduced which appealed to the experience and interests of his pupils (a practice also found in Carolingian texts), and the content of the *Excerptiones* was modified by the incorporation of a more comprehensive treatment of paradigms, and the exclusion or drastic reduction in material of the more rhetorical and metrical elements. The result is a practical working *Grammar*, well adjusted to local need, simpler than the Latin *Excerptiones*, but not as basic as the *Ars Minor*, which the boys had already mastered. What we do not know, of course, is the extent to which the changes had already been made in the "*scola Æthelwoldi*", where they could have been stabilised either in written form for reference, or orally by constant repetition in a recurrent pedagogical context such as gave rise to Winchester vocabulary.[24] Nor do we know whether Ælfric's own teacher Æthelwold, whose traditions he expressly embodies in the *Grammar*, had already developed some of the vernacular technical terms which the *Grammar* employs. The *Vita Æthelwoldi* describes a context in which this would be possible since it records that:

> Dulce namque erat ei adolescentes et iuuenes semper docere, et Latinos libros Anglice eis soluere, et regulas grammaticae artis ac metricae rationis tradere, et iocundis alloquiis ad meliora hortari.

---

[23] *Epistola de litteris colendis*, ed. A. Boretius, in: *Capitularia regum Francorum*, ed. A. Boretius and V. Krause, 2 vols. (Hannover, 1883–97: MGH, Capitularia regum Francorum I–II), I, No. 29, pp. 78–79, at p. 79. *Admonitio generalis*, ed. Boretius, in: *Capitularia regum Francorum* I, No. 22, pp. 52–62.

[24] H. Gneuss, "The origin of standard Old English and Æthelwold's school at Winchester", *ASE* 1 (1972), pp. 63–83; W. Hofstetter, *Winchester und der spätalt-englische Sprachgebrauch: Untersuchungen zur geographischen und zeitlichen Verbreitung altenglischer Synonyme* (Munich, 1987: Texte und Untersuchungen zur Englischen Philologie 14); idem, "Winchester and the standardization of Old English vocabulary", *ASE* 17 (1988), pp. 139–61.

It was always agreeable to him to teach young men and the more mature students, translating Latin texts into English for them, passing on the rules of grammar and metric, and encouraging them to do better by cheerful words.[25]

The *Glossary*, as a word-list for extending vocabulary, is also, of course, a bilingual text, by its very nature; it is arranged as a class-glossary (i.e. words are alphabetised within subject-groups), an organisational principle which would be convenient for initial learning, the development of subsequent practice dialogues and later reference.

The *Colloquy*, which exercises what has been learnt in the more abstract form offered by the *Grammar* and *Glossary*, is necessarily monolingual, the Old English interlinear gloss-translation through which it has become famous not being by Ælfric.[26] The tradition in which it stands is that of the schoolroom dialogue for a learnt language familiar from classical times.[27] In these dialogues it is normal for roles to be adopted by the scholars and their teacher, for there to be extensive lists which exercise vocabulary, for much of the dialogue to describe daily activities through a question and answer exchange and, in the more developed examples, for there to be a debate, which is adjudicated by some kind of *consiliarius* figure. Ælfric's *Colloquy* is a very well constructed example of the genre, but he has developed the tradition in a distinctive way by extending the breadth of the occupational reference: the typical scholastic colloquy at this level is more commonly concerned with the practicalities of the scholars' own daily lives. Ælfric's *Colloquy* has this dimension – the dialogue begins and ends in the schoolroom and the daily life of the young monk is given prominence – but we also move beyond the cloister in hearing about the occupations of the ploughman, shepherd, oxherd, hunter, fisher, fowler, merchant, leather-worker (shoemaker), salter, baker, and cook, with a few additional occupations being introduced as the colloquy progresses. The variety has the pedagogical advantages of broadening the linguistic range, allowing for a high level of participation, and providing stimulating and challenging opportunities for changes of register, levels of discourse, and even dramatic characterisation of a modest kind. It is also an excellently constructed practice text in that the boys' answers to the basic questions about the occupations naturally include lists inevitably arranged by subject, which thus exercise vocabulary in a way which is straightforwardly related to the *Glossary*, whilst at

[25] Wulfstan of Winchester, *The Life of St Æthelwold*, ed. M. Lapidge and M. Winterbottom (Oxford, 1991), pp. 46–49 (Latin and English). Ælfric produced an abbreviated version of Wulfstan's *vita* but regarded the information that Æthelwold used the vernacular when teaching as important enough to be retained, although he does not specify that the books are Latin ones (the implication is clear enough, however), and he omits the reference to Æthelwold's teaching of the rules of grammar and metre (p. 77: Ælfric's chap. 20, drawing on Wulfstan's chap. 31).

[26] On this point and on the *Colloquy*'s pedagogical principles, which are summarised in this paragraph, see: J. Hill, "Winchester pedagogy and the *Colloquy* of Ælfric", *LSE* n.s. 29 (1998), pp. 137–52.

[27] See n. 15 above. For the texts of prose colloquies from Anglo-Saxon England, with introductory studies of the tradition, see: *Latin Colloquies from Pre-Conquest Britain*, ed. S. Gwara (Toronto, 1996); *Anglo-Saxon Conversations: The Colloquies of Ælfric Bata*, ed. S. Gwara, translated with an introduction by D.W. Porter (Woodbridge, 1997).

the same time this variety is carefully counterbalanced with a repetitious exercising of the common bases of Latin grammar, with dramatically justifiable changes of case, person, tense and mood, embodied where possible in the sample vocabulary through which these features were abstractly presented in the *Grammar*. Ælfric does not, for example, concern himself with lexical diversity when dealing with common actions such as "to speak", "to sing", and "to catch", but uses, in their various forms as required by the dialogue, the verbs "*loquor*", "*cantare*" and "*capere*", which are the models in the *Grammar*. This is the interconnectedness which I referred to earlier, and which defines the context of the *Colloquy* as being primarily textual, within a linguistically self-referential instructional sequence.

Yet there have been many times when *The Colloquy* has been read at face value as a simple sociological document. In 1838 it was cited (and partly translated) by Henry Wadsworth Longfellow in order to comfort the suffering students of his own day by offering a selective reading intended to demonstrate that, if school was a grim business in the mid-nineteenth century, it was nevertheless a great deal better than it had been in Anglo-Saxon times.[28] If this reading, at a distance of nearly two hundred years, seems too remote, we can turn to a publication of 1920, reissued in 1975, which cites the *Colloquy* in order to prove that flogging was a time-honoured (and therefore presumably justifiable) tradition in English schools.[29] In 1915, driven by the then common tendency to idealise the Anglo-Saxon period as the time when Englishmen were budding egalitarians and were as yet mercifully untainted by the feudalising Normans, the *Colloquy* was taken as evidence that education was available to all, secular as well as religious, unfree as well as free.[30] The wonderful assumption was made that the master was a layman since his questions about the monastic life were taken to indicate that he could not himself be a monk. And to cap it all, it was deduced that the occasion was that most beloved of Victorian and Edwardian institutions, the Sunday School, since the hunter explains that, whilst he went hunting yesterday, he has not been hunting today, because today, when he is in school, is Sunday.

We may well be amused by these naive approaches – and I admit that I have chosen some extreme examples – but it is a striking fact that a substantial proportion of the bibliography on Ælfric's *Colloquy* consists of the whimsical and the misleading, together with repetitious summaries and translations which add nothing to our understanding of the nature of the text, the traditions to which it relates, or the techniques that it deploys. More of a problem, however, are the various editorial treatments of the *Colloquy*, for, as Norman Blake once reminded us, the editor of a text is the most influential critic one reads.[31]

---

[28] H. Wadsworth Longfellow, "Anglo-Saxon literature", *North American Review* 47 (1838), pp. 90–134, at pp. 132–33 (often reprinted, for example in his: *Poets and Poetry of Europe* (Cambridge, 1845; New York, 1857; 2nd edn 1871), and his: *Collected Prose* (Boston, 1857; rev. edn 1866; repr. 1886, 1894)).

[29] A.W. Parry, *Education in England in the Middle Ages* (London, 1920; repr. New York, 1975), pp. 37–38.

[30] A.F. Leach, *The Schools of Medieval England* (London, 1915), pp. 88–91. The book was reissued in New York in 1968 and 1969.

[31] N.F. Blake, *The English Language in Medieval Literature* (London, 1977), p. 55.

[Hill's essay continues with close discussion of modern editions of Ælfric's *Colloquy*, pointing out their constructed nature and their tendency to highlight not Ælfric's text itself, but rather the Old English gloss on it that is uniquely interlineated in a single surviving manuscript (London, British Library MS Cotton Tiberius A.iii). She also discusses the medieval amplifications of Ælfric's *Colloquy* that are found in certain manuscripts, including Cambridge, St John's College MS 154, fols. 204r–215r. This early eleventh-century version, which was greatly augmented by Ælfric Bata, includes examples of hermeneutic Latin, a precious style that Ælfric of Eynsham shunned but that Ælfric Bata revelled in. Our excerpt resumes at p. 22 of Hill's essay, where she speaks of the Tiberius manuscript and then the St John's manuscript; and to conclude this section we skip to her concluding paragraph.]

The tinkering with the lists and the hermeneutic indulgence in the epilogue are probably attributable to Ælfric Bata. But, if this is so, his intervention here is quite restrained, by comparison with the major rewriting which we find in the St John's manuscript. This Latin-only text draws heavily upon glossaries to augment the lists, taking us into an improbable world where the Anglo-Saxon hunter's prey includes elephants, camels, lions and snails. Ælfric Bata's amplified version is in fact a display-text and it rightly takes its place in the manuscript amongst other abstruse colloquies by the same author, which are similarly vehicles for parading Ælfric Bata's own erudition. If these colloquies have a pedagogical function, and it is probable that they do, it is as exercises in lexical variation in support of the *recherché* hermeneutic tradition, rather than being practice dialogues of the fundamental kind we see in Ælfric's original.[32]

[…] Of course we do not know what manuscripts have been lost, but if the surviving evidence is at all indicative, it suggests that Ælfric's *Colloquy* had relatively little use outside Ælfric's immediate circle and that his pupil Ælfric Bata was its chief exploiter, drawing it, by his successive modifications, more and more into the hermeneutic orbit, a realignment which raises interesting questions about the status and function of written colloquies in late Anglo-Saxon England. Given the tendency to use question and answer even within formal grammatical instruction[33] and the demand for an active

---

[32] Ælfric Bata's pedagogical techniques are discussed by: D.W. Porter, "The Latin syllabus in Anglo-Saxon monastic schools", *Neoph* 78 (1994), pp. 463–82, and in his introduction to *Anglo-Saxon Conversations*, as well as by Gwara in the introduction to *Latin Colloquies*. For two hermeneutic dialogues in verse form, composed at Winchester in Æthelwold's school or soon after his death, see: M. Lapidge, "Three Latin poems from Æthelwold's school at Winchester", *ASE* 1 (1972), pp. 85–137. The relevant texts are the *Altercatio magistri et discipuli* and the *Responsio discipuli*. The *Carmen de libero arbitrio*, also hermeneutic, is not a dialogue. For discussion of one of the important study-texts for the hermeneutic tradition see: P. Lendinara, "The third book of the *Bella Parisiacae Urbis* by Abbo of Saint-Germain-des-Près", *ASE* 15 (1986), pp. 73–89; idem, "The Abbo glossary in London, British Library, Cotton Domitian i", *ASE* 19 (1990), pp. 133–49. On the origins of the hermeneutic style in England, see: M. Gretsch, *The Intellectual Foundations of the English Benedictine Reform* (Cambridge, 1999: *Cambridge Studies in Anglo-Saxon England* 25).

rather than simply a passive understanding of Latin within the monastic life, it is difficult to believe that teachers did not make frequent use of practice dialogues. But these, in the more basic stages of language learning, were likely to have been of the moment and oral, for what would have been the purpose of expending time and resources on writing them down? A colloquy of this kind which was written out would, by that very act, acquire a different status and function, being transformed into an example to be learnt or a model of what could be achieved, a standard for others to emulate.[34] Perhaps this is how Ælfric's *Colloquy* should be understood, representing an essentially transient element in basic language teaching, which may have been widely used (though perhaps with less skill than this carefully thought out written version displays), but of which we inevitably have very little surviving evidence. By contrast, the colloquies which generally achieved the status of *written* texts were those which were essentially part of a bookish tradition – media for displaying and developing the hermeneutic style, an altogether more specialised and *recherché* register than Ælfric was striving for in his grammatical works, or than he ever personally employed when writing Latin himself.[35] Ælfric recreated – and at the same time developed – the classical model of the colloquy, and its existence as an exemplar within a carefully prepared pedagogic set alongside the *Grammar* and *Glossary* makes good sense. But whereas the *Grammar* and *Glossary* were the 'permanent' tools of instruction and were much used in the form issued, the value of the *Colloquy* as a written text to be handed on was much less obvious, except to Ælfric's pupil, who adopted it for another tradition, of which Ælfric was not a part. We can appreciate Ælfric's intellectual position and pedagogical skill by examining the traditions and techniques of his grammatical texts, but the variations in response to them, as also to his other reforming works, point to Ælfric's distinctive individuality as a scholar and define him, yet again, as someone who, though a committed exponent of the Reform, bears witness to its diversity.

---

[33] As in Ælfric's own *Grammar* and as in the grammatical dialogues which are found in some of the manuscripts. See: Law, "The study of grammar", pp. 92–95, for comment on the use of the question and answer form in elementary language teaching (pp. 134–36 in *Grammar and Grammarians*). M. Bayless, "*Beatus quid est* and the study of grammar in late Anglo-Saxon England", *Historiographia Linguistica* 20 (1993), pp. 67–110, provides an extended example.

[34] The learning of a set dialogue has some pedagogic value in instilling patterns and building up confidence, but within a manuscript culture the gains are not likely to have been seen as great enough to justify the production of more copies, from which the master would in any case have to teach his pupils orally. Similarly, one can understand that there might be some reluctance to spend resources on copying a text which was purely exemplary. Ælfric had provided exemplary material before, in the form of the *Catholic Homilies*, intended to combat the bad example of other preaching material in circulation, but these homilies – like the *Grammar* and *Glossary* – could also actually be used directly and so were copied.

[35] For an important assessment of Ælfric as a Latinist, see: C.A. Jones, "*Meatim Sed et Rustica*: Ælfric of Eynsham as a medieval Latin author", *The Journal of Medieval Latin* 8 (1998), pp. 1–57.

3

Textuality and Cultural Transformations

Christianity is a religion built on paradox. As George Hardin Brown writes in his 1986 essay 'Old English Verse as a Medium for Christian Theology':[1]

> The creed of Christian faith consists of paradox and an astounding resolution of opposites. It holds that the incomprehensible, transcendent, spiritual, eternally blissful God beyond history became flesh as an historical, mortal, affective, touchable, agonized man. It claims the son preexisted his own creation and his mother. This woman is a virgin before and after being a mother, simultaneously the humble Galilean handmaid and the empress queen of the universe. Mankind, for whom the God-man dies, is a creature of God but he is likewise His enemy. Man is vicious and depraved but worthy of the sacrificial death of the Son of God; he is a disobedient, worthless servant but an adopted son and co-heir with Christ, sharing his Body. Man is a wandering exile in earth's vale of tears; he is a secure citizen in the New Jerusalem. The Church is ruled by the Holy Spirit; the Church is ruled by all too fallible men. The Christian faith affirms these and many more naturally irresolvable antitheses.

Among the many additional paradoxes alluded to by Brown at the end of this passage is the relation of Christian teachings to the written word. Although Jesus of Nazareth left behind no writings, preferring instead to reach out to others through his voice and his charismatic presence, Christianity is a religion of the book. Indeed, as organized Christianity gradually took on the character of a world religion during the first millennium AD, the Book became one of its two leading symbols, sharing that role with the Cross. The capitalization of those words in that last sentence underscores this symbolism, which transcended the making of any individual book or cross.

---

[1] George Hardin Brown, 'Old English Verse as a Medium for Christian Theology', in *Greenfield Studies*, 15–28 (at 17–18).

Old English Literature: A Guide to Criticism with Selected Readings, First Edition. John D. Niles.
© 2016 John D. Niles. Published 2016 by John Wiley & Sons, Ltd.

The most venerated of all books copied during the early Middle Ages were the four Gospels written by the evangelists Matthew, Mark, Luke and John, for these works were taken to record the words of the Saviour himself, along with accounts of his teachings as recorded by men who either personally had witnessed his miracles and his agony or else were close companions of those who did. In addition to the Gospels, Christianity was built on the whole inherited body of what Jews regarded as Holy Scripture, as well as on a large body of newer writings that either depended directly on Scripture, as books of biblical exegesis did, or that augmented it in crucial ways. Writings in this latter category included works by authors, including the Church Fathers, who were not just leading spokesmen for the Christian faith, but were also learned custodians of the ancient Greek, Latin, and Hebrew heritage of letters.

To say that Christianity is a religion of the book, however, and that in addition we owe to Christian authors and scribes a great part of our knowledge of the writings of Greek and Latin antiquity, is still only half the story. The material books on which Christian doctrine rests are in a constant give-and-take relationship with modes of speech. This is true now and it was even truer in Anglo-Saxon times, whether one thinks of the reading of books aloud, or of the ceremonial language and songs of the liturgy, or of the somewhat less formal register of preaching. There were also the more relaxed speaking environments of the classroom, the workplace, or the home, when room was found there for prayer, other acts of devotion, and discourse on religious topics.

When we study the manuscript records of Anglo-Saxon England, then, we are looking at material objects produced in a society where the contents of books were routinely made accessible through oral performance. This was only natural at a place and time when most people used spoken English for virtually all communicative purposes, including the use of books written out in Latin, even if those books were composed in a language that was only known to a clerical elite. The clergy were expected to communicate the gist of those books to unlearned members of society, including men and women of high rank, some of whom were patrons of Christianity and the arts. When Brian Stock and other medievalists speak of the 'textual communities' of the Middle Ages, then, what they are referring to are groups of people who both used books and talked about them. While many of those persons were members of the clergy, not all of them were.[2]

The culture of the book in Anglo-Saxon England therefore involves both textual and oral dimensions. Moreover, in the later part of the period, as literacy in the vernacular became more common, the pages of books became a ground where Latin writings visibly intersected with English ones. This can often be seen even when what we are looking at seems at first glance to be a straightforward example of 'a medieval Latin book'. This intersection might result either from the writing out of an English text side by side with a Latin one or from the use of English to gloss Latin words or phrases.

The present chapter reviews recent critical approaches to the textuality – or, more precisely, the evolving textualities – of Anglo-Saxon literature. First of all, this requires

---

[2] Note Stock's concise book *Listening for the Text: On the Uses of the Past* (Philadelphia: University of Pennsylvania Press, 1990), as well as his prior volume *The Implications of Literacy: Written Language and Models of Interpretation in the Eleventh and Twelfth Centuries* (Princeton: Princeton University Press, 1983).

looking at critics' engagements with the work of scribes and with the deployment of scripts and images on the handwritten page. Second, it involves consideration of cultural transformations of the kind that occurred when, for example, a work of classical literature was reworked into a Christian idiom in the course of its medieval transmission. A well-known instance is the conversion of Ovid's great poem the *Metamorphoses* into the rhymed French octosyllabic poem known as the *Ovide moralisé*, which was widely disseminated during the later Middle Ages. To cite an analogous instance from the period before the Conquest: when Boethius's prosimetric treatise *De consolatione philosophiae* was translated into Old English by persons working to fulfil King Alfred the Great's programme for the advancement of learning, English-language equivalents had to be found for Boethius's philosophical terms. Some of this new lexicon bore native associations, as when Boethius's personified abstractions *Philosophia* and *Fortuna* were converted into the translator's *Wisdom* and *Wyrd*, two words that had a history of prior use outside the intellectual framework of Christianity. With their use, a subtle shift occurs that transports the reader from the urbane world of fifth-century Ravenna to the alternative culture of northern European *eorlas* and *ceorlas* ('noblemen and freemen'). A comparable shift can be observed when this same translator speaks of a wagon wheel as an equivalent to the Boethian image of the concentric circles of the spheres.[3]

Accordingly, the present chapter will address both textuality per se and those issues of cultural transformation that have to do with the making of Anglo-Saxon books and texts.

The Anglo-Saxon Book: Icon or Pragmatic Object?

The Lindisfarne Gospels (London, British Library MS Cotton Nero D.iv), an acknowledged masterpiece, is a suitable starting point for discussion of high-end book-making during the early Middle Ages.[4] No other manuscript that is known to have been produced in an Anglo-Saxon scriptorium more clearly illustrates the role of the Book as a leading symbol of Christianity.

Research by Michelle P. Brown, the former curator of illuminated manuscripts at the British Library, has tended to confirm that this priceless manuscript was written out some time around the year 700 – that is, during the lifetime of the Venerable Bede – by a single scribe working alongside a team of artists and artisans at the Northumbrian monastery of Lindisfarne. The character of the book's script, as well as its lavish ornamentation, reflects the character of Lindisfarne as a locus where multiple cultural impulses coalesced. While by

---

[3]   This passage, which was singled out for discussion by Milton McC. Gatch, *Loyalties and Traditions: Man and His World in Old English Literature* (New York: Bobbs-Merrill, 1971), 103–10, is the subject of extensive analysis by Adrian Papahagi, 'From Boethius's *Orbes* Simile to the Wheel of Fate Metaphor in the Old English Version of the *Consolatio Philosophiae* (IV, prose 6.15)', *Scriptorium* 63 (2009): 3–29. A comprehensive analysis of the prose version of the Old English Boethius, seen in relation to its Latin original, is offered by Nicole Guenther Discenza, *The King's English: Strategies of Translation in The Old English Boethius* (Albany: State University of New York Press, 2005).

[4]   For basic information see Janet Backhouse, *The Lindisfarne Gospels* (London: Phaidon, 1981).

the year 700, Lindisfarne was lodged firmly within the orbit of Roman Christendom, the monastery had been founded by Irish-speaking monks whose mother church was the abbey of Iona, in the Inner Hebrides. Iona, in turn, was influenced by contacts involving Ireland and the early Christian communities of the Middle East and Coptic Egypt. As Brown emphasizes in her 2003 book *The Lindisfarne Gospels: Society, Spirituality, and the Scribe*, the making of the Lindisfarne Gospels therefore involved a rich fusion of cultures:[5]

> The volume's decoration conjures up a world in which the old order was giving way to the new, an uneasy, reckless time during which one of the great shifts in world history was taking place and cultures were metamorphosing and melting into one another, giving birth to new identities. There are echoes of the vigour of prehistoric societies – Celts, Picts and the Germanic/Scandinavian peoples – whose secrets are shrouded in the mists of time and are still being yielded up to the archaeologist's trowel, and of encoded symbolism and ostentatious visible consumption of wealth. There are, woven into its pages, testimonies to the learning and culture of the Graeco-Roman world, of early Byzantium, papal Rome, Lombardic and Ostrogothic Italy and Frankish Gaul. The pivotal role of the Middle East, of Jerusalem, Palestine and Coptic Egypt (home of the ascetic desert fathers, the 'hard men' of the early Christian church) is acknowledged and celebrated within its pages too.

The complexity of the cultural interchanges mentioned by Brown is consistent with the weight that scholars have recently been putting on the cosmopolitan character of Anglo-Saxon culture from its very inception, once the early Saxon settlements were in place and Christianity had been reintroduced to Britain by Irish and Roman missionaries. A greater contrast to nineteenth-century stereotypes of the 'primitive Germanic' character of early Anglo-Saxon England can scarcely be imagined.

Of special interest to literary scholars is the section of Brown's book headed 'Script as Icon: The Book as Teacher, Preacher and Cult Focus' (pp. 66–78). Here books with a powerful religious content are discussed as 'embodiments of divinity' (p. 69) that were valued for their apotropaic value as well as their power of prophylaxis (that is, their healing power, if laid on an ill person's chest, for example). As Brown points out, very precious books, like holy relics, might be kept for the most part unseen as part of a church's treasury of icons. They thus partook of the mystique that pertains to hidden sources of power. Sacred calligraphy as well, much as in Islamic tradition, was a feature of the design of certain books. A famous instance is the 'Chi/Rho' page of the Lindisfarne Gospels, with its group of stylized letters, both Greek and Roman in origin, that record the incipit of the gospel of Matthew and that stand for the name of Christ (fol. 29r; see Brown pp. 334–36 and her plate XII). The 'carpet' pages of this same manuscript – pages that face the incipit pages of the four Gospels and that contain nothing but ornament – participate in the book's symbolism. 'The *crux gemmata* ("jewelled Cross") and the Gospelbook', writes Brown, referring to two major symbols of early Christianity, 'combine in an electrifying symbiosis in the magnificent diptychs of cross-carpet page and decorated incipit in the Lindisfarne Gospels,

---

5   Michelle P. Brown, *The Lindisfarne Gospels: Society, Spirituality, and the Scribe* (Toronto: University of Toronto Press, 2003), at pp. 1 and 4. Note also Brown's more recent study *The Lindisfarne Gospels and the Early Medieval World* (London: British Library, 2011).

where, I would suggest, the crosses and adorned words embody the Godhead and we are presented with the physical embodiment of the Word' (p. 75).

Ordinary manuscripts, too, are not without their interest. A critic's interest in a manuscript may be heightened if the book shows signs of use, even to the point of appearing disorderly. An example is the 'Commonplace Book' of Wulfstan the homilist, the major ecclesiast and law-maker of the late Anglo-Saxon period who served first as Bishop of London (996–1002) and then concurrently as Bishop of Worcester (1002–16) and Archbishop of York (1002–23). The term 'Commonplace Book' is used of a collection of canonical, liturgical, and homiletic writings thought to have been put together originally either by or for Wulfstan at Worcester in the early years of the eleventh century. In her 1942 study 'Archbishop Wulfstan's Commonplace Book', Dorothy Bethurum regards this anthology as an attempt to regulate the practices of both bishops and lesser clergy under Wulfstan's supervision.[6] In one form or another, miscellanies of a textually related kind were used to similar purpose, though with changes of detail and emphasis, through the twelfth century and into the thirteenth, and at least eleven such manuscripts are identified as one or another instantiation of the 'Commonplace Book'. Certain of these manuscripts are casual in appearance and include annotations and insertions that indicate their practical use. One of them, London, British Library MS Cotton Nero A.i, includes interpolations and additions made by Wulfstan himself, in addition to an assortment of marginalia, scribbles, and doodles that appear to date from as late as the beginning of the fourteenth century.[7] As a group, as Bethurum observes, the 'Commonplace Book' manuscripts feature not just definable works that can be attributed to known authors, but also short chapters and sentences interspersed fairly much at random, including fragmentary sentences and paragraphs.[8]

Only in the most tenuous sense could Wulfstan's 'Commonplace Book' be said to call up the idea of the Book as an icon of the faith. Rather, study of its textual history, starting with Wulfstan himself and continuing over a period of almost three centuries, provides evidence that the culture of the book in Anglo-Saxon England could also be personal, pragmatic, dynamic, and contested, as well as remarkably persistent over time. Current scholarship has been equally concerned with these two coexisting sides of Anglo-Saxon textuality, the hieratic and the dynamic.

---

[6]   Dorothy Bethurum, 'Archbishop Wulfstan's Commonplace Book', *PMLA* 57 (1942): 916–29, at 916–17.

[7]   *A Wulfstan Manuscript: London, British Library MS Cotton Nero A.i*, ed. Henry R. Loyn, EEMF 17 (Copenhagen: Rosenkilde & Bagger, 1971). With this facsimile can be compared *The Copenhagen Wulfstan Collection: Copenhagen Kongelige Bibliotek Gl. kgl. sam. 1595*, ed. James E. Cross and Jennifer Morrish Tunberg, EEMF 25 (Copenhagen: Rosenkilde & Bagger, 1993). Facsimile pages from other Commonplace Book manuscripts are included in Mildred Budny, *Insular, Anglo-Saxon, and Early Anglo-Norman Manuscript Art at Corpus Christi College, Cambridge: An Illustrated Catalogue*, 2 vols (Kalamazoo: Medieval Institute Publications, 1997), vol. 1, pp. 535–44 and 599–608, and vol. 2, plates 456–60 and 550–59.

[8]   The stemmatic relationship of the Commonplace Book manuscripts has been charted by Hans Sauer, 'The Transmission and Structure of Archbishop Wulfstan's *Commonplace Book*', in *Readings: OE Prose*, 339–93. A preliminary version of this article appeared as 'Zur Überlieferung und Anlage von Erzbischof Wulfstans "Handbuch"', *Deutsches Archiv für Erforschung des Mittelalters* 36 (1980): 341–84.

Writerly Self-Reflexivity

There is reason to think that members of the Anglo-Saxon clergy were fascinated by their own literacy, even to the point that one can speak of the workings of a 'mythology of script' at that time.[9] Literacy meant more than the ability to read books; it was also a power by which people could make books, rework them, gloss them, fashion them in new configurations, or fill in their marginal spaces with sketches or writings that had anything or nothing to do with their original contents. Literate people also engaged with – and played with – the *idea* of books as elements of their social world, and with script itself as a special medium with potentially arcane associations.

The self-reflexivity of writers is especially evident in the genre of the riddle, as exemplified by the ninety-five or so Old English riddles of the Exeter Book. As Laurence K. Shook points out in his 1974 article 'Riddling Relating to the Anglo-Saxon Scriptorium', a number of these have as their solution one or another object associated with the activity of scribes. These solutions include the feather or quill pen, the inkwell, parchment, the writer's fingers, the book itself, or (in one droll riddle) the book's eternal foe, the bookworm.[10] An example is K-D 51, which can be solved just as well either in Old English as *feðer* or in Latin as *penna*, for both these common nouns have the double meaning 'pen' or 'bird's feather'.[11] This riddle depends on that avian pun, for it speaks of an object that swiftly 'flew aloft' (the quill pen) and then 'dove beneath the wave' (the ink of the inkwell) before then leaving black 'footprints' on the page. Another riddle that pertains to the scriptorium is K-D 60. Though some critics do not include this poem in the genre of the riddle proper, to my mind it is one, and it is best solved in the Old English tongue as *hreod*, a word whose semantic field can include either 'reed', 'reed pipe or flute', or 'reed pen'. The riddler plays on the triple ambiguity of this word, for the speaking object first tells how it grew up in isolation in a watery homeland by the shore of the sea; it then refers to a period of its life when it was able to 'speak' (even though 'mouthless') over the mead-bench; and it then tells how, in a third incarnation, it has been cut by a knife in such a manner as to be able to deliver a silent message 'to you, for the two of us alone'. The riddle's answer is thus the *hreod* in its three modes of existence as reed, reed pipe, and reed pen. One intriguing aspect of this text is that its shape-changing speaker turns out to be the very pen that has written the verse riddle that the reader is trying to solve. The text thus involves the conceit whereby a text that was written at any time or place whatsoever can still be read as if it were an intimate

---

[9] Seth Lerer's book *Literacy and Power in Anglo-Saxon Literature* (Lincoln: University of Nebraska Press, 1991) has already been mentioned in this connection.

[10] Laurence K. Shook, 'Riddling Relating to the Anglo-Saxon Scriptorium', in *Essays in Honour of Anton Charles Pegis*, ed. J. Reginald O'Donnell (Toronto: Pontifical Institute of Mediaeval Studies, 1974), 215–36. See further chap. 3, 'The Riddle and the Book' (pp. 97–125), of Lerer's study *Literacy and Power*, as well as my book *Old English Enigmatic Poems and the Play of the Texts* (Turnhout: Brepols, 2006) at 117–22, 126–27, 130–32, and 148 n. 26.

[11] The abbreviation 'K-D' refers to the numbers assigned to the Exeter Book riddles in vol. 3 of the collective ASPR edition, whose joint editors are George Philip Krapp and Elliott Van Kirk Dobbie.

communication meant for the present reader alone. Although critics have often assumed that the normal way in which Old English poetry was received was via the voicing of texts,[12] this particular riddle is of interest for its allusion to silent reading.

The device of the 'speaking object', known in the schools as prosopopoeia, was evidently popular both in Latinate and Germanic cultural contexts, for there are examples of it in inscriptions on Anglo-Saxon sculpture, metalwork, and jewellery.[13] In a 2005 study on Anglo-Saxon scribal colophons, prefaces, and similar texts, Peter Orton devotes particular attention to texts where the books of this period purport to speak to the reader in the first person singular voice.[14] A leading example is the latter part of the metrical preface to King Alfred's Old English translation of St Gregory the Great's *Cura pastoralis*, a book regulating the conduct of bishops. In this short poem, which is rhetorically more venturesome than the didactic text that it prefaces, Gregory's book recounts in its own voice, as it were, what its mission was once it had been brought from Rome over the salt sea to the island of Britain. 'After that', the book tells its reader, 'King Alfred translated each and every word of me into English and sent me to his scribes south and north; he commanded that additional copies be made according to this exemplar, so that he could send them on to his bishops.'[15] Orton argues that the device of prosopopoeia lends King Alfred's translation heightened authority. In addition, of course, whoever composed this text must have had a riddler's penchant for play involving an inanimate object's point of view.

It has by now become a critical commonplace that language and letters themselves can be the subject of play in Anglo-Saxon literature. Sometimes what is involved is play on the sound of words – the figure called paronomasia in the schools, or what in modern terminology is called punning, though the modern word implies a comic element that is not necessarily present in medieval examples. In her influential 1972 article 'Some Uses of Paronomasia in Old English Scriptural Verse', Roberta Frank calls attention to many examples of this type of wordplay.[16] Other linguistic games to be found in Anglo-Saxon literature are meant for the eye as well as the ear, for they involve manipulation of the letters of the alphabet. An example is the medieval Latin genre of the acrostic poem, of which Dunstan, one of the founders of the tenth-century Benedictine Reform, wrote a

---

[12] For example, R.D. Fulk and Christopher M. Cain emphasize 'the orality of the medium' of Old English poetry in general, adding that 'all Old English poems were sung, or capable of being sung, to the accompaniment of a stringed instrument, a lyre or harp': R.D. Fulk and Christopher M. Cain, *A History of Old English Literature* (Oxford: Blackwell, 2003), 28.

[13] See for example David A. Hinton, *The King Alfred Jewel and Other Late Anglo-Saxon Decorated Metalwork* (Oxford: Ashmolean Museum, 2008).

[14] Peter Orton, 'Deixis and the Untransferable Text: Anglo-Saxon Colophons, Verse-Prefaces and Inscriptions', in *Imagining the Book*, ed. Stephen Kelly and John J. Thompson (Turnhout: Brepols, 2005), 195–208.

[15] *The Anglo-Saxon Minor Poems*, ed. Elliott Van Kirk Dobbie, ASPR 6 (New York: Columbia University Press, 1942), 110, lines 11–15a (my paraphrase).

[16] Roberta Frank, 'Some Uses of Paronomasia in Old English Scriptural Verse', *Speculum* 47 (1972): 207–26, repr. in *Readings: Junius MS*, 69–98. For discussion of thematically significant wordplay in *The Seafarer* by the critic Stanley B. Greenfield, see Chapter 6 below.

notoriously difficult example.[17] Earlier in the present chapter mention was made of the arcane lettering on certain pages of the Lindisfarne Gospels, for example the 'Chi-Rho' page that begins the Gospel of St Matthew. The highly stylized Greek and Latin letters used on this page would have heightened its hieratic value. Another example is the use of runes for certain inscriptions carved into the perimeters of the shaft of the Ruthwell Cross, a Northumbrian stone sculpture that appears to have been made at about this same time (though the date of all its parts is disputed).[18] As is well known, the words spelled out by these runes closely parallel the wording of parts of the tenth-century poem *The Dream of the Rood*, the visionary work in which the True Cross is imagined to speak to the dreamer (and reader) in the first person singular voice. The runes of the Ruthwell Cross throw a veil of mystery over the cross's words. Only a learned 'docent' conversant with both the runic alphabet and Christian iconography, it could be argued, could have explicated the meaning of this monument to its viewers.

Most present-day runologists tend to assume that runes and paganism did not neces-sarily have anything to do with one another, despite what modern writers have sometimes had to say about rune-magic.[19] Unclouded thinking on this topic is offered in R.I. Page's study *An Introduction to English Runes*.[20] One of Page's leading assumptions is that runes that are recorded in manuscript sources (rather than being inscribed on metal or stone) reflect an interest in the letters of the runic alphabet qua letters, seen as an alternative to the Roman alphabet. Since each rune of the futhorc (the runic alphabet) had a name as well as a phonetic value (for example, the runic letter F traditionally stood for both the phoneme <f> and the word *feoh* 'wealth'), runes could be deployed either as letters or logographs, or as both these things at once. This double capacity opened up prospects for linguistic play. The Old English *Rune Poem*, for example, consists of little more than a list of runic letters accompanied by short versified passages, each of which begins with the name of the rune (which must be supplied by the reader). Though this poem is sometimes spoken of as if it were 'archaic' or 'primitive' on the grounds that runes pertain to ancient Germania, it can also be approached as an expression of the learning of the Anglo-Saxon scriptorium.

---

[17] See the appendix (pp. 108–11) to Michael Lapidge's study 'The Hermeneutic Style in Tenth-Century Anglo-Latin Literature', *ASE* 4 (1975): 67–111. In the Anglo-Latin context, the term 'hermeneutic' refers to an author's use of highly recondite diction, often involving Greek lexical roots.

[18] For full discussion of this monument and its inscriptions, with illustrative photographs, see *The Ruthwell Cross: Papers from the Colloquium Sponsored by the Index of Christian Art*, ed. Brendan Cassidy (Princeton: Princeton University Press, 1992). A diagrammatic sketch of the runes is reproduced at p. 115 of *The Anglo-Saxon Minor Poems* (ASPR 6), with transcription.

[19] See for example R.W.V Elliott's study *Runes: An Introduction* (Manchester: Manchester University Press, 1959), as well as two articles by that same author on Cynewulf's runic signatures that are reprinted in *Readings: Cynewulf*, 281–307. Elliott often construes Anglo-Saxon runic writings in such a manner as to reveal what he considers to be their ancient and ultimately pagan content.

[20] R.I. Page, *An Introduction to English Runes* (London: Methuen, 1973); 2nd edn, Boydell Press, 1999. Page's chap. 5 ('*Runica Manuscripta* and the Rune-Names') and chap. 12 ('More Manuscript Runes') are of special interest to students of Old English literature, as is his chap. 8 ('How to Use Runes').

Whatever their motives were, Anglo-Saxon writers sometimes chose to mystify their readers by incorporating runic letters into passages of ordinary script.[21] Cynewulf is a noteworthy example, with his use of runic letters to encode his name into the text of four extant Old English religious poems. In her 1975 article 'The Art of Cynewulf's Runic Signatures', Dolores Warwick Frese points out the literary finesse of this rhetorical stratagem while also giving a sympathetic account of Cynewulf's devotional purposes.[22] Cryptography involving either runic letters or the letters of the roman alphabet is a feature of the Exeter Book riddles, as well, while an enigmatic cluster of runes figures importantly in the Exeter Book poem *The Husband's Message*.[23] Moreover, the Old English dialogic poem *Solomon and Saturn I* offers an arresting example of scribal play involving the futhorc, for at lines 84–140 of this poem the letters that are required to spell out the Paternoster are introduced one by one as if each were a warrior capable of striking blows against the devil.[24] In one of the two extant copies of this work (namely Cambridge, Corpus Christi College MS 422, Part A), the letters are written out in runes as well as in roman capitals, while in the other they are written in roman capitals alone. In the view of this poem's most recent editor, Daniel Anlezark, the runes in CCCC 422 were probably added as an expression of 'a highly literate playfulness'.[25]

Cryptographic texts such as the ones just mentioned problematize the question of audience. Were Old English cryptographic poems written down so that they might be voiced aloud? Or were they meant for private reading? The question of the prospective audience of Old English literary works has attracted increasing attention in recent years as long-held assumptions about the aural reception of Old English poetry have been interrogated.[26] Rather than speaking of a work's singular 'audience', as if it were a timeless document addressed to persons who had no embodied location in time or space, critics are now more likely to speak in the plural of the work's prospective 'audiences', thus acknowledging that a work may

---

[21] See Robert DiNapoli, 'Odd Characters: Runes in Old English Poetry', in *Verbal Encounters: Anglo-Saxon and Old Norse Studies for Roberta Frank*, ed. Antonina Harbus and Russell Poole (Toronto: University of Toronto Press, 2005), 145–61. Cryptography in the Exeter Book riddles is discussed as well by Dieter Bitterli, *Say What I Am Called: The Old English Riddles of the Exeter Book and the Anglo-Latin Riddle Tradition* (Toronto: University of Toronto Press, 2009), chaps 4–6 (pp. 83–131).

[22] Dolores Warwick Frese, 'The Art of Cynewulf's Runic Signatures', in *Anglo-Saxon Poetry: Essays in Appreciation for John C. McGalliard*, ed. Lewis E. Nicholson and Dolores Warwick Frese (Notre Dame: University of Notre Dame Press, 1975), 312–34, repr. in *Cynewulf: Readings*, 323–45.

[23] Discussion of this crux is central to my article 'The Trick of the Runes in *The Husband's Message*', *ASE* 32 (2003): 189–223, repr. with revisions in my *Old English Enigmatic Poems*, 213–50.

[24] For the text of this passage see *The Old English Dialogues of Solomon and Saturn*, ed. Daniel Anlezark (Cambridge: D.S. Brewer, 2009), 68–70; for commentary, see pp. 28–31 of Anlezark's Introduction to this volume as well as F. B. Jonassen, 'The Pater Noster Letters in the Poetic Solomon and Saturn', *Modern Language Review* 83 (1988): 1–9.

[25] Anlezark, *The Old English Dialogues*, 29.

[26] Note for example Hugh Magennis, 'Audience(s), Reception, Literacy', in Pulsiano & Treharne, 84–101.

have had multiple readers or listeners at different times.[27] Critics' recent engagements with arcane elements in the manuscript records of Old English verse have contributed to a shift away from a perception of that verse as public, voiced, and declamatory – and hence, in the minds of some, as essentially primitive or Germanic – towards a perception of certain specific poems as being learned, artistically complex, and intellectually demanding, much like the Latin verse that was produced during this same period.

Reading Old English Texts in their Manuscript Context

A turning point in the recent criticism of Old English literature was reached in the year 1982 with the publication of Fred C. Robinson's essay 'Old English Literature in Its Most Immediate Context'.[28] At the start of that essay, Robinson expresses his thesis as follows (p. 11):

> My thesis is that when we read an Old English literary text we should take care to find out what precedes it in its manuscript state and what follows it. We should know whether it is an independent text or part of another, larger text. We should have some sense of the poem's *mise en page* and some conception of the manuscript as a whole. For medieval books often constituted composite artefacts in which each component text depended on its environment for part of its meaning. If a text is detached from its codicological environment (as texts normally are in our modern editions), we risk losing that part of its meaning.

Robinson supports his argument for a contextualist approach to Anglo-Saxon manuscript culture with reference first of all to a minor poem that has been imperfectly understood. This is a scribal colophon, or address to the reader, known to readers of ASPR as 'The Metrical Epilogue to Manuscript 41, Corpus Christi College, Cambridge'. Study of this poem opens up consideration of scribes as agents who sometimes made meaningful interventions in the works they copied. Robinson broadens his claims by taking into account the poem known as *Maxims II* or *The Cotton Gnomes*, showing the significance of the position of this work at the head of the handsome manuscript in which it is uniquely written out (London, British Library MS Cotton Tiberius B.i). Here it directly precedes first the poem known as the *Menologium* (an account of the seasons and festal days of the Christian year) and then a major version of the Anglo-Saxon Chronicle (version C, also known as the Abingdon Chronicle II). These three works, written out by the same hand, are shown to have a coherent relation to one another as the reader proceeds from the timeless realm (that of the maxims), to cyclical time (the liturgical year), to historical time

---

[27] This is the practice adopted in chap. 2 ('Date, Provenance, Author, Audiences') of the *Beowulf Handbook*, for example.

[28] Fred C. Robinson, 'Old English Literature in Its Most Immediate Context', in Niles, 11–29 and 157–61, repr. in Robinson's essay collection *The Editing of Old English* (Oxford: Blackwell, 1994), 3–24, and in *Readings: Shorter Poems*, 3–29 (there without photographic plates).

(the particular events noted in the Chronicle). Robinson offers this as just one example of the collaborative processes that resulted in meaningful collocations of texts in manuscripts of the Anglo-Saxon period.

Robinson's seminal essay served to direct critical attention away from modern editions of Old English literary works so as to take into account the ways in which such works were written out, and were received, in the Anglo-Saxon manuscript records. Certain more recent publications direct attention to the art and craft of writing itself, in the most literal sense (palaeography). Others focus on how whole books or segments of books were compiled out of individual sheets or clusters of parchment (codicology). A valuable resource in the first of these subdisciplines is *The Historical Source Book for Scribes*, by Michelle P. Brown and Patricia Lovett.[29] This offers hands-on instruction as to how to write like a medieval scribe, using virtually identical writing materials, techniques, and letter-forms. Another invaluable sourcebook for palaeography is Jane Roberts's 2005 *Guide to Scripts Used in English Writings up to 1500*.[30] This includes photographic facsimiles of handwritten pages, meticulously accurate transcriptions of scribal texts, and a well-informed commentary. A third welcome resource is Michelle P. Brown's 2007 book *Manuscripts from the Anglo-Saxon Age*. This volume, which represents a thorough revision of an earlier publication by Brown on that same subject, includes facsimile pages beautifully reproduced in colour, with an informed commentary.[31] Another essential publication is Raymond Clemens and Timothy Graham's 2007 *Introduction to Manuscript Studies*.[32] The two authors offer an informed discussion of types of parchment, pigments, scribal corrections, glossing, rubrication, punctuation, and abbreviations, among other topics. They also discuss the medieval production of different types of manuscript, from deluxe gospels and psalters to more pragmatic texts such as charters and cartularies. While neither this book nor the others just mentioned has a direct bearing on the criticism of Old English literature, each contributes to a growing body of scholarship about medieval manuscript culture, familiarity with which has become a sine qua non for present-day criticism.

Not by coincidence, the 'back to the manuscripts' movement of recent decades coincides with the increasing availability of high-quality facsimile images of the pages of medieval manuscripts. Certain recent books have been published in conjunction with an independently marketed optical disc. An example is Kevin Kiernan and Andrew Prescott's 1999 publication *Electronic Beowulf*, which consists of two discs providing high-quality digital images of each page of the *Beowulf* manuscript, together with ancillary materials that include facsimiles of the two Thorkelin transcripts of *Beowulf* dating from the late

---

[29] Michelle P. Brown and Patricia Lovett, *The Historical Source Book for Scribes* (London: British Library, 1999).

[30] Jane Roberts, *Guide to Scripts Used in English Writings up to 1500* (London: British Library, 2005).

[31] Michelle P. Brown, *Manuscripts from the Anglo-Saxon Age* (Toronto: University of Toronto Press, 2007); this represents a much expanded version of her book *Anglo-Saxon Manuscripts* (London: British Library, 1991).

[32] Raymond Clemens and Timothy Graham, *Introduction to Manuscript Studies* (Ithaca: Cornell University Press, 2007).

eighteenth century.[33] Two electronic publications of comparable value are *A Digital Facsimile of Oxford, Bodleian Library, MS. Junius 11*, produced by Bernard J. Muir and Nick Kennedy in 2004,[34] and 'The Exeter DVD', otherwise known as *The Exeter Anthology of Old English Poetry*, produced by Muir and Kennedy in 2006 as a companion to Muir's print edition of the poems of the Exeter Book.[35]

At least as significant as such individual publications as these are the efforts being made by a number of libraries to publish systematic sets of online digital images of their medieval manuscript holdings, whether free of charge or through individual or institutional subscription. Among the libraries that have taken a leading role in this process are the Bodleian Library, Oxford; the British Library, London; and the Parker Library of Corpus Christi College, Cambridge. Details about these and other online publishing projects need not be given here, given how rapidly this dimension of medieval studies is changing. Searches on the World Wide Web that focus on individual libraries will yield up-to-date information.

One of the most ambitious current projects in Anglo-Saxon manuscript studies is Anglo-Saxon Manuscripts in Microfiche Facsimile (ASMMF),[36] a series, that is intended to make readily available a photographic record of each and every page containing Old English writings. Individual fascicles in the series, each of which is edited by a distinguished scholar (or scholarly team), feature a cluster of related manuscripts such as 'psalters', 'gospels', or 'anonymous homilies'. Each fascicle includes an expert description of the manuscripts it contains. The first fascicle was published in 1994, while almost two dozen others, out of a projected total of about forty, had appeared in print by the end of 2014. While the use of microfiches as a medium for facsimile images is less than ideal – high-quality digital images would be preferred – this aspect of the ASMMF production was governed by licensing restraints.

Among other noteworthy publications pertaining to manuscript studies,[37] two stand out for their value as reference works. One of these is the 2014 publication *Anglo-Saxon*

---

[33] *Electronic Beowulf*, ed. Kevin Kiernan with Andrew Prescott (London: British Library, 1999). This publication supplements (and can be used independently of) Kiernan's book *Beowulf and the Beowulf Manuscript*, 2nd edn (Ann Arbor: University of Michigan Press, 1996; first published 1981).

[34] Bernard J. Muir and Nick Kennedy, *A Digital Facsimile of Oxford, Bodleian Library, MS. Junius 11*, Bodleian Digital Texts 1 (Oxford: Bodleian Library, 2004), CD-ROM.

[35] Bernard J. Muir and Nick Kennedy, *The Exeter Anthology of Old English Poetry* (Exeter: Exeter University Press, 2006); this supplements the two-volume edition abbreviated as 'Muir' in the present book.

[36] The chief editor of ASMMF over the years has been A.N. Doane, now Professor Emeritus of English at the University of Wisconsin–Madison. The series is presently co-edited by Matthew T. Hussey of Simon Fraser University, Vancouver.

[37] Four of these deserve mention here, if only in passing: these are *Anglo-Saxon Manuscripts and their Heritage*, ed. Phillip Pulsiano and Elaine M. Treharne (Aldershot: Ashgate, 1998); *Old English Literature in its Manuscript Context*, ed. Joyce Tally Lionarons (Morgantown: West Virginia University Press, 2004); *The Genesis of Books: Studies in the Scribal Culture of Medieval England in Honour of A.N. Doane*, ed. Matthew T. Hussey and myself (Turnhout: Brepols, 2011); and *Readings: MSS*.

Manuscripts: A Bibliographical Handlist, compiled by Helmut Gneuss and Michael Lapidge. This lists every book known to have been in circulation in Anglo-Saxon England whether composed in Latin or English (or in both languages) and whether extant now or not.[38] The other is Michael Lapidge's 2006 study *The Anglo-Saxon Library*, the most systematic attempt yet made to describe the libraries of Anglo-Saxon England's monasteries and cathedrals and to itemize their known or probable holdings.[39] Thanks to these two publications alone, researchers can now speak with far greater assurance than before about actual Anglo-Saxon textual communities and the books that were available to their members.

It is impossible to predict what additional insights into the literature of Anglo-Saxon England will be gained as a result of this surge of attention to the manuscript itself as a primary source of knowledge. Recent research, for example, has drawn attention to the contributions of individual scribes to the 'flux of texts' in the Anglo-Saxon period. It is now becoming possible to ascribe some kind of identity to those scribes, together with evidence about their dates and places of activity, even if only via a number such as 'Hand no. 176d' rather than by a more personal designation. The most significant publication in this area is Donald Scragg's 2012 book *A Conspectus of Scribal Hands Writing English*,[40] which represents a distillation of results from several major research projects involving the identification of individual scribes of the late Anglo-Saxon period. Paradoxically, perhaps, we may soon know more about the scribes of individual works of Old English literature than we know about their authors. Concurrently, long-held assumptions regarding authorship and authority in the Old English context have been brought into question.

Authors and Scribes: The Flux of Texts

Research into almost any aspect of the manuscript culture of the Middle Ages provides evidence for the radical instability of texts, or what certain theorists have called *mouvance*.[41] As we have seen, for example, Ælfric's *Colloquy* was transmitted in several different forms, one of which was greatly augmented by Ælfric Bata. Likewise we have seen how complex and unstable the manuscript transmission was of Wulfstan's 'Commonplace Book'. These examples illustrate the point that only a relatively few medieval authors, such as the early Church Fathers, were granted the status of authorities whose works were not subject to

---

[38] Helmut Gneuss and Michael Lapidge, *Anglo-Saxon Manuscripts: A Bibliographical Handlist of Manuscripts and Manuscript Fragments Written or Owned in England up to 1100* (Toronto: University of Toronto Press, 2014).

[39] Michael Lapidge, *The Anglo-Saxon Library* (Oxford: Oxford University Press, 2006).

[40] Donald Scragg, *A Conspectus of Scribal Hands Writing English, 960–1100* (Cambridge: D.S. Brewer, 2012).

[41] A leading theorist in this area is the Swiss-French and Canadian medievalist Paul Zumthor, one of whose influential studies is 'Intertextualité et mouvance', *Littérature* 41 (1981): 8–16. Pursuing closely related research is William Tim Machan, author of *Textual Criticism and Middle English Texts* (Charlottesville: University of Virginia Press, 1994). Machan's expertise is in the *mouvance* (or fluidity) of texts during the Middle English period.

alteration.[42] One may well ask: Is it possible to reconstruct the original form of a book such as Wulfstan's 'Commonplace Book' from the flux of manuscript records that pertain to it? Or is there much justification for doing so, as opposed to drawing on the transmission history of that work as evidence for trends in intellectual history, church discipline, or the like? One is probably wise not to have preconceptions about such matters, but rather to approach each work or cluster of works as a separate problem.

While vernacular writings were particularly subject to instability in their transmission, the same is true of many Latin works. Even Bede's Latin *Historia ecclesiastica*, which today seems a monument of early English historiography, was subject to change and augmentation, as Joanna Story has shown in her 2009 article 'After Bede: Continuing the *Ecclesiastical History*'.[43] Story traces how Bede's foundational account of the English was supplemented during the later eighth century, when additional historical material was added so as to bring it up to date. It was then translated into Old English some time around the year 900, with adaptations. Later on, during the post-Conquest period, Bede's Latin text was emended, augmented, and adapted on an ambitious scale as Anglo-Norman historians drew on Bede's authority so as to trace the origins of the English from their own perspective.

Manuscript copies of Ælfric's works, too, including his major collection the Catholic Homilies, were reworked during the centuries after that author's death. Although Ælfric mandates that his writings be copied exactly as he wrote them – 'Now I pray and implore in God's name, if anyone wants to copy this book, that he correct it carefully against the exemplar'[44] – his texts were in fact subject to scribal alterations that extended even to the rewriting of whole homilies, as recent research has shown.[45] Jonathan Wilcox

[42] See on this topic A.J. Minnis, *Medieval Theory of Authorship: Scholastic Literary Attitudes in the Later Middle Ages* (London: Scolar Press, 1984). Mary Swan, 'Authorship and Anonymity', in Pulsiano & Treharne, 71–83, discusses the means by which Anglo-Saxon authors tried to assert their authority even though their wish to preserve the integrity of their work was 'ultimately unrealizable' (p. 79).

[43] Joanna Story, 'After Bede: Continuing the *Ecclesiastical History*', in *Early Medieval Studies in Memory of Patrick Wormald*, ed. Stephen David Baxter et al. (Aldershot: Ashgate, 2009), 165–84. See also R.H.C. Davis, 'Bede after Bede', in *Studies in Medieval History Presented to R. Allen Brown*, ed. Christopher Harper-Bill (et al.) (Woodbridge: Boydell, 1989), 103–16, and Sharon Rowley, 'Bede in Later Anglo-Saxon England', in *The Cambridge Companion to Bede*, ed. Scott DeGregorio (Cambridge: Cambridge University Press, 2010), 216–28.

[44] 'Nu bydde ic and halsige on Godes naman, gif hwa þas boc awritan wylle, þæt he hi geornlice gerihte be ðære bysene': see Jonathan Wilcox, 'Transmission of Literature and Learning: Anglo-Saxon Scribal Culture', in Pulsiano & Treharne, 50–70 (at 64). For discussion see Wilcox's edition *Ælfric's Prefaces*, Durham Medieval Texts, 9 (Durham, UK: Department of English Studies, 1994), at 70–71.

[45] Note Joyce Hill, 'Ælfric, Authorial Identity and the Changing Text', in *The Editing of Old English: Papers from the 1990 Manchester Conference*, ed. D.G. Scragg and Paul E. Szarmach (Woodbridge: D.S. Brewer, 1994), 177–89; Mary Swan, 'Old English Made New: One Catholic Homily and its Reuses', *LSE* n.s. 28 (1997): 1–18; Hugh Magennis, 'Ælfric's Lives of Saints and Cotton Julius E.vii: Adaptation, Appropriation and the Disappearing Book', in Kelly and Thompson, *Imagining the Book*, 99–110; and Elaine Treharne, 'Making their Presence Felt: Readers of Ælfric, c. 1050–1350', in Magennis & Swan, 399–422.

thus concludes that 'Ælfric's sense of his work as an authorized and fixed text was not compatible with the practice of early medieval vernacular textual transmission.'[46]

Scripture was another matter. While the text of Holy Writ was not subject to change – to be sure, no scribe would have dared to alter it – any individual book containing religious texts might still be subject to influences that affected its appearance and character. Even the Lindisfarne Gospels was not exempt from this tendency. During the late tenth century, a scribe named Aldred added a small but distinct continuous interlinear Old English gloss to the Latin lettering of that masterpiece.[47] There is no reason to think that this was regarded as an act of desecration. On the contrary, from what we know of Aldred he was both a careful scribe and a prominent member of his community, for in later years he became bishop of the monastic community at Chester-le-Street, near Newcastle-upon-Tyne, where the Lindisfarne Gospels resided at that time. So this deluxe book, too, seems to have been valued not just as an iconic relic dating from a former age, but also as an object of continuing use in an environment where bilingual literacy had become the norm.

Old English verse texts present a special problem from this perspective. Thanks to their prosodic features, poems can be memorized more easily than prose texts. Were they relatively stable in their transmission or not? Such a question might well be posed of the unique manuscript copy of *Beowulf*, which dates from approximately the year 1000 although some specialists argue for a date of composition of the poem itself as early as the late seventh or early eighth century. Those who favour that view have to reckon with a time-span of at least two centuries, and possibly more, during which its written text was potentially subject to scribal alteration in the course of recopying.

The stability of the transmission of Old English poetry has been investigated recently by Jonathan Wilcox and others, including Peter Orton in his wide-ranging book *The Transmission of Old English Poetry*.[48] To sum up the main conclusion to which the research of these scholars points: close study of poetic texts that happen to survive in more than one medieval manuscript suggests that none of these copies can be taken as reliable evidence of 'the poem itself'. As Orton points out, obvious scribal errors occur with some frequency in poetic texts, as is unsurprising given the linguistic difficulty of Old English verse, which tends to employ a specialized diction involving unusual compound words and arresting metaphors. In the course of transmission, moreover, some whole lines of verse can drop out and new lines can be added, while other lines are rewritten in a creative manner. In her influential 1990 book *Visible Song*, Katherine O'Brien O'Keeffe shows that Anglo-Saxon

---

[46] Wilcox, 'Transmission of Literature and Learning', 63.

[47] Aldred's gloss is visible on practically every page of the Lindisfarne Gospels: see for example Brown, *The Lindisfarne Gospels*, plates 3–5, 11–13, 15, 17, 21, and 25.

[48] Wilcox, 'Transmission of Literature and Learning', 55–63; Peter Orton, *The Transmission of Old English Poetry* (Turnhout: Brepols, 2000). A seminal study in this area of research is Kenneth Sisam's 'The Authority of Old English Poetical Manuscripts', *RES* 22 (1946): 257–68, repr. in that author's essay collection *Studies in the History of Old English Literature* (Oxford: Clarendon Press, 1953), 29–44, as well as in Stevens & Mandel, 36–51. In addition, Roy Michael Liuzza, 'The Texts of the Old English Riddle 30', *JEGP* 87 (1988): 1–15, offers a focused comparison of two different manuscript versions of what is usually spoken of as a single poem, though the two versions differ markedly from one another.

scribes exercised some freedom when copying 'Cædmon's Hymn', which survives in multiple copies either as a gloss on Bede's Latin text of the *Historia ecclesiastica* or in the Old English translation of that work.[49] The minor changes made by scribes to that nine-line poem resist the name of 'error', however, seeing that one variant may be just as satisfactory as another in terms of its versification and other formal properties. O'Brien O'Keeffe suggests that Anglo-Saxon scribes too, like Cædmon and other poets who may have learned their craft as participants in an oral tradition, could have been conversant with the style and the generative grammar of Old English verse.[50]

In keeping with these findings as well as with general trends in criticism, present-day Anglo-Saxonists are less likely than before to speak with assurance as to what constitutes 'the text' of a given work. In her 1995 book *The Textuality of Old English Poetry*, Carol Braun Pasternack mounts a radical critique of modern critical editions of medieval texts for being quasi-dictatorial in their efforts to manufacture a single 'clean' text of a work out of a jumble of conflicting manuscript readings. Adopting a stance that recalls the postmodern resistance to traditional notions of the centre versus the periphery, Pasternack expresses the wish – while quickly recognizing its impracticality – that modern scholarly editions could be 'cast aside' so that each and every variant of a medieval text, since it is 'as authentic as any other', could be allotted its own critical edition.[51] This might be called the 'constellation' approach to editing, as opposed to the 'star' approach that has long been in favour. While practical problems stand in the way of the realization of such an ideal, and while the attractiveness of the ideal itself is subject to debate, Pasternack gives voice to scholars' growing appreciation that each manuscript record of a literary work can have its own validity or interest, especially if that copy can be ascribed to a particular textual community.[52]

Research into the scribal transmission of Anglo-Saxon texts has a potential impact on the customary division of early English literature into two periods labelled 'Old English' and 'Middle English'. If Old English texts were copied until long after the Conquest, and if moreover they were revised, rewritten, glossed, and apparently used for practical purposes, then it is natural to ask what the justification is for drawing a sharp line at the year 1066, or

---

[49] Katherine O'Brien O'Keeffe, *Visible Song: Transitional Literacy in Old English Verse* (Cambridge: Cambridge University Press, 1990); note also O'Brien O'Keeffe's prior study 'Orality and the Developing Text of Cædmon's *Hymn*', *Speculum* 62 (1987): 1–20, repr. in *Readings: MSS*, 221–50 and in Liuzza, 79–102.

[50] Scribal variations of the kind pointed out by O'Brien O'Keeffe can be accounted for in multiple ways, however, as is maintained by Douglas Moffat, 'Anglo-Saxon Scribes and Old English Verse', *Speculum* 67 (1992): 805–27, and Peter Orton, 'The Transmission of the West Saxon Versions of *Cædmon's Hymn*: A Reappraisal', *Studia Neophilologica* 70 (1998): 153–64.

[51] Carol Braun Pasternack, *The Textuality of Old English Poetry* (Cambridge: Cambridge University Press, 1995), at pp. 28 and 26, respectively. Chap. 1 of this study is reprinted in Joy & Ramsey, 519–45.

[52] Worth note in this connection is the recent collective edition *La Chanson de Roland / The Song of Roland: The French Corpus*, gen. ed. Joseph J. Duggan, 3 vols (Turnhout, Brepols, 2005). Here six independent versions of 'a single work' receive even-handed editorial treatment. The time, labour, and expense involved in the production of an outstanding multi-volume edition like this, however, are not easily calculated.

even a blurry one at 'about the year 1100', so as to mark the end of the Old English period. This question is raised in two recent books that address the afterlife of Old English literature during the post-Conquest period, namely the 2000 essay collection *Rewriting Old English in the Twelfth Century* and Elaine Treharne's 2012 book *Living through Conquest: The Politics of Early English, 1020–1220*.[53] When one takes into account analogous questions about periodization that have been raised by specialists in the Middle English period,[54] there seems to be little reason to take the year of the Conquest as anything more than a decisive date in political history. In terms of literature and the history of the English language, scholars are increasingly hesitant to venture any date at all for the 'end' of the Old English period. One's perspective on this question is likely to differ, of course, depending on whether one has in mind Old English verse, very little of which was written down after about the year 1000, or Old English prose, especially legal texts and homilies, which continued to be copied and used long after the Conquest, especially in those pockets of the country such as Worcester where a sense of English identity remained strong.[55]

From Latin to Old English: Translation or Transformation?

If the scribal transmission of works written in either Latin or the vernacular was subject to instability, then what can be said about the transfer of textual materials across the linguistic divide that separates those two languages? Were significant changes involved when a work of Latin literature was translated into Old English? Moreover, what kind of changes occurred when either rhetorical figures or thematic *topoi* that were well-known features of the Latinate tradition were adopted by authors composing in English?

Janet M. Bately addresses the first of these questions, the one pertaining to translation, in her landmark 1980 essay 'The Literary Prose of King Alfred's Reign: Translation or Transformation?'[56] Her focus in this study is a set of three translations traditionally dated to the late ninth century and ascribed either to King Alfred the Great or to scholars

---

[53] *Rewriting Old English in the Twelfth Century*, ed. Mary Swan and Elaine M. Treharne (Cambridge: Cambridge University Press, 2000); Elaine M. Treharne, *Living through Conquest: The Politics of Early English, 1020–1220* (Oxford: Oxford University Press, 2012).

[54] Note in this connection Christopher Cannon, *The Grounds of English Literature* (Oxford: Oxford University Press, 2004), and 'Between the Old and the Middle of English', *New Medieval Literatures* 7 (2005): 203–21, and see further the discussion of the politics of periodization offered by Kathleen Davis, *Periodization and Sovereignty: How Ideas of Feudalism and Secularization Govern the Politics of Time* (Philadelphia: University of Pennsylvania Press, 2008).

[55] Of special interest has been the glossing of English-language manuscripts at twelfth- and thirteenth-century Worcester. See Christine Franzen, *The Tremulous Hand of Worcester: A Study of Old English in the Thirteenth Century* (Oxford: Clarendon Press, 1991); and two studies by Wendy E.J. Collier: '"Englishness" and the Worcester Tremulous Hand', *LSE* 26 (1995): 35–47, and 'A Thirteenth-Century User of Anglo-Saxon Manuscripts', *BJRL* 79 (1997): 149–65.

[56] Janet M. Bately, *The Literary Prose of King Alfred's Reign: Translation or Transformation?* Old English Newsletter Subsidia 10 (Binghamton, NY: CMERS, 1984), repr. in *Readings: OE Prose*, 3–27; the quotation in the following paragraph is from the Subsidia publication. Note also Bately's edition *The Old English Orosius*, EETS s.s. 6 (London: Oxford University Press, 1980).

working at his behest. These are the Old English prose psalms of the Paris Psalter; the earliest Old English version of Boethius's *De consolatione philosophiae*; and the Old English version of Paulus Ososius's early fifth-century history of the ancient world, the *Historiarum adversum paganos libri VII*. The ascription of this latter translation to Alfred's immediate circle of scholars is now doubted by many, including Bately. Indeed, the role of King Alfred in the production of the translations that have often been attributed to him or to his patronage has become a matter of sharp critical dispute. While Malcolm Godden has questioned the king's participation in the making of any of these translations, other authoritative specialists, including Bately, continue to see Alfred's role as both personal and significant.[57] The intriguing question of authorship, however, is peripheral to the one I am addressing here, which has to do with the substantive character of the translations.

Bately finds that considerable freedom of expression characterizes the wording of the Old English prose translation of the psalms. She likewise points out that the translator of the psalms incorporated into his text some materials drawn from a medieval commentary on the Psalter, thus changing the work's character. The translators of Boethius and Orosius, too, took significant liberties by adding explanatory or supplementary materials to their sources. Bately concludes that the most apt term to use for the making of these texts is indeed 'transformation' rather than 'translation'. Rather than offering literal versions of their sources, the translators 'transformed the Latin into what may be called independent English prose' (p. 21).

Similar conclusions have been reached by other researchers. While key elements of the source-text may remain stable, many changes of detail and emphasis can be noticed, and some of these innovations have ideological as well as rhetorical force. In his 1987 study 'Adaptation and *anweald* in the Old English Orosius', for example, William A. Kretzschmar, Jr, points out that the translator of Orosius tones down that author's polemical defence of early Christianity while still emphasizing a providential pattern in world history.[58] The translator achieves this end in part by dwelling on the role of *anweald*, or 'God-given authority to rule', in the course of human events, as contrasted to the raw exercise of power. Like the Anglo-Saxon Chronicle and the Old English translation of Bede's *Historia ecclesiastica* – two other major historical works whose generation is often linked to King Alfred's circle – the Old English Orosius served to characterize the English people and their rulers as 'part of a Grand Design which had not ended with Rome' (Kretzschmar, p. 143).

---

[57] Malcolm Godden, 'Did King Alfred Write Anything?', *MÆ* 76 (2007): 1–23, questions whether any surviving Old English texts should be ascribed to Alfred himself. Writing in response, Janet Bately, 'Did King Alfred Actually Translate Anything? The Integrity of the Alfredian Canon Revisited', *MÆ* 78 (2009): 189–215, has reasserted her view that the earliest version of the Old English Boethius can be attributed to Alfred, as can the Old English prose translation of the psalms, while likewise to be attributed to Alfred's sponsorship are the Old English versions of Gregory the Great's *Cura pastoralis* and of Augustine's *Soliloquies*. For a capsule overview of the Old English texts commonly known as 'Alfredian', see Nicole Discenza, 'Alfredian Texts', in *Blackwell Encyclopaedia*, 29–30; but cf. Godden, 'The Alfredian Project and its Aftermath: Rethinking the Literary History of the Ninth and Tenth Centuries', *PBA* 162 (2009): 93–122.

[58] William A. Kretzschmar, Jr, 'Adaptation and *anweald* in the Old English Orosius', *ASE* 16 (1987): 127–45.

The translation of Orosius is thus 'a piece of Alfredian revisionism' that had 'the welfare and quite possibly the justification of the state at its foundation' (p. 145).

A comparable argument relating to the translation of Bede's *Historia ecclesiastica* has been made by Nicole Discenza in her 2002 article 'The Old English *Bede* and the Construction of Anglo-Saxon Authority'.[59] Bede's work was evidently translated into Old English during the Alfredian period or thereabouts by a scholar (or perhaps several scholars) of Mercian origin. Discenza shows that the translator downplayed elements of the text that had lost their urgency, such as the controversy over the dating of Easter. In addition, Bede's deference to the authority of Pope Gregory the Great is minimized. Instead, the translator projects Bede himself into a position of authority, thereby adding lustre to that scholar's reputation while at the same time setting the isle of Britain and the English people at centre stage. As she concludes, 'The translation [...] dramatically recentres the text' (p. 77). Similarly, Sharon Rowley has observed that the translator reduced his source by about a third, making changes that decentre Roman authority, among other effects.[60] Whether or not one concludes that Bede's history was 'transformed' through these changes, clearly it was adapted in a deliberative manner that contributed to English identity-formation.

Translation, however, is just one of the means by which culture is transmitted across language barriers. Scholars have also asked if the rhetorical figures and tropes that were part of the Latin school curriculum were absorbed into works composed in the vernacular, and if so, what adaptations were involved.

In a pair of articles published in 1967 and 1978, Jackson J. Campbell demonstrated that writers of Old English prose of the later Anglo-Saxon period, Ælfric and Wulfstan in particular, frequently made use of rhetorical figures that were taught in the schools as part of the curriculum in *grammatica*.[61] This is only to be expected seeing that well-educated members of the clergy would have learned the craft of writing through such means. Such figures of speech as antithesis, anaphora, polysyndeton, and zeugma can readily be located in the work of these authors, to name just a few of the rhetorical devices that were taught as a means of structuring a discourse in an eloquent and persuasive manner. Moreover, Campbell traces the presence of a number of examples of recognized figures of speech in select examples of anonymous Old English verse, including the Exeter Book poems *The Phoenix*, *The Seafarer*, *The Wanderer*, and the first of the riddles.[62] Indeed it is easy enough

---

[59] Nicole Guenther Discenza, 'The Old English *Bede* and the Construction of Anglo-Saxon Authority', *ASE* 31 (2002): 69–80.

[60] Sharon Rowley, *The Old English Version of Bede's Historia Ecclesiastica* (Cambridge: D.S. Brewer, 2011), at p. 4.

[61] Jackson J. Campbell, 'Knowledge of Rhetorical Figures in Anglo-Saxon England', *JEGP* 66 (1967): 1–20, and 'Adaptation of Classical Rhetoric in Old English Literature', in *Medieval Eloquence: Studies in the Theory and Practice of Medieval Rhetoric*, ed. James J. Murphy (Berkeley: University of California Press, 1978), 173–97.

[62] Other scholars active at that time who called attention to the use of Latinate rhetorical figures in Old English verse include Ann S. Johnson, 'The Rhetoric of *Brunanburh*', *PQ* 47 (1968), 363–72; Milton McC. Gatch, *Loyalties and Traditions: Man and His World in Old English Literature* (New York: Pegasus, 1971), 98–99; and Marie Nelson, 'The Rhetoric of the Exeter Book Riddles', *Speculum* 49 (1974): 421–40.

to point to examples in these poems of such devices as paronomasia (wordplay on homophonic syllables of words thought to have an etymological connection), or personification (the ascription of human attributes to inanimate things), or synonomia (the close juxtaposition of different words that are nearly identical in meaning), to cite just three familiar ones. In her more recent book *Verse and Virtuosity*, Janie Steen has raised this matter anew in a detailed and nuanced way, concentrating her attention on *The Phoenix*, *Judgment Day II*, two of the Exeter Book riddles (nos. 35 and 40), and the signed poems of Cynewulf. Steen concludes that whether or not Old English poets learned Latinate schemes and tropes directly from rhetorical manuals used in the classroom, they very likely 'imbibed these devices from the actual Latin texts they were reading, mainly Christian Latin and Anglo-Latin authors'.[63]

Not all figures of speech deployed in Old English poetry can be assumed to be a product of the schools, however, seeing that Old English verse is permeated by a native rhetoric that was not necessarily reliant on Latinate models. For a modern reader of Old English verse to account for its system of versification by reference to 'paromoeon' (the Latin term for 'alliteration'), for example, might seem to be beside the point, even though that rhetorical term may be technically correct. Some of the metaphorical language that is characteristic of Old English poetry can plausibly be ascribed to the native poetic tradition, as well, especially the kennings, as when, for example, the ocean is called 'the gannet's bath', 'the cup of waves', or 'the courtyard of the winds'. Litotes, too, can assume a grimly northern aspect in Old English verse, as Roberta Frank points out in her 2006 article 'The Incomparable Wryness of Old English Poetry',[64] as when poets composing in Old English make use of the heavily accented negative prefix '*un-*' (still favoured in modern German). An example drawn from *Beowulf* is the *unfæger* light (literally the 'un-pretty light') that flames from Grendel's eyes as he enters the hall Heorot, where his intended victims lie sleeping (*Beowulf* 727). Such an idiom as this is unlikely to be borrowed from Latin school texts, even if it could be shown to have parallels there.

As Campbell wisely observes, the exact set of influences that lie behind an Old English poet's use of a known rhetorical figure may thus be impossible to determine, for 'there is always the possibility that a given figure may equally well be the result of the poet's instinctive use of his native linguistic tradition as the product of his following learned precepts acquired during his education.'[65] The point to be kept in mind is that it is just as unsafe to assume that a given Old English text was composed in conscious imitation of a Latinate rhetorical model as it is to assume that it was not. What is of special interest is the manner in which the figure is realized. Still, if a definite model for a particular figure can be identified in the Latinate rhetorical tradition, then this might help to fill in our understanding of the intellectual context in which the work was produced, and hence to sharpen our understanding of the work itself.

---

[63] Janie Steen, *Verse and Virtuosity: The Adaptation of Latin Rhetoric in Old English Poetry* (Toronto: University of Toronto Press, 2008), 139.

[64] Roberta Frank, 'The Incomparable Wryness of Old English Poetry', in *Inside Old English: Essays in Honour of Bruce Mitchell*, ed. John Walmsley (Oxford: Blackwell, 2006), 59–73.

[65] Campbell, 'Adaptation of Classical Rhetoric', 190.

Source Studies and the Culture of Translation

This question of possible learned influences on the rhetoric of Old English poetry can serve as an entry point to discussion of source studies, one of the more active areas of Old English literary research in recent years. This is a field of inquiry that offers both frustrations and the thrill of discoveries, and its payoff for literary criticism can be significant.[66]

Almost any reader of early medieval literature will be struck by its derivative character. One can scarcely identify a work of Anglo-Latin or Old English literature for which several possible sources or analogues cannot be named for certain of its parts, at least.[67] Paradoxically, however, much of this same literature may strike one as original, at times even markedly so. The great difference between the literature of the medieval period and that of our own times is that virtually no medieval author shows signs of having *striven* for originality. Instead, the constant tendency among authors of prose works was to claim that one's work was in alignment with prior writings that were well known and highly regarded. As for Old English verse texts, their uniform medium – the four-stress alliterative line – breathes conventionality. So too does their frequent use of the gnomic voice, as well as their invocations of the somewhat misty authority of oral tradition, as in variations on the phrase 'we have heard' or 'I have heard'.

Sometimes a learned author makes no secret at all about what source or sources he is using. This is true of those Old English homilies where the pericope (the biblical passage assigned to a particular feast day) is announced and quoted at the start. At other times an author like Ælfric may make clear that he is rewriting someone else's previous narrative. An example is the beginning of Ælfric's life of St Edmund, king and martyr (d. 869).[68] Ælfric informs the reader that he is retelling an account of the death of St Edmund that a monk named Abbo, whom we know to be a French monk who became abbot of Fleury in 988, wrote out in Latin after hearing the story told. Since Abbo's *Passio sancti Eadmundi* survives, Ælfric's life can readily be compared with its Latin source. In other instances, however, instances of indebtedness have to be sought out. Possible source-texts can often be identified, often plural in number, but the intertextual relations of similar works or passages might be so obscure as to be impossible to chart. Exacerbating this problem are uncertainties involving the dating of texts, hence their priority. In addition, it may be a matter of educated guesswork whether a hypothetical source-text would have been available, whether in whole or in part, to a particular Anglo-Saxon author.

---

[66] See the lucid overview by D.G. Scragg, 'Source Study', in O'Brien O'Keeffe, 39–58. Two additional studies are recommended for their practical applications of the principles involved in source studies: Katherine O'Brien O'Keeffe, 'Source, Method, Theory, Practice: On Reading Two Old English Verse Texts', *BJRL* 76 (1994): 51–73, repr. in *Toller Lectures*, 161–81 with an updated bibliography, and Joyce Hill, 'Authority and Intertextuality in the Works of Ælfric', *PBA* 131 (2005): 157–81.

[67] A useful resource in this connection is *Sources and Analogues of Old English Poetry* (Cambridge: D.S. Brewer, 1983). Volume 1 of this two-volume publication, ed. Daniel G. Calder and Michael J.B. Allen, is subtitled *The Major Latin Texts in Translation* (Cambridge: D.S. Brewer, 1976), while volume 2, ed. Calder et al., is subtitled *The Major Germanic and Celtic Texts in Translation*.

[68] *Ælfric: Lives of Three English Saints*, ed. G.I. Needham, 2nd edn (Exeter: University of Exeter Press, 1976), 43–59; in addition, a good teaching edition is available in Mitchell & Robinson, 203–11.

Despite these potential uncertainties, a great deal of productive research has by now been undertaken in this area, thereby clarifying the ways in which Old English prose and verse relate to a much larger body of medieval literature composed in Latin and other languages. Much of this research deals with homilies and saints' lives. As Charles D. Wright states in his 2007 study 'Old English Homilies and Latin Sources',[69] 'the recovery of these devotional sources has been one of the great undertakings – and one of the great successes – of Old English literary scholarship since the late nineteenth century.' Wright adds the cautionary remark, however, that 'it is still unfinished business' (pp. 15–16).

While part of that unfinished business has to do with the reliable tracking down of sources, another part concerns what to do with the prize once the hunt has come out well. Wright makes clear that the main business of source studies can be said to begin, not to end, once the source or sources of an Anglo-Saxon text are identified, for the implications of these discoveries for textual criticism, literary history, intellectual history, and stylistic analysis still need to be explored (pp. 59–60):

> Source identification resolves the discrete voices, words, and works that a homilist has compiled and appropriated (whether overtly or covertly), enabling us to observe how they have been transformed in the process, and helping us to assess what the homilist wrote (textual criticism), when he wrote it and for whom (literary history), what kind of intellectual milieu, library, and ideological position he wrote from (intellectual history), and how he rewrote the rhetorical and verbal fabric of a Latin text in his own language (stylistic analysis) [...]. The business of interpreting and contextualizing these discoveries, moreover, is not merely unfinished; it has hardly begun, and new approaches and new questions will undoubtedly enable Anglo-Saxonists to exploit them in new ways.

Donald Scragg makes much the same point: 'The best scholars have always recognized that of far greater moment than the sources themselves is the use that an author, named or otherwise, made use of the inherited material.'[70] I would only add, speaking in my own voice, that whenever an Anglo-Saxon author 'rewrote the rhetorical and verbal fabric of a Latin text in his own language', as Wright puts it, critics who study that act of rewriting might soon find themselves involved in a good deal more than what Wright terms 'stylistic analysis'. Cultural transformations too can be involved, ones that involve power, ideology, and identity-formation, just as can happen when a whole work composed in Latin is translated into the vernacular.

In his 2002 book *The Culture of Translation in Anglo-Saxon England*, Robert Stanton has proposed that 'translation' can serve as 'an overarching idea to explain Anglo-Saxon literary culture'.[71] Stanton suggests that translation 'defines an attitude to received authority and sets the terms under which authority can be reproduced and shifted from one institution or

---

[69] Charles D. Wright, 'Old English Homilies and Latin Sources', in *The Old English Homily: Precedent, Practice, and Appropriation*, ed. Aaron J. Kleist (Turnhout: Brepols, 2007), 15–66.

[70] Scragg, 'Source Study', 45.

[71] Robert Stanton, *The Culture of Translation in Anglo-Saxon England* (Cambridge: D.S. Brewer, 2002), 2.

social group to another' (p. 1). In this light, although English was at first used only to gloss or otherwise interpret more authoritative Latin texts, in the course of time, 'English acquired a hermeneutic status and authority in its own right' (p. 2). From such a perspective, source studies naturally converges with translation theory, which interrogates the 'cultural translations' that were involved when Latinate materials were adapted into the vernacular.

Two major sourcing projects are in progress at the present time, one based on either side of the Atlantic. Their two approaches are essentially the converse of one another. *Fontes Anglo-Saxonici*, an Oxford-based database, sources Anglo-Saxon texts passage by passage, sentence by sentence, or phrase by phrase, identifying the probable source-passages used for each segment of text. Annotations identify the works in which verbal correspondences are found, while sigla denote how close or how remote the connection is judged to be.[72] *Sources of Anglo-Saxon Literary Culture* (abbreviated *SASLC*) is a North-American-based database that documents the availability in Anglo-Saxon England of texts that are likely to have influenced the literary culture of that period. Notice is taken of evidence that derives from surviving Anglo-Saxon manuscripts, entries in Anglo-Saxon booklists, and references by Anglo-Saxon authors, as well as the use of the words of source-texts in translations, quotations, or citations by later authors. A trial version of *SASLC* was published in 1990, and the first volume in a projected multi-volume series appeared in 2001.[73] If no other *SASLC* volumes have appeared as of the time of this writing (2015), this is perhaps a sign of the magnitude of the task taken on by this consortium of scholars. In the meantime, researchers can make use of the section titled 'Catalogue of Classical and Patristic Authors and Works Composed before AD 700 and Known in Anglo-Saxon England' included in Lapidge's *The Anglo-Saxon Library* (at 275–342).

Most source studies have focused on prose texts rather than verse. There is a reason for this priority other than the sheer bulk of prose that figures in the Old English corpus compared with the slender amount of verse. While the authors of homilies and other prose texts were clearly learned persons schooled in a range of Latin Christian texts, it is unsafe to make the same assumption with regard to the makers of Old English verse texts, even though it might be valid in certain instances. Nevertheless, as we have seen, a persuasive case has been made that certain thematic or rhetorical elements of certain poems can plausibly be traced to Latinate sources. This opens up the possibility that at least some verse texts, and perhaps many of them, are best interpreted within the same intellectual context as is assumed for works of learning composed in prose.

One scholar who gained high regard for his contributions to this dimension of Old English literary criticism is James E. Cross. In a series of articles and notes published over

---

[72] For more information on *Fontes Anglo-Saxonici* see: http://fontes.english.ox.ac.uk.

[73] See *Sources of Anglo-Saxon Literary Culture: A Trial Version*, ed. Frederick M. Biggs, Thomas D. Hill, and Paul E. Szarmach (Binghamton: Center for Medieval and Early Renaissance Studies, 1990). Helpful in its explanation of the rationale, methods, assumptions, terms, and problematic aspects of source studies is the Introduction to that book (pp. xv–xxxiii), written by Thomas D. Hill. The single volume published in this series thus far is *Sources of Anglo-Saxon Literary Culture*, vol. 1: *Abbo of Fleury, Abbo of Saint-Germain-des-Prés, and Acta Sanctorum*, ed. Frederick M. Biggs et al. (Kalamazoo: Medieval Institute Publications, 2001). For further information see the web site for the project at: https://saslc.nd.edu.

a half-century starting in the 1950s, Cross pointed out numerous examples of the use of Latin *topoi* in Old English verse and prose, developing methods of analysis that others too have used with success.[74] One of Cross's seminal essays, his 1956 study '*Ubi Sunt* Passages in Old English', takes as its point of departure fourteen passages in Old English verse and prose where variations are played on the formula '*Hwær syndon?*' These expressions, he shows, are indebted to formulaic passages employing the phrase '*Ubi sunt?*' that were widely disseminated in the Latin literature of the early Middle Ages, often in imitation of Isidore of Seville's use of the phrase towards the end of his *Synonyma*. Although doubts had earlier been expressed that the famous elegiac passage near the end of *The Wanderer* that begins at lines 92–93, beginning '*Hwær com?*', was indebted to this Latinate tradition, Cross points out the existence of very comparable phrasing in the eighth Blickling homily, which in turn is a fairly close rendering of a prior Latin sermon. Cross concludes: 'The poet chooses [Old English] poetic words and they have a distinct flavour on that account but the ideas they represent can all be found in "ubi sunt" passages in the popular [Latin] sources' (p. 41).

This conclusion alone, it could be argued, is no more than a starting point for a well-developed critical understanding of *The Wanderer*. In other publications, however, Cross made clear that what he aimed to do in essays such as this is not just to identify the sources underlying Old English poems, but also to cast light on the clusters of ideas that are active in them. As he writes in his 1972 essay 'The Literate Anglo-Saxon' (originally presented as a lecture to the British Academy), 'the student of sources obviously contributes to the understanding of the intellectual environment from which literature springs and of which each individual work of literature is a part' (p. 71). Cross and other scholars pursuing source studies have succeeded in anchoring the study of a good part of Old English literature, including such well-known poems as *The Wanderer* and *The Seafarer*, in the thought-world of medieval Christianity. This is no small achievement, given the strong tendency of nineteenth- and early twentieth-century critics to focus on the Germanic, or pagan, or 'wild' aspects of Old English poetry while having little to say about its Christian content.

What Cross did not try to do, and what in some instances might still profitably be done, is to account for the cultural shifts or transformations that were involved when familiar Christian topoi were expressed in the medium of Old English verse, which was saturated with ancient native associations.[75] The long-standing custom whereby native poetry was performed orally for the enjoyment and education of listeners was bound to have at least a

---

[74] Note in particular J.E. Cross, '*Ubi Sunt* Passages in Old English – Sources and Relationships', *Vetenskaps-Societeten i Lund Årsbok* (1956): 23–44; 'Aspects of Microcosm and Macrocosm in Old English Literature', in *Brodeur Studies*, 1–22; and 'The Literate Anglo-Saxon – On Sources and Disseminations', *PBA* 58 (1972): 67–100. Cross likewise pioneered the search for the specific versions of sources used by Old English writers, for example in his 1986 essay 'Identification: Towards Criticism', in *Greenfield Studies*, 229–46.

[75] See however Andy Orchard, 'Re-Reading *The Wanderer*: The Value of Cross-References', in *Via Crucis: Essays on Early Medieval Sources and Ideas in Memory of J.E. Cross*, ed. Thomas N. Hall (Morgantown: West Virginia University Press, 2002), 1–26. Taking up the '*ubi sunt*' theme in *The Wanderer*, Orchard approaches this Exeter Book text as one that 'retains an intense interest in worldly, not to say "heroic," affairs' (p. 2). His essay represents a fitting tribute to Cross by extending source studies into more complex interpretive ground.

residual effect on texts, like *The Wanderer* and *The Seafarer*, that we know now only through writing. While the intellectual tenor of this verse is dominantly Christian, its poetic idiom and cultural associations represent a fusion of learned and oral-traditional elements. The oral dimension of Old English literature, however, is best explored in the next chapter.

A Selection from the Criticism

The critical excerpt that follows is from an essay by Malcolm Parkes that appeared in 1976 in volume 5 of *Anglo-Saxon England*, the first journal to be devoted entirely to research on Anglo-Saxon themes. Parkes (1930–2013) was a fellow at Keble College, Oxford, during the years 1965 to 1997 and held the Chair in Palaeography at the University of Oxford. Among his noteworthy publications is *Their Hands before Our Eyes: A Closer Look at Scribes*.[76]

While Parkes's 1976 essay has no direct bearing on literary criticism, its implications for the understanding of Anglo-Saxon literary culture are profound. For one thing, Parkes traces the development of a form of insular handwriting, square minuscule, that became the norm for Anglo-Saxon scribes writing in the vernacular. As has been mentioned, the evolution of that script can be correlated with the development of a standard form of the written vernacular itself, namely 'standard late West Saxon'. By far the majority of pre-Conquest manuscripts are composed in this standard or something like it. In the course of time, as well, a particular lexicon, 'the Winchester vocabulary', came to be associated with both these developments.[77]

Just as significant are the implications of Parkes's essay for the understanding of early English historiography. His essay takes as its subject the Parker manuscript, which contains the 'A' version of the Anglo-Saxon Chronicle (Cambridge, Corpus Christi College MS 173). This is now also known as the Winchester recension of the Chronicle since, as Parkes shows, it was begun at the Old Minster, Winchester, towards the end of the reign of King Alfred the Great. The manuscript also contains an early version of the laws of Alfred and Ine. Although CCCC 173 includes a number of texts in addition to the Chronicle and the laws of Alfred and Ine, Parkes shows that these additional texts (including the 'Sedulius' of his title) were bound together with the others only at a relatively late date. One of Parkes's main tasks is thus to reconstruct, through palaeographical and codicological analysis, what the state of the manuscript was at a certain key period of its earlier existence. His conclusions are of great potential interest not only for early English historiography and legal studies, but also for persons interested in the use of books in the construction of English national identity.

---

[76]   M.B. Parkes, *Their Hands before Our Eyes: A Closer Look at Scribes* (Aldershot: Ashgate, 2008), a volume based on a series of lectures delivered by Parkes at the University of Oxford in 1999.

[77]   These interconnected developments in palaeography, the Old English lexicon, and the literary standard are discussed by Helmut Gneuss, 'The Origin of Standard Old English and Æthelwold's School at Winchester', *ASE* 1 (1972): 63–83, and Mechthild Gretsch, 'Winchester Vocabulary and Standard Old English: The Vernacular in Late Anglo-Saxon England', *BJRL* 83 (2001): 41–87; see also Gretsch, 'Ælfric, Language and Winchester', in Magennis & Swan, 109–37.

Readers who have a facsimile of the Parker Library manuscript close to hand stand to profit the most from Parkes's analysis. Fortunately an EETS facsimile is readily available, and many research libraries provide access to a digital facsimile via Parker Library on the Web.[78]

For Further Reading

Brown, Michelle. 2001. 'Anglo-Saxon Manuscript Production: Issues of Making and Using'. In Pulsiano & Treharne, 102–17.

Crick, Julia. 'The Art of Writing: Scripts and Scribal Production'. In the *Cambridge History*, 50–72.

Discenza, Nicole Guenther, and Paul E. Szarmach, eds. 2015. *A Companion to Alfred the Great*. Leiden: Brill.

Irvine, Martin. 1991. 'Medieval Textuality and the Archaeology of Textual Culture'. In *Speaking Two Languages*, 181–210 and 276–84.

Irvine, Susan. 2013. 'English Literature in the Ninth Century'. In the *Cambridge History*, 209–31.

Lees, Clare A. 1991. 'Working with Patristic Sources: Language and Context in Old English Homilies'. In *Speaking Two Languages*, 157–80 and 264–76.

Sauer, Hans. 2009. 'Language and Culture: How Anglo-Saxon Glossators Adapted Latin Words and their World'. *Journal of Medieval Latin* 19: 437–68.

---

[78]   *The Parker Chronicle and Laws: A Facsimile*, ed. Robin Flower and Hugh Smith, EETS o.s. 208 (London: Oxford University Press, 1941). For Parker Library on the Web, see: http://parkerweb. stanford.edu.

M.B. Parkes, 'The Palaeography of the Parker Manuscript of the *Chronicle*, Laws, and Sedulius, and Historiography at Winchester in the Late Ninth and Tenth Centuries' (1976).[1]

The Parker manuscript, Cambridge, Corpus Christi College 173,[2] is generally recognized to be the earliest surviving copy of the compilation known as the *Anglo-Saxon Chronicle*. It cannot be the original since it contains various scribal errors including dislocation in the chronology, yet its physical characteristics reflect all the major divisions in the text recognized by modern scholars: it seems to reflect the nature and sometimes even the format of the various exemplars from which it was copied. The purpose of this article is to draw attention to these and other palaeographical features and to survey some of the questions arising from them.

---

[1]   Excerpted from M.B. Parkes, 'The Palaeography of the Parker Manuscript of the *Chronicle*, Laws, and Sedulius, and Historiography at Winchester in the Late Ninth and Tenth Centuries', *ASE* 5 (1976): 149–71. Used with permission from Cambridge University Press.

[2]   N.R. Ker, *Catalogue of Manuscripts Containing Anglo-Saxon* (Oxford, 1957), nos. 39 and 40. Wherever possible my references to the manuscript are to the facsimile edition of fols. 1–56 by Robin Flower and Hugh Smith, *The Parker Chronicle and Laws*, EETS o.s. 208 (London, 1941, repr. 1973). When citing the facsimile I follow the year numbers given there.

[Parkes goes on to describe the five separate booklets that comprise the Parker manuscript as it exists today. The two booklets of greatest interest with regard to the manuscript's early history are no.1 (fols. 1–25), which contains the annals of the Chronicle from the first entries to the year 924, these annals being prefaced by a genealogy of the West Saxon royal house to the time of King Alfred; and no. 3 (fols. 33–52), containing the laws of Alfred and Ine, along with a capitulary (a list of chapter titles). Three scribes were at work in booklet 1, and Parkes describes the contribution made by each of them.]

The history of this manuscript is therefore a complicated one and in this article I propose to concentrate on those stages which will throw most light on the origins of the *Anglo-Saxon Chronicle* and upon the different criteria which affected the history of the compilation in the tenth century [...].

The first two quires of booklet 1 originally formed a single independent booklet copied by a single scribe (scribe 1) writing all at one time. His exemplar must have been extremely close to the original – the revision which Plummer called the 'common' recension ending in 891. First, the date of the original must be close to 891: it represents a revision which must have taken place after Alfred's accession because of the reference in the annal for 853 to Alfred's 'hallowing' at Rome, a reference which makes sense only if the annalist were writing with hindsight; if the annal had been written contemporaneously with the event, there could have been no ambiguity about what happened to a four-year-old boy who was at the time no closer than fourth in line of succession to the throne. Secondly, the language of the common recension seems to be consistent: there is no substantial difference between that used in earlier annals and that used in the one for 891, and the language seems to me to be appropriate to 891. Thirdly, this date is also consistent with what we know about the circulation of other early copies.[3]

The handwriting of scribe 1 is consistent with the end of the ninth century and his booklet was therefore probably contemporary with the revision itself. Changes in the layout on fols. 1v and 4v represent decisions taken by this scribe: he began iv with four long lines but changed to a layout of two columns, which he maintained until 4v where he began the page with the two-column layout in mind, but reverted to long lines with the annal for 449. The survival of the superfluous years in quite this form suggests that his exemplar was based closely either on something resembling Easter tables or on a collection of material abstracted from notes to Easter tables.[a] The change in the layout on 4v suggests that at this point the state of the exemplar reflected an increase in the amount of material available from such sources as the chronological epitome of Bede, or from such local sources as those which provided the account of the foundation of Wimborne in 718 and the story

[3]   Summarized by Dorothy Whitelock, *The Anglo-Saxon Chronicle*, trans. Dorothy Whitelock with David C. Douglas and Susie I. Tucker (London, 1961), p. xxi.

[a]   [Easter tables: during the Middle Ages, tables were drawn up listing the date of Easter in successive years. Brief historical entries were sometimes added opposite the dates.]

of Cynewulf and Cyneheard inserted into the annal for 755. Moreover, leaves 2 and 7 of the second quire are two singletons instead of a bifolium.[b] The arrangement of material on this second singleton (fol. 14) leads us to suspect that it is a cancel.[4] By contrast with the arrangement of the material on the verso where he has spread out the material – spaced it to fill up the page – the compression of material on the recto suggests that either new material has been added on this page or existing material has been rearranged here. It is the page dealing with the accession of Alfred. Finally the blank entry for 892 on 16r suggests that the exemplar stopped at this point.

The independent booklet thus prepared by scribe 1 was extended by scribe 2, who added a new quire, and was completed by scribe 3. Scribe 2 began on 16v and continued until the end of the entry for 912, six lines from the foot of 21r. Scribe 3 took over at the beginning of the next entry, ignored the year numbers inserted by his predecessor and continued to the end of the booklet (25v), with short passages interpolated by other scribes.[5] Scribe 3 modelled his hand closely on that of scribe 2 (an important feature to which I shall return later), but the two scribes consistently did certain things in different ways and my identification of these hands is based on these crucial differences of habit. First, scribe 2 indicated omissions by placing either a single dot or two vertical dots on or below the line and inserting the omitted letters above,[6] whereas scribe 3 used a 'comma'-shaped stroke below the line instead of dots.[7] Secondly, scribe 2 formed the bottom left-hand limb of the letter **x** by means of a firm stroke made in a single movement, whereas scribe 3 formed this feature by means of a hairstroke made in two movements: the first placed at a more pronounced angle followed by a second, return movement on the underside. The different **x** forms can be seen on 21r.[8] Once these criteria have been used to determine the respective stints it is possible to observe further differences between the two hands: for example, scribe

---

[b]   [Bifolium: a sheet of vellum folded in half so as to make two leaves (four pages) of equal size. A singleton is one of the halves produced in this manner (two pages).]

[4]   If the scribe had wished to cancel the first leaf he would have been able to replace the whole bifolium.

[5]   Ker, *Catalogue*, p. lix, emphasizes the difficulty of identifying different scribes in this particular part of the manuscript. Although I disagree with his suggestion (*Catalogue*, no. 39) that there was only one main scribe, I agree with his identification of different features in the handwriting of the following passages: 23v12–15, 24v22–25 and 25r1–7. I suspect that the first and last passages represent lapses from standard on the part of scribe 3.

[6]   See esp. 16v1, 17r24 (with dots omitted), 17v19, 19v10 and 20v8.

[7]   See esp. 22r4, 22v3, 24r5, 24v3 and 8 and 25r23. All the corrections listed here and in the preceding note are unmistakably in the hands of the main scribes: they were all made at the time of writing. Not only is the colour of the ink the same as that used for the text but also the amount of ink in the pen at the time is appropriate. By contrast all other corrections (e.g. at 17v1 and 24, 20v20 and 23r14) have been made by other hands at different times.

[8]   That of scribe 2 is visible at lines 14, 20 and in the year numbers, that of scribe 3 at lines 24 and 26.

2 left a slightly larger space before **m** or **n** when they did not occur in ligatures;[9] scribe 3 used 'f'-shaped **y** consistently.

These two scribes not only supplemented an independent booklet left by scribe 1 but seem to have been copying from exemplars which were themselves 'booklets' and which must have been close to the originals if not the originals themselves. Scribe 2 began by adding a supplement to the annal for 891 and continued with entries for 892 and 893 on the verso of 16, the supplementary leaf of the first scribe's booklet. (The year numbers were altered by somebody else later.) In this way he was forced to use the ruling of scribe 1. However, from fol. 17 onwards, the first leaf which he was able to rule and lay out for himself, there is a striking change: at the first opportunity (18r) he centred each year number on a line of its own with space above and below, and copied the entries in long lines which fill the whole width of the written space. After the account of Alfred's wars with the Danes ending in 897 scribe 2 reverted to the layout established by scribe 1, and on 20r apparently emulated the form of enlarged **H** used by his predecessor at the beginning of each entry. The exemplar of the account of Alfred's wars with the Danes seems itself to have been a separate 'booklet', with a layout different from that normally used for annals. It is a 'history' layout (compare that of the Old English Orosius or the Old English Bede) and not an 'annals' layout. This change in layout corresponds to a change in literary style. Cecily Clark has argued that the style of the *Chronicle* from 892 to 897 differs from that of the annals up to that point: instead of merely recording events the writer of this section often goes into the question of motivation.[10] Moreover, there is a cancel: leaves 3 and 6 of this third gathering are two singletons instead of a bifolium. On the verso of the second singleton (fol. 22) begins the unique copy of the account of the last campaigns of Edward the Elder. Scribe 3 cancelled the only leaf to contain material already entered and substituted a new leaf (22) to receive this new material. Because the parchment was very thick he ruled the remaining leaves of the prepared quire (23 and 24) on the recto to coincide with his predecessor's original ruling on the verso. A further change in the layout at this point (22v) suggests that the new material was copied from another separate 'booklet', because scribe 3 altered the style and position of the year numbers, adding vertical bounding lines to contain them. He also altered the layout from twenty-six lines to the page to twenty-five, leaving the last ruled line blank.[11] The acquisition of new material and the new layout caused him to overshoot the quire, making it necessary to add a supplementary leaf (25) to complete the by now extended 'booklet'.

---

[9]   As, e.g., in *stemn gesetenne* (17r1) and *wifum* (17r18).

[10] 'The Narrative Mode of *The Anglo-Saxon Chronicle* before the Conquest', *England Before the Conquest: Studies in Primary Sources presented to Dorothy Whitelock*, ed. Peter Clemoes and Kathleen Hughes (Cambridge, 1971), pp. 215–35, esp. 221–24.

[11] The vertical ruling is visible in the facsimile on 22r, 23r and 24r and the unused last ruled line is visible on 24v.

Changes in layout and format suggest that the exemplars from which this booklet was copied were the originals or very close to them (seemingly independent booklets which perhaps represented the first fair copies on parchment). By the time we get to the other later copies all such discrepancies had been eliminated.[12] The cancels suggest that new material came to hand or was reworked in the scriptorium in which these scribes worked. It is likely, therefore, that the scriptorium (or perhaps scriptoria) responsible for this first extended booklet was also the home of the originals. We must therefore examine other manuscripts which are associated with the work of scribes 1 and 2 to see whether it is possible to establish a connection between them.

Scribe 1 was also responsible for filling lacunae in the bifolium (fols. 57–58) added to the eighth-century Latin booklet now bound up with the rest of the Parker manuscript, [...] and for filling lacunae in the text of Sedulius contained in this booklet. As T.A.M. Bishop has observed, his handwriting is very similar to that of the second scribe of Cambridge, Trinity College 368, a copy of the *Etymologiae* of Isidore of Seville. Bishop argued that the scribes worked in the same scriptorium: he drew attention to details such as capital **T** with a descender in final positions and to a distinctive form of **r** in the combination **or**, and illustrated similarities of style and aspect in his plates.[13]

Scribe 2 was also responsible for the Tollemache Orosius (London, British Library, Add. 47967), since the habits which characterize his handwriting in the Parker manuscript are also present in that of the Orosius.[14] This manuscript contains elaborate initials in outline which are by the artist responsible for those in the Junius Psalter (Oxford, Bodleian Library, Junius 27).[15] The initials of these two manuscripts are

---

[12] As, e.g., in London, British Library, Cotton Tiberius A. vi (s. x²) and Cotton Tiberius B. i (s. xi¹–s. xi²).

[13] 'An Early Example of the Square Minuscule', *Transactions of the Cambridge Bibliographical Society* 4 (1964–68), 246–52, esp. plates xviii and xix.

[14] Facsimile edition, *The Tollemache Orosius*, ed. Alistair Campbell, EEMF 3 (Copenhagen, 1953). Examples of the characteristic method of indicating omissions can be seen at pp. 31 line 11 (*bie*), 95 line 31 (*nu*) and 150 line 16 (*mar-*). Examples of the gap before **m** or **n** when not in ligature can be seen at pp. 102 line 26 (*fæstenne*), 128 line 8 (*ongunnen*) and 140 line 10 (*be tæcan*).

[15] Facsimile, New Palaeographical Society, *Facsimiles of Ancient Manuscripts...* 2nd series (London, 1913–30), plate 62; see Francis Wormald, 'Decorated Initials in English MSS from AD 900 to 1100', *Archaeologia* 91 (1945), 107–35, esp. 118, and Otto Pächt and J.J.G. Alexander, *Illuminated Manuscripts in the Bodleian Library, Oxford*, vol. 3 (Oxford, 1973), no. 21. I suspect that scribe 2 was also responsible for the Junius Psalter. However this was clearly a special book and since all the corrections were made over erasure, and since the scribe was more careful in his placing of the strokes (hence less likely to leave the characteristic gaps before **m** and **n**), I cannot demonstrate the identity of the scribe on the criteria already adduced. Nevertheless a careful comparison of the main hand of the psalter with the work of scribes 2 and 3 and with hands of related style (e.g., those of the additions to Bern, Burgerbibliothek, 671; cf. O. Homburger, *Die illustrierten Handschriften der Burgerbibliothek Bern* (Bern, 1962), p. 31)

closely related to those in the earliest surviving copy of the Old English version of Bede (Oxford, Bodleian Library, Tanner 10).[16] Thus we have two manuscripts by the same scribe and two manuscripts by the same artist.

> has convinced me that the hand of the Junius Psalter is most closely related to that of scribe 2. If the chronology of his work is to be based on his progress in achieving standardization of the handwriting, I would conjecture that the manuscripts were produced in the order Tollemache Orosius, Junius Psalter, Parker *Chronicle*.

[16] Facsimile, Ker, *Catalogue*, pl. I; see Francis Wormald, 'The "Winchester School" before St Æthelwold', *England Before the Conquest*, ed. Clemoes and Hughes, pp. 305–13, esp. 305–7, and Pächt and Alexander, *Illuminated Manuscripts in the Bodleian Library*, vol. 3, no. 22.

[Parkes offers evidence indicating that at one time all the just-mentioned manuscripts were together in the same place. He then demonstrates that features of the manuscripts in this group reflect the successive stages of a pattern of palaeographical evolution. This pattern is one of gradual standardization, as can be traced through three factors: (1) adoption of a prototype of the square minuscule type of insular script, (2) the use of square capitals as the basis for a display script, and (3) the adoption of continental practices with regard to the arrangement and ruling of the parchment sheets. Parkes concludes that the manuscripts of this group were produced at the same scriptorium, namely Winchester; and, moreover, that this scriptorium 'seems to have pioneered and propagated new standards and new models of handwriting' (p. 163). Parkes then shows that ecclesiastics from the Continent exerted a strong influence on these developments at Winchester, and he attributes to their influence the strong interest in historiography shown in the Winchester manuscripts.]

> The continental elements in the palaeography of these early manuscripts produced in a revived scriptorium at Winchester suggest the influence of Alfred's continental helpers. If we can trust the evidence of tradition, Winchester also had the right man to revive a scriptorium with such a distinctive style – Grimbald of St Bertin. According to Grierson's analysis of the evidence,[17] Grimbald came to England from Rheims where he was at that time a trusted servant of the archbishop, Fulk. The tradition records that in England he lived in a *monasteriolum* at Winchester, which the monks of Hyde Abbey clearly regarded as the ancestor of New Minster their earlier foundation. Although I suspect twelfth-century Benedictine hagiography in this tradition, there is no reason to doubt that Grimbald

---

[17] Philip Grierson, 'Grimbald of St Bertin's', *EHR* 55 (1940), 529–61.

was closely associated with Winchester. Although other manuscripts of the *Anglo-Saxon Chronicle* record the year of Grimbald's death, only in the Parker manuscript (20r) has a tenth-century hand most skilfully inserted the actual day and month – the obit of Grimbald. Moreover Edmund Bishop has suggested on the basis of liturgical evidence that the 'practical' calendar which lies behind the extracts found in that of the Junius Psalter and in the other later Winchester calendars had been brought to England by Grimbald.[18]

Grimbald came from Rheims where there was a flourishing and highly disciplined scriptorium. He would have been well equipped to revive a scriptorium at Winchester by imposing continental scribal principles and by introducing continental scribal practices. In the ninth-century products of the Rheims scriptorium the pattern of standardization had been so rigorously applied that a modern scholar has described the script as 'distinguished by its very traitlessness', 'there seems to have been a conscious effort to abolish [ligatures]' and 'the letters are usually carefully formed and stand fairly straight'.[19] Square capitals were used at Rheims as a 'secondary' display script in much the same way as in the manuscripts at Winchester[20] and there is a remarkable parallel between the first line of the genealogy of the Parker manuscript and the first line of Rheims 99.[21] But on the continent such forms and usages were by no means confined to the Rheims scriptorium: what is important in the context of my argument is that these forms and usages are present in Rheims manuscripts and not absent from them.

Fulk's predecessor as archbishop of Rheims from 845 to 882 had been the redoubtable Hincmar, trained in the historiographical centre of St Denis, the Frankish 'royal' monastery. Hincmar's interest in historiography and hagiography are well known.[22] Grimbald came therefore from a centre in which the tradition of Frankish historiography was still alive and he would have been equally well equipped to promote the revision and transmission of historical texts. Of the six manuscripts from this early Winchester scriptorium no less than three – the earliest surviving copy of the annals of the house of Wessex, the earliest surviving copy of the Old English translation of Orosius's world history against the pagans and the earliest surviving copy of the Old English translation

---

[18] Bishop, *Liturgica Historica* (Oxford, 1918), p. 256.

[19] Frederick M. Carey, 'The Scriptorium of Reims during the Archbishopric of Hincmar', *Classical and Mediaeval Studies in honor of Edward Kennard Rand*, ed. Leslie Webber Jones (New York, 1938), pp. 41–60, esp. 48.

[20] E.g., Rheims, Bibliothèque Municipale, MSS 296, 384, 385, 390, 414, 425 and 438.

[21] In each case the first line of the text begins with an initial followed by a series of square capital forms. In each case the first line ends with a divided word and uncial forms are used for that part of the word needed to complete the first line.

[22] The best account is by J.M. Wallace-Hadrill (*The Long-Haired Kings* (London, 1962), pp. 100–5). Further details, M. Manitius, *Geschichte der lateinischen Literatur des Mittelalters*, vol. 1 (1911), 339.

of Bede's ecclesiastical history of the English – demonstrate a very strong interest in history in this scriptorium in the early tenth century at a time when some parts of the *Chronicle* (at the very least the account of Edward the Elder's last campaigns) were being written. The influence of Grimbald seems to be reflected in the contents of the surviving manuscripts of this scriptorium as well as in their palaeography.

In the late ninth century, therefore, Winchester provided the right milieu for the revision of a set of earlier annals and the compilation of a chronicle. Moreover a text of the *Chronicle* was available at Winchester during the tenth century, which enabled a later Winchester scribe to correct a defect in the first booklet of the Parker manuscript. This correction – the insertion of the annal for 710 – is of particular importance: a comparison of this inserted annal with other versions of the *Chronicle* indicates that it must have been part of the original text.[23] I suggest that this now lost Winchester witness to the original was the very collection of booklet exemplars whose existence is indicated by the palaeographical evidence of layout and cancels in the first booklet of the Parker manuscript. I suggest that this collection of booklet exemplars with their added material and reworked passages constituted perhaps the first fair copies on parchment of the original drafts and that Winchester was the home of this collection.[24]

With Grimbald's background it is reasonable to suppose that he would not only have introduced discipline, organization and a taste for historical texts into the Winchester scriptorium but also that he would have exerted some influence on the compilation of the *Anglo-Saxon Chronicle*, if only by introducing a concept of 'dynastic' history. Like others before me,[25] I think I can detect traces of such influence behind the common recension of the annals to 891. I shall select two instances. The first is the controversial reference in the annal for 853 to Alfred's

[23] See Whitelock, review of the facsimile of the Parker manuscript, *EHR* 57 (1942), p. 121.

[24] I am not convinced by Sir Frank Stenton's suggestion ('The South-Western Element in the Old English Chronicle', repr. *Preparatory to 'Anglo-Saxon England'*, ed. Doris Mary Stenton (Oxford, 1970), pp. 106–15) that the *Chronicle* was compiled somewhere in the Somerset area. Although south-western sources must have provided much of the material on which the recension was based, on Stenton's own evidence there is a strong case for Winchester as the centre where the reworking took place. The more obvious explanation for the evidence he cites in support of his suggestion, and in particular that of Æthelweard's chronicle, is that Æthelweard's collection of the annals had been annotated by somebody in the south-west in much the same way as the Parker manuscript was annotated at Winchester and Canterbury.

[25] E.g., Grierson, 'Grimbald of St Bertin's'. Eric John (*Orbis Britanniae* (Leicester, 1966), p. 39) hints at a 'Frankish' annalist.

hallowing at Rome. I have already argued that this passage was written after Alfred's accession and I think that the most obvious explanation of this reference is that it was written under the supervision of someone who was conversant with the Frankish practice of consecrating kings.[26] Janet L. Nelson has adduced a Frankish parallel for this story in Hincmar's treatment of Clovis's baptism.[27] I would see the passage in the annal for 853 not as crude propaganda but as an attempt to explain in contemporary historical terms both the survival of a sickly boy and the successes of a sick man. Secondly, the annal for 885 shows a close awareness of what was happening on the continent, and that for 887 shows a detailed knowledge of the complicated descent of the line of Frankish kings. Finally, Wallace-Hadrill has called attention to similarities between the *Anglo-Saxon Chronicle* and the *Annals of St Bertin* composed by Hincmar and to the possibility of Grimbald's influence upon Asser.[28] I suggest that Grimbald, a man trained in a Frankish historiographical centre, was responsible for a tradition of West Saxon historiography based on a revived scriptorium at Winchester and that this tradition could well have influenced much of the earlier part of the *Anglo-Saxon Chronicle*.

Moreover, the surviving manuscripts suggest that this tradition outlived him for a time and reached its culmination at the second stage in the history of the Parker compilation, represented by the state of the manuscript in the mid-tenth century. At this time, as the quire signatures 'c' on 25v and 'e' on 42r show, the present third booklet containing the laws of Alfred and Ine was added to the first.[29] The booklet

---

[26] On which see P.E. Schramm, 'Die Krönung bei den Westfranken und Angelsachsen', *Zeitschrift für Rechtsgeschichte* 54, Kan. Abt. 23 (1934), 117–242.

[27] 'The Problem of King Alfred's Royal Anointing', *Journal of Ecclesiastical History* 18 (1967), 145–63, esp. 158, where is cited Hincmar's *Adnuntiatio* preceding the consecration of Charles the Bald as king of Lorraine in 869 (MGH, Capitularia II, ed. Alfred Borelius and Victor Krause (1897), 340); cf. also Hincmar's *Vita Remigii* (MGH, Scriptores rerum Merovingicarum III, ed. Bruno Krusch (1896), 298).

[28] J.M. Wallace-Hadrill, 'The Franks and the English in the Ninth Century: Some Common Historical Interests', *History* 35 (1950), 202–18, esp. 213 ff. Marie Schütt, 'The Literary Form of Asser's *Vita Alfredi*', *EHR* 72 (1957), 209–20, demonstrates Asser's independence of Einhard. Note also the curious scribal error in the lost manuscript as recorded in the transcript used by Wise (*Asser's Life of King Alfred*, ed. W.H. Stevenson (repr. with contr. by D. Whitelock, Oxford, 1959), p. 22, n.): in the heading 'Anno Dominicae Incarnationis DCCCLXVII, nativitatis Ælfredi praefati regis decimo nono' the original scribe had written 'Karoli' instead of 'Ælfredi'. On the general background of kingship and on the consecration of Judith by Hincmar on the occasion of her marriage to Æthelwulf, see J.M. Wallace-Hadrill, *Early Germanic Kingship in England and on the Continent* (Oxford, 1971), pp. 133–36.

[29] The leaf which must have contained the quire signature 'd' is now missing (after fol. 32) from the beginning of quire v, which forms the first quire of booklet 3.

containing the laws was copied by two scribes, both of whom used a later version of the new minuscule: one who was responsible for the first page of the list of capitula and one who was responsible for the rest of the booklet. The second hand resembles (but is not identical with) that of the scribe of several Winchester charters (Pierre Chaplais's 'scribe 3')[30], and especially Sawyer 552.[31,c]

But it is the activity of the compiler responsible for adding this booklet to the first which is most relevant. In this mid-tenth-century form the contents of the compilation were as follows:

• The genealogy of the West Saxon royal house down to Alfred;
• Annals to 891;
• Chronicle of Alfred's wars with the Danes 892–97;
• Annals 898–918;
• Account of the last campaigns of Edward the Elder 919–25;
• Laws of Alfred and Ine.

The compilation thus consisted of a record of the achievements of the West Saxon royal house in war – down to the last campaign of Edward the Elder, and in peace – down to the legislation of Alfred. It is as though the compiler had in mind Alfred's high regard for the kings before him as expressed in the letter which accompanied the exemplars of the *Cura Pastoralis* – how they heeded both God and his messengers, how they prospered both in martial prowess and in knowledge, how they extended their native territory outwards and maintained their peace, their morality and their authority within the realm. It suggests a conscious attempt on the part of this compiler, active some time during or after the reign of Athelstan, to preserve the tradition of the West Saxon royal house in its purest form. Other sources portray Athelstan as the culmination of this tradition of dynastic achievement: in the Latin panegyric used by William of Malmesbury in the *Gesta Regum* Athelstan is described in the following terms: 'Regia progenies produxit nobile stemma.'[32] The form of the compilation of the Parker manuscript in the mid-tenth century emphasizes the previous achievements of this dynasty.

That the compilation should have taken this form in a centre like Winchester is hardly surprising.

---

[30] 'The Origin and Authenticity of the Royal Anglo-Saxon Diploma', *Journal of the Society of Archivists* 3 (1965), pp. 59–60.

[31] Facsimile, Edward A. Bond, *Facsimiles of Ancient Charters in the British Museum*, 4 vols (1873–78), vol. 3, no. 16.

[c] [Sawyer 552: Parkes's reference is to the standard numeration of Anglo-Saxon charters as set forth in P.H. Sawyer, *Anglo-Saxon Charters: An Annotated List and Bibliography* (London: Royal Historical Society, 1968).]

[32] *De Gestis Regum Anglorum*, ed. W. Stubbs, Rolls Series (1887–89), vol. 1, 145.

[In the remainder of the article, Parkes shows reasons why it is unsurprising that a book like CCCC 173 was produced at Winchester, especially seeing that both King Alfred and his son, King Edward the Elder, were buried there. 'The resemblance [...] to the Frankish royal house of St Denis is striking', he comments, while noting that at both places 'there is the same interest in dynastic achievement' (pp. 167–68). Parkes concludes with an analysis of the manuscript's later history, during the course of which the three additional booklets of the present compilation were added.]

4

Orality

If the question were posed, 'Is there any one area of research in literary studies that underwent a conspicuous transformation during the twentieth century, a gain in real knowledge where a state of relative ignorance had previously prevailed?', then a considered response would be to point to the progress made, in practically all parts of the world, in the understanding of oral poetry and oral poetics.

In Anglo-Saxon studies, understanding of the system of Old English poetics, including its stylized diction and the relation of that diction to the Old Germanic alliterative metre, has been significantly advanced through research into the verbal and formal resources by which living traditions of oral poetry are sustained. The key factor in the longevity of such traditions in one or another part of the world, it has been shown, is the existence of singers so skilled in the art of oral performance – and so dedicated to its practice – as to be able to draw on a repertory of traditional songs so as to recreate those materials anew while in the act of performing them aloud, and to repeat such performances again and again when given the opportunity. Among these creative persons are the 'singers of tales' whose training, compositional techniques, and repertoires of heroic songs were lucidly analysed by Albert B. Lord (1912–91) in a series of books and articles published beginning in the year 1960.[1]

A focal point for Lord's research was ancient Greek epic poetry, as it had been for his mentor, the Homerist Milman Parry (1902–35),[2] whom Lord assisted in fieldwork in the Balkans during the 1930s, resuming that research on his own in the early 1950s once political circumstances permitted. In addition, Lord had a special interest in Old

---

[1]   Albert B. Lord, *The Singer of Tales* (Cambridge, MA: Harvard University Press, 1960; 2nd edn, 2000, prepared by Stephen Mitchell and Gregory Nagy, with CD); *Epic Singers and Oral Tradition* (Ithaca: Cornell University Press, 1991); *The Singer Resumes the Tale*, ed. Mary Louise Lord (Ithaca: Cornell University Press, 1995).

[2]   After Parry's untimely death in 1935, his son Adam gathered together his published and unpublished papers in *The Making of Homeric Verse: The Collected Papers of Milman Parry*, ed. Adam Parry (Oxford: Oxford University Press, 1971).

Old English Literature: A Guide to Criticism with Selected Readings, First Edition. John D. Niles.
© 2016 John D. Niles. Published 2016 by John Wiley & Sons, Ltd.

English literature and wrote on that topic thoughtfully from time to time, directing his attention especially to *Beowulf, The Battle of Maldon*, Cynewulf's *Elene*, and the figure of Cædmon. His writings have a bearing on the criticism of Old English poetry that is manifest even when oblique. Despite the controversies that his research has sometimes inspired, it is that body of work, more than that of any other single scholar, that has set the comparative study of oral heroic poetry on a sound and rational basis where previously much ignorance and guesswork had prevailed.

While Parry, Lord, and scholars inspired by their work have taught us much about the formal artistry and the generative skills of singers of tales, research into oral poetry and oral poetics involves much more than this. Anthropological research into the cultural and mental world in which singers and storytellers practise their art in sundry parts of the globe, too, has had an impact on our conception of the corresponding world in which at least some Old English literature is rooted. In addition, the interface of literacy and orality, in societies where those two means for the transmission of knowledge coexist, has been of interest to medievalists. Whatever oral traditions were cultivated by the early Germanic-speaking peoples of Europe including the Anglo-Saxons, these traditions must have met and merged with the culture of the book that was such a distinct feature of early medieval Christianity. Such historical interactions as these are potentially illuminated through study of comparable processes of cultural synthesis in more recent times. Research into Anglo-Saxon England naturally has a significant place in any such investigations, for in no other part of northern Europe does a large body of vernacular poetry survive from a period before the year 1000. The special character of this verse calls for explanation, as does the very fact of its existence.

Among the numerous ramifications of recent research into oral poetry and poetics in Old English literary studies and related areas of scholarship, four stand out.[3]

First of all, the texture of the verse form used by virtually all Anglo-Saxon poets is now recognized not just to feature a certain number of fixed formulas, as has long been recognized, but also to be based throughout on complex interlocking patterns of formulaic diction. These patterns, it has been argued, are precisely of the kind that would have enabled poets schooled in an oral technique to perform in the medium of Old Germanic verse for hours, drawing on their repertoires in a flexible fashion so as to suit a particular occasion, much as present-day singers of tales have been shown to be able to do.[4] In other words, the verbal texture of Anglo-Saxon poetry is what it is not just for aesthetic reasons, nor out of sheer clumsiness or some kind of primitive instinct (as some critics used to think), but also

---

[3] A wide range of scholarship on orality is assembled in the critical anthology *Medieval Oral Literature*, ed. Karl Reichl (Berlin: de Gruyter, 2012); this features twenty-seven individual contributions by distinguished scholars.

[4] It is the flexibility of the formulaic system of Old English poetic diction (as opposed to the use of fixed epithets in Homer's verse) that was emphasized in two important articles by Donald K. Fry: 'Old English Formulas and Systems', *ES* 48 (1967): 193–204, and 'Variation and Economy in Beowulf', *MPh* 65 (1968): 353–56. For discussion see chap. 5, 'Formula and Formulaic System', and chap. 6, 'Compound Diction', of my book *Beowulf: The Poem and Its Tradition* (Cambridge, MA: Harvard University Press, 1983). Many additional references to research on Old English formulaic diction are noted by Andy Orchard, *A Critical Companion to Beowulf* (Cambridge: D.S. Brewer, 2003), 85–91.

for reasons of utility. Although Christian terms and concepts are present throughout the extant verse, scholars have argued that the verse-making system in which all poets worked must date back to a period of prehistory when oral performance would have been the one means by which native verse was produced.

Second, despite any number of critical controversies that remain unresolved, the substantive understanding of certain individual texts of the Anglo-Saxon period has been permanently affected by this direction of research. This is certainly true of *Beowulf*, with its highly stylized formulaic language, its unique structure (which is so different from that of classical epic), its gestures to the many-storied legendary past of the Germanic-speaking peoples, and its fusion of heroic and Christian perspectives. Research into the cultural world of oral poetry has obvious relevance also to the Old English metrical charms, some of whose striking features fall into place when one views these sometimes rough-and-ready texts as products of a monastic culture that was by no means isolated from the oral transmission of knowledge in society at large, including age-old medical beliefs and practices.[5] Research along these lines has likewise had an impact on the critical understanding of texts pertaining to related bodies of early medieval literature, including Old Norse eddic poetry, certain Old Irish texts, certain Old High and Middle High German texts including the *Hildebrandslied* and the *Nibelungenlied*, a number of Old French *chansons de geste* including the *Chanson de Roland* song-complex, and a considerable body of Middle English popular romances, among other post-Conquest texts.[6] Even certain Old English prose texts, such as the sermons of Wulfstan, can now be understood in a new light as the expression of a special kind of oral-formulaic technique, as Andy Orchard has pointed out in his 1992 article 'Crying Wolf'.[7]

Just as importantly, research by such scholars as the classicist Eric Havelock (1903–88) and the cultural historian and philosopher Walter J. Ong (1912–2003) has clarified the structures of thought that are characteristic of people living in societies where literacy is not the norm.[8] Their work has led to new ways of looking at certain Old English verse texts as

---

[5]   The intersections between popular and formal modes of knowledge in the Old English metrical charms, with attention to the respective dynamics of orality and literacy, are studied by Karen Louise Jolly in her book *Popular Religion in Late Saxon England: Elf Charms in Context* (Chapel Hill: University of North Carolina Press, 1996).

[6]   The extension of Parry's and Lord's methods of research into a number of different medieval literary traditions is reviewed by John Miles Foley in *The Theory of Oral Composition: History and Methodology* (Bloomington: Indiana University Press, 1988). Mark C. Amodio discusses the interplay of orality and literacy in both Old English and Middle English verse in *Writing the Oral Tradition: Oral Poetics and Literate Culture in Medieval England* (Notre Dame: University of Notre Dame Press, 2004).

[7]   A.P. McD. (Andy) Orchard, 'Crying Wolf: Oral Style and the *Sermones Lupi*', *ASE* 21 (1992): 239–64.

[8]   Note particularly Eric A. Havelock, *The Muse Learns to Write: Reflections on Orality and Literacy from Antiquity to the Present* (New Haven: Yale University Press, 1967), and Walter J. Ong, *Orality and Literacy: The Technologizing of the Word* (New York: Methuen, 1988). See also Ong, 'Writing is a Technology that Restructures Thought', in *The Written Word: Literacy in Transition*, ed. Gerd Baumann (Oxford: Clarendon Press, 1986), 23–50. Of related interest are the writings of the social anthropologist Jack Goody, including *The Interface Between the Written and the Oral* (Cambridge: Cambridge University Press, 1987).

products of a mentality that differs in key ways from our own. Research along such lines is a natural extension of approaches to the poetry of the Anglo-Saxons, like that of other peoples of the ancient world, as, in its origins, an expression of the time-tested lore and wisdom of a people.[9]

Finally, research into the interface of orality and literacy has had a bearing on the understanding of Anglo-Saxon manuscript culture, which some scholars now approach as a kind of extension of oral modes of the transmission of knowledge into the material realm.[10] One particular area of research that has implications in this regard is study of the means by which, in present-day cultures, songs and stories that normally circulate only in oral performance have been taken down in writing through acts of oral dictation or other means, undergoing inevitable change as a result of that process.[11] Research into such acts of textualization can provide a comparative context for our understanding of similar phenomena that may have occurred during the Middle Ages, thus leading to the preservation of 'oral-like' texts, ones that show a significant residue of oral features. Research along these lines suggests that the distinction between oral tradition and literary artefact is hardly an oppositional one involving 'pure' entities on either side of a cultural divide. Rather, just as the modes of oral discourse in a society where literacy is at all widespread will be influenced by literate models, the same is true in reverse. Scholars no longer assume that poetry that survives from the early medieval period, therefore, even if fixed in manuscript form, was the product of a literate practice and a literate mentality alone.[12]

In order to understand these developments, it will be worth taking a somewhat closer look at the history of recent scholarship in this area, considered especially in its impact on the criticism of Old English literature. Although some scholars speak of this kind of research as exemplifying oral-formulaic theory, or what elsewhere has been called the Oral Theory or just the Theory (with those latter titles capitalized so as to lend this mode of research a quasi-mythological stature), my own preference is to speak more neutrally of 'research into oral poetry and poetics'. This leaves room for a multiplicity

---

[9]   This point is developed by Morton W. Bloomfield and Charles W. Dunn in their jointly authored book *The Role of the Poet in Early Societies* (Cambridge: D.S. Brewer, 1989).

[10]   Of particular interest in this context are the writings of Brian Stock, including *Listening for the Text: On the Uses of the Past* (Philadelphia: University of Pennsylvania Press, 1990).

[11]   The textualization of oral literature is studied from a variety of critical perspectives in the anthology *Oral Art Forms and their Passage into Writing*, ed. Else Mundal and Jonas Wellendorf (Copenhagen: Museum Tusculanum Press, 2012). My own thinking on the topic is expressed in a chapter on 'Orality' in *The Cambridge Companion to Textual Scholarship*, ed. Neil Freistat and Julia Flanders (Cambridge: Cambridge University Press, 2013), 205–23, and in my essay 'From Script to Print – and Beyond', *Western Folklore* 72 (2013), 229–51. This latter study serves as the Introduction to a special issue of *Western Folklore* on the textualization of oral forms.

[12]   The interpenetration of oral and literate modes of thought and expression is studied by Katherine O'Brien O'Keeffe in her book *Visible Song: Transitional Literacy in Old English Verse* (Cambridge: Cambridge University Press, 1990), as well as in the essays included in *Vox Intexta: Orality and Textuality in the Middle Ages*, ed. A.N. Doane and Carol Braun Pasternack (Madison: University of Wisconsin Press, 1991).

of theoretical positions, any one or more of which may be found to have relevance to a given singer, text, or tradition.[13]

Parry, Lord, and their Legacy

Much as nineteenth-century Anglo-Saxonists tended to follow in the footsteps of classicists, the main twentieth-century scholarly impetus for research into Old English oral poetics has come from Homeric studies. Pursuing the long-standing question as to how the two great Homeric epics, the *Iliad* and the *Odyssey*, could have been produced in a period near the dawn of Greek literature, when the arts of literacy were still barely known, Milman Parry, then a young professor of Classics at Harvard University, set out to see how this question could be illuminated through field research into living traditions of oral heroic poetry. In this choice he was strongly influenced by prior ethnographic fieldwork undertaken in different parts of Eurasia. One of the early specialists in research of this kind was the German-born Russian scholar Wilhelm Radloff (1837–1918), a foundational figure in Turkic studies, who had recorded and published a large body of traditional heroic literature from singers in present-day Kyrgyzstan and other parts of Central Asia. Another pioneer was the Serbian scholar Matija Murko (1861–1952), who had made a smaller but comparable collection of South Slavic oral poetry and whose 1929 book *La poésie populaire épique en Yougoslavie au début du XXe siècle* ('Popular Epic Poetry in Yugoslavia at the Beginning of the Twentieth Century') made a strong impression on Parry at the time when he defended his doctoral dissertation in Paris. Eventually, on the basis of a comparison of the formulaic style of Homer with that of epic singers in the Balkans, Parry believed that he had found a key to answering 'the Homeric question', as the puzzle of the origins of the *Iliad* and the *Odyssey* was then called. Homer too, Parry concluded, must have been a singer of tales, a poet adept in the art of performing epic poetry aloud in the highly stylized language of his poetic tradition.

Parry's great insight, which was left to Lord to develop and refine, was the realization that singers who grow up in an active oral culture can internalize and master the techniques of oral composition just as surely as persons growing up in a society where literacy is well established can master the techniques of literary composition. In either context, the person naturally develops such skills not just through the memorization of prior examples – though memorization is a factor – but also through ever-increasing competence in the art of composition-in-performance. The key factor that accounts for the facility of singers of tales, Parry found, is their ability to deploy, in an apparently spontaneous fashion, a specialized 'language within the language' that consists largely of set formulas and formula-like phrases. These are the building blocks through which longer and more supple passages of verse can be composed. In like manner, entire poems, including ones of great length, can be built up from constituent themes (or set pieces) whose chief appeal has to do with their traditionality.

---

[13] The diversity of the oral poetic traditions of the world, and hence the futility of trying to reduce them to any one system, is emphasized by Ruth Finnegan in her book *Oral Poetry: Its Nature, Significance, and Social Context* (Cambridge: Cambridge University Press, 1977; augmented edn, 1992).

Since the art of composition-in-performance is not one that most people are necessarily conscious of today (even though they may employ something similar to it every day in the course of normal conversation), it deserves a few additional words of clarification.

In a literate society, as any novelist or short-story writer knows, writing can take on many forms that are original to a particular work and that at the same time are bound by the conventions of print culture. These conventions include matters of diction, grammar, form, genre, and style. In an oral culture, the analogous art of composition is called 'singing', or 'storytelling', or 'the art of oral performance'. What Parry and Lord were able to document is that the art of oral poetic composition, too, is at the same time both creative and bound by tradition. In part, the difference between these two modes of 'performance', that of the lone writer and that of the singer of tales with his live audience, has to do with the degree to which each one is bound by convention. While most well-regarded authors disparage mere conventionality, the singer of tales and his audience tend to delight in the fulfilment of expectations. There is also the factor of fluency. The writer in the act of composition may labour over a page for hours, stopping and starting again so as to find just the right words in just the right sequence; and later on, the same writer may revise that page so as to get it just right. The singer's words, by contrast, follow closely upon one another in a rhythmic pulse that is unceasing, at least until the next musical interlude or period of rest. At heightened moments, what the singer may produce is a kind of cascade of language. The only way the singer can 'perfect' or 'revise' his song, correspondingly, is by performing a new version of it. Another factor that sets the art of the singer of tales apart from his lettered counterpart is the communal nature of oral performance. While an author can write in an isolated room or cabin so as to please either himself, or a small circle of friends, or a hoped-for future imagined readership, the singer of tales lives in and for the moment of performance. He sings for a group of people whose physical presence is a crucial ingredient in this art form, just as it is with live drama; and in an important sense he serves as the voice of those people, enunciating key aspects of their history, their codes of social behaviour, and their ethics in a manner that invites (and often receives) immediate approbation. Without that warm and animated symbiosis between audience and performer, the art of the singer of tales cannot exist. Only its shadow self can persist in the form either of audio recordings or of transcribed texts, which are routinely edited before being 'published' on either vellum or the printed page.

To return to the bearing of this line of research on Old English studies: among the scholars who were stimulated by Milman Parry's and Albert B. Lord's researches were Anglo-Saxonists who hoped to be able to capitalize on this research so as to ascertain if their own 'Beowulfian question' could be resolved. They wished to find out if, through study of the formulaic language of a range of different texts, Old English poems that were the work of orally improvising poets (if any of them were) could be distinguished from the work of learned authors.

The major initiative in this direction was taken by one of Lord's senior colleagues at Harvard, Francis Peabody Magoun, Jr (1895–1979) in a pair of articles published in 1953 and 1955.[14] In the second of these, 'Bede's Story of Cædman: The Case History of an

---

[14] Francis P. Magoun, Jr, 'The Oral-Formulaic Character of Anglo-Saxon Narrative Poetry', *Speculum* 28 (1953): 446–67, repr. in Nicholson, 189–221, Fry, 83–113, Fulk, 45–65, and *Essential Articles*, 319–51; and Magoun, 'Bede's Story of Cædman: The Case History of an Anglo-Saxon Oral Singer', *Speculum* 30 (1955): 49–63.

Anglo–Saxon Oral Singer', Magoun directed attention to the Northumbrian cowherd Cædmon, whom Bede (in 4: 24 of his *Historia ecclesiastica*) celebrates as what might be called a 'singer of tales' of the eighth century: that is to say, a person whose initial dream-vision, together with his subsequent career as a composer of verse on religious themes, provides a parallel to the life histories of singers who have been recorded in the field.[15] Of particular interest in Bede's account, as Magoun points out, is the sympathetic portrayal of an act of collaboration between an unlettered singer and the highly educated members of a monastic community. According to Bede, this meeting of cultures resulted in the recording of a significant body of orally composed devotional verse.

It is Magoun's earlier article, however, 'The Oral-Formulaic Character of Anglo–Saxon Narrative Poetry', that proved to be of crucial importance in discussions of orality in the Anglo–Saxon context. Here Magoun advanced the thesis that study of the precise language used by the *Beowulf* poet and other Anglo–Saxon poets can go a long ways towards answering the question of the mode of composition of Old English verse. 'Oral poetry, it may be safely said', he writes, 'is composed entirely of formulas, large and small, while lettered poetry is never formulaic, though lettered poets occasionally consciously repeat themselves or quote verbatim from other poets in order to produce a specific rhetorical or literary effect' (p. 447). Magoun supported this claim through an initial analysis of the first fifty verses of *Beowulf* so as to show that they are a tissue of formulas of one kind or another. He takes this verse to be representative of Old English poetic language as it was at a relatively early stage (the earlier eighth century), even though by then it had already been permeated by Christian thought and sentiments. He then compares with this Beowulfian passage lines 512–35 of *Christ and Satan*, a poem of later date (as is widely assumed) from the Junius manuscript of Old English poetry. His point in doing so is to show how thoroughly, with the passage of years, Anglo–Saxon poets had come to be able to sing 'in a slightly adjusted traditional language' on Christian themes that had come to pervade the literature. A point emphasized by Magoun is that despite the differences in style that are evident from such a comparison as this, one can point to 'a marked uniformness or unity of style' in Old English poetry (p. 458). In an earlier article, he had associated this common style with Old West Germanic verse as a whole, as others too had done.[16] In his 1953 article he accounts for this uniformity with reference to the formulaic language used by Anglo–Saxon singers, calling attention to 'a continuity that seems to live until the Norman Conquest' (p. 458).

Magoun's aim in in this seminal article, then, was to proclaim the existence of a method – the detailed charting of the presence of formulaic diction in a poem, or else the demonstration that the poem lacks such formulas – that can serve as a test for orality. This method, in his mind, could serve as 'a touchstone with which it is now possible to determine to

---

[15] Of interest in this connection is Albert B. Lord's 1993 study 'Cædmon Revisited', in *Bessinger Studies*, 121–37. Cædmon's initiatory dream-vision has worldwide parallels; indeed, in Central Asia, seldom will a novice singer of epic songs set out to perform in public until he has had a dream-vision calling him to that vocation.

[16] Francis P. Magoun, Jr, 'A Note on Old West Germanic Poetic Unity', *MPh* 43 (1945): 77–82. Cf. Robert L. Kellogg, 'The South Germanic Oral Tradition', in *Franciplegius: Medieval and Linguistic Studies in Honor of Francis Peabody Magoun, Jr.*, ed. Jess B. Bessinger, Jr, and Robert P. Creed (New York: New York University, 1965), 66–74.

which of the two great categories of poetry a recorded text belongs: to the oral or to the lettered tradition' (p. 449). In addition, Magoun sought to use such tools to chart the evolutionary history of Old English poetry, starting from a period of prehistoric oral origins and continuing to the end of the Anglo-Saxon period, when poetry of a semi-traditional kind was still being composed even in a society where the arts of literacy were well advanced. As his discussion of Cynewulf makes clear, Magoun recognized that a poet who was obviously lettered could also compose verse in a traditional manner (p. 460):

> Mention of Cynewulf raises a question concerning the relation between lettered persons and orally performed poetry. Not all Anglo-Saxon Christian poetry needs to have been composed by lettered singers – witness the story of Cædman. Any good unlettered singer who had translated for, or expounded to, him the *Apocryphal Gospel of St. Matthew and St. Andrew* could easily have composed *Andreas*. But Cynewulf was surely a lettered person, else how could he have conceived a plan to assure mention of his name in prayers by means of runic signatures which depend on a knowledge of spelling and reading for their efficacy? If, however, the narrative parts of his poems prove on testing to be formulaic, one must assume that those parts at least he composed in the traditional way. That he subsequently got them written down, whether dictating to himself, as it were, or to another person – possibly a more convenient procedure – is beside the point. In any event there would be no conflict with, or contradiction to, tradition.

I dwell on this passage because subsequent critics have commonly, though erroneously, stated that Magoun advanced sweeping claims about the oral character of Old English poetry. What his 1953 article actually emphasizes is the *traditional formulaic character* of this verse, with this characteristic seen as an inheritance from an earlier common Germanic period when oral composition was the norm.

In any event, it was not long before a scholarly debate ensued regarding Magoun's bold proposition that 'lettered poetry is never formulaic.' While such a generalization might withstand scrutiny with regard to the elite poetry of our own time, the Anglo-Saxon period is another matter. A persuasive rebuttal to this part of Magoun's argument was made by Larry D. Benson – another of Lord's Harvard colleagues – in his 1966 essay 'The Literary Character of Anglo-Saxon Formulaic Poetry'.[17] In a manner that was at the same time respectful of Magoun's scholarship and forceful in its alternative interpretation of the evidence, Benson used the same technique of formulaic analysis to show that Old English poems that are of indubitably learned origin, such as the Christian allegorical poem *The Phoenix*, Exeter Book Riddle 35 (which is a translation of Aldhelm's riddle 'De Lorica'), the Old English metrical paraphrases of the first fifty of the psalms, and the Old English metrical versions of the lyric poems in Boethius's *De consolatione philosophiae*, are all manifestly formulaic in their style. The inescapable conclusion to which his observations lead is that 'literate poets could quite easily write in a formulaic style.' In his own neatly formulated view, 'To prove that an Old English poem is formulaic is only to prove that it is an Old English poem' (p. 336).

---

[17] Larry D. Benson, 'The Literary Character of Anglo-Saxon Formulaic Poetry', *PMLA* 81 (1966): 334–41.

Benson's article is often read as a refutation of Magoun's, and in part it is that. When the two studies are read side by side in an unbiased manner, however, what they confirm is that there is indeed 'a marked uniformity of style' in Old English poetry, in Magoun's words. As a result of the stylistic conservatism of Old English verse, the unlettered singers of this period were able to compose in this style (as with the example of Cædmon), and lettered writers were able to do so just as well (as with Benson's multiple exhibits). Benson is therefore justified in his main conclusion, namely, that 'We must use the greatest caution in assuming the oral composition of any surviving Old English poem' (p. 340). Upon reflection, this can be seen to be only half the story, however. What also can be said, though Benson does not say it, is that we should use equally great caution in assuming the *literate* authorship of any surviving Old English poem that is not demonstrably the product of a learned pen. The 'Beowulfian question' that had been animating critics for some while thus remained unresolved by this debate.

Oral Poetics and Noetics

Criticism on the oral dimension of Old English literature has taken a variety of forms in recent decades, some of it in a direct line of intellectual descent from the work of Parry and Lord and some of it less so. Taken as a whole, the very significant amount of research into the world's oral literatures that has been undertaken in the past half-century has led to the conclusion that each tradition presents its own special features of language, versification, genre, and style. Among the different performers working in any one linguistic tradition, as well, or among the different genres of that tradition, the relative importance of rote memorization versus the art of composition in performance may differ. No touchtone for distinguishing the oral style from its literary counterparts has yet turned up, therefore, and none is likely to do so, despite hopes that have sometimes been expressed to the contrary.

The work of the medievalist and Africanist Jeff Opland is illustrative of these developments. A native of South Africa who conducted extensive fieldwork in that country before teaching for some while in the USA and eventually settling in the UK, Opland edited and translated several volumes of South African oral poetry in addition to completing a major critical study, *Xhosa Oral Poetry*, based largely on his field research.[18] In addition, his 1980 book *Anglo-Saxon Oral Poetry* represents a sustained engagement with Old English traditions of oral poetry that apparently developed out of a common Germanic heritage.[19] Opland's expertise in these two very different traditions put him in the unusual situation of being able

---

[18] Jeff Opland, *Xhosa Oral Poetry: Aspects of a Black South African Tradition* (Cambridge: Cambridge University Press, 1983).

[19] Jeff Opland, *Anglo-Saxon Oral Poetry: A Study of the Traditions* (New Haven: Yale University Press, 1980). Among Opland's more specialized studies, his 1980 article 'From Horseback to Monastic Cell: The Impact on English Literature of the Introduction of Writing', in Niles, 30–43 and 161–63, offers a brief but incisive discussion of the transition from oral to literate modes of literary production in the Anglo-Saxon context. See also Opland's studies '*Imbongi Nezibongo*: The Xhosa Tribal Poet and the Contemporary Poetic Tradition', *PMLA* 90 (1975): 185–208, and 'On Anglo-Saxon Poetry and the Comparative Study of Oral Poetic Traditions', *Acta Germanica* 10 (1977): 49–62.

to explore the possible bearing of the oral traditions of the Bantu peoples of southern Africa on the study of Old English poetry and poetics. Focusing on the praise poet (*imbongi*) who is a fixture of Bantu tribal societies, Opland pointed out that the corpus of Anglo-Saxon verse includes encomiastic elements that bear comparison with what we see in South Africa. His publications question the Parry/Lord model of composition based on his experience with singers who, even if well educated, were capable of performing long improvised poems that combined eulogy with social critique. The *imbongi*, he shows, produces nothing that could be called a 'song' with its own name, shape, and relatively stable content. Instead, each poem that the *imbongi* performs is unique even if its language is permeated by convention. Opland advances the hypothesis that eulogistic poetry was the norm in Germanic-speaking lands until, with the coming of Christianity and Christian learning, models of extended narrative were introduced. This is not, of course, a proposition that is subject to proof, but it remains an intriguing speculation. It serves to cast doubt on the assumption, entrenched in the early years of *Beowulf* criticism and still attractive to some, that the short narrative lay, or *Lied*, was a primary oral genre in the early northern European context.

A very different perspective on Old English oral traditions is offered by another Anglo-Saxonist who has taken up the challenge of field research, the German scholar Karl Reichl. Working with skilled oral poets in a part of the world that was closed off to Parry and Lord in the 1930s for geopolitical reasons but that had been open to Wilhelm Radloff in the previous century, Reichl has devoted much of his professional career to documenting the oral poetic traditions of the Turkic-speaking peoples of Central Asia. His editions and translations of oral epic poetry from Uzbekistan – the epics *Alpomish* and *Edige*, in particular, which are central to Uzbek or Karakalpak identity – are scholarly models of their kind. So too is his wide-ranging 1992 book *Turkic Epic Poetry*, the only survey of its kind.[20] Drawing inspiration from Lord's *Singer of Tales*, in the course of time Reichl has become the leading authority on the world's most vital living traditions of oral heroic poetry, the Central Asian, and he has been making accessible to an international audience a large body of traditional literature from that region that has been recorded in the field.

As a philologist whose chief training is in the languages and literatures of early northern Europe, Reichl has made sustained efforts to apply insights gained from his fieldwork to the critical understanding of such works as *Beowulf*, *The Battle of Brunanburh*, *The Fight at Finnsburh*, the *Chanson de Roland*, and the *Nibelungenlied*, approaching these heroic poems as grounded in the art of oral poetic composition regardless of exactly how their extant texts were composed and recorded. In his 2002 comparative study *Singing the Past*, Reichl explores the manner in which the heroic poetry of medieval Europe and contemporary Central Asia both preserves and transforms history, thus contributing to a people's sense of

---

[20] Karl Reichl, *Turkic Epic Poetry: Traditions, Forms, Poetic Structure* (New York: Garland, 1992). See also Reichl, *Das usbekische Heldenepos Alpomish: Einführung, Text, Übersetzung* (Wiesbaden: Harrassowitz, 2001), and his exemplary English-language edition *Edige: A Karakalpak Heroic Epic as Performed by Jumabay Bazarov*, FF Communications 141 (Helsinki: Academia Scientiarum Fennica, 2007), with CD–ROM. Reichl is presently at work on a translation into English of the Kyrgyz epic *Manas* (Jüsüp Mamay's version).

cultural identity.[21] When assessing how much light the study of Turkic epic can contribute to the understanding of the anonymous medieval heroic poetry of northern Europe, Reichl adopts a cautious stance, recognizing both differences and parallels between these different traditions. The attitude towards history that he discerns in *Beowulf*, for example, differs from what he finds in Uzbek epic. While Uzbek singers and their audiences are strongly focused on 'tribal roots', the same cannot be said of *Beowulf* and other extant Germanic poems. These, Reichl observes, tell of an ancient past and of heroes 'too distant to be seen as "our ancestors" by a contemporary audience'.[22] At the same time, Reichl has confirmed beyond any shadow of doubt that in a society where the arts of oral poetry are prized, skilled singers, whether illiterate or literate, can spin out long narrative songs for hour after hour, usually to their own accompaniment on a stringed instrument, without recourse to anything other than their own memory and their competence in a stylized oral poetic medium. Like Lord's or Opland's research, Reichl's research into Central Asian epic poetry offers no master key to the understanding of Old English poetry and its oral antecedents. Still it provides an invaluable perspective on that early anonymous verse based on study of living traditions of oral poetry that until recently have remained little known in the West, despite their cultural centrality in their home regions.[23]

Among other Anglo-Saxonists who have made significant original contributions to the understanding of Old English verse in the light of oral poetry and poetics, three will be singled out for attention here. These are Edward B. Irving, Jr, Ward Parks, and John Miles Foley.

In his 1989 book *Rereading Beowulf*, Edward B. Irving, Jr, took a marked turn away from the New Critical methods that had characterized his earlier study *A Reading of Beowulf*.[24] Instead, he embraced certain aspects of oral theory as providing an entry point to understanding both that poem's emphatically conventional artistry and its poet's mental world. As he writes in the first page of the preface to *Rereading Beowulf*, 'My critical imagination was fired a few years ago by the "oral" theory of Old English literature, and as a result my whole point of view toward the poem shifted. What used to seem like troublesome flaws in a remarkable poem, cracks to be anxiously papered over, now seem merely structural features

---

[21] Karl Reichl, *Singing the Past: Turkic and Medieval Heroic Poetry* (Ithaca: Cornell University Press, 2000). Among Reichl's many articles, one that is of special interest is 'Turkic Bard and Medieval Entertainer: What a Living Epic Tradition Can Tell Us about Oral Performance of Narrative in the Middle Ages', in *Performing Medieval Narrative*, ed. Evelyn Birge Vitz et al. (Cambridge: D.S. Brewer, 2005), 167–78. Another is 'Silencing the Voice of the Singer: Problems and Strategies in the Editing of Turkic Oral Epics', in *Textualization of Oral Epics*, ed. Lauri Honko (Berlin: Mouton de Gruyter, 2000), 103–27, an essay that emphasizes the impossibility of representing more than select aspects of a singer's performance in the ontologically different medium of script or print.

[22] Reichl, *Singing the Past*, 150.

[23] In order to enhance appreciation of the importance of Inner Asian traditions for the comparative study of oral heroic poetry, I have recently edited a special issue of *Journal of American Folklore* on the topic 'Living Epics of China and Inner Asia' (forthcoming summer 2016). Receiving special attention there are the Kyrgyz epic *Manas* and the Tibeto-Mongolian epic *Gesar*, two epic cycles that exist in multiple versions and that, in the millions of lines of their recorded texts, vastly exceed in magnitude the epic poems of the Western tradition.

[24] Edward B. Irving, Jr, *Rereading Beowulf* (Philadelphia: University of Pennsylvania Press, 1989). His earlier book *Reading Beowulf* is discussed in Chapter 1 above.

of this kind of early poetry' (p. ix). Irving goes on to state his readiness 'to accept the poem as a most distinguished descendant of a long and skillful oral tradition' (p. 2).

In *Rereading Beowulf*, Irving takes issue with those critics (including Larry D. Benson) who regarded the high aesthetic quality of *Beowulf* as a reason to rule out that poem's oral composition. Instead, turning this view on its head, Irving argues that 'we must move from seeing the oral-derived style as a crippling restriction to perceiving it as generating through its very conventions the unmistakably high quality of the verse' (p. 8). Of particular interest is Irving's attempt in the first chapter of his book, titled 'The Approach to Heorot', to show the pervasive workings in *Beowulf* of an oral 'noetics' (from Greek *nous* 'mind'). He borrows this term from the writings of Walter J. Ong, whose work in this area represents a fresh turn in an intellectual tradition going back to early twentieth-century attempts to distinguish modern scientific thinking from what was once called the 'primitive mind'.[25] Central to both Ong's approach to oral poetry as a general phenomenon and Irving's approach to *Beowulf* is an emphasis on the 'mnemonic base' that underlies oral art forms. Irving sees this as a defining influence on the patterned nature of story-plots, the uninhibited repetition of formulaic phrases and themes, and the frequent use of 'didactic maxims that restate the ethos of the work' (p. 16). Additionally, Irving traces in *Beowulf* specific instantiations of the general tendency, in the thought-world of oral poets, to favour an aggregative or copious style of narration; to develop the action in terms of agonistically toned black-and-white opposition; and to favour situational rather than abstract thinking, among other features of a comparable kind, working his way through a list of nine 'oral' characteristics that had previously been identified by Ong. Whether or not one believes that the presence in *Beowulf* of such features as these proves that poem to be the result of oral composition – a thesis that Irving is careful never to advance – *Rereading Beowulf* goes far towards undermining anachronistic criticism that would view the greatest of Anglo-Saxon poems as 'defective' because it departs so decisively from modern aesthetics and current analytical modes of thought.

Ward Parks is perhaps best known for his 1990 study *Verbal Dueling in Heroic Narrative*.[26] Building on the work of Ong as well as on that of of contemporary folklorists, Parks takes account of the important role of flyting, or ritualized verbal combat, in the cultures depicted in such poems as the *Iliad*, the *Odyssey*, *Beowulf*, and *The Battle of Maldon*, seeing this age-old aspect of the heroic ethos as contributing to 'the heroic vindication of self through the winning of honor' (p. 26). Unferth's verbal challenge to the young hero Beowulf, together with the hero's crushing response to that provocation, is only one example of this widespread confrontational mode, which Parks shows to be characteristic of oral cultures the world over. The power of insight that Parks brings to the topic of verbal duelling is evident also in his 1987 essay 'The Traditional Narrator and the "I Heard" Formulas in Old English Poetry'.[27] Here he calls attention to those formulaic phrases whereby the narrator of *Beowulf* claims to be repeating knowledge that he has gained through oral report. In Parks's view, these 'I heard' formulas 'attest to a conception of the poetic narrator as one who re-creates,

---

[25] Important studies by Ong are cited in note 8 above.

[26] Ward Parks, *Verbal Dueling in Heroic Narrative: The Homeric and Old English Traditions* (Princeton: Princeton University Press, 1990).

[27] Ward Parks, 'The Traditional Narrator and the "I Heard" Formulas in Old English Poetry', *ASE* 16 (1987): 45–66. Of related interest is Stanley B. Greenfield's well-regarded essay 'The Authenticating Voice in *Beowulf*', *ASE* 5 (1976): 51–62, repr. in *Readings: Beowulf*, 97–110.

who re-enacts, who remembers the sayings (utterances) of the past and through his own acts of poetic discourse makes them present again' (p. 47). In another essay published at about this same time, 'Interperformativity and *Beowulf*',[28] Parks plays off a term, 'intertextuality', that figures importantly in the vocabulary of recent criticism and uses it as an entry point to the question of how a given text serves as a nexus of allusions to others. His term 'interperformativity' refers to 'the chain of oral performances' that is reenacted in each new performance of a work of oral literature (p. 25). Through the so-called digressions of *Beowulf* in particular, he argues, the poet 'situates his story of Beowulf in a world of songs' (p. 32), doing so in such a manner that the larger-than-life men and women who figure in the poem's legendary episodes are coinhabitants with the hero in the realm of memory. Parks's research, like Irving's, makes a significant contribution to what might be called oral literary theory. Skirting the problematic question of the mode of composition of particular works including *Beowulf*, Parks concentrates instead on how to read these works in terms consistent with the oral culture that underlies them.

Before his untimely death in 2012, John Miles Foley made a series of significant contributions to 'oral literary theory' and the comparative study of oral traditions. As the editor of a number of critical anthologies on oral literature, the author of a major bibliography on that topic, the author of several related guides, and the founding editor of the journal *Oral Tradition*, Foley dedicated his career to promoting, extending, and refining the line of research initiated by Milman Parry and Albert B. Lord. Foley's personal contributions to the development of oral theory, all of which have a potential bearing on the critical understanding of Old English poetry, find expression in three books in particular. These are his 1990 study *Traditional Oral Epic*, his 1991 book *Immanent Art*, and his 1995 study *The Singer of Tales in Performance*.[29] In the first of these he develops original models of how traditional phraseology is employed and how stylized thematic structures operate in three separate traditions of European epic poetry, namely the Greek, the Anglo-Saxon, and the Serbo-Croatian. In *Immanent Art*, he dwells on the *pars pro toto* principle of 'traditional referentiality' by which any single incident in an oral epic poem has the potential to call to mind all other incidents of this kind that figure in the tradition. It is through the memories of the performer and his listeners, Foley argues, that 'the tradition' is present in immanent form in any of its innumerable instantiations. In *The Singer of Tales in Performance*, Foley makes an ambitious effort to fuse Parry/Lord oral theory with contemporary performance theory as well as with the movement known as ethnopoetics, an approach to the representation of orality that aspires to give voice to the singer or storyteller even in the mute medium of print. A key term by which Foley unites these different strands of research is 'word-power', which he defines as 'that particular mode of meaning [made] possible only by virtue of the enabling event of performance and the enabling referent of tradition' (p. xiv). While this is a compact definition, Foley's elucidation of the term in the main body of his book demonstrates its value.

---

[28]   Ward Parks, 'Interperformativity and *Beowulf*', *Narodna Umjetnost* 26 (1989): 25–35.

[29]   John Miles Foley, *Traditional Oral Epic: The Odyssey, Beowulf, and the Serbo-Croatian Return Song* (Berkeley: University of California Press, 1990); *Immanent Art: From Structure to Meaning in Traditional Oral Epic* (Bloomington: Indiana University Press, 1991); and *The Singer of Tales in Performance* (Bloomington: Indiana University Press, 1995). Note also his book *The Theory of Oral Composition* (n. 6 above).

Perhaps brief notice of my 1997 book *Homo Narrans* will not be thought out of place here, as well.[30] The large claim of this book is that the narrative capability – the ability to tell stories – is a trait that, more than any other, defines human beings as such, in part because of its power to generate counterfactual worlds. Taking inspiration from Lord and other scholars who have cultivated the comparative method in oral literary research, I explore connections between the 'dead texts' of Anglo-Saxon England and the living singing and storytelling traditions of Scotland, based on field research undertaken there during the period 1984–91. Individual chapters take as their respective themes 'somatic communication', or meaningful connections that depend on the bodily presence of performers and listeners and not just the exchange of words; 'oral poetry acts', or staged events whose chief purpose – and whose potentially trans-formative effect – is to generate written and/or printed versions of songs or stories that are normally only performed aloud; and 'the strong tradition-bearer', a term that I use to refer to gifted singers and storytellers who not only perpetuate an oral tradition, but also actively shape it into new forms through their creativity and charisma. A study of related interest is my 2003 essay 'The Myth of the Anglo-Saxon Oral Poet'.[31] Here I argue that the idea of oral poetry served the people of pre-Conquest England as a cultural myth: that is, that the people of that time prized the image of the 'bard of ancient days' as a counterpart to the actual learned authors and scribes whose role in society was becoming ever more important.

A good deal of recent scholarship on orality has concentrated not on the act of oral com-position, but rather on the voicing of literature regardless of its compositional origins. Drawing on the work of the French-Canadian critic Paul Zumthor in particular, Ursula Schaefer uses the term 'vocality' to refer to this dimension of the recorded literature of Anglo-Saxon England, particularly in her 1992 book *Vokalität*.[32] Likewise, A.N. Doane, in his 1994 article 'The Ethnography of Scribal Writing and Anglo-Saxon Poetry' and other essays, has written of 'scribal performance', seen as a bodily act that can be compared to the art of the oral performer but that takes place in the medium of ink and vellum. Doane sug-gests, controversially, that a scribe's apparent aural perception of a text can be replicated through the editorial handling of that text.[33] Much of Katherine O'Brien O'Keeffe's

---

[30] John D. Niles, *Homo Narrans: The Poetics and Anthropology of Oral Literature* (Philadelphia: University of Pennsylvania Press, 1997).

[31] John D. Niles, 'The Myth of the Anglo-Saxon Oral Poet', *Western Folklore* 62 (2003): 7–61. A revised version of this essay is included as chap. 4 of my book *Old English Heroic Poems and the Social Life of Texts* (Turnhout: Brepols, 2007). The essay draws inspiration from Roberta Frank's study 'The Search for the Anglo-Saxon Oral Poet', *BJRL* 75 (1993): 11–36, repr. with a postscript in *Toller Lectures*, 137–60. Frank demonstrates the workings of a similar cultural myth in eighteenth- and nineteenth-century Europe, when bards were all the go.

[32] Ursula Schaefer, *Vokalität: Altenglische Dichtung zwischen Mündlichkeit und Schriftlichkeit*, ScriptOralia 39 (Tübingen: Gunter Narr, 1992); note also her study 'Ceteris Imparibus: Orality/ Literacy and the Establishment of Anglo-Saxon Literate Culture', in *The Preservation and Transmission of Anglo-Saxon Culture*, ed. Paul E. Szarmach and Joel T. Rosenthal (Kalamazoo: Medieval Institute Publications, 1997), 287–311.

[33] A.N. Doane, 'The Ethnography of Scribal Writing and Anglo-Saxon Poetry: Scribe as Performer', *Oral Tradition* 9 (1994): 420–39. Among others of Doane's studies, worth special note is 'Oral Texts, Intertexts, and Intratexts: Editing Old English', in *Influence and Intertextuality in Literary History*, ed. Jay Clayton and Eric Rothstein (Madison: University of Wisconsin Press, 1991), 75–113.

scholarship as well, including her 2012 essay 'Orality and Literacy: The Case of Anglo-Saxon England', focuses on the intersection of scribal practices with oral modes of knowledge.[34] Correspondingly, a good deal of attention has shifted towards 'vestigial orality', or the traces of oral tradition that can be discerned in texts of the early medieval English tradition, with these texts seen as influenced by an oral culture regardless of their exact mode of composition, which will never be known. Mark C. Amodio's 2004 book *Writing the Oral Tradition* is of sustained interest in this regard.[35] A shorter study that is representative of scholarship in this area is Katherine Lynch's 2011 essay 'The *Wiþ Dweorh* Charms in MS Harley 585: A Union of Text and Voice'.[36]

A Selection from the Criticism

The selection that follows, Donald K. Fry's essay 'The Memory of Cædmon', could be characterized as a prospectus for a book-length study that never appeared in print. Thanks to Fry's lucid presentation of large ideas, the essay stands well on its own as a stimulus to thought about the relationship of orality and literacy. Among the topics addressed by Fry are the formulaic nature of oral poetry; individual memory and 'social memory'; and the cultural role of oral poetry, with attention to both ancient Greece and Anglo-Saxon England. Fry directs attention first to the age of Bede and then to the reign of King Alfred, by which time Christian verse drawing on an inherited formulaic style was being produced fairly widely.

Fry (b. 1937), a native of North Carolina, attended Duke University as an undergraduate and received the PhD in English in 1966 from the University of California, Berkeley, writing a dissertation on the aesthetics of the oral-formulaic style in the Old English poem *Judith*. Mention was made earlier in this chapter of the important research he published on Old English formulaic diction at that time. Fry taught for three years at the University of Virginia before joining the faculty of the State University of New York, Stony Brook, where for fifteen years he held the position of Professor of English and Comparative Literature. In 1984 he took on the position of Associate at the Poynter Institute for Media Studies, a non-profit school for journalism. Among his other noteworthy publications is his edition *Finnsburh: Fragment and Episode*, and he served as one of the co-editors of the major reference work *Medieval Scandinavia: An Encyclopedia*.[37]

---

[34]   Katherine O'Brien O'Keeffe, 'Orality and Literacy: The Case of Anglo-Saxon England', in Reichl, *Medieval Oral Literature*, 121–40; note also her influential book *Visible Song* (n. 12 above).

[35]   Mark C. Amodio, *Writing the Oral Tradition* (cited in n. 6 above). Note also Amodio's study 'Res(is)ting the Singer: Towards a Non-Performative Anglo-Saxon Oral Poetics', in *New Directions in Oral Theory*, ed. Mark C. Amodio (Tempe, AZ: ACMRS, 2005), 179–208.

[36]   Katherine E. Lynch, 'The *Wiþ Dweorh* Charms in MS Harley 585: A Union of Text and Voice', in *The Genesis of Books: Studies in the Scribal Culture of Medieval England in Honour of A.N. Doane*, ed. Matthew T. Hussey and John D. Niles (Turnhout: Brepols, 2011), 51–68.

[37]   *Finnsburh: Fragment and Episode*, ed. Donald K. Fry (London: Methuen, 1974); *Medieval Scandinavia: An Encyclopedia*, ed. Phillip Pulsiano, co-edited by Kirsten Wolf, Paul Acker, and Donald K. Fry (New York: Garland, 1993).

For Further Reading

Acker, Paul. 1998. *Revising Oral Theory: Formulaic Composition in Old English and Old Icelandic Verse.* New York: Garland.

Creed, Robert P. 1963. 'The Singer Looks at His Sources'. In *Brodeur Studies*, 44–52.

Foley, John Miles. 1991. 'Texts that Speak to Readers who Hear: Old English Poetry and the Languages of Oral Tradition'. In *Speaking Two Languages*, 141–56 and 259–64.

Orchard, Andy. 1997. 'Oral Tradition'. In O'Brien O'Keeffe, 101–23.

Renoir, Alain. 1988. *A Key to Old Poems: The Oral-Formulaic Approach to the Interpretation of West-Germanic Verse.* University Park, PA: Pennsylvania State University Press.

Riedinger, Anita. 1985. 'The Old English Formula in Context'. *Speculum* 60: 294–317.

Russom, Geoffrey R. 1978. 'Artful Avoidance of the Useful Phrase in *Beowulf, The Battle of Maldon*, and *Fates of the Apostles*'. *SPh* 75: 371–90.

Scholes, Robert, and Robert Kellogg. 1966. 'The Oral Heritage of Written Narrative'. In their co-authored book *The Nature of Narrative*, 17–56. London: Oxford University Press.

Sorrell, Paul. 1992. 'Oral Poetry and the World of *Beowulf*'. *Oral Tradition* 7: 28–65.

Donald K. Fry, 'The Memory of Cædmon' (1981)[1]

I am honored to contribute to a *Festschrift* for Professor Albert Lord, whose scholarship has influenced my thinking for the last fifteen years. This paper builds on the seminal insights of Lord, Milman Parry, and F.P. Magoun, attempting to propose a new model for Old English literary history on a formulaic basis. What do we mean by "formulaic"? I think we mean the typical traditionally expressed. We mean that traditional poets sound like the poets of their past, like their contemporaries, and like their own previous performances. They tell stories familiar to their audiences, organized in narrative and imagistic patterns familiar to their audiences, and expressed in diction familiar to their audiences. Even when they incorporate new stories and concepts requiring new vocabulary, they manipulate the old formal patterns to preserve the impression of traditional and familiar continuity. In short, they constantly play against their audiences' memory of poetry.

We all think we know how memory works: like a computer, of course, storing bits of data and recalling them in original form whenever we need them. In fact, psychologists generally reject that model, preferring instead a reconstructive theory

---

[1] Donald K. Fry, 'The Memory of Cædmon', in *Oral Traditional Literature: A Festschrift for Albert Bates Lord*, ed. John Miles Foley (Columbus: Slavica Publishers, Inc., 1981), 282–93. Used with permission from Slavica Publishers Inc.

along lines suggested by F.C. Bartlett in his classic book, *Remembering, A Study in Experimental and Social Psychology.*[2] Bartlett divides memory into perception and recall, proposing that the process of perception itself organizes material to be memorized into general impressions accompanied by a few striking details, both then stored. Such perception patterns vary according to the individual, but with a countertendency toward standardized patterns determined by social groups. Memorizing proves quite simple when the memorizer's perception patterns fit the material closely, and difficult when they do not. Bartlett observes:

> In certain cases of great structural simplicity, or of structural regularity, or of extreme familiarity, the immediate data are at once fitted to, or matched with, a perceptual pattern which appears to be pre-existent so far as the particular perceptual act is concerned. This pre-formed setting, scheme, or pattern is utilised in a completely unreflecting, unanalytical and unwitting manner. Because it is utilised the immediate perceptual data have meaning, can be dealt with, and are assimilated. In many other cases no such immediate match can be effected. Nevertheless, the subject ... casts about for analogies with which to subdue the intractibility of the perceptual data. (p. 45)

Bartlett also found that these perceptual grids group together through associations drawn from past experience:

> A study of the actual facts of perceiving and recognizing suggests strongly that, in all relatively simple cases of determination by past experiences and reactions, the past operates as an organised mass rather than as a group of elements each of which retains its specific character. (p. 197).

In recall, we reconstruct the perceived material by combining the stored general patterns and some details, although we may not recognize the discrepancies between the original and this reconstruction. Bartlett comments:

> Human remembering is normally exceedingly subject to error. It looks as if what is said to be reproduced is ... really a construction, serving to justify whatever impression may have been left by the original. It is this "impression," rarely defined with much exactitude, which most readily persists. So long as the details which can be built up around it are such that they would give it a "reasonable" setting, most of us are fairly content, and are apt to think that what we build we have literally retained. (pp. 175–76)

And Bartlett summarizes:

> Remembering is not the re-excitation of innumerable fixed, lifeless and fragmentary traces. It is an imaginative reconstruction, built out of the relation of our attitude towards a whole active mass of organized past reactions or experience, and to a little outstanding

---

[2]   Cambridge, 1932.

detail which commonly appears in image or in language form. It is thus hardly ever really exact, even in the most rudimentary cases of rote recapitulation. (p. 213)[3]

The mind, according to Bartlett, consists of interconnected patterns of organization, which control perception and recall. We might express his theory in a visual metaphor: the mind organizes itself in certain associated shapes. Perception is a screen pierced by holes shaped like the mind's forms, a screen we hold up to outside material. Data which fits enters easily through a hole; data which does not fit must be altered to the shape of an opening. In recall, we reconstruct the original material by means of these shapes. Put another way, we could say that perception compresses material into abstract patterns containing selected details; in recall, we supplement those selected details with reconstructed details sufficient to re-inflate the abstraction back into the full-blown shapes of external experience. If you are skeptical about this model, try a little experiment. Recall something you see every day: your own face. Got the picture? Did you forget the ears? Put them in. Are all the bumps and moles in place? Put them in. Did you remember to color the eyes? You see, Bartlett is right. We recall generalities and congratulate ourselves on our precise memory, and we can reconstruct the details if we want to. But the key word is "reconstruct."

Bartlett's model sounds familiar, for it parallels current notions of formulaic poetry. The stereotyped phrases we call formulas cluster into families, whose abstract structures we label "systems." These substitution systems are analogous to the grids of perception, abstract shells filled out with other words. At the narrative level, type-scenes function as the abstract patterns with plot details fleshing them out. Stories and themes tend toward the typical, toward general patterns of behavior modified for specific applications. These traditional organizations of formulaic material fit Bartlett's standards for easy memorizing: "great structural simplicity, ... structural regularity, ... extreme familiarity" (p. 45), allowing a simplified perception stage. The mind does not have to abstract perceived formulaic material because such material is already organized into familiar abstract patterns. To return to my visual metaphor, the formulaic phrases are already shaped like the holes in the perceptual grid.[4] Furthermore, just as material stored in the memory has an internal structure of associations, so do the formulaic wordhoard and scenehoard and storyhoard structure themselves around ties of association. Certain formulas and systems cluster thematically with others, certain ideas and images cohere, certain scenes tend to include certain details, etc. Material formulaically organized is easily memorized, and easily recalled for members of a traditionally-oriented culture. Hence traditional poets can

---

[3]   He admits the presence of rote recall as well (pp. 203, 264).

[4]   For similar imagery, see, for example, John Miles Foley, "Formula and Theme in Old English Poetry," in Benjamin Stoltz and Richard S. Shannon, eds., *Oral Literature and the Formula* (Ann Arbor, 1976), pp. 207–32; and Michael Nagler, *Spontaneity and Tradition: A Study in the Oral Art of Homer* (Berkeley: University of California Press, 1974).

recall millions of formulaic phrases and thousands of systems and hundreds of scenes and storiess. And so can their audiences.

We profess astonishment at such memory feats, but in fact powerful memories characterize nonliterate societies, indeed usually function as the primary device for education of the young and for ethical reinforcement in adults. Early Greek civilization proves a case in point.

The best evidence points toward the introduction of the Greek alphabet about 700 BC; Homer, who lived about this time or a generation earlier perhaps, probably composed his epic poems without the aid of writing, by formulaic means. Marcel Jousse characterizes Homeric man as a "mnemotechnician,"[5] whose practical and intellectual life turned on memorized cultural values, defined and reinforced by oral poetry. James Notopoulos puts it this way:

> The oral poet as a mnemotechnican preserved the useful by binding it in verse, by forging a metrical pattern which facilitated and guarded against mistake the information to be preserved. Memory therefore is equally important in conserving the useful as well as perpetuating the immortal in oral literature; the poet is the incarnate book of oral peoples.[6]

In a daring hypothetical reconstruction of early Greek culture, Eric Havelock differentiates the social function of oral verse from modern notions of art:

> Greek society before 700 BC was non-literate. In all such societies experience is stored in the individual memories of the members of the society and the remembered experience constitutes a verbal culture. The verbal forms utilized for this purpose have to be rhythmic to ensure accurate repetition, and the verbal syntax has to be such that statements, reports, and prescriptions are cast in the forms of events or acts. The Homeric poems, and to an equal degree the Hesiodic, exhibit these symptoms. They constitute not literature in the modern sense, but orally stored experience, the content of which incorporates the traditions of a culture group and the syntax of which obeys the mnemonic laws by which this kind of tradition is orally preserved and transmitted.[7]

The introduction of writing about 700 BC brought about changes, but probably not so drastic as we might expect. Writing remained a difficult art to master, a craft skill for the few, with widespread popular reading far in the future.[8] In fact, this transition period probably lasted until Socrates's lifetime (died 399 BC). Havelock believes that the first Greek texts written down were *The Iliad* and *The Odyssey*, as one of

---

[5] *Le Style oral rhythmique et mnémotechnique chez les Verbo-moteurs* (Paris, 1925).

[6] "Mnemosyne in Oral Literature," *Transactions of the American Philological Association*, 69 (1938), 469.

[7] "Pre-literacy and the Pre-Socratics," *Bulletin of the Institute of Classical Studies*, 13 (1966), 50.

[8] Eric A. Havelock, *Preface to Plato* (rpt. New York, 1967), p. ix, hereafter cited as *Preface*.

the measures taken by a non-literate culture to preserve its corporate tradition in an enclave of language existing apart from the vernacular, metrically contrived to preserve an extensive statement in the memories of the members of the culture. To transcribe this enclave became the first business to which the alphabet was put. And so we reach in the first instance the poems that pass under the name of Homer.[9]

The transition period involved authors such as Pindar, Hesiod, and even the Athenian dramatists, writing for essentially nonliterate audiences. Again, Havelock proposes:

> For a long time after the resources of transcription became available, they would be used still to transcribe what had previously been orally composed, … the transcription would be made in the first instance for the benefit of the composers themselves rather than their public, and … the products of the Greek poets who followed Homer would be devised for memorization by listening audiences, not for readership by literates. ("Prologue," p. 362)

Conservative tendencies would prevail, both in style and social functions of poetry; as Havelock puts it,

> Composers of the contrived word originally … allowed their compositions to be taken down by a listener. Later they took to writing them down themselves at dates which cannot easily be settled. But whichever they did, their initial proclivity would be to use the script now available only to record what was already previously composed according to oral principles. That is, the oral habit would persist and would remain effective to a varying degree, even in the case of composers whom we would style writers. This habit, after all, had not been personally chosen by themselves; it was a conditioned response to the needs of an audience who still demanded of the compositions offered that they be memorisable. ("Prologue," p. 388)

Although these literate poets took advantage of the new writing techniques to modify their own compositional methods, they still lacked any significant reading public. So the authors probably produced only one copy of their works, or at most just a few; families and authorities stored such copies in archives, even sometimes engraved the poems on temple walls.[10] Transmission and diffusion of the texts depended almost completely on memory and public recitation.

The Greeks memorized the early poets as a part of their education, and Homer emerged as "the Hellenic educational manual *par excellence*" (*Preface*, p. 28). Tutors recited Homer for their pupils to memorize. Poetry held a position, says Havelock,

> central in the educational theory … a position held apparently not on the grounds that we would offer, namely poetry's inspirational and imaginative effects, but on the ground

---

[9] "Prologue to Greek Literacy," in *University of Cincinnati Classical Studies*, vol. 2 (Norman, 1973), p. 361, hereafter cited as "Prologue."

[10] J.A. Davison, "Literature and Literacy in Ancient Greece," chap. 4 of his *From Archilochus to Pindar* (New York, 1968), pp. 86–128.

that it provided a massive repository of useful knowledge, a sort of encyclopedia of ethics, politics, history and technology which the effective citizen was required to learn as the core of his educational equipment. Poetry represented not something we call by that name, but an indoctrination which today would be comprised in a shelf of textbooks and works of reference. (*Preface*, p. 27)

Memory and performance dominated education, both public and private:

A purely poetic *paideia*, to be effectively transmitted, requires only regular occasions for performance, whether professional or amateur. The youth would be required to repeat and to match their memories against each other and against their elders. Everything that was to be absorbed and remembered was communicated to them as the deeds and thoughts of their great ancestors. (*Preface*, p. 124)

In summary, after 700 BC, Homer's poems were written down and memorized for educational purposes, and later writers composed in a form suitable for recitation and memorization. Thus oral poetry continued to exert its influence as a device for preserving cultural values throughout the semi-literate era of Greek history.

The Anglo-Saxons remained semi-literate, or more accurately nonliterate, both in English and in Latin, throughout their history, at all levels of society. For example, V.H. Galbraith counts exactly four literate Old English kings (Sigbert, Aldfrith, Alfred, and perhaps Ceolwulf);[11] Cædmon, although he became a monk, never seems to have learned to read or write. Even after Christian missionaries introduced writing in England in 597, no popular reading audience ever developed. Yet the Church faced the difficult twin problems of attaining and strengthening converts. I propose here that, after about 680, the English church used written poetry as an educational device, transmitted largely in memorized form.[12] And Cædmon and his memory began the whole process.

Cædmon extemporizes exactly once, creating the original hymn in his dream; after that moment, he becomes exclusively a memorial poet. In his *Ecclesiastical History*, 4: 24, Bede tells us:

When [Cædmon] awoke, he remembered (*memoriter retenuit*) all that he had sung while asleep and soon added more verses in the same manner, praising God in fitting style.[13]

---

[11] Galbraith, "The Literacy of the Medieval English Kings," in L.S. Sutherland, ed., *Studies in History* (London, 1966), pp. 78–111; Rosalind Hill, "Bede and the Boors," in G. Bonner, ed., *Famulus Christi* (London, 1976), pp. 93–105; C.P. Wormald, "The Uses of Literacy in Anglo-Saxon England and Its Neighbours," *Transactions of the Royal Historical Society*, 5th series, 27 (1977), 95–114.

[12] Alan Jabbour, "Memorial Transmission in Old English Poetry," *Chaucer Review*, 3 (1969), 174–90.

[13] All references to Bede's Latin version cite *Bede's Ecclesiastical History of the English People*, ed. and trans. by B. Colgrave and R.A.B. Mynors (Oxford, 1969). For the ninth-century Alfredian translation, I cite T. Miller, ed. and trans., *The Old English Version of Bede's Ecclesiastical History of the English People*, EETS 95–96 (London, rpt. 1959). This quotation appears on p. 417.

He recites these verses from memory the next morning to Abbess Hild and "a number of the more learned men." They read him "a passage of sacred history or doctrine, bidding him make a song out of it, if he could, in metrical form. He undertook the task and went away; on returning the next morning he repeated the passage he had been given, which he had put into excellent verse."[14] Cædmon memorized what the scholars read to him and also memorized his own resultant poem in order to recite it the following day. Later, Bede describes the poet's procedure explicitly:

> He learned all he could by listening to them and then, memorizing (*rememorando*) it and ruminating over it, like some clean animal chewing the cud, he turned it into the most melodious verse: and it sounded so sweet as he recited it that his teachers became in turn his audience. (Colgrave and Mynors, p. 419)

The Old English translator expands that last clause:

> and his song and his leoð wæron swa wynsume to gehyranne, þætte seolfan his lareowas æt his muðe wreoton and leornodon.

> (and his song and his music were so delightful to hear, that even his teachers wrote down the words from his lips and learnt them.) (Miller, pp. 346–47)

The scholars did not memorize the poems and then write them down. Rather they wrote them down from Cædmon's memory in order to memorize them for themselves. Abbess Hild, I believe, recognized immediately that Cædmon's invention of Christian vernacular verse had broad applications as an educational device. In Bede's narrative, before our very eyes, we see her turn Cædmon, as it were, into a teaching machine. The scholars feed Cædmon sacred narrative and/or doctrine, and he manufactures palatable verse, which they record and memorize. Bede tells us two subsequent effects of Cædmon's invention:

> By his songs the minds of many were often inspired to despise the world and to long for the heavenly life. It is true that after him other Englishmen attempted to compose (*facere*) religious poems, but none could compare with him. (Colgrave and Mynors, p. 415).

Cædmon's songs brought about conversions and started others writing such verse, including Bede himself. Elsewhere I have suggested that later Anglo-Saxon poets, whether they composed in writing or orally, used the forms of the inherited oral poetry, simply because no other poetic existed for them.[15] Now I wish to propose

---

14 Colgrave and Mynors, p. 419. Cp. "sacrae historiae *sive* doctrinae sermonem" with "sum halig spell *and* godcundre lare word" ("a holy narrative *and* some word of divine doctrine," my italics; Miller, pp. 344–45). The Old English translator substitutes "and" for "or," suggesting that Cædmon melded history and doctrine; see my "Cædmon as a Formulaic Poet," in J.J. Duggan, ed., *Oral Literature: Seven Essays* (Edinburgh, 1975), p. 43.

15 See my "Cædmon as a Formulaic Poet" and "Themes and Type-Scenes in *Elene* 1–113," *Speculum*, 44 (1969), 35–44.

another reason for such conservative loyalty to tradition: Old English poets used formulaic techniques because, as I argued in the first section of this paper, formulaic poetry is easy to memorize. The pre-formed units (formula, type-scene, known story), already organized for easy memorization by poets, also aid the memory of the audience. I suggest that, as in early Greece, memorized poetry formed a large part of the education of an essentially nonliterate populace. Such poetry easily moved about, penetrating all classes of society, lay and clerical, spreading by word of mouth to remote areas. It promoted proper behavior, conveyed the basic Christian message for conversion, and strengthened the faith of new converts and old, all in entertaining, familiar form, requiring no elaborate training in Latin or theology. Such poetry also had the latitude to absorb new subject matter while making it sound like old familiar poetry; thus Christ becomes a warrior with a *comitatus* of apostles,[16] Adam talks like a thane, etc. So churchmen could inject doctrine into narrative, raising the theological sophistication not only of the laymen, but also of clerics, whose average formal learning never reached very high. Indeed, the Anglo-Saxon poetry we possess ranges from the simple paraphrase of the *Lord's Prayer* to the rich density of *Christ I*, from the flat piety of *Juliana* to the whirling allegories of *Phoenix*, from the astonishing Patristic virtuosity of *Exodus* to the inexpressible genius of *Beowulf*, a mirror for princes and Christians alike.

Much evidence exists for this memorial transmission and its educative function, but I shall confine myself here to a brief discussion of King Alfred. His contemporary biographer Asser tells us:

> Alas, by the unworthy carelessness of his parents and tutors, he remained ignorant of letters until his twelfth year, or even longer. But he listened attentively to Saxon poems day and night, and hearing them often recited by others committed them to his retentive memory....

When, therefore, his mother one day was showing him and his brothers a certain book of Saxon poetry which she held in her hand, she said: "I will give this book to whichever of you can learn it most quickly." And moved by these words, or rather by divine inspiration, and attracted by the beauty of the initial letter of the book, Alfred said in reply to his mother, forestalling his brothers, his elders in years though not in grace: "Will you really give this book to one of us, to the one who can soonest understand and repeat it to you?" And, smiling and rejoicing, she confirmed it, saying: "To him will I give it." Then taking the book from her hand he immediately went to his master, who read it. And when it was read, he went back to his mother and repeated it.[17]

---

[16]   See C.J. Wolf, "Christ as Hero in *The Dream of the Rood*," *NM*, 71 (1970), 202–10.

[17]   *Asser's Life of King Alfred*, trans, by Dorothy Whitelock, in her *English Historical Documents c. 500–1042* (New York, 1955), p. 266; quoted from W.H. Stevenson, ed., *Asser's Life of King Alfred* (Oxford, 1904), chaps 22–23.

Illiterate Alfred memorizes vernacular poems "recited by others" constantly. Alfred must have the book read to him by a tutor in order to memorize it. Since he did not learn to read until about the age of forty, he continued learning by memorizing vernacular books. Asser continues:

> Meanwhile the king, in the midst of wars and frequent hindrances of this present life, and also of the raids of the pagans and his daily infirmities of body, did not cease … to recite Saxon books, and especially to learn by heart Saxon poems, and command others to do so. (Asser, chap. 76, p. 267)

Alfred took the church's educational technique, used it for his own continuing education, and later applied it to secular education as well.

In summary, the formulaic techniques explored by Parry, Lord, and Magoun allow us to account for the phenomena of the surviving Old English poetic material. Anglo-Saxon Christian poets, inspired by Cædmon, wrote in the inherited formulaic style, whose familiarity and formal properties made the poems easy to memorize. Christian learning spread through an illiterate population by means of memory and recitation, all radiating from an author's original manuscript. The Vikings and Henry the Eighth no longer need to shoulder all the blame for our present scarcity of surviving Anglo-Saxon poetic manuscripts. There simply were not very many in the first place. Indeed, the manuscript of a traditional society, of the nonliterate Anglo-Saxons, was memory.

5

Heroic Tradition

Ever since the eighteenth and early nineteenth centuries, when the surviving poetic records from the Anglo-Saxon period began to be published in modern editions, scholars and critics have been specially drawn to those poems that allude to the kings and heroes of the Heroic Age of the Germanic peoples, or that are otherwise expressive of a heroic ethos on the field of war.[1] While attention has naturally gravitated towards *Beowulf*, which is by far the longest and most accomplished of these poems as well as the one richest in allusions to the legendary history of the northern peoples, a good deal of criticism has also focused on a handful of shorter poems that survive, two of them in the Exeter Book and two from other sources.

A brief account of these poems may be found helpful.[2] One of these is the Exeter Book poem *Widsith*, long ascribed a very early date because what it largely consists of is catalogues of the names of kings and peoples of antiquity, including many legendary figures of the northern world. The catalogues are linked by a first-person narrative set in the voice of a singer, 'Widsith' by name, who claims to have visited certain of these figures in person. The most noteworthy of these is Eormanric, the famed king of the East Goths (known to Latin historians as Ermanaricus, d. 375, and in Old Norse tradition as Jǫrmunrekr), at whose court he performed songs of praise and received gifts from the king's and queen's own hands. Another of these poems is *Waldere*, a heroic narrative about the flight of Waldere (alias Waltharius, Walther, or Walter of Aquitaine) and his betrothed lover from the court of Ætla, king of the Huns (the historical Attila, d. 453). Also featured in the two fragments

---

[1] On the basis of historical writings composed in Latin, the Heroic Age, also known as the Migration Age (or in German scholarship, the *Völkerwanderungszeit*) can be dated to ca. AD 375–575.

[2] A convenient teaching edition is available: *Old English Minor Heroic Poems*, ed. Joyce Hill, Durham Medieval and Renaissance Texts 2, 3rd edn (Toronto: Pontifical Institute of Mediaeval Studies, 2009). Still valuable is Frederick Norman's survey 'The Early Germanic Background of Old English Verse', in *Medieval Literature and Civilization: Studies in Memory of G.N. Garmonsway* (London: Athlone, 1969), 3–27.

Old English Literature: A Guide to Criticism with Selected Readings, First Edition. John D. Niles.
© 2016 John D. Niles. Published 2016 by John Wiley & Sons, Ltd.

of *Waldere* that happen to survive is Guðhere, the fifth-century king of the Burgundians (alias Guntharius, Gundaharius, Gunther, or Old Norse Gunnar). Importantly, the narrative style of *Waldere* is so leisurely and so highly ornamented that one can infer that the poem as a whole, had it survived, would have been of a length comparable to *Beowulf*, thus providing evidence that *Beowulf* was not a one-off production. A third short poem with legendary content is *Deor*, a strophic poem that is normally classified among the Exeter Book 'elegies'. *Deor* makes somewhat cryptic allusions to Eormanric; to a shadowy figure named Geat, perhaps the eponymous founder of the tribe known as the Geatas; and to a certain Ðeodric, plausibly identified as the Gothic king Theodoric the Great (d. 526), who ruled over much of Italy in some splendour from his royal seat in Ravenna. The fourth of these poems is *The Fight at Finnsburg*, a fragment of what was once a somewhat longer poem telling of deadly combat at the stronghold of a certain Finn, king of the Frisians. Since this same incident is the subject of one of the inset songs in *Beowulf* ('the Finnsburg episode', at lines 1063–1160a), *Beowulf* and *The Fight at Finnsburg* are sometimes edited as companion pieces.

Often discussed alongside these poems are two poems that tell of historical battles of the Anglo-Saxon period in a heroic style. The earlier of these, *The Battle of Brunanburh*, serves as the annal for the year 937 in multiple recensions of the Anglo-Saxon Chronicle. This is a panegyric of King Æthelstan and his English troops on the occasion of what was apparently a decisive victory over a coalition of Dalriadan Scots and Dublin-based Vikings. The other is *The Battle of Maldon*, widely admired as an idealized narrative account, with many set speeches, of the heroic resistance of warriors led by Byrhtnoth, ealdorman of Essex, to an assault by Viking marauders. The actual battle dramatized in this way is mentioned in several recensions of the Chronicle and was apparently fought in the year 991.

While Old English poems set in the Heroic Age tended in former times to be approached as expressions of a 'Dark Age' culture centring on an ancient Germanic warrior code, and while *The Battle of Brunanburh* and *The Battle of Maldon*, as well, were seen as presenting reflexes of that ethos in a contemporary setting, the more recent critical tendency has been to read all of these poems such as we have them, including *Beowulf*, as participants in the dominant Christian culture of Anglo-Saxon England. Their heroic themes and sentiments are seen as being compatible with a Christian worldview, rather than representing some prior or alternative culture associated with the pre-Christian past. Although some questions pertaining to each of these poems remain unresolved, recent critical work tends to see each one as contributing to the shaping of English identity within its period of transmission, however that period is defined for each text.

One reason for this change of perspective has been an erosion of confidence in the authority of the Roman historian and ethnographer Tacitus, whose treatise the *Germania*, which dates from about AD 100, was once taken as a sound guide to the character and mores of the Germanic peoples of Europe from Roman imperial days through the time of the Anglo-Saxon settlement of Britain.[3] The biases and special interests underlying Tacitus's treatise are now generally acknowledged. In her 1996 article 'Tacitus, Old English Heroic Poetry, and Ethnographic Preconceptions', M.J. Toswell has noted that 'the parallel,

---

[3]   *Tacitus: Germania*, trans. J.B. Rives (Oxford: Clarendon Press, 1999), with an excellent introduction and commentary.

so frequently drawn, to Tacitus's *Germania* as a kind of analogy for or even explanation of the ethical code of the Anglo-Saxon warrior is a great deal more tenuous tha[n] it might appear.'[4] During the nineteenth century – the great era of competing nationalisms – the *Germania* became required study in German schools, as Toswell points out, eventually serving as 'one of the principal texts of Arian xenophobic nationalism and part of the honour code by which war was to be pursued' (p. 503). What Tacitus has to say about the Germanic peoples of the northern European regions lying outside the Empire's control – the purity of their race, the physical strength of their men, the special regard in which their women were held, the culture of fame and shame that motivated many aspects of their social behaviour, and the cult of loyalty among their warriors on the field of battle (the *comitatus* ideal, to use Tacitus's Latin term for it) – all these matters have become subject to questioning by recent scholars, who are inclined to see in the *Germania* an implied critique of degenerate Roman mores as well as some elements of accurate ethnography.

Correspondingly, it is the unique character of many of the ingredients of *Beowulf*, not their traditionality, to which Larry D. Benson calls attention in his 1970 essay 'The Originality of *Beowulf*'.[5] Rather than taking otherwise unattested elements that figure in that poem as part of 'the tradition', invoked as a vague yet powerful entity, Benson poses the question (as it were), 'How would our critical response to *Beowulf* differ if, instead, we assume that these elements are the poet's invention?' In his view, considerable misapprehension may have resulted from critics' unquestioning acceptance of two assumptions: 'First, we assume that the central fable of *Beowulf* must have been based on extensive previous sources; second, we assume that our poet must have treated those sources with considerable respect, preserving them largely unchanged' (p. 4). The force of Benson's argument (many details of which remain subject to dispute) is to call attention to the *Beowulf* poet as a traditional artist who was, still, 'definitely an artist', so that 'the work that he created by his traditional means is a unique, "original" work of art' (p. 31). The poem's originality is seen especially in the figure of the hero Beowulf himself, who in Benson's view was probably close to unknown before this poet told of him and who could therefore serve as an ideal narrative subject 'not despite but because of his very obscurity' (p. 33). The poet thus essentially invented the hero's career, including the dragon fight featured in the poem's latter part.

In her characteristically stylish essay 'Germanic Legend in Old English Literature', Roberta Frank directs attention in an analogous manner to innovative aspects of *The Fight at Finnsburg*, *Waldere*, *Widsith*, and *Deor*, as well as *Beowulf*, rather than reiterating the notion of the traditionality of these works.[6] In her view, Germanic legend was of interest to the Anglo-Saxons because it had utility for them. Rather than simply possessing and retelling legends of the Heroic Age as a part of their heritage, the Anglo-Saxons 'tried harder

---

[4]   M.J. Toswell, 'Tacitus, Old English Heroic Poetry, and Ethnographic Preconceptions', in *Studies in English Language and Literature: 'Doubt Wisely', Papers in Honour of E.G. Stanley*, ed. M.J. Toswell and E.M. Tyler (London: Routledge, 1996), 493–507, at 493.

[5]   Larry D. Benson, 'The Originality of Beowulf', in *The Interpretation of Narrative: Theory and Practice*, ed. Morton W. Bloomfield (Cambridge, MA: Harvard University Press, 1970), 1–43.

[6]   Roberta Frank, 'Germanic Legend in Old English Literature', in Godden & Lapidge, 82–100. Page references in the present paragraph refer to the second (2013) edition of this guide.

and harder with each passing century to establish a Germanic identity' (p. 82). Frank emphasizes that a considerable historical distance separated the people of later Anglo-Saxon England from either the Migration Age or the yet more remote period about which Tacitus wrote. The past that these poems speak of, in her view, is a largely 'imaginary' one (p. 83). Rather than assuming that the Anglo-Saxons had always cherished memories of their pagan past, she traces an increasing interest in that sector of the past in the translations of the Alfredian period. As she points out, 'the literary category we call "Germanic" is ours, not theirs' (p. 86). Frank shows reason to believe that what she calls 'Gothicism', or 'the desire to forge ancestral links with the people of Ermanaric and Theodoric' (p. 87), became fashionable around 800 in the multicultural empire of Charlemagne and his successors, and in time it became an English vogue as well. Tracing one's descent from legendary kings of the Goths or other great figures of the northern past became a favourite pastime of the West Saxon dynasty of kings, whose pseudo-genealogy was fashioned along such lines.[7] Frank's study raises the question whether a plausible reading context for these poems set in the Heroic Age should be sought not in the earlier centuries of Anglo-Saxon England, as used to be assumed, but rather in the ninth and tenth centuries, a period not so far removed from the date of the manuscript copies that survive. While the dating of Old English poetry remains a vexed question, such an approach invites a fresh reconsideration of these heroic works and their role in a changing society.

Short Poems on Legendary Themes

The poem known as *Widsith* exemplifies certain of these newer critical currents.[8] This has often been taken to be a very old poem (even perhaps the oldest in the English language) on the grounds that its three constituent metrical lists of names of kings and peoples represented, fairly much intact, the sort of lore that ancient poets had passed down from generation to generation. Kemp Malone, one of the poem's two chief twentieth-century editors, therefore refers to these metrical lists as *thulas*, making use of that Old Norse-derived word in this connection (as Andreas Heusler had done before) so as to direct attention to the role of ancient Germanic poets as performers of rote lists presenting genealogies and the like.[9] Malone also relegates certain lines of *Widsith* to small font so as to mark them out as probable

---

[7]   See the studies by Craig R. Davis and Audrey L. Meaney cited in notes 85 and 86 of the present chapter.

[8]   Muir, vol. 1: 238–43 and vol. 2: 542–49. There are two older freestanding editions of the poem, each of which contains a wealth of information about related Germanic history and legends: R.W. Chambers, *Widsith: A Study in Old English Heroic Legend* (Cambridge: Cambridge University Press, 1912), and *Widsith*, ed. Kemp Malone, revised edn (Copenhagen: Rosenkilde & Bagger, 1962), first published 1936. The two editors disagree about a number of points; Chambers's judgements are more often trustworthy, in my view.

[9]   The Old Icelandic word *þula* originally denoted a harp-like musical instrument; in time it came to denote strings of rhymes running on without strophic division. The etymologically related OE noun *þyle* is used twice in *Beowulf* to refer to Hunferth (alias Unferth) in his role as a kind of court orator (*Beowulf* 1165, 1456).

interpolations into a hypothetical original text, a procedure that was typical for his time but that most editors would be wary of adopting today.

Such a conception of *Widsith* as a direct expression of the ancient Germanic past has been challenged. In his 1980 article 'Two Voices in *Widsith*', Donald K. Fry called attention to the manner in which the poet interweaves two narrative voices: that of the speaker Widsith, the imagined *scop* ('wandering or court poet') of ancient pagan times whose discourse is the main content of the poem, and that of the narrator, whose voice is heard in the poem's first nine and last nine lines.[10] This latter more detached speaker (who can be compared with the detached narrator whose voice is heard in the first and last lines of *The Wanderer*) knows of the divine dispensation of the world and calls implicit attention to an afterlife of salvation, as opposed to the Germanic *scop*'s ideal of an afterlife of fame. Through this juxtaposition of voices, two different time frames and fields of mental reference are contrasted – that of pagan past and Christian present.

Although Fry does not attempt to assign a date to *Widsith*, his approach to the poem's Christian authorial perspective is consistent with Gösta Langenfelt's ascription of *Widsith* to the first half of the tenth century, a re-dating of the poem that is based chiefly on internal evidence having to do with the names that figure in the poem's lists.[11] Fry's approach is consistent as well with the argument raised by Joyce Hill, in her 1984 article 'Widsiđ and the Tenth Century', that so many additions were made to the poem's original lists in the course of its scribal transmission that the best reading context for the poem as we have it today is the tenth century, when the Exeter Book was written down.[12] For my own part, in my 1999 study 'Widsith and the Anthropology of the Past', I argue that the poem as a whole was probably invented on the basis of a miscellany of knowledge during a period, from the late years of the reign of King Alfred (r. 871–99) to the later tenth century, when the English 'were constructing their historical present, with its various ethnic constituencies, out of a series of gestures to the past'.[13] If thinking along such lines is accepted, then *Widsith* takes on the aspect of one of the most original of Old English poems, not one of the most conservative, whether in its striking narrative design or as regards the creative ethnicities that are laced into its allusions to historical or legendary characters.

A connection to Anglo-Saxon political consciousness has been traced in *The Fight at Finnsburg*, as well, when this fragment is read alongside the corresponding episode in *Beowulf*.[14] This shard of a poem telling of a battle at the stronghold of Finn, king of the

---

[10]   Donald K. Fry, 'Two Voices in *Widsith*', *Mediaevalia* 6 (1982 for 1980): 37–56.

[11]   Gösta Langenfelt, 'Studies in *Widsith*', *Namm och Bygd* 47 (1959): 70–111. Contrary arguments in favour of the traditional early dating of the poem, however, have been advanced by Leonard Neidorf, 'The Dating of *Widsiđ* and the Study of Germanic Antiquity', *Neoph* 97 (2013): 165–83.

[12]   Joyce Hill, 'Widsiđ and the Tenth Century', *NM* 85 (1984): 305–15, repr. in *Readings: Shorter Poems*, 319–33.

[13]   '*Widsith* and the Anthropology of the Past', *PQ* 78 (1999): 171–213. A revised version of this essay, titled 'Widsith, the Goths, and the Anthropology of the Past', is included in my book *Old English Heroic Poems and the Social Life of Texts* (Turnhout: Brepols, 2007), 73–109, followed by an addendum, 'Some New Interest in the Goths'. Quotation from p. 78 of the 2007 publication.

[14]   For a recent edition see *Klaeber's Beowulf*, 273–90, and cf. Donald K. Fry, *Finnsburh: Fragment and Episode* (London: Methuen, 1984). Note also J.R.R. Tolkien, *Finn and Hengest: The Fragment and the Episode*, ed. Alan Bliss (London: Allen & Unwin, 1982), a book that Bliss produced from Tolkien's papers after his death.

Frisians, used to be read as a prime example of the 'heroic lay' that critics once attributed to the early Germanic peoples as a primary oral genre, though assumptions of that kind are best viewed with scepticism, as Eric G. Stanley makes clear in his 1987 essay 'The Germanic "Heroic Lay" of Finnesburg'.[15] The inference that the poem had a role to play in an emergent sense of Anglo-Saxon identity rests on the proper name 'Hengest', which is used with reference to a warrior-chief who is introduced at line 17 of the poem as *Hengest sylf* ('Hengest himself'). This manner of speaking of the man is a more emphatic one than we find with any of the other characters introduced in the poem, though eight other men on the Danish side are named. In the corresponding part of *Beowulf*, an equivalent warrior named Hengest is mentioned no fewer than four times (at 1083a, 1091a, 1096b, and 1127b). He takes on the role of leadership of this band of Danes (or *Healfdene* 'Half-Danes', as they are called here) after the death of their original leader, Hnæf. It does not take a long leap of the imagination to identify the Hengest named in both these poems with the Hengest who is famed in Anglo-Saxon historical sources, going back to Bede,[16] as one of the two founding figures in the mid-fifth-century conquest of Britain by Angles, Saxons, and Jutes. This Hengest was celebrated in later times as the founder of the royal dynasty of the kingdom of Kent, and his name figures in other Anglo-Saxon royal genealogies as well. True, the Hengest of *Beowulf* is associated with the 'Half-Danes' (*Healfdene*), but ethnic labels are notoriously slippery in the early medieval context and the modifier 'Half' leaves his identity rather up in the air. There are no other 'Hengests' in the legendary history of the north. Experts who have studied the question have lined up on either side of an interpretive divide as to whether or not the Hengest of *Finnsburg* and *Beowulf* is the same man as the Hengest of the Migration Myth, with about twenty scholar-critics convinced of this equation and about half that number doubting it.[17] If the 'yeas' have it right, then the Finnsburg story would have been of special interest to an Anglo-Saxon audience for the sake of this insular connection. *The Fight at Finnsburg* might then be subtitled (as it were) 'The Youthful Deeds of Hengest, when He First Became a Chief'. The appeal of such a theme to an audience of Anglo-Saxons can readily be imagined.

Deor too is now generally read in a tenth-century context, seeing that the design of that poem has been shown to rely on elements of Boethian philosophy of a kind that were circulating in tenth-century England thanks to the production of English translations of Boethius's *De Consolatio philosophiae* by King Alfred or his successors.[18] The poem's one-line intermittent refrain – *þæs ofereode; þisses swa mæg* – reiterates the speaker's main theme, namely 'this too shall pass.' The refrain arguably bears scriptural echoes that were deeply

---

[15] E.G. Stanley, 'The Germanic "Heroic Lay" of Finnesburg', in his volume *A Collection of Papers with Emphasis on Old English Literature* (Toronto: Pontifical Institute of Mediaeval Studies, 1987), 281–97.

[16] Bede, *Historia ecclesiastica* 1: 15; *Bede's Ecclesiastical History of the English People*, ed. Bertram Colgrave and R.A.B. Mynors (Oxford: Clarendon Press, 1969), 48–53.

[17] My count is based on information presented in *Klaeber's Beowulf*, p. 182, esp. notes 1 and 2.

[18] Note for example Murray F. Markland, 'Boethius, Alfred, and *Deor*', *MPh* 66 (1968–69) 1–4, and Kevin S. Kiernan, '*Deor*: The Consolations of an Anglo-Saxon Boethius', *NM* 79 (1978): 333–40. For two complementary recent editions, with commentary, see Klinck, 43–46, 90–91, and 158–68, and Muir, vol. 1: 281–83 and vol. 2: 597–602.

embedded in the tradition of medieval learning.[19] The place of this poem in the Exeter Book, a chiefly devotional anthology, is surely not fortuitous.

Waldere is naturally read with close reference to the medieval Latin *Waltharius* saga whose composition was ascribed, during the Middle Ages, to Ekkehard of St Gall (d. 973), though that ascription may or may not be reliable.[20] In a remarkable example of parallel cultural traditions involving Latin and a vernacular language, this poem tells in full what appears to be the same story as is told in the *Waldere* fragments, doing so in Latin hexameters of a Virgilian cast. Since the dates when the *Waltharius* saga and *Waldere* were composed are difficult to ascertain, the relationship of one text to the other cannot be declared with confidence.[21] It is of interest, however, that the two poems were in circulation at the same time, seeing that the stray manuscript leaves that preserve the two fragments of *Waldere* are dated to around the year 1000. The existence of *Waltharius* provides emphatic corroboration that by the tenth century, the 'matter of Germania' was percolating into the Christian, Latinate culture of the clergy. This cultural shift is illustrated by *Waldere*, *Widsith*, *Deor*, *Finnsburg*, and *Beowulf* alike, for all these texts survive in manuscripts, probably monastic in origin, that were copied out during the period roughly 975–1010, regardless of when each poem was originally composed.

Brunanburh, Maldon, and the Critics

Much of the scholarly literature on *The Battle of Brunanburh* published during the past hundred and fifty years has focused on that poem's relation to history, geography, politics, and the like.[22] The most stimulating of such approaches from a literary critic's point of view are likely to be those that engage with the poem's ideological dimension. In her 1994 essay '*The Battle of Brunanburh* and the Matter of History', Janet Thormann argues that

---

[19]   A plausible reading of the refrain has been offered by Joseph Harris, with additional discussion and bibliography: '*Deor* and Its Refrain: Preliminaries to an Interpretation', *Traditio* 43 (1987): 23–53. In 'The Refrain in *Deor*', in *Old English Heroic Poems and the Social Life of Texts*, 189–93, I advocate a manner of reading the refrain that takes close account of its calculated grammatical ambiguity.

[20]   The Old English poem has been edited by Arne Zettersten, *Waldere* (Manchester: Manchester University Press, 1979), and more recently by Jonathan B. Roper, *The Old English Epic of Waldere* (Newcastle upon Tyne: Cambridge Scholars, 2009). An older edition by Frederick Norman is still worth consulting: *Waldere* (London: Methuen, 1933). A convenient translation of the *Waltharius* epic is included in *Waltharius and Ruodlieb*, ed. and trans. Dennis M. Kratz (New York: Garland, 1984).

[21]   For discussion see Ute Schwab, 'Nochmals zum ags. *Waldere* neben dem *Waltharius*', *Beiträge zur Geschichte der deutschen Sprache und Literatur* 101 (1979): 229–51, 347–68. Note also, writing from the perspective of oral-formulaic theory, Alexandra Hennessey Olsen, 'Formulaic Tradition and the Latin *Waltharius*', in *Bessinger Studies*, 265–82.

[22]   There is a freestanding edition by Alistair Campbell: *The Battle of Brunanburh* (London: Heinemann, 1938). Study of historical and legendary sources that relate to the battle itself has been facilitated through publication of *The Battle of Brunanburh: A Casebook*, ed. Michael Livingston (Exeter: University of Exeter Press, 2011).

Brunanburh served as a means of consolidating the people of the realm of England into a single nation, one with a proud martial heritage going back to the fifth-century English Conquest.[23] It is significant in this regard that the poem is unlikely to have been composed right after the battle; rather, it almost surely dates from the 950s, as Donald Scragg has argued in his 2003 article 'A Reading of *Brunanburh*'.[24] What the poem therefore appears to represent is a self-conscious use of heroic verse, absorbed into the surrounding prose of the Anglo-Saxon Chronicle, for essentially propagandistic purposes on behalf of the royal family of Wessex, who had become rulers of a united England by the 950s.

Brunanburh has attracted the attention of translators, including Alfred Lord Tennyson, whose 1880 translation of the poem into a kind of drum-beating trochaic metre, replete with verbal archaisms, represents a quintessence of late nineteenth-century medievalism. Tennyson's version of the poem has doubtless exemplified 'the poetry of the Anglo-Saxons' for modern readers who do not read Old English. It has been praised by one late twentieth-century critic as 'the first modern translation of Anglo-Saxon poetry with much claim to readability and poetic merit', though such a judgement may reflect current tastes rather than transhistorical aesthetics.[25]

One feature of *Brunanburh* that has attracted the attention of both translators and critics is the poem's extravagantly poetic style, including its bold metaphorical conceits. In his 1986 study '*Brunanburh* 12b–13a and Some Skaldic Passages', for example, Joseph Harris has suggested that this aspect of the poem may reflect the influence of Old Norse skaldic poetry on the Old English verse tradition.[26] There is nothing improbable about this suggestion seeing that skalds were apparently active at English courts, as well as elsewhere in the British Isles, during the period extending from the eighth century through the reign of King Cnut (r. 1016–35); and in terms of its genre, *The Battle of Brunanburh* can be viewed as a kind of court poem.

---

[23] Janet Thormann, '*The Battle of Brunanburh* and the Matter of History', *Mediaevalia* 17 (1994 for 1991): 5–13. Note also, on closely related topics, Thormann's study 'The *Anglo-Saxon Chronicle* Poems and the Making of the English Nation', in *Anglo-Saxonism and the Construction of Social Identity*, ed. Allen J. Frantzen and John D. Niles (Gainesville: University Press of Florida, 1997), 60–85, and Mercedes Salvador-Bello, 'The Edgar Panegyrics in the *Anglo-Saxon Chronicle*', in *Edgar, King of the English 959–975: New Interpretations*, ed. D.G. Scragg (Woodbridge: Boydell, 2008): 252–72.

[24] Donald Scragg, 'A Reading of *Brunanburh*', in *Unlocking the Wordhord: Anglo-Saxon Studies in Memory of Edward B. Irving, Jr*, ed. Mark C. Amodio and Katherine O'Brien O'Keeffe (Toronto: University of Toronto Press, 2003), 109–22.

[25] Edward B. Irving, Jr, 'The Charge of the Saxon Brigade: Tennyson's *Battle of Brunanburh*', in *Literary Appropriations of the Anglo-Saxons from the Thirteenth to the Twentieth Century*, ed. Donald Scragg and Carole Weinberg (Cambridge: Cambridge University Press, 2000), 174–93 (at p. 174). See also Michael Alexander, 'Tennyson's *Battle of Brunanburh*', *Tennyson Research Bulletin* 4 (1985): 151–61, and Michael P. Kuczinski, 'Translation and Adaptation in Tennyson's *Battle of Brunanburh*', *PQ* 86 (2007): 415–31.

[26] This is a line of inquiry pursued in different ways by both Harris, *Brunanburh* 12b–13a and Some Skaldic Passages', in *Magister Regis: Studies in Honor of Robert Earl Kaske*, ed. Arthur Groos et al. (New York: Fordham University Press, 1986), 61–68, and myself in 'Skaldic Technique in *Brunanburh*', *Scandinavian Studies* 59 (1987): 356–66.

Among the shorter Old English poems composed on legendary or martial themes, the one that has aroused by far the most critical interest is *The Battle of Maldon*, a poem that figures larger in the recent criticism of Old English literature than any other save only *Beowulf*.[27] Since the poem can be dated to some time after the year 991, when the battle itself was fought, it is of interest for showing the persistence of heroic ideals into the late Anglo-Saxon period. Chief of these is the ideal of *comitatus* loyalty, or the loyalty of the members of a war band (Tacitus's *comitatus*) to their leader. The poem is not, however, composed in the many-faceted 'jewelled style' that is characteristic of *Beowulf* and that is on display in *Waldere* as well, poems set in a fabled world of the past. Rather, its more straightforward style serves as a fairly transparent medium for a narrative of heroism and sacrifice on the part of individual men in an actual battle fought on English soil. Since no few of the men named in the poem are known to have been historical persons,[28] one of the poet's purposes may have been to honour the memory of men who died in battle that day while also declaring the ignominy of certain named men who fled. The poem thus serves as a forceful reminder of the longevity of the culture of 'fame and shame' that is put on display in *Beowulf* and that arguably persists in attenuated form still today.

Still, *The Battle of Maldon* can scarcely be taken as a straightforward account of what happened on the field of battle at the coast of Essex in 991. As Edward B. Irving argued in his 1961 article 'The Heroic Style in *The Battle of Maldon*', the narrative is highly stylized in a manner that enhances its heroic theme.[29] This is particularly true as regards use of the conventions of dialogue to report the 'last dying words' of a number of men, including the aged Byrhtwold, whose speech is frequently cited as a succinct and moving expression of the heroic ethos: 'Mod sceal þe mare, þe ure mægen lytlað!' ('Our courage must be greater as our might diminishes', 313). Through a number of speeches expressive of a similar theme, the poem modulates towards moral exemplum as well as heroic narrative.

Critics have naturally wondered if the *Maldon* poet was influenced by literary precedents or models. In her 1976 article 'The Ideal of Men Dying with their Lord in the *Germania* and in *The Battle of Maldon*', Rosemary Woolf called attention to 'a well-known resemblance between the heroic behaviour described in [Tacitus's] *Germania*' and in this Old English poem.[30] While Tacitus says of the code of honour of the Germanic warrior, 'To survive the leader and retreat from the battlefield is a lifelong disgrace and infamy', in *Maldon*, in Woolf's words, 'the poet has the followers of Byrthnoth affirm one after the other that it would be a disgrace to leave the battlefield now that their lord lies dead' (p. 63). Although Woolf sees this resemblance as a significant one, she also acknowledges that 'the

---

[27]   The chief freestanding edition is *The Battle of Maldon*, ed. D.G. Scragg (Manchester: Manchester University Press, 1981). An indispensable adjunct to this publication is *The Battle of Maldon AD 991*, ed. Donald Scragg (Oxford: Blackwell, 1991), a volume published on the occasion of the millenary of the battle. This includes the text of the poem, a literal translation, contributions by eighteen experts, and a comprehensive bibliography.

[28]   See Margaret A.L. Locherbie-Cameron, 'The Men Named in the Poem', in Scragg, *The Battle of Maldon AD 991*, 238–49.

[29]   Edward B. Irving, Jr, 'The Heroic Style in *The Battle of Maldon*', *SPh* 58 (1961): 457–67.

[30]   Rosemary Woolf, 'The Ideal of Men Dying with their Lord in the *Germania* and in *The Battle of Maldon*', *ASE* 5 (1976): 63–81, at 63.

harking back to Tacitus by students of Anglo-Saxon history and literature has been shown to be fallacious, originating in the ethnic romanticism of German scholars in the late nineteenth century' (p. 63). As a way of accounting for the poem's apparent thematic parallel to the *Germania*, she posits not direct continuity from the Roman imperial world to late tenth-century England, but rather indirect influence coming to England via Danes of the Viking Age, for 'it was in the long unconverted Scandinavian countries that highly primitive traditions survived into the Christian literary era' (p. 80). She revives the suggestion, first voiced by Bertha Phillpotts in 1929,[31] that the *Maldon* poet was influenced by the lost Scandinavian poem known as *Bjarkamál*, which, from what we know of it, gave memorable voice to this same theme of 'a retainer's semi-suicidal resolve not to outlive his lord' (p. 80). Woolf posits that *Bjarkamál* became known in England through the presence of Danish settlers there, so that the author of *Maldon* was able to draw upon it: indeed, 'he was deeply impressed by it and borrowed from it the major theme and mood of his poem' (p. 79).

Woolf's argument would seem to be a difficult one to sustain, however, for *Bjarkamál* is known only from a paraphrase of it made long after 991 by the historian Saxo Grammaticus (ca. 1150 – ca. 1220), who turned that Danish poem into Latin hexameters. In a rejoinder to Woolf published in 1990, Roberta Frank calls attention to the precariousness of her hypothesis seeing that *Bjarkamál* may not have been in circulation before the twelfth century.[32] Frank argues that the *Maldon* poet's representation of the ideal of loyalty unto death, even after one's lord has been killed, is actually forward-looking rather than atavistic. She cites a good deal of evidence from Old Norse skaldic poetry and from the Old French *chansons de geste* to show that a concept of loyalty much like what is articulated in *Maldon* was gaining prominence in Europe from the end of the tenth century into the thirteenth, being absorbed into the creed of feudalism and Christian vassalage. In particular, she finds close parallels to the *Maldon* story in a cluster of accounts of the death in 1086 of King Knútr Sveinsson the Saint, his brother Benedikt, and Knútr's loyal retainers. Frank maintains that the ideal that Woolf saw as a 'born again' Germanic survival 'seems here – as in *Maldon* – the by-product of individual, voluntary Christian fidelity' (p. 105). Much of the interest of this article resides in Frank's demonstration that a work of Old English heroic literature could have so many affinities with intellectual currents that were just emerging in Europe at around the turn of the first millennium. One does not have to look back to Tacitus or to the Heroic Age of the Germanic peoples in order to locate parallels to the ideal of loyalty that finds expression in this poem.

The question of how fully the poem celebrates a purely secular ideal of loyalty has been raised by others as well. Taking issue with the idea that *Maldon* is a 'secular' poem, for example, A.N. Doane in his 1978 article 'Legend, History, and Artifice in *The Battle of Maldon*'

---

[31] B.S. Phillpotts, '*The Battle of Maldon*: Some Danish Affinities', *Modern Language Review* 24 (1929): 172–90.

[32] Roberta Frank, 'The Ideal of Men Dying with Their Lord in *The Battle of Maldon*: Anachronism or *Nouvelle Vague*?', in *People and Places in Northern Europe 500–1600: Essays in Honour of Peter Hayes Sawyer*, ed. Ian Wood and Niels Lund (Woodbridge: Boydell, 1991), 95–106. A broad comparative reading context for *Maldon* is developed in a second study by Roberta Frank that appeared in that same year, '*The Battle of Maldon* and Heroic Literature', in Scragg, *The Battle of Maldon AD 991*, 196–207.

maintains that 'In the time when *Maldon* could have been composed [...] nothing was only secular, of this world, cut off completely from other realities and higher spheres.'[33] Doane calls attention to Ealdorman Byrhtnoth's posthumous reputation as a '*vir religiosus*' (a man of deep devotion') who was 'one of the great benefactors and protectors of monasticism', adding a reminder that 'Hero and saint are not mutually exclusive categories' (p. 44). Provocatively, Doane refers to *Maldon* as 'England's first and only "chanson de geste"' (p. 43), in an allusion to the Old French *Chanson de Roland* and its crusading ethos as well as to the *Maldon* poet's characterization of the Viking enemies of the English as heathen savages (they are called *wælwulfas* 'wolves of slaughter', 96a). Writing along comparable lines in Chapter 5, 'Triumphant Lordship and New Retainership in *The Battle of Maldon*', of his 2000 book *The Anglo-Saxon Warrior Ethic*, John M. Hill discovers a fusion of worldly and spiritual ideals in the noble self-sacrifice of the loyal retainers at Maldon, seeing in their decisions 'a politically inspired, Christian transvaluation of retainer loyalty from a secular to a transcendental plane'.[34] Like Frank and Doane, Hill sees no evidence of there having existed 'a code of glorious death' (p. 128) in the earlier heroic literature of the Anglo-Saxons, including *Beowulf*. Only in *Maldon* does he discern an ideal of 'suicidal' heroism (an adjective he employs three times, at pp. 112 and 128); and he associates this new ethic of war with Christian attitudes that were crystallizing at about the turn of the first millennium.

The question of how fully the poet integrates a Christian perspective into his narrative has been debated back and forth. For every expert who has praised the poem as a straightforward celebration of loyalty and courage on the field of war, as George Clark did in his 1968 study '*The Battle of Maldon*: A Heroic Poem',[35] another has emphasized the poem's religious dimension, as Richard Hillman did in his 1985 study 'Defeat and Victory in *The Battle of Maldon*', even to the point of finding the poet's representation of Byrhtnoth and his retainers 'reminiscent of Christ's mission to mankind and the special role of his disciples'.[36]

A noteworthy attempt to define a middle ground in these debates was made by Fred C. Robinson in his 1974 essay 'God, Death, and Loyalty in *The Battle of Maldon*'.[37] The focal point of Robinson's essay is Ealdorman Byrthnoth's final speech before the Vikings cut him down (lines 172–80). For a moment, at this point in the stylized narrative, all action ceases while Byrhtnoth prays that his soul be spared the torments of devils so that angels may bear

---

[33] A.N. Doane, 'Legend, History, and Artifice in *The Battle of Maldon*', *Viator* 9 (1978): 39–66, at 44. Doane takes issue with the views of J.E. Cross, 'Oswald and Byrhtnoth: A Christian Saint and a Hero Who is Christian', *ES* 46 (1965): 93–109, who affirms the traditional view that *Maldon* is 'a secular poem' that illustrates 'secular virtues and motives' (Cross, p. 109).

[34] John M. Hill, *The Anglo-Saxon Warrior Ethic: Reconstructing Lordship in Early English Literature* (Gainesville: University Press of Florida, 2000), at 112.

[35] George Clark, '*The Battle of Maldon*: A Heroic Poem', *Speculum* 43 (1968): 52–71.

[36] Richard Hillman, 'Defeat and Victory in *The Battle of Maldon*: The Christian Resonances Reconsidered', *English Studies in Canada* 11 (1985): 385–95, at 387.

[37] Fred C. Robinson, 'God, Death, and Loyalty in *The Battle of Maldon*', in *J.R.R. Tolkien, Scholar and Storyteller: Essays in Memoriam*, ed. Mary Salu and Robert T. Farrell (Ithaca: Cornell University Press, 1979), 76–98, repr. in Robinson, 105–121, and in Liuzza, 425–44.

it to the Lord unscathed. Following up on a note by Morton Bloomfield, Robinson identifies a specific allusion in this scene to what was known in the Middle Ages as the *judicium particulare*; that is, 'a literal, physical struggle between devils and angels for possession of the soul as it leaves the body of a dying man' (p. 80).[38] Unlike Bloomfield, however, who cites this passage as an example of how an awareness of patristic ideas can illuminate one's appreciation of Old English literature, Robinson shows that the idea was current in popular religious belief. Moreover, he emphasizes its associations with real terror of the unknown, rather than with unruffled faith in the beneficence of a kindly Lord. One aspect of Robinson's argument is that the period when *Maldon* was composed, the late tenth or early eleventh century, was marked by a crisis of faith for the English, as this was a time when 'pessimism and uncertainty over the Divine scheme of things were not uncommon' (p. 87). The heroic spirit summoned up by Byrhtnoth and his loyal retainers, Robinson argues, is enhanced when we take into account the atmosphere of fear and desperation that afflicted society at this time. The English warriors who stand firm 'decide to die', in Robinson's view, not for God or country, nor for the sake of their immortal souls, nor even in the hope of victory, but so as to uphold to the utmost a principle of loyalty 'which underlay all that was positive and good in life as they understood it' (p. 97). While a weak version of Robinson's argument might seem reminiscent of late nineteenth-century attitudes toward chivalry and the English gentleman,[39] Robinson's strong statement of it, in a volume of essays honouring the memory of J.R.R. Tolkien, affirms Tolkien's concept of the poem as expressing the most defiant rays of idealism in the darkest of times.

Another question about *Maldon* that has been the subject of debate is Byrhtnoth's culpability for the deaths of his men and for the defeat of the English. Was it wise or foolish for Byrhtnoth to refuse to grant tribute to the Vikings, preferring to offer spears 'point first' instead? Does the poet suggest that Byrhtnoth was tricked into granting the Vikings *landes to fela* ('too much land', 90a), when they sought leave to cross the causeway at Maldon so that a pitched combat could ensue, or was this decision an expression of open-eyed courage on his part? Most importantly, when we are told that Byrhtnoth made this decision *for his ofermode* (89b), what exactly does this phrase mean? 'In his overmastering pride', as Tolkien construed it? Or is the phrase less pejorative, so that its sense is 'in his great boldness' or even 'in his supreme courage'?

This last question in particular has occupied the critics. Although the OE simplex *mod* could have either positive or negative associations (it can denote either 'pride', 'arrogance', or 'courage'), *ofermod* does sound like too much of what in different circumstances might have been a good thing. In an article that is a model of the philological

---

[38] The essay by Morton W. Bloomfield is 'Patristics and Old English Literature: Notes on Some Poems', in *Brodeur Studies*, 36–43 (at 37–38), repr. in Nicholson, 367–72, and in *Essential Articles*, 63–73. Another key contribution to the critical literature on *Maldon* is Fred C. Robinson's slightly later study 'Some Aspects of the *Maldon* Poet's Artistry', *JEGP* 75 (1976): 25–40, repr. in Robinson, 122–37. Here Robinson identifies the poet's apparently self-conscious use of Scandinavian locutions as 'the first literary use of dialect in English' (p. 26). If accepted, this point must be considered another aspect of the poem's innovative character.

[39] My allusion here is to Mark Girouard's fine book *The Return to Camelot: Chivalry and the English Gentleman* (New Haven: Yale University Press, 1987).

precision for which he is known, Helmut Gneuss has made clear that *ofermod* carries negative associations in the other contexts in which that word occurs, being used (in the same manner as Latin *superbia*) as a term of criticism or reproach to denote 'pride' or perhaps 'arrogant pride'.[40]

Critics have judged Byrhtnoth's behaviour in *The Battle of Maldon* in a manner consistent with their way of reading the poem as a whole. While Robinson, for example, has no doubt that the poet's use of *ofermod* 'signals a criticism of Byrhtnoth's generalship' (p. 93), he also argues somewhat paradoxically that what he characterizes as Byrhtnoth's error or blunder – the ealdorman's decision to allow the Vikings to advance so that a pitched battle can ensue – enhances the poignancy of the poet's representation of the heroic ideal. Although the men who remain at the front have reason to reassess 'the force of their own sworn loyalties' (p. 94), they still choose to stand firm. Others critics have pursued a negative vein of criticism that goes back to J.R.R. Tolkien's admired 1953 publication 'The Homecoming of Beorhtnoth Beorhthelm's Son'.[41] While the main part of this artful study consists of Tolkien's poetic dramatization of an imagined scene pertaining to the aftermath of the battle fought at Maldon, appended to this verse-drama is an influential critical essay, titled '*Ofermod*', in which Tolkien critiques Byrhtnoth's heroic choice, attributing it to self-destructive pride.

Correspondingly, Thomas D. Hill, in his 1969 article 'History and Heroic Ethic in *Maldon*',[42] wrote of Byrhtnoth as a leader who 'sacrificed his own army' (p. 291) because of an 'error' that had as a consequence his 'failure' as a leader (terms that Hill repeats a number of times). What Hill emphasizes in this article is 'the needless waste of life which could result from the attempt to live heroic ethic within history' (p. 294). Heather Stuart, writing in 1982, was yet more emphatic in discerning an anti-heroic theme in *Maldon*.[43] Byrhtnoth in his pride, in her view, is 'solely responsible for the course of events' (p. 129) and 'sends his loyal men to a useless and unnecessary death' (p. 130). In the view of some, the first part of that judgement may seem to give little credit to the Vikings for having some influence in the matter; and one might also wonder if the flight of the cowardly retainers should be factored in. In any event, Stuart argues that the English warriors who choose to stand and fight are 'trapped [...] in their heroic fantasy' (p. 135). In the end, what makes the poem worth reading is that 'it depicts, with sympathy and insight, man's ability to deceive himself' (137). Stuart's post-Gallipoli reading of the poem is a provocative one that, whether commanding assent or not, provides a pedagogically stimulating riposte to the more positive assessments of the poem's warrior ethos that have so long been heard in the criticism.

A closing assessment of these matters can be left to Hugh Magennis. His considered view, in an essay published in 2010, is as follows: 'In the poem's ideologically charged depiction of battle, heroism is allied with Christian faith and with attachment to country, to the

[40] Helmut Gneuss, '*The Battle of Maldon* 89: Byrhtnoð's *ofermod* Once Again', *SPh* 73 (1976): 117–37, repr. in *Readings: Shorter Poems*, 149–72, with a bibliographical postscript.
[41] J.R.R. Tolkien, 'The Homecoming of Beorhtnoth Beorhthelm's Son', *Essays and Studies* 6 (1953): 1–18. The same essay is discussed later in the present chapter and in Chapter 11 below.
[42] T.D. Hill, 'History and Heroic Ethic in *Maldon*', *Neoph* 54 (1969): 291–96.
[43] Heather Stuart, 'The Meaning of *Maldon*', *Neoph* 66 (1982): 126–39.

extent of making Byrhtnoth a saint-like defender of *Æthelredes eard* ("the land of [king] Æthelred").[44] This, one feels, is a judicious word on the subject but is unlikely to be the final one.

As one can infer, *The Battle of Maldon* has been both a magnet for critics and a kind of magic mirror for them, whether they know it to be so or not. More than any other Old English poem with the exception of *Beowulf*, *Maldon* has a way of refracting and reflecting the viewer's gaze regardless of the angle from which one views it. While the text, of course, is always itself, presenting very few problems of literal interpretation, the poem as an act of communication has a remarkable ability to take on something of the personality and the convictions of its individual readers. It seems now pious, now secular, in its system of values. At one moment the poet seems passionately idealistic as regards the value of courage and sacrifice on the field of battle, and then again he seems painfully cognizant of the human cost of war. The result of this 'existential indeterminacy', as it might be called, is that there are almost as many *Maldons* as there are readers of Old English verse.[45]

Beowulf and the Critics

It would defy any writer's powers of compression to do justice, within the compass of a few pages, to the criticism of *Beowulf* that has seen print in the past half century or so. Fortunately that impossible task has been made unnecessary since a number of guides to the criticism on that poem are available. Some of these are listed in the Select Bibliography at the end of the present book.[46] These include two complementary annotated bibliographies on the poem compiled by Douglas D. Short (1980) and Robert J. Hasenfratz (1993), plus the 1997 *Beowulf Handbook*, which offers a chapter-by-chapter guide, partly chronological in organization, to the modern criticism on particular aspects of the poem including its style, sources, structure, symbolism, and theme. Then there is Andy Orchard's 2002 *Critical Companion to Beowulf*, which offers an informed commentary on nearly all aspects of the poem, well stocked with bibliographical citations. Of substantial value as well is the

---

[44] Hugh Magennis, 'Germanic Legend and Old English Heroic Poetry', in Saunders, 85–100, punctuation adjusted. As might be discerned from this quotation, another question raised in the critical literature is whether or not the poem's allusions to King Æthelred are to be taken ironically, given that king's dismal reputation in the eyes of posterity. Fred C. Robinson, 'Some Aspects of the *Maldon* Poet's Artistry', p. 28, sees a strong possibility of irony in these allusions; Magennis evidently does not. This latter view tends to be held by those who date the poem's composition to a time not long after the battle was fought, before there was time for the king's ill repute to be established.

[45] My own leading thoughts on *Maldon* are published elsewhere, and I would not exempt them from this mirroring effect: '*Maldon* and Mythopoesis', *Mediaevalia* 17 (1994 for 1991): 89–121, repr. in Liuzza, 445–74. This essay presents the revisionist view that, perhaps paradoxically, this heroic poem serves to reinforce the need for some other response to the Viking threat than a military one, seeing that the brave stand made by Byrhtnoth and his warriors ended in such grievous loss. A revised version of that essay is included as chap. 6 of my book *Old English Heroic Poems and the Social Life of Texts*, where it is accompanied by two supplementary notes.

[46] That section includes bibliographical details pertaining to the books cited in the present paragraph.

Introduction to *Klaeber's Beowulf* (2008), with its jointly-authored discussion of many topics of importance and its section on 'Some Trends in Literary Criticism' (pp. cxxii–cxxix). Especially recommended is the section of the Introduction headed 'Christian and Heroic Values' (pp. lxvii–lxxix). In the initial chapter of his 1990 book-length study of the poem, as well, George Clark provides a judicious evaluation of prior *Beowulf* criticism, while Howell D. Chickering, Jr, weaves many allusions to recent criticism into the discursive parts of his 2006 book *Beowulf: A Dual-Language Edition*.

The discussion I offer here will be restricted to certain landmark studies published since 1950, with passing mention of additional books and articles. Singled out for attention are studies that address the poem's religious content and its representation of the heroic ideal, especially if these publications have provided a stimulus to subsequent criticism by establishing the ground on which key aspects of the poem's meaning have been discussed.

Perhaps the largest issue debated in the nineteenth- and twentieth-century critical literature on *Beowulf* is how to interpret the poem's intermixture of Christian and heroic elements. As we have seen, Klaeber laid the foundation for sound judgements in this area by making a comprehensive inventory of the poem's Christian passages and allusions while at the same time arguing that all of the poem is of a single piece, rather than being a patchwork of parts of different origin, as advocates of *Liedertheorie* had maintained. Dorothy Whitelock, as well, in her 1951 book *The Audience of Beowulf*,[47] laid the foundation for subsequent criticism of the poem by arguing that one cannot understand *Beowulf* without taking into account the close relationship that must have existed between the mind-set of the author, whom she unhesitatingly refers to as 'the *Beowulf* poet', and that of its audience. These persons, in her view, must have been Christians whose conversion was 'neither partial nor superficial' (p. 5). As she states at the start of her book (p. 4):

> The Christian element is not merely superimposed; it permeates the poem. It is not confined to a few – or even a number – of pious ejaculations in the author's own person or in the mouths of his characters; an acceptance of the Christian order of things is implicit throughout the poem. It pervades the very imagery: the sun is 'heaven's candle' or 'the bright beacon of God', the spring thaw comes when 'the Father unbinds the fetters of the pool.' If there once was an original *Beowulf* from which all this was lacking, a poet – no mere scribe – has gone to the trouble of completely re-thinking and revising the work, and it is with the audience for whose benefit he did this that I am concerned, not with the hypothetical audience of a postulated earlier work.

Whitelock's emphasis on the kind of audience that can be inferred for the poem went far to delineate what kind of criticism is appropriate for a poem of this character. She infers, for example, that members of the audience had full trust in the Christian deity, though they may not have been deeply learned; were familiar with conventional poetic epithets for the devil and other elements of religious belief; believed in the reality of monsters and devils; were conversant with biblical stories and had some knowledge of how the Bible was construed in the medieval exegetical tradition; accepted the duty of blood vengeance, in the sense of extracting retribution for crimes perpetrated against members of one's kin-group; and had enough knowledge of Germanic history and legend to recognize the main historical

---

[47]   Dorothy Whitelock, *The Audience of Beowulf* (Oxford: Clarendon Press, 1951).

or legendary figures mentioned in the narrative, for example King Offa of the continental Angles or King Hygelac of the Geatas. These factors lead her to postulate a lay audience for the poem, yet one that was 'steeped in Christian doctrines' (p. 21). As for when this audience lived, or in what part of Britain, she prefers not to narrow the range of possibilities overmuch; her sense of the matter is that the poem probably dates from any time during the late seventh through the eighth centuries. Although she rules out a date later than that because of the generally positive character of the poet's representation of the Danes, not all subsequent critics have followed her in that inference. She surmises that if we knew more about the reign of Offa the Great (757–96), the eighth-century Mercian king who ruled over all of central Britain, we might find reason to associate *Beowulf* with his court. This suggestion has been endorsed by some others, though it remains speculative.

Whitelock's argument that *Beowulf* was composed for an audience separated by some lapse of time from the period of the initial conversion of the English people prepared the way for the revisionist thesis advanced by Larry D. Benson in his 1967 study 'The Pagan Coloring in *Beowulf* '.[48] Inverting the idea, heard so often in the earlier criticism, that the poem's religious passages represented a kind of 'Christian colouring' added to the work in the course of its monastic transmission,[49] Benson pointed out that there are actually only a few passages in the poem that allude to heathen customs. These are the ship funeral of Scyld Scefing near the start; a passing allusion to the observation of omens, at verse 204b; and three passages that tell of cremation funerals. In addition, there is the much-discussed passage near the start of the poem – suspected by some, including Tolkien, to be a later interpolation – in which some of the Danes resort to pagan sacrifice in a desperate effort to ward off Grendel's evil (lines 178–88). Benson suggests that the same poet who created a polished, unified Christian poem out of older story materials could have added these details, too, so as to enhance the poem's historical verisimilitude while impressing upon members of the audience that the characters in the story were indeed pagans living in pre-Christian times.

Benson concurs with what was then a consensus opinion that *Beowulf* was composed sometime from the late seventh through the eighth century, a time when English mission-aries, including Boniface (ca. 675–754), were engaged in intense missionary activity on the Continent. Benson argues, moreover, that the poet viewed the pagan characters of his poem in much the same way as the missionaries viewed the peoples whom they wished to convert. That is, the poet regarded those characters with 'compassion', and even, in the passage where certain ones turn to idol worship, with 'intense sympathy with their plight' (p. 201). Benson concludes his study by reiterating that 'one cannot imagine *Beowulf* in anything like its present state without its Christian basis, but one can easily conceive of it without its few touches of paganism' (p. 207).

Not all parts of Benson's essay have been found equally persuasive. Subject to particular doubt is his construction of the passage in which the Danes offer sacrifice to idols. Most

---

[48] Larry D. Benson, "The Pagan Coloring in *Beowulf* ", in *Old English Poetry: Fifteen Essays*, ed. Robert P. Creed (Providence: Brown University Press, 1967), 193–213, repr. in *Readings: Beowulf*, 35–50.

[49] The phrase 'Christian colouring' recurs with some frequency in the earlier criticism; note for example F.A. Blackburn, 'The Christian Coloring in the *Beowulf* ', *PMLA* 12 (1897): 205–25, repr. in Nicholson, 1–21.

specialists agree that, in the manner of certain homiletic writings of the later Anglo-Saxon period including sermons by Wulfstan, this passage excoriates idolatry and predicts damnation for its practitioners. According to this view, the poet is declaring 'the hope of the heathens' (*hæþenra hyht*, 179a) to be a tragic illusion, if heathens believe that by offering sacrifice to false gods they will gain anything other than an eternity of torment.[50] Accordingly, in his 1987 essay 'Hæþenra Hyht in *Beowulf* ', Eric G. Stanley emphasizes the orthodox Christian view that unbaptized heathens were damned even if virtuous, as Beowulf was.[51] On the other hand, Stanley B. Greenfield offers a rejoinder to Stanley in his 1985 essay '*Beowulf* and the Judgement of the Righteous'.[52] Crucial to Greenfield's view is a passage from the last part of the poem when, after the dragon fight, the poet states that the hero's soul departs from his body 'to seek out the judgement of the righteous' (*secean soðfæstra dom*, 2820). This phrase, Greenfield plausibly maintains, can scarcely mean that Beowulf's soul is damned, whatever exact fate we are to imagine for it.

Nor is there agreement that *Beowulf* should be read within the context of seventh- and eighth-century Anglo-Saxon missionary work. While a connection of this kind is possible, it does not necessarily follow from the poet's preoccupations as a whole, which have to do with matters other than Christian conversion. The chief importance of Benson's article is that it served to focus attention on *Beowulf* as simultaneously both a heroic and a devout work. By reading the poem as the work of a Christian author who introduced 'local colour' to his story, Benson cast a spotlight on the *Beowulf* poet's artful retrospective characterization of his characters as, in essence, virtuous heathens. The main characters Beowulf and Hrothgar could thus be admired, up to a certain point, as men who followed 'the natural law' (that is, the law of nature, from which binding rules of moral conduct could be deduced) and who therefore lacked 'only the knowledge of God necessary for salvation' (p. 204). That is to say, though the characters in the poem speak frequently of God, they do not know of Christ or the Redemption.

Other critics writing in recent years have inferred that the poet intended to portray the main actors in the poem – Beowulf and Hrothgar in particular – as virtuous pagans, potentially redeemable through action of God's grace. Such a suggestion was made by Charles Donahue in a pair of articles in which he pointed out that not all Christians of the early medieval church, particularly in Ireland, shared the orthodox view that salvation was available only to those redeemed through Christ.[53] 'Virtuous pagan' is not, however, a term that one would use of all the characters in the poem, seeing that some of them, such as Hunferth/

---

[50]   See the notes on lines 175–88, 177, 179, and 183b in *Klaeber's Beowulf*, as well as the discussion in Andy Orchard, *A Critical Companion to Beowulf* (Cambridge: D.S. Brewer, 2003), 152–53.

[51]   Eric G. Stanley, 'Hæþenra Hyht in *Beowulf* ', in *Brodeur Studies*, 136–51, repr. in Stanley, *A Collection of Papers with Emphasis on Old English Literature*, 192–208.

[52]   Stanley B. Greenfield, '*Beowulf* and the Judgement of the Righteous', in *Learning and Literature in Anglo-Saxon England: Studies Presented to Peter Clemoes on the Occasion of His Sixty-Fifth Birthday*, ed. Michael Lapidge and Helmut Gneuss (Cambridge: Cambridge University Press, 1985), 393–407. This and twenty other essays by Greenfield on topics relating to Old English poetry are reproduced in his posthumously published collection *Hero and Exile: The Art of Old English Poetry*, ed. George H. Brown (London: Hambledon, 1989).

[53]   Charles Donahue, '*Beowulf*, Ireland, and the Natural Good', *Traditio* 7 (1949–51), 263–77; '*Beowulf* and Christian Tradition: A Reconsideration from a Celtic Stance', *Traditio* 21 (1965): 55–116.

Unferth or the murderous princess whom King Offa of the Angles is said to have married, serve as models to avoid. Following suggestions made by others in passing, including Tolkien in his 1936 essay on the poem, Gernot Wieland argues in his 1988 article 'Moses and *Beowulf*' that the audience would have viewed the characters of *Beowulf* much as they viewed the characters of Old Testament narratives, as known either directly through the Bible or through verse paraphrases of the kind included in the Junius manuscript of Old English poetry.[54] That is to say, the audience would have seen them as figures of great stature, ranging widely in moral rectitude, some of whom enjoyed favour as 'God's chosen ones' even if their vision was unenlightened by a knowledge of Christ.

A significant minority of critics has maintained that the poem embodies a Christian perspective through and through. A cluster of studies of such an orientation is included in the 1963 essay collection *An Anthology of Beowulf Criticism*, edited by Lewis E. Nicholson.[55] Though diverse in its contents, this anthology of reprinted essays has long served as a landmark publication for those interested in the poem's religious dimension. Among the distinguished medievalists represented here are Morton W. Bloomfield, who identifies specific passages where the influence of patristic thinking can be seen in *Maldon*, *Beowulf*, and other Old English poems;[56] D.W. Robertson, Jr, who locates scriptural influence in the description of Grendel's mere, which he views as a kind of hellish perversion of the *locus amoenus* or 'earthly garden-paradise' of religious texts;[57] Allen Cabaniss, who relates the episode featuring Grendel's mother to the solemn liturgical ceremonies of Easter week, including the rites and symbols of baptism;[58] Margaret E. Goldsmith, who argues that the narrative of *Beowulf* is permeated by scriptural and patristic allusions that add up to a powerful condemnation of earthly pride and covetousness;[59] and M.B. McNamee, SJ, who argues that *Beowulf* as a whole represents an allegory of salvation, or that it could have been construed as such by members of its original audience.[60] Goldsmith advances her thesis in terms that are largely allegorical in mode and Augustinian in intellectual content, as she does in her 1970 book *The Mode and Meaning of Beowulf*. Her underlying assumption is that the audience of *Beowulf* must have been learned enough in patristics and in medieval practices of allegorical reading to be able to discern in the text a complex network of Christian allusions and parallels. It is perhaps chiefly for this reason that her approach has not found much favour, particularly among those who,

---

[54] Gernot Wieland, '*Manna mildost*: Moses and Beowulf', *Pacific Coast Philology* 23 (1988): 86–93.

[55] *An Anthology of Beowulf Criticism*, ed. Lewis E. Nicholson (Notre Dame: University of Notre Dame Press, 1963), elsewhere abbreviated 'Nicholson'.

[56] Bloomfield, 'Patristics and Old English Literature' (n. 38 above).

[57] D.W. Robertson, Jr., 'The Doctrine of Charity in Medieval Literary Gardens: A Topical Approach through Symbolism and Allegory', *Speculum* 26 (1951): 24–49, repr. in Nicholson, 165–88.

[58] Allen Cabaniss, 'Beowulf and the Liturgy', *JEGP* 54 (1955): 195–201, repr. in Nicholson, 223–32.

[59] Margaret E. Goldsmith, 'The Christian Perspective in *Beowulf*', *Brodeur Studies*, 71–90, repr. in Nicholson, 373–86, and in Fulk, 103–19; Goldsmith, *The Mode and Meaning of Beowulf* (London: Athlone Press, 1970). See also Goldsmith's prior study 'The Christian Theme of *Beowulf*', *MÆ* 29 (1960): 81–101.

[60] Maurice B. McNamee, '*Beowulf* – An Allegory of Salvation?', *JEGP* 59 (1960): 190–207, repr. in Nicholson, 331–52, and in Fulk, 88–102. McNamee develops a similar thesis in his book *Honor and the Epic Hero: A Study of the Shifting Concept of Magnanimity in Philosophy and Epic Poetry* (New York: Holt, 1960), 86–117.

following Whitelock, hesitate to think of the poem's audience in such terms; for one wonders why persons so committed to mainstream patristic learning would have wanted to preserve a poem of this out-of-the-way character at all.[61] Worth comparing with Goldsmith's approach is the one adopted by Bernard F. Huppé in his 1984 book *The Hero in the Earthly City*.[62] Huppé offers a reading of *Beowulf* from a thoroughgoing Augustinian perspective without, however, regarding the poem as an allegory. His more gently modulated discussion helps to establish an orthodox Christian reading context for the poem whether or not it offers the final word on particular matters of interpretation.

McNamee's summary of the poem's chief Christian elements is worth citing. The particular construction that he puts on these elements is of course his own:[63]

> The god referred to throughout by Hrothgar and Beowulf alike is the one, providential God of the Christians, the Creator and Lord of the whole universe and the Creator and Final Judge of man as well. Idolatry and especially devil worship are looked upon as aberrations hateful to the true God and subject to divine punishment. Man's whole life is represented as under the providential care of this one, true God. [...] The joyful hymn which is sung at Hrothgar's court and which particularly enrages the jealous Grendel is a hymn of creation telling the story of the beginnings of all things, not unlike the Creation poem of Cædmon. Besides this [...] there is frequent reference to the judgment to come. The human situation as a race fallen from grace is hinted at too, in the fact that Grendel is represented as a monstrous offspring of the murderer Cain; and the flood sent by God to destroy the sinful race is shadowed forth in the carvings of the flood on the hilt of the magic sword which Beowulf brings back from the mysterious mere.

The elements that McNamee speaks of here pertain to the poem's main narrative and cannot well be ignored. One still may hesitate to adopt the next step in McNamee's argument, which is that anyone reading the poem who knows of the Redemption will be struck by 'the remarkable parallel that exists between the outline of the *Beowulf* story and the Christian story of salvation' (p. 335). While Klaeber discerned the hint of such a parallel, he exercised great circumspection in speaking of it.[64] McNamee, by way of contrast, finds the parallel

---

[61]   Note in this connection W.F. Bolton, *Alcuin and Beowulf: An Eighth-Century View* (New Brunswick: Rutgers University Press, 1978). Bolton poses the question: 'How would a learned, orthodox eighth-century member of the clergy such as Alcuin have regarded *Beowulf*?' He makes clear that Alcuin would have scorned it. Often cited in this connection is Alcuin's rhetorical question, posed in a letter written to a Northumbrian bishop in the aftermath of the Viking sack of Lindisfarne in AD 793, 'What has Ingeld to do with Christ?' In Alcuin's view, churchmen who patronized songs about heathen heroes were inviting God's wrath.

[62]   Bernard F. Huppé, *The Hero in the Earthly City: A Reading of Beowulf* (Binghamton: State University of New York Press, 1984). Of related interest is Huppé's earlier more wide-ranging study *Doctrine and Poetry: Augustine's Influence on Old English Poetry* (Binghamton: State University of New York Press, 1959).

[63]   Quotation from McNamee, '*Beowulf* – An Allegory of Salvation?', 333–34, omitting the footnotes.

[64]   See for example p. lxxix of *Klaeber's Beowulf*, where the wording to be found in Klaeber's prior editions is repeated almost verbatim: 'We might even feel inclined to recognize features of the Christian Savior in the destroyer of hellish fiends, the warrior brave and gentle, the king who dies for his people.... Though delicately kept in the background, such an inflection of the story lends the tale a rewarding religious dimension.'

'remarkable', and he goes on to argue that 'it would take no stretch of the imagination for an audience familiar with the Christian story of salvation and with an innate taste for the allegorical and riddles in general to see in Beowulf an allegorization of Christ the Savior.' For McNamee, the hero 'exemplifies the virtues of humility and charity which Christ Himself had come to preach' (pp. 337–38).

Not all readers have been convinced of these points. When McNamee speaks of the hero's 'humility', for example, one wants to cry out that the young hero is explicitly called *wlanc* 'proud' at 341a and *goldwlanc* 'proud in his gold trappings' at 1881a; while whatever the source of strength is that enables him to kill in succession Grendel, Grendel's mother, and the dragon, it is assuredly not the virtue of humility.[65] *Beowulf* has seemed to most critics to resist an allegorical reading even if the basic parallel that McNamee presents is acknowledged.[66] What to me seems both credible and important to take into account is McNamee's argument that a medieval audience *could well have interpreted* the main thrust of the narrative along such lines. Medieval readers might have found Christian echoes in many of the story's incidental details as well, such as the specification that the Danish warriors gave the hero up for dead and abandoned their spot overlooking Grendel's mere at precisely 'the ninth hour (*non dæges*, 1600a), the hour when Jesus is said to have given up the ghost.[67] After all, 'reading like a Christian' is exactly what any novice member of the clergy was trained to do when encountering either Old Testament narratives or classical epic poems like Virgil's *Aeneid* or Statius's *Thebaid*. It is this emphasis on what the *Beowulf* story 'represented to the Anglo-Saxon imagination' (p. 343) that establishes McNamee's study as a landmark in *Beowulf* criticism; for it is this aspect of the poem that could have led to its being copied and preserved in a monastic setting.

Although McNamee interprets the hero of *Beowulf* as a model of magnanimity and fortitude, other critics have dwelled on dark shadows in the narrative, even to the point of seeing the hero as flawed beyond redemption and his society as equally imperfect. The seeds of such a view were planted by J.R.R. Tolkien in his 1936 essay 'Beowulf: The Monsters and the Critics' as well as in the critical essay, titled '*Ofermod*', that forms the second part of his 1953 publication 'The Homecoming of Beorhtnoth Beorhthelm's Son'. In this he discusses the hero's pride in *The Battle of Maldon* and *Beowulf* in parallel terms.[68] Tolkien had his own intellectual and aesthetic reasons, however, for mistrusting power as something

---

[65] The value set on pride in *Beowulf* and other works of Old English literature is explored by Levin L. Schücking, *Heldenstolz und Würde im Angelsächsischen* (Leipzig: S. Hirzel, 1933).

[66] Alvin A. Lee, for example, in his chapter on 'Symbolism and Allegory' in the *Beowulf Handbook* (pp. 233–54), treats this subject in a subtle way, maintaining that 'although a consensus has emerged that *Beowulf* is not an allegory in a formal, structural way, there is a wide recognition that it is strongly thematic and that it shows allegorical tendencies' (p. 233). Elsewhere Lee develops his own complex mode of reading the poem in a symbolic manner, particularly in his books *The Guest-Hall of Eden: Four Essays on the Design of Old English Poetry* (New Haven: Yale University Press, 1972) and *Gold-Hall and Earth-Dragon: Beowulf as Metaphor* (Toronto: University of Toronto Press, 1998).

[67] For discussion of this possible scriptural echo and other comparable ones, see Andy Orchard, *A Critical Companion to Beowulf*, 148, with references.

[68] See the earlier discussion in the present chapter, where this same essay is discussed in connection with the theme of pride in *The Battle of Maldon*.

that inevitably leads to moral decay. In his own fiction, he celebrated diminutive heroes of a most unprepossessing kind. An example from *The Lord of the Rings* is Frodo's friend Samwise, whose moral superiority to other characters, including Frodo at certain points, resides precisely in his innocence and his lack of either ambition or pretension.

Perhaps the leading spokesman for a view of the hero of the poem as flawed is John Leyerle in his 1965 essay 'Beowulf the Hero and the King'.[69] In Leyerle's view, the poem exposes 'the fatal contradiction at the core of heroic society'. The hero strives for glory, but glory leads to pride, and the end result of this process is that Beowulf is responsible for the destruction of the Geatas after he becomes king (p. 89, pp. 101–02):

> The hero follows a code that exalts indomitable will and valour in the individual, but society requires a king who acts for the common good, not for his own glory. The greater the hero, the more likely his tendency to imprudent action as king. [...] All turns on the figure of Beowulf, a man of magnificence, whose understandable, almost inevitable pride commits him to individual, heroic action and leads to a national calamity by leaving his race without mature leadership at a time of extreme crisis, facing human enemies much more destructive than the dragon.

Leyerle's assessment of the hero's pride has exerted a powerful influence on later critics, despite contrary views that have sometimes been expressed.[70] Part of the reason for this effect may be the vatic force with which Leyerle pronounces his judgements: like other 'strong' critics of that time, he speaks in an oracular mode that seems to leave no room for dissent. I have gone on record myself as opposing Leyerle's views as expressed in this article,[71] and this is no place to repeat that argument, especially since my own reading of the poem has shifted somewhat over time in the direction of greater alertness to its complex layering of voices representing different perspectives. The point to be made here is that Leyerle's forceful anti-heroic approach, when coupled with Tolkien's sensitivity to the poem's darker tones, has had a powerful impact on subsequent criticism. It is rare these days that one reads about *Beowulf* without hearing of the hero's pride, or his hopelessness, or his 'defeat' at the end of the poem, with this last term voiced again and again in the critical literature despite the hero's success in killing the dragon that was threatening to destroy his people.

A related idea that is often expressed in the criticism of the past forty years is that the society depicted in *Beowulf* is plagued by violence, materialism, hopelessness, and manifold

---

[69]   John Leyerle, 'Beowulf the Hero and the King', *MÆ* 34 (1965): 89–102.

[70]   Among critics who, following Klaeber and others, have seen the hero as a model of courage, magnanimity, and even wisdom are Robert E. Kaske, '*Sapientia et Fortitudo* as the Controlling Theme of *Beowulf*', *SPh* 55 (1958): 423–56, repr. in Nicholson, 269–310; Edward B. Irving, Jr, *A Reading of Beowulf* (New Haven: Yale University Press, 1968); and George Clark, *Beowulf* (Boston: Twayne, 1990). Stanley B. Greenfield, '*Beowulf* and the Judgement of the Righteous' (n. 52 above), sees the hero's only flaw as one of judgement, while even Eric G. Stanley, 'Hæþenra Hyht' (n. 51 above), does not doubt the hero's virtue even though he sees him as necessarily damned on theological grounds.

[71]   I offer a critique of Leyerle's arguments in my book *Beowulf: The Poem and Its Tradition* (Cambridge, MA: Harvard University Press, 1983), at 237–47.

other failings. Thus in their 1974 co-authored essay 'Social Structure as Doom: The Limits of Heroism in *Beowulf*',[72] Harry Berger, Jr, and H. Marshall Leicester, Jr, spoke of 'raid, plunder, slaughter, feud, vengeance, envy, resentment, and treachery' as elements finely woven into the structure of the Dark Age society depicted in the poem (p. 51). These serve as the 'specific institutional bases' of the conflict and disorder that the flawed hero tries unsuccessfully to overcome, little knowing that he is a victim of the heroic milieu, not its master (p. 40). Similarly, in his 1972 article 'Feuds in *Beowulf*: A Tragic Necessity?',[73] Stanley J. Kahrl stressed that endemic violence plagues the society depicted in the poem. In his view, 'Even with wisdom and fortitude the hero can only do so much […]. For in the affairs of men violent solutions lead only to further violence, to a train of revenge that leads finally to the extermination of one of the feuding parties' (p. 198). A subtler exposition of such a theme is offered by Linda Georgianna in her 1987 article 'King Hrethel's Sorrow and the Limits of Heroic Action in Beowulf'.[74] Georgianna emphasizes 'the hopelessness of the heroic cycle of battle and vengeance' (p. 846) and discerns a general state of 'confusion and paralysis at the heart of heroic society' (p. 848), seeing an emblem of this paralysis in King Hrethel's suicidal grief after the accidental death of one of his sons at the hands of another.

Such approaches as these differ materially from Tolkien's, for Tolkien saw the hero as locked in a tragic struggle, reminiscent of Old Norse myths of Ragnarǫk and of Wagner's *Götterdämmerung*, against mythologized forces of doom in the universe. Berger and Leicester, Kahrl, and Georgianna write about the hero's being enmeshed in the violence and the flawed peace-keeping mechanisms of Dark Age society, not about his struggles against monstrous and unholy adversaries. It is worth remarking that none of these post-1970 authors takes into account the medieval Christian perspective whereby all earthly societies are subject to violence and destruction because of the fallen state of humankind. Christian pessimism about the possibility of lasting happiness in this world, one would think, ought to be close to any critic's consciousness when writing about the representation of human society in a long and serious medieval poem that leads to a tragic outcome. This religious attitude, however, often goes unmentioned in recent writings about *Beowulf*. When for example Daniel Anlezark comes close to giving voice to the perspective of Christian pessimism in the chapter on *Beowulf* he contributed to a collection of essays published in 2010,[75] he does not name this worldview as such. Instead, while identifying *Beowulf* as a poem 'about the glorious potential of society' that is at the same time 'also about the limits of human beings to maintain happiness' because of the 'disastrous potential'

[72]   Harry Berger, Jr, and H. Marshall Leicester, Jr, 'Social Structure as Doom: The Limits of Heroism in *Beowulf*', in *Old English Studies in Honour of John C. Pope*, ed. Robert B. Burlin and Edward B. Irving, Jr (Toronto: University of Toronto Press, 1974), 37–79.

[73]   Stanley J. Kahrl, 'Feuds in *Beowulf*: A Tragic Necessity?', *MPh* 69 (1972): 189–98. In 'The Myth of the Feud in Anglo-Saxon England', *JEGP* 114 (2015): 163–200, I argue against conceiving of the world of *Beowulf* as a feud culture, in the sense in which medievalists commonly deploy that term.

[74]   Linda Georgianna, 'King Hrethel's Sorrow and the Limits of Heroic Action in *Beowulf*', *Speculum* 62 (1987): 829–50.

[75]   Daniel Anlezark, 'Old English Epic Poetry: *Beowulf*', in Saunders, 141–60.

of individual kings to fail and young warriors to go wrong (pp. 158–59), he presents the poet's vision as an essentially secular one rather than relating it to a Christian worldview that, in Whitelock's considered opinion, would have been second nature to members of the poet's audience.

One of the influential critics to adopt a sceptical view of the seemingly glorious world of *Beowulf* is Fred C. Robinson in his 1985 book *Beowulf and the Appositive Style*. In Robinson's view, the poet develops his narrative in such a way as to establish a sharp distinction between the violent world of the characters and the more enlightened one inhabited by the narrator and his Christian audience.[76] In this regard Robinson builds on Marijane Osborn's persuasive 1978 article 'The Great Feud: Scriptural History and Strife in *Beowulf* '.[77] Osborn contrasts what the characters in the poem know or do not know versus what we in the audience know. This difference of perspective, she shows, results in a number of structural ironies. The Danes have no knowledge that Grendel is descended from Cain and is literally diabolical, for example, but we as members of the audience do. We can therefore understand the hero's mission as part of a cosmic struggle of good against evil (the 'Great Feud' of scriptural history), but the Danes only know of a blood-thirsty monster and a bold young stranger who is willing to risk his life for their cause. Robinson develops a comparable line of thought while emphasizing, as Osborn does not, the 'hopeless plight' of the hero, who is 'benighted in a violent world' since he is deprived of revelation.

Moreover, Robinson posits an analogy, though it remains only a loose one, between the appositive syntactic style of *Beowulf* – that is, the doubling or trebling effect whereby the poet juxtaposes two, three, or even more words or phrases that are roughly synonymous in meaning – and what he terms the poem's 'artfully ambiguous' religious diction (p. 43). Members of the audience, he argues, must always ask what a given religious expression means to the pagan characters in the poem, as opposed to what it means to Christians who are able to understand what that expression means in the light of revelation. A dual reading practice of this kind is required, he argues, because much of the poet's religious vocabulary was carried over from pagan days (pp. 37–38):

> The poet and his audience lived after that renovation of the Old English poetic language initiated by Cædmon, and for them terms like *ælmihtiga, alwealde, frea, metod*, and *sigora waldend* ['the almighty', 'the ruler of all', 'the lord', 'the lord', and 'the determiner of victories', respectively] inevitably suggested the Christian God. But in *Beowulf* the poet is returning that traditional diction of Old English poetry to a pre-Cædmonian, pre-Christian setting where it could have none of the Cædmonian meanings. Therefore, each time the poet's audience heard a character in the poem utter a Christianized Germanic word for a higher being, they would necessarily have had two apposed meanings in mind: the pre-Christian meaning, which was the only one the pagan characters could know, and the postconversion meaning which had become dominant by the time of the poet.

---

[76] Fred C. Robinson, *Beowulf and the Appositive Style* (Knoxville: University of Tennessee Press, 1985).

[77] Marijane Osborn, 'The Great Feud: Scriptural History and Strife in *Beowulf* ', *PMLA* 93 (1978): 973–81, repr. in *Readings: Beowulf*, 111–25.

Robinson's claim is somewhat different, then, from the observation that neither the characters nor the narrator ever speak of God in terms specific to Christ or the Trinity. That point, granted by all, has been taken to indicate an effort on the poet's part to avoid anachronism of the sort that one does find, for example, in the scriptural poem *Judith* from the same manuscript, where the ancient Hebrew heroine Judith at one point prays to 'the God of creation, the Holy Ghost, and the almighty Son, [...] the glory of the Trinity' (*frymða god ond frofre gæst,/ bearn alwaldan, [...] ðrynesse ðrym*, 83–86a). Rather, what Robinson calls for is a way of reading the poem such that no religious expression that is set into the mouth of one of the characters, as opposed to the voice of the narrator, can be taken as referring in its primary sense to the God in whom Christians trust. This is a very different way of reading the poem from McNamee's, Whitelock's, or Klaeber's, or from that of a long line of other critics who have understood the religious language of *Beowulf* to be similar to what is found in other poems of the corpus.

As James Cahill points out in his 2008 article 'Reconsidering Robinson's *Beowulf*',[78] the reasoning that underlies Robinson's claim is impeccably circular. Once one accepts the premise that no pagan character can use the religious language of Christianity, then there is no alternative but to adopt the conclusion that no pagan character ever does. Since there are points in the text, however, where Robinson's interpretation is incompatible with what would seem to be a natural reading of the poet's words, Cahill concludes that Robinson's main premise must be flawed.

Since the stakes in this debate are high in terms of the poem's overall interpretation, its terms are worth taking up somewhat more closely. Robinson's reasoning can be paraphrased as follows. Since the characters in the poem are depicted as pagans living in pre-Christian times, they can have no knowledge of the God of the Christian faith. Those characters do, however, speak of deity, judgement, damnation, and the like. When they do so, then, we must assume that they are only speaking of 'some god', 'some kind of judgement', 'some kind of punishment after death', and the like. When King Beowulf, for example, is near death and is gazing on the dragon's hoard that he has won for his people, he gives thanks (in appositional manner, at lines 2794–96) to 'the Lord/lord of all' (*frean ealles*) 'the King/king of glory' (*wuldurcyninge*), and 'the 'eternal Lord/lord' (*eceum dryhtne*). To Robinson, that last phrase, an inflected form of *ece dryhten*, must be construed to mean no more than 'some manner of long-lasting deity', for the king cannot know of the true God. When on numerous other occasions, however, it is the narrator who uses that same nominal phrase *ece dryhten*, it can be taken to denote 'the eternal Lord'. The same principle holds true of the other words for deity, including the word *God* itself. To put the matter another way: a Robinsonian critic who was given the task of re-editing Klaeber's text would presumably choose to capitalize the nouns 'God' or any of its synonyms when these words are spoken

---

[78] James Cahill, 'Reconsidering Robinson's *Beowulf*', *ES* 89 (2008): 251–62. A brusque dismissal of Robinson's approach is offered by Edward B. Irving, Jr, in his 1997 overview 'Christian and Pagan Elements', in the *Beowulf Handbook*, 175–92, at 187–88. Also finding reasons for scepticism is Geoffrey Russom, 'History and Anachronism in *Beowulf*', in *Epic and History*, ed. David Konstan and Kurt A. Raaflaub (Oxford: Wiley-Blackwell, 2010), 243–61, at 252–54.

by the narrator, but only then, and not when they are put into the mouth of any of the poem's characters.[79]

In countering Robinson's approach, Cahill points out that the phrase *ece drihten* (to keep to that example) occurs elsewhere ninety-three times in the Anglo-Saxon poetic records, always with the sense 'the eternal Lord'. He believes the chances are strong that any Anglo-Saxon reader or listener who was competent in the formulaic language of Old English poetry would automatically have taken that phrase to mean 'the eternal Lord' in this part of *Beowulf*, as well, just as any reader today will most naturally do, given the conventional nature of the verse. Cahill notes as well that fourteen instances of this same phrase occur in the poems of the Junius manuscript. Indeed it is a commonplace for the characters in the Old English verse paraphrases of Genesis, Exodus, and Daniel to speak of God using essentially the same formulaic vocabulary as we hear in the speeches of Hrothgar and Beowulf, even though these Old Testament characters cannot know of Christ. In the Christian view, the God of Moses is the same deity that Christians worship today, for there is just one true God. Correspondingly, from this perspective, it would be natural for readers to construe the speeches in *Beowulf* much as one construes the speeches in the Old English poems *Exodus* or *Daniel*, confident that the 'noble pagans' depicted in *Beowulf*, including Hrothgar and Beowulf himself, are like Moses and Daniel in their ability to perceive the true God through their own spiritual insights, even if their knowledge remains only partial.

To read the religious language of *Beowulf* in the manner advocated by Robinson therefore seems problematic. While I have no reputation as a prognosticator, I would hazard a guess that in future years, Robinson's manner of construing the religious language in *Beowulf* will increasingly come to seem period-specific to the 1980s. As Roy M. Liuzza has remarked in passing in his discerning 1994 essay 'The Return of the Repressed',[80] one of the two driving wheels of Robinson's book, the desire to locate 'artfully ambiguous terminology' in this poem (p. 43), is an outgrowth of New Critical impulses of the kind that were particularly favoured during the period from about 1945 to 1985. This was a time when William Empson's classic study *Seven Types of Ambiguity* was found on every critic's shelf.[81] The book's second driving wheel, the desire to discover in *Beowulf* the hopeless plight of persons benighted in a violent world shot through with deceit, treachery, and betrayal, might also be called an expression of twentieth-century intellectual currents, ones that pertain especially to the last four decades of the century. This was an era of Cold War tensions, civil unrest, conspicuous assassinations, the Vietnam War, and recurrent social malaise relating to espionage, conspiracies, cover-ups, and the corrupt exercise of power.

---

[79] This is not in fact the practice followed by Robinson and by Bruce Mitchell in their jointly authored student edition *Beowulf: An Edition with Relevant Shorter Texts* (Oxford: Blackwell, 1998). Here, as is also the standard practice in the six ASPR volumes, none of the Old English words for 'God', including 'God', are capitalized. This practice has the possible advantage of not overdetermining the reader's response to the religious language of the text.

[80] Roy Michael Liuzza, 'The Return of the Repressed: Old and New Theories in Old English Literary Criticism', in *Readings: Shorter Poems*, 103–47, at 133 n. 20.

[81] William Empson, *Seven Types of Ambiguity* (London: Chatto & Windus, 1930); 2nd edn, 1947; 3rd edn, 1956.

Robinson sees the pagan world depicted in *Beowulf* as permeated with corrupt impulses and the poet himself as someone who, though partly sympathetic to that world, 'wished to affirm the distance between Christian contemporaries and noble pagan ancestors' (p. 41).

An alternative to this view is that the poem we call *Beowulf* came into being in large measure so as to affirm cultural *connections* between Christian contemporaries and pagan ancestors, despite the fact that those people had not lived under the Christian dispensation. An argument to that effect was advanced by the British legal historian Patrick Wormald in his well-regarded 1978 study 'Bede, *Beowulf* and the Conversion of the Anglo-Saxon Aristocracy'.[82] Other scholar-critics have taken it up with differences of individual perspective.[83] While Wormald attributes to the Age of Bede the poet's apparent attempt to reconcile Christian values with the traditional ethos of the Anglo-Saxon warrior aristocracy, others have seen no strong reason to ascribe this effort at cultural synthesis to an eighth-century date, for this assimilative process seems to have been a continuing one that, if anything, became more pronounced during the tenth century, when bilingual literacy became the norm. Of interest in this regard is Roberta Frank's 1982 article 'The *Beowulf* Poet's View of History'.[84] This study, among others, has been influential in shifting critics' attention to the first Viking Age of the ninth and tenth centuries as a time when major cultural syntheses were taking place, ones that involved Danes as well as Englishmen and that resulted in a new vision of the past such as is embodied in the narrative of *Beowulf*. Craig R. Davis, too, has traced particular instances of cultural assimilation – ones relevant to the genealogy of the Scylding kings introduced at the start of *Beowulf* – in his 1992 essay 'Cultural Assimilation in the Anglo-Saxon Royal Genealogies'.[85] These Beowulfian connections are taken up as well by Audrey L. Meaney in her 1989 study 'Scyld Scefing and the Dating of *Beowulf* – Again', where they serve in Meaney's view to confirm a date for the

---

[82] Patrick Wormald, 'Bede, *Beowulf* and the Conversion of the Anglo-Saxon Aristocracy', in *Bede and Anglo-Saxon England*, ed. R.T. Farrell, BAR British series 46 (Oxford: British Archaeological Reports, 1978), 32–95.

[83] On the poem as anchoring contemporary values in an imagined past, see Charles J. Donahue, 'Social Function and Literary Value in *Beowulf*', in *The Epic in Medieval Society: Aesthetic and Moral Values*, ed. Harald Schöller (Tübingen: Niemeyer, 1977), 382–90, and cf. my essay 'Locating *Beowulf* in Literary History', *Exemplaria* 5 (1993): 79–109, repr. with revisions and addenda in my *Old English Heroic Poems and the Social Life of Texts* (Turnhout: Brepols, 2007), 13–58, at 56–57 in particular. The essay is also reprinted in Joy & Ramsey, 131–61, and in the collection of reprinted essays titled *Beowulf: Updated Edition*, ed. Harold Bloom (New York: Chelsea House, 2007), 35–62.

[84] Roberta Frank, 'The *Beowulf* Poet's Sense of History', in *The Wisdom of Poetry: Essays in Early English Literature in Honor of Morton W. Bloomfield*, ed. Larry D. Benson and Siegfried Wenzel (Kalamazoo: Medieval Institute Publications, 1982), 53–65, 271–77, repr. in Donoghue, 167–81, and in Howe, 98–111. Of related interest is Frank's article 'Skaldic Verse and the Date of *Beowulf*', in *The Dating of Beowulf*, ed. Colin Chase (Toronto: Toronto University Press, 1981), 123–39, repr. in *Readings: Beowulf*, 155–80.

[85] Craig R. Davis, 'Cultural Assimilation in the Anglo-Saxon Royal Genealogies', *ASE* 21 (1992): 23–36, repr. as chap. 3 of his book *Beowulf and the Demise of Germanic Legend in England* (New York: Garland, 1996).

composition of at least this part of the poem no earlier than the late ninth century and probably in the early decades of the tenth.[86]

One critic who, while inclined to ascribe the poem to an earlier date than that, has been especially productive in pursuing points of continuity between past and present in the poem's system of values is John M. Hill. Writing in the tradition of the Danish scholar Vilhelm Grønbech and other early twentieth-century scholars who today might be called cultural historians, Hill has authored a noteworthy series of studies of the heroic economy put on display in *Beowulf*. His major publication in this area is his 1995 book *The Cultural World in Beowulf*, which includes chapters on such subjects as 'Feud Settlements in *Beowulf*', 'The Jural World in *Beowulf*', and 'The Economy of Honour in *Beowulf*'.[87] Hill seeks to uncover the inner logic of the society whose workings are put on display in the poem. Since the *Beowulf* poet's treatment of such themes as gift-exchange, marital arrangements, inheritance, blood vengeance, raiding, and booty are sometimes bafflingly allusive, Hill casts light on these matters through evidence drawn from comparative social anthropology. In accord with a fundamental premise of anthropological field research, Hill adopts a non-judgemental attitude when dealing with social institutions that might be thought repugnant or barbaric. His premise is that the customs and behaviours to which reference is made in *Beowulf* must have been functional in the society in question. He shows, for example, that in certain societies of the current world, blood vengeance can play a jural role in resolving disputes when undertaken within limits and in accord with conventional norms of behaviour. Likewise the threat of retaliation can serve as a peacekeeper, helping to keep a lid on violence that might otherwise disturb social equilibrium. While this cluster of ideas may seem alien to people accustomed to living in a society where legitimate violence is the monopoly of what is assumed to be a benevolent state, Hill demonstrates its possible relevance to the management of disputes in the world of *Beowulf*. His research is based on the premise that no great gulf separated the imagined world of *Beowulf* from the actual society of the members of the poet's audience, at least in terms of the pragmatics of maintaining social equilibrium. Involved in the poet's story of fabulous adventure set in the Heroic Age, therefore, was an element of social modelling.

Hill is not alone in drawing on the literature of social anthropology in an attempt to clarify the inner workings of 'the economy of honour' in *Beowulf*. Critics who have pursued analogous approaches include Robert E. Bjork in his 1994 study 'Speech as Gift in *Beowulf*';[88] Jos Bazelmans in his 1999 book *By Weapons Made Worthy*;[89] and Peter S. Baker in his 2013 book *Honour, Exchange and Violence in Beowulf*.[90] In a brilliant approach to the

---

[86]   Audrey L. Meaney, 'Scyld Scefing and the Dating of *Beowulf* – Again', in *Toller Lectures*, 23–73; this 2003 publication represents a significantly augmented version of Meaney's earlier article 'Scyld Scefing and the Dating of *Beowulf*', *BJRL* 71 (1989): 7–40. Compare the argument mounted by Frank, 'Skaldic Verse'.

[87]   John M. Hill, *The Cultural World in Beowulf* (Toronto: University of Toronto Press, 1995). See also Hill, 'Social Milieu', chap. 13 (pp. 255–69) of the *Beowulf Handbook*.

[88]   Robert E. Bjork, 'Speech as Gift in *Beowulf*', *Speculum* 69 (1994): 993–1022.

[89]   Jos Bazelmans, *By Weapons Made Worthy: Lords, Retainers, and Their Relationship in Beowulf* (Amsterdam: Universiteit van Amsterdam, 1999).

[90]   Peter S. Baker, *Honour, Exchange and Violence in Beowulf* (Cambridge: D.S. Brewer, 2013).

predominant role of dialogue in *Beowulf,* Bjork approaches the exchange of speeches between the characters in the poem as a form of gift-exchange, one that is undertaken with certain conventional rules of engagement. Bazelmans writes persuasively on the role of arms, armour, and other forms of material wealth in confirming the bonds of loyalty in society through a system of gift-exchange centring on the king. Baker takes an unsentimental look at the violent tenor of life as represented in *Beowulf,* including predatory kingship, which he views as a leading aspect of the institutionalized violence that was typical of this period. He attempts to approach his topic free from either the moral biases or the sugar-coating that can blur one's critical judgement.

Other new directions in *Beowulf* studies deserve brief mention here, though it is impossible to do justice to them all.[91] Helen Damico's 1984 book *Beowulf's Wealhtheow and the Valkyrie Tradition,* for example, seeks to bring out the power and interest of certain of the female characters of *Beowulf,* including the cup-bearing figure of Wealhtheow, by exploring their mythological affinities.[92] Damico is one of a number of critics of *Beowulf,* including Tolkien, who have discerned a similarity between aspects of the poem and features of Old Norse mythology. The poem's stark close, in particular, has called the myth of Ragnarǫk to mind; while the hall Heorot with its cosmological associations has been likened to Ásgarð (Asgard), the hall of the Old Norse gods and heroes.[93] None of these parallels, however, have seemed to most critics central to the poet's design, as opposed to being distant echoes of ancient beliefs.

Jane Chance's 1986 book *Woman as Hero in Old English Literature,* too, bypasses familiar stereotypes of the 'woman mourner' or of 'woman as victim' so as to direct attention to female figures as active agents in the Old English narratives in which they play a role.[94]

---

[91] Two additional books deserving the attention of serious students of the poem have been influential in directing attention to the age of Cnut and to eighth-century East Anglia, respectively, as possible contexts for the poem's composition. These are Kevin S. Kiernan, *Beowulf and the Beowulf Manuscript,* 2nd edn (Ann Arbor: University of Michigan Press, 1996; first published 1981), and Sam Newton, *The Origins of Beowulf and the Pre-Viking Kingdom of East Anglia* (Cambridge: D.S. Brewer, 1993).

[92] Helen Damico, *Beowulf's Wealhtheow and the Valkyrie Tradition* (Madison: University of Wisconsin Press, 1984). Damico's most recent contribution to *Beowulf* studies, her book *Beowulf and the Grendel-kin: Politics and Poetry in Eleventh-Century England* (Morgantown: West Virginia University Press, 2015), has appeared in print too recently to be taken into account here.

[93] Ursula Dronke, '*Beowulf* and Ragnarǫk', *Saga-Book of the Viking Society* 17 (1969): 302–25; Paul Beekman Taylor, 'Heorot, Earth, and Asgard: Christian Poetry and Pagan Myth', *Tennessee Studies in Literature* 11 (1966): 119–30. Note further Taylor's book *Sharing Story: Medieval Norse-English Literary Relationships* (New York: AMS Press, 1998), and for topics of mythological interest, Richard North, *Heathen Gods in Old English Literature* (Cambridge: Cambridge University Press, 1997).

[94] Jane Chance, *Woman as Hero in Old English Literature* (Syracuse, NY: Syracuse University Press, 1986). Chap. 7 of this book, 'Grendel's Mother as Epic Anti-Type of the Virgin and Queen', is reprinted in Fulk, 251–63. Compare in this connection Joyce Hill's 1990 article '"Þæt Wæs Geomuru Ides!" A Female Stereotype Examined', in Damico & Olsen, 235–47, repr. in Howe, 153–66; and Helen Bennett, 'The Female Mourner at Beowulf's Funeral: Filling in the Blanks/ Hearing the Spaces', *Exemplaria* 4 (1992): 35–50, repr. in Howe, 167–78.

With regard to *Beowulf*, this aim entails finding a place on centre stage for Grendel's mother, whose crucial though horrific role had been minimized in the earlier criticism. Both Damico's and Chance's books can be associated with what Clare A. Lees, in her 1997 study 'Old English and Feminist Criticism', has called 'first phase' feminism.[95] This term has been used of scholarship, chiefly dating from the mid-1980s, that chiefly set out to call attention to the existence of celebrated and exceptional women either in history or in the literary imagination while still, in the view of some, leaving male-sanctioned gender paradigms intact.

Gillian R. Overing's 1990 book *Language, Sign, and Gender in Beowulf* could be said to represent 'second phase' feminism in that it adopts a semiotic and gender-oriented approach to *Beowulf*, one that is strongly influenced by deconstructive critical methods.[96] The book is one of several significant ones published at about this same time that introduced the tropes of postmodern critical discourse to Old English studies, often including an emphasis on the indeterminacy of literary texts and the collusion of individual critics, with their inevitable preconceptions and biases, with texts in the act of critical interpretation.[97] The focus of Overing's analysis is thus not on what the poem means, but rather *how* it means – that is to say, how any search for its meaning is caught up in a spiral of words and interpretations that has no final resolution. Her book demonstrates what it means to 'read like a (postmodern) woman', as opposed to 'reading like a (positivist) man', as was once the settled norm, or 'reading like a Christian', as has been tried with *Beowulf* on various occasions with partial success. Her book is illuminating of something, but readers will have to judge for themselves how fully they find that 'something' to be the Anglo-Saxon poem of *Beowulf*, as opposed to late twentieth-century intellectual currents that surge and eddy around this archaic poem, bringing some of its neglected elements to the surface. An element that serves as a leitmotif in Overing's book is the female figure (introduced at lines 1931b–62) referred to most often as 'Modthryth' in the critical literature.[98] As both King Offa's docile queen and a formerly murderous princess who threatened her male suitors with death, Modthryth is a model of ambivalent feminine power and hence a figure of special interest from a contemporary feminist perspective. From Overing's point of view, as 'one of the least conclusive elements of the poem', Modthryth is by virtue of that fact 'an affirmation of process in interpretation' (p. 112) – a phrase that may perhaps be taken to refer to the fraught process involved in anyone's understanding of anything.

---

[95]   Clare A. Lees, 'At a Crossroads: Old English and Feminist Criticism', in O'Brien O'Keeffe, 146–69. There is a more recent survey by Mary Dockray-Miller, 'Old English Literature and Feminist Theory: A State of the Field', *Literary Compass* 5/6 (2008): 1049–59.

[96]   Gillian R. Overing, *Language, Sign, and Gender in Beowulf* (Carbondale: Southern Illinois University Press, 1990). The last chapter of this book is reprinted with revisions in *Readings: Beowulf*, 219–60, under the title 'The Women of *Beowulf*: A Context for Interpretation'.

[97]   A landmark publication along such lines is the 1991 anthology of critical essays *Speaking Two Languages*. Of related interest is Allen J. Frantzen's book *Desire for Origins: New Language, Old English, and Teaching the Tradition* (New Brunswick: Rutgers University Press, 1990), chap. 6 of which is reprinted in Joy & Ramsey, 92–129.

[98]   The Old English passage in which she is introduced is somewhat obscure. In *Klaeber's Beowulf* this figure's name is reconstructed as 'Fremu', in an editorial decision that may or may not meet with the assent of time. See *Klaeber's Beowulf*, the note on 1931b (pp. 224–26).

The indeterminacy of the text and the subjectivity that is necessarily involved in one's reading of it are embraced by James W. Earl in his 1994 book *Thinking about Beowulf*,[99] one of the most original and entertaining contributions to Old English studies made in recent years. Earl draws on psychoanalytic models, chiefly of a Freudian kind, to stimulate thought about such large matters as kinship and kingship, the men's hall as symbol and as ritual space, and the threat, in his view, that 'women and the ancient claims of the kindred' were once felt to pose to 'the civilizing work of men'. Rather than attempting a conventional explication of the poem, Earl relies on imagery drawn from *Beowulf*, as well as on knowledge of the material world of the early Anglo-Saxons, so as to contribute to a psychohistory of the race. That is to say, Earl analyses aspects of the historical evolution of human civilization in terms like the ones used by Freud to describe the developmental stages of an individual person from infancy on. This is an ambitious scheme, as well as a risky one that may be thought to savour of outmoded nineteenth- and earlier twentieth-century evolutionary models, and of course Earl only sketches it in. By the rules of his own game, Earl cannot draw on *Beowulf* as more than a point of mental reference, for he insists that '*we cannot safely use the poem to help us interpret Anglo-Saxon history; we cannot assume the poem is representative of any period, or even, finally, representative of anything at all*' (p. 17, his italics). Accordingly, he ends his book not with conventional conclusions, but rather with a self-reflective account of 'the neuroses I bring to *Beowulf*'. This account is enlivened by a summary and explication of two dreams he claims to have had that relate to the poem. One of these features 'a sphinx, not quite buried in the desert sand'. This image serves as a suitable emblem for *Beowulf*, especially given Earl's frequent references to Oedipus and the Oedipus complex, for we all know of Oedipus's penchant for riddles.

Both Overing and Earl thus shift attention from the poem *Beowulf*, in the sense in which that term has had meaning to prior critics, to something else potentially related to that older concept, namely the late twentieth-century reading subject in the act of contemplating *Beowulf*, whether at one's desk or from the soft surface of an analyst's couch.[100] The experience of the individual reader is likewise a central concern of Seth Lerer in the chapter on 'Hrothgar's Hilt and the Reader in *Beowulf*' that forms an important part of his 1991 book *Literacy and Power in Anglo-Saxon Literature*.[101] While forty years before, Dorothy Whitelock had shone a spotlight on the early medieval *audience* of that poem as the entry point to its critical understanding, Overing, Earl, Lerer and like-minded late twentieth-century critics have directed attention to the contemporary *reader* as the gateway to the poem's sphinx-like presence. One is therefore not surprised to note that Johann Köberl's

---

[99]   James W. Earl, *Thinking about Beowulf* (Stanford: Stanford University Press, 1994).

[100]   A representative chapter from each of these two books is featured in Joy & Ramsey, an anthology that highlights the impact of modern critical theory on Old English literary studies. These are Overing's chap. 2, 'Swords and Signs: Dynamic Semeiosis in *Beowulf* ', in Joy & Ramsey, 547–85, and Earl's chap. 6, '*Beowulf* and the Origins of Civilization', in Joy & Ramsey, 259–85. Earl's chapter was originally published in somewhat different form as a contribution to *Speaking Two Languages*, 65–89 and 239–41.

[101]   Seth Lerer, 'Hrothgar's Hilt and the Reader in Beowulf', chap. 5 of *Literacy and Power in Anglo-Saxon Literature* (Lincoln: University of Nebraska Press, 1991), repr. in Joy & Ramsey, 587–628.

2002 book on the poem has the title *The Indeterminacy of Beowulf*.[102] The content of that book serves as proof (if any were needed) that a good critic, like a good lawyer, can speak elegantly and persuasively for some while to the effect that there are no conclusions to be drawn.

Implicit in almost any critical reading of a work of literature is a concept of the historical culture to which it pertains, including the question of its date. *Beowulf* is no exception, even though experts differ greatly in their conclusions other than agreeing that the poem was composed and recorded in writing somewhere in England at some point between the late seventh and the early eleventh centguries. On palaeographical grounds, the unique manuscript copy of *Beowulf* can be dated to about the year 1000, plus or minus a decade or two, and that approximate date provides a *terminus ad quem* for the composition of the poem itself. As for the time and place of the poem's composition – or better, perhaps, the *process* of its composition – arguments can only proceed by inference, whether by appeal to philological, stylistic, or social-historical evidence or on the basis of theories of literary influence nested within an overall concept of Anglo-Saxon literary history. Fortunately there is no need to review critics' conflicting arguments here, for pertinent discussion can be found in the Introduction to *Klaeber's Beowulf* (at pp. clxii–clxxx), though those pages should not be taken to foreclose debate. Representative views are mentioned in passing in earlier parts of the present chapter.[103] Those who wish to examine the theoretical underpinnings and the critical implications of such arguments are referred to a pair of judicious essays that review the problem of dating without trying to resolve it. One of these studies, by Nicholas Howe, serves as the Afterword to the reprinted edition of the 1981 volume *The Dating of Beowulf*, a book that greatly stimulated scholarly debate.[104] The other essay, more bracing in its critique of the methods (especially philological ones) that critics have brought to bear on the dating question, is Roy Michael Liuzza's 1995 study 'On the Dating of *Beowulf*'.[105] In the present writer's view – one that makes no claim to be a disengaged one – the most recent substantial publication in this area, the 2014 volume of critical essays titled *The Dating of Beowulf: A Reassessment*, is too one-sided in its approach to provide a satisfactory resting point for more than a relatively circumscribed cluster of critics who have concerned themselves with this issue.[106]

---

[102] Johann Köberl, *The Indeterminacy of Beowulf* (Lanham, MD: University Press of America, 2002).

[103] See in particular the references in prior parts of this chapter to studies by Patrick Wormald (n. 82), Roberta Frank (n. 84), Craig R. Davis (n. 85), Audrey L. Meaney (n. 86), John M. Hill (n. 87), Kevin Kiernan (n. 91), Sam Newton (n. 91), and Helen Damico (n. 92).

[104] Nicholas Howe, 'The Uses of Uncertainty: On the Dating of *Beowulf*', published as an Afterword (pp. 213–20) to the reprinted edition of *The Dating of Beowulf*, ed. Colin Chase (Toronto: University of Toronto Press, 1997; first published 1981); the essay is repr. in Howe, 179–89.

[105] Roy Michael Liuzza, 'On the Dating of *Beowulf*', in *Readings: Beowulf*, 281–302.

[106] *The Dating of Beowulf: A Reassessment*, ed. Leonard Neidorf (Cambridge: D.S. Brewer, 2014). Interested readers are referred to my review of this volume (forthcoming in *Speculum* ca. 2016), as well as to the conclusions drawn in my two essays 'Locating *Beowulf* in Literary History' (cited in n. 83 above) and 'On the Danish Origins of the *Beowulf* Story', in *Anglo-Saxon England and the Continent*, ed. Hans Sauer and Joanna Story (Tempe, AZ: ACMRS, 2011), 41–62.

Indeterminacy and its Discontents

Before concluding the present chapter, I will turn briefly to a single more recent book on *Beowulf*, Scott Gwara's 2008 study *Heroic Identity in the World of Beowulf*.[107] Signs are in evidence in this ambitious book, as well as in two other recent studies mentioned in the preceding pages (those by Daniel Anlezark, which dates from 2010, and Peter S. Baker, which dates from 2013), that the tidal wave of postmodernism that broke on the shores of literary studies during the decade of the 1990s had subsided somewhat by the middle of the following decade, leaving the landscape of Old English studies significantly altered but still recognizable.

Gwara sets into careful balance with one another the main strands of *Beowulf* criticism that have been outlined in the previous pages: Christian versus secular perspectives, indeterminate readings versus potentially determinate ones, admiring versus condemnatory views of the hero's character, neutral versus condemnatory views of the hero's society. A preliminary section of Gwara's book, titled 'Two Beowulfs' (pp. 8–12), takes account of claims made on either side of these last two questions. Noting that a number of critics have identified the hero's pride as a major failing (whether or not they see his society as equally flawed), Gwara dwells on that issue in particular. While his own views tend to fall into alignment with Leyerle's, he also detects (at 23–25) a 'general ambivalence' in the poet's use of the words *wlonc* 'proud' and *wlenco* 'pride', two terms that cover a wide semantic spectrum from the positive ('dignified') to the derogatory ('arrogant'). Tipping the scales towards a negative assessment of the hero's pride, in Gwara's view, is the existence of a considerable body of Anglo-Saxon 'wisdom' literature, chiefly from the Exeter Book, that emphasizes the danger of excessive zeal, seeks to curb immoderation, and recommends self-restraint. In a section of his book headed 'The *Oferhygd* Complex', Gwara approaches *Beowulf* in the light of that cautionary literature (p. 36):

> Germanic 'wisdom' [that is, wisdom literature] promotes ideal kingship by advocating methods preventing recklessness associated with leadership. For Germanic kings, ambition can yield 'overconfidence' or 'immoderation', concepts expressed by the term *oferhygd* in *Beowulf*. *Oferhygd* defines a kind of Germanic psychosis specific to leaders. Superficially, it means 'excessive spirit' or 'impetuosity', although it may be best to think of it as a leader's excessive ambition. Casting a long semantic shadow over Beowulf's heroic mentality in the first half of the poem, OE *oferhygd* in *Beowulf* reflects a specific propensity for something like arrogant overconfidence. In the context of Beowulfian kingship, it is expressed in warfare and in relations with the comitatus. The prospect of Beowulf's *oferhygd* would handicap his leadership because excessive zeal in a king translates into blind intolerance that portends fatal misjudgments.

The difference between Gwara's post-postmodern analysis and Leyerle's essay dating from the 1960s is that while Leyerle states with bold assurance just what he thinks the poem means, Gwara leaves ample room for multiple conclusions, as when using the subjunctive mood in the sentence just quoted: it is the *prospect* of Beowulf's dangerous pride that *would* handicap his leadership were he to succumb to 'the kingly reflex of excessive ambition' (p. 53). Whether the hero does succumb to that reflex or not is left up in the air. Gwara expresses the

---

[107]   Scott Gwara, *Heroic Identity in the World of Beowulf* (Leiden: Brill, 2008).

view, as well, that in both the Grendel fight and the dragon fight, the limits of heroic excess are debated rather than being determined in a judgemental way. 'Indeterminacy' is thus a keyword in his analysis, overruling his inclination to perceive the hero as flawed.

Personally, as might be guessed by now, I believe that as far as the hero's supposedly overweening pride is concerned, Gwara is wise not to rush to embrace conclusions that are not clearly articulated in the text. In particular, a body of wisdom literature that we know of chiefly from the Exeter Book – a compilation that is plausibly linked to the ideology of the late tenth-century Benedictine Reform – does not necessarily provide an apt reading context for *Beowulf*, which most critics take to be expressive of an 'unreformed' culture and which has been thought to express with greatest eloquence something other than orthodox Christian doctrine. Maxims, as well, are often cautionary the whole world round: Look before you leap; Blind men rush in where angels fear to tread; Better safe than sorry. And yet in the performative world of 'duelling proverbs' that folklorists have documented, for every proverb that advises caution, there is another one urging decisive action: Opportunity only knocks once; He who hesitates is lost; Seize the day. The existence of maxims of a cautionary kind has never precluded heroic poems from existing.

An approach to the question of the hero's pride in *Beowulf* by way of a body of wisdom literature would be more convincing, in my eyes, if it were based on gnomic elements that find expression *within* the poem, of which there are no few. An example is the phrase *swa sceal man don* ('so ought one do!'), used at 1534b with reference to the hero's effort to win 'everlasting praise' (*longsumne lof*, 1536a) through his exploits in the depths of Grendel's mere. As for Gwara's identification of the '*oferhygd* complex' as a crucial critical framework for our understanding of *Beowulf*, such a claim would be more persuasive if the poet ever used the noun *oferhygd* with direct reference to the hero. In fact, it is only the patriarchal figure King Hrothgar, who is no longer capable of heroic action, who uses that word (twice, at 1740a and 1760b) while warning the hero of the evils that can arise when a king succumbs to avarice, greed, a violent disposition, and *oferhygd* and therefore dies an outcast, hated by his people. This is good advice and the young hero Beowulf takes it, to judge from what we know of his later beneficent rule over the Geatas and of their love for him at his death. Still the fact that a reader of Gwara's perceptivity is inclined to read the poem as an indictment of pride points to the possibility that *Beowulf* could well have been understood in that same way, by some readers or listeners at least, among members of its original audiences.

The main point that ought to emerge from this discussion is that an acknowledgement of the possibility of multiple voices in *Beowulf* is now deeply engrained in the criticism. This is true even though, personally, I dislike the notion of indeterminacy. It savours too much of trendiness for my taste. It offers a refuge for those who lack the stupidity to make up their minds. All the same, the fact that *Beowulf* has meant so many different things to so many different readers, all of whom have a fair claim to literacy, learning, and enlightenment, does seem to point to something real about the kind of poem that this is.

For one thing, the poem does not stay still. This is true in part because trends in the criticism change over time. Reading *Beowulf* over the decades is like looking at a fixed object from a moving train; the object may seem to be in steady movement, though of course it is the observer who is lapping the miles. Moreover, those observers themselves are not fixed entities; they are animate beings subject to change over time. Tolkien's views about the poem evolved over time; why should not yours or mine? The heroic *Beowulf* that I admired when in my twenties is not the same brooding, reflective *Beowulf* that I mull over today. The world itself has changed, so why should the poem stay still? Facebook rules the social world, Wikipedia the realm of knowledge; 'Unferth' has become 'Hunferth' again, in certain publications at least;[108] Hrothgar's court poet just might have recently recovered his proper name, 'Healgamen', after a long period of anonymity.[109] This ferment would be dizzying for scholars of the generation of Friedrich Klaeber to contemplate, could they now be in a position to observe it.

Moreover, like Shakespeare's plays – and we will not talk about *their* indeterminacy – *Beowulf* was in its own time a work of popular literature, we may surmise, rather than having been meant for the appreciation of an educated elite alone. In its own time, the poem offered something for everyone. Members of the warrior class would naturally have identified with its astounding story of brave deeds, as well as with its gleaming mead-hall setting, even if they themselves inhabited a far less showy world. Persons of a religious vocation too could have admired it for its polarized struggle of good versus evil and its manifold spiritual insights: Hrothgar's 'sermon', for example, must be one of the most effective discourses on pride ever composed. Ethnic Englishmen of the late ninth or the tenth centuries, right from the start of the poem with its story of the founding of the Scylding dynasty, could have picked up on genealogical connections of importance to the royal dynasty of Wessex;[110] while if any ethnic Danes were in the audience, they could have done the same as regards Danish genealogical connections, much as they could have gloried in the Age of Gold of the Scandinavian peoples through images of the gilded hall Heorot and its courtly displays. Young thegns could have absorbed lessons in courage and loyalty from the poem;[111] grizzled commanders could have studied its problem points as regards prudent leadership. Courtiers could have learned from it proper court etiquette;[112] public speakers could have learned from it much about the use of *sententiae* amidst other oratorical arts;[113] poets could have studied from it almost all they needed to know about the art of vernacular verse-making. Anglo-Saxons of an antiquarian disposition could have had a field day contemplating its representations of material culture, just as their modern-day counterparts do.[114] Children, or anyone with a delight in fantasy,

---

[108] The Danish un-hero *Hunferth* is named consistently as such by the scribe, with an emphatically bold initial capital H- at line 499, which is the beginning of fitt VIII. Modern editors began emending the name to *Unferth* in the later nineteenth century under the influence of philological positivism (since initial *Hun-* does not seem to provide acceptable alliteration); and a return to MS *Hunferth* is now favoured by certain scholars out of respect for the readings of medieval manuscripts as witnesses to how a text was received in its own time.

[109] On this innovation see *Klaeber's Beowulf*, the note on lines 1066–70 (at pp. 180–81).

[110] On this dynastic connection, see Audrey L. Meany, 'Scyld Scefing and the Dating of *Beowulf* – Again' (n. 86 above).

[111] See Peter R. Richardson, 'Making Thanes: Literature, Rhetoric, and State Formation in Anglo-Saxon England', *PQ* 78 (1999): 215–32.

[112] Note in this regard Malcolm M. Brennan, 'Hrothgar's Government', *JEGP* 84 (1985): 3–15.

[113] See Peter S. Baker, 'Beowulf the Orator', *Journal of English Linguistics* 21 (1988): 3–23.

[114] Those interested in the *Beowulf* poet's representations of material culture may wish to consult *Beowulf: An Illustrated Edition* (New York: Norton, 2008), which features Seamus Heaney's translation of the poem along with facing-page photographs of scenes and material objects that offer a counterpoint to the text. My Afterword to that book (pp. 213–45) consists of an archaeological commentary along with relevant bibliography.

would have been thrilled by its ghoulish and suspenseful elements.[115] Women could have learned lessons in how to pull the strings in society even when those strings are invisible to men.[116] Aged persons, perhaps sadly, could have seen something of their physical deterioration in the poet's portrait of the aged King Hrothgar, so weak except in wisdom;[117] and any parents who happened to be in the audience could have prayed that they would never see their own image reflected in that of the bereaved father whose son has been hanged as the perpetrator of some unknown crime.[118]

When contemplating the different approaches that have been taken to the critical interpretation of *Beowulf* in the past half-century or so, I am reminded of the fable of the blind men and the elephant. You know the story, I am sure; it seems to have been in circulation in Jain, Buddhist, Sufi Muslim, Hindu, and Western versions for a number of centuries. A group of blind men have the task of describing an elephant through the sense of touch alone. Each man is only able to feel one part of the animal – the trunk, the foot, the side, the ear, the tail, or the tusk, for example – and, on the basis of that limited knowledge, each one tries to define the animal's true nature. The results are predictably laughable. The point of the fable is that, could we but see ourselves aright, we are all like blind people groping our way towards knowledge. We live in hope of ascertaining the true nature of matters that are often so large, and so alien to our customary lifeworld, as to be beyond our powers of comprehension, even when our sense of touch is good and our insights are pooled. I am fond of this parable not just because of a partiality towards elephants, a species so clearly superior to our own in dignity and morals, but also because the elephant is the hero of the fable, while the blind men can only inspire amusement.

The point of my calling this fable to mind, of course, is to suggest that *Beowulf*, too, is both too large and too alien for our comprehension. It is the elephant in the closet of English literature. In addition, *Beowulf* is best thought of as something that, in its Anglo-Saxon setting, was wholly conformed to its habitat. By 'habitat' I mean to refer to a mental world and a social system that were exactly suited to sustain it, but that can be reconstructed today only with difficulty if at all. The best we can do is to make educated guesses about the inner logic of the poem and the working mechanisms of the society it depicts, rather like looking at a ticking pocket-watch from the outside when we live in a digital age. While some of us may be top-shelf philologists, historians, theologians, metrists, or social anthropologists, we may still be flattering ourselves if we believe we have the mental equipment to enter into the thought-world of the poem and make it our own. Much of what passes for criticism of *Beowulf*, as a result, is little more than a paraphrase of that poem into inferior language of our own.

---

[115] Alain Renoir, 'Point of View and Design for Terror in *Beowulf*', *NM* 63 (1962): 154–66, repr. in Fry, 154–66, offers a persuasive account of what he finds to be the poet's 'cinematic technique'. See also Michael Lapidge, 'Beowulf and the Psychology of Terror', in *Bessinger Studies*, 373–402, repr. in Howe, 134–53.

[116] John M. Hill, '*Beowulf* and the Danish Succession: Gift Giving as an Occasion for Complex Gesture', *Medievalia et Humanistica* n.s. 11 (1982): 177–97, offers sharp insights into Wealhtheow's exercise of power behind the scenes in Heorot.

[117] Note Edward B. Irving, Jr, on 'What to Do with Old Kings', in *Comparative Research on Oral Traditions*, ed. John Miles Foley (Columbus, OH: Slavica Publishers, 1988), 259–68.

[118] See *Beowulf* 2444–62a, the passage known as 'The Father's Lament'.

A Selection from the Criticism

The selection that follows, by the Swiss scholar Ernst Leisi, was originally published in German over sixty years ago. Since it has retained much of its value and deserves to be better known, it has been made available here in English translation. Leisi's theme is gold in *Beowulf*, and by extension the whole system of material wealth and exchange in the ancient Germanic world. Gold is seen as a substance of material value, a sign of a person's rank and standing, and a means by which the members of society can be bound to one another in a network of mutual obligations and trust. Leisi attempts to give a philologically exact account of the nature and function of treasure in the world of *Beowulf*, drawing on the Anglo-Saxon law codes as a leading source of information.

As persons will be aware who have visited the early medieval collections of the national museums of Denmark, Sweden, and neighbouring countries, northern Europe during the period when *Beowulf* is set – the Age of Migration or *Völkerwanderungszeit*, now also fittingly referred to by some as the Age of Attila – was literally an age of gold. Thanks to the achievements of a warrior elite who either served the Roman emperors as mercenaries or clients, or raided on the Empire's borders, or in the course of time conquered whole portions of it, more gold was apparently in open circulation then in those northern lands than at any other time before or since. Much of this wealth took the form of beautifully crafted ornaments, including gilded weapons. Wealth also circulated in the form of gold coins, or of coin-like medallions worn as pendants in an economy of gift-exchange. The *Beowulf* poet makes frequent allusion to this wealth, for he tells almost exclusively of the top echelon of society: the inhabitants of the king's hall and the members of a prince's *gedryht*, or 'war band'. This elite society is presented in superlative terms, if not morally than at least as regards their finery.

Gold, still, does not necessarily have a uniformly positive value in *Beowulf*, as more than one critic has observed. The poet makes a point of speaking of the 'useless' treasures of the dragon's hoard (or at least the 'unused' ones – *unnyt*, 3168a). Through many allusions to disastrous events, as well – the tragic fate threatening the Geatas after their king's death, or the fate of the magnificent necklace that Wealhtheow bestows on the hero (1202–14a) – the poet reminds his audience of the transitory nature of wealth. And indeed, any Anglo-Saxons reading or listening to the poem would have been aware that the Age of Gold that is depicted in the poem did come to an end, leaving in its traces diminished societies that more closely resembled their own. Gold has thus seemed to many modern critics to have a double value in *Beowulf*, as one might expect in a poem where Christian and heroic values intersect. While it is not part of Leisi's purpose to dwell on Christian perspectives of transience, they too need to be taken into account in a balanced critical understanding of the poem and its semantics of material wealth.

Ernst Leisi (1918–2001) was awarded the degree of PhD at the University of Zurich. An expert in *Anglistik*, he authored several books on the English language, including *Praxis der englischen Semantik* (1985). From 1952 to 1956 he taught at the University of Kiel, West Germany, thereafter serving on the faculty of the University of Zurich until his retirement in 1984.

Leisi's essay will gain in resonance if it is read alongside certain other classic studies of treasure and gift-exchange in ancient or non-Western societies, including Marcel Mauss's

The Gift and M.I. Finley's *The World of Odysseus*.[119] Among many studies on gold and its moral valence in *Beowulf*, two stand out: Michael Cherniss's chapter on treasure in his 1972 book *Ingeld and Christ*, and Patricia Silber's 1977 study 'Gold and its Significance in *Beowulf*'.[120] Persons with an interest in the archaeology of gold in the insular context will want to study the Sutton Hoo treasures, available for viewing at the British Museum website and expertly published in the Museum's multi-volume publication *The Sutton Hoo Ship Burial*.[121] A vivid witness to the importance of loot in the early Anglo-Saxon context is the recently discovered Staffordshire Hoard, for which one can now consult both the British Museum guidebook and Leslie Webster's study 'Imagining Identities: The Case of the Staffordshire Hoard'.[122]

For Further Reading

Bremmer, Rolf H., Jr. 2013. 'Across Borders: Anglo-Saxon England and the Germanic World'. In the *Cambridge History*, 185–208.

Busse, W.G., and R. Holtei. 1981. '*The Battle of Maldon*: A Historical, Heroic and Political Poem'. *Neoph* 65: 614–21. Repr. in *Readings: Shorter Poems*, 185–98.

Clark, George. 1997. 'The Hero and the Theme'. In the *Beowulf Handbook*, 271–90.

Davis, Craig R. 1999. 'Cultural Historicity in *The Battle of Maldon*'. *PQ* 78 (1999): 151–69.

Haarder, Andreas. 1975. *Beowulf: The Appeal of a Poem*. Viborg: Akademisk Forlag.

Hill, Thomas D. 1994. 'The Christian Language and Theme of *Beowulf*'. In Aertsen & Bremmer, 63–77. Repr. in Donoghue, 197–211.

Hunter, Michael. 1974. 'Germanic and Roman Antiquity and the Sense of the Past in Anglo-Saxon England'. *ASE* 3: 29–50.

Lendinara, Patrizia. 2001. 'The Germanic Background'. In Pulsiano & Treharne, 121–34.

Magennis, Hugh. 2010. 'Germanic Legend and Old English Heroic Poetry'. In Saunders, 85–100.

O'Brien O'Keeffe, Katherine. 2013. 'Values and Ethics in Heroic Literature'. In Godden & Lapidge, 101–19.

Orchard, Andy. 2013. '*Beowulf*'. In Godden & Lapidge, 137–58.

Overing, Gillian R. 2013. '*Beowulf*: A Poem in Our Time'. In the *Cambridge History*, 309–31.

---

[119] Marcel Mauss, *The Gift: The Form and Reason for Exchange in Archaic Societies*, trans. W.D. Halls (New York: Norton, 1990), first published 1925; M.I. Finley, *The World of Odysseus*, 2nd edn (London: Chatto and Windus, 1977), first published 1954.

[120] Michael Cherniss, 'Treasure: The Material Symbol of Human Worth', chap. 4 of his book *Ingeld and Christ: Heroic Concepts and Values in Old English Christian Poetry* (The Hague: Mouton, 1972); Patricia Silber, 'Gold and its Significance in *Beowulf*', *Annuale Mediaevale* 18 (1977): 5–19. Note also, on treasure and covetousness, the studies by Goldsmith cited in n. 59 of the present chapter. The theme of treasure as an aspect of the system of Old English poetics per se is touched on in the next chapter, 'Style'.

[121] Rupert Bruce-Mitford, *The Sutton Hoo Ship Burial*, 3 vols in 4 (London: British Museum Publications, 1975–83).

[122] Kevin Leahy and Roger Bland, *The Staffordshire Hoard*, 2nd edn (London: British Museum, 2014); Leslie Webster, 'Imagining Identities: The Case of the Staffordshire Hoard', in *Anglo-Saxon England and the Visual Imagination*, ed. Stacy S. Klein, Jonathan Wilcox, and myself (Tempe, AZ: ACMRS, forthcoming 2016).

Ernst Leisi, 'Gold and Human Worth in *Beowulf*', first published as 'Gold und Manneswert im *Beowulf*' (1952).[1]

The author of *Beowulf* shows great admiration for his protagonist. Beowulf is showered with epithets honouring him; indeed, he is often simply called *se gōda* – the good one. Thus he is evidently a role model of morality for the author, as well as, generally, for the society of the time when the work was composed.

Once Beowulf has freed Hrothgar and his court from the monsters, the king rewards him with riches. He demonstrates an unusual joy about this: *Gūðrinc goldwlanc græsmoldan træd / since hrēmig* ('Proudly arrayed in gold, the warrior strode through the meadow, rejoicing in the treasure', 1881–82a). This jubilation about the goods that he has received causes us some discomfiture, for we otherwise imagine the people of ancient Germania as idealistic and averse to material pleasure and luxury.[a,b] But there is more: when Beowulf, wounded by the dragon, senses that his end is near, he dispatches his companion as follows: 'Make haste, so that I may see the hoard and die all the more easily' (2747 ff.). Finally, he even thanks God for the favour of having been allowed to see the gold again before his death (2794 ff.).

From these passages, we have the sense that Beowulf is unusually greedy. However, since (as we know) he is a role model, this cannot be counted as a vice; rather, there must be special circumstances surrounding these riches and wealth in general. Indeed, this conclusion can be inferred from the Old English words that express the concept 'rich'. The words for wealth in the Old English poetic language are very numerous, and yet (we feel) they are at the same time peculiarly ambiguous: *ēadig* must sometimes be translated as 'rich', sometimes as 'fortunate'; the same applies to *sǣlig*; *wlonc* means 'rich', but in other passages 'proud'; *rīce* sometimes 'rich', sometimes 'powerful'; *blǣd* means both 'wealth' and 'fame'; *ār* denotes 'possession', 'good deed', or 'honour'; *spēd* means 'wealth', 'success', or 'virtue'; *duguð* means 'wealth', 'fame', or 'virtue'.[2] We note that there is not a single word that encompasses wealth as a merely economic

---

[1] Ernst Leisi, 'Gold und Manneswert im *Beowulf*', *Anglia* 71 (1952): 259–73. Used with permission from Walter de Gruyter GmbH. Translated into English by John D. Niles with the assistance of Shannon A. Dubenion-Smith, 2016.

[a] [Leisi's notes are lightly filled out and updated for the present publication but are otherwise unchanged, except that his references to translations into German of a work originally published in a foreign language are generally replaced by references to English translations of those same works. In n. 2, a reference is omitted to a work in progress that seems never to have been published.]

[b] [Leisi writes of *die Germanen*, a term that harkens back to the Roman historian Tacitus's book *Germania*, in which much is made of the austere virtues of the German peoples living at the northern frontiers of the Roman Empire.]

[2] Cf. the dictionaries by Grein and Bosworth-Toller. See also B. von Lindheim, 'Neue Wege der Bedeutungsforschung', *Neuphilologische Zeitschrift* 3 (1951), with its very valuable commentary on *spēd* and *sǣlig*.

fact. In Old English, it is impossible to say about someone 'He is rich, but a bad and unhappy person', because virtue or happiness, or both, are already subsumed in the concept 'rich'. This can only mean that by definition, wealth means happiness, and that the relationship between wealth and virtue is so close that one who is rich is also virtuous, and vice versa.

The question of how we arrive at this state of affairs may first of all be answered with the counter-question: How does one acquire wealth in the world of Old English epic poetry? And here it basically appears that all present-day means of acquiring wealth are excluded. Not only is there no increase in wealth through interest; there is also neither individual trade nor industry. That the concepts 'purchase', 'sale', and 'wages' must have originally been unknown can be inferred from the Old English language.[3] The relevant words are either borrowings from Latin, such as *cēap* 'purchase', or are developed from other concepts through semantic shift; thus in the whole body of Old English poetry *sellan* means 'to give as a gift', while *bycgan* means 'to pay with one's life' or 'to buy a person'. In the same manner, no one earns income by following a trade. To the extent that people are free and are not the property of an overlord, they are directly dependent on the king who provides their means of support but who does not remunerate them in the modern sense. While there do exist words, such as *lēan* and *mēd*, that are generally translated as 'reward', here we are always dealing with 'reward' in the moral sense: reward or payback for a good or evil deed.

How then, in Old English poetry, does one come by wealth, since one is barred from all the resources to which we are accustomed? Beowulf receives treasures for killing Grendel and his mother; that is, for liberating the king's court at its moment of great crisis. Wiglaf becomes rich by being the only warrior not to abandon his lord during the battle with the dragon. Beowulf's companions, who have traversed the sea with him, also receive rewards, as do court entertainers for raising the spirits of the men. From time to time riches are also distributed in advance, as it were, resulting in an obligation on the part of the recipient to distinguish himself in battle. In sum, one can say that in the world of Old English epic poetry, no one acquires wealth in a quotidian or petty way. Rather, one is enriched exclusively as a result of extraordinary achievements, of having proved to the highest degree one's value as a person. The rich man is also always the brave one, the proud one, the happy one, and this explains why the terms 'rich', 'virtuous', 'proud', and 'happy' merge in a manner that we find so strange.

What do these riches consist of in material terms? In some instances, horses are given away or even land, but usually it is treasures. Though this term can encompass precious weapons, above all it denotes actual pieces of jewellery. Among these, it is the 'rings' (*hringas* and *bēagas*, Old High German *bauge*) that make the most frequent appearance and that, with some qualifications, can almost be called currency.[4] Thus,

---

[3]   Bernhard Fehr, *Die Sprache des Handels in Altengland* (St Gall: Honegger'sche Buchdrukkerei, 1909).

for the most part, these gifts are not commodities but luxury items. It might be expected that their beauty and physical appearance would be described in the literature with some precision. In reality, however, when these pieces are mentioned, their aesthetic aspect is mentioned only in very general terms. On the other hand, again and again it is made clear that what we are dealing with are old, valued heirlooms (*lāf, ealdgestrēon, ǣrgestrēon*) that are of distinguished or magical origins (they may be called *Wēlandes geweorc* 'Wayland's work' or *enta geweorc* 'the works of giants'). So these are things that are laden with prestige, so to speak, and that impart this prestige to their owners as well. Thus Beowulf presents a sword decorated in gold to the man who has guarded his boat 'so that he was henceforth all the more respected on the mead-bench because of that gift, that heirloom'.[5] That this is not an isolated example can be seen in the use of *weorðian*. What this verb means is 'to pay tribute', 'to treasure, cherish', first of all in a very general sense (e.g. 1959), though one who is *geweorðod* is especially the recipient and wearer of treasure (250, 331, 1038, 1450, 2176). For this reason, the dictionaries also give the meanings 'to give a present', 'decorate' for *weorðian*, though this usage is imprecise to the extent that the most important semantic value of the term, namely the enhancement of personal worth, thereby becomes blurred. It is precisely there that the meaning of wealth resides. Its main purpose is not to provide the possessor with aesthetic pleasure: it is impossible for Beowulf to wear all the rings he has received, and also one never hears mention of men who are richly adorned. In addition, a rich person does not lead a more comfortable life than a poor one; rich people cannot convert their wealth as they please since there is nothing to be bought. Even the obligation to pass wealth on to a third person becomes associated with the receipt of riches, as will be discussed below.

The position of the king, who can still be imagined as a sort of tribal ruler, is obviously important. He supports a retinue of a couple of dozen men who live with him in the lords' hall. The liegemen with their attendants are the core troupe of the king and thus they play the most important role in waging war and, for that matter, in the state, which we apparently have before us *in statu nascendi* ('in an incipient form'). When the king, as we have seen, showers his men with gifts, then he must have great resources at his disposal. Indeed, his Old English names confirm this fact. The king is the *goldwine gumena* 'the gold friend of men', the *sincgifa* 'the giver of riches', the *bēaga brytta* 'the distributor of rings', or simply *se rīca* 'the rich one'. His throne is the *gifstōl* 'the gift-throne'; the phrase *sinc brytnian* 'to distribute treasure' basically means 'to rule'.[6] All of these expressions indicate that gift-giving is a function without which a ruler cannot be imagined; it is something that belongs to the essence

---

4   A. Hansen, *Angelsächsische Schmucksachen: Eine kultur-geschichtlich-etymologische Untersuchung*, dissertation Kiel, 1913. On the concept of 'rings' as a form of currency, see Karl von Amira, *Grundriss des germanischen Rechts*, 3rd edn (Strassburg: Trübner, 1913), section 63 (p. 199).

5   'Hē þǣm bātwearde bunden golde / swurd gesealde, þæt hē syðþan wæs / on meodubence māþme þý weorþra, / yrfelāfe' (1900–03a).

6   A. Bartels, 'Rechtsaltertümer in der angelsächsischen Dichtung', dissertation Kiel, 1913, esp. at pp. 36 and 47.

of kingship, not just to its peripheral components. For many passages also demonstrate that the king stands or falls by virtue of his power to give. Even as a youth, Hrothgar's grandfather had an open hand (21 ff.) and thus acquired a large, willing retinue. On the other hand, King Heremod, whom Hrothgar names as an example to avoid, 'gave no rings' (1719); and thus he became a loner and also one who 'fiercely hoards his riches' (1749) and comes to a bad end, while another person who 'unhesitatingly distributes gifts' (1756) assumes the throne. There is even a technical term, (*be*)*wennan*, which means that one garners the favour of liegemen through the gifts to which they are accustomed.[c]

All this should not be understood, though, as if there were a sort of contractual relationship between the king and his retinue, so that the king paid his men for their service in the modern sense. What in reality keeps the king and his retinue together is not a contract, nor a law, but a traditional, self-evident custom, one that is characterized by a word that until now has seemed – quite annoyingly – to have various divergent meanings, namely *duguð* 'virtue'. In certain passages, *duguð* must be translated as 'morality', while in others it clearly denotes 'bravery' (or, alternatively, 'the tried and tested part of the retinue', a sense that can easily be explained as 'bravery put into concrete terms'). In yet other passages, what it means is 'generosity' or 'wealth'. In the light of the social background that has been described, these seemingly incompatible meanings may now be harmoniously integrated into a whole: *duguð* designates the moral relations that are supposed to exist between the king and his retinue. Thus that word can often be translated simply as 'morality', but this morality has a different effect on these two sides. The retinue fulfils the duty of *duguð* if the men are brave, hence the meaning 'bravery'. On the part of the king, however, what *duguð* means is 'generosity' and thus also the prerequisite for generosity, 'wealth'. The same two-sidedness also applies to the verb *dugan* 'to be worthy, to be of use'. A brave man such as Beowulf 'is worthy' (e.g. 526); on the other hand he can also say to Hrothgar, after he has received his gifts: *ðū ūs wēl dohtest*, 'you certainly did well by us', that is 'you were generous towards us' (1821). Most likely the adjective *til* (along with the adverb *tela*), which until now has been translated as 'good, brave, upright', also has this double meaning of 'generous' and 'virtuous'.

Just as the relationship between the king and his retinue is not overtly contractual, so the act of royal gift-giving has rather irrational characteristics. The king does not offer gifts at regular intervals, but only on special festive occasions. These celebrations are the well-known Old Germanic feasts. Contrary to what is sometimes assumed, however, these are not feasts for the purpose of material pleasure. It is characteristic of the literature that one never can be quite sure what the men are drinking, for *bēor* 'beer', *medu* 'mead', and *wīn* 'wine' get conflated in a single scene. At one moment there is talk of a 'mead-bench', at the next moment of the 'wine hall', and at yet

---

[c]   [See the *DOE*, s.v. *be-wennan*, glossed as 'to attend to, entertain (someone)', a verb with two occurrences in the corpus of OE, both of them in *Beowulf*.]

another moment of 'the enjoyment of beer'. Nothing is said about whether these drinks taste good. Apparently they are not drunk for their own sake, but are only the prerequisite for an intoxicatingly heightened feeling of being alive – an atmosphere, far removed from daily life, of ambition, male pride, and boasting. Contributing to this atmosphere is the *scop* – the singer – who praises the glorious deeds of former days. It is in this manner that what the poets call *hæleða drēam* 'the men's festive jubilation' comes into being.[7] In this elevated atmosphere a large part of the life of the state takes place. The king gives away his riches during boastful speeches: *on gylp seleð fǣtte bēagas* ('proudly he gives away ornamented rings', 1749); he 'gives rings to increase his fame' (1720; cf. *Widsith* 70). And it is especially this that earns him the loyalty of his retinue. In this same intoxicated mood, the retainers commit themselves to service in return: they not only boast about past feats (such as Beowulf and his swimming competition with Breca), but they also utter the *bēot*, a commitment (usually declared in a state of inebriation) to a single great feat, or a declaration of their intent to win victory or else die alongside their king in battle.[8] This *bēot* is taken very seriously, as one can see not only from *Beowulf*, but also from the poem *The Battle of Maldon*, where after the death of his leader, one man after another recalls his *bēot* and stands firm in hopeless battle until death. This whole mode of behaviour – the boastful giving of gifts, the impetuous willingness to provide service in return – can be much better understood when one knows that gifts are not of economic or material value, but rather are a token of honour. Not only do they indicate where virtue resides, they also call for it.

As has been mentioned, the king does not earn and maintain his prestige so much by possessing riches as by giving them away. To a certain extent this also holds true for the next owner. 'Everyone must share gifts generously who wishes to gain honour before the Lord', the first verse of the Old English *Rune Poem* declares.[9] Æschere, one of Hrothgar's foremost warriors, is likewise called a *sincgifa* 'giver of riches' who 'did well' by the others (1342–44). And Beowulf himself no sooner returns to his homeland than he passes on most of the gifts he has received to his own lord, King Hygelac (2144–99). This is in no way a mere handing over of what he has won. Beowulf received these gifts from Hrothgar with the usual formula of gift-giving *tō sylfes dōme* 'for use as you see fit' and with the advice *brūc ealles wēl* 'enjoy everything

---

[7] Compare B. von Lindheim, 'O.E. *Dréam* and its Subsequent Development', *RES* 22 (July 1946).

[8] L.L. Schücking, *Heldenstolz und Würde im Angelsächsichen*, Abhandlungen der Sachsische Akademie der Wissenschaft, Phil.-histor. Klasse, 17, part 5 (Leipzig, 1933), was the first to point out the special meaning of *bēot* and *gylp* within the Old English social system, just as in general in his works he lays down the foundations for a thorough explication of Old English word meanings.

[9] Precisely on the grounds of this connection, it seems more correct to take *dryhten* to mean not 'God' here, but rather 'secular lord', as Helmut Arntz does in his *Handbuch der Runenkunde* (Halle: Niemeyer, 1944).

properly'.[10] Clearly, the enjoyment of these things is maximized when they are passed on to another person so as to increase one's own honour. Yet another aspect of the scene between Beowulf and Hygelac is worth noting. Evidently, honour requires that one does not 'sit on' a gift. The king, for instance, tries immediately to trump Beowulf with counter-gifts, and he is successful in doing so since he has even greater means at his disposal. Something similar happens in *Widsith* (88 ff.): the singer receives a precious ring from the king of the Goths, passes it on to his own rulers, and receives from his princess an even greater gift in return.

Any doubts concerning the trophy-like character of precious objects are all the more decisively dispelled when one contemplates the word with which they are most often denoted.[d] *Māðm* (or *māðum*) is usually translated 'treasure'. There is no reason for this, however. Gothic *maiþms* clearly means 'gift'; in addition, there is a clear connection between Latin *mutuus* 'reciprocal' and several other Indo-European words with the meaning 'retaliation'. Thus Old English *māðm* apparently does not denote just any treasure, but one that functions as a gift (especially a gift presented in return for services rendered). The earliest modern translators of Old English poetry disapproved of the fact that an object, even when nothing is said about gift-giving, can always be called a 'gift' (especially in light of the common compound words *māðm-swēord, -fæt, -æht*, etc.), and thus they ascribed to that word a meaning different from what it has in Gothic. The justification for this practice evaporates as soon as one recognizes that objects of this kind always remain gifts.[11]

To sum up these points, we have arrived at an ethnic, economic, and political system that can best be named the *honour-price system*. The 'money' that has not yet been minted, but that exists in the form of jewellery and the like, is not yet an economic instrument; rather, it is an index of value and virtue, a token of honour. A man's prestige, and with that his power, depends on his wealth. Prestige is measured not in terms of how much one possesses, but how much one gives away. Thus we see a tendency to pass gifts on, so that valuable objects by definition always remain gifts and move on from owner to owner. This system of exchange, which does not rest on established law but rather on unconsciously maintained customs, also helps to maintain the integrity of the primitive state in which men vow their loyalty to a gift-giving ruler in reciprocal service to him. Beneficence and vows of loyalty clearly show their privileged emotional character in that they take place in the intoxicated atmosphere of the feast.

---

[10]   A single item of weaponry is entrusted to Beowulf by Hrothgar to be handed over directly to Hygelac; at least it is possible to interpret line 2157 in this way, though it is somewhat obscure.

[d]   [Leisi uses the German term *Wanderpreischarakter* to refer to trophy objects of this kind. A *Wanderpreis* is a prize that, in certain athletic competitions, is handed on from winner to winner depending on who is victorious in a given year.]

[11]   Hence the designation *gifsceattas* 'gift-riches' (378).

Still, a question arises as to what extent the circumstances described in the literature are based on historical fact. It must be emphasized that what *Beowulf* conveys to us is not a mere set of details, but rather a complete, self-contained system in which each element presupposes the others. The invention of such a system from scratch would be completely alien to the spirit of Old English poetry. The authors of these works do not manifest even the slightest ability to disregard their own sociological reality and immerse themselves in that of other peoples. Indeed, in the Old English paraphrases of the Bible, words such as *dryhten*, *dryht*, *drēam*, and *gylp* transfer typically Germanic features onto biblical peoples, and even onto the kingdom of heaven.[12] In the early Middle Ages it is practically unheard of for someone to want to make his personal opinions known in a work of literature. The author almost always expresses only those views that are generally accepted, while concealing his individual personality. This same tendency finds external expression in the characteristic anonymity of medieval literary works. As a result, the Old English poetry that is known to us, when compared with later works, is amazingly uniform not only stylistically, but also ideologically. Most important for our analysis, the meaning of words like *duguð*, *māðm*, and the words for wealth remains constant throughout the literature. To think that a sharply defined and characteristic social vocabulary, used by several authors in the same sense, should refer to things that have no existence outside the literary realm seems improbable, at the very least.

It is also significant to observe that, from a sociological standpoint, there is no difference between those works of literature that feature fantastic or fictitious contents and those whose contents are historical or didactic. 'The king shall distribute rings in the hall', states one of the *Cotton Gnomes*. In the historical poem *The Battle of Maldon* (AD 991), the leader of the English troops is called 'the richest' and 'the ring-giver', a tribute of golden rings is demanded, and the warriors recall the *bēotas* they uttered on the mead-bench. Even into the tenth century, the Anglo-Saxon Chronicle speaks of the English king as a *bēag-gifa*, 'ring-giver'. Even if here, almost one hundred years after King Alfred, we might be dealing with titles and representations that are merely traditional, it is next to impossible that such a tradition is only based on poetic fictions and lacks an historical foundation.

Of special value among direct historical sources are the Old English laws, which date back to about AD 600.[13] From them one gets the impression that the 'honour-price system' as a whole had already by that time been supplanted by another system, but that it still lived on in numerous traces. What is new and different is that already

---

[12] K. Guntermann, 'Herrschaftliche und genossenschaftliche Termini (für Gott, Christus, den Teufel und ihre Umgebung) in der geistlichen Epik der Westgermanen', dissertation Kiel, 1910.

[13] F. Liebermann, *Die Gesetze der Angelsachsen* (Halle: Niemeyer, 1903–16); especially useful are the glossaries of legal terms and topics in the second half of vol. 2.

from about 680 on there is mention of purchasing and merchants.[14] A prerequisite to developed trade is a money economy in which money is a purely economic, ethically indifferent instrument that can be earned and spent more or less prosaically. And such an economic system is fundamentally incompatible with the 'honour-price system' in which wealth represents human distinction in the absence of an economic function.[15]

On the other hand, the afterlife of the old order can be inferred on many grounds. The long-lasting, complete identity of ownership and class is remarkable. *Ēadig* and *earm* (as in *Æthelrēd VI*, ca. 1008) are still translated in a Latin paraphrase as *nobili*, *ignobili* with reference to class standing. Not until a translation of the *Laws of Cnut* in the *Quadripartitus* of AD 1114 do those two terms find purely economic expression in Latin *dives* and *pauper*. For a long time, the function of money remains more ideal than that, more ethical. The following things can be bought, according to Liebermann: 'The serf and the wife [... and] intercession from God, from the court, and the authorities'. Moreover, according to that same authority, 'The criminal buys off imprisonment or corporal punishment by paying a fine. By paying wergild, a killer and his kin-group buy off the blood vengeance that is threatened by the kin-group of the slain person. [...] The civil servant who has been dismissed buys back his office from the king.'[16] The place for gift-giving or economic exchange long remains the feast (*Leges Henrici*, section 81, at 1114–18), and the feast enjoys special protection, as we see from the phrases *grið on ealahūse* or *pax que dabitur in ealahūs* 'the peace that prevails in the drinking-hall' (*III Æthelrēd*, section 1.2). Other historical evidence points in the same direction as the laws.[17]

Thus the residual effects of an older economic order can be clearly recognized. It is obvious, though, that this order can no longer have existed in its pure form at the time of the oldest laws; similarly, the *Beowulf* poet does not depict his contemporary world, but rather things from the past that were still comprehensible. Just how long the 'honour-price system' really prevailed is difficult to say, but there are several reasons to see it as common Germanic and, therefore, to date it back to the continental

---

[14] Other sources indicate that trading was active at this time; see F.M. Stenton, *Anglo-Saxon England* (Oxford: Oxford University Press, 1943), 55–56 and 219.

[15] Still, trade is not something quotidian in its beginnings, but is presented as a more or less dangerous, heroic undertaking whereby (for example) hostages are taken, as in Alfred's treaty with King Guthrum's Danes, AD 880–90, so that a person who had become rich through trade was at the same time also distinguished in a moral sense. Indeed, a certain degree of economic success is one of the prerequisites to elevation to the rank of the nobility: see Liebermann, *Gepyncðo, Ehrenrang*, section 6 (ca. AD 1029–60).

[16] Liebermann, glossary, s.v. *Handel*, 2.

[17] Compare D. Whitelock, *The Beginnings of English Society* (Harmondsworth: Penguin, 1952) on the king's presentation of gifts to thegns; the king's dependence on his power of giving (p. 34); large representative expenditures on festive occasions (pp. 58–59); the special prestige of old weapons (p. 95); and presentations of tribute (p. 69).

Germanic period, that is before AD 450, at least in terms of its origins and heyday. Evidence drawn from Tacitus, Old Germanic literature, and various pan-Germanic institutions supports this conclusion.

As is often remarked, the sociological image that Tacitus's *Germania* presents is very similar to what we see in *Beowulf*. Interest on loans is unknown, while offerings of tribute (weapons, horses, jewellery) are made by neighbouring peoples. The peoples of ancient Germania do accept coinage, but it remains foreign to them. The feast is at the centre of political life. The ruler showers his retinue with gifts and gains the means to do so through wars aimed at acquiring loot.[18]

Within Old Germanic literature, the traces of the honour-price system are definitely not restricted to Anglo-Saxon England. When in *Widsith* the generosity and excellence of the Burgundian, Gothic, and Langobardic kings come in for special praise (at lines 66, 89, 70 ff.), one might be tempted to understand this theme as a projection of local English conditions onto the other Germanic regions. Standing in the way of this interpretation is the fact that corresponding phenomena are to be found in Old High German and Old Norse literature. The *Hildebrandslied* makes mention of rings that are presented as gifts of a lord;[19] the Eddic *Hávamál* gives instructions regarding the reciprocal nature of gift-giving; and the kings named in skaldic poetry are likewise given the honorary titles 'ring-givers' or even 'squanderers of gold'.[20]

---

[18] 'To loan out capital at interest and extend it into interest payments is unknown' (chap. 26). 'They take particular pleasure in the gifts of neighbouring tribes … choice horses, splendid weapons, ornamental discs and torques; we have now taught them to take money also' (chap. 15). 'But the mutual settlement of feuds, the forging of marriage bonds, the adoption of leaders, even peace and war are often discussed at their feasts' (chap. 22). 'The means for this munificence comes from robbery and war' (chap. 14). *Tacitus: Germania*, trans. J.B. Rives (Oxford: Clarendon Press, 1999). Cf. Rudolf Much, *Die Germania des Tacitus* (Heidelberg, 1937), esp. the subject index s.v. the entries *Gold* and *Geschenke* and the discussion of how trustworthy the *Germania* is.

[19] Old High German *truhtīn*; cf. OE *dryhten* 'lord'.

[20] A systematic survey of Old Germanic literature lies beyond the scope of this essay. However, there already exist several studies that approach our problem from the point of view of cultural history, sociology, or economic history. Vilhelm Grønbech, *Kultur und Religion der Germanen*, 2 vols (Hamburg, 1937) [trans. into English as *The Culture of the Teutons*, 2 vols (London: Oxford University Press, 1931)], offers rich material drawn from Nordic literature. The sociologist Marcel Mauss, *The Gift: Forms and Functions of Exchange in Archaic Societies* (London: Cohen & West, 1954) provides a perceptive, comprehensive study of the obligation of gift-giving as a predecessor to the contract, together with a study of *monnaie de renommé* (or what here is called 'honour-price') in which evidence from Germanic sources, among others, is mentioned. Wilhelm Gerloff, *Die Entstehung des Geldes und die Anfänge des Geldwesens*, 2nd edn (Frankfurt am Main: Klostermann, 1943) touches repeatedly on the ancient Germanic world, for example with regard to the honorary titles of Nordic kings (p. 37) and 'hoard money' (or 'honour price') among the peoples of ancient Germania (p. 74).

Finally, what speaks for the existence of the honour-price system among the peoples of ancient Germania is the fact that various Germanic institutions that may repel us today are only comprehensible when one sees them as stemming from this old order. Relevant here is the well-known harshness of Germanic law vis-à-vis theft (which may be punishable by the death penalty, enslavement, or banishment). This harshness becomes comprehensible when we have arrived at the perception that property served as an index of moral worth. When the early Germanic thief stole something, what he took into his possession was not only a thing; he also adorned himself with virtue, honour, power, and general human value to which he had no right. In addition, he robbed another person of this same part of his prestige; thus he acted in the same manner as a plagiarist does today. For this reason, in a society that had the highest regard for those values, he had to face the prospect of most serious punishment.[21]

When we today contemplate the institution of wergild, we may find dubious the idea that a human life can be completely paid for with gold and goods.[22] If, however, wealth is the measure of a person's worth, then the killer or his kin-group is paying penance though a loss of prestige, a grievous loss in Germanic society. Also the widespread custom of 'purchasing' a bride is no longer to be understood as a degradation of the woman to the status of an economic object (an idea that runs counter to the otherwise elevated status of women in Germanic society).[23] Instead, we may grasp that only a man of high honour can take the bride as his own.

One source of royal wealth is tribute.[24] The more tribute a ruler receives, the greater his honour. All peoples across the sea are compelled to pay tribute to Scyld, the ancestor of Hrothgar, and thus he is called 'a good king'. Before the battle of Maldon the Vikings demand tribute not in the form of commodities or items of normal economic exchange, but rather golden rings.

Since the value of items of jewellery is more ideal than material, the rich burial deposits that one encounters in the course of archaeological excavations become more intelligible. In a certain sense, these things are the embodiment of the praiseworthy deeds of the deceased, who retains them in the other world as a sign of honour and a confirmation of his or her personal identity. In any event, they are much more strongly connected to the moral identity of the deceased than goods of a merely economic nature could be.

---

[21] These circumstances still have an effect today on English law, which, influenced only slightly by Roman law, has maintained the Germanic legacy with greater fidelity. There theft is classified as a felony. Until 1828, instances of theft above the value of 12 pence were in principle punishable by death. Still today, English law calls for lifetime imprisonment for theft of official documents (see the *Encyclopaedia Britannica*, s.v. 'larceny'). These examples are in complete accord with public opinion, which, in Germanic countries, generally condemns crimes involving property much more harshly than is seen elsewhere.

[22] Cf. Liebermann; Grønbech, vol. 2: 293.

[23] *Exeter Maxims*, line 82; Liebermann; Grønbech, vol. 2: 283.

[24] Whitelock, *Beginnings of English Society*, 69; Gerloff, *Die Entstehung*, 74; Tacitus.

It is not impossible, indeed it is even probable, that the function of wealth as a sign of distinction, and hence the 'honour-price system' as a whole, is not a unique historical phenomenon limited to the peoples of ancient Germania, but is a general characteristic of archaic cultures. As Wilhelm Gerloff has written, 'One of the most age-old and common means to satisfy the desire for admiration that dominates social life is the hoarding of certain goods and, on certain occasions, their conspicuous expenditure. The origins of money are to be found in the dedication of certain goods for such purposes.'[25] Indeed, phenomena parallel to the social order that is represented in *Beowulf* can be found in the Homeric world, as well as among the people of present-day Polynesia, not to mention many other peoples both past and present.[26]

---

[25] Gerloff, *Die Entstehung*, 24.

[26] For details concerning the honour-price, the firm connection between virtue, power, and wealth, and the obligation of wealthy members of society to give gifts, see Mauss, *The Gift*; Bronislaw Malinowski, *Argonauts of the Western Pacific* (London: Routledge 1922); J. Huizinga, *Homo Ludens* (London: Routledge, 1949); and H.M. Chadwick, *The Heroic Age* (Cambridge: Cambridge University Press, 1912).

Part III
Other Topics and Approaches

6

Style

The study of style has long held a central place in Old English literary studies.[1] One reason for this fact is the exceptional character of Old English poetry, and certain examples of early Middle English verse as well, when compared with almost any verse in the later history of English literature from Chaucer to the late nineteenth century. Much of this special character relates to the alliterative verse form that Old English poets shared with poets composing in the Old Saxon, Old High German, and Old Norse traditions and that is almost certainly a legacy from the common Germanic era, when all northern poetry was oral poetry. This legacy was strong enough to exert a conservative influence on Old English verse, regardless of what must often have been its written mode of composition, up to the end of the Anglo-Saxon period, when new poetic forms came increasingly into favour through both French and Latinate influences. Indeed, a case can be made that the special rhythmic character of English-language poetry in general, when compared with the rhythm of verse composed in the Romance languages of Europe, derives from its Germanic alliterative substrate.

Such stylistic features of Old English verse as the use of special poetic diction, much of it metaphorical, including the particular device known as the kenning;[2] frequent verbal

---

1. Daniel G. Calder offers an historical survey, 'The Study of Style in Old English Poetry: A Historical Introduction', in *Old English Poetry: Essays on Style*, ed. Daniel G. Calder (Berkeley: University of California Press, 1979), 1–65.

2. One study that remains essential, though dated in some ways, is Henry Cecil Wyld, 'Diction and Imagery in Anglo-Saxon Poetry', *Essays and Studies* 11 (1925): 49–91, repr. in *Essential Articles*, 183–227. Yet more authoritative is Arthur Gilchrist Brodeur's chapter 'The Diction of *Beowulf*', chap. 1 of his book *The Art of Beowulf* (Berkeley: University of California Press, 1959). Note also Thomas Gardner, 'The Old English Kenning: A Characteristic Feature of Germanic Poetical Diction?', *MPh* 67 (1969): 109–17.

repetitions based on flexible systems of formulaic diction;[3] a generous use of compound diction, compound nouns and adjectives in particular;[4] and the syntactic device known as variation, or grammatical apposition – 'the very soul of the Old English poetical style'[5] – are now seen as effortlessly wedded to the old alliterative verse form, as opposed to being awkward features of a primitive style. Each of these stylistic features has received ample attention in the critical literature. Stanley B. Greenfield and Daniel G. Calder offer a succinct account of them, with illustrative examples, in their *New Critical History of Old English Literature*,[6] while Andy Orchard devotes a key chapter of his *Critical Companion to Beowulf* to a richly elaborated discussion of the *Beowulf* poet's deployment of alliteration, assonance, rhyme, synonyms, compounds, and formulaic verbal repetition, among other stylistic elements, with *Beowulf* taken as a supreme representative of the 'classic' mode of Old English verse.[7] Other subjects of attention in the critical literature are such characteristic non-structural features of the verse as litotes, which is often used for ironic effect, and the use of superlatives.[8] The use of rhetorical figures and tropes derived from the Latin school tradition, as is discussed in Chapter 3, has likewise been of interest in the critical literature, as is also true of types of rhetorical patterning that are practically inescapable in literary composition, including parallelism, antithesis, and chiasmus, but that take on special characteristics in the stylized medium of Old English verse.[9]

---

[3]   On formula and formulaic system in Old English verse see Chapter 4 above, 'Orality', esp. n. 4, where reference is made to studies by Donald K. Fry and others.

[4]   In addition to chap. 1 of Arthur G. Brodeur's *The Art of Beowulf*, note Appendix B to that book (pp. 254–71), where Brodeur analyses the compounds formed in Old English poetry on fifty-seven different base-words. In 'Compound Diction and the Style of *Beowulf*', *ES* 62 (1981): 489–503, repr. with revisions as chap. 6 of my book *Beowulf: The Poem and Its Tradition* (Cambridge MA: Harvard University Press, 1983), I relate this poem's handling of compound diction to the oral-formulaic tradition in which it is grounded.

[5]   *Klaeber's Beowulf*, p. cxviii; the jointly authored fourth edition repeats the phrase as it appears in Klaeber's prior editions. See on this topic the astute observations of Arthur G. Brodeur, 'Variation', chap. 2 of his *The Art of Beowulf*, repr. in Fulk, 66–87; and Fred C. Robinson, 'Two Aspects of Variation in Old English Poetry', in Calder, *Essays on Style*, 127–45, repr. in Robinson, 71–86. Note also Robinson's book *Beowulf and the Appositive Style* (Knoxville: University of Tennessee Press, 1985), from which significant excerpts are reprinted in Howe, 73–98.

[6]   Greenfield & Calder, chap. 5, 'Some Remarks on the Nature and Quality of Old English Poetry'.

[7]   Andy Orchard, *A Critical Companion to Beowulf* (Toronto: University of Toronto Press, 2003), chap. 3 (pp. 57–97).

[8]   See most recently Roberta Frank, 'The Incomparable Wryness of Old English Poetry', in *Inside Old English: Essays in Honour of Bruce Mitchell*, ed. John Walmsley (Oxford: Blackwell, 2006), 59–73; cf. Leslie Harris, 'Litotes and Superlative in *Beowulf*', *ES* 69 (1988): 1–11.

[9]   In a study that has retained much of its value, Adeline Courtney Bartlett, *The Larger Rhetorical Patterns in Old English Poetry* (New York: Columbia University Press, 1935), discussed such stylistic features as these as a means of organizing whole blocks of verse. In my article 'Ring Composition and the Structure of *Beowulf*', *PMLA* 94 (1979): 924–35, I propose that chiasmus is of particular importance as a stylistic and structural principle in *Beowulf*, sometimes taking on complex 'layered' forms. Others too have made such claims, which admittedly can rely to some extent on subjective judgements as regards what constitutes balance and symmetry in a literary composition.

The exceptional power of convention in the corpus of Old English verse is brought out by Elizabeth M. Tyler in her 2006 article 'Poetics and the Past', as well as in her book *Old English Poetics*, published that same year.[10] In Tyler's view, the study of poetic diction – the language of treasure, in particular – helps to open up to view 'the social and political ideologies of Old English secular poetry in late Anglo-Saxon England' ('Poetics and the Past', p. 225). The language of treasure is 'a part of the fabric of poetic discourse in a manner analogous to stylistic phenomena such as formulas, variation, and kennings: you almost cannot have an Old English poem without it' (p. 228). She develops the thesis, as well, that the traditional poetics of Old English verse continued to be used as late as the beginning of the eleventh century not as a form of nostalgia, but because 'it played a vital role in shaping the Anglo-Saxon relationship with the past' (p. 250).[11]

Old English prose, too, has increasingly been subjected to analysis in terms of its stylistic tendencies and effects. The homiletic style of Wulfstan, which was expertly analysed by Angus McIntosh in his 1949 study 'Wulfstan's Prose', calls out for attention seeing how oratorical that author could be, particularly in his *tour de force* 'The Sermon of Wolf to the English' (*Sermo Lupi ad Anglos*).[12] Ælfric's more limpid and elegant prose has not lent itself so readily to stylistic analysis except as regards his use, particularly in his saints' lives though also elsewhere, of a rhythmic and alliterative form that can equally well be described as poetic prose or prose-like poetry, for it has a loosely four-stress rhythmic pulse and also observes, though again somewhat loosely, the structural alliteration that goes far to define Old English verse as such. Ælfric, however, shuns Old English poetic diction, with its martial associations. Correspondingly, he rarely employs the syntactic device of variation, a generative engine of Old English verse as well as an unmistakable element of its conventional style.

The character of Ælfric's alliterative prose was discussed at some length by John Collins Pope in the Introduction to his 1966–67 edition of certain of Ælfric's sermons.[13] Pope concluded that Ælfric's sermons might best be printed as a kind of verse, rather than as prose, though the latter practice continues to be favoured by most editors. More recently, in

---

[10] Elizabeth M. Tyler, 'Poetics and the Past: Making History with Old English Poetry', in *Narrative and History in the Early Medieval West*, ed. Elizabeth M. Tyler and Ross Balzaretti (Turnhout: Brepols, 2006), 225–50; and Tyler, *Old English Poetics: The Aesthetics of the Familiar in Anglo-Saxon England* (York: York Medieval Press, 2006).

[11] Compare the somewhat different arguments advanced by Renée R. Trilling, *The Aesthetics of Nostalgia: Historical Representation in Old English Verse* (Toronto: University of Toronto Press, 2009), on the relationship between poetic form and historical consciousness during the Anglo-Saxon period.

[12] Angus McIntosh, 'Wulfstan's Prose', *PBA* 35 (1949): 109–42, repr. in *British Academy Papers on Anglo-Saxon England*, ed. E.G. Stanley (Oxford: Oxford University Press, 1990), 111–44. Cf. Andy Orchard's study 'Crying Wolf: Oral Style and the *Sermones Lupi*', *ASE* 21 (1992): 239–64. A text of the *Sermo Lupi* is included in Mitchell & Robinson at pp. 329–36, and there is a valuable stand-alone edition: *Sermo Lupi ad Anglos*, ed. Dorothy Whitelock, 3rd edn (Exeter: Exeter University Press, 1976, first published 1939).

[13] *Homilies of Ælfric: A Supplementary Collection*, ed. John Collins Pope, 2 vols, EETS 259–60 (London: Oxford University Press, 1967–68), vol. 1: 105–35. See also Haruko Momma, 'Rhythm and Alliteration: Styles of Ælfric's Prose up to the *Lives of the Saints*', in *Anglo-Saxon Styles*, 253–69.

his 2005 essay 'The Relation between Old English Alliterative Verse and Ælfric's Alliterative Prose', Bruce Mitchell has pointed out that there are parallels to Ælfric's style in certain poems of the Anglo-Saxon tradition, thus showing that Ælfric was not wholly an innovator in this regard.[14] And breaking yet more sharply with the view that Ælfric wrote in a kind of 'verse-like' hybrid form of prose, Thomas A. Bredehoft has argued that Ælfric may have looked upon himself as a poet working, though at a relatively late date, within a continuing Old English verse tradition.[15]

The style of the Anglo-Saxon Chronicle, too, has come under scrutiny. As Cecily Clark pointed out in her 1971 study 'The Narrative Mode of *The Anglo-Saxon Chronicle* before the Conquest', a distinction can usefully be made between the abbreviated style of most of the Chronicle's annals and the expansive style adopted in certain blocks of years, including those entries that tell of the Viking wars of King Alfred the Great and of the troubled reign of King Æthelred the Unready.[16] Likewise Richard P. Horvath, in his study 'History, Narrative, and the Ideological Mode of *The Peterborough Chronicle*',[17] has called attention to stylistic disjunctions in the Peterborough Chronicle (the E version of the Chronicle), particularly at those points where Norman atrocities are recounted. Horvath argues that in these post-Conquest entries the mode of historiography varies 'from annal and chronicle', seen as dispassionate modes of narrative, 'to what we might regard as interpretive history', which is sometimes passionately emotive and has an ideological dimension (p. 123). More recently, in his book *Textual Histories*, Thomas A. Bredehoft has offered an integrated analysis of the Chronicle in its manuscript context, discussing (among other topics) the problematic distinction between prose and verse in certain late entries.[18]

When deployed with care, the stylistic analysis of a given work has the potential to resolve questions about that work's authorship, date, or geographical provenance, and scholarship along such lines has always been valued for that reason. The poems that were once attributed

---

[14]   Bruce Mitchell, 'The Relation between Old English Alliterative Verse and Ælfric's Alliterative Prose', in *Latin Learning and English Lore: Studies in Anglo-Saxon Literature for Michael Lapidge*, ed. Katherine O'Brien O'Keeffe and Andy Orchard, 2 vols (Toronto: University of Toronto Press, 2005), vol. 2: 284–304.

[15]   Thomas A. Bredehoft, *Early English Metre* (Toronto: University of Toronto Press, 2005) 81–98. Cf. Bredehoft, 'The Boundaries Between Verse and Prose in Old English Literature', in *Old English Literature in Its Manuscript Context*, ed. Joyce Tally Lionarons (Morgantown: West Virginia University Press, 2004), 139–72, and Bredehoft, *Authors, Audiences, and Old English Verse* (Toronto: University of Toronto Press, 2009), 146–70.

[16]   Cecily Clark, 'The Narrative Mode of *The Anglo-Saxon Chronicle* before the Conquest', in *England before the Conquest: Studies in Primary Sources Presented to Dorothy Whitelock*, ed. Peter Clemoes and Kathleen Hughes (Cambridge: Cambridge University Press, 1971), 215–35.

[17]   Richard P. Horvath, 'History, Narrative, and the Ideological Mode of *The Peterborough Chronicle*', *Mediaevalia* 17 (1994 for 1991): 123–48.

[18]   Thomas A. Bredehoft, *Textual Histories: Readings in the Anglo-Saxon Chronicle* (Toronto: University of Toronto Press, 2001). Additionally, in his study 'History and Memory in the Anglo-Saxon Chronicle', in Johnson & Treharne, 109–21, Bredehoft explores the effect of annalists' frequent use of superlative expressions. A recent collection of critical essays offers many valuable insights into the narrative style of different parts of the Chronicle: this is *Reading the Anglo-Saxon Chronicle: Language, Literature, History*, ed. Alice Jorgensen (Turnhout: Brepols, 2010).

to the late seventh-century poet Cædmon on the basis of their inclusion in the Junius manuscript (Oxford, Bodleian Library MS Junius 11), whose contents are reminiscent of the types of poetry attributed to Cædmon by the Venerable Bede, for example, are now no longer ascribed to that author since their language and style must pertain to a later date. In like manner, in his 1986 article 'Contrasting Features in the Non-Ælfrician Lives', Hugh Magennis demonstrates that four works of prose hagiography included in the major medieval collection of Ælfric's saints' lives (London, British Library MS Cotton Julius E.vii) cannot have been written by Ælfric himself, for they are stylistically distinct as regards such matters as syntax, vocabulary, the handling of direct speech, and the treatment of sources.[19] Their exclusion from the Ælfrician canon is thereby confirmed. Moreover, Magennis demonstrates that each of these anonymous lives must be of separate authorship, for they show no stylistic or linguistic unity among themselves. Although comparisons of this kind may seem to exclude exceptionalism, or the possibility that a given author experimented now in one style and now in another, a cautious analysis will take this possibility into account.

In retrospect, an alertness to the stylistic effects in play in individual Old English poems seems to have been at its peak during the 1960s and 1970s, as New Critical impulses filtered into the criticism of Old English literature from other periods of literary studies. This was a period of discontent with the notion that the meaning of a poem could be discerned without precise attention to the aesthetic effects of particular lexical choices. Such matters as tone, aural patterning, and verbal ambiguity were at the forefront of critics' consciousness. One leading scholar-critic of this orientation was Stanley B. Greenfield, who in his 1972 book *The Interpretation of Old English Poems* presented a series of probing inquiries into the linguistic bases for interpreting Old English texts.[20] Chapter 4 of this study, entitled 'The Play of Sound and Sense', identifies many examples of verbal ambiguity, while in other parts of the book Greenfield discusses poetic diction, the formula, variation, the verse form, and syntax. A single passage from this chapter can serve as an example of this method, with its occasional problematic aspects.

The example is taken from Greenfield's discussion of wordplay in *The Seafarer*, where, in his view, 'different word repetitions', ones that involve play on two or more different meanings of a word, 'cohere into a pattern of meaning for the poem' (p. 88). Study of this poem's style thus unlocks its meaning:[21]

> In lines 41b and 43a, *dryhten* is repeated with two different referents, an earthly lord and God: '[There is no man] whose *lord* [*dryhten*] is so dear to him that he will never have a care as to

[19] Hugh Magennis, 'Contrasting Features in the Non-Ælfrician Lives in the Old English Lives of Saints', *Anglia* 104 (1986): 316–48. The works in question are *The Legend of the Seven Sleepers*, *The Life of St Mary of Egypt*, *The Life of St Eustace*, and *The Life of St Euphrosyne*. These same non-Ælfrician saints' lives are discussed from different perspectives by the contributors to *Anonymous Interpolations in Ælfric's Lives of Saints*, ed. Robin Norris, Old English Newsletter Subsidia 35 (Kalamazoo, MI: Medieval Institute Publications, 2011).

[20] Stanley B. Greenfield, *The Interpretation of Old English Poems* (London: Routledge & Kegan Paul, 1972).

[21] Greenfield, *The Interpretation*, 88–89. Omitted from the passage as quoted here are Greenfield's inset quotations of the Old English text. Instead, the key OE vocabulary is inserted between square brackets.

what the *Lord* [*dryhten*] will assign him on his sea journey.' Somewhat later in the poem, in lines 64b–88, the words *dream, blæd* and *duguð* are similarly used in two distinct senses, with reference to heavenly joys and consortium on the one hand, and with references to departed social communion on the other. The speaker, reaffirming his decision to embark upon his voyage, will do so 'because dearer to me are the joys [*dreamas*] of the Lord than this dead life, transitory on earth'. It is best for a man, he says, to fight against the devil to achieve 'the glory [*blæd*] of eternal life, joy [*blæd*] among the hosts [*dugeðum*]'. These *dreamas*, this *blæd*, are of the divine variety, and the *duguð* is the host of angelic comrades. But immediately following this last phrase, the speaker reminisces in elegiac mood about the days that have departed: 'The days have departed, all the pomp of earth's kingdom. [...] This host [*duguð*] has all fallen, joys [*dreamas*] have departed, the weaker live on and possess this world, possess it with toil. Glory [*blæd*] is laid low.'

Greenfield goes on to argue that the wordplay in the latter part of this passage cuts against the poem's intellectual content, which in his view affirms the need of the Christian to renounce earthly pleasures for the sake of salvation (pp. 89–90):

> The pattern thus established serves to emphasize, it seems to me, an ambivalence of feeling in the emotional or tonal quality of the poem: it is certainly the speaker's recognition of the transience of earthly life that urges him to seek the security [of heaven], [...] but the repetitive use of the same words with earthly referents suggests that he is still wistful in his backward glance at a departed golden age. It is wrong, I think, for us to ignore or to twist this aspect of the poem's meaning to bring, as some critics would insist, tonal unity into harmony with its intellectual direction.

Greenfield's analysis reveals the complexities and, to some extent, the self-contradictory dimensions of *The Seafarer*. Still, as in much New Critical scholarship, his conclusions rest to some extent on what remains a subjective reading of the text. Is the poet indeed 'wistful in his backward glance' at the things of the earth? Indeed, when allusion is made to the ruined civilizations of the past, does the poet mean for us to think of these civilizations in terms of 'a departed golden age', as Greenfield asserts? Or do they illustrate the ultimate vanity of earthly things? While the pattern of linguistic wordplay to which Greenfield calls attention ought to be evident enough to any vigilant reader of the poem, the tone of this passage, and hence the poem's meaning, would still seem to be open to question.

A Selection from the Criticism

The critical selection that follows, by J.R. Hall, explores the style and meaning of the Old English poem known as *The Rune Poem*. Unlike *The Seafarer*, this poem had attracted only occasional attention in the prior critical literature even though it had long been studied as a chief source of knowledge about Old English runes and their names. Hall approaches this work just as he might any other poem in the Anglo-Saxon corpus despite its unusual form, by which one rune after another of the Old English runic alphabet is set on the page, each one initiating a short versified statement in which that name, or that concept, is given some apt characterization. Pointing out numerous examples of verbal ambiguity in the poem, Hall argues that such wordplay allows the poet to shift rapidly between antithetical aspects of the created world. Ambiguity can even take the form of punning, as when the noun *treow* is used in a manner that denotes both 'wood' (cf. modern English *tree*) or 'faith' (cf. modern English *truth*). Characteristic of this poet's riddle-like art are thus lightning-like shifts in perspective.[22]

One incidental aspect of Hall's essay that might be overlooked is that, unlike many critics of a secular orientation, he unobtrusively affirms his personal alignment with the Christian worldview that underlies *The Rune Poem* and virtually all other Old English literature that survives. This is so not just when he quotes the poet's closing allusion to *godes dom* ('God's judgement' or 'eternal life'), but also when he speaks of God's 'allowing the earth' to bring forth its fruits for rich and poor, or when he speaks of the oak tree as being 'made part of the world by God' as a benefit, ultimately, to humankind. His criticism of Old English literature thus has a double perspective, as he is in a position to see it both as a sympathetic insider, as it were, and as a dispassionate scholar trained in twentieth-century modes of critical analysis.

J.R. Hall taught for many years on the faculty of the Department of English at the University of Mississippi before recently retiring from his position there. He was awarded the PhD in English from the University of Notre Dame in 1973 after having previously studied economics at St John Fisher College in Rochester, New York. A leading specialist in the poems of the Junius manuscript, he has also written authoritatively on the history of editing Old English texts and the history of Anglo-Saxon scholarship, especially in nineteenth-century America. Several of his important critical studies are cited elsewhere in the present book.[23]

For Further Reading

Beechy, Tiffany. 2010. *The Poetics of Old English*. Burlington: Ashgate.
Calder, Daniel G. 1986. 'Figurative Language and its Contexts in *Andreas*: A Study in Medieval Expressionism'. In *Greenfield Studies*, 115–36.
Dance, Richard. 2010. 'The Old English Language and the Alliterative Tradition'. In Saunders, 34–50.
Davies, Joshua. 2013. 'The Literary Languages of Old English'. In the *Cambridge History*, 257–77.
Godden, Malcolm. 1992. 'Literary Language'. In *The Cambridge History of the English Language, vol. 1: The Beginnings to 1066*, ed. Richard Hogg, 490–535. Cambridge: Cambridge University Press.

---

[22] Studies of Old English runes and/or *The Rune Poem* with a bearing on Hall's essay are cited above in Chapter 3, notes 19–24; the writings of R.I. Page are indispensable in this regard. The chief edition of the poem is *The Old English Rune Poem: A Critical Edition*, ed. Maureen Halsall (Toronto: University of Toronto Press, 1981). See further Margaret Clunies Ross, 'The Anglo-Saxon and Norse *Rune Poems*: A Comparative Study', *ASE* 19 (1990): 23–39, and, on a related set of texts, Roberta Dewa, 'The Runic Riddles of the Exeter Book: Language Games and Anglo-Saxon Scholarship', *Nottingham Medieval Studies* 39 (1995): 26–36.

[23] At Chapter 1, n. 2; Chapter 9, n. 34; and Chapter 11, n. 23.

Howe, Nicholas. 2003. 'What We Talk About When We Talk About Style'. In *Anglo-Saxon Styles*, 169–78.

Leslie, R.F. 1959. 'Analysis of Stylistic Devices and Effects in Anglo-Saxon Literature'. In *Stil- und Formprobleme in der Literatur*, ed. Paul Böckmann, 129–36. Heidelberg: C. Winter, 1959. Repr. in *Essential Articles*, 255–63.

Momma, Haruko. 2013. 'Old English Poetic Form: Genre, Style, Prosody'. In the *Cambridge History*, 278–308.

O'Brien O'Keeffe, Katherine. 1997. 'Diction, Variation, the Formula'. In the *Beowulf Handbook*, 85–104.

Scragg, Donald G. 2013. 'The Nature of Old English Verse'. In Godden & Lapidge, 50–65.

Stanley, E.G. 1956. 'Old English Poetic Diction and the Interpretation of *The Wanderer, The Seafarer*, and *The Penitent's Prayer*'. *Anglia* 73 (1956): 413–66. Repr. in his volume *A Collection of Papers with Emphasis on Old English Literature* (Toronto: Pontifical Institute of Mediaeval Studies, 1987), 234–80.

J.R. Hall, 'Perspective and Wordplay in the Old English *Rune Poem*' (1977)[1]

The poet of the *Rune Poem* uses a tight formal structure. He takes up, in order, twenty-nine letters of the runic alphabet and briefly describes the object or concept that each letter signifies. Despite the limitations of this form, the poet often manages to suggest multiple aspects of the created world through wordplay and the use of comparison and contrast. Some scholars believe that early Germanic peoples regarded the runes as possessing magical or religious power.[2] The power vitalizing this poem, however, is the power of the human intellect itself to see the realities that the rune-names designate in shifting perspective.

The wordplay begins in the second stanza:

> ᚢ (ur) byþ anmod   and oferhyrned,
> felafrecne deor,   feohteþ mid hornum,
> mære morstapa;   þæt is modig wuht.[3]   (4–6)

[The wild ox is resolute and is over-horned (surmounted with towering horns?); it is an extremely dangerous beast, it uses its horns for fighting, that famed moorland-dweller; that is one brave creature!]

---

[1] J.R. Hall, 'Perspective and Wordplay in the Old English *Rune Poem*', *Neophilologus* 61 (1977): 453–60. Used with permission from Springer Print and Business Media. Where editorial translations are provided, they are set between square brackets.

[2] For a list of studies on this question, see the select bibliography compiled by A. Hacikyan, "The Runes of Old English Poetry," *Revue de l'Université d'Ottawa*, 43 (1973), 74.

[3] Citation of the *Rune Poem* is from the edition by Elliott V.K. Dobbie, *The Anglo-Saxon Minor Poems*, ASPR 6 (New York, 1942). Citation of other OE poems is also to texts in ASPR.

To stress the resolute ferocity of the wild ox, the poet employs an envelope pattern, *anmod ... modig*, which is perhaps best captured in translation as "single-minded ... tough-minded." The double reference to horns, *oferhyrned ... mid hornum*, reinforces this pattern. Scholars have long differed, however, on the precise meaning of Divide as 'ofer-hyrned'. unattested elsewhere in OE. According to one interpretation, the word means "having horns above," a reading that is etymologically defensible and aptly descriptive.[4] But the same can be said for the alternate interpretation, "having great horns," a detail that bears on the use of the horns as a weapon.[5] That both aspects of the horns – their location and character – would have been important to an Anglo-Saxon audience is shown by an OE gloss of *unicornis*, which brings together the same two features:

> Þæt deor hæfþ ænne horn bufan þam twam eagum, swa strangne and swa scearpne þæt he fiht wið þone myclan ylp, and hine oft gewundaþ on ðære wambe oþ dead.[6]

> [That wild beast has a single horn up above his two eyes, such a strong and sharp one that he fights against the massive elephant and often pierces its belly with a mortal wound.]

Each of the proposed meanings of *oferhyrned* conveys accurate and valuable information. I suggest that the word was coined by the poet himself and that he intended it to be understood in both senses. The capacity of *oferhyrned* to evoke different aspects of the creature accords with the capacity of the wild ox itself not only to be dangerously equipped (*byþ*, *is*) but also to act dangerously (*feohteþ*). Translating the unique compound quite literally as "over-horned" preserves an ambiguity used to good purpose.

The stanza should not be considered simply by itself, however. In describing the next rune-word, the poet exploits a humorous juxtaposition:

> ᚦ (ðorn) byþ ðearle scearp;   ðegna gehwylcum
> anfeng ys yfyl,   ungemetun reþe
> manna gehwylcun   ðe him mid resteð.   (7–9)

> [The thorn is exceedingly sharp; it is an evil thing for anyone to grasp; its savagery against those who lie down amidst them knows no limit.]

---

[4] For this reading see Bosworth-Toller, s.v. *oferhyrned;* J.R. Clark Hall's *Dictionary*, s.v. *oferhyrned*; and Theodor Grienberger, "Das ags. Runengedicht," *Anglia*, 45 (1921), 206.

[5] For this interpretation see Bruce Dickins, *Runic and Heroic Poems* (Cambridge 1915), p. 13; R.I. Page, *An Introduction to English Runes* (London, 1973), p. 73 ("huge horns"); and cf. Grein-Köhler, s.v. *oferhyrned* "alte cornutus."

[6] London, British Library MS Cotton Julius A.ii; see Thomas Wright, ed., *Anglo-Saxon and Old English Vocabularies*, 2nd edn revised by Richard Wülcker (London, 1884), vol. 1: 319–20.

Horns and thorns: two objects of a decidedly different yet similar nature. As the double meaning of *oferhyrned* indicates, horns come from above and are very large; on the other hand, thorns come from below (as the man accidentally resting among them soon discovers) and are of course very small. Although posing a less apparent threat than horns, thorns do present a danger, one that must not be overlooked. To drive home the point, the poet, with obvious hyperbole, describes thorns as though he is still describing the wild ox. Thorns are "evil ... immeasurably savage." The word used for "savage," *reðe*, occurs elsewhere in OE in reference to wild animals.[7]

The effectiveness of the stanzas on the wild ox and the thorn depends in part on a contrast in content between the stanzas themselves. In the *rad* or "riding" stanza, the contrast is internal:

> ᚱ (rad) byþ recyde   rinca gehwylcum
> sefte, and swiþhwæt   ðam ðe sitteþ on ufan
> meare mægenheardum   ofer milpaþas.   (13–15)

[Horseback-riding is an easy thing for warriors in the hall, and very strenuous for one who is mounted on a hardy steed on paths that stretch for miles.]

Here the poet, apparently alluding to the custom of warriors boasting of their prowess in the mead-hall, suggests that to talk of bold feats of riding is one thing, but to perform them is an entirely different matter. Just as a man must be wary in his dealings with different elements of nature, so must he be careful not to misjudge his own ability. Reality sometimes diverges from one's expectations, a lesson reflected in a poetic technique of the stanza itself. The yoking of *sefte* "easy" with *swiþhwæt* "very difficult" by both alliteration and the use of *and* – instead of a disjunction – implies a parallel, but the two words in fact have contrasting semantic values.

Antithesis between different aspects of the same concept or object is fundamental to the poet's mode of thought. In lines 19–31, in fact, the technique of double focus informs four of five stanzas. *Gyfu* "a gift" brings not only honor to the generous man but also assistance to the destitute (19–21); *hægl* "hail," a grain when it falls from heaven in storms, later turns to water (25–26); *nyd* "trouble" is oppressive to the heart, yet it may become a help for man (27–28); *is* "ice," though very cold and slippery, glistens like jewels (29–31).

The *hægl*, *nyd*, and *is* stanzas merit further consideration as a group. Ralph V.W. Elliott has observed that, in the ancient Germanic alphabet, the *fuþark*, the rune for *nyd* may have been placed between the runes for *hægl* and *is* because these two natural elements are major causes of "trouble" for mankind.[8] The same idea seems implicit in the OE poet's treatment of the three runes. Hail comes in storms, and ice is very

---

[7]   See Bosworth-Toller, s.v. *reðe*, II; see also s.v. *reðness*, II.
[8]   *Runes: An Introduction* (Manchester, 1959), p. 58.

cold and slippery; either, like trouble, is oppressive. But the poet does not focus exclusively on the negative aspects of these rune-words. In the second part of each stanza, he points to mitigating or redemptive aspects: hail changes to water; trouble may become a help; ice is fair to the gaze.[9] Moreover, the grouping of *hægl*, *nyd*, and *is* is itself flanked on either side by runic images – *wen* "joy" and *ger* "year" – which the poet so defines as to compensate for the three intervening challenges to human serenity. Men experience joy when they have *byrga geniht* "the (material) abundance of cities" (24b), and at the fertile time of the year God allows the earth to bring forth *beorhte bleda* "bright fruit" for rich and poor (34a). Hence, the perils of hail, trouble, and ice are offset by strategically placed images of plenitude, as well as by moderating features of their own.

Similarly, in the stanza on the yew the poet presents an instance in which a tree of coarse appearance is transformed into a source of material comfort for man:

> ᛇ (eoh) byþ utan   unsmeþe treow,
> heard, hrusan fæst,   hyrde fyres,
> wyrtrumun underwreþyd,   wyn on eþle.   (35–37)

[The yew is a rough tree on its exterior; it is a hard wood, planted firmly in the ground, a keeper of fire, undergirded by roots; it is a joy to have on one's property.]

The poet dramatizes the transformation of the yew, from a tree into firewood, by a sudden shift of perspective. After describing the yew as an object of nature for three hemistichs, he abruptly calls the yew "a keeper of fire." Thus personified, the rough and immobile tree assumes a new dimension. But before this image is resolved, the poet, in another sudden shift, again focuses on the yew in its natural setting, *wyrtrumun underwreþyd* "supported by roots." Only then does he complete the stanza with another reference to firewood. The yew as tree, as firewood, as tree, as firewood: such an intertwining of references occurs nowhere else in the poem. The key to the poet's purpose is found in the insertion of *wyrtrumun underwreþyd* after *hyrde fyres*, a contrast that turns on the idea of dependency. In the hearth the yew as "a keeper of fire" sustains flame; in the ground the yew as a tree is itself "supported by roots." Although more imposing as an object of nature, the yew is, paradoxically, more independent when working in the service of man. The final half-line celebrates the transformation, completing the stanza on an upbeat. The yew becomes a "joy in the home." The description of the yew, begun in the realm of nature, concludes in the realm of spirit.

---

[9] The special relationship between the hypermetric *hægl* and *nyd* stanzas is discussed in detail by Frederick G. Jones, "The Hypermetric Lines of the *Rune Poem*," *Neuphilologische Mitteilungen*, 74 (1973), 224–31.

The runic stanza for the oak also focuses on a tree in its various manifestations. Here the distinction is between the oak as a producer of acorns and as a source of ship timber:

ᚪ (ac) byþ on eorþan   elda bearnum
flæsces fodor,   fereþ gelome
ofer ganotes bæþ;   garsecg fandaþ
hwæþer ac hæbbe   æþele treowe.   (78–80)

[The oak, on land, provides nourishment for meat for the children of men; it often travels over the gannet's bath [the high seas]; the ocean will test whether or not the oak keeps admirable faith.]

The first three half-lines refer to the contribution that fallen acorns make to the human food supply. Men do not eat them, but swine do; and men feed on this *flæsc*.[10] Hence, *on eorþan* may fittingly be rendered "on the ground," from which swine eat mast: "Acorns on the ground are the swine's food for the sons of men." In this sense *on eorþan* contrasts with the oak on the sea in the second half of the stanza. *On eorþan* also elicits a long-range perspective, however. For as a constituent element of the universe, the oak is "on earth" – made part of the world by God – as a benefit ultimately for mankind: "The oak is on earth, for the sons of men, food for the swine." *On eorþan* is richly ambiguous, evoking complementary aspects of the same reality.

The poet employs a similar dual sense in the second part of the stanza, where *ac* is to be understood as material for ship-making. The paronomasia turns on two words: "The ocean tests whether the oaken vessel *hæbbe* excellent *treowe*." *Habban* can be construed as "to keep" or "to have." *Treow* can mean either "faith" or "wood," a fact which OE poets elsewhere have exploited to good effect.[11] In the form *treowe*, as here, the word literally means "faith"; in the sense "wood," *treow* is neuter and of

---

[10] To stress this idea, Dickins, p. 21, translates: "(the oak) fattens the flesh (of swine) for the children of men." Dickins also cites Anglo-Saxon illustrations of swine feeding in an oak forest. Page, p. 84, gives a similar translation: "The oak feeds the pig for meat for the sons of men."

[11] *Treow* wordplay is employed in the Exeter *Maxims* (159–60), in the Cotton *Maxims* (32b–34a), and in *The Dream of the Rood* (4b–25b). For a detailed treatment of the first instance, see J.E. Roesch, "*Hygecræft:* Scriptural Allegory in *Maxims* I and II," dissertation, University of Wisconsin, 1971, pp. 150–56; for the second instance, see R. MacGregor Dawson, "*The Structure of the Old English Gnomic Poems,*" *JEGP*, 61 (1962), 21; for the third, see P.B. Taylor, "Text and Texture of *The Dream of the Rood*," *NM*, 75 (1974), 194–95. The last instance is especially germane to the wordplay in the *Rune Poem*, for in both the pun is on the accusative forms *treow* "tree" and *treowe* "faith."

course takes no inflection in the accusative. Yet the reason prompting three scholars to construe *treow* in the passage as "wood" is not to be discounted.[12] It is natural to expect a discussion of the oak as nautical timber to refer to its excellence in with-standing water; it is the notion of the oak keeping faith that seems remote. As with the wordplay on *on eorþan* in the first part of the stanza, however, *treow* "faith" and *treow* "wood" are meanings of mutual reinforcement, pointing ultimately to the same reality. Precisely by testing whether the oaken vessel "keeps excellent faith" (*hæbbe æþele treowe*), the ocean also tests whether the oaken vessel "has excellent wood" (*hæbbe æþele treow*).

The case for this pun is also supported by the fact that *treow* is non-alliterative in the context. The poet could have employed a synonym, for example *wær* (occurring fourteen lines later in the plural), and not have disturbed his poetic line[a]. The poet's use of *treow* "faith," despite the evocation of *treow* "wood," suggests that he intended a double meaning. So, too, with *habban*. Earlier the poet uses the formulaic expres-sion *healdan trywa* "to hold faith," which phrase, if repeated here, would have reduced the reader's inclination to understand *treow* as "wood." Unlike *healdan*, *habban* accords equally well with either sense of *treow*, inviting the reader to see a double sense in the passage.

In the stanza devoted to the ash rune, immediately following the lines on the oak, the poet again summons a twofold perspective. In OE *æsc* can mean "ash tree" or "spear" of ash wood; the poet chooses terms applying to either sense:

> ᚫ (æsc) biþ oferheah,   eldum dyre,
> stiþ on staþule,   stede rihte hylt,
> ðeah him feohtan on   firas monige.   (81–83)

R.I. Page translates: "The ash, precious to men, is very tall. Firm in its base, it keeps its place securely though many men attack it."[13] The picture of a tree under attack is also found in other OE passages in which a tree characterizes woodchoppers as ene-mies or in which a felled tree is described as a war-captive.[14] Some commentators, however, understand the last line and a half of the runic stanza as a reference, not to the ash tree, but to the ash spear.[15] But these critics do not go far enough in their analysis, for the whole stanza fittingly describes the weapon. *Oferheah*, occurring only

---

[12] See Wilhelm Grimm, *Ueber deutsche Runen* (Göttingen, 1821), pp. 224, 232; J.M. Kemble, "On Anglo-Saxon Runes," *Archaeologia*, 28 (1840), 224; and L. Botkine, *La Chanson des runes* (Le Havre, 1879), p. 14.

[a] [OE *wær*: the word can mean 'faith' and is usually translated 'covenant' or 'pledge'.]

[13] *An Introduction to English Runes*, p. 84; Dickins, p. 23, has a similar translation.

[14] For woodchoppers as a tree's enemies, see *The Dream of the Rood* (28–33a) and *Riddle* 73 (1–7); for a tree described as a war-captive, see *Riddle* 53 (1–8a).

[15] See Dobbie's note to line 81 in his edition, p. 159.

here in OE, recalls the poet's earlier use of *oferhyrned* and suggests a similar multiple reference. In one sense the word refers to the "very tall" ash tree. But *heah*, as a simplex or in compounds, can also be a value-term with the sense "excellent" or "exalted."[16] So understood, *oferheah* provides an apt parallel to *dyre* in reference to a highly valued weapon: "The ash spear is much exalted, precious to men; firm in position, it rightly holds place though many men fight against it." Read one way, the stanza depicts the struggle between nature and men attempting to appropriate a tree for their use; read another way, the lines refer to the use to which men put the wood. Implicit in this double focus is the transformation of the ash from tree to spear, a transformation closely paralleled in *Riddle 73*, in which the ash itself is the speaker.[17] But whether tree or spear, the durability of its wood is the ash's chief characteristic. The resistance challenging woodcutters provides security for warriors.[18]

Elliott observes that it would be technically more correct if the rune cited last in the poem were used, instead, in penultimate position.[19] But the poet deviates from the expected order and, in his longest stanza, ends the poem with an image of finality:

> ᛠ (ear) byþ egle   eorla gehwylcun.
> Ðonn fæstlice   flæsc onginneþ,
> hraw colian,   hrusan ceosan
> blac to gebeddan,   bleda gedreosaþ,
> wynna gewitaþ,   wera geswicaþ.[20]   (90–94)

---

[16] See Bosworth-Toller, s.v. *heah, heahness, heahcræft, heahgesceaft, heahmiht, heahnama, heahpungen, heahtreow.*

[17] See Frederick Tupper, Jr, ed., *The Riddles of the Exeter Book* (Boston, 1910), pp. 211–12; Tupper quotes the runic stanza in connection with this riddle.

[18] For another passage in which a rune-word itself has a double sense throughout the description, see the *os* stanza (10–12). Scholars have long debated whether *os*, "the source of every language" (10), should be interpreted as Lat. *os* "mouth" or as OE *os* "god" (found only in compounds). But Stanley B. Greenfield, *A Critical History of Old English Literature* (New York, 1965), p. 193, is almost certainly correct in suggesting that the poet is using a *double entente.*

[19] *Runes: An Introduction,* pp. 53–54. Elliott points out that *ear* "the grave" belongs to the first extension of the alphabet; *ior* "eel," the rune preceding *ear* in the poem, came later historically.

[20] I have altered Dobbie's punctuation in this passage to accord with my view that the clausal series beginning with *ðonn* (91–93a) depends upon the last three clauses (93b–94), not on the first clause in the stanza (90). "The grave is loathsome to each man" is a general statement, true even before the approach of death; but only "when the flesh, the pale body, quickly begins to cool, to choose the earth as its bed-partner," then "prosperity vanishes, joys perish, pledges end."

[The grave[b] is loathsome to everyone. When the flesh, the pallid corpse, begins to grow cold once and for all, to choose the earth as its bed-fellow, then the fruits of earthly life vanish, joys depart, covenants come to an end.]

These lines function as a *memento mori*, with the density of verbs underscoring the rapidity of corporeal disintegration. The imagery of sexual union lends powerful irony. The body goes to meet its "bed-partner," not with flushed anticipation, but with the flesh pale and cold.[21] Instead of a joyous wedding feast, this union is marked by the end of prosperity and joy; instead of marriage vows, the uniting of a man's flesh with the earth signals the end to all pledges.[22]

But this concluding stanza is not itself conclusive. Set off against the stark fact of human mortality so graphically portrayed here is much of the rest of the poem; for images of comfort in human life (as in the lines on "joy" and "year") occur in more than half of the twenty-eight earlier stanzas. The first lines of the poem offer particular contrast to the last:

> ᚠ (feoh) byþ frofur fira gehwylcum.
> Sceal ðeah manna gehwylc miclun hyt dælan
> gif he wile for drihtne domes hleotan. (1–3)

[Wealth is a comfort to each and every person. Still everyone must give it out freely if he wishes to be allotted salvation in the presence of the Lord.]

Although God's *dom* – eternal life – is conditional, it can be attained by generously disposing of the wealth which, as the second last line of the poem reminds the reader, vanishes with the grave.[23] The reference to eternal life in these introductory lines

---

[b] [Although, following other critics, Hall takes 'earth', and hence by extension 'the grave', to be the sense of the OE word *ear*, which in turn is taken to be the name of the rune that heads the present verse paragraph, this interpretation is by no means secure. For an alternative approach to the problem of the meaning of this rune in this particular context, see my study *Old English Enigmatic Poems and the Play of the Texts* (Turnhout: Brepols 2006), 271–77. There can be no disagreement, however, about the gist of this stanza, which concerns the finality of death.]

[21] The word used for "bed-partner," *gebedda*, is otherwise used in OE only in reference to women. See Bosworth-Toller, s.v. *gebedda*; Grein-Köhler, s.v. *bed* (*gebedda*).

[22] For *wær* as a term for a nuptial vow, see the Exeter *Maxims* 100: *Wif sceal wið wer wære gehealdan* [a wife must keep her marital vow]....

[23] I follow Grein-Köhler, s.v. *dom*, 10, in reading the word here as a reference to heaven. For a similar use of the phrase *dom hleotan* (*hlutan*), see the *Menologium* 192b–93a, where *dom* is varied by *eadigne upweg* [the blessed path upwards]. The phrase *for drihtne* in the runic stanza may be an allusion to judgment "before the Lord," at which the generous man will "obtain glory."

combines with the final image of corporeal death to constitute a frame enclosing the many scenes of daily existence in the intervening stanzas.

A primary concern of the poet was to induce his audience to perceive the complexity of creation and the multiple aspects of realities within it. Many of the runic stanzas resemble riddles.[24] And like a riddle-master, the rune-poet uses wordplay, antithesis, and ambiguity to challenge the reader to enlarge his perspective and deepen his sensitivity to the world in which he lives and moves and has his being. The manner in which the poet overcomes the limitations of his strict poetic form is itself a lesson in overcoming the limitations of a single point of view. It may be, as Bruce Dickins asserts, that the *Rune Poem* has "no great literary value"; but it is surely misleading to say that the poem is "exactly parallel, indeed, to the old nursery rhyme:

> A was an Archer who shot at a frog;
> B was a Butcher who had a big dog."[25]

Perhaps the main purpose of the *Rune Poem* was to assist the memory in retaining the names of the various characters of the runic system.[26] Yet the poet, wishing to teach more than simply an alphabet, made his poem memorable in more ways than one.

---

[24] Scholars have often noted this quality in certain runic stanzas. See Grienberger, pp. 209–10, 214; Dobbie, pp. xlviii–xlix; Greenfield, p. 193; and Page, pp. 77, 84. Tupper cites runic stanzas to elucidate certain Exeter riddles; see his edition pp. xiv, 142, 191. 212.

[25] *Runic and Heroic Poems*, p. v.

[26] See Page, p. 73.

7

Theme

The leading purpose of thematic approaches to Old English literature has been to ascertain key elements of the thought-world of the Anglo-Saxons, as expressed in the stylized media of poetry and prose. Such approaches typically cut across the boundaries of genre. They may embrace more than one historical period, if indeed their authors venture to make historical distinctions at all, seeing how difficult it is to date almost any of the poetry and some of the prose. By definition, thematic approaches are thus open-ended, though in practice they may be based on a particular set of texts chosen so as to yield insightful conclusions.

Especially since the field of vision adopted in a given thematic study may be restricted to verse, with prose either taken into account or not depending on the critic's aims and methods, the thought-world that such studies open up for our inspection should not be confused with that of ordinary reality; rather, it is one of the imagination.[1] Thematic studies of the literature deal with a world parallel to the 'real world' that social historians try to document through legal documents, funerary archaeology, place-name evidence, archaeobotany, and other means. This makes that world of the imagination all the more interesting, for it is inhabited by kings and heroes, devils and beasts, torturers and saints, sages and exiled wanderers, not to mention cannibals, angels, and spooks who berate their bodies after death. These sundry figures find their way onto the manuscript page among such other stylized elements as mead-halls, barrows, ruins, fabulous treasures, shipwrecks, bone-chilling weather, carrion birds, and literally eye-popping miracles. The relation of these things to the actual life-world of the Anglo-Saxons is an inherent problem in such research, as well as one of its main points of interest.

Thematic approaches to Old English literature have not always been in vogue. During the heyday of the New Criticism – a movement that arrived later to Old English studies than to other sectors of the literary establishment – critics tended to zero in on individual poems and

---

[1] It is the thought-world pertaining to ordinary reality that Daniel Anlezark sets out to describe in his chapter 'The Anglo-Saxon World View', in Godden & Lapidge, 66–81; to this end he relies chiefly on prose sources of a scientific, historical, or geographical kind.

Old English Literature: A Guide to Criticism with Selected Readings, First Edition. John D. Niles.
© 2016 John D. Niles. Published 2016 by John Wiley & Sons, Ltd.

their particular artistic qualities. Questions pertaining to style and language received exquisite scrutiny, while the pursuit of ideas or idea-clusters cutting across textual boundaries was likely to be considered a form of cheating. Thus it is that in 1968, when two specialists in the field, Martin Stevens and Jerome Mandel, assembled an anthology of reprints of critical essays under the title *Old English Literature: Twenty-Two Analytical Essays*,[2] their book included an initial section on style, language, and versification; then a short section on individual prose works or authors; and then twelve essays devoted to individual poems, from *Cædmon's Hymn* to *Beowulf*. Likewise, a major critical anthology published in 1975, *Anglo-Saxon Poetry: Essays in Appreciation*,[3] contained twenty-five original essays, twenty-one of which were devoted to analysis of one or another individual poem, from *Beowulf* to *Widsith*. Three of the remaining essays took as their subjects a pair of related poems, like *The Wanderer* and *The Seafarer*, while a single essay was devoted to Cynewulf's runic signatures. Poetic craft or nuance was in the air; ideas or idea-clusters were not.

Studies devoted to a particular theme in Old English literature figure on occasion in the early criticism, though not with great frequency. One topic of recurrent interest to nineteenth- and early twentieth-century critics was Wyrd, or the relationship between Wyrd and Providence, with Wyrd generally characterized at that time as the embodiment of an inscrutable power, heavy with pagan associations, whose doom no hero could evade though his spirit could remain undaunted.[4] In his 1941 article 'Wyrd in Anglo-Saxon Prose and Poetry', B.J. Timmer mounted a strong critique of that earlier critical conception, showing that in King Alfred's translation of Boethius's *De Consolatione philosophiae*, the term *wyrd* has no associations with heathen belief in a superhuman, blind, and hostile power; instead, when God's Providence is carried out, then 'it is called *wyrd*.'[5] In poetry (including *Beowulf*), Timmer shows, God and *wyrd* are basically parallel in conception, not hostile powers.

One poetic theme that has been a magnet for critics, given its imputed pagan overtones, is that of the 'beasts of battle'. A survey of Old English verse turns up some fourteen instances of this topos, which alludes to the role of carrion creatures (wolves, ravens) in devouring or threatening to devour the corpses of the slain. Poets employ the theme either to signal the approach of a battle or to characterize its bloody aftermath, whether this is seen in a tragic or a gloating light. In his wide-ranging 2007 article 'Beasts of Battle, South and North', Joseph Harris shows this theme to have both Old Norse and continental parallels and reviews its treatment in the critical literature ever since the time of Jacob Grimm, who saw it as '*durch und durch heidnisch*' ('pagan through and through').[6] As with Wyrd, however, most

---

[2]   *Old English Literature: Twenty-Two Analytical Essays*, ed. Martin Stevens and Jerome Mandel (Lincoln: University of Nebraska Press, 1968), abbreviated elsewhere as 'Stevens and Mandel'.

[3]   *Anglo-Saxon Poetry: Essays in Appreciation for John C. McGalliard*, ed. Lewis E. Nicholson and Dolores Warwick Frese (Notre Dame: University of Notre Dame Press, 1975).

[4]   See Chapter 1 above for discussion of *wyrd* in books by Stopford Brooke and G.K. Anderson, and cf. Bertha S. Phillpotts, 'Wyrd and Providence in Anglo-Saxon Thought', *Essays and Studies* 13 (1928): 7–27, repr. in Fulk, 1–13.

[5]   B.J. Timmer, 'Wyrd in Anglo-Saxon Prose and Poetry', *Neoph* 26 (1941): 24–33 and 213–28, repr. in *Essential Articles*, 124–58; quotation from the latter source, p. 131. Of related interest is Alan H. Roper, 'Boethius and the Three Fates of *Beowulf*', *PQ* 41 (1962): 386–400.

[6]   Joseph Harris, 'Beasts of Battle, South and North', in *Source of Wisdom: Old English and Early Medieval Latin Studies in Honour of Thomas D. Hill*, ed. Charles D. Wright, Frederick M. Biggs, and Thomas N. Hall (Toronto: University of Toronto Press, 2007), 3–25; quotation from p. 15.

critics these days would see the theme's possible associations with the god Woden/Oðin and his attendant ravens as no more than vestigial at best. Perhaps the most influential earlier study of the theme was that by Francis P. Magoun, Jr, in his 1955 article 'The Theme of the Beasts of Battle in Anglo-Saxon Poetry'.[7] Magoun identified it in its various permutations as a prime illustration of the oral-formulaic type-scene, seen as a conventional building block of oral narrative. In a rejoinder to Magoun, Adrien Bonjour, in his 1957 essay '*Beowulf* and the Beasts of Battle', countered this view by calling attention to the powerfully individual way in which the *Beowulf* poet deploys the theme – once only, towards the end of that poem (at 3024b–27) – as opposed to the more routine ways in which it is used by other poets.[8] To my mind there is no contradiction between these two approaches, seeing that skilled oral poets are the masters of their tradition rather than its slaves.

Also attracting the attention of critics has been the devil, always a figure of insidious allure. To judge from the frequency with which he makes an appearance in the Old English narrative poetry that survives, no other figure was so ubiquitous in the Anglo-Saxon popular imagination. Perhaps this is because the devil and his minions were thought to be constant presences in the actual world, more intimately involved in the affairs of human beings than divine powers tend to be. In her 1953 article 'The Devil in Old English Poetry', Rosemary Woolf takes stock of many poems and passages in which the devil plays a role, pointing out counterparts to the devil in the god Loki of northern mythology and in the figure of the wicked counselor Bikki in *Vǫlsunga Saga* and other Old Norse texts.[9] She suggests that Anglo-Saxon authors had no difficulty fitting the Christian concept of the devil into their pre-Christian system of beliefs, with its category of the faithless retainer. Adopting a different outlook in his 2001 book *Satan Unbound*, Peter Dendle opens up the field of vision to take in prose homilies, prose saints' lives, and Bede's *Historia ecclesiastica* as well as verse texts.[10] Dendle argues that rather than simply being a tempter or a negative moral exemplar, the figure of the devil serves an ontological function in this literature by engaging the audiences of these narratives in a debate, conducted most often between the prince of darkness and one or another saint, concerning the legitimacy of God's just rule by force. It is not an argument that the devil wins.

In another ambitious study, *Allegories of War*, John P. Hermann has traced the many ways in which insular poets made use of the Pauline theme of spiritual warfare (the armour of God, the breastplate of righteousness, the sword of the word of God).[11] Drawn from Ephesians 6.11–17 and based on the standard military equipment of the Roman legionary soldier, this

---

[7] Francis P. Magoun, Jr, 'The Theme of the Beasts of Battle in Anglo-Saxon Poetry', *NM* 56 (1955): 81–90.

[8] Adrien Bonjour, '*Beowulf* and the Beasts of Battle', *PMLA* 72 (1957): 563–73, repr. with additional comments in his *Twelve Beowulf Papers: 1940–1960* (Neuchâtel: Faculté des lettres, 1962), 135–49. An authoritative overview of the topos is offered by Mark Griffith, 'Convention and Originality in the Old English "Beasts of Battle" Typescene', *ASE* 22 (1993): 179–99.

[9] Rosemary Woolf, 'The Devil in Old English Poetry', *RES* n.s. 4 (1953): 1–12, repr. in *Essential Articles*, 164–79.

[10] Peter Dendle, *Satan Unbound: The Devil in Old English Narrative Literature* (Toronto: University of Toronto Press, 2001).

[11] John P. Hermann, *Allegories of War: Language and Violence in Old English Poetry* (Ann Arbor: University of Michigan Press, 1989).

extended figure of speech was forcefully developed by the fourth/fifth-century Roman Christian poet Prudentius in his allegorical poem the *Psychomachia*. Hermann traces how such Anglo-Saxon authors as Aldhelm, Alcuin, and Ælfric drew on this theme. This learned tradition exerted a strong influence on Cynewulf and the anonymous authors of other Old English Christian poetry, serving to endow the austere path of renunciation with the ideology of active heroism. If Hermann is right, certain authors of Old English works may have savoured the manner in which the theme of spiritual warfare lends itself to scenes of sanctioned violence – 'sanctioned' because the figures that are brutally and sometimes grotesquely quelled are the Vices or their spiritual allies. In Hermann's view, which he develops with reference to Jacques Lacan and other leading theorists of a psychoanalytical orientation, 'the Old English representation of spiritual life as a violent conflict is complicitous with social violence' (pp. 1–2) rather than being dissociated from the life-world of the Anglo-Saxons.

Other themes crucial to Old English literary consciousness that have been taken up to good effect in the critical literature are *exile*, seen by Stanley B. Greenfield as a controlling theme in the elegies, where it is attended by conventional imagery;[12] *the hall*, considered by Kathryn Hume and others as a central image and symbol in heroic poetry and, perhaps, in the Anglo-Saxon psyche more generally;[13] the concept of *home*, seen by Anita Riedinger and by Nicholas Howe as an elusive object of desire in the early medieval context because of concurrent longings for a secure home in this world and an eternal one beyond it;[14] and *treasure*, seen by many critics as an ubiquitous feature in the poetry, one that can carry an ambiguous moral valence.[15] Other studies of a comparable kind are less closely linked to particular images or clusters of imagery. Topics singled out for attention include *the operations of the mind*, studied by Malcolm Godden with specific reference to the semantic field of the word *mod*, which modulates in connotation from positive 'courage' to neutral 'mind' or

---

[12] Stanley B. Greenfield, 'The Formulaic Expression of the Theme of "Exile" in Anglo-Saxon Poetry', *Speculum* 30 (1955): 200–6, repr. in *Essential Articles*, 352–62. Cf. Stacy S. Klein, 'Gender and the Nature of Exile in Old English Elegies', in *A Place to Believe in: Locating Medieval Landscapes*, ed. Clare A. Lees and Gillian R. Overing (University Park: Pennsylvania State University Press, 2006), 113–31.

[13] Kathryn Hume, 'The Concept of the Hall in Old English Poetry', *ASE* 3 (1974): 63–74. The large literature on the hall includes James W. Earl, 'The Role of the Men's Hall in the Development of the Anglo-Saxon Superego', *Psychiatry* 46 (1983): 139–60, repr. with revisions as chap. 4 of his book *Thinking about Beowulf* (Stanford: Stanford University Press, 1994); and chap. 2 ('The Hall') of Daniel Donoghue's book *Old English Literature: A Short Introduction* (Oxford: Blackwell, 2004). Archaeological evidence for actual halls dating from the Heroic Age of the Scandinavian peoples is presented in my book *Beowulf and Lejre* (Tempe, AZ: ACMRS, 2007), which features contributions by Marijane Osborn (who also served as co-editor) and by the Danish archaeologist Tom Christensen.

[14] Anita R. Riedinger, '"Home" in Old English Poetry', *NM* 96 (1995): 51–59; Nicholas Howe, 'Looking for Home in Anglo-Saxon England', in *Home and Homelessness in the Medieval and Renaissance World*, ed. Nicholas Howe (Notre Dame: University of Notre Dame Press, 2004), 143–63. Of related interest is Howe's book *Writing the Map of Anglo-Saxon England: Essays in Cultural Geography* (New Haven: Yale University Press, 2008), with its chapter on 'Home and Landscape' (pp. 47–72).

[15] A noteworthy study of treasure and its significance in *Beowulf* is the essay by Ernst Leisi translated into English as the reading selection for Chapter 5 above. See also the works by Marcel Mauss and M.I. Finley cited in Chapter 5, n. 119, and the studies by Elizabeth M. Tyler cited in Chapter 6, n. 10.

'spirit' to negative 'dangerous, rebellious inner force';[16] *the Anglo-Saxon myth of migration*, seen by Nicholas Howe as a culturally central cluster of ideas that the Anglo-Saxons culti-vated about their past;[17] *the ethic of war*, analysed by James E. Cross in both its literary and its real-life dimensions;[18] and *the poet*, investigated by Emily Thornbury as both a real-life figure and a cultural icon.[19] Certain of the studies just mentioned are firmly seated in the idealized mental world of verse, while others draw on a wide range of sources composed in either verse or prose so as to illuminate Anglo-Saxon social history. The relationship between these two worlds, one of which consists of ideas while the other pertains to life as it was lived, constitutes a large part of the interest of this mode of criticism.

Thankfully, criticism of a particular theme in a given historical period is never limited to a single approach. The fact that one critic has done a brilliant job of illuminating a particular theme by no means exhausts the subject. For example, in his 1993 article 'The Cultural Construction of Reading in Anglo-Saxon England', Nicholas Howe draws on ethnographic and historical sources so as to show how reading was 'a communal act' and 'a performative event' in Anglo-Saxon England.[20] From Howe's perspective, reading practices were undertaken in the midst of a predominantly oral culture, and the act of reading (from the Old English verb *rædan*, meaning in its core sense 'to give advice') was linked by deep cultural associations with the voicing of counsel in the sphere of public life. By way of contrast, in his 1997 article '*Rædan, Areccan, Smeagan*: How the Anglo-Saxons Read',[21] M.B. Parkes draws on his deep knowledge of Anglo-Saxon manuscript culture to show how the scribes of this period used 'a complex of new graphic conventions' (p. 5), including specific marks of punctuation, so as to facilitate the careful silent reading of texts – undertaken very possibly in private – in addition to the reading of those texts out loud. One can scarcely imagine two approaches to the same topic that differ so sharply in perspective. Those who study the two essays together will have much to learn.

A Selection from the Criticism

Among recent critics who have pursued thematic approaches to Old English litera-ture, Hugh Magennis stands out as having done so repeatedly and productively, defining through his critical practice a set of methods that others can aspire to

---

[16] M.R. Godden, 'Anglo-Saxons on the Mind', in *Learning and Literature in Anglo-Saxon England: Studies Presented to Peter Clemoes on the Occasion of His Sixty-Fifth Birthday*, ed. Michael Lapidge and Helmut Gneuss (Cambridge: Cambridge University Press, 1985), 271–98. Broader in scope is Antonina Harbus's book *The Life of the Mind in Old English Poetry* (Amsterdam: Rodopi, 2002), and, yet more so, Leslie Lockett, *Anglo-Saxon Psychologies in the Vernacular and Latin Traditions* (Toronto: University of Toronto Press, 2011).

[17] Nicholas Howe, *Migration and Mythmaking in Anglo-Saxon England* (New Haven and London: Yale University Press, 1989), repr. 2001 with a new Introduction.

[18] James E. Cross, 'The Ethic of War in Old English', in *England before the Conquest: Studies in Primary Sources presented to Dorothy Whitelock*, ed. Peter Clemoes and Kathleen Hughes (Cambridge: Cambridge University Press, 1971), 269–82.

[19] Emily V. Thornbury, *Becoming a Poet in Anglo-Saxon England* (Cambridge: Cambridge University Press, 2014).

[20] Nicholas Howe, 'The Cultural Construction of Reading in Anglo-Saxon England', in *The Ethnography of Reading*, ed. Jonathan Boyarin (Berkeley: University of California Press, 1993), 58–79; quotations from p. 59.

[21] M.B. Parkes, '*Rædan, Areccan, Smeagan*: How the Anglo-Saxons Read', *ASE* 26 (1997): 1–22.

emulate.[22] In the essay that follows, Magennis identifies laughter first of all as a gesture, when alluded to in the literature, rather than being an upwelling of emotion, as we think of it being in life. Developing a brief typology of laughter in Old English verse and prose, he outlines what he finds to be its five types. In addition, he relates the various image-complexes involving laughter to two different but intertwined settings or traditions: on the one hand that of the hall, with its conviviality, and on the other hand that of Christian spiritual discipline, where laughter is associated with worldly vanities. Taking the Exeter Book poem *The Seafarer* as the focal point of his analysis, he finds in this poem 'a dynamic interaction of contrasting significances' for the laughter of men – laughter that the poem's imagined speaker finally rejects.

The extensive modern critical literature on *The Seafarer* can best be accessed via two expert publications: Anne L. Klinck's critical edition *The Old English Elegies*, and Bernard J. Muir's edition *The Exeter Anthology of Old English Poetry*.[23] No one who sets out to study the meaning or the modern critical reception of that poem will want to ignore Dorothy Whitelock's brilliant 1950 study 'The Interpretation of *The Seafarer*'.[24] Whitelock revolutionized understanding of *The Seafarer* by establishing its links to the historical practice of exile-pilgrimage *pro amore dei* 'for the love of God', well attested in the early medieval context in Ireland as well as elsewhere. This historical connection complements the poem's intellectual links to the medieval topos that human life itself, especially as lived by monks, is a kind of exile-pilgrimage whose desired resting point is heaven.

Hugh Magennis received the PhD in English in 1981 from The Queen's University, Belfast. Before his recent retirement, he taught at that University for many years as Professor of Old English Literature, and he also served for a time as director of the Institute of Theology. He has written importantly on Ælfric and Old English hagiography, and, with Mary Swan, he is one of the two co-editors of the invaluable compilation *A Companion to Ælfric*. A critic of great versatility and insight, he is the author of *Images of Community in Old English Poetry*, which includes important discussion of the hall and feasting in *Beowulf* and other Old English texts. Magennis is also the author of the comprehensive survey *The Cambridge Introduction to Anglo-Saxon Literature*. His recent book *Translating Beowulf* analyses translations of that poem that have appeared in print during the past two hundred years.[25]

---

[22] See e.g. Hugh Magennis, 'The Cup as Symbol and Metaphor in Old English Literature', *Speculum* 60 (1985): 517–36; '"No Sex Please, We're Anglo-Saxons"? Attitudes to Sexuality in Old English Prose and Poetry', *LSE* 26 (1995): 1–27; 'Treatments of Treachery and Betrayal in Anglo-Saxon Texts', *ES* 76 (1995): 1–19; and *Anglo-Saxon Appetites: Food and Drink and Their Consumption in Old English and Related Literature* (Dublin: Four Courts Press, 1999).

[23] Klinck, 35–40, 79–83, 126–45; Muir, vol. 1: 229–33, vol. 2: 522–36.

[24] Dorothy Whitelock, 'The Interpretation of *The Seafarer*', in *The Early Cultures of North-West Europe*, ed. Cyril Fox and Bruce Dickins (Cambridge: Cambridge University Press, 1950), 261–72, repr. in *Essential Articles*, 442–57, and in Stevens & Mandel, 198–211.

[25] Full references: *A Companion to Ælfric*, ed. Hugh Magennis and Mary Swan (Leiden: Brill, 2009); *Images of Community in Old English Poetry* (Cambridge: Cambridge University Press, 2006); *The Cambridge Introduction to Anglo-Saxon Literature* (Cambridge: Cambridge University Press, 2011); *Translating Beowulf: Modern Versions in English Verse* (Cambridge: D.S. Brewer, 2011).

For Further Reading

Caie, Graham D. 1976. *The Judgment Day Theme in Old English Poetry*. Copenhagen: Nova, 1976.

Green, Martin. 1975. 'Man, Time, and Apocalypse in *The Wanderer, The Seafarer,* and *Beowulf*'. *JEGP* 74: 502–18. Repr. in *Readings: Shorter Poems*, 281–302.

Hume, Kathryn. 1976. 'The "Ruin Motif" in Old English Poetry'. *Anglia* 94: 339–60.

Kabir, Ananya. 2001. *Paradise, Death, and Doomsday in Anglo-Saxon Literature*. Cambridge: Cambridge University Press.

Magennis, Hugh. 2007. 'The Solitary Journey: Aloneness and Community in *The Seafarer*'. In *Text, Image, Interpretation: Studies in Anglo-Saxon Literature and its Insular Context in Honour of Éamon Ó Carragáin*, ed. Alastair Minnis and Jane Roberts, 303–18. Turnhout: Brepols.

Renoir, Alain. 1976. 'Oral Themes and Written Texts'. *NM* 77: 337–46.

Renoir, Alain. 1989. 'The Hero on the Beach: Germanic Theme and Indo-European Origin'. *NM* 90: 111–16.

Tristram, Hildegard L.C. 1978. 'Stock Descriptions of Heaven and Hell in Old English Prose and Poetry'. *NM* 79: 102–13.

Hugh Magennis, 'Images of Laughter in Old English Poetry, with Particular Reference to the *Hleahtor Wera* of *The Seafarer*' (1992)[1]

In a well-known article Susie Tucker presents a survey of references to laughter in Old English poetry and shows laughter to be more widespread and more varied in significance in this poetry than might perhaps be expected.[2] She does not, however, set out to discuss these references and the attitudes which they display in the contexts of the larger frameworks of ideas on which they depend. Some images of laughter, of course, are fairly well self-explanatory in their significance, but others take on their full meaning only when interpreted as parts of larger complexes of imagery. This article presents one analysis of the different 'types' of laughter found in Old English poetry and also – where relevant – it describes briefly the complexes of imagery to which they belong and the specific sources upon which they draw.

A particular focus of interest in the present examination is provided by the powerful lines in *The Seafarer* in which the speaker contrasts the bleakness of life at sea in winter with the ease of life in the company of men on land. At sea, he declares, he had only the song of the swan for his pleasure – 'to gomene' (20) – and he develops this

---

[1] Hugh Magennis, 'Images of Laughter in Old English Poetry', *English Studies* 73 (1992): 193–204. Used with permission from Taylor and Francis. Where editorial translations are provided, they are set between square brackets.

[2] S.I. Tucker, 'Laughter in Old English Literature', *Neoph*, 43 (1959), 222–26. See also G. Wahrig, 'Das Lachen im Ae. und Mittelenglischen', *Zeitschrift für Anglistik und Amerikanistik*, 3 (1955), 274–304 and 385–418 (this article, not known to Tucker, makes the significant distinction between laughter against someone – *Gegeneinanderlachen* – and laughter with someone – *Miteinanderlachen*); G.H. Reinhold, *Humoristische Tendenzen in der englischen Dichtung des Mittelalters* (Tübingen, 1953); L.R. McCord, 'A Study of the Meanings of *Hliehhan* and *Hleahtor* in Old English Literature', University of Missouri PhD dissertation, 1979.

ironic image by typifying the desired pleasures on land, which he missed, as the laughter of men and the drink of mead: in this lonely life he had

> ganetes hleoþor
> ond huilpan sweg   fore hleahtor wera,
> mæw singende   fore medodrince.[3]   (20–22)

[… the gannet's cry and the curlew's call in place of men's laughter, the gull singing in place of mead-drinking.]

As Susie Tucker says of these lines, 'laughter suggests company, not loneliness, warmth, not cold, relaxation, not tension.'[4] But it is the association of laughter with drinking and *gomen* which gives this picture its definition and significance. This association makes us think of scenes of joy and revelry in the bright world of the Germanic hall, the great place of happy laughter in the Old English secular tradition. Our passage indeed is rightly celebrated as representing a particularly compelling evocation of the joys of the hall. The overall message and outlook of *The Seafarer*, however, encourage the audience, stimulated by their experience of a different strand of imagery of laughter current in the early Middle Ages, to perceive a further level of meaning in these lines, as the desired pleasures symbolized by the hall are themselves brought into question. This different strand has its source in the traditions of Christian Latin literature.[5] The suggestive resonance of the passage from *The Seafarer* derives from a dynamic interaction of contrasting significances for images of laughter.

In Old English poetry as a whole images of laughter are employed in a number of ways. An outline of the 'types' of laughter which are found in the poetry serves to bring out the variety and richness of this imagery. The essentially symbolic and gestural nature of laughter in the range of images which occur is highlighted by the absence in Old English poetry of incidental laughter or qualified laughter: images of laughter are characteristically in the foreground in Old English poetry and appear without descriptive elaboration.

Laughter as a Symbol of Joy or Relief

In one group of references in Old English poetry images of laughter are found at times of joy or relief. This is perhaps the most basic meaning of laughter in the poetry, and indeed it could be argued that other strands of significance ultimately depend on

---

[3]   All references to Old English poetry are to *The Anglo-Saxon Poetic Records*, ed. G.P. Krapp and E.V.K. Dobbie, 6 vols (New York and London, 1931–53).

[4]   'Laughter in Old English Literature', p. 223.

[5]   On Christian attitudes to laughter see E.R. Curtius, *European Literature and the Latin Middle Ages*, trans. R.W. Trask (London, 1953), Excursus IV, 'Jest and Earnest in Medieval Literature', 417–35. See also H. Adolf, 'On Medieval Laughter', *Speculum*, 22 (1947), 251–53.

the universal appeal of this primary image of unrestrained happiness. It is an image which requires no knowledge of background ideas to be fully understood, being immediate in its impact and complete in itself. Nonetheless, it is a stylized, not a realistic image: in the real world a joyful state of mind makes people laugh easily, but they seldom actually laugh at a moment of intense relief – indeed, as some Old English prose writers realize,[6] they are more likely to weep. In Old English poetry there are no occurrences of the idea of weeping for joy. Instead, in this poetry which exploits so much the demonstrative significance of contrasting physical gestures and actions,[7] laughter acts as an eloquent expression of the joy of men and women at decisive moments of good news or good fortune.

This laughter is thus, unlike the 'hleahtor wera' of *The Seafarer*, the laughter of a particular time and of reaction to particular events, rather than being seen as reflecting a continuing state of mind. In *The Descent into Hell* in the Exeter Book it is the laughter of the imprisoned souls when Christ comes down to free them:

> Open wæs þæt eorðærn, æþelinges lic
> onfeng feores gæst, folde beofode,
> hlogan helwaran. (19–21)

[Wide open was that earthly vault; the prince's corpse received the breath of life; the ground shook, the inhabitants of hell laughed aloud.]

And it is the laughter of the joy in heaven at Christ's ascension in *Christ II*:

> þa wæs engla þreat
> on þa halgan tid hleahtre bliþe
> wynnum geworden. (738–40)

[... then in that happy hour the throng of angels became enraptured in their laughter, their jubilation.]

It is the laughter of glad tidings at the finding of the true Cross (*Elene*, 992–94) and of the relief felt by Christ's disciples when he calms the storm at sea (*Andreas*, 454–57). In none of these cases can the image of laughter be traced in the sources, where available for comparison: this image is distinctive of the vivid climactic style of narrative in

---

[6] In *Ælfric's Lives of Saints*, ed. and trans. W.W. Skeat, EETS o.s. 76, 82, 94, 114 (London, 1881–1900; repr. as two vols, 1966) see 'Legend of the Seven Sleepers', lines 823–25 (vol. 1: 538); and 'Life of St Eustace', lines 280–81 (vol. 2: 206) and 364 (vol. 2: 212); see also *Apollonius of Tyre*, ed. P. Goolden (Oxford, 1958), p. 38 line 12.

[7] Aspects of gesture are discussed further in my article, '*Monig oft gesæt*: Some Images of Sitting in Old English Poetry', *Neoph*, 70 (1986), 442–52. For a fuller study see W. Habicht, *Die Gebärde in englischen Dichtungen des Mittelalters*, Bayerische Akademie der Wissenschaften, Philosophisch-historische Klasse, Abhandumgen, Neue Folge, 46 (Munich, 1959).

Old English poetry and it contrasts with the less immediate language of the Latin and Old English prose analogues. The passage in *Andreas* indeed, on Christ's calming of the storm, appears to substitute the image of the laughter of relief for a different idea altogether, for the source of this poem (although it does not survive in the exact form which the *Andreas* poet used) probably would have spoken instead of the *fear* which the disciples felt at the power of Christ's hand: the Old English prose *Life of St Andrew* has at this point, 'Hi hine ondredon ealle þa þe his weorc gesawon' [All those who saw his deed were struck by fear of him].[8]

Laughter of Triumph, Hostility and Scorn

In many ways similar to this first kind of laughter in Old English poetry is laughter which expresses triumph, or hostility, or scorn. This again is laughter prompted at a specific time by specific circumstances, but unlike the laughter of joy or relief this laughter has an opponent who is its object, who is derided or defeated: it is an exultant laughter at someone else's expense. In *The Battle of Maldon* Byrhtnoth laughs having killed a Viking enemy:

> Him æt heortan stod
> ætterne ord.   Se eorl wæs þe bliþra,
> hloh þa, modi man,   sæde metode þanc.   (144–46)

[The deadly spear-point lodged at his heart. The ealdorman was all the happier; he laughed then, that brave man, he spoke thanks to God.]

Evil characters too rejoice in their wicked work: the devil who has tempted Adam and Eve laughs at his success:

> Hloh þa and plegode
> boda bitre gehugod.   (*Genesis*, 724–25)

[Sharply aroused in his spirit, the messenger then laughed aloud and rejoiced.]

The heathen Eleusius laughs that Juliana is helpless in his power:

> Ahlog þa se hererinc,   hospwordum spræc.   (*Juliana*, 189)

[The soldier then laughed out loud, he spoke words of scorn.]

---

[8]   *The Blickling Homilies*, ed. and trans. R. Morris, EETS o.s. 58, 63, 73 (London, 1874–80; repr. as one vol, 1967), p. 235.

Grendel, of course, attacking Heorot, laughs in gloating anticipation of his crimes – 'þa his mod ahlog' (*Beowulf*, 730): the laughter is inward but the image functions as a manifestation to the audience of his exultant evil. In a striking image the poet of Exeter Book *Riddle 33* speaks of the sound of a crashing iceberg as menacing laughter:

> Hlinsade hlude;   hleahtor wæs gryrelic,
> egesful on earde.   (3–4)

[It made a huge din; its laughter in that place was horrible, terrifying.]

This personification gives a startling representation of the sound of the iceberg but also suggests overtones of Grendel-like threat. In *Genesis A* Ham laughs at the nakedness of his father, Noah (*Genesis*, 1582–84), Abraham and his followers laugh at their defeat of the Four Kings (2065–67), and the poet even refers to scorn – 'husce' (2384) – treating Sarra's disbelieving laughter at God's announcement that she is to bear a child in her old age (2382–89).

Scornful laughter is the most characteristic kind of laughter found in Old Norse and other heroic poetry[9] and indeed in hagiography.[10] It is also the most common kind of laughter which occurs in the bible.[11] The biblical references to laughter are

---

[9] Derisive, often cruel, laughter, recalling the 'Homeric laughter' of the *Iliad* and the *Odyssey*, is widely exemplified in the Old Norse *Poetic Edda* (references here are to *Edda. Die Lieder des Codex Regius nebst verwandten Denkmälern*, ed. G. Neckel, vol. 1: *Text*, 4th edn, rev. H. Kuhn (Heidelberg, 1962): see *Reginsmál*, stanza 15 (p. 177); *Brot af Sigurðarqviðo*, stanza 10 (p. 199); *Guðrúnarhvǫt*, stanza 7 (p. 265) (Guðrun laughs in exulting anticipation); *Hamðismál*, stanza 6 (p. 269). In *Atlaqviða* laughter provides a spectacular expression of defiance: at stanza 24 Hǫgni laughs aloud as his heart is cruelly cut out (p. 244); in *Hamðismál*, stanza 20 (p. 272) Iǫrmunreccr laughs in his hall as he awaits his final, fatal battle. Outside the Norse tradition reckless laughter from Germanic heroes in the face of danger can be seen in *Waltharius* (ed. K. Strecker, 2nd edn (Berlin, 1924)), lines 1044 and 1424. On laughter in heroic poetry see further C.M. Bowra, *Heroic Poetry* (London, 1952), pp. 493–501.

[10] In the tradition of early medieval hagiography it is not only the wicked who laugh at the innocent, as in *Juliana* line 189, quoted above. The saints themselves laugh heroically in their defiance of torture and suffering and in their scorn for their obdurate oppressors. Thus, in Ælfric's saints' lives, Saints Simon and Jude laugh at the devil and his followers (*Ælfric's Catholic Homilies: The Second Series: Text*, ed. M. Godden, EETS s.s. 5 (London, 1979), XXXIII, line 26 (p. 281)), St Polycarp finds the idea of buying a miracle laughable (*Lives of Saints*, V, line 199 (vol. 1: 128), St Lawrence laughs as he is stoned (*The Homilies of the Anglo-Saxon Church: The First Part, Containing the Sermones Catholici, or Homilies of Ælfric*, ed. and trans. B. Thorpe, 2 vols (London, 1844–46), XXIX (vol. 1: 426, 428)), and St George smiles – 'smearcode' – at his time of torture (*Lives of Saints*, XIV, line 126 (vol. 1: 314)), as does St Vincent (*Lives of Saints*, XXXVII, line 140 (vol. 2: 434)). For other examples of laughter in hagiographical writings see Curtius, 'Jest and Earnest in Medieval Literature', pp. 425–28.

[11] See also the following (references are to the Vulgate text): IV Kings 19:21; II Paralipomenon 30:10; Nehemias 2:19; Job 5:22, 12:4, 29:24; Psalms 2:4, 21:8, 36:13, 43:14, 58:9; Proverbs 1:26, 29:9; Ezechiel 23:32.

extensively commented on by the patristic exegetes: for example, the exegetes contrast the laughter of Sarra at being told she is to have a child, interpreted as the laughter of doubt, with that of Abraham, the laughter of thankfulness, and they emphasize that the name Isaac means 'laughter'.[12] It is not the exegetical significance of laughter which attracts Old English poets, however, but the gestural: characters reveal themselves through it in a direct and concrete way. Derisive laughter is also characteristic of the related tradition of biblical poetry in Old Saxon. Indeed this is the only kind of laughter found in the *Heliand*: images of joy in the *Heliand* do not specifically mention laughter.[13]

In inverted form the laughter of triumph or scorn becomes the absence of laughter, which appears in Old English poetry as an image of ignominious defeat. Typically we are told of the defeated that they had no occasion – *ne þurfan* – to laugh, an expression which with fine understatement reveals the completeness of defeat and by implication suggests the exultation of the victors. In *The Battle of Brunanburh*, for example, the poet exclaims of the defeated Scots and Vikings that

> mid heora herelafum   hlehhan ne þurftun
> þæt heo beaduweorca   beteran wurdun
> on campstede   cumbolgehnastes.   (47–49)

[… in the midst of the remnants of their army they had no need to laugh that they had been superior in martial deeds, at the clash of standards, on that battlefield.]

Similar images occur in *Genesis A* (72–75), *Andreas* (1702–4), and *Elene* (918–19).

Laughter as a Symbol of Happiness and Prosperity

Sometimes it is clear, however, that reference to the absence of laughter is not so much an inversion of the idea of the laughter of triumph as an allusion to a different strand of the imagery of laughter. In this, laughter is a symbol of happiness and prosperity in life rather than of sudden elation. The end of this happiness and prosperity is seen as a giving up of laughter. Of the grieving Egyptians in *Exodus* we are told,

---

12   On the laughter of Sarra and Abraham see Bede, *In Genesim*, ed. C.W. Jones, CCSL, 118A (Turnholt, 1967), 207–8 and 217; Alcuin, *Interrogationes et Responsiones in Genesin*, PL, 100, 539–40. On the name Isaac as meaning 'laughter' see Jerome, *Hebraicae Questiones in Libro Geneseos*, ed. P. Antin, CCSL, 72 (Turnholt, 1959), 22, and *Liber Interpretationis Hebraicorum Nominum*, also ed. Antin, CCSL, 72, 67.

13   The *Heliand* has two references to the suffering Christ as the object of jeering laughter: see *Heliand und Genesis*, ed. O. Beghagel and B. Taeget, 9th edn (Tübingen, 1984), lines 5300 and 5639–40. In these instances the aspect of derision in the laughter is emphasized by the accompanying adverbial phrases, 'mid hoscu' and 'the hosce' respectively. In the *Heliand* joy in the hall is loud – 'hlud' – but the poet does not use the verb 'to laugh': see 2741–42.

wæron hleahtorsmiðum handa   belocene. (43)

[... the hands of those laughter-smiths were stayed.]

In Old English poetry the image of laughter as a symbol of happiness and prosperity is concentrated above all in the hall. Laughter can be seen, along with drinking, music, and the giving of gifts, as an essential expression of the *dream* [merriment] associated with the hall. The central hall activity is feasting, and it is at the feast that laughter and these other elements of life in the hall have their proper setting. They are the recurrent motifs by which the concept of the ideal feast is defined.

Thus when, in the passage quoted at the beginning of this article, the poet of *The Seafarer* refers to laughter and drinking, this poet is not presenting a vague picture of well-being but is alluding to the concept of the feast in the Germanic hall with its rich associations of communal joy and harmony. Such laughter at the feast is vividly exemplified in *Beowulf*, where there is 'hæleþa hleahtor' [laughter of men] at Heorot (611) and where Beowulf's death is presented as a giving up of hall joys:

> 'Nu se herewisa   hleahtor alegde,
> gamen and gleodream.'[14]   (3020–21)

['Now (that) the leader of armies has laid aside laughter, revelry, and the joys of music.']

In *The Rune Poem* too we hear of 'plega and hleahter' [merriment and laughter] (38)

> ðær wigan sittað
> on beorsele   bliþe ætsomne.   (39–40)

[... where warriors sit in the beer-hall, happy together.]

The elaboration of this aspect of hall imagery (which is not typical of Old Norse and is not found in Old Saxon) may have been encouraged by the small number of biblical references to the laughter of a life of joy: Job is told that once more God will fill his mouth with laughter (Job 8:21), and there is a number of biblical texts which contrast the laughter of joy with the tears of unhappiness.[15] But usually such passages have a monitory significance – 'Woe upon you who laugh now; you shall mourn and weep' (Luke 6:25, etc.) – which is not apparent in the Old English analogues, and certainly the commentators insist on the anagogical meaning of laughter in such passages in a way which would be inappropriate in most of the Old English passages mentioned in this section.

---

[14]   The same formula occurs in *Guthlac A*, 229, 'hleahtor alegdon', where it expresses the ignominy and tribulation of the devils ejected by Guthlac from their remote stronghold. Needless to say, there is no corresponding image of laughter in Felix's life of Guthlac.

[15]   Compare the image of tears and laughter – 'wop and hleahtor' – in the Old English poem *Solomon and Saturn* (348–49).

Disordered, Riotous Laughter

There is one passage in Old English poetry which stands out as presenting laughter in the hall without these suggestions of harmony and trust. This is the passage in *Judith* in which the drunken Holofernes engages in riot and disorder:

> Hloh ond hlydde,   hlynede ond dynede.   (23)

[He laughed and bawled, he roared and made a din.]

Here the poet presents a perversion of the ideal feast as seen in *Beowulf*, and instead of courtesy and nobility gives us uproar. Feasting *as such* is not censured, but this particular feast is shown to be a sad travesty of what feasting should be.

In this scene the criterion of heroic dignity – the good feast – combines with that of Christian moral teaching on moderation to condemn the behaviour of Holofernes, not least his excessive laughter. References to the necessity of avoiding excessive laughter are commonplace in the Christian literature of the early Middle Ages, going back ultimately to biblical texts like Ecclesiasticus 21:23, with its reference to the loud laughter of the fool. Some of the classic pronouncements from the bible (including this one) and from the fathers are collected in Defensor's *Liber Scintillarum*.[16] For example, Defensor adapts Jerome's praise of Nepotian, when he says that the wise man should temper his gravity of character with the cheerfulness of his looks. As Jerome says of Nepotian, laughter, but not guffawing, was the sign that he felt glad – 'Gaudium risu, non cachinno, intellegeres.'[17] The comments on excessive laughter which Defensor culls from the pseudo-Basilian *Admonitio ad Filium Spiritualem*, especially in the form in which they occur in the Old English interlinear version of the *Liber Scintillarum*, 'wodnys witodlice ys mid cyrme hlyhhan' (*amencia namque est cum strepido ridere*),[18] provide a direct condemnation of behaviour such as that of Holofernes.[a] According to the view exemplified by such statements laughter should be tempered always with moderation. In his *Rule* St Benedict bade his monks 'risum multum aut excussum non amare' [not to be fond of extended or explosive laughter].[19]

---

[16]   *Defensoris Liber Scintillarum*, ed. D.H.M. Rochais, CCSL, 117 (Turnholt, 1957), lv, 'De risu et fletu' (pp. 179–81); for the Old English interlinear translation see E.W. Rhodes, ed., *Defensor's Liber Scintillarum*, EETS o.s. 93 (London, 1899), pp. 171–73.

[17]   *Epistolae*, LX, x, 6, ed. I. Hilberg, CSEL, 54 (Vienna and Leipzig, 1910), 560–61; for *Liber Scintillarum* see CCSL, 117, lv, 14 (p. 180); Rhodes, p. 172.

[18]   Rhodes, p. 172; CCSL, 117, lv, 22 (p. 180).

[a]   [Both the Old English and the Latin statements have the same meaning: 'Indeed, to laugh in a loud outburst is a kind of madness.']

[19]   *Benedicti Regula*, ed. R. Hanslik, CSEL, 75 (Vienna, 1960), iv, 53–54 (p. 32). The corresponding passage in the Old English translation of the *Rule* has 'ne hleahter ne sceal he lufian' [nor shall he be fond of laughter] (omitting the epithets qualifying *laughter*), *Die angelsächsischen Prosabearbeitungen der Benedictinerregel*, ed. À. Schröer, Bibliothek der angelsächsischen Prosa, 2 (Kassel, 1888; repr. with appendix by H. Gneuss, Darmstadt, 1964), p. 18, lines 8–9.

Writers of Old English homilies follow these patristic sentiments in condemning those who are, as it is put in two of the homilies edited in Napier's *Wulfstan Sammlung*, 'to hlagole' [too apt to laugh].[20] The Old English version of the *Theodulfi Capitula* speaks against 'unnytte hleahtor' [pointless laughter] and 'micelne ond ungemetlicne cancettende hleahtor' [loud and immoderately cackling laughter].[21] And according to the writer of the account of John the Baptist in the *Old English Martyrology*, it was 'for … scondfulles gebeorscypes hleahtreo and for druncenes kyninges wordum' [on account of laughter at a disgraceful feast and the words of a drunken king] that John was beheaded.[22] It is clear that by his uncontrolled laughter as by other elements of his behaviour Holofernes identifies himself as disorderly and contemptible, both in terms of the idealized world of heroic poetry and in terms of Christian moral teaching.

Sublime Laughter

In *Solomon and Saturn* Saturn acknowledges by his happy laughter his defeat in the debate and the enlightenment which Solomon has provided for him:

> Hæfde ða se snotra   sunu Dauides
> forcumen and forcyðed   Caldea eorl.
> Hwæðre wæs on sælum   se ðe of siðe cwom
> feorran gefered;   næfre ær his ferhð ahlog.   (175–78)

[The wise son of David had overcome the Chaldean chief and put him to shame. He who had journeyed there travelling from afar was happy indeed; never before had his spirit laughed aloud.]

The darkness of ignorance is dispelled by the light of truth, and the pagan's reaction to the sublimity of this truth is one of unrestrained spiritual joy.

This is the only occurrence in Old English poetry *or* prose of this kind of striking image of the recognition of truth. Sublime laughter is not mentioned elsewhere, not

---

[20] *Wulfstan: Sammlung der ihm zugeschriebenen Homilien nebst Untersuchungen über ihre Echtheit*, ed. A. Napier, Sammlung englischer Denkmäler in kritischen Ausgaben, 4 (Berlin, 1883; repr. with bibliographical supplement by K. Ostheeren, Dublin, 1967), V, p. 40, line 18, and X, p. 70, line 13.

[21] See *Theodulfi Capitula in England: Die altenglischen Übersetzungen, zusammen mit dem lateinischen Text*, ed. H. Sauer, Münchner Üniversitäts-Schriften, Institut für Englische Philologie, Texte und Untersuchungen zur Englischen Philologie, 8 (Munich, 1978), p. 329, line 71, and p. 331, lines 72–73. This is also in *Ancient Laws and Institutes of England*, ed. and trans. B. Thorpe, 2 vols (also published in one-vol. folio edition) (London, 1840), vol. 1: 416 (one-vol. edn, p. 477).

[22] *Das altenglische Martyrologium*, ed. G. Kotzor, Bayerische Akademie der Wissenschaften, Philosophisch-historische Klasse, Abhandlungen, Neue Folge, 88: 1–2, 2 vols (Munich, 1981), vol. 2, p. 192, line 14; p. 193, line 3.

even laughter in heaven,[23] even though this is a not-uncommon theme in the exegesis of biblical texts like Luke 6:21 ('Blessed are you who weep now; you will laugh for joy'). Gregory the Great, discussing the reference to future laughter in Job 8:21, says that this is the laughter of the blessed in the 'aeterna patria' [eternal homeland],[24] and similarly Alcuin, speaking of the passage in Ecclesiastes commending mirth (8:15), declares that this refers to the (future) mirth of those who are poor now and to spiritual food and drink.[25] In Old English there are several references to future weeping,[26] but the image of future laughter makes no further appearance in extant Old English literature. There is, however, an episode in the Latin *Life of King Edward* in which in a dream the king laughs with sublime joy when he has a vision of the Seven Sleepers of Ephesus turning over onto their left sides.[27] Although this episode is supplied only from later revised versions of the text it may well have been present in truncated form in the original version of the life.[28]

Laughter as a Symbol of Vanity

We have seen that according to one important strand of Christian teaching, laughter should be enjoyed only in moderation. Man might be *risus capax* [prone to laughter] (Alcuin is among those who take up this Aristotelian *dictum*)[29] but too much unrestrained laughter brings negligence of the soul and of its well-being. But it is possible to discern another strand of Christian writing about laughter which goes much further than this and presents laughter as a central symbol of the vain pleasures of the

---

[23] As noted above, in the reference to laughter in heaven in *Christ II*, 738–40, the emphasis is on the joy felt at the moment of Christ's Ascension rather than on a continuing sense of heavenly bliss.

[24] *In Expositionem Beati Job Moralia*, ed. M. Adriaen, CCSL, 143–143B (Turnholt, 1979–85), viii, lii, 88.

[25] *Commentaria super Ecclesiaten*, PL, 100, 701D–702A. Here Alcuin follows Jerome, *Commentarius in Ecclesiasten*, CCSL, 72, 320.

[26] For example, a homily edited by Thorpe in 'Ecclesiastical Institutes' in *Ancient Laws and Institutes of England* contrasts the shortness of present laughter with the endlessness of tears in hell: 'for swa sceortum hleahter to swa langum & biterum tearum' [for such short laughter, to such long-lasting and bitter tears] (vol. 2: 57; one-vol. edn, p. 467); in *Blickling Homilies* V we read of the 'wop & hream' [weeping and howling] of hell (p. 61); in VII Christ releases the captive souls: 'Nis nu nænig heaf gehyred' [Now no lamentation is heard] (p. 85).

[27] *Vita Ædwardi Regis Qui apud Westmonasterium Requiescit*, ed. F. Barlow (London, 1962), pp. 66–71.

[28] See Barlow, pp. xxxix–xli.

[29] *De Dialectica*, xiii, PL, 101, 966D–967A. For the background to the idea of man as *risus capax* see H. Adolf, 'On Medieval Laughter'.

world, which must be rejected altogether. It is this renunciatory strand which brings us back to the resonant lines from *The Seafarer* with which we began.

This strand would find its origin in the words of Christ, already quoted, that those who laugh now will weep hereafter (Luke 6:21; see too James 4:9). The idea of future weeping – linked to an image of diabolic laughter – is illustrated particularly graphically in the account of Dryhthelm's vision of hell given in Bede's *Ecclesiastical History*. In the confused noise of hell Dryhthelm is unable to distinguish clearly between the weeping of men and the laughter of devils: 'fletum hominum et risum daemonorum clare discernere nequirem' [I was unable to distinguish clearly the weeping of human beings and the laughter of devils].[30]

In some Old Testament texts too laughter is repudiated: 'I said of laughter it is mad', declares Ecclesiastes (2:2), and in Ecelesiasticus the laughter of the wicked is seen as wanton sin (27:14).

---

[30]   *Bede's Ecclesiastical History of the English People*, ed. and trans. B. Colgrave and R.A.B. Mynors (Oxford, 1969), 5: 12 (p. 492); the Old English version has 'ic ðone wop þara manna & þone hleahtor þara diofla sweotolice geheran ne meahte', *The Old English Version of Bede's Ecclesiastical History of the English People*, ed. and trans. T. Miller, 4 vols, EETS o.s. 95, 96 [Part 1], 110, 111, [Part 2] (London, 1890–98), Part 1, p. 428, lines 5–6 [...].

[Omitted here are two paragraphs, with their notes, that provide support for Magennis's claim that laughter is often repudiated in ancient and medieval texts.]

In the writings of the early medieval church laughter often occurs together with feasting [...]. When laughter and feasting are mentioned together in these writings it is in the context of the castigation of the empty seductions of the world. Bede's *De Die Iudicii*, for example, lists some of the world's injurious pleasures which will cease in eternal torment:

> Noxia nunc huius cessebunt gaudia saeculi:
> Ebrietas, epulae, risus, petulantia, iocus ...[31]

[The foul pleasures of this world will then come to an end: drunkenness, sumptuous foods, laughter, wantonness, joking.]

---

[31]   Ed. D. Hurst, CCSL, 122 (Turnholt, 1955), 443.

In the Old English paraphrase of this poem, *Judgement Day II*, this is rendered,

> þonne drancennes gedwineð mid wistum,
> and hleahter and plega hleapað ætsomne ...   (234–35)

[... then drunkenness will vanish along with feasting, and laughter and gaming will make off together.]

One of the pseudo-Augustine *Sermones ad Fratres in Eremo*, used as a source for *Blickling Homilies* VIII, declares that the banquets of the foolish rich man are characterized by 'saltationes et jocos in ebrietatibus' [dancing and jesting in bouts of drunkenness];[32] in the *Blickling Homilies* this becomes 'wiste ond plegan ond oferdrync' [feasting and games and drinking to excess].[33] *Blickling Homilies* V speaks of 'þa symbelnessa ond þa idelnessa ond þa ungemetlican hleahtras'.[34] Here 'hleahtras' [Translation: 'feasts and periods of idleness and outbreaks of immoderate laughter] is qualified by 'ungemetlican', but in other sources it is clear that the whole idea of feasting and laughter is reproved. *Vercelli Homilies* IV speaks of the 'unglædlic hleahter' [unhappy laughter] of this world, contrasting it to the 'ungeendoda heaf' [unending lamentation] of suffering in hell, and it has the soul declare to the body, 'Ic wæs þin gamen ond þin gladung ond þin hleahtor ond þin myrhð' [I was thy gaming and thy merriment and thy laughter and thy mirth].[35]

In this renunciatory tradition, feasting and laughter have a significance directly antithetical to that which we saw in discussing the symbolism of the Germanic hall. If such a renunciatory view of feasting and laughter were introduced into the presentation of the secular world of the Old English heroic tradition it would clearly have the effect of undermining the whole value system associated with the hall.

The Seafarer is a poem which explicitly teaches the embracing of the inspiring joys of the Lord and the rejection of the transitory attractions of 'þis deade lif' [this dead life] (65). The connotations of renunciation in the imagery of laughter which we have seen in other early medieval literature become relevant in the context of the homiletic message of this poem, and these connotations interact potently with those of laughter as an image of hall joys. This interaction reflects the whole approach of *The Seafarer*, which uses the elements of secular heroic poetry in a dynamic and imaginative way.

In the passage from *The Seafarer* on the laughter of men and the drinking of mead laughter functions at a primary level as a representation of the good things which the speaker must go without on his solitary journey, and these good things are seen in the terms of the Germanic hall with all its suggestions of *dream* [joy]: the poet is thus

---

[32] PL, 40, 1341.

[33] Morris, p. 99.

[34] Morris, p. 59.

[35] *Die Vercelli-Homilien. I: I–VIII Homilie*, ed. M. Förster, Bibliothek der angelsächsischen Prosa, 12 (Hamburg, 1932), IV, lines 29–30 (p. 74), 311 (p. 99).

able to express the appeal of worldly pleasures with a real sense of longing. But at the same time, by virtue of the other connotations of laughter and feasting, which derive from writings in Christian literature, the poet is able to prompt the audience to reflection on the intrinsic values of such pleasures. The poet employs the language of secular tradition to present the seductiveness of the world, but knows, with the author of Ecclesiastes (but unlike the land-dweller in the poem, who, 'wlonc ond wingal' [proud and flushed with wine] (29),[b] sees no further than present pleasure), that the house of feasting brings distraction from essential truth. Laughter for the poet of *The Seafarer* is a symbol [of] the bright world of the Germanic hall but it is simultaneously a symbol of vanity.

Laughter and drinking appear elsewhere in Old English poetry, of course, without such connotations, but for the monastic reader 'ruminating' on the words of this contemplative poem it would be natural not only to consider the concepts of heroic poetry suggested by these lines, but also to think of the other commonplace collocation of laughter and feasting in early medieval literature, in the tradition of Christian writing on the vain pleasures of the world. The significance of laughter and drinking in *The Seafarer* is thus double-sided: it suggests relief from the 'cearselda fela' [many roomfuls of anxiety] (5) of the poem's opening lines, but it also suggests that such relief is illusory.

Thus in Old English poetry it is always the symbolic rather than the realistic dimension of the imagery of laughter which is the essential one. Laughter, a universal sign of human joy, is taken up and employed by Old English poets both in an immediate sense which requires no special knowledge of background to be understood fully, and also in more specific senses which are dependent on larger frameworks of ideas. In *The Seafarer* two conceptions of laughter, one provided by the coherent body of imagery associated with the Germanic hall, the other deriving directly from the symbolism of homiletic literature with its condemnation of all worldliness and vanity, meet in fruitful opposition as the speaker thinks longingly of the 'hleahtor wera' and the accompanying 'medodrinc'. There is no suggestion of riot or scurrility in this poem's evocation of the joys of the hall, but underlying it is an awareness that, attractive though these joys may appear to be, they are short-lived and that true and enduring joy is to be found elsewhere. The poem's appreciation of the brightness of the world, as compellingly symbolized by laughter and feasting, gives power and depth to its renunciatory message.

---

[b] [While, in keeping with the spirit of Magennis's essay, the translation 'proud and flushed with wine' has been provided here, an alternative translation is 'flown with insolence and wine' (see Bosworth-Toller, s.v. *wingal*). Such a more negative interpretation of this arresting OE phrase would tend to undermine Magennis's conclusion, as expressed in his final paragraph, that 'There is no suggestion of riot or scurrility in this poem's evocation of the joys of the hall.' Regardless of this question, there is no doubt that the poem's speaker renounces and transcends the limited worldview of the land-dweller in his cups.]

8

Genre and Gender

The category of genre, always a slippery one in literary criticism, is exceptionally treacherous in the context of Old English literature, especially as regards texts composed in verse. Genre customarily implies a conspiracy of expectations between authors and readers or, in the oral context, between performers and listeners. Generic expectations can be relatively unproblematic in the area of Old English prose; we know quite well what a sermon is (or what one was in the medieval context), and we can likewise easily recognize as such a prose saint's life, an annal or a chronicle, a law code, an example of scientific or pseudo-scientific literature like the Old English prognostics,[1] or a prose romance like the Old English version of the Greek and Latin romance of *Apollonius of Tyre*.[2] We venture into deep waters, however, when we try to infer what the generic expectations were that attended the reception of most Old English verse. Few poems of this period that are composed in the vernacular bear obvious generic markers. Moreover, most are anonymous compositions whose relation to Latin tradition is subject to debate. All but a few survive only in unique manuscript copies that are at an unknown remove from the originals, and we are accustomed to reading them in the medium of editions that date from a thousand years or more later. It is a challenge to know if the generic terms used by present-day critics when speaking about Old English poetry correspond to anything in the Anglo-Saxons' own experience of these texts.

---

[1] Although long neglected in the critical literature, prognostics – texts that claim to present means of predicting the future – have been discussed of late by Laszlo Sandor Chardonnens, *Anglo-Saxon Prognostics, 900–1100: Study and Texts* (Leiden: Brill, 2007) and by Roy M. Liuzza, *Anglo-Saxon Prognostics: An Edition and Translation of Texts from London, British Library, MS Cotton Tiberius A.iii* (Cambridge: D.S. Brewer, 2010). This is in keeping with a recent increase of critical interest in Anglo-Saxon scientific or pseudo-scientific writings.

[2] *The Old English Apollonius of Tyre*, ed. Peter Goolden (London: Oxford University Press, 1958). This work, which is the unique example of its kind in Old English, is the subject of an insightful study by Anita R. Riedinger, 'The Englishing of Arcestrate: Women in *Apollonius of Tyre*', in Damico & Olsen, 292–306.

Old English Literature: A Guide to Criticism with Selected Readings, First Edition. John D. Niles.
© 2016 John D. Niles. Published 2016 by John Wiley & Sons, Ltd.

Intersecting with concepts of literary genre are ideas pertaining to the respective roles of the two sexes in literary representation. Regardless of what the actual biological and psychological complexities of gender in life may be (or may once have been, in ancient societies), literary representations of human beings have long tended to fall into two major categories, male and female. This distinction is enshrined in law codes and other legal documents as well as in imaginative literature. We can thus almost say that there are two "genres" of human beings represented in Old English literature, male and female, with mention of either one triggering its own conspiracy of expectations. Needless to say, the male gender is the more ubiquitous one both in Old English literature and in the modern critical reception of that body of writings, even though representations of women have received close critical scrutiny of late.

At the risk of conflating matters whose full exposition would require extended treatment on their own, the present chapter will therefore discuss the two categories of genre and gender side by side. Likewise the reading selection with which the chapter concludes will call attention to a genre of Old English literature, namely the metrical charms, in which, unusually, the voices and experiences of women figure with occasional prominence.

Genre

Since no examples of 'Anglo-Saxon literary criticism' survive, it is quite possible that a precise native vocabulary to distinguish one poetic genre from one another was never developed. If it was not, this is perhaps because no need for one was felt. The chief native term for poetry, *giedd* (or *gied*), is used in the corpus of Anglo-Saxon writings with reference to many things, from poetry, to prophecy, to healing charms, to riddles, to heightened speech.[3] Other Old English terms for poetry or song that are used on occasion, such as *leoþ* 'poem, verse', *song* 'song', and *spell* 'story' or 'performance', are almost impossible to pin down in terms of generic distinctions.[4]

Certain types of verse, those that are imitative of Latin models, are unproblematic as regards their generic conventions. This is true of the Exeter Book riddles, which are clearly inspired by the Latin riddle collections of Aldhelm and other learned authors. Still, the anonymous Old English poets who took up this genre did so with considerable originality, as Jonathan Wilcox has made clear in an incisive overview of the Exeter Book riddle collection,

---

[3] For discussion see Karl Reichl, 'Old English *giedd*, Middle English *yedding* as Genre Terms', in *Words, Texts and Manuscripts: Studies in Anglo-Saxon Culture Presented to Helmut Gneuss on the Occasion of His Sixty-Fifth Birthday*, ed. Michael Korhammer, Karl Reichl, and Hans Sauer (Woodbridge: D.S. Brewer, 1992), 349–70. In chap. 1 of *Homo Narrans: The Poetics and Anthropology of Oral Literature* (Philadelphia: University of Pennsylvania Press, 1999), at 16–30, I suggest that *giedd* was a keyword in the Anglo-Saxons' cultural vocabulary and that the word denoted 'sentensious, rhythmically charged speech … uttered in a heightened register' (p. 30).

[4] See Jeff Opland, 'The Words for Poets and Poetry', in his *Anglo-Saxon Oral Poetry: A Study of the Traditions* (New Haven: Yale University Press, 1980), 230–56, and more recently Emily V. Thornbury, *Becoming a Poet in Anglo-Saxon England* (Cambridge: Cambridge University Press, 2014), with its close discussion of words for 'poet'.

focusing on how the riddles operate rhetorically rather than on the question of definition.[5] Similar independence from and dependency on Latinate models is characteristic of the Old English versified saints' lives, as well, for the poems that take saints as their subject are remarkably original in their conception. As Michael Lapidge has remarked when speaking of six Old English poems that are often referred to as examples of verse hagiography, namely Cynewulf's three poems *Elene, Juliana,* and *The Fates of the Apostles* plus *Guthlac A, Guthlac B,* and *Andreas,* only one of them – *Juliana* – 'could properly be described as a saint's life' in the sense in which that term is best understood.[6]

A perennial issue in *Beowulf* criticism is, 'What is its genre'? Few critics have been happy with the term 'epic', given how sharply the poem departs in form and style from epics of the Greek and Latin tradition as well as from modern epics, like *Paradise Lost,* that rely on those same classical conventions. As we have seen, J.R.R. Tolkien called *Beowulf* 'a heroic-elegiac poem', a hybrid term that suits a leisurely narrative whose action falls into two distinct parts, first the two Grendel episodes and then the dragon fight. Stanley B. Greenfield favoured the term 'epic tragedy', which has its own appeal.[7] It is uncertain, however, if either of these two modern terms denotes a type of poetry known in Anglo-Saxon times for which there could have been a 'conspiracy of expectations'. Robert Hanning prefers to speak of *Beowulf* as an example of 'heroic history', a term that calls to mind how closely history and heroic fantasy are interwoven in the historical writings of the early Middle Ages.[8] The poem's folktale-like structure and ghoulish elements, however, scarcely recall the medieval Latin pseudo-histories to which Hanning compares it. Joseph Harris approaches Beowulf as a kind of *summa litterarum,* adopting that term to denote a unique work that summarizes and transcends the literary forms of a prior era – the prior era, in this case, being that of Germanic oral song.[9] 'Anthology-like', Harris writes, *Beowulf* contains at least the following genres: genealogical verse, a creation hymn, elegies, a lament, a heroic lay, a praise poem, historical poems, a flyting, heroic boasts, gnomic verse, a sermon or paternal advice, and perhaps less formal oral genres' (p. 163). This is an attractive proposition; and yet as Harris presents it, it rests on the conception that a learned *Beowulf* poet self-consciously worked these elements into a single composition, rather like Chaucer assembling his *Canterbury Tales.* If it is valid to compare *Beowulf* with oral epic poems that are in circulation still today in Central Asia, all long songs of this kind are compendia. As a singer of tales draws out a heroic narrative to substantial length, he naturally incorporates into it any number of lesser genres. Perhaps, when attempting to characterize the genre of *Beowulf* as well as other Old English poems, it

---

5   Jonathan Wilcox, '"Tell Me What I Am": The Old English Riddles', in Johnson & Treharne, 46–59. In a study that is as well researched as it is well written, Patrick J. Murphy, *Unriddling the Exeter Riddles* (University Park: Pennsylvania State University Press, 2011), brings out the original qualities of the riddles while pursuing their affinities with both the *enigmata* of the Latinate tradition and popular riddles of the kind known to folklorists.

6   Michael Lapidge, 'The Saintly Life in Anglo-Saxon England', in Godden & Lapidge, 251–72, at 267.

7   Stanley B. Greenfield, '*Beowulf* and Epic Tragedy', in *Brodeur Studies,* 91–105.

8   Robert W. Hanning, *Beowulf* as Heroic History', *Medievalia et Humanistica,* n.s. 5 (1974): 77–102.

9   Joseph Harris, 'Beowulf as Epic', *Oral Tradition* 15 (2000): 159–69. See too his related study '*Beowulf* in Literary History', *Pacific Coast Philology* 17 (1982): 16–23, repr. in Fulk, 235–41.

is less important to fasten on a single critical term than to engage in discussion of the many conventional features that contribute to the poem's success.

This can certainly be said of the poems customarily known as elegies. 'Elegy' too is a term with which few critics are comfortable in the Old English context, though no very satisfactory alternatives have been proposed. The most nuanced and informative discussion of the matter is that by Anne L. Klinck in part 3, 'The Nature of Elegy in Old English' (pp. 220–51), of her 1992 book *The Old English Elegies: A Critical Edition and Genre Study*.[10] The nine poems identified by Klinck as examples of the type are *The Wanderer*, *The Seafarer*, *The Riming Poem*, *Deor*, *Wulf and Eadwacer*, *The Wife's Lament*, *Resignation*, *The Husband's Message*, and *The Ruin*. All of these are preserved uniquely in the Exeter Book, and most are set in the first-person singular voice. The key elements in the Old English elegiac genre, in Klinck's view, is that of separation from an object of desire, together with a corresponding feeling of longing, combined in certain of the poems with a movement towards some kind of consolation. As she writes: 'The essential element of elegy as it is found in these Exeter Book poems is the sense of separation: a distance in time or space between someone and their desire.' She adds: 'Longing that springs from unsatisfied desire is the product of separation, and pervades all the poems, *The Wife's Lament* and *Wulf and Eadwacer* most painfully, *The Husband's Message* with hope for reunion' (p. 225). Exile is the form typically taken by this state of separation. In four of these poems, as well, 'the ordered human society is juxtaposed with an eternal order, the desire for which transcends all feelings of human loneliness', while a few of the poems introduce the theme of *consolatio*, or a movement towards reassurance, 'the assertion that the separation from what is loved in this world is not permanent [...] or will be transcended by a union in the next' (p. 233). Still, this pattern of loss and consolation 'is not fulfilled in all of the elegies' (p. 234). As one can see from Klinck's carefully considered remarks, it is hard to formulate generalizations that apply to these poems equally well across the board. Perhaps part of the 'conspiracy of expectations' that hovered about them, if there was one, was that no one of them should be too much like the others.

Some critics would absorb the 'elegies' into a larger category, that of 'wisdom literature', as was first suggested by Morton W. Bloomfield in his wide-ranging 1968 essay 'Understanding Old English Poetry'.[11] A similar argument was advanced by Thomas Shippey in his 1976 book *Poems of Wisdom and Learning in Old English Literature*, which

---

[10] Note also Stanley B. Greenfield, 'The Old English Elegies', in *Continuations and Beginnings: Studies in Old English Literature*, ed. E.G. Stanley (London: Nelson, 1966), 142–75, and Martin Green's Introduction (pp. 11–28) to an anthology of critical essays that he edited, *The Old English Elegies: New Essays in Criticism and Research* (Rutherford, NJ: Fairleigh Dickinson University Press, 1983). María José Mora, 'The Invention of the Old English Elegy', *ES* 76 (1995): 129–39, identifies this genre as, in effect, a creation of the critical literature. On the other hand, Joseph Harris has speculated that Old English and Old Norse elegiac poems alike are rooted in a common Germanic literary culture that pre-dated the conversion, one that had to do with laments for the dead; see in particular his 'Elegy in Old English and Old Norse: A Problem in Literary History', in *The Vikings*, ed. R.T. Farrell (London: Phillimore, 1982), 157–64.

[11] Morton Bloomfield, 'Understanding Old English Poetry', *Annuale Mediaevale* 9 (1968): 5–25, repr. in his essay collection *Essays and Explorations: Studies in Ideas, Language, and Literature* (Cambridge, MA: Harvard University Press, 1970), 59–80.

offers texts and translations, with an informed commentary, of ten Old English poems that pertain to the loose category of 'wisdom'; and Shippey has taken up the matter again in his 1994 essay '*The Wanderer* and *The Seafarer* as Wisdom Poetry'.[12] By now there is general agreement that 'wisdom literature' is an important category, or 'super-genre', into which many examples of traditional gnomic, philosophical, or hortatory verse can be grouped. Less certainty attends the question of which Old English works pertain to that category in a core sense – as, for example, collections of gnomes such as the *Exeter Maxims* and the *Cotton Maxims* clearly do – as opposed to sharing certain general features of a 'wisdom tradition'. Elaine Tuttle Hansen discusses this matter in the Introduction to her 1988 book *The Solomon Complex: Reading Wisdom in Old English Poetry* without trying to resolve it.[13]

Another subtype of 'wisdom literature', what is customarily called the 'charm', is just as problematic a category as is 'epic' or 'elegy'. In common parlance, a charm is an object worn on the body for its imagined medical properties or its apotropaic effects, if not just for the sake of its … well, its charm. The same term is commonly used for medical procedures that are not thought to be consistent with rational cause and effect, for procedures thought to be scientific are simply called 'cures'. On one hand, not all Anglo-Saxon healing texts can be called 'charms', for this would efface their practical and scientific side, which is the dominant one.[14] To distinguish only certain curious cures as 'charms', on the other hand, is to impose a modern scientific mentality on a body of medical lore that constitutes a single system of knowledge and praxis in the manuscript culture in which it comes down to us. Altogether it seems safest to restrict the term 'charm' to those texts or passages that can properly be called incantations: those, that is, that were evidently meant to be spoken or chanted aloud and that tend to employ structural alliteration, though the result is often 'verse-like' rather than metrical in a strict sense. Given their non-orthodox content, incantations of this kind can fairly readily be distinguished from prayers, which also are spoken or chanted aloud but are liturgical in nature. None of these distinctions is hard and fast. The ambitious cure known as *Æcerbot* ('Field Remedy'), for example, which is directed against the workings of witchcraft, is *sui generis* in its mixture of liturgical and non-liturgical ritualistic actions, as well as in its combination of both orthodox and startlingly unorthodox prayers.[15] The cures discussed in the

[12]   T.A. Shippey, *Poems of Wisdom and Learning in Old English* (Cambridge: D.S. Brewer, 1976); '*The Wanderer* and *The Seafarer* as Wisdom Poetry', in Aertsen & Bremmer, 145–58.

[13]   Elaine Tuttle Hansen, *The Solomon Complex: Reading Wisdom in Old English Poetry* (Toronto: University of Toronto Press, 1988). Compare Carolyne Larrington, *A Store of Common Sense: Gnomic Theme and Style in Old Icelandic and Old English Wisdom Poetry* (Oxford: Clarendon Press, 1993), and Paul Cavill, *Maxims in Old English Poetry* (Cambridge: D.S. Brewer, 1999). Thomas D. Hill, 'Wise Words: Old English Sapiential Poetry', in Johnson & Traherne, 166–82, argues that 'careful and sympathetic study of these texts can enable us to understand the values and the thought-world of the Anglo-Saxons more immediately than [can] the study of other literary texts' (p. 179).

[14]   It is the scientific and possibly efficacious side of the Anglo-Saxon medical tradition that is emphasized by M.L. Cameron in his book *Anglo-Saxon Medicine* (Cambridge: University Press, 1993). Previous discussions of the medical literature tended to focus on its magical elements within the context of worldwide folk practices and ancient Germanic mythological beliefs, an approach that is exemplified in Godfrid Storms, *Anglo-Saxon Magic* (The Hague: Nijhoff, 1948). Neither Cameron's approach nor Storms's need be thought to exclude the other.

[15]   For discussion see Thomas D. Hill, 'The *Æcerbot* Charm and its Christian User', *ASE* 6 (1977): 213–21, and my own 1980 essay 'The *Æcerbot* Ritual in Context', in Niles, 44–56 and 163–64.

reading selection that concludes the present chapter feature charms in this more narrow sense. With their unparalleled instructions to a woman who fears losing her child, these remedies open up the realm of popular religion to our view.[16]

Gender

When one takes account of the Old English 'elegies' in particular, it is clear that one factor that cuts across the notion of genre is that of gender. It is not by chance that *Wulf and Eadwacer* and *The Wife's Lament*, two poems of the Old English poetic corpus that are set into the voices of women and that deal poignantly with female separation, longing, and loss, are core examples of the genre known as 'elegy'. Indeed, these two poems go far to define the leading characteristics of that genre. In her 1990 essay 'Women's Songs, Women's Language', Patricia A. Belanoff reads two elegiac poems of the Exeter Book as reflexes of an ancient Germanic genre of *Frauenlied* 'women's song'. Drawing on the writings of the French feminist critic Julia Kristeva, she argues that these poems employ a kind of language that is specific to women, regardless of whether or not a woman composed them.[17]

Critics have often noted that when women's experience is called to mind in Old English poetry, this is often in the context of mourning and loss.[18] It is as if each of the two sexes, male and female, has its own generic characteristics, with mention of men readily encouraging the 'conspiracy of expectations' that they will be engaged in the active pursuit of *lof* ('a good reputation') or *dom* (either 'glory' or 'salvation'), while mention of women is more likely to call up scenarios of suffering and loss.

It is possible, however, that contemporary critics wishing to dramatize representations of women in the arts of the Anglo-Saxon period have been drawn towards interpretations of sources that are also amenable to non-gender-based analyses. To cite one possible example: in her 2003 essay 'Broken Bodies and Singing Tongues', the distinguished art historian and literary critic Catherine E. Karkov explores the intersections of gender and violence in the

---

[16] Most extant Old English medical texts are preserved in two major manuscript collections. One of these, the so-called 'Lacnunga' manuscript (or 'Book of Cures'), contains many cures of a folkloric character. It has recently been well edited by Edward Pettit: *Anglo-Saxon Remedies, Charms, and Prayers from British Library MS Harley 585: The Lacnunga*, 2 vols (Lewiston: Edward Mellen Press, 2001). The other collection, known as 'Bald's Leechbook' in recognition of the Anglo-Saxon physician who evidently assembled it, contains a greater proportion of cures of a scientific nature. Karen Louise Jolly, *Popular Religion in Late Saxon England: Elf Charms in Context* (Chapel Hill: University of North Carolina Press, 1996), offers a critical framework for understanding how Anglo-Saxon charms of a folkloric kind functioned within a Christian worldview.

[17] Patricia A. Belanoff, 'Women's Songs, Women's Language: *Wulf and Eadwacer* and *The Wife's Lament*', in Damico & Olsen, 193–203. Note also Marilynn Desmond, 'The Voice of Exile: Feminist Literary History and the Anonymous Anglo-Saxon Elegy', *Critical Inquiry* 16 (1990): 572–90; and on the question of 'women's language' more generally, Gillian R. Overing, 'On Reading Eve: *Genesis B* and the Reader's Desire', in *Speaking Two Languages*, 35–63 and 232–39, with allusions to a wide critical literature.

[18] The theme of female mourning and loss is central to the studies by Joyce Hill and Helen Bennett cited in Chapter 5 above, n. 94.

illustrations that accompany a particular Anglo-Saxon manuscript copy of Prudentius's *Psychomachia*, namely Cambridge, Corpus Christi College MS 23.[19] Finding that 'gender is crucial to any reading of the *Psychomachia*' (p. 121), Karkov characterizes the allegorical battles recounted in this text as 'sexualized battles' in which the Virtues 'quite clearly become male in order to triumph, piercing the bodies of the Vices with their enormous phallic swords' (pp. 128–29). The Vices, she finds, are all shown as 'female in death'. Female Ira ('Wrath'), in particular, is shown as 'uncontrolled and uncontainable', for she 'foams at the mouth and shows her teeth' (p. 127). Karkov finds the illustrations in CCCC MS 23 to be disturbing, for they depict the defeat of the Vices in terms of graphic violence directed against women – women who, in their death-throes, are in turn allied with monsters. John Hermann's argument (mentioned in the previous chapter) that the motif of spiritual warfare is complicitous with social violence in the Anglo-Saxon context would thus seem to be confirmed with a vengeance.

Whether one finds Karkov's argument convincing or not, however, will rest on whether or not one accepts her gendering of the figures of the Vices and Virtues in these illustrations. Another distinguished art historian, Mildred Budny, genders the figures differently. In Budny's meticulously annotated catalogue of the illustrated manuscripts in the Parker Library,[20] the gender of these figures from CCCC MS 23 is found to be problematic. Sometimes it is simply hard to discern. Moreover, the gender of an individual Vice can switch from 'probably male' to 'probably female' from one illustration to the next.[21] The figure of Ira is sexed as 'male' in Budny's catalogue, not as female, as Karkov has it.[22] While Karkov, without giving further specifics, characterizes Budny's identifications as 'inaccurate',[23] the matter is not necessarily resolved so easily. If Budny does have it right – and readers are invited to make up their own minds through scrutiny of the images themselves – then female Patientia 'Patience' dispatches a male-like, somewhat deranged-looking Ira 'Wrath' while maintaining a measure of philosophical serenity. Correspondingly, one might be content to construe Patientia's sword as, after all, St Paul's sword of the Word rather than a phallic symbol; and the social relevance of these illustrations would seem to diminish to the point of no return.

---

[19] Catherine E. Karkov, 'Broken Bodies and Singing Tongues: Gender and Voice in the Cambridge, Corpus Christi College 23 *Psychomachia*', *ASE* 30 (2001): 115–36.

[20] Mildred Budny, *Insular, Anglo-Saxon, and Early Anglo-Norman Manuscript Art at Corpus Christi College, Cambridge: An Illustrated Catalogue*, 2 vols (Cambridge: The Parker Library, Corpus Christi College, 1997). CCCC MS 23 is discussed at length as no. 24 in the catalogue (vol. 1, pp. 275–437, along with plates 222–95 in vol. 2). Plates in this publication are paralleled by ones included in Karkov's article; in addition, high quality digital images of CCCC MS 23 are available, via subscription, at Parker Library on the Web: http://parkerweb.stanford.edu.

[21] This is true of Avaritia 'Avarice', in Budny's account.

[22] Budny, *Illlustrated Catalogue*, 333. The grammatical gender of the words denoting the Vices was not a determining factor for the artist. While for example Latin *ira* is a feminine noun, OE *yrre*, the cognate noun that accompanies the Latin text, is neuter. While *fides* (Latin 'faith') is feminine, the corresponding Old English term written out by the scribe, *se geleafa*, is masculine. One could argue that inconsistencies in grammatical gender contributed to the Anglo-Saxon artist's reluctance to present the sex of these figures in an unambiguous way.

[23] Karkov, 'Broken Bodies', p. 119, n. 20.

When two expert art historians are in flat-out disagreement with one another in such a seemingly straightforward matter as sexing a human figure, then it might savour of presumption for persons who lack special training in this field to try to resolve the matter. It is fair to raise the question, however: did the artist of CCCC MS 23 deliberately depict these allegorical figures in such a way as to avoid their being identified with flesh-and-blood men and women? In other words, did the distinction of allegorical *virtues versus vices* trump the distinction of *male versus female bodies*, as crucial as that latter distinction may seem to many critics of the present day? This question, which I will not venture to answer, raises in turn a more general one, namely: how safe is the assumption that we ourselves are free from period-specific biases analogous to the ones that are so obvious to us when, with the advantage of hindsight, we read literary criticism that dates from long ago? Although this question applies across the board to all the critical studies mentioned in the present chapters, it has particular relevance to those whose ideological dimension is conspicuous.

In recent years, heralded by the landmark critical anthology *New Readings on Women in Old English Literature* as well as by Gillian R. Overing's feminist-oriented study *Language, Sign, and Gender in Beowulf*,[24] scholarship on gender and women in Old English literature has burgeoned, branching out so as to include research into sexuality, same-sex relations, and medieval masculinities. Certain influential studies along these lines are cited elsewhere in the present book.[25] Among other significant publications, four can be said to stand out. These are Allen J. Frantzen's 1998 book *Before the Closet*, which includes analysis of same-sex relations in the early medieval period, particularly in saints' lives and works of pastoral advice;[26] Clare A. Lees and Gillian R. Overing's 2001 co-authored book *Double Agents*, which shifts attention away from the social history of Anglo-Saxon women so as to engage with the male biases involved in how the cultural record concerning women has been formed;[27] the 2004 anthology *Sex and Sexuality in Anglo-Saxon England*, edited by Carol Braun Pasternack and Lisa M.C. Weston, which includes eight new essays on a topic seldom treated in a forthright manner in the earlier criticism, together with a valuable Introduction;[28] and Stacy S. Klein's 2006 book *Ruling Women: Queenship and Gender in Anglo-Saxon Literature*, which demonstrates how the discourse of queenship in the

---

[24] The first of these, abbreviated 'Damico & Olsen' in the present book, has been cited several times; Overing's book is discussed in my Chapter 5.

[25] Note previous references to the work of Jane Chance (Chapter 5 n. 94), Helen Damico (Chapter 5 n. 92), Stacy S. Klein (Chapter 5 n. 12), Claire Lees (Chapter 5 n. 64 and n. 95), and Anita Riedinger (Chapter 8 n. 2); cf. also the article by Karma Lochrie cited in Chapter 9 (n. 22) and the studies by Shari Horner cited in Chapter 10 (notes 22–23).

[26] Allen J. Frantzen, *Before the Closet: Same-Sex Love from Beowulf to Angels in America* (Chicago: University of Chicago Press, 1998).

[27] Clare A. Lees and Gillian R. Overing, *Double Agents: Women and Clerical Culture in Anglo-Saxon England* (Philadelphia: University of Pennsylvania Press, 2001).

[28] *Sex and Sexuality in Anglo-Saxon England: Essays in Memory of Daniel Gillmore Calder*, ed. Carol Braun Pasternack and Lisa M.C. Weston (Tempe, AZ: ACMRS, 2004). Note also Pasternack's complementary study 'Negotiating Gender in Anglo-Saxon England', in *Gender and Difference in the Middle Ages*, ed. Sharon Farmer and Carol Braun Pasternack (Minneapolis: University of Minnesota Press, 2003), 107–42, and her chapter on 'Sex and Sexuality' in Stodnick & Trilling, 181–96.

writings of this period sheds light on Anglo-Saxon thinking about a broad range of social issues including conversion, social hierarchy, and male heroism.[29]

One incidental aspect of this last-named book is that Klein is led to the conclusion (at p. 195) that, however important the distinction of male versus female gender was to Anglo-Saxon authors, other distinctions – she mentions pagan versus Christian religion, or combatant versus non-combatant status in warfare – might at times have mattered to those writers more. Examples of such distinctions could be multiplied: one might think of high versus low social rank; of clerical versus lay status; or of English versus Welsh, Danish, or Norman ethnicity, to cite just three additional possibilities. Although my thinking on this subject should not be confused with Klein's, I am inclined to interpret her remark as a premonition that gender studies would soon be so fully integrated into mainstream Anglo-Saxon scholarship that the primacy of gender as a lens through which Old English literature is studied need not be insisted upon to the exclusion of other perspectives.

A Selection from the Criticism

In the critical selection that follows, Lisa M.C. Weston discusses three related Old English metrical charms that are intended to ensure the safe delivery of a child and the successful nourishing of the child after birth. Charms of such a kind must have had a crucial importance for women living at a time when, as the social historian Sally Crawford has written, 'An Anglo-Saxon mother could never have felt confident that her new baby would survive in the difficult and dangerous environment out of the womb, and her practical experience must have been that the child she was caring for was as likely to die as to live.'[30]

Born in England, Weston was raised there and in Canada before immigrating to the United States. She was awarded the PhD in 1982 from UCLA, where she studied Old and Middle English, Medieval Latin, Old Norse, and Celtic literatures, and she has subsequently taught at the California State University at Fresno. Her publications take as their subject Old English wisdom poetry, magico-ritual texts, the works of medieval women writers, and constructions of gender and sexuality, especially in hagiography. Readers are directed in particular to her recent chapter on saintly lives and sexuality in the 2013 *Cambridge History of Early Medieval English Literature*.[31]

Weston begins her essay on the women's childbirth charms by establishing a set of binary oppositions: Latin and Greek versus Germanic, learned versus oral, male versus female, priest versus shaman, normative versus non-normative, the men's hall versus the home. She then subverts the reader's expectation that what will follow, with specific reference to the metrical childbirth charms, will be an exploration of the second side of the opposition 'rational versus irrational'. Instead, she suggests that 'women's cures' could involve empirical

---

[29]   Stacy S. Klein, *Ruling Women: Queenship and Gender in Anglo-Saxon Literature* (Notre Dame: Notre Dame University Press, 2006). Cf. Klein's essay 'Centralizing Feminism in Anglo-Saxon Literary Studies: *Elene*, Motherhood, and History', in Johnson & Treharne, 149–65.

[30]   Sally Crawford, *Childhood in Anglo-Saxon England* (Stroud: Sutton Publishing, 1999), 75.

[31]   L.M.C. Weston, 'Saintly Lives: Friendship, Kinship, Gender and Sexuality', in the *Cambridge History*, 381–405.

knowledge that, while scientific, was unknown to male physicians. She distinguishes between the female creators and practitioners of childbirth charms and the male transmitters of knowledge who were chiefly responsible for the manuscript culture through which these cures are known to us today. Part of the value of Weston's essay resides in its demonstration that what we know as researchers into any historical period is conditioned by the channels – chiefly male-dominated – by which knowledge of the past has come down to us. In this regard, Weston's essay is representative of a large body of late twentieth-century and early twenty-first-century literary criticism that is devoted to recovering the voices, and the cultural experience, of early medieval women.

For Further Reading

Ashurst, David. 2010. 'Wisdom Poetry'. In Saunders, 125–40.

Battles, Paul. 2014. 'Toward a Theory of Old English Poetic Genres: Epic, Elegy, Wisdom Poetry, and the "Traditional Opening"'. *PQ* 111: 1–33.

Cross, J.E. 1961. 'On the Genre of *The Wanderer*'. *Neoph* 45: 63–75.

Davis, Kathleen. 2013. 'Old English Lyrics: A Poetics of Experience'. In the *Cambridge History*, 332–56.

Fell, Christine, with Cecily Clark and Elizabeth Williams. 1984. *Women in Anglo-Saxon England and The Impact of 1066*. London: British Museum. [Two books in one, the first of which is authored by Fell while the second is co-authored by Clark and Williams.]

Foley, John Miles. 2003. 'How Genres Leak in Traditional Verse'. In *Unlocking the Wordhord: Anglo-Saxon Studies in Memory of Edward B. Irving, Jr*, ed. Mark C. Amodio and Katherine O'Brien O'Keeffe, 76–108. Toronto: University of Toronto Press.

Glosecki, Stephen O. 2007. 'Stranded Narrative: Myth, Metaphor, and the Metrical Charm'. In *Myth in Early Northwest Europe*, ed. Stephen O. Glosecki, 47–70. Turnhout: Brepols.

Klein, Stacy S. 2012. 'Gender'. In Stodnick & Trilling, 39–54.

Meaney, Audrey L. 1989. 'Women, Witchcraft and Magic in Anglo-Saxon England'. In *Superstition and Popular Medicine in Anglo-Saxon England*, ed. D.G. Scragg, 9–39. Manchester: Manchester Centre for Anglo-Saxon Studies.

Lees, Clare A., and Gillian Overing. 2010. 'Women and the Origins of English Literature'. In *The History of British Women's Writing, 700–1500*, ed. Liz Herbert McAvoy and Diane Watt, 31–40. Basingstoke, UK: Palgrave.

Weston, L.M.C. 'The Language of Magic in Two Old English Metrical Charms', *NM* 86 (1985): 176–86.

Lisa M.C. Weston, 'Women's Medicine, Women's Magic: The Old English Metrical Childbirth Charms' (1995)[1]

What remains to us of Anglo-Saxon medicine is less a unified system than a palimpsest (or perhaps a collage) of traditions Greco-Roman and Germanic, literate and oral, Christian and pagan. The creators of the manuscripts usually called *Lacnunga* (Harley 585) and *Leechbook* (Regius 12 D xvii), which contain between them the bulk of extant medical remedies, consciously situate their works within a classical scientific tradition. *Leechbook* cites Pliny; both it and *Lacnunga* draw upon Alexander of Tralles.[2] The first two of *Leechbook*'s three parts follow the pattern of classical texts by listing prescriptions for external and internal disorders from the head down; *Lacnunga* accompanies an Old English translation of the *Herbarium* of Apuleius.

Within these frames – classical and scientific even in their project of systematically compiling remedies as written texts – the manuscripts place empirical prescriptions based on local as well as originally Mediterranean *materia medica*, and a number of nonscientific charms and amulets both Greco-Roman and Germanic. These magical remedies, especially numerous in *Lacnunga*, locate the manuscripts at the point where oral and textual traditions meet even more explicitly than do the scientific prescriptions. Their talismans need to be literally reinscribed on parchment, cloth, or wax: the written text itself constitutes *materia medica*. Other charms and prayers lie dormant on the page until said aloud: their efficacy is wholly oral and performative.

Such magical formulas invoke both Christ and Woden – sometimes, as with the Nine Herbs Charm, in the same incantation. Earlier commentators like Godfrid Storms spoke of Christian interpolations; more recent scholars locate the charms within a tradition of Christian magic, the rise of which has been documented most recently by Valerie Flint.[3] Internal evidence suggests *Lacnunga*'s monastic origin: J.H.G. Grattan and Charles Singer attribute the piecemeal compilation of the text to, among others, "the medicus of a monastery" and "the inmate of some small monastery in the North in which Irish influence survived."[4] The prevalence of Christian liturgy as well as the repeated inclusion of masses and paternosters in its charms leads Karen Jolly to conclude that the most likely Anglo-Saxon magico-medical practitioner was, as often as not, a village priest. She notes that most of the rituals using

[1]   L.M.C. Weston, 'Women's Medicine, Women's Magic: The Old English Metrical Childbirth Charms', *Modern Philology* 92 (1995): 279–93. Used with permission from The University of Chicago Press.
[2]   Godfrid Storms, *Anglo-Saxon Magic* (The Hague, 1948), pp. 14–15, 19. For a more detailed account of Anglo-Saxon medicine's debt to classical science, see M.L. Cameron, "The Sources of Medical Knowledge in Anglo-Saxon England," *Anglo-Saxon England* 11 (1983): 135–55. Both Harley 585 (*Lacnunga*) and Regius 12 D xvii (*Leechbook*) are manuscripts in the holdings of the British Library.
[3]   Valerie I.J. Flint, *The Rise of Magic in Early Medieval Europe* (Princeton, NJ, 1991).
[4]   J.H.G. Grattan and Charles Singer, *Anglo-Saxon Magic and Medicine* (London, 1952), pp. 19, 21.

masses or litanies are pitted against illness of supernatural origin; a priest and only a priest, she posits, could bring against evil spirits his authority as mediator between God and man, this world and the other.[5] Less obviously Christian charms, however, seem to invoke the presence of that other magical technician, the shaman. For Stephen Glosecki, the charm "Against a Sudden Stitch" offers the most pronounced instance of shamanic healing, for "whoever composed this charm – a preliterary and pre-Christian doctor, most likely – recounts direct experience of the dreamtime" and of spiritual combat against otherworldly enemies.[6]

Among these contrasting influences, however, we should identify yet one more: gender. Both manuscripts encode a male textual tradition. This is particularly true of *Leechbook*, where a Latin poem names an owner, Bald, and his scribe, Cild, who combined previous books compiled by editors named Oxa and Dun. *Lacnunga*, too, invokes the male as the normative voice, except in its metrical childbirth charm(s). In these verses, known to modern scholars as "For a Delayed Birth,"[7] as nowhere else, a woman speaks on her own behalf, suggesting that we might well ask who, among the Anglo-Saxons, had the primary responsibility for healing, and most especially for managing childbirth.

These responsibilities are less documented than those of male doctors like Bald, Oxa, and Dun, at least partly because female healing practices constituted less a professional specialty than an inseparable part of everyday domestic duties and participation in the community of women. Despite the masculine ordering principle responsible for the preservation of the medical remedies as we now have them in the *Leechbook* and *Lacnunga*, and despite the identification by name of three physicians, all male, it seems at least possible that women contributed much to medical wisdom, with the metrical childbirth charms being only the most obvious instance. We may, indeed, go so far as to suggest the existence of an identifiable female medical tradition, one which came to be partially appropriated by male authorities even as it was viewed with suspicion. Audrey Meaney documents women's healing function within the household, and documents, too, the less benign view of this healing, especially where it involved charming, taken by churchmen like Ælfric.[8] Glosecki,

5   Karen Louise Jolly, "Anglo-Saxon Charms in the Context of a Christian World View," *Journal of Medieval History* 11 (1985): 279–93; see also her later "Magic, Miracle, and Popular Practice in the Early Medieval West: Anglo-Saxon England," in *Religion, Science and Magic: In Concert and in Conflict*, ed. Jacob Neusner, Ernest S. Fredrichs, and Paul Virgil McCraken Flesher (New York, 1989), pp. 166–82.

6   Stephen Glosecki, *Shamanism and Old English Poetry* (New York, 1989), p. 14.

7   E.V.K. Dobbie, *The Anglo-Saxon Minor Poems* (New York, 1942), pp. 123–24; all citations of the charms are from this edition. These charms have also been edited by Felix Grendon, *The Anglo-Saxon Charms* (New York, 1909), pp. 206–9; Storms, pp. 196–203; and Grattan and Singer, pp. 189–91.

8   Audrey L. Meaney, "Women, Witchcraft and Magic in Anglo-Saxon England," in *Superstition and Popular Medicine in Anglo-Saxon England*, ed. D. G. Scragg (Manchester, 1989), pp. 9–40. For a discussion of medieval women's participation in their own healing, see Monica Green, "Women's Medical Practice and Health Care in Medieval Europe," in *Sisters and Workers in the Middle Ages*, ed. Judith M. Bennett (Chicago, 1989), pp. 39–78.

though identifying his shaman as normatively male (and connecting him to similarly male warriors and smiths), notes the existence of shamankas and indeed "the apparent association of shamanizing with women in saga lore."[9]

We may assume, however, that women's healing would not have consisted wholly of belief in and service to supernatural powers. M.L. Cameron, championing the commonsense rationality of many of *Leechbook*'s and *Lacnunga*'s herbal remedies, argues that use of copper or iron utensils displays not superstition but an empirical knowledge of chemical reactions. Cameron assumes the masculinity and professionalism of the healer. He speaks of "materials available to the Anglo-Saxon physician, drawn from both his ancestral pagan Teutonic background and from the Mediterranean culture introduced by Christian missionaries."[10] But who else, we may ask, would have known such chemical reactions? Women – at least some of them – could have gained the kind of common sense to which Cameron has drawn our attention from everyday experience with health problems, in the same way that they learned, for example, the unfortunate consequences of using an iron pot to preserve fruit or the necessity of using one if onion skins are to yield an olive green dye. A few potions and charms found their way into medical texts. Many more healing salves and strengthening brews for women in labor were no doubt passed on through oral tradition, from mother to daughter, along with recipes, instructions for cheese-making, pickling and preserving, and making dye and soap.

While such empirical remedies escape their original gendered social context once they are transcribed into a manuscript, the metrical childbirth charms – indeed any remedies incorporating ritual or otherwise requiring performance – retain more of their gendered speaking voice and their connection to an oral tradition. Granted, this connection is not a simple one. The very presence of oral "texts" in a manuscript marks them as appropriated; so does the existence of women's texts in an otherwise male context. They are by no means pristine remains of a primary oral tradition, though we can only speculate about how they found their way into *Lacnunga*. Should we posit a female scribe as first source, or a double monastery as their first home?[11] How many transcriptions have the charms seen? These questions remain unanswerable in the present state of our knowledge, which depends, of course, on the accessibility of written texts. We can, nevertheless, hear a woman's voice behind the words that the charm records.

---

[9] Glosecki, p. 100.

[10] M.L. Cameron, "Anglo-Saxon Medicine and Magic," *Anglo-Saxon England* 17 (1988): 191–215, 211.

[11] Elsewhere in *Lacnunga* a mostly Latin prayer-remedy against pestilence begs God *libera illam* (free this woman). The Latin is followed by a passage of garbled Irish prefaced *brigitarum*. Grattan and Singer suggest that the plural nominative *brigitae* ("brigits") are perhaps nuns of Saint Brigit (p. 201).

The manuscript offers five metrical passages divided by accompanying ritual instructions in prose and by three parallel introductory formulas, each repetition marked by an initial capital:

> Se wifman se hire cild afedan ne mæg ...
> Se wifmon se hyre bearn afedan ne mæge ...
> Se wifman se ne mæge bearn afedan ...

The woman's inability to *afedan hire cild* may be variously translated "nourish her child in her womb," "bring her child to term," and "nurse her child" after its birth. Though E.V.K. Dobbie, Felix Grendon, Godfrid Storms, and J.H.G. Grattan and Charles Singer all edit them as one, the evidence would suggest that the scribe has in fact gathered together three separate but related remedies. Their shared rubric subsumes all of childbearing from conception to weaning, the entire period during which the child depends upon the nurturance and potency of its mother's body. While the manuscript commonly collects alternative remedies under repeated headings, it does not elsewhere conflate multiple complaints in this fashion. The conflation as well as the rubric implies that these are women's concerns, things beyond the male physician's domain.[12] However much scribal intervention divides the texts from their original performance, then, the metrical childbirth charms nevertheless evoke a female oral tradition existing alongside of and in dialogue with the dominant male traditions – shamanic, priestly, and scientific – within the manuscript and within the greater context of Anglo-Saxon England.

The history of gender relations in the middle ages is a complex one. Nevertheless, as close students of the period like Judith Bennett have shown, we can generalize that men and women formed effectively two communities within the greater village whole, and we may deduce that the separation would have had profound ideological and psychological consequences.[13] James W. Earl suggests some of the effects on the male community as he addresses "The Role of the Men's Hall in the Development of the Anglo-Saxon Superego" and the definition of heroic behavior.[14] By such definitions,

---

[12] A section now unfortunately missing from *Leechbook* is described as containing "remedies against natural obstruction of women and all infirmities of women," thus similarly separating women's medicine from the main body of the text. The rubric continues "if a woman cannot bear a child or if the child is dead in the woman's womb, or if she cannot bring it forth, place on her girdle the prayers that are mentioned in these leechbooks" (Storms (n. 2 above), pp. 202–3). The physician/priest is thus distanced from his patient through the proxy of a talisman. Another entry in *Lacnunga*, headed "gif wif ne mæge bearn beran," contains only a Latin formula, "solve iube deus ter catenis." Grattan and Singer construe it as "Rejoice, loose their chains, O Lord' thrice" (pp. 186–87). They also disregard the caption and consider it part of the previous charm for an elf-shot horse.

[13] Judith M. Bennett, *Women in the Medieval English Countryside* (New York, 1987).

[14] James W. Earl, "The Role of the Men's Hall in the Development of the Anglo-Saxon Superego," *Psychiatry* 46 (May 1983): 139–60.

for example, *Beowulf*'s Scyld Sceafing can be judged *god cyning*, and the Cotton Maxims can decree that

> Ellen sceal on eorle,   ecg sceal wið hellme hilde gebidan.

(Courage shall be in the warrior, edge[a] shall against helmet experience battle.)[15]

As Mary Douglas points out, "ideas about separating, purifying, demarcating and punishing transgressions have as their main function to impose a system on an inherently untidy experience. It is only by exaggerating the difference between within and without, above and below, male and female, with and against, that a semblance of order is created."[16] Where the men's hall occupies the cultural center and defines that "semblance of order," women and women's lives outside the hall in the places where they cooked the food, wove the cloth, and bore the children – all processes, as Sherry Ortner argues, transforming nature into culture – represent a potentially dangerous ambiguity.[17] Given the logical oppositions male/female and human/nonhuman, if the norm for human is male, where does woman stand if not on the boundary between the human hall and the nonhuman wilderness? The women's world may thus appear like the shaman's in its liminality, but this liminality is constant rather than transitory, literal rather than metaphorical.

Indeed, to define women's reality as liminal at all may be to stand at the (male) cultural center and look out at women, not to look with women. So Caroline Walker Bynum argues against Victor Turner's paradigm, noting how often the imagery and narratives of later medieval female spirituality are marked by continuity or intermediacy, how rarely they invoke reversals and the oppositional structure upon which depends the genuine liminality of religious conversion, of the warrior's or the wise man's initiation, and of the shaman's magical battles.[18] Bynum's critique prompts us to inquire about the negotiation

---

[a]   [Weston uses the noun 'edge' to mean 'sword', just as in the Old English text.]

[15] Dobbie, pp. 55–57, lines 16–17a.

[16] Mary Douglas, *Purity and Danger: An Analysis of Concepts of Pollution and Taboo* (London, 1966), p. 4.

[17] Sherry B. Ortner, "Is Female to Male as Nature Is to Culture?" in *Woman, Culture and Society*, ed. Michelle Zimbalist Rosaldo and Louise Lamphere (Stanford, CA, 1974), pp. 67–87.

[18] Caroline Walker Bynum, "Women's Stories, Women's Symbols: A Critique of Victor Turner's Theory of Liminality," in *Anthropology and the Study of Religion*, ed. Robert L. Moore and Frank E. Reynolds (Chicago, 1984), pp. 105–25. Following Nancy Chodorow, Bynum finds psychological correlates for cultural and social paradigms: male oppositional definitions and consequent liminalities reinforce the experience of separation from the world of the mother and an artificial initiation into the world of adult men. Female continuity reiterates the continuance of life in the mother's world and natural initiation into womanhood. Female religious life melds spirituality with ordinary domestic and social reality: "Women's rather 'structureless' religion simply continued their ordinary lives (whose ultimate status they usually did not control), just as the economic work of 'holy women' – weaving, embroidery, care of the sick and small children – continued women's ordinary experience" (p. 117).

of cultural paradigms by women (specifically the creators and performers of the metrical childbirth charms) as well as by men (including the compilers of *Lacnunga* and *Leechbook*) who construe female behavior. How do women negotiate the healer/shaman's link to the warrior? To what extent do the words of women not only express female experience but also recognize (and perhaps use or even subvert) women's images in the men's hall?

Anglo-Saxon wise men, both priests and shamans, working from the symbolic center to distinguish the known from the unknown and thus to control the world around them, set women's indeterminacy within and yet against their own distinctions. The only woman in the Cotton Maxims, for example, appears with the thief and the thurse (or troll) as threats to the order established by the rest of the wise man's utterance. Her crime, seeking a lover *þurh dyrne cræfte* (by secret craft), Audrey Meaney suggests, may in fact be witchcraft, using magical means to take control of her own sexuality.[19] The poem calls her an *ides*, a poetic epithet for a human woman cognate with the Old Norse *dísir* and the Old High German *idisi*, both of which denote supernatural creatures.

This is one of many references that confound human and supernatural women. *Helrunas* may be human sybils or evil spirits. *Burgrunas* may be wisewomen of the community, but they may also be supernatural guardian spirits. Human *wicce* may possess inherent, possibly hereditary magical powers; or they may simply practice sorcery. Then again, they may be fully supernatural hags. When Wulfstan, for example, couples *wicce* with *wælcyrge*, perhaps echoing a traditional alliterative collocation, his witch seems supernatural; yet both nouns designate human beings.[20,b]

Truly, fear and awe before the possibility of women's inherent contact with the supernatural are deep-rooted. Much – probably too much – has been made of Tacitus's assertions about the prophetic power and prestige of Germanic women. Glosecki speculates that "with Germanic as with many other tribal peoples, women were considered gifted in supernatural arts partly because of menstruation, which connects them with the cosmic rhythm of lunar cycles."[21] As Jenny Jochens notes, a reputation

---

[19] Audrey L. Meaney, "The *Ides* of the Cotton Gnomic Poem," in *New Readings on Women in Old English Literature*, ed. Helen Damico and Alexandra Hennessy Olsen (Bloomington, IN, 1990), pp. 158–75.

[20] Christine Fell, *Women in Anglo–Saxon England* (Bloomington, IN, 1984), p. 31; Meaney, "Women, Witchcraft and Magic in Anglo-Saxon England" (n. 8 above), p. 15.

[b] [A brief account of the literal meaning of the OE words cited here by Weston may be found helpful. The noun *wælcyrge*, cognate with 'valkyrie', has the root meaning 'chooser of the slain'; its meaning in the context of Wulfstan's sermons is apparently 'witch or sorceress'. As for the terms cited earlier in this paragraph, *hell-run* appears to denote 'sorceress', while *burh-rune* or *burh-runan* are OE glosses on Latin *parcae* or *furiae* ('fates' or 'furies', respectively). The OE feminine noun *wicce* denotes 'witch' or 'sorceress'; there is a corresponding masculine noun *wicca* that is taken to mean 'wizard, soothsayer, sorcerer, magician'. See Bosworth-Toller or the *DOE* on this vocabulary, none of which is transparent, as Weston emphasizes.]

[21] Glosecki (n. 6 above), p. 100.

for supernatural knowledge may stem less from social deification than from difference: "Unable to choose between political alternatives or fearful of their outcome, men occasionally sought advice from 'the others.'"[22] Paul Bauschatz likewise sketches the mythological and symbolic linkage of women and prophecy: "Women were more in touch with the forces beyond this life," the forces of the natural, animal world and of Urd's Well, the world of Wyrd, the realm of the unknown and uncontrolled.[23]

According to continental sources, some wandering wives join in "wild hunts" with night-flying hags and spirits of the dead. Or so texts like the *Canon Episcopi* record: "Some wicked women perverted by the devil, seduced by illusions and phantasms of demons, believe and profess themselves, in the hours of the night, to ride upon certain beasts with Diana, the goddess of pagans, and an innumerable multitude of women, and in the silence of the dead of night to traverse great spaces of earth."[24] Burchard of Worms likewise asks women in his *Corrector*: "Do you believe ... that, in the silence of the night, when you are stretched out upon your bed with your husband's head upon your breast you have the power, flesh though you are, to go out of the closed door and traverse great stretches of space with other women?"[25] He gives Diana a Germanic identity, that of Holda, a vague supernatural figure who, with Percht and other similar "Winter Goddesses" as well as the Celtic Cailleach, the earlier continental Matronae, and perhaps the Anglo-Saxon Mothers of Bede's *modranecht*, inhabits storm, night, and the wild places whence she dispenses knowledge of female mysteries such as spinning and midwifery.[26] In references like these Carlo Ginzburg sees evidence of archaic shamanistic practices surviving into medieval folk-belief in the form of "a primarily female ecstatic religion, dominated by a nocturnal goddess."[27] Whatever the reality of Holda cults, or even the reality of dreams of riding with Holda, there can hardly be a better image of the female community as separate, as other.

The *mihtigan wif* (powerful women) battled and exorcised in the Anglo-Saxon charm "Against a Sudden Stitch" first appear riding over the *hlæwe*, "the burial mound" – symbolically marking the limits of human (or at least male) life and knowledge. Even the identity of the charm's riders defies easy knowledge and control: they may be *ylfa* (elves), or *esa* (æsir) [high gods], or *hægtessan* (hags). By "æsir" could be meant valkyries,

[22] Jenny Jochens, "*Voluspa*: Matrix of Norse Womanhood," *JEGP* 88 (1989): 344–62, quote on 360.
[23] Paul Bauschatz, *The Well and the Tree: World and Time in Early Germanic Culture* (Amherst, MA, 1982), p. 65.
[24] Henry C. Lea, *Materials toward a History of Witchcraft* (New York, 1957), pp. 178–79.
[25] Flint (n. 3 above), p. 123.
[26] For Germanic "Winter Goddesses," see Lotte Motz, "The Winter Goddess: Percht, Holda, and Related Figures," *Folklore* 95 (1984): 151–66, and her earlier "Sister in the Cave: The Stature and the Function of the Female Figures of the Eddas," *Arkiv for nordisk Filologi* 95 (1980): 168–82. For Celtic analogues, see Anne Ross, "The Divine Hag of the Pagan Celts," in *The Witch Figure*, ed. Venetia Newall (London, 1973), pp. 139–64.
[27] Carlo Ginzburg, *Ecstasies: Deciphering the Witches' Sabbath* (New York, 1991), p. 122; cf. Flint, pp. 122–25.

or perhaps a figure like the Old Norse Freyja who, valkyrie-like, commands a portion of the slain and, witch-like, rules the magic of the *seiðr* [sorcery].[28] In the glosses, as Katherine Morris observes, *hægtesse* overlaps with *wælcyrige*, especially in naming a creature of uncontrollable fury or frenzy. Other glosses like *ganea* (whore) link witches' fury with female sexuality, the area of female life most remote from male control and consequently that most fraught with danger.[29] We may well wonder whether such images, replete with such dangerous and frightening ambiguity from the perspective of the men's hall, might not contrarily empower the women outside, especially for the management of their own pregnancies and childbirths.

As Adrian Wilson has documented, until the advent of "modern medicine," child-bearing followed "a pervasive popular ritual that was maintained by (and probably had been created by) the women of England."[30] The actual birth was an exclusively female ceremony: the mother-to-be selected a number of women to attend her under the direction of the presiding midwife. Their preparation of the lying-in chamber re-created it as sacred space. The caudle (a mixture of ale, milk, honey, and herbs effective in inducing labor and easing pain) provided a sacred drink.[31] The woman remained secluded within this female-constituted world until her "churching," an official (and male-managed) ecclesiastical ceremony. Though later explained as an act of thanksgiving, the churching has its liturgical roots in Leviticus's injunction that

---

[28] Lotte Motz, "Freyja, Anat, Ishtar and Inanna: Some Cross-Cultural Comparisons," *Mankind Quarterly* 23 (1982): 196.

[29] Katherine Morris, in "Witch Words: The Origin and Background of German *Hexe*," *General Linguistics* 27 (1987): 82–95, in fact champions an etymological connection between *hægtesse*, earlier **hagazussa*, not just with the widely accepted "hedge-woman" but also with a postu-lated **haga(na)*, (female) genitalia (p. 92). Her later "The Lascivious Witch," *Mankind Quarterly* 26 (1986): 285–303, further discusses the yoking of witchcraft and fornication. Motz sees Freyja's association with sexual union as linked less with the procreation we might expect from a "fertility" goddess than with sex for its own sake or perhaps for the sake of the frenzy arising from intercourse as an inducement to shamanic ecstasy ("Freyja, Anat, Ishtar and Inanna," pp. 201–2). In this she follows Peter Buchholz's speculations in "Shamanism – the Testimony of Old Icelandic Literary Tradition," *Medieval Scandinavia* 4 (1971): 7–20, concerning the nature of *ergi* [unmanliness] and its function in regard to the *seiðr*. Glosecki (n. 6 above) takes pains to refute Eliade's earlier assertions that the *seiðr* was a female spe-cialty, though he wonders whether, given women's proverbial connection with magic, "rather than being *beneath* men, the *seiðr* may not have been above them, originally" (p. 101).

[30] Adrian Wilson, "Patient or Participant? Seventeenth Century Childbirth from the Mother's Point of View," in *Patients and Practitioners: Lay Perceptions of Mediane in Preindustrial Society*, ed. Roy Porter (Cambridge, 1985), pp. 129–44, 133.

[31] For discussion of caudles, see Jacques Gelis, *History of Childbirth* (Boston, 1991), pp. 114–15 and 152–53. Hillary Spurling, *Elinor Fettiplace's Receipt Book* (London, 1986), pp. 86–87 and 217, provides two examples preserved within a commonplace book collection of recipes, for-mulas, and domestic advice bequeathed from mother to daughter in one Renaissance English family.

the childbearing woman needs ritual purification: birth renders her impure and therefore dangerous or (from a different perspective) powerful.

Hence, by looking through female-defined rituals, by looking with women at images of female ambiguity and power, we can best interpret the women's metrical charms which appear in *Lacnunga* amid other, more male-identified, incantations and remedies.

The first charm requires three ritual acts, each accompanied by ceremonial speech. The first incantation must be repeated by the woman three times as she steps over the grave of a dead man:

> Ðis me to bote   þære lapan lætbyrde,
> þis me to bote   þære swæran swærbyrde,
> þis me to bote   þære laðan lambyrde.

> (This my remedy for hateful slow birth,
> this my remedy for heavy difficult birth,
> this my remedy for hateful imperfect birth.)

The verbal magic lies in the triple (actually, ninefold) repetition of "þis me to bote … -byrde," the echo and alliteration of *lapan læt-* and *laðan lam-*, the polyptoton of *swæran swær-*. This verbal technology is common to other metrical charms, irrespective of gender.[32] Marie Nelson interprets the formula as an act of defiance, a naming and exorcism of "the three great threats to the life of her unborn child."[33] By stepping over the grave, Nelson suggests, the mother transfers the influence of evil spirits away from herself. But the woman names no evil spirits, and her words turn her magical force not outward, as in other charms, but back upon herself: "þis me to bote." The ritual will bear a different interpretation, one based in female negotiations of the mythic images discussed above. Passing over the grave, she makes herself a benign *mihtigan wif* (to borrow a phrase from "Against a Sudden Stitch"). Those who lead the wild hunts also protect birth; perhaps the souls of the unborn issue from the same Otherworld of the dead.[34] The grave marks a boundary between the living and the non-living, this human world and the other: the woman bearing a not-yet-living child embodies a similar boundary within herself.

---

[32] See, among other articles, Judith Vaughan-Sterling, "The Anglo-Saxon *Metrical Charms:* Poetry as Ritual," *JEGP* 82 (1983): 186–200; and L.M.C. Weston, "The Language of Magic in Two Old English Metrical Charms," *NM* 86 (1985): 176–86.

[33] Marie Nelson, "A Woman's Charm," *Studia Neophilologica* 57 (1985): 3–8, quote on 3.

[34] Gelis discusses continental folklore concerning Holda's wild hunt as embracing the souls of both dead and unborn children. For this reason, "before the human intercourse which would humanize and 'familiarize' the future offspring came a coupling of the woman with the forces of nature. A woman paying her visit to the blessed spring, the sacred stone or the holy tree was attempting to capture the essence, the principle of the child" (p. 36).

In the next part of the charm a complementary act completes her passage with her child from potential to actual life. Here she steps over a living man (her husband) saying,

> up ic gonge, ofer þe stæppe
> mid cwican cilde, næles mid cwellendum,
> mid fulborenum, næles mid fægan.

> (Up I go, step over you
> with a living child, not a dead one,
> with a full-born one, not a doomed one.)

The woman and the child within her womb cross another boundary; indeed, the woman herself becomes the boundary her child will pass through by moving from nonlife to life. Her formula once more depends for its magical force upon the phrase-initial adverbs in "up ic gonge, ofer þe stæppe," the repetition of *mid ... næles mid*, the alliteration and chiastic endings of *cwican* and *cwellendum*, *fulborenum* and *fægan*.

The third and final part of this charm reinforces the ritual's private, unofficial character even as it places the woman within a larger (and explicitly Christian) community. When she feels that the child lives, the mother – and for the first time she is so named, *seo modor* rather than *þæt wif* – goes to the church. Standing before the altar she announces, "Criste, ic sæde, þis gecyþed" (by Christ, I have said, this is manifested)[c]. All previous actions have been in the present, the tense of process and becoming; here *gecyþed* and even *sæde* (which should logically be present) are in the past, the tense of what has become established. Her actions, verbal and nonverbal, look ahead to the churching which will end her confinement. Through her charm the mother has bespoken herself potent and fertile; her words have made her womb a site of transformation, of the nonliving becoming living, the inchoate taking form.

The second childbirth charm is less complex. The woman who cannot bring a child to term, that is, who has had a stillbirth, "genime heo sylf hyre agenes cildes gebyrgenne dæl" (takes herself some earth[d] from her own child's grave). The instructions thus underscore the woman's agency and personal power. She wraps this earth in black wool and sells it to a merchant. Her words, like those of the first charm, pronounce the action they accompany:

> ic hit bebicge, ge hit bebicgan,
> þas sweartan wulle and þysse sorge corn.

> (I sell it, you buy it,
> this black wool and this sorrow's seed.)

---

[c] [An alternative translation is possible: 'To Christ I have spoken, I have made this known.']
[d] [An alternative translation of the first part of this recipe is possible, one that takes into account the subjunctive form of the OE verb *genime*: 'Have the woman herself take some earth ...']

Alliteration binds *sweartan* to *sorge* in the second line, and interlaced word-endings -*e* and -*n* tie both lines together. The repetition of *bebicgan*, both "sell" and "buy," marks the present movement of what has happened (the past stillbirth) beyond the boundaries of the village, into the unknown – the merchant's marginality answering the woman's own. Does the black wool suggest a woman's spinning and weaving?[35] It surrounds the "seed" of her sorrow; perhaps this metaphorically re-creates her pregnancy. If so, this gesture returns her to potent possibility.

The third and last childbirth charm aids the woman who cannot breastfeed her child. First she must take up in her own hand the milk of a cow of one color, sip it, and carry it in her mouth to a stream of running water. She must spit the milk out, then drink a mouthful of water from the same hand, swallowing it this time. The cow and the stream both provide nurturing liquids; by sipping the milk she feeds herself as she wishes to feed her child, and by transferring the milk to the water she physically enacts the desire that milk will flow as abundantly as the stream. The woman makes herself an intermediary to her own desire: she swallows the water's abundance. As in the first charm, the woman moves between two places: the cow in the byre at home and the stream that perhaps marks the boundary of the settlement.

After swallowing she announces,

> gehwer ferde ic me þone mæran   maga þihtan,
> mid þysse mæran   mete þihtan;
> þonne ic me wille habban   and ham gan.

> (Everywhere I carried with me the famous strong son,
> with this famous strong meat,
> then I want to possess myself and go home.)[e]

---

[35] Evidently some churchmen feared that weaving, a traditionally female occupation carried out in the bowers away from male control, could become the occasion for illicit magic. Burchard, e.g., inquires, "Have you been present at, or consented to, the vanities which women practice in their woolen work, in their weaving, who, when they begin their weaving, hope to be able to bring it about that with incantations and with their own actions that the threads of the warp and the woof become so intertwined that unless someone makes use of their other diabolical counter-incantations he will perish totally?" (Flint (n. 3 above), p. 227). In chapter 157 of *Njal's Saga* (Einar Sveinsson, ed., vol. 12 of *Íslenzk Fornrit* (Reykjavik, 1954); Magnus Magnusson and Herman Pálsson, trans. (Harmondsworth, 1960)), valkyries weave the destinies of fighting men before the Battle of Clontarf; and in Chapter 11 of the *Orkneyinga Saga* (Finnbogi Gudmundsson, ed., vol. 34 of *Íslenzk Fornrit* (Reykjavik, 1965); Hermann Pálsson and Paul Edwards, trans. (Harmondsworth, 1978)), Earl Sigurd's sorceress mother embroiders him a banner which brings victory to her son but death to his unfortunate standard-bearers.

[e] [The exact meaning of the passage quoted here is somewhat obscure, though its gist is clear. An alternative translation is as follows: 'Everywhere I have carried with me the glorious one strong in its stomach, along with the glorious one strong in its feeding; I intend to keep him and go home.' This alternative reading depends on taking *maga-pihtan* and *mete-pihtan* as compound adjectival forms (here functioning as nouns) referring to the child, or perhaps to

Her words gain power through repeating *mæran ... þihtan*, while varying *maga* with *mete*. They also vary past and present tenses: the past carrying of the child, which she *ferde*, and the present desired possession of the milk, what she *wille habban*. Nelson draws attention to the reflexive *me habban* in the final line and paraphrases, "I want to have control over my own body."[36] This reading is apt: the mother does desire control, the power within herself to create and provide milk as she has created the life of her child.

Physically this desire translates into further motion. Without looking back, the charm says, she has gone to the stream, and without looking back she must return home, going to a house other than her own home and receiving food there. Carrying within herself the power of flowing nurturance and sharing, too, some of the stream's symbolic marginality, she becomes the recipient of some other woman's nurturing. As in the final stage of the first charm, she rejoins the community while still embodying her potent ambiguity.

Individually, each of these charms empowers the childbearing woman and, indeed, the female community to which she belongs. She takes responsibility for her own healing; she speaks words no one else can speak for her. But these charms are exceptions in the magico-medical manuscript tradition. Their oral and female healing practices have been appropriated and segregated within male writing and male classification of knowledge in hierarchical systems. Their difference from male healing practices is all the more visible when these vernacular charms from *Lacnunga* are contrasted with the Latin childbirth charm found in MS Junius 85.[37] There someone else – perhaps a priest – must write magical words upon virgin wax; the resulting amulet is bound under the mother's right foot. A literate authority thus acts for and upon his patient. The Junius text itself invokes biblical models for safe deliveries:

Maria virgo peperit Christum, Elisabet sterelis peperit Iohannem baptistam.
Adiuro te infans, si es masculus an femina, per Patrem et Filium et Spiritum sanctum,
     ut exeas et recedas, et ultra ei non noceas neque insipientiam illi facias. Amen.
Videns dominus flentes sorores Lazari ad monumentum lacrimatus est coram Iudeis et
     clamabat:
Lazare veni foras.
Et prodiit ligatis manibus et pedibus qui fuerat quatriduanus mortuus.

(Mary, virgin, brought forth Christ; Elizabeth, sterile, brought forth John the Baptist.
I adjure you, infant, whether you be masculine or feminine, by the Father and the Son

---

the child and the uterus, respectively. (See Boswoth-Toller on these two OE words.) The form *þonne* could then be taken as a variant spelling of the pronoun *pone*, referring to the child rather than the milk. If a reading along such lines is favoured, then the charm may address the problem of bringing an unborn child to full term rather than that of successfully breast-feeding an infant.]

36   Nelson, "A Woman's Charm," p. 5.
37   Charms from British Library manuscript Junius 85 are edited by Storms (n. 2 above), p. 283, and Grendon (n. 7 above), p. 159.

and the Holy Spirit, that you awaken and move, and no longer do any injury or foolishness.[f] Amen. The Lord, seeing the sisters of Lazarus weeping at the tomb, wept in the presence of the Jews and cried out: Lazarus come forth. And he came forth with hands and feet bound who had been four days dead.)

The healing charm – "prayer" might be more accurate – finds its model in exorcism: the child to some extent "possesses" his mother (the child's models, Christ, John, and Lazarus, are all male, so she is rightly *his* mother) and thus must be induced to depart by biblical precedents and the innate force of Latin as the language of the sacred. The as yet unborn child is poised, liminally like the figure of Lazarus, between life and death; the woman has become more a vessel than a participant. Indeed birth here partakes of the miraculous, not the natural, and if the child is to come forth like Lazarus, the woman must be his tomb. Far from actively managing the birth, the women around the mother become, like sisters of Lazarus, audience rather than actors. Only the Lord acts: His words, inscribed by His vicar on the talisman, accomplish the miracle. Ironically, however, even as the charm grants the power of the priest's male world, it reinforces his exclusion from the female realm; he enters the birth chamber only through the proxy of the talisman.

The contrasts are clear. Through the vernacular charms' magically powerful alliteration and repetition the female speaker creates desired situations for herself. Her charms recognize and use boundaries between the human and the nonhuman for their power, but they are not exorcisms: no elf or demon is battled or blamed. This feature in itself makes the metrical childbirth charms quite different from not only the Latin but also other vernacular charms embodying underlying structures of opposition and spiritual warfare, as Nigel Barley, Stephen Glosecki, Karen Jolly, and Marie Nelson all observe. Barley notes that "for the Anglo-Saxons ... there is a strong opposition between the cultural sphere of the village and the wild areas beyond, especially uninhabited marshes and forests – uninhabited by humans that is – because this is the home of the giants, monsters, elves and dwarves" who cause disease.[38] *Lacnunga* therefore prescribes "a holy drink against tricks of elves and against every temptation of the fiend," and *Leechbook* a salve "against the race of elves and nightwalkers." Often the charms oppose female magic: the malign creatures to be battled in "Against a Sudden Stitch" are supernatural women, and another *Lacnunga* charm against tumors,

---

[f]   [The exact meaning of this passage too is somewhat obscure. While Storms (and Weston, who quotes from Storms's edition) provides the reading 'ut exeas et recedas', Grendon locates a negative adverb here: 'ut exeas et non recedas'. Grendon's edition of the passage would yield the translation 'that you [the unborn child] issue forth and not turn back', i.e. 'that you exit the womb'. The following clause, taking account of the Latin pronouns *ei* and *illi* (which Weston leaves untranslated), could then be construed 'and moreover that you do not injure her nor do her any foolishness', with evident reference to the pregnant woman. It is hard to say how these philological matters might affect Weston's argument.]

[38]   Nigel Barley, "Anglo-Saxon Magico-Medicine," *Journal of the Anthropological Society of Oxford* 3 (1972): 67–76, quote at 68. See also Marie Nelson, *Structures of Opposition in Old English Poems* (Atlanta, 1989).

scrofula, and worms describes the swellings as Noththe's nine sisters. To Glosecki such spirits, sisters to *disir* and valkyries, "are vaguely female, unpredictable, mostly evil, able to materialize out of nowhere and then disappear, usually after causing or predicting trouble."[39]

Those who enact these charms see themselves as warriors fighting supernatural foes, and when we look through their eyes we may find it difficult to see any other reality. After all, we ourselves often envision medicine as a battle against disease, and so it is not without cause that even the most recent critics notice only an Anglo-Saxon medical man. But even as we read his traces in essentially male manuscripts, we must recognize the influence of gender on paradigms and modes of perception. When we find a woman speaking and acting within a gendered manuscript "frame" we must recognize both voice and frame for what they are. From *Lacnunga's* childbirth charms we can learn to discern the differences in imagery and magical acts which mark women's utterances, women's negotiation of the complex healing traditions of Anglo-Saxon England.

---

[39]   Glosecki (n. 6 above), p. 66.

9

Saints' Lives and Christian Devotion

What is arguably the most pervasive shift in the criticism of Old English literature that has occurred within the past fifty years has to do with how that literature is perceived in relation to the Christian culture of its time. As we have seen, nineteenth- and early twentieth-century critics of Old English verse tended to mine it for its Germanic or pre-Christian elements, often working in the assumption that its overtly Christian elements were late and artistically inferior. As for the Christian passages to be found in poems of a presumed early date and secular character, they were often attributed to scribal interpolation or reworking. Prose was fairly categorically neglected except as a source for political, religious, social, and legal history. While mid-twentieth-century critics, influenced by the New Criticism, focused attention on the artistic integrity of Old English literary works, they too often concentrated on those aspects of Old English literature that had to do with secular values rather than the spirit of devotion. They too usually wrote on verse as opposed to prose, since verse has long been a prestigious genre whose nature lends itself to close formal analysis.

By the close of the twentieth century, much had changed in these regards. The prose literature of the Anglo-Saxons, most of which is obviously Christian in inspiration, was being given sustained attention as a crucial witness to the culture of the Anglo-Saxons taken as a whole. Correspondingly, the late Anglo-Saxon period, especially the period from the late ninth century through the reign of King Cnut (ca. 890–1035), was attracting lively interest as the period when the educational reforms spearheaded by King Alfred and the leaders of the Benedictine Reform were made, when the great ecclesiastical writers Ælfric and Wulfstan were active, and when the bulk of Old English literature was written down in manuscript form. Imaginative literature on religious themes, as well, was receiving sustained attention, whether for its literary value or as a source for cultural studies of the kind that were emergent during the 1980s and 1990s.

The result of this major shift of perspective is that Old English literature is now generally perceived to be a Christian literature. Writings that deal directly with religion and those that address one or another aspect of 'the world', broadly conceived, now tend to be read as expressions of a single culture. Not excluded from this generalization is such a favourite poem as *The Wanderer*, which even into the mid-twentieth century had been read

Old English Literature: A Guide to Criticism with Selected Readings, First Edition. John D. Niles.
© 2016 John D. Niles. Published 2016 by John Wiley & Sons, Ltd.

as one 'where pagan negation is artistically triumphant' rather than as one offering a message of Christian consolation.[1] *Beowulf* too now tends to be seen as a poem that 'echoes and uses (within limits) the normal discourse of Christianity'.[2]

In previous parts of this book, mention has been made of writings by several scholar-critics who helped to lay the foundations for an integrated view of Anglo-Saxon literature taken as a whole.[3] Arguably the most influential proponent of such a view during the past half-century has been Paul E. Szarmach, who over the course of his professional career from the 1970s to the 2010s has edited or co-edited a number of valuable anthologies of critical essays on such topics as Old English prose homilies, prose saints' lives, prose writings of the Alfredian era, and, most recently, the lives of female saints of Anglo-Saxon England.[4] This is in addition to his services to the profession as, among other things, the long-term editor of the *Old English Newsletter* (1976–96); the Director of the Medieval Institute of Western Michigan University, Kalamazoo (1995–2007); and the Executive Director of the Medieval Academy of America and editor of *Speculum* (2006–11). Szarmach has been particularly active in promoting Anglo-Saxon source studies and has published widely on Old English saints' lives, religious prose, and related topics. His career has had a perceptible impact on a shift of gravity in the field of Anglo-Saxon literary studies away from the isolated analysis of individual poems and towards an integrated understanding of all Old English literature as the expression of a single culture, Christian in faith and broad in intellectual compass.

While no more than a few areas of literary research that have been impacted by these developments can be mentioned here, it will be helpful to take note of certain post-1950s developments in the study of Old English homilies, saints' lives, and Old Testament verse paraphrases. At the end of this chapter, notice will be taken of one of the most compelling of all works of English devotional literature, *The Dream of the Rood*.

An attractive entry point to the critical understanding of Old English homiletic literature is offered by Mary Swan in her 2004 essay '*Men ða leofestan*: Genre, the Canon, and the Old English Homiletic Tradition'.[5] Swan accepts that many modern readers may encounter 'uneasiness and resistance' to Old English homiletic prose on account of 'its committed, polemical nature'. As she sagely remarks,

---

1 Recalled here are the words of G.K. Anderson as quoted in Chapter 1 above.

2 Paul Cavill, 'Christianity and Theology in *Beowulf*', in Cavill, 15–39, at 37.

3 See Chapter 1 for discussion of Milton McC. Gatch's *Loyalties and Traditions*, with brief mention in Chapter 5 of two books by Bernard F. Huppé (cited in n. 62).

4 Volumes edited by Szarmach up to the present time include *The Old English Homily and Its Backgrounds*, co-edited by Bernard F. Huppé (Albany: State University of New York Press, 1978), and another four titles edited by Szarmach alone: these are *Studies in Earlier Old English Prose* (Albany: State University of New York Press, 1986); *Holy Men and Holy Women: Old English Prose Saints' Lives and Their Contexts* (Albany: State University of New York Press, 1996, hereafter abbreviated as '*Holy Men & Women*'); *Old English Prose: Basic Readings* (New York: Garland, 2000); and *Writing Women Saints in Anglo-Saxon England* (Toronto: University of Toronto Press, 2013).

5 Mary Swan, '*Men ða leofestan*: Genre, the Canon, and the Old English Homiletic Tradition', in Cavill, 185–92.

> The common opening of Old English homilies: *men ða leofestan* 'most beloved men',[6] confronts the modern reader from the very first words with a rhetoric that refuses to allow us any critical distance or disengagement from the community of belief on which the preacher's voice insists: it sets up for the reader a relationship with the speaker of shared ideology, when the relationship we want is one of critical scrutiny. (p. 186)

Swan suggests, however, that the very alterity of sermon literature can be used to pedagogical advantage, since students cannot well use the critical strategies devised for interpreting modern literature and must seek out other avenues. One productive approach, she argues, is through the general notion of 'performance', for 'the repetition of preaching constantly re-presents basic Christian doctrine; participation in the Mass, including listening to the homily, repeatedly frames the preacher and the congregation as Christian, and the individual churchgoer as a Christian' (p. 190). Readily folded into such an approach to Old English homilies, in her view, is cultural and queer theory, for this can help to elucidate how 'a masculine-gendered Christian identity' is constructed by the same phrase *men ða leofestan* and other conventional phrasing. Swan expresses her debt, in formulating these ideas, to the research of Clare Lees in her 1999 book *Tradition and Belief*, which in turn draws on the feminist scholarship of Judith Butler, speech-act theory, and the notion of 'performativity' in the context of Old English religious writings.[7]

Scholarship on Old English homiletic literature has been significantly advanced by the 2007 essay collection *The Old English Homily: Precedent, Practice, and Appropriation*, edited by Aaron J. Kleist, with its multiple chapters treating close to all aspects of this genre.[8] The up-to-date bibliographical citations in this book make unnecessary any attempt to duplicate that ground here. In addition, Kleist's judicious Introduction to that volume provides a sound entry point to research being done in this field. This publication makes for an apt companion to the newer editions of Ælfric's homilies that have been mentioned in previous chapters, as well as to the standard edition of the homilies of Wulfstan, while anonymous homilies too, receive close attention here.

Welcome as well is a set of recent publications on the Vercelli Book, one of the major sources for the devotional verse as well as the homiletic prose of the Anglo-Saxon period. Donald Scragg's 1992 edition *The Vercelli Homilies and Related Texts* represents the first complete modern edition of the twenty-three anonymous prose works written out in the Vercelli Book.[9] Scragg emphasizes that 'in no sense is the book a homiliary', for what it consists of is a mixture of sermons, saints' lives, and religious narratives; these constitute 'a

---

[6]   An alternative translation of this phrase is 'most beloved people' or 'dearly beloved people'. OE *men* is often non-specific as to gender, though the word can denote male persons alone.

[7]   Clare A. Lees, *Tradition and Belief: Religious Writing in Late Anglo-Saxon England* (Minneapolis: University of Minnesota Press, 1999).

[8]   *The Old English Homily: Precedent, Practice, and Appropriation*, ed. Aaron J. Kleist (Turnhout: Brepols, 2007).

[9]   *The Vercelli Homilies and Related Texts*, ed. D.G. Scragg, EETS o.s. 300 (Oxford: Oxford University Press, 1992). See also Scragg, 'The Compilation of the Vercelli Book', *ASE* 2 (1973): 189–207; a revised version of this article is included in *Readings: MSS*, 317–43.

uniform collection of pious reading, although one for which no exact parallel has been found either in English or in Latin' (p. xix). Thanks to Scragg's edition, plus translations of those same Vercelli Book prose works made available by Lewis E. Nicholson on the basis of work done by his students at the University of Notre Dame,[10] one can now examine the poems recorded in the Vercelli Book with easy reference to the prose contents of this same manuscript, and vice versa.[11] Study of this unique devotional anthology is likewise facilitated by the 1976 EEMF facsimile volume prepared by Celia Sisam.[12] As for critical evaluation of the contents of the Vercelli Book, many topics of interest are explored in the 2009 essay collection *New Readings in the Vercelli Book*, edited by Samantha Zachar and Andy Orchard,[13] as well as in Zachar's book *Preaching the Converted*, published that same year.[14] Research on the anonymous Old English homilies has also been advanced through Richard J. Kelly's 2003 publication *The Blickling Homilies*, a convenient (though less than definitive) edition and translation of the eighteen anonymous Old English sermons written out a single manuscript now located at Princeton University (Princeton, Scheide Library 71).[15]

Another growth area in Old English literary studies is hagiography. The overview of this genre offered by Hugh Magennis in his 2004 chapter 'Approaches to Saints' Lives' provides a solid basis for criticism in this area while also serving as a guide to resources currently available to researchers.[16] Like homilies, saints' lives present distinct challenges to current readers – and have a distinct appeal, as well – on account of the alterity of their aesthetics when compared with literature of other genres. By far the most important collection of saints' lives written in Old English is the one produced by Ælfric; the major set of lives written in Latin is by Bede, whose *Historia ecclesiastica* incorporates one after another example of this genre, each one artfully told, as is discussed by E. Gordon Whatley in his 1996

---

10   *The Vercelli Book Homilies: Translations from the Anglo-Saxon*, ed. Lewis E. Nicholson (Lanham, MD: University Press of America, 1991).

11   Six Old English poems are written out in the Vercelli Book, namely *Andreas*, *The Fates of the Apostles*, *Soul and Body I*, *Homiletic Fragment I*, *The Dream of the Rood*, and *Elene*. They are edited as a group in *The Vercelli Book*, ed. George Philip Krapp, ASPR 2 (New York: Columbia University Press, 1932).

12   *The Vercelli Book*, ed. Celia Sisam, EEMF 19 (Copenhagen: Rosenkilde & Bagger, 1976).

13   *New Readings in the Vercelli Book*, ed. Samantha Zacher and Andy Orchard (Toronto: Toronto University Press, 2009). Note also Elaine Treharne, 'The Form and Function of the Vercelli Book', in *Text, Image, Interpretation: Studies in Anglo-Saxon Literature and its Insular Context in Honour of Éamon Ó Carragáin*, ed. Alastair Minnis and Jane Roberts (Turnhout: Brepols, 2007), 253–66.

14   Samantha Zacher, *Preaching the Converted: The Style and Rhetoric of the Vercelli Book Homilies* (Toronto: University of Toronto Press, 2009).

15   *The Blickling Homilies: Edition and Translation*, ed. and trans. Richard J. Kelly (London: Continuum Books, 2003). Note in addition Jonathan Wilcox's discerning study 'The Blickling Homilies Revisited: Knowable and Probable Uses of Princeton University Library, MS Scheide 71', in *The Genesis of Books: Studies in the Scribal Culture of Medieval England in Honour of A.N. Doane*, ed. Matthew T. Hussey and myself (Turnhout: Brepols, 2011), 97–115.

16   Hugh Magennis, 'Approaches to Saints' Lives', in Cavill, 163–83. Still of value is Rosemary Woolf's earlier survey 'Saints' Lives', in *Continuations and Beginnings*, ed. E.G. Stanley (London: Nelson, 1960), 37–66.

survey 'Introduction to the Study of Old English Prose Hagiography' and by Paul E. Szarmach in his 2009 article 'Æðeldreda in the Old English Bede'.[17]

Versified saints' lives, in particular, have had a distinct appeal in recent Old English literary criticism. These include the two poems *Andreas* and *Elene* from the Vercelli Book, *Juliana* from the Exeter Book, and two Exeter book poems about the eighth-century Mercian cenobite, St Guthlac. Sharing certain generic characteristics with these poems is the Old English biblical paraphrase *Judith*, a spirited narrative that, though surviving only as a fragment, retells the core narrative of the biblical Book of Judith in a manner reminiscent of a Christian heroic saint's life. In part, the appeal of these poems rests on their intellectual and artistic complexity, for those who hope to understand them properly must remain alert to medieval systems of allegoresis and exegetical commentary. This aspect of their art has been foregrounded by Thomas D. Hill and others beginning with Hill's seminal 1969 study 'Figural Narrative in *Andreas*'.[18] The workings of figural narrative in the two saints' lives authored by the poet whom we know as 'Cynewulf', namely his poems *Elene* and *Juliana*, have been explicated in several of the contributions to the 1996 anthology *Cynewulf: Basic Readings*, edited by Robert E. Bjork (elsewhere in this book abbreviated as *Readings: Cynewulf*).[19] Other reasons why critical interest has gravitated to the saints' lives in recent years include their adaptation of the heroic ethos, as Edward B. Irving, Jr, emphasized in his 1983 article 'A Reading of *Andreas*';[20] their scenes of raw or grotesque violence, as is discussed by John P. Hermann in his 1989 book *Allegories of War*;[21] their portrayals of active or powerful women, as various critics have discussed including Karma Lochrie in her 1994 study 'Gender, Sexual Violence, and the Politics of War in the Old English *Judith*';[22] and their bearing on Anglo-Saxon practices of the religious life, as Christopher A. Jones has

---

[17]   E. Gordon Whatley, 'An Introduction to the Study of Old English Prose Hagiography: Sources and Resources', in *Holy Men & Women*, 3–32; Paul E. Szarmach, 'Æðeldreda in the Old English Bede', in *Poetry, Place, and Gender: Studies in Medieval Culture in Honor of Helen Damico*, ed. Catherine E. Karkov (Kalamazoo: Medieval Institute Publications, 2009), 132–50.

[18]   Thomas D. Hill, 'Figural Narrative in *Andreas*', *NM* 70 (1969): 261–73. Of closely related interest is James W. Earl, 'The Typological Structure of *Andreas*', in Niles, 66–89 and 167–70. See also Hill, '*Imago Dei*: Genre, Symbolism, and Anglo-Saxon Hagiography', in *Holy Men & Women*, 35–50, and Earl, 'Typology and Iconographic Style in Early Medieval Hagiography', in *Typology and English Medieval Literature*, ed. Hugh T. Keenan (New York: AMS Press, 1992), 89–120.

[19]   Note particularly Joseph Wittig, 'Figural Narrative in Cynewulf's *Juliana*', *ASE* 4 (1975): 37–55, repr. in *Readings: Cynewulf*, 147–69; and Thomas D. Hill, 'Sapiential Structure and Figural Narrative in the Old English *Elene*', *Traditio* 27 (1971): 159–77, repr. in a revised version in *Readings: Cynewulf*, 207–28. Responses to the vexed questions of who Cynewulf was, when he lived, and what the canon of his works consists of are offered in two other contributions written for this same anthology: these are R.D. Fulk, 'Cynewulf: Canon, Dialect, and Date', pp. 3–21, and Patrick W. Conner, 'On Dating Cynewulf', pp. 23–55.

[20]   Edward B. Irving, Jr, 'A Reading of *Andreas*: The Poem as Poem', *ASE* 12 (1983): 215–37.

[21]   John P. Hermann, *Allegories of War: Language and Violence in Old English Poetry* (Ann Arbor: University of Michigan Press, 1989).

[22]   Karma Lochrie, 'Gender, Sexual Violence, and the Politics of War in the Old English *Judith*', in *Class and Gender in Early English Literature: Intersections*, ed. Britton J. Harwood and Gillian R. Overing (Bloomington: Indiana University Press, 1994), 1–20.

argued in his 1995 article 'Envisioning the *Cenobium* in the Old English *Guthlac A*'.[23] Another feature of these versified narratives that has appealed to critics is their vigorous style, as is brought out for example by Howell D. Chickering in his 2009 study 'Poetic Exuberance in the Old English *Judith*'.[24] Also of interest is the humour that plays about certain hyperbolic features of their narrative, as no few current readers may have experienced when reading, for example, of blithe saints, frustrated devils, and angry tormentors foaming at the mouth.

While devoting his chief attention to the last of these features, humour, in his 2003 article 'Eating People Is Wrong: Funny Style in *Andreas* and its Analogues', Jonathan Wilcox has offered a splendid summary of the conventions that govern the genre of saints' lives as a whole.[25] 'Saints' lives are an awkward genre to define', he writes. One of the main problems they present for the modern reader is that their authors 'demonstrably work to flatten out the potential for human interest in the stories they recount', emphasizing instead their edifying content. This content 'is best explained in typological terms', Wilcox argues, for certain incidents replicate incidents in the life of Christ, while others can be understood as allusions to the liturgy. Popular interest in the genre often comes from 'the pleasure of [its] surface narrative', which frequently has to do with extreme and violent details (torture, decapitation, raging persecutors, defiant virgins, spectacular miracles, and the like). Wilcox maintains that one reason for the appeal of saints' lives is that they are 'fundamentally ironic, being premised on a duality of vision: [...] the tormenters and the worldly see things one way, the saint and the saved (and the perceptive audience) see them in another'. Though the tortured and martyred saint 'has a rough time of it indeed', still, 'all such torment is ultimately irrelevant, as the saint well recognizes' (p. 202). Wilcox calls attention to the interrelatedness of genre and style in the saint's life, with style pertaining to the linguistic surface of the tale and genre pertaining to audience expectations — two elements that are inextricably linked.

Given their multiple sources of appeal, it is no surprise that Old English narratives of holy men and women have been subject to diverse interpretations in the critical literature. An instructive example is *Judith*, as that poem is approached in the essay by Karma Lochrie that is mentioned shortly above and by Hugh Magennis in his 2002 study 'Gender and Heroism in the Old English *Judith*'.[26] Lochrie and Magennis come to incompatible conclusions about a number of aspects of *Judith* while still agreeing that the heroine of this narrative represents a strong female character. For Lochrie, the poem

---

[23]   Christopher A. Jones, 'Envisioning the *Cenobium* in the Old English *Guthlac A*', *Mediaeval Studies* 57 (1995): 259–91.

[24]   Howell D. Chickering, 'Poetic Exuberance in the Old English *Judith*', *SPh* 106 (2009): 119–36, repr. in *On the Aesthetics of Beowulf and Other Old English Poems*, ed. John M. Hill (Toronto: University of Toronto Press, 2010, 24–42.

[25]   Jonathan Wilcox, 'Eating People Is Wrong: Funny Style in *Andreas* and its Analogues', in *Anglo-Saxon Styles*, 201–22.

[26]   Hugh Magennis, 'Gender and Heroism in the Old English *Judith*', in *Writing Gender and Genre in Medieval Literature: Approaches to Old and Middle English Texts*, ed. Elaine Treharne (Cambridge: D.S. Brewer, 2002), 5–18.

undermines the Anglo-Saxon heroic ethos by reducing it to a form of male sexual aggression. Her attention centres on the Assyrian warlord Holofernes, Judith's persecutor, who operates within 'a masculine warrior economy bound by a homosocial network' – the culture of the hall – 'and a code of violence' (p. 8). When Judith succeeds in beheading the drunken Holofernes and then rallies her people to battle, Lochrie sees her in psychoanalytical terms as a woman who has appropriated 'the masculine fantasies of rape and violence' (p. 14). To paraphrase Lochrie's argument, the male code of sexual and military violence thus remains unsubverted at the end of the poem, even though the poem still serves as a cutting critique of that same male code, whose influence Lochrie traces, though with no attempt at scholarly documentation, in America's late-twentieth-century military establishment. Magennis, on the other hand, anchors his analysis of the poem not in psychoanalytical theory, nor in contemporary cultural critique, but rather in the Book of Judith, the biblical work of which the Old English poem is a free adaptation. Magennis identifies the heroine of the Old English poem as 'an exception to the norm' in Old English literature, in that she engages in violence and 'takes upon herself a terrifying heroic task' (p. 8). She is therefore ascribed heroic epithets, such as *ellenrof* 'valourous', that one would normally expect only to be applied to men. In his view, the Old English poet departs from his Latin source in depicting Judith in such a manner that she takes on a heroic role 'without losing her femaleness': she is not, for example, ascribed an Old English equivalent to the Latin adjective *viriliter* 'manly'. Magennis emphasizes that 'Judith is guided by her faith in God' (at lines 6, 89, and 344), and that it is this faith that enables her to carry out her act of deliverance.

Two different poems named *Judith* thus seem to be discussed in these articles, published eight years apart on either side of the Atlantic, one of them written by a North American feminist scholar contributing to a book on class and gender, the other by a senior male scholar contributing to a leading British journal of literary studies. Without trying to adjudicate these differences myself, I will refer the reader to a third scholar-critic, Malcolm Godden, who concludes his own analysis of the poem with the following summary remark: 'Though the traditional vision of the heroic society seems to be mildly ironized or subverted in the picture of the Assyrian army, in the representation of Judith and the Hebrews there seems to be a full-hearted acceptance of heroic values within the context of a citizen army and the defence of the native land.'[27]

Another focal point for recent critics has been the Junius manuscript of Old English poetry, which contains the biblical paraphrases *Genesis A*, *Genesis B*, *Exodus*, and *Daniel*, plus the poem known as *Christ and Satan*, which has no one model and bears a resemblance to Anglo-Saxon homiletic literature. Although, as has been mentioned, Cædmon is no longer thought to have authored any poems of the Junius manuscript, his nine-line 'Hymn' continues to arouse interest as the earliest example of Old English verse that has survived, thanks to scribal additions to the Latin text of Bede's *Historia ecclesiastica* and to the inclusion of a West Saxon version of the 'Hymn' in the Old English translation of

---

[27] Malcolm Godden, 'Biblical Literature: The Old Testament', in Godden & Lapidge, 214–33, at pp. 229–30.

Bede's history. Those with an interest in the 'Hymn' and its scribal transmission will find an invaluable resource in the form of Daniel Paul O'Donnell's 2005 book *Cædmon's Hymn: A Multi-Media Study, Edition and Archive*, with an accompanying CD-ROM.[28] As for modern criticism on Cædmon and his 'Hymn', elsewhere I have assembled an annotated guide to it covering the period up to about the year 2008.[29]

A major point of interest as regards the poems of the Junius manuscript has been *Genesis B*, with its arresting account of the temptation of Eve by Satan.[30] Alain Renoir's 1990 article 'Eve's I.Q. Rating: Two Sexist Views of *Genesis B*', brings both wit and insight to bear on this episode from one of the most admired of Old English poems, which survives in a fragment consisting of 851 poetic lines.[31] A number of additional essays on the poems of the Junius manuscript are reprinted in Roy M. Liuzza's anthology *The Poems of MS Junius 11*.[32] Noteworthy among these is James W. Earl's essay 'Christian Tradition in the Old English *Exodus*', which analyses how medieval Christian exegetical material is incorporated into an Anglo-Saxon poet's retelling of the story of Moses and the flight of the Jews from Egypt.[33] In another groundbreaking study, 'The Old English Epic of Redemption', J.R. Hall argues that the Junius manuscript as a whole, including its last section, is organized according to a unified Christian eschatological worldview as expressed in writings of the Augustinian tradition, a thesis that has provoked debate in the critical literature.[34] The attention of art historians, too, has been drawn to this manuscript. Since the poetic texts comprised in Junius 11 are accompanied by expressive line drawings showing scenes and characters from Old Testament history or other sources, critical interest has centered on the relation of these illustrations to the texts, as is discussed by Catherine E. Karkov in her 2001 book *Text and Picture in Anglo-Saxon England*.[35]

---

[28] Daniel Paul O'Donnell, *Cædmon's Hymn: A Multi-Media Study, Edition and Archive* (Cambridge: D.S. Brewer in association with SEENET and the Medieval Academy, 2005). There is also an older but still useful Methuen edition: *Three Northumbrian Poems: Cædmon's Hymn, Bede's Death Song and the Leiden Riddle*, ed. A.H. Smith (London: Methuen, 1933), reissued with corrections in 1968.

[29] This is the entry for 'Cædmon' in *Classical and Medieval Literature Criticism* (Detroit: Gale Research Co., ca. 2011). Included in that resource, which is now available online, are extracts from sixteen modern critical studies accompanied by an introduction and a select bibliography.

[30] See *The Saxon Genesis: An Edition of the West Saxon Genesis B and the Old Saxon Vatican Genesis*, ed. A.N. Doane (Madison: University of Wisconsin Press, 1991).

[31] Alain Renoir, 'Eve's I.Q. Rating: Two Sexist Views of *Genesis B*', in Damico & Olsen, 262–72.

[32] *The Poems of MS Junius 11: Basic Readings*, ed. R.M. Liuzza (London and New York: Routledge, 2002), hereafter abbreviated as *Readings: Junius MS*.

[33] James W. Earl, 'Christian Tradition in the Old English *Exodus*', *NM* 71 (1970): 541–70, repr. in *Readings: Junius MS*, 137–72.

[34] J.R. Hall, 'The Old English Epic of Redemption: The Theological Unity of MS Junius 11', *Traditio* 32 (1976): 185–208, repr. in *Readings: Junius MS*, 20–52. Note also Hall's complementary essay '"The Old English Epic of Redemption": Twenty-Five-Year Retrospective', in *Readings: Junius MS*, 53–68.

[35] Catherine E. Karkov, *Text and Picture in Anglo-Saxon England: Narrative Strategies in the Junius 11 Manuscript* (Cambridge: Cambridge University Press, 2001).

A Selection from the Criticism

Beyond any doubt, the devotional poem from the Vercelli Book that has been of sharpest interest to critics is *The Dream of the Rood*. While this is arguably the earliest example of the genre of 'dream vision' that is so well attested in medieval French and Middle English literature, the Old English poem can scarcely be understood via that later tradition. In the following selection, Edward B. Irving, Jr, approaches *The Dream of the Rood* as if from the inside, setting aside, initially, the whole body of knowledge about Christ and the Crucifixion that a reader still inevitably brings to that poem. Irving does this in an effort to grasp, and thereby help us share in, the harrowing psychological experience of the poem's nameless speaker, the figure whom Irving aptly calls 'Dreamer'. We are led through the process of that person's emergence from a 'dark night of the soul' into a state of enlightenment, thanks to the first-person speech of the personified Rood. A set of correspondences is thus established between the dreamer, the personified cross of the Crucifixion, and Christ himself, all of whom pass through a period of acute doubt and suffering before finding redemptive release from that agony. A similar trajectory of doubt and release is experienced by the reader of the poem, who is led, through Irving's analysis, to a vicarious understanding of the *via crucis*, or 'way of the Cross'.

One would not want to take Irving's essay as the only guide to the meaning of *The Dream of the Rood*. Irving clearly has little to say about the entire second half of the poem, with its closely braided theological allusions. Indeed, one could argue that the 'dramatic interaction' between the dreamer and the personified cross on which Irving fixes his attention serves as no more than a long and artistically moving prelude to the doctrinal points that follow, as the cross itself delivers a 'sermon' touching on major tenets of the faith and as the dreamer accepts his apostolic mission as a follower of Christ. Other critics besides Irving have done much to clarify the early medieval religious context in which the poem as a whole is best understood. As John V. Fleming demonstrated in his 1966 article '*The Dream of the Rood* and Anglo-Saxon Monasticism', both of the two main parts of the poem present unmistakable allusions to the monastic way of life: clearly the poem is meant to proclaim its message specifically to monks as well as to all Christians.[36] Equally significant are the poem's associations with the medieval institution of the veneration of the cross and with the liturgy of Holy Week, as Earl R. Anderson pointed out in his 1989 study 'Liturgical Influence in *The Dream of the Rood*' and as others too have since discussed.[37] In addition, Andy Orchard's 2009 article '*The Dream of the Rood*: Cross References' develops a reading context for the poem by tracing its apparent influence among writers of the Anglo-Saxon period,[38] while Éamonn Ó Carragáin's magisterial 2005 volume *Ritual and the Rood* conjoins study of this

---

[36]   John V. Fleming, '*The Dream of the Rood* and Anglo-Saxon Monasticism', *Traditio* 22 (1966): 43–72.

[37]   Earl R. Anderson, 'Liturgical Influence in *The Dream of the Rood*', *Neoph* 73 (1989): 293–304; and see Sarah Larret Keefer's more recent study 'The Dream of the Rood at Nones on Good Friday', in *Poetry, Place, and Gender: Studies in Medieval Culture in Honor of Helen Damico*, ed. Catherine E. Karkov (Kalamazoo: Medieval Institute Publications, 2009), 38–60.

[38]   Andy Orchard, '*The Dream of the Rood*: Cross-References', in Zachar and Orchard, *New Readings in the Vercelli Book*, 225–53.

poem, together with its companion piece the great Northumbrian stone monument Ruthwell Cross, to extensive research into the iconography of the cross in early medieval Europe.[39] In its own terms, still, Irving's study is a stunning example of the power of artfully crafted criticism to help current readers gain access, through a poet's visionary language, to the most profound mysteries of human existence.

Edward B. Irving, Jr (1923–1998) received the PhD from Yale University in 1951. He was soon after appointed to the faculty of English at the University of Pennsylvania, where he remained for the rest of his professional career. His two books *Reading Beowulf* (1968) and *Rereading Beowulf* (1989), discussed in previous chapters, merit a lasting place in the history of criticism of that poem. Among his other important publications on Old English literature are his essays 'Image and Meaning in the Elegies', 'Heroic Experience in the Old English Riddles', and 'The Advent of Poetry: *Christ I* '.[40]

For Further Reading

Anlezark, Daniel. 2010. 'Old English Biblical and Devotional Poetry'. In Saunders, 101–24.

Clayton, Mary. 2013. 'Preaching and Teaching', In Godden & Lapidge, 159–79.

Gatch, Milton McC. 1977. *Preaching and Theology in Anglo-Saxon England: Ælfric and Wulfstan.* Toronto: University of Toronto Press.

Hall, Thomas N. 2001. 'Biblical and Patristic Learning'. In Pulsiano & Treharne, 327–44.

Hall, Thomas N. 2005. 'Old English Religious Prose: Rhetorics of Salvation and Damnation'. In Johnson & Treharne, 136–48.

Jones, Christopher A. 2013. 'Performing Christianity: Liturgical and Devotional Writing'. In the *Cambridge History*, 427–50.

Keefer, Sarah Larratt. 2005. 'Old English Religious Poetry'. In Johnson & Treharne, 15–29.

Marsden, Richard. 2013. 'Biblical Literature: The New Testament'. In Godden & Lapidge, 234–50.

Remley, Paul G. 1996. *Old English Biblical Verse: Studies in Exodus, Genesis and Daniel.* Cambridge: Cambridge University Press.

Scheil, Andrew. 2013. 'Sacred History and Old English Religious Poetry'. In the *Cambridge History*, 406–26.

---

[39] Éamonn Ó Carragáin, *Ritual and the Rood: Liturgical Images and the Old English Poems of the 'Dream of the Rood' Tradition* (London: British Library and Toronto: University of Toronto Press, 2005).

[40] Edward B. Irving, Jr, 'Image and Meaning in the Elegies', in *Old English Poetry: Fifteen Essays*, ed. Robert P. Creed (Providence: Brown University Press, 1967), 153–66; 'Heroic Experience in the Old English Riddles', written for *Readings: Shorter Poems*, 199–212; and 'The Advent of Poetry: *Christ I*', *ASE* 25 (1996): 123–34.

Edward B. Irving, Jr, 'Crucifixion Witnessed, or Dramatic Interaction in *The Dream of the Rood*' (1986)[1]

Very few of the countless artistic representations of the Crucifixion in the Middle Ages have the capacity to seize our imaginations like the Old English poem we call *The Dream of the Rood*.[2] Probably it is rivalled only in the visual arts. Other literary attempts in English to express the complex experience of suffering and witnessing that dominates the event seem to fall short of *The Dream of the Rood*'s special intensity. I think specifically of the later religious lyrics where the listener or reader is urged to meditate on the catalogued afflictions of Christ; or the more dramatic renditions where the listener or reader, taken into the scene as spectator or passer-by, is movingly addressed directly by a reproachful Christ from the cross (particularly in the 'O vos omnes' theme),[3] or where pain is inflicted on Christ's passive body by a squad of irritable soldiers (York Crucifixion play) or (a close analogue) literary or dramatic works where the listener or reader is invited to share the helpless agony of Mary on Golgotha – this last often a dialogue between Christ's two natures, with Mary representing the suffering human and the majestic son on the cross the divine.[4]

This essay will explore the process of dramatization and the psychology of the two main characters in the poem, especially in the first half of it, trying to isolate more clearly what, despite many excellent critical attempts, have never yet been quite

---

[1]   Edward B. Irving Jr., 'Crucifixion Witnessed, or Dramatic Interaction in *The Dream of the Rood*', in *Modes of Interpretation in Old English Literature: Essays in Honour of Stanley B. Greenfield*, ed. Phyllis R. Brown et al. (Toronto: University of Toronto Press, 1986), 101–13. Used with permission from Judith Moffett and from the University of Toronto Press.

[2]   Since the critical literature on the poem is so voluminous, I mention here only a few key essays. Introduction to the two recent separate editions should be consulted: that of Bruce Dickins and Alan S.C. Ross, *The Dream of the Rood*, 4th edn (London, 1954, rpt. 1963; New York, 1966), and that of Michael Swanton, *The Dream of the Rood* (Manchester, 1970). A brief but thoughtful critical essay is J.A. Burrow, 'An Approach to *The Dream of the Rood*', *Neophil* 43 (1959) 123–33. On the poem's doctrinal content especially, see H.R. Patch, 'Liturgical Influence on *The Dream of the Rood*', *PMLA* 24 (1919) 233–57; J.V. Fleming, '*The Dream of the Rood* and Anglo-Saxon Monasticism', *Traditio* 22 (1960) 43–72; Faith H. Patten, 'Structure and Meaning in *The Dream of the Rood*', *ES* 49 (1968) 394–401; Robert B. Burlin, 'The Ruthwell Cross, *The Dream of the Rood* and the Vita Contemplativa', *SPh* 65 (1968) 23–43; N.A. Lee, 'The Unity of *The Dream of the Rood*', *Neophil* 56 (1972) 469–86.

[3]   See Rosemary Woolf, *The English Religious Lyric in the Middle Ages* (Oxford 1968) 42–5 and elsewhere, for discussion of the use of this theme, derived ultimately from Lamentations 1:12, 'O vos omnes qui transitis per viam, attendite et videte si est dolor sicut dolor meus' (oh all you who pass by the way, take heed and see if there is grief like mine), always taken to be a speech of Christ, usually from the Cross.

[4]   See Woolf's *English Religious Lyric* and also her study *The English Mystery Plays* (London, 1972), esp. 238–68.

satisfactorily defined: the operative elements in *The Dream of the Rood*'s massive emotional power. This attempt will not be quite satisfactory either, it goes without saying, but I hope it may advance our understanding and appreciation a small way by taking a slightly different approach; in any encounter with such a masterpiece, that may be worth doing.

From the very beginning of the poem and all the way on to its ending, we can see a clear process under way, a development away from confusion, or even from down-right befuddlement, towards clarity, confidence, and certainty. A poem of progressive enlightenment must begin in the dark. It should be noted that this vision-poem starts with total non-vision, the blackness of sleep and midnight, though the enthusiastic tone of the opening lines in itself hints strongly at the prospect of ultimate success.

> Hwæt! Ic swefna cyst   secgan wylle
> h[w]æt me gemætte to   midre nihte,
> syðþan reordberend   reste wunedon.   (1–3)[5]

Listen to me, I wish to tell the very best of visions, what I dreamed at midnight, when speech-bearers dwelt in their beds.

At once this darkness becomes semi-darkness, the dubious and impeded vision of the subjunctive: 'Þuhte me þæt ic gesawe / syllicre treow' ('it seemed to me that I might have seen a very strange tree'). This subjunctive form of the verb 'to see' later clarifies itself, as the features of the objects seen become more distinct, into the firmer indica-tives of lines 14 and 21: 'geseah ic' ('I clearly saw') (giving the perfective prefix 'ge-' full value). There is still much paradox here, of course, since the more plainly the object is seen, the more details are made out, the less its nature seems to be understood.

It is a very strange Tree that the character I will henceforth call simply Dreamer thinks he might have seen, a Tree first perceived as an almost formless upward surge of light and power into the air, becoming some kind of signalling object, a 'beacen', covered with brightly radiant gold and gems. That Dreamer does not yet know him-self what this object is is implied by the very fact that he is at once contrasted with, and feels himself inferior to, certain others who do know – who identify it and show their reverence towards it. Hosts of angels behold it and know it, angels we see only after his (and our) eyes have been steadily guided upward to the cross-beam and then above. The angels thus seem to appear in that 'heavenly' space above the cross-bar where we see them depicted in early Christian art, bending towards or cradling Christ's serene and divine head, while below the cross-beam, in the mortal or 'earthly' space, blood flows from Christ's wounds or his legs may be twisted in pain.[6]

---

5   Quotations from the text are taken from Swanton's edition; macrons are omitted.

6   See Swanton, 52–5, and Adolf Katzenellenbogen, 'The Image of Christ in the Early Middle Ages', in *Life and Thought in the Early Middle Ages*, ed. Robert S. Hoyt (Minneapolis, 1967) 66–84.

This tree is then a public sight, drawing the attentive gaze of many. Yet it is not the most common kind of public sight that it might at first superficially resemble, the gallows of an ordinary criminal. Like Anglo-Saxon poets elsewhere, Dreamer proceeds in his definition of what he is looking at by first eliminating what the thing is *not*. If it were a mere gallows, it could never be the cynosure of the admiring gaze of the fair and the holy, and of all men and all nature.

But repetition of the word 'syllic' ('strange') in line 13 recalls us to the state of mind of the puzzled Dreamer who cannot view the tree as the rest of the universe apparently does; they know something he does not yet know. The tree's uncomfortable strangeness takes on new meaning through the way it now makes impact on Dreamer (an impact reinforced effectively by the alliteration of 'syllic' and 'synnum'):

> Syllic wæs se sigebeam,   ond ic synnum fah,
> forwundod mid wommum.   (13–14a)

> Strange was that potent tree and I stained with sins, desperately wounded with
> corruptions.

All that we have so far been told is that Dreamer sees the glorious beauty of the tree. Why then, from where, does he get this sudden overwhelming sense of sin? One might call it an abrupt and startling sense of self, as if the object of his vision had turned without warning into a mirror of blinding clarity. It would be much too rational to say flatly that he thinks along such lines as these: 'Because I'm not able to *see* what those angels are obviously looking at, since I don't know what it can be, I must be stained and sick with sin.' But that connection of ideas must be some part of it. Part of it too is his apparent intuition that beneath all that gold and glory is hidden something uglier, blood and wounds like his own, an ugliness he seems to sense the presence of even before we are told that he actually sees it. I am fumbling without much success after something important here. Perhaps Dreamer's puzzlement, and insight, and the flickering ambivalence of what he is straining so hard to see clearly (yet perhaps also resisting the implications of) are all better reflected in strictly poetic form resistant to paraphrase: for example, in pun-like turns on words and paradoxical echoes that bring out both positive and negative meanings, in 'fah' ('bright-coloured') and 'fag' ('marked with evil'), or in 'bewunden' ('wound about, adorned') and 'forwundod' ('desperately wounded').[7] Despite the difficulties of vision, or because of the effort they demand, or because of Dreamer's new self-knowledge, it is at this point, as I remarked earlier, that he shifts fully into the indicative and can analyse with more assurance the mysteries before him, or at least take them more firmly into his range of vision.

---

[7]   Swanton, 64

He looks hard at the object. He sees a tree of glory, covered with *clothing* (can it then be a human figure, somehow?), shining with joys (emotionally electrifying and positive), drenched in the light and jewels of honour and reverence. Words wrenched slightly askew from their expected meanings (like 'wædum', 'clothing') keep telling us that this is a riddle-object before us, and that there are rules to the guessing-game one must play in identifying it. One rule is that the object is not to be called by its proper name, Rood, until the Rood itself, in lofty heroic style, names itself proudly, at the very moment when it ceases entirely to be a forest-tree and rises symbolically to become a cross, The Cross: 'Rod wæs ic aræred' ('Rood was I raised up', 44). It reminds us of how, at the appropriate stage in his advance into Denmark to take on the task of fighting the monster Grendel, another riddling heroic figure proclaims his identity: 'Beowulf is min nama' (*Beowulf*, 343).

Now, though still far from being able to guess the riddle, Dreamer peers and scrutinizes anxiously, and not altogether in vain. His vision penetrates some distance.

> Gimmas hæfdon
> bewrigene weorðlice   weald[end]es treow.[8]
> Hwæðre ic þurh þæt gold   ongytan meahte
> earmra ærgewin,   þæt hit ærest ongan
> swætan on þa swiðran healfe.   (16b–20a)

Jewels had covered beautifully the tree of the ruler. But still I could perceive *through* that gold the ancient agony of wretched men, could perceive that it first began to bleed on the right side.[a]

Dreamer speaks almost as if he had solved the riddle, breaking through a deceptive façade (jewels) to the bitter and ugly truth within. Not only does he seem to see through this mask of outward beauty in space, he seems also to peer back through time to some past history of suffering, as if the very past began to betray itself by bleeding, at the very moment when he saw it. The intense effort of perception has its immediate effect. His intuition forces him to confront himself in this glimpse of blood and agony. He is now, as he must be, paradoxically terrified of the beautiful sight: 'forht ic wæs for þære fægran gesyhðe' [I was stricken with fear in the presence of that beautiful sight] (21a).

---

[8] Probably the usual emendation of 'wealdes' to 'wealdendes' ('of the Ruler') should be made here for the sake of the metre; yet 'wealdes treow' might possibly stand in contrast to 'wuldres treow' (14), anticipating the clarifying 'Haelendes treow' (25).

[a] [An alternative translation of the last clause is as follows: 'I could perceive … the ancient agony of wretched men when it first began to bleed on the right side.' In other words, the dreamer's vision of the bleeding cross leads to his perception that this beautiful object was once associated with dreadful agony.]

Yet at this point he must stop. Without other help, he can see no more and can go no further in understanding either what is in front of him or the obscure emotions seething inside him. He can only lie passively watching the glimmering rapid transmutations of the lovely/hideous riddle-object before him: its changing of clothes and colours (hinting, though Dreamer does not yet know this, at Christ's garments, bruised skin, streaming blood); its abrupt shift from being soaked in blood-wetness to gleaming with treasure (with perhaps some constant quality of shininess as a common visual ground); its state of being 'fus', restlessly unstable and always ready to be converted into something else at any moment.

To have the Rood itself (or, to name and personify our second character, Rood himself) furnish the needed help by explaining his own meaning to Dreamer seems to require, theologically speaking, that Dreamer first be in a state of repentance, as Robert Burlin has pointed out, citing the word 'hreowcearig' in line 25 as meaning 'repentant'.[9] Such repentance involves complex feelings: Dreamer's bafflement, and his anxiety about his lack of understanding; his admiration for the Tree's remote and dazzling beauty; his flinching back from what he does partly discover about what is in front of him and what is within him; his silent childlike waiting in hope of some further guidance.

There is a clear and important transition from Dreamer's confused state to the beginning of Rood's autobiographical narrative, one that links the two characters. Rood seems at the outset of his story more than a little like Dreamer, unable to make full sense of the ironies and paradoxes of his own experience – or at least telling his story in a way to give that impression, for Rood always speaks in the present dramatic moment and without retrospective and authoritative understanding of the full meaning of the events in which he participates.

The first lines of Rood's speech place him in a somewhat misleading context:

> Ðæt wæs geara iu,   (ic þæt gyta geman),
> þæt ic wæs aheawen   holtes on ende,
> astyred of stefne minum.   (28–30a)

> That was very long ago – I still remember it – that I was hewn down at the forest's edge, moved from my trunk.

The first line is formulaic in an old tradition of heroic poetry. It is reminiscent, for example, of the opening of Beowulf's long speech before his doomed fight with the dragon, where the hero falls back on his early memories to strengthen himself for present action:

> Fela ie giogoðe   guðræsa genæs,
> orleghwila;   ic þæt eall gemon.   (2426–27)[10]

---

[9] See the article by Burlin cited above, esp. 30.
[10] Quoted from Fr. Klaeber, *Beowulf and the Fight at Finnsburg*, 3rd edn (Boston, 1951).

I survived many warlike encounters in youth, times of fighting. I remember all that.

The associations of such a formula might prepare us to think of Rood as a heroic figure but, as he tells what happened to him, we wonder whether he indeed plays any heroic role at all, for he seems disturbingly passive for a hero, allowing others to cut him down (warriors are 'hewn down' in Old English poetry just as trees are), carry him, make evil use of him. His history thus is a close parallel to the preceding vision, where the glorious (heroic) Tree as Dreamer sees it is half the time scarred and blurred by marks of defeat and bloody agony. The placing of verbs at the crucial beginnings of verses in lines 30–33 ('astyred', 'genamon', 'geworhton', 'heton', 'bæron', 'gefæstnodon') relentlessly stresses the series of brutal actions carried out *on* him, ironically reminding us of the many actions this hero is *not* carrying out himself. When Rood at last sees Christ approaching him to be crucified, the exertion of heroic will is largely transferred from the passive Rood to Christ ('he me wolde on gestigan', 'he wanted to climb up on me', 34).

But it is important to see that, if Rood begins in some sense from where Dreamer is, there is almost immediately a movement in his case from merely inert passivity towards a tense and deliberate willing of such inaction, a willing so strong as to be a kind of action, as Rood comes to understand the incredible situation in which he has been placed. To the extent (a large extent) that he partakes of the role of hero, he must now endure the hardest fate a hero can suffer: to be blocked completely from taking any action. Action is the natural mode of the hero's being and his essential definition. To be thus blocked from it is to feel great pain. Familiar examples from *Beowulf* are King Hrothgar seething with helpless anger under Grendel's unrelenting attacks on his hall, or Hengest enduring the long winter in a foreign hall, prevented for a time by complex circumstances from avenging his king's death. Rood can neither defend his king nor avenge his death. Worse yet, unimaginably terrible, God his king has ordered him to be an accomplice, chief agent even, in the very torture and murder of God: Rood is given the technical term 'bana' ('bane', or 'slayer') in line 66. Though Rood now feels this pain, he does not yet fully understand that what he now suffers is the new Christian heroism of the martyr rather than the old Germanic heroism. Literally uprooted Tree – a hero not allowed to be a hero – and figuratively uprooted Dreamer thus share a sense of disorientation.

Such a parallel between Rood and Dreamer seems a compelling one. The way Rood speaks at first shows full sympathy with Dreamer's confusion, as if he were implying something like: 'Even though I myself actually went through this experience, at first I couldn't understand it.' In Dreamer's original vision, the same paradox of blood and glory was laid out in spatial terms, side by side, or so nearly simultaneous as to seem to overlap in time; this is now matched by the more clearly temporal, step-by-step experience of Rood himself. Possibly there is a further parallel to Dreamer's humiliating sense of being stained by sins in Rood's compulsive returning to the topic of what he feels as his 'heroic sin', that is, his failure to act to protect or avenge his lord. One might imagine Rood saying: 'I too have felt miserably guilty, just as you are feeling now.' Though Rood's narrative now moves rapidly into the heart of mystery, it must not move so rapidly that the merely human Dreamer cannot follow.

Although up till now I have been doggedly insisting on viewing the interaction between these two fictional characters on the level of literal drama and assuming that this level is of primary importance in the poem's effect on its audience, this artificially limited way of looking at the poem is bound to become intolerably strained, for obviously we cannot go on pretending that we really do not know anything about the symbolic (that is, 'real') meaning of the text. This is only to say, to put it in theatrical terms, that the dramatic irony of the scene is too highly developed to be ignored. If Dreamer and Rood do not know – or do not know clearly and fully at this point in the narrative time-line of the poem – we know, although it is not easy to state discursively and explicitly all that we know when we begin to lay out all the complexities the dramatic situation implies within a new and 'proper' framework of theological meaning. What does the Rood stand for?[11] We can enumerate some things: Christ as man, a human sufferer pierced by dark nails and racked by conflicts and doubts; as son (an Isaac type dumbly obedient to the inexplicable demands of a father who seems to have forsaken him); as the innocent Paradisal world of non-human nature (the Tree as Peaceable Kingdom), violated and appalled by man's cruelty and forced, against nature, to torture nature's own creator; as a dignified and proud participant and witness/martyr; as an apostle-preacher giving us the most literally 'inside' version of the Crucifixion we could imagine; as an object-lesson in how this pride and this new kind of heroic achievement can grow precisely out of the enduring of abasement and humiliation. As has come to be generally recognized, making the figure of the Rood represent chiefly the passively suffering human dimension of Christ allows the actual character of Christ who appears in the poem to be one of pure heroic will, in part human courage but chiefly God's intense will to save mankind. Yet the theological information the poem provides is nothing Christians do not already know. In that sense they hardly need the poem. What makes the poem needed is the way it leads to understanding not through ideas but through feelings about ideas as they are acted out in dramatic time. The knowledge we gain must be experiential: like Dreamer and Rood, we come to know through sharing in suffering and suspense.

One chief way the nature, duration, and intensity of Rood's suffering is brought out is by the stylistic feature that is most striking in the first part of Rood's speech (28–73): extraordinarily heavy repetitions of certain words and phrases. Use of so rigorously limited a set of words in itself creates a feeling of psychological entrapment. As part of a spoken utterance, the repetitions vividly imitate the obsessive and reiterative mumblings of a shock-victim. 'I saw ... but I didn't dare ... I could have ... but I didn't ... I trembled ... but I couldn't ... they hurt me ... but I couldn't hurt them.' Four times in only 13 lines the phrase 'ic ne dorste' (with minor variations) appears; each time it does, we are brought back from some new detail of horror and

---

[11] See the works listed in note 2.

outrage to the small prison of paralysed action, Rood's tormented inability to take vengeance. Rood's every wish to act is blocked by the stern adversatives of necessity, 'hwæðre', 'ac', in a way at least vaguely analogous to the frustration of Dreamer's attempts to seize on the security of a single meaning for his vision of the Tree. However Rood feels, whatever occurs, he must remain fixed in his standing position. He cannot bow, or break, or use his strength to crush the insolent 'enemies' who torment him and his beloved king. He must always stand fast, his only movement an anguished trembling in resonance with the anguished trembling of the earth itself convulsed in earthquake. The movements that surround Rood emphasize his immobility: Christ hurries to climb up and embrace him; dark nails are driven into him; blood streams down. Only at the end he moves just a little, bowing forward to let the disciples lift Christ's body down from the remorseful clutch of its wretched murderer and most faithful retainer.

Enduring physical and emotional pain is only part of Rood's role in this scene. He must also play the important role of eyewitness. Here again the repetitions are many: not only the 'geseah ic' of lines 33 and 51 and the 'ic þæt eall beheold' of 58, but Rood's showing forth of his deep wounds, still there to be inspected as evidence by Dreamer (here briefly playing the part of doubting Thomas to the resurrected Christ); the witnessing crowd of 'many' who observe Christ's courage in mounting the 'high gallows'; the watch or wake of the mourning disciples over Christ's cooling body; Rood's own witnessing (and this is surely an original detail) of the carving of the sepulchre from 'bright stone'. At all points, the event of the Crucifixion experience must be fully attested and publicly authenticated.

And its implications must be understood. Like Dreamer (as I have been arguing), Rood seems to move gradually towards such understanding, first from frightened passivity to violent conflict and horror, which reaches a climax in lines 46–49 describing the nailing, wounding, mocking, bleeding of Rood and King together, and then on towards summary statement, a stage that may begin in line 50:

> Feala ic on þam beorge   gebiden hæbbe
> wraðra wyrda.   Geseah ic weruda God
> þearle þenian.   (50–52a)

I have experienced many angry fates on that hill. I saw the God of Hosts stretched out in agony.

Such verses suggest at least some small measure of distance from the immediate pain, and a clearer and calmer view of what has been happening. As Rood looks about him in the lines that follow – is now *able* to look about him and beyond his own pain – he sees that darkness has fallen and that all Creation weeps, lamenting the King's fall. We recognize the 'cosmic' setting in which Rood first appeared in Dreamer's vision. Now Rood is able to name Christ for the first time in the poem, seeing and naming this scene as we ourselves see it: 'Crist wæs on rode' ('Christ was on the cross', 56).

This same phrase is, incidentally, given special prominence in the runic verses from the poem selected to be carved on the Ruthwell Cross: it appears at the top of the west face. We should recall that that great stone cross is personified; all the passages on it come from Rood's speech.

Now the narrative slows down markedly in pace and intensity. Rood watches gravely as the disciples come to remove, mourn over, and bury Christ's body. Since they fill our field of vision while this goes on, they shift our attention away from Rood's vivid experiences towards what he is watching. After singing their own sorrow-song, the three personified crosses stand alone in a weeping group reminiscent of the three Marys of many pictures of the Crucifixion scene and of the later religious drama. Like Christ, the crosses are then brought to ground and buried; like Christ, Rood undergoes later resurrection and receives great honour. The actions here are spaced out and fewer; feelings are given more leisure for expression. We are moving towards Rood's calm interpretation of his own passionate story and his application of it to Dreamer, as the poem shifts down very noticeably from the intense narrative mode to the discursive and hortatory. Both modes would certainly have seemed equally important to the original poet and audience, but for many modern readers the interesting part of the poem is over at this point. Older editors often tried to jettison the last half as inept later addition or interpolation. But the poem cannot truly be over until Dreamer's questions are concretely answered, the dialogue is completed, and Dreamer's own response to the explanation made to him is registered. And so, point by point, the mysteries of the initial vision are explicitly made clear.

The experience undergone by Rood himself in being first lowered (humiliated, wounded, buried) and then raised to glory is first summarized for Dreamer as a 'personal' experience before it is explicitly extended to the experience of Christ and combined with it:

> On me Bearn Godes
> þrowode hwile.   Forþan ic þrymfæst nu
> hlifige under heofenum,   ond ic hælan mæg
> æghwylcne anra   þara þe him bið egesa to me.   (83b–86)

On me God's son suffered for a time, and so now glorious I tower under the heavens, and I can heal everyone who is in awe of me.

Here the Tree we saw in the earlier vision towering towards heaven and worshipped by all Creation reappears, but now we can see and understand why it soars so high – because God's son went so low. The suffering is exactly what brings the glory; there is no way pain can be separated from the splendour that inheres in the Incarnation. The rhythms of the pattern are compelling. I fell, I rose; I was tormented, I am worshipped, with the alliteration strongly marking this contrast of pain and glory in 'þrowode'/'þrymfæst' (84) and in 'leodum laðost'/'lifes weg' (88). The wounded and bewildered Rood has now become, despite and because of his own suffering, a healer and a guide for all men who seek him, enlightened and able to give enlightenment through his own ordeal. He makes his final reference to his natural origin in the forest in a crucial identification of himself with Mary, the natural member of the race of women who was, like him, elected by God to be 'theotokos', God-bearer. Three strong epithets for God ('wuldres Ealdor', 'heofonrices Weard', 'ælmihtig God') are massed in the sentence to emphasize the divine power that fused itself with these two earthly beings, woman and tree, in the Incarnation and in the Crucifixion.

The parallel with Mary seems to bring the Rood down closer to the world of men. Certainly for the rest of his speech his attention is entirely human-directed. Dreamer is instructed to describe the vision he has had to men and to identify to them the object of his vision ('þæt hit is wuldres beam', 'that it is the tree of glory', 97) in explicit terms. God suffered on the rood expressly for the many sins of 'manncyn' and of Adam (98–100). God rose from death to help men, and he will return on Doomsday to seek mankind. He will search out and he will find each individual man on that day. Then the normal response of each person will be fear, exactly like – now we understand it! – the fear felt by Dreamer in the vision as he became conscious that his sins were exposed to God's view. In the new context we see such anxiety as an experience all must go through. Yet the scene of Judgment is put in consoling terms. Such fear is not to be feared. There will be no person there who will not be afraid, because every man was afraid to volunteer to die on the Cross. Against this background, the Rood's courage stands out absolutely. He has managed to transcend and vanquish the fear inherent in all ordinary beings, and has thus now become the true source of courage for all, worn as a crucifix on each man's breast at Judgment Day. Every soul can seek heaven through that symbol. The whole immense story, as in *Paradise Lost*, has now been internalized. Cosmic narrative and myth are contracted into one small but all-powerful talisman, the Rood as the Key to the Kingdom.

Dreamer's final lines can best be seen, in contrast with his profound disorientation at the opening, as a new orientation, a repointing and redirection of himself. As God's (and the Rood's) full attention is now blazingly directed upon the Dreamer, he is at once pulled magnetically towards the Rood, and continues to point towards it:

> Gebæd ic me þa to þam   beame bliðe mode,
> elne mycle,   þær ic ana wæs
> mæte werede.   Wæs modsefa
> afysed on forðwege;   feala ealra gebad
> langunghwila.   (122–126a)

I prayed earnestly towards that tree with happy heart and great zeal, where I was alone with a tiny band. My mind was ready for the journey outward; I had lived through a great many times of misery.

It should be noted that Dreamer not only prays to and towards Rood but he is also 'imitating', that is, he is using language that recalls Rood's story. The body of Christ was also abandoned by its friends, as Dreamer says he is, and left 'with a tiny band' (69); Rood too told us what he had lived through ('gebiden', 79). Dreamer is now intent on seeking the fulfilment of his life's hope in the 'sigebeam' and realizes that his protection depends entirely on the Rood ('geriht to þære rode', 131). His friends having already passed on to heaven, Dreamer waits for the time his friend Rood will return in reality, not merely in the mists of dream as before, and will bring him back to the great feast in God's hall. By viewing the Rood as rescuer, the Dreamer can place himself appropriately among those fabled waiters-in-hell, the Old Testament patriarchs who expect the arrival of Christ on the great day of the Harrowing of Hell. To those so long in burning and darkness (and Dreamer's painful experience during his vision may include him among these), the heroic Son appears to open up hell and lead them all in triumph back to his native land. That same young hero Rood once saw hastening fearlessly towards his execution is now the young king assuming his birthright in his own kingdom and sharing that birthright in glory with his ecstatic followers. All the elements of the initial vision are now in place and fully lighted. The poem ends here on a satisfactorily resolving chord.

I have tried to show that *The Dream of the Rood* differs from the common medieval lecture-dialogue of Platonic ancestry (Lady Philosophy explaining the universe to the prisoner Boethius, or Beatrice instructing Dante, or – in parody – the Eagle suffocating the hapless Chaucer in verbiage in *The House of Fame*) in that the lecturer is entitled to speak with ultimate authority only when he has first shared with his listener similar acute bewilderment and pain. In this poem the essential experience, the Crucifixion, is thus seen from two angles that meet in a single image of unparalleled spiritual and psychological richness.

10

Ælfric

The one known author of the late Anglo-Saxon period whose polished writings would stand out as exceptional in any period of English literature is Ælfric (ca. 950 – ca. 1010), known as Ælfric of Eynsham since he served as abbot of the newly refounded Oxfordshire abbey of Eynsham for the last five or so years of his life. Previously, from 987 to 1005, he had been a monk and priest at the abbey of Cerne Abbas, Dorset. It is there, in the peaceful Cerne valley in the Dorset downs, that he is thought to have written most of his works, doing what he could within the span of one lifetime to set the devotional life in England on a sound basis from his orthodox Christian perspective. His achievement is especially impressive when viewed against the dark clouds of political turbulence that increasingly disrupted the realm during the long and troubled reign of Æthelred the Unready (r. 978–1016).

The identity of Ælfric is now firmly established after a long period of uncertainty and misapprehension in that regard; likewise the corpus of his genuine works is now well defined.[1] Interest still attends the question of how the canon of his works was subject to revision during the period of two to three centuries after his death.[2] Ælfric is now seen

---

[1] See Joyce Hill, 'Ælfric: His Life and Works', in Magennis & Swan, 35–65; or for a capsule summary of current knowledge, Malcolm Godden, 'Ælfric of Eynsham', in *Blackwell Encyclopaedia*, 8–9. The determination of the corpus and chronology of Ælfric's works owes much to the research of Peter Clemoes, 'The Chronology of Ælfric's Works', in *The Anglo-Saxons: Studies in Some Aspects of their History and Culture Presented to Bruce Dickins*, ed. P.A.M. Clemoes (London: Bowes & Bowes, 1959), 212–47, repr. in *Readings: OE Prose*, 29–72.

[2] This and related questions having to do with the posthumous use of Ælfric's writings are discussed by Aaron J. Kleist, 'Assembling Ælfric: Reconstructing the Rationale behind Eleventh- and Twelfth-Century Compilations', in Magennis & Swan, 369–98, and by Elaine Treharne, 'Making their Presence Felt: Readers of Ælfric, c. 1050–1350', in Magennis & Swan, 399–422.

Old English Literature: A Guide to Criticism with Selected Readings, First Edition. John D. Niles.
© 2016 John D. Niles. Published 2016 by John Wiley & Sons, Ltd.

not just as a pious Christian author, capable of writing English prose that is a model of clarity and elegance, but also as the leading spokesman for the late tenth-century Benedictine Reform of English monasticism.[3] While this term is used in a broad way to refer to the revival of organized English monasticism after the period of devastation caused by the ninth-century Viking wars, more narrowly it refers to the ecclesiastical reforms instituted by churchmen connected with the royal court at Winchester, particularly during the reign of King Edgar the Peaceable (r. 959–75). The leading ecclesiasts of the Reform included Dunstan, who was abbot of Glastonbury from the mid-940s on and was then named Archbishop of Canterbury (959–88), and Æthelwold, who served successively as abbot of Abingdon (ca. 954–63) and bishop of Winchester (963–84) and who founded a school at the Old Minster, Winchester, that was a model for other schools established during this period of reorganization. Ælfric can be seen as a 'second generation' product of the Reform and the person who brought it most fully to fruition in the realms of learning and education.

As Mechthild Gretsch has remarked in her 1999 book *The Intellectual Foundations of the English Benedictine Reform*, the Latin language and the English language were 'the two pillars on which Æthelwold's school rested'.[4] It is natural that in the context of the bilingualism of this period, Ælfric composed his major works in English, even though he must have regarded Latin as his chief language of literacy. In many ways his broad literary output reminds one of Bede's, dating from two and a half centuries earlier, with the difference that Bede wrote his works in Latin for a clerical elite, while Ælfric directed the great bulk of his writings – his homilies and saints' lives, in particular – to a mixed audience that could have included regular clergy, secular clergy, and members of the laity. His leading purpose in many of his writings seems to have been to make the essentials of orthodox Christian doctrine and learning available to all English-speaking persons with a desire for education or enlightenment, in language that they could understand and that they could profit from, both intellectually and in the moral conduct of their lives. Ælfric was thus a leading figure in the 'culture of translation' of Anglo-Saxon England, never striving for innovation or originality and yet also never merely derivative in his use of Latinate sources.

---

[3] For a succinct overview of the historical processes involved in the Reform, see Michael Lapidge, 'Monasticism', in *Blackwell Encyclopaedia*, 320–22; more detail is provided by George Hardin Brown, 'The Anglo-Saxon Monastic Revival', in *Renaissances before the Renaissance: Cultural Revivals of Late Antiquity and the Middle Ages*, ed. Warren Treadgold (Stanford: Stanford University Press, 1984), 99–113. The best social history of the church in early England is John Blair's *The Church in Anglo-Saxon Society* (Oxford: Oxford University Press, 2005). For a revisionist view of what was involved in the Reform, see Christopher A. Jones, 'Ælfric and the Limits of "Benedictine Reform"', in Magennis & Swan, 67–108.

[4] Mechthild Gretsch, *The Intellectual Foundations of the English Benedictine Reform* (Cambridge: Cambridge University Press, 1999), 2. Gretch addresses the Reform's impact on English schools and on the development of a specialized 'Winchester vocabulary', as does Joyce Hill, 'The Benedictine Reform and Beyond', in Pulsiano & Treharne, 151–69. See also the studies by Gretsch cited in Chapter 3 above, at n. 77.

Since Ælfric was a prolific author of homilies, saints' lives, and pedagogical works, among incidental writings some of which are of great interest,[5] the character of his achievements resists being summarized in just a few paragraphs. One entry point to his thought, particularly as regards the practice of translation from Latin sources into English, is afforded by the prefaces he appended to his leading works. These include Latin and English prefaces to his two series of Catholic Homilies; Latin and English prefaces to his lives of the saints; Latin and English prefaces to his *Grammar*; and his 'Preface to Genesis', which introduces his English translation of the first part of the Vulgate Genesis. In this latter preface he explicates in brief the system of figural exegesis by which Christians, departing from Jewish practice, were to read the books of the Old Testament.[6] All these prefaces and a few related texts have been gathered together by Jonathan Wilcox in a teaching edition equipped with a glossary, notes, and modern English translations of the Latin.[7] Their leading ideas are explored by Mary Swan in her 2009 study 'Identity and Ideology in Ælfric's Prefaces'.[8] Swan calls particular attention to Ælfric's use of first-person rhetoric, a form of address that, while asserting his authority as a spokesman for orthodoxy, also establishes positions for his addressees which either 'identify them as fellow-members' of the community of reformed monks or 'allow them the possibility of joining this circle by correct belief and practice' (p. 269).

Since Ælfric's works of a pedagogical or a homiletic character are touched on in earlier chapters of the present book, my focus here will be on his collection known in modern times as his *Lives of Saints*, though its contents are in fact somewhat miscellaneous.[9] As Malcolm Godden discusses in his 1996 study 'The Saints' Lives in Ælfric's Catholic Homilies',[10] Ælfric incorporated about twenty-six narratives of a hagiographical kind in his two series of Catholic Homilies. Clearly his engagement with hagiography was both deep and sustained, for he drew on saints' lives again and again to illustrate points relating to doctrine, morality, and church history. To judge from Godden's analysis, he gradually perfected the mature narrative style that he employs with confidence in his later collection the *Lives of Saints*.

---

5   Note in particular *Ælfric's Letter to the Monks of Eynsham*, ed. Christopher A. Jones (Cambridge: Cambridge University Press, 1998); this letter sets forth the Benedictine rule as it was to be observed at Ælfric's monastery of Eynsham. For an edition of Ælfric's long treatise on the Old and New Testaments known as his Letter to Sigeweard, see *The Old English Heptateuch and Ælfric's Libellus de Veteri Testamento et Novo*, ed. Richard Marsden, vol. 1, EETS o.s. 330 (Oxford: Oxford University Press, 2008), 201–30. For a modern English translation of that latter text – one dating from 1623 – see pp. 15–75 of *The Old English Version of the Heptateuch, Ælfric's Treatise on the Old and New Testament, and his Preface to Genesis*, ed. S.J. Crawford, EETS 160 (London: Oxford University Press, 1922), repr. with additions, 1969.

6   Marsden, *The Old English Heptateuch*, 3–7. A convenient teaching edition of the 'Preface to Genesis' is available in Mitchell & Robinson, 202–7.

7   Jonathan Wilcox, *Ælfric's Prefaces*, Durham Medieval Texts, 9 (Durham: Department of English Studies, 1994).

8   Mary Swan, 'Identity and Ideology in Ælfric's Prefaces', in Magennis & Swan, 247–69.

9   *Ælfric's Lives of Saints*, ed. Walter W. Skeat, 2 vols, EETS o.s. 76, 82, 94, 114 (London: Oxford University Press, 1881–1900), with facing-page translations.

10   Malcolm Godden, 'Experiments in Genre: The Saints' Lives in Ælfric's Catholic Homilies', in *Holy Men & Women*, 261–87.

From a modern critical perspective, Ælfric's saints' lives have proved to be by far his most engaging works, for in them he not only uses a prose style that is deliberately reminiscent of Old English alliterative verse, though devoid of its stylistic embellishments. He also recounts narratives that are both devout and distinctly heroic, in the broad sense of that term. Moreover – though Ælfric's writings are scarcely sensational, and though he does almost nothing to individualize his saints – these stories have an appeal that rests on their deployment of miracles, wonders, stark and vivid contrasts, forceful dialogue, graphic violence, and other narrative elements of an arresting kind. Like all saints' lives, as well, his lives astonish one with the power of holy men and women to triumph over each and every challenge or ordeal, to the glory of God and to the abasement of the powers of evil on earth – a theme capable of offering hope to mortals in any dark time.

The appeal of these stories could thus to some extent be characterized as escapist, though Ælfric himself would never have thought of them in that way. In any event, they rely at every moment on the conventions of their genre. As Thomas D. Hill has pointed out in his 1996 study 'Genre, Symbolism, and Anglo-Saxon Hagiography',[11] their appeal can be likened to that of medieval romance literature – another genre where wonders and marvels abound. Hill thus suggests using the term 'sacral romance' to refer to them in acknowledgement that they feature non-naturalistic plots that are often of an emblematic kind. One might add that just as in the *Zaubermärchen* or 'wondertale' of Europe in its classic form, the audience's delight in the genre of saints' lives is not diminished by the flatness of the characters depicted.[12] As Hugh Magennis has written in his 1996 article 'Ælfric and the Legend of the Seven Sleepers',[13] the saints in Ælfric's version of the 'Sleepers' legend 'are not shown as people with whom the audience can identify or sympathize'. Rather, 'they exist on a rarified and emotionless level, on which there is no concern with worldly need or with fears. In their transfigured state at the end of the narrative their faces may shine like the sun, but the saints are also in a sense transfigured from ordinary life in the rest of the narrative as well, being presented as changeless icons rather than as striving human beings at a time of trial' (p. 326). The protagonists of these tales can thus suffer gruesome ordeals or punishments without one necessarily being repelled in horror, for their eventual transfiguration is assured. Michael Lapidge makes a similar point in his 2013 study 'The Saintly Life in Anglo-Saxon England', a chapter that offers a masterful overview of the genre of hagiography. Lapidge finds a rationale for the stylization of these tales in Ælfric's devotional purposes:

> Certainly Ælfric regarded himself as the apologist of the universal Church: and it would have been no compliment to tell him that his hagiography imparted individual characteristics to individual saints. On the contrary, Ælfric would wish his saints to be seen merely as vessels of God's divine design on earth, indistinguishable as such one from the other, all worthy of our veneration and all able to intercede for us with the unapproachable deity.[14]

---

[11] Thomas D. Hill, '*Imago Dei*: Genre, Symbolism, and Anglo-Saxon Hagiography', in *Holy Men & Women*, 35–50.

[12] Cf. the remarks by the Swiss literary scholar and folklorist Max Lüthi as regards the abstract style of the classic fairy tale of the Grimm type: *The European Folktale: Form and Nature*, trans. John D. Niles (Philadelphia: Institute for the Study of Human Issues, 1982), esp. chap. 2, 'Depthlessness' (pp. 11–23).

[13] Hugh Magennis, 'Ælfric and the Legend of the Seven Sleepers', in *Holy Men & Women*, 317–31.

[14] Michael Lapidge, 'The Saintly Life in Anglo-Saxon England', in Godden & Lapidge, 251–72, at 269.

Compared with other collections of saints' lives that we know of from the early Middle Ages, Ælfric's compilation seems inclusive almost to the point of making up a canon, especially when one takes into account the additional lives incorporated into his Catholic Homilies. One finds nothing comparable to this in the English-language tradition until the late thirteenth century, when the major anthology known as the *South English Legendary* was compiled. 'After Ælfric', as Lapidge drily remarks, 'there was not much left for other Old English hagiographers to do' (p. 266). Still, Ælfric was only one among very many early medieval hagiographers, and another twenty or so additional prose *vitae* have come down to us in Old English. While many saints who figure in Ælfric's *Lives of Saints* (such as St Eugenia, St Sebastian, St Apollinarius of Ravenna, St Eustace, and St Martin) had a cult that spanned Europe, Ælfric also had a clear interest in saints native to Britain. Examples from the early Anglo-Saxon period are St Alban, St Oswald, and St Æthelthryth (or Etheldreda), three saints who previously had been celebrated by Bede. Among the holy men and women of the later Anglo-Saxon period who figure in Ælfric's collection, one is St Edmund king and martyr (d. 869); another is St Swithin (d. 863), a somewhat obscure bishop of Winchester whose posthumous cult was promoted by the leaders of the Benedictine Reform. As is argued by the historian David Rollason in his 1989 study *Saints and Relics in Anglo-Saxon England*,[15] the political dimension of saints' lives is a point of perennial interest. Ælfric's retelling of the story of the martyrdom of St Edmund at the hands of marauding ninth-century Danes, for example, has an obvious relevance to the Viking wars of Ælfric's own late tenth-century period day. Likewise the canonization of St Swithin, together with the publishing of an authorized *vita* of that saint, has an equally transparent relation to the establishment of Winchester as the capital city of a united tenth-century Christian kingdom.

A portion of the recent criticism on Ælfric's saints' lives has focused on two related themes: their relation to the pre-existing Anglo-Saxon heroic tradition, and their attitude towards the notion of 'justified violence'. The first of these topics is taken up by Jocelyn Wogan-Browne in her article 'The Hero in Christian Reception: Ælfric and Heroic Poetry'.[16] Arguing against critics' prior tendency to regard Ælfric's concept of heroism as a Christian transformation of the Germanic heroic ethos, she interprets it with reference to prior Christian tradition alone. In her view, 'The social relations and values of the Germanic heroic ethos' – the value put on vengeance, treasure-giving, and loyalty, in particular – are simply 'not present' in these lives (p. 218). Responding to that view in his 2006 article 'Ælfric and Heroic Literature', Hugh Magennis argues that the social and ethical value-system of heroic literature is not just 'irrelevant' to Ælfric's project; it is 'counterproductive' to it, and so Ælfric actively works to avoid it.[17] Ælfric's soldier saints, in particular, in striking contrast to Byrhtnoth in *The Battle of Maldon*, 'take no pleasure' in acts of war (p. 41). To this end

---

[15] David Rollason, *Saints and Relics in Anglo-Saxon England* (Oxford: Blackwell, 1989), esp. chap. 5 ('The Politics of Sainthood') and chap. 6 ('The Cult of Saints and the Unification of England').

[16] Jocelyn Wogan-Browne, 'The Hero in Christian Reception: Ælfric and Heroic Poetry', in *La funzione dell' eroe germanico: storicità, metafora, paradigma*, ed. Teresa Pàroli (Rome: Il Calamo, 1995), 323–46, repr. in Liuzza, 215–35.

[17] Hugh Magennis, 'Ælfric and Heroic Literature', in *The Power of Words: Anglo-Saxon Studies Presented to Donald G. Scragg*, ed. Hugh Magennis and Jonathan Wilcox (Morgantown: West Virginia University Press, 2006), 31–60, at 36.

Ælfric employs diction that, while sometimes formulaic, is studiously 'non-Germanic' in its formulaic character, even when, in his paraphrase of the Books of Maccabees, he portrays fierce and ruthless warriors who defend their land against heathen invaders.

Likewise, the question of Ælfric's attitude to warfare in general has been a subject of critical controversy. In the article just cited as well as in his earlier study 'Warrior Saints, Warfare, and the Hagiography of Ælfric of Eynsham',[18] Hugh Magennis emphasizes that Ælfric both softens the violence of his warrior saints and reads Old Testament narratives in a spiritual sense, so that what might at first seem like the advocacy of just warfare can be seen upon reflection to refer to the topos of the *miles Christi*, 'the soldier of Christ', of whom the monk is the supreme exemplar. James W. Earl, in his 1999 study 'Violence and Non-Violence in Anglo-Saxon England',[19] goes yet further in the direction of seeing Ælfric as an advocate of Christian non-violence. Earl's view has been contested, however, by John Edward Damon in his 2003 book *Soldier Saints and Holy Warriors*,[20] as well as by E. Gordon Whatley in his 2007 study 'Hagiography and Violence: Military Men in Ælfric's Lives of Saints'.[21] Damon holds that Ælfric worked towards a synthesis of potentially irreconcilable attitudes about the legitimacy of violence through reference to the medieval doctrine of the three estates: 'following the divine will', in this understanding, 'leads the cleric to abstain from war, the warrior to wage war, and the king to lead both orders in accord with the will of God' (p. 244). In Damon's view, Ælfric's lives of martial saints thus form 'an important part of the prehistory of crusading ideology' (p. 246). In like manner, Whatley sees the 'sanitized violence' of these tales as a symptom of something new in the Europe of this time, namely 'the church's incorporation of violence into Christian thought and practice' (p. 230). In view of critics' conflicting responses to these questions, it is possible that Ælfric composed his lives in such a manner as not to seem doctrinaire on any point other than one: namely, that members of the clergy were not to bear arms or take a personal role in acts of violence of any kind, whatever others did.

A point of special interest has been Ælfric's depiction of holy women, a topic discussed by Shari Horner in her 2001 book *The Discourse of Enclosure*.[22] Relying in part on recent

---

18 Hugh Magennis, 'Warrior Saints, Warfare, and the Hagiography of Ælfric of Eynsham', *Traditio* 56 (2001): 27–51. Cf. Damian Fleming, 'A Demilitarized Saint: Ælfric's *Life of St. Sebastian*', *Anglia* 127 (2009): 1–21.

19 James W. Earl, 'Violence and Non-Violence in Anglo-Saxon England: Ælfric's *Passion of St. Edmund*,' *PQ* 78 (1999): 125–49.

20 John Edward Damon, *Soldier Saints and Holy Warriors: Warfare and Sanctity in the Literature of Early England* (Aldershot: Ashgate, 2003), chap. 6: 'Ælfric: Path of the Holy Christian Warrior'.

21 E. Gordon Whatley, 'Hagiography and Violence: Military Men in Ælfric's Lives of Saints', in *Source of Wisdom: Old English and Early Medieval Latin Studies in Honour of Thomas D. Hill*, ed. Charles D. Wright, Frederick M. Biggs, and Thomas N. Hall (Toronto: University of Toronto Press, 2007), 217–38.

22 Shari Horner, 'Bodies and Borders: The Hermeneutics of Enclosure in Ælfric's Lives of Female Saints', chap. 4 (pp. 131–72) of her *The Discourse of Enclosure: Representing Women in Old English Literature* (Albany: State University of New York Press, 2001). Of related interest though different in their approach are two studies by Mary Clayton: 'Ælfric's *Judith*: Manipulative or Manipulated?', *ASE* 23 (1994): 215–27, and 'Ælfric's *Esther*: A *Speculum Reginae*?', in *Text and Gloss: Studies in Insular Learning and Literature Presented to Joseph Donovan Pheifer*, ed. Helen Conrad O'Brian, Anne Marie D'Arcy, and John Scattergood (Dublin: Four Courts Press, 1999), 89–101.

scholarship by such feminist theorists as Elaine Scarry and Carolyn Dinshaw, Horner examines how Ælfric's representations of female saints and their bodily torments contributes to the creation of a gendered social system, doing so in part through a 'corporeal hermeneutics' by which 'sacred texts are interpreted either literally (through the body) or spiritually' (p. 136). Pursuing this line of thought in her 2000 article 'Gender, Humor, and Discourse in Ælfric's Lives of Saints', Horner writes against the stereotype that Old English literature is 'predominantly harsh' and is preoccupied with 'the pain and sorrow of this world'.[23] She shows on the contrary that the commonplace whereby 'the young, apparently powerless virgin' is confronted by 'her physically and politically powerful persecutor' is sometimes exploited in Ælfric's saints' lives for incongruous and even humorous effect (p. 130).

Incidentally, at the start of this last-named essay, Horner calls attention to a rather remarkable misstatement made by two respected contemporary specialists in women's literature. This is that 'Anglo-Saxon culture, which predated Christianity in England, was oblivious of or hostile to women.'[24] One sees signs here not just of a fissure between the relative perceptions of most Anglo-Saxonists and certain modernists, but of a gaping chasm. While one is not surprised to learn that certain late twentieth-century scholars believe the Anglo-Saxons to have been categorically misogynist, one wonders what Ælfric would have thought if he had known that posterity would think of him as pre-Christian.

The question of who made up the audience for these lives is another one of current interest. Modern readers of Ælfric's saints' lives have naturally wondered: 'Who did he write them for?' Clearly not just for his two chief lay patrons, Æthelweard and his son Æthelmær, who were successively ealdormen of the western provinces and leading figures at the court of King Æthelred the Unready.[25] In his 2006 article 'The Audience of Ælfric's Saints' Lives', Jonathan Wilcox reviews the evidence with a bearing on this matter and arrives at a complex answer: namely, that the *Lives of Saints* 'probably saw use, either through reading or listening, in many or all of the following circumstances':[26]

- As private reading by the literate and pious nobles Æthelweard and Æthelmær;
- For public recital (in a pseudo-liturgical context or over meals) to the extended household of Æthelweard and Æthelmær, incorporating both men and women of different social ranks and different ages;
- As private reading by other secular nobles, including those with whom Ælfric corresponded;

---

[23] Shari Horner, '"Why Do You Speak So Much Foolishness?" Gender, Humor, and Discourse in Ælfric's *Lives of Saints*', in *Humour in Anglo-Saxon Literature*, ed. Jonathan Wilcox (Cambridge: D.S. Brewer, 2000), 127–36.

[24] Quotation by Horner (at her p. 127) of a passage in *The Norton Anthology of Literature by Women: The Traditions in English*, ed. Sandra M. Gilbert and Susan Gubar, 2nd edn (New York: Norton, 1996), p. 5.

[25] See Catherine Cubitt, 'Ælfric's Lay Patrons', in Magennis & Swan, 165–92.

[26] Jonathan Wilcox, 'The Audience of Ælfric's *Lives of Saints* and the Face of Cotton Caligua A.xiv, fols. 93–130', in *Beatus Vir: Studies in Early English and Norse Manuscripts in Memory of Phillip Pulsiano*, ed. A.N. Doane and Kirsten Wolf (Tempe, AZ: ACMRS, 2006), 228–63, at 258–59. I have repunctuated Wilcox's list, adding bullets and capitals but otherwise leaving it unchanged.

- For public recital to the households of those other secular nobles incorporating both men and women of different social ranks and different ages;
- As private reading by the bishops with whom Ælfric corresponded;
- For reading aloud to the episcopal household of the bishop's palace;
- As pious private reading by a monastic audience not fully literate in Latin, especially that in a female monastic house;
- For edifying public reading, to be recited over meals, to a monastic audience not fully literate in Latin, especially that in a female monastic house;
- As pious private reading by a non-monastic religious community not fully literate in Latin, especially that in a minster of secular priests;
- For edifying public reading, to be recited over meals or elsewhere, to a non-monastic corporate audience not fully literate in Latin, especially that in a minster of secular priests;
- For private devotional reading by an isolated priest in the community;
- As potentially uplifting reading to a complete village community by the isolated priest out in the field.

Interestingly, Wilcox identifies women as making up an important portion of the target audience for these tales. The gist of his non-tendentious conclusions is that 'multiple reading communities' are implicit in the idea that these *vitae* are narrative reading pieces; and that correspondingly, 'the lives were likely heard and interpreted in different ways by different folks and served multiple purposes' (p. 259). It is tempting to extend Wilcox's pluralistic conclusions to other examples of Old English literature, even if each author or manuscript collection represents a special case.

A Selection from the Criticism

When conducted astutely and with due attention to historical factors that impinge upon an author, modern criticism can be revealing of both a writer and his times; moreover, it can shed light on the unplanned and emergent ways in which an author has responded, over a period of years, to the impact of events. This is true of the following excerpt from an essay by Malcolm Godden dating from 1994. Godden analyses the response of two leading members of the Anglo-Saxon intelligentsia – Ælfric of Eynsham and Wulfstan the homilist – to the approach of the millennial year 1000, with its possible apocalyptic overtones, and to the unrelated arrival on the shores of Britain, beginning in the year 991, of armies of Viking raiders, chiefly Norwegians, who very quickly devastated the realm, humiliating and impoverishing the English through their increasingly extortionate demands of tribute, or 'protection money'.

Only the first part of Godden's essay, the part that deals with Ælfric, is reproduced here. Readers are encouraged to seek out on their own the essay's remainder, which tells of Wulfstan's resistance to – and accommodation with – the Vikings into the earlier years of the reign of King Cnut (r. 1017–35). At this point, in a remarkable and instructive turnaround, Wulfstan took on a leading role as advisor to the Danish-born king, much as he had previously served as a key advisor to King Æthelred. The second half of Godden's essay focuses on the changing status of the manuscript records of Wulfstan's most famous sermon, his *Sermo Lupi ad Anglos*, during these turbulent years and into the twelfth century.[27]

In the present excerpt, Godden analyses Ælfric's reliance on three different intellectual paradigms as a way of accounting for the appearance of the Vikings on English shores, namely that the Norsemen have come (1) as precursors to the apocalypse; or (2) as agents of God's wrath being visited on the people for their sins; or (3) as heathen agents of the devil. Each paradigm implied a different role for the clergy at this critical moment in English national history, and Ælfric is shown shifting from one paradigm to another, gradually coming to emphasize the need for a staunch military response to Viking aggressions, as the unforeseeable disasters taking place during his lifetime took their course.

From 1991 until his retirement in 2013, Malcolm Godden (b. 1945) held the position of Rawlinson and Bosworth Professor of Anglo-Saxon at the University of Oxford and was concurrently a fellow of Pembroke College, Oxford. He received the PhD at the University of Cambridge in 1970 under the direction of Peter Clemoes, writing a thesis that was subsequently published as *Ælfric's Catholic Homilies: The Second Series, Text*. As has been mentioned in earlier chapters, this was the first volume of what eventually became a three-volume set, the second volume of which was the work of Clemoes. In the year 2000 Godden completed the set's third and final volume, *Ælfric's Catholic Homilies: Introduction, Commentary and Glossary*.[28] In its 850 or so printed pages, this arguably represents the most distinguished single-volume achievement in recent Anglo-Saxon scholarship. Godden is also the author of *The Making of Piers Plowman* (1990); the co-editor, with Susan Irvine, of the stellar edition *The Old English Boethius* (2009); and the co-editor, with Michael Lapidge, of *The Cambridge Companion to Old English Literature*.[29] Covering the same historical period as the essay that is excerpted here is Godden's 1990 article 'Money, Power and Morality in Late Anglo-Saxon England'.[30]

---

27 Although this sermon has attracted the lion's share – or should we not say the wolf's share? – of modern criticism on Wulfstan's life and works, a wide range of additional topics are explored in the essay collection *Wulfstan, Archbishop of York: The Proceedings of the Second Alcuin Conference*, ed. Matthew Townend (Turnhout: Brepols, 2004). Three additional Wulfstan studies are worth special note: Stephanie Hollis, 'The Thematic Structure of the *Sermo Lupi*', *ASE* 6 (1977): 175–95, repr. in Liuzza, 182–203; Patrick Wormald, 'Archbishop Wulfstan and the Holiness of Society', in his essay collection *Legal Culture in the Early Medieval West* (London: Hambledon, 1999), 225–51, repr. in *Anglo-Saxon History: Basic Readings*, ed. David A.E. Pelteret (New York: Garland, 2000), 191–224; and Jonathan Wilcox, 'The Wolf on Shepherds: Wulfstan, Bishops, and the Context of the *Sermo Lupi ad Anglos*', in *Readings: OE Prose*, 395–418.

28 *Ælfric's Catholic Homilies: The Second Series, Text*, ed. Malcolm Godden, EETS s.s. 5 (London: Oxford University Press, 1979); *Ælfric's Catholic Homilies: The First Series, Text*, ed. Peter Clemoes, EETS s.s. 17 (Oxford: Oxford University Press, 1997); Malcolm Godden, *Ælfric's Catholic Homilies: Introduction, Commentary and Glossary*, EETS s.s. 18 (Oxford: Oxford University Press, 2000).

29 Malcolm Godden, *The Making of Piers Plowman* (London: Longman, 1990); *The Old English Boethius: An Edition of the Old English Versions of Boethius's De Consolatione Philosophiae*, ed. Malcolm Godden and Susan Irvine, 2 vols (Oxford: Oxford University Press, 2009); *The Cambridge Companion to Old English Literature*, 2nd edn, ed. Malcolm Godden and Michael Lapidge (Cambridge: Cambridge University Press, 2013), first published 1991.

30 M.R. Godden, 'Money, Power and Morality in Late Anglo-Saxon England', *ASE* 19 (1990): 41–65.

For Further Reading

Clemoes, Peter. 1966. 'Ælfric'. In *Continuations and Beginnings: Studies in Old English Literature*, ed. E.G. Stanley, 176–209. London: Nelson.

Cubitt, Catherine. 2000. 'Memory and Narrative in the Cult of Early Anglo-Saxon Saints'. In *The Uses of the Past in the Early Middle Ages*, ed. Yitzahak Hen and Matthew Innes, 29–66. Cambridge: Cambridge University Press.

Gneuss, Helmut. 2009. *Ælfric of Eynsham: His Life, Times, and Writings*. Old English Newsletter Subsidia 34. Kalamazoo: Medieval Institute Publications.

Godden, Malcolm. 1985. 'Ælfric's Saints and the Problem of Miracles'. *LSE* n.s. 16: 83–100. Repr. in *Readings: OE Prose*, 287–309.

Gretsch, Mechthild. 2005. *Ælfric and the Cult of Saints in Late Anglo-Saxon England*. Cambridge: Cambridge University Press.

Hill, Joyce. 2000. 'Ælfric and Wulfstan: Two Views of the Millennium'. In *Essays on Anglo-Saxon and Related Themes in Memory of Lynne Grundy*, ed. Jane Roberts and Janet Nelson, 213–35. London: King's College.

Keynes, Simon. 2000. 'Apocalypse Then'. In *Not Angels, but Anglicans: A History of Christianity in the British Isles*, ed. Henry Chadwick et al., 41–47. Norwich: Canterbury Press.

Lazzari, Loredana, Patrizia Lendinara, and Claudia di Sciacca, eds. 2014. *Hagiography in Anglo-Saxon England: Adopting and Adapting Saints' Lives into Old English Prose (c. 950–1150)*. Turnhout: Brepols.

Phelpstead, Carl. 2009. 'King, Martyr and Virgin: *Imitatio Christi* in Ælfric's *Life of St. Edmund*'. In *St. Edmund, King and Martyr: Changing Images of a Medieval Saint*, ed. Anthony Bale, 27–44. Woodbridge: York Medieval Press in association with the Boydell Press.

Whatley, E. Gordon. 2002. 'Pearls before Swine: Ælfric's Vernacular Hagiography and the Lay Reader'. In *Via Crucis: Essays on Early Medieval Sources and Ideas in Memory of J.E. Cross*, ed. Thomas N. Hall, 158–84. Morgantown: West Virginia University Press.

Malcolm Godden, 'Apocalypse and Invasion in Late Anglo-Saxon England' (1994)[1]

The moral and theological problems posed by successful invasion, and particularly invasion of a sophisticated Christian civilization by heathen barbarians, were a recurrent issue in Anglo-Saxon writings. Bede took up the issue briefly in his *Historia Ecclesiastica*, suggesting that the Anglo-Saxon invaders were agents of the divine wrath against the slothful and sinful Britons: 'the fire kindled by the hands of the heathen executed the just vengeance of God on the nation for its crimes.'[2] Alcuin touched on the issue again in his

---

[1] Excerpted from Malcolm Godden, 'Apocalypse and Invasion in Late Anglo-Saxon England', in *From Anglo-Saxon to Early Middle English: Studies Presented to E.G. Stanley*, ed. by Malcolm Godden, Douglas Gray, and Terry Hoad (Oxford: Clarendon Press, 1994), 130–62. Used with permission from Oxford University Press. Where editorial translation are added, they are set between square brackets.

[2] *Bede's Ecclesiastical History of the English People*, ed. B. Colgrave and R.A.B. Mynors (Oxford, 1969), 1: 15.

letters on the sack of Lindisfarne by the Vikings, suggesting a parallel with the earlier Anglo-Saxon invasions and hinting that the attack might have been divine punishment for fornication, adultery, incest, avarice, robbery, or perhaps bad judgements.[3] It was a major concern in Alfredian prose, and seems to have influenced the choice of Latin works to translate. Alfred hinted at the idea of divine punishment as an explanation for the Vikings in his preface to the *Pastoral Care* but explored the issue much more fully and profoundly in his version of Boethius: he introduced the discussion with his own account of the barbarian invasion of Italy and the imprisonment of Boethius, and then used that as a basis for questioning the apparent dominance of evil in a world supposedly ruled by a benevolent God.[4] The Old English version of Orosius's history of the world engaged centrally with the same topic, taking as its starting point the barbarian sack of Rome and trying to place both it and the whole history of empires and warfare in the context of a Christian scheme: the translator, following but modifying his source, noted the possibility that barbarian invasion of Christian communities could be seen as divine punishment for their sins, but argued more strongly that the comparative mildness of such invasions in the Christian era was evidence of the ultimate benevolence of the Christian dispensation: 'It is disgraceful for us to complain, and call it warfare, when strangers and foreigners come to us and rob us of some little thing and immediately leave us again.'[5]

When Viking raiding resumed at the end of the tenth century it prompted writers such as Ælfric and Wulfstan to take up this issue once again, no doubt in awareness of all their predecessors. Both became increasingly involved in advising the king and his council, as well as attempting to offer guidance to a wider public, and their writings show them exploring and adapting a number of different ways of coming to terms with the Viking problem. Not the least of their intellectual problems was that they wrote in the shadow of eschatological expectations, and had somehow to face the question of the relationship between those two very different kinds of threat.

Ælfric

A recent historical study remarks of Ælfric that 'for the most part he wrote for monks, and his view looks inward to the monastery not outwards to the larger kingdom'.[6] If the first statement was never true of Ælfric, the second both reflects a common view of him and has a degree of justice for his early career. But however cloistered he may

3   Letter to Ethelred of Northumbria, in *Alcuini Epistolae*, ed. E. Dümmler, Monumenta Germaniae Historica, Epistolae Carolini Aevi, II, 1895, 42–44; translated in *English Historical Documents*, vol. 1: *c. 500–1042*, ed. D. Whitelock (2nd edn, London, 1979), 842–44.
4   *King Alfred's West-Saxon Version of Gregory's Pastoral Care*, ed. H. Sweet, EETS o.s. 45 and 50 (London, 1871), 5, lines 5–13; and *King Alfred's Old English Version of Boethius De Consolatione Philosophiae*, ed. W.J. Sedgefield (Oxford, 1899).
5   *The Old English Orosius*, ed. J. Bately, EETS s.s. 6 (London, 1980), 83.
6   J. Campbell, E. John, and P. Wormald, *The Anglo-Saxons* (Oxford, 1982), 202.

have been at Cerne, his election as abbot of Eynsham in 1005 would have brought him into close contact with national politics and external events even if he had not needed to care about them before. Recent work by historians has increasingly emphasized the political roles played by his patrons Æthelweard and Æthelmær.[7] The fact that Ælfric's new community at Eynsham included Æthelmær himself might suggest it had a role as a place of pastoral or cloistered retreat from the political turmoil. But Barbara Yorke argues that Eynsham was designed by Æthelmær as a place of temporary exile rather than permanent retreat.[8] Æthelmær was back in political life a few years later. Conversation between Ælfric and his patron may have been entirely about the doctrine of the Trinity and the knottier aspects of predestination theory; but it is just as likely that it was about the concept of the three estates and the precedents for warfare. Certainly Ælfric's writings show an increasing concern with political and national issues, even before he went to Eynsham; and by the end of his life he had become strikingly outspoken on such matters. That it involved a shift of emphasis for himself is evident from the way in which he reinterpreted, in a more political way, biblical texts and stories which he had earlier treated in a far less topical sense.

There are two main points to make about his early work: first, its use of an apocalyptic setting; secondly, the absence of reference to the Viking threat. In the preface to his first series of *Catholic Homilies*, written around 990, Ælfric announces the approaching end of the world and the coming of the reign of Antichrist, as a context for his own writing.[9],[a] The series ends with a homily on the signs that are to accompany the ending of the world – of which some, Ælfric insists, have already been seen and the others are not far distant. One of these signs, according to the Bible, is that nation shall rise up against nation and kingdom against kingdom. Ælfric notes that this has happened in recent times, more severely than in previous ages, but gives no more detail and passes on immediately to other signs.[10] He may not in fact have been thinking of particularly recent events: the next sign which he discusses is earthquakes, and his examples of recent occurrences are actually from the time of the emperor Tiberius. Certainly there is no explicit reference to the Vikings. Similarly, when he returns to that biblical verse in the context of a different Gospel reading, in the homily on martyrs in his second series of *Catholic Homilies*, written probably two or three years later, he gives it the

---

[7]   See especially B. Yorke, 'Æthelmær: The Foundation of the Abbey at Cerne and the Politics of the Tenth Century', in *The Cerne Abbey Millennium Lectures*, ed. K. Barker (Cerne Abbas, 1988), 15–25.

[8]   Ibid. 20.

[9]   *The Homilies of the Anglo-Saxon Church: The First Part, containing the Sermones Catholici or Homilies of Ælfric*, ed. B. Thorpe, vol. 1 (London, 1844), 2–6. (Subsequent references to this text will be in the form CH I (= First Series of Catholic Homilies) and page number in Thorpe's edition.)

[a]   [The edition by Thorpe used by Godden and cited in his note 9 has subsequently been superseded by the 1997 publication *Ælfric's Catholic Homilies: The First Series, Text*, ed. Peter Clemoes as is noted elsewhere in the present volume.]

[10] CH I. 608.

briefest of comments and moves on to the evidently more interesting subjects of the early persecution of the martyrs and the possibilities for a kind of spiritual martyrdom within the security of the monastic cloisters.[11] When he does engage with the question of why God might permit a heathen *here* [warband] to oppress His followers, it is primarily to introduce a series of comforting stories from Old and New Testament times showing how God has in fact saved and protected his people:

> Oft hwonlice gelyfede menn smeagað mid heora stuntan gesceade, hwi se Ælmihtiga God æfre wolde þæt þa hæðenan his halgan mid gehwilcum tintregum acwellan mos- ton; ac we wyllað nu eow gereccan sume geswutelunge of ðære ealdan æ, and eac of ðære niwan, hu mihtiglice se Wealdenda Drihten his halgan wið hæðenne here ... gelome ahredde. (CH I. 566)

> Often people of little faith ask with their foolish reasoning why the Almighty God would ever allow the heathens to kill his saints with every kind of torment; but we will now give you some demonstrations, both from the old law and the new, of how mightily the powerful lord has often protected his saints from the heathen *here*.

By the time he completed the Second Series however, probably in 994–95, the Viking threat had already begun to impinge on his writing and the apocalypse becomes less prominent. The preface to this series, evidently written after the work was completed, says nothing of the world's ending but does mention the Vikings, if only as a hindrance to writing. And in subsequent works the Vikings and the problem of invasion become important issues. They are particularly frequent in his next major collection, the so-called *Lives of Saints*.[12]

The key discussion here, though a deeply puzzling one, is a homily called *De Oratione Moysi*, 'On the Prayer of Moses' (LS xiii), in which Ælfric attempts to place the Viking attacks in terms of the divine will and the end of the world. This is one of the most politically charged of all Ælfric's writings, though much of the charge is just below the surface and the implications are at times puzzling and at times naïve. The collection in which it appears was begun after 995 and completed by 1002, and tex- tual and linguistic evidence suggests that this item was composed earlier than most of the others in the collection; one should perhaps think of a date not long after 995, though a little earlier is possible.[13]

---

[11] *Ælfric's Catholic Homilies: The Second Series, Text*, ed. M. Godden, EETS s.s. 5 (London, 1979), 311. Subsequent references to this text will be in the form CH II (= Second Series of Catholic Homilies) plus homily number and line number.

[12] *Ælfric's Lives of Saints*, ed. W.W. Skeat, EETS o.s. 76, 82, 94, 114 (London, 1881–1900, reprinted as two volumes 1966). References to this text will be in the form LS plus item and line number.

[13] See P. Clemoes. 'The Chronology of Ælfric's Works', in *The Anglo-Saxons: Studies presented to Bruce Dickins*, ed. P.A.M. Clemoes (London, 1959), 212–47, at 222–25; and M.R. Godden, 'Ælfric's Changing Vocabulary', *ES*, 61 (1980), 206–23, at 211.

The text begins, appropriately and positively enough, by describing how the Hebrews defeated their enemies in battle. Joshua led the army and Moses prayed; as long as Moses lifted his arms in prayer Joshua was successful, but whenever Moses' arms drooped Joshua was driven back. The story evidently offers a paradigm for the relations between military power and the Church: the military success of the general is entirely dependent on the intercessory efforts of Moses, whose contemporary equivalent were the clergy, or perhaps more specifically the monks; and this is a theme to be developed later. But at this point Ælfric limits himself to a more restricted message:

> Be þisum we magon tocnawen þæt we cristene sceolan
> on ælcere earfoðnisse æfre to gode clypian .
> and his fultumes biddan mid fullum geleafan .
> gif he ðonne nele his fultum us don
> ne ure bene gehyran . þonne bið hit swutol
> þæt we mid yfelum dædum hine ær gegremedon .
> ac we ne sceolon swaðeah geswican þære bene .
> oðþæt se mild-heorta god us mildelice ahredde .
>
> (LS xiii. 30–37)

> From this we can recognize that we Christians should in every distress call to God and ask for his help [in complete faith]; if he will not give us help nor hear our petition it will be clear that we have angered him previously with our evil deeds. But nevertheless we should not cease from prayer until the merciful God mercifully saves us.

In his earlier homilies Ælfric had offered much more complex analyses than this, recognizing that there were many reasons why God might allow his people to be afflicted, and anger with them for their sins was only one of those.[14] But the emphasis on divine anger turns out to have a part to play in contemporary polemic later in the text. Ælfric then steers away from the topical implications of the Joshua and Moses story and draws a spiritual meaning out of it: 'Now we have warfare against the fierce devil' (line 41). He then drifts into a rather rambling discussion of prayer, fasting, penance, and the twelve abuses of the world. But then he suddenly introduces the contemporary situation:

> Wel we magon geðencan hu wel hit ferde mid us .
> þaða þis igland wæs wunigende on sibbe .
> and munuc-lif wæron mid wurð-scipe gehealdene .
> and ða woruld-menn wæron wære wið heora fynd .
> swa þæt ure word sprang wide geond þas eorðan .

---

14   See e.g. CH I. 470–76 and 574.

Hu wæs hit ða siððan ða þa man towearp munuc-lif .
and godes biggengas to bysmore hæfde .
buton þæt us com to cwealm and hunger .
and siððan hæðen here us hæfde to bysmre .
Be þysum cwæð se ælmihtiga god . to moyse on þam wæstene .
Gif ge on minum bebodum farað . and mine beboda healdað .
þonne sende ic eow ren-scuras on rihtne timan symble .
and seo eorðe spryt hyre wæstmas eow .
and ic forgife sibbe and gesehtnysse eow .
þaet ge butan ogan eowres eardes brucan .
and ic eac afyrsige ða yfelan deor eow fram .
Gif ge þonne me forseoð and mine gesetnyssa awurpað .
ic eac swyðe hrædlice on eow hit gewrece .
ic do þæt seo heofen bið swa heard eow swa isen .
and seo eorðe þær-to-geanes swylce heo æren sy .
Þonne swince ge on idel . gif ge sawað eower land
ðonne seo eorðe ne spryt eow nænne wæstm .
And gif ge þonne git nellað eow wendan to me .
ic sende eow swurd to and eow sleað eowre fynd .
and hi þonne awestað wælhreowlice eower land .
and eowre burga beoð to-brocene and aweste .
Ic asende eac yrhðe into eowrum heortum .
þæt eower nan ne dear eowrum feondum wið-standan .
Þus spræc god gefyrn be þam folce israhel .
hit is swa ðeah swa gedon swyðe neah mid us .
nu on niwum dagum and undigollice.

(LS xiii. 147–77)

We can well consider how well things fared with us when this island was living in peace, and monasteries were treated with honour and the laity were vigilant against their enemies, so that our fame sprang widely throughout this world. What happened then afterwards, when people overthrew the monasteries and treated God's services with contempt, but that disease and hunger came upon us, and afterwards a heathen army treated us with contempt. Almighty God spoke to Moses about this in the wilderness: 'if you walk in my commandments and keep my commandments, I will send you rain at the right time and the earth will produce its crops for you, and I will give you peace and harmony, so that you may enjoy your land without fear and I will drive the evil beasts from you. If you scorn me and reject my laws, I will very swiftly avenge it on you. I will cause the heavens to be as hard as iron to you, and the earth beneath it like brass. Then you will toil in vain if you sow your land, and the earth will produce no crops for you, and if you will still not turn to me, I will send a sword to you and your enemies will strike you, and they will savagely lay waste your land, and your cities will be ruined and laid waste. I will send cowardice into your hearts so that none of you will dare to resist your enemies.' Thus said God of old concerning the people of Israel, but it has now very nearly happened to us, in recent times quite openly.

Hunger, pestilence, and the heathen *here* are here seen as divine punishment for the English nation's destruction of the monastic life and their contempt for the monks' services to God. Ælfric's nostalgic reference in another text to the times of Edgar when the monastic life flourished and no foreign *scip-here* was seen, makes it clear that his reference here is not to the distant past but to the very recent Viking raids, of the 980s and early 990s, which he interprets as a divine punishment for English attacks on the monastic movement occurring since the time of Edgar, presumably in the reign of Ethelred himself.

Ælfric is clearly drawing here on a long tradition of viewing invasion as divine punishment, but in a particularly personal form. It is a thoroughly monastic, one might say cloistered, point of view. He then gives a long series of Old Testament examples of God punishing sinners in his anger but being willing to spare them if proper intercession is made. The contemporary and political resonance of his argument is again hard to miss:

> Be ðysum man mæg tocnawan þæt micclum fremiað
> þam læwedum mannum . þa gelæredan godes ðeowas .
> þæt hi mid heora ðeow-dome him ðingian to gode .
> nu god wolde arian eallum ðam synfullum .
> gif he þær gemette tyn riht-wise menn .
>
> (LS xiii. 216–20)

From this one can see that the learned servants of God[15] greatly benefit the laity when they by their offices intercede for them with God, now that God was willing to spare all the sinful if he met ten righteous people there [that is, in Sodom].

Both by their intercession and by their mere presence in the kingdom the monks save the laity from the divine anger that they have deserved. That part of the message is clear enough. But what are we to make of the story Ælfric then tells of David, whose people are destroyed by God because of the king's own sin (240–72)? Is there a suggestion that the Viking attacks relate to the specific sins of Ethelred or Edgar? The political bite of this text is striking.

Finally at the end of the text Ælfric introduces the topic of the end of the world:

> Fela ungelimpa beoð on ende ðissere worulde .
> ac ge-hwa mot forberan emlice his dæl .
> swa þæt he ðurh ceorunge ne syngie wið god .
> and for ðære woruld-lufe him wite ge-earnige .

---

[15] By *gelæredan*, 'learned', Ælfric probably means specifically the monks.

Þes tima is ende-next and ende þyssere worulde .
and menn beoð geworhte wolice him betwynan .
swa þæt se fæder winð wið his agenne sunu .
and broðor wið oþerne to bealwe him sylfum .
                              (LS xiii. 290–97)

There will be[16] many misfortunes at the end of this world, but everyone must bear his
lot patiently, so that he does not sin against God by complaining and earn punishment
for his love of this world. This time is last and the ending of this world, and people will
be made evil towards each other, so that the father fights with his own son and brother
with his brother, to their own destruction.

It is not clear how if at all Ælfric meant this apocalyptic note to relate to the earlier
mention of Viking armies or to the general theme of divine wrath and mercy. The
final words draw on Christ's words foretelling the last days in Mark 13: 12:

Tradet autem frater fratrem in mortem, et pater filium.

[Brother will betray brother unto death, and a father his son.]

But Ælfric does not use the earlier verses from Mark foretelling wars and the rising
of nation against nation as signs of the approaching end, and makes no reference here
to warfare or invasion. His emphasis is rather on misfortunes that must be patiently
born, and on internal conflict. It is indeed hard to see how his interpretation of the
Vikings could have been fitted into an apocalyptic framework. The listing of historical precedents, and the suggestion that monastic intercession can ward off the danger,
are at odds with any notion that the invasions might be part of a final and inevitable
apocalypse. We seem to be dealing here with two different paradigms for explaining
the contemporary situation.

This is clearly an important and politically significant text, but the different ways
of explaining invasion are hard to reconcile: there is first the biblical paradigm of
divine aid against the foreign enemy; then the alternative biblical paradigm of divine
wrath and punishment for sins; and finally the apocalyptic paradigm of tribulations
marking the end of the world. The need to find a way of comprehending and explaining Viking attacks in a context of religious belief and institutions is strongly felt; but
the answers are as yet unclear and Ælfric seems to be trying out several different
historical models.

This piece, as I have said, is possibly an early one within the *Lives of Saints* collection.
Elsewhere in that collection Ælfric seems to have been developing a very different
and more positive view of the situation, associated with a search for a different kind

---

[16]   *Beoð* is present in form but probably future in meaning.

of historical model or analogue. The paradigm which offered itself immediately was Abbo of Fleury's account of the martyrdom of St Edmund at the hands of the Vikings in 871.[17] Abbo wrote his version in 985–87 and a few years later Ælfric produced his own English version of it, which he included in the *Lives of Saints* collection (LS xxxii). The gap in time was short, but enough for Viking raids to have become a much more typical and urgent issue; Ælfric recalls that for us when he remarks that the Danes in 871 went with their *scip-here* harrying and killing widely throughout the land, *swa heora gewuna is* ('as their custom is', line 28). Edmund and his subjects are here seen not as sinners but as innocent victims – the Danes killed men and women and simple children, says Ælfric, and shamefully treated the innocent (*bilewitan*, 42) Christians. The Vikings are the bloodthirsty agents of the devil – *geanlæhte þurh deofol*. The attack is conceived as a religious conflict culminating in an act of martyrdom: Edmund's rejection of Viking political domination is closely identified with his refusal of the Viking demands to forsake his God, and his murder imitates the deaths of Christ and St Sebastian. While God apparently permits the heathen persecution, He is seen to be protecting the king's body from a succession of attempted violations of his sanctity, as an explicit guarantee and symbol of Edmund's spiritual salvation. As a model for comprehending the Viking troubles it is strikingly different from the piece *De Oratione Moysi*: neither the wrath of God nor the approach of apocalypse has any place here, and the emphasis is on heroic resistance or patient endurance of afflictions instigated by the devil and his heathen agents rather than monastic intercession to ward off an attack instigated by a wrathful God.

The theological implications of this narrative are explored in a discursive passage in another text from this collection, *Natale Quadraginta Militum* (LS xi). After telling the story of the forty soldiers who were martyred in the days of the emperor Licinius for their refusal to sacrifice to pagan gods, Ælfric adds a long discussion of the implications. One of the main points that he makes is that though God permits the heathens to persecute his followers it is the devil who incites them and God will punish them; the use of present tense suggests that he is thinking of his own time:

> þa hæðenan hynað and hergiað þa cristenan
> and mid wælhreowum dædum urne drihten gremiað .
> ac hi habbað þæs edlean on þam ecum witum .
> (LS xi. 353–55)

The heathens oppress and harry the christians and anger our lord with cruel deeds, but they will have their repayment for this in eternal torments.

There is divine anger here, but it is directed against the heathen raiders not their victims. What Ælfric seems to be developing here is a way of viewing the Viking

---

[17] Edited by M. Winterbottom in *Three Lives of English Saints* (Toronto, 1972).

raids quite different from that seen in the *De Oratione Moysi*, one that uses the paradigm of martyrdom: the Viking attacks reflect neither divine wrath nor apocalypse but the age-old conflict between the forces of the devil and the followers of God, and can be paralleled by all the stories of heathen persecutions of the early Church which form the bulk of the *Lives of Saints* collection, and indeed by some Old Testament stories. That, perhaps, is the major point of the collection, apparently instigated as it was by two leading members of the military aristocracy, ealdorman Æthelweard and his son Æthelmær.

This way of placing the Viking troubles is developed further in one of the latest of Ælfric's writings, a homily dated approximately around 1009.[18] In the midst of an exposition of the Gospel story of the disciples' fishing, Ælfric launches into a sudden attack on those Englishmen who sided with the Danes, arguing that this was the work of the devil and a betrayal of their own nation:

> Swa fela manna gebugað mid ðam gecorenum
> to Cristes geleafan on his Gelaðunge,
> þæt hy sume yfele eft ut abrecað,
> and hy on gedwyldum adreogað heora lif,
> swa swa þa Engliscan men doð þe to ðam Deniscum gebugað,
> and mearciað hy deofle to his mannrædene,
> and his weorc wyrcað, hym sylfum to forwyrde,
> and heora agene leode belæwað to deaðe.
>
> (128–35)

So many people turn with the elect to the faith of Christ within his church that some of them, the evil ones, break out again, and live their life in false doctrine, as do those English people who turn to the Danes, and mark themselves with the devil, in allegiance to him, and do his works, to their own destruction, and betray their own nation to death.

There is nothing to prompt this outburst in the sources and the sharpness is perhaps rather surprising, but the perspective is that developed earlier in the *Lives of Saints*: once again the Vikings are the agents of the devil rather than divine wrath, and national and political opposition to them is identified with the true faith. The connection with the *Lives of Saints* is underlined when Ælfric goes on to draw a parallel with the victims and traitors of the early persecutions of the Church:

> Swa dydon eac hwilon sume þa Cristenan
> on anginne Cristendomes: þa ða man acwealde
> þa halgan martiras huxlice mid witum,

---

18 *Homilies of Ælfric: A Supplementary Collection*, ed. J.C. Pope, EETS o.s. 259, 260 (London, 1967–68), no. xiv (pp. 511–27).

for Cristes geleafan, þa cyddon wel fela
heora ungetrywðæ, and wiðsocon Criste,
and hine forleton, þæt hy libban moston,
ac heora lif wæs syððan wyrse þonne deað.
(140–46)

So did also formerly some Christians at the beginning of Christianity: when the holy
martyrs were shamefully killed with torments for their faith in Christ, those showed
well their untruth, and forsook Christ, and abandoned him, so that they might live, but
their life was afterwards worse than death.

One of the important implications of this hagiographic model for the Viking raids
is the political one that resistance is imperative. For if we look back at the life of
Edmund, one can note how the question of military resistance is delicately worked
out. Edmund's first impulse is to resist the Vikings in battle and it is only when
the bishop convinces him that military resistance is impossible that he turns to the
Christian ideal of passive endurance. There is also possibly a hostile allusion to
the contemporary issue of Danegeld: Hinguar's demand that the royal or national
treasure-hoard be opened to him is coupled with his demand for political submission,
and the two are linked by Edmund with the concept of submission to heathen
domination. This implicit concern with justifying military resistance to the Vikings
in a religious context is also explored further in a digression in his account of the
Maccabees (LS xxv); Ælfric enunciates the concept of the just war and defines it as
war against the cruel seamen (*reðan flotmen*). The point is then developed further
with a discussion of the doctrine of the three estates of society, identifying the
landowning class as a warrior class, the *bellatores*.

Ælfric's later writings also show him exploring further the possibilities of Old
Testament narrative as a paradigm for the Viking problem. When he produced his prose
rendering of the story of Judith, perhaps around 1002–5, he offered a variety of ways of
interpreting the story, or seeing its contemporary relevance, such as taking Judith herself
as a type of the Church in conflict with the devil, or as a type of the nun, but he did not
propose a political or military reading.[19] When, however, he wrote his long treatise on
the Old and New Testaments some time after he became abbot of Eynsham in 1005, it
was the military and political implications of the Judith story that he emphasized:

Iudithe seo wuduwe, þe oferwann Holofernem þone Siriscan ealdormann, hæfð hire
agene boc betwux þisum bocum be hire agenum sige; seo ys eac on Englisc on ure wisan
gesett eow monnum to bysne, þæt ge eowerne eard mid wæ[p]num bewerian wið
onwinnendne here.

---

[19] *Angelsächsische Homilien und Heiligenleben*, ed. B. Assmann, Bibliothek der angelsächsischen Prosa, 3, repr. with a supplementary introduction by P.A.M. Clemoes (Darmstadt,
1964), 102–16.

Judith the widow who overcame the Syrian ealdorman Holofernes has her own book among the others, about her victory; this is also set down in English in my fashion, as an example for you people, that you should defend your land with weapons against the invading *here*.[20]

The shift of emphasis is perhaps partly to be explained by the fact that the treatise is formally addressed to a secular landowner, Sigeweard of East Heolon, and a member of what Ælfric would call the class of *bellatores*. But as a note at the head of the text explains, the work was read, and no doubt intended, as an address to a wider readership than just one, and the passage itself uses *eow monnum* in the plural. The shift of readership is itself significant. When Ælfric wrote his version of Judith he thought of a religious-minded readership including nuns; now it was the fighting class that was on his mind, and he was looking to the Old Testament for historical parallels to the Viking attack.

It would have been easy, perhaps natural, for someone in Ælfric's position to find in the Judith story support for the argument which he had made much earlier in the piece *De Oratione Moysi*, that God lets the heathen army oppress his people when they fail to honour him and that intercession by the Church is what will save them, rather than military means. For in the biblical Book of Judith Achior tells Holofernes that the Israelites have in the past only been defeated when they angered their God; Judith's intercession with God is an important theme of the biblical story, and, as we have seen, Ælfric had previously interpreted her as the Church. But that is not in fact the way he invites Sigeweard to read the story: his suggestion is much more in line with the Old English poem on Judith, which presents her as a heroic figure and emphasizes the importance of warfare. Ælfric's decision to read the story in a topical sense, and with militaristic implications, is an interesting straw in the wind.

It is, though, with reference to the Maccabees that he reserves his sharpest comments on the national and political scene. When he produced his *Lives of Saints* collection, perhaps around 1000, the longest single item was his account of the wars of the Maccabees against the heathen invaders of Israel, and in his comments on the just war and the three classes of society he implicitly drew out the relevance to his own time. Now, writing in 1006 or later, he draws Sigeweard's attention sharply to the lessons of their story:

hig wunnon mid wæ[p]num þa swiðe wið þone hæðenan here, þe him on wann swiðe, wolde hig adilegian and adyddan of þam earde, þe him God forgeaf, and Godes lof alecgan. Hwæt, þa Mathathias, se mæra Godes þegen, mid his fif sunum, feaht wið þone

---

[20] *The Old English Heptateuch*, ed. S.J. Crawford, EETS o.s. 160 (London, 1922), 49, lines 772–80.

here miccle gelomlicor ðonne þu gelyfan wylle, and hig sige hæfdon þurh þone soðan God, þe hig on gelyfdon æfter Moyses æ. Hig noldon na feohtan mid fægerum wordum anum, swa þæt hi wel spræcon, and awendon þæt eft, þe læs ðe him become se hefigtima cwyde, þe se witega gecwæð be sumum leodscipe þus: *Et iratus est furore Dominus in populo suo et abhominatus est hereditatem suam, et cetera:* "Drihten wearð yrre mid graman his folce, and he onscunode his yrfewerdnisse, and he betæhte hig on hæþenra handum, and heora fynd soðlice hæfdon heora geweald, and hig swiðe gedrehton þa deriendlican fynd, and hig wurdon ge-eadmette under heora handum." Nolde Machabeus, se mæra Godes cempa, habban þisne dom ðurh his Drihtenes yrre, ac him wæs leofre, þæt he mid geleafan clipode on his eornost to Gode þisne oðerne cwyde: *Da nobis, Domine, auxilium de tribulatione, quia uana salus hominis, et cetera:* 'Syle us, leof Drihten, þinne soðan fultum on ure gedrefednisse and gedo us strengran, for þan ðe mannes fultum ys unmihtig and idel. Ac uton wyrcean mihte on þone mihtigan God, and he to nahte gedeð urne deriendlican fynd.' Machabeus þa gefylde ðas foresædan word mid stranglicum weorcum, and oferwann his fynd, and sint for ði gesette his sigefæstan dæda on ðam twam bocum on biliothecan Gode to wurðmynte, and ic awende hig on Englisc and rædon gif ge wyllað eow sylfum to ræde! (Crawford, 49–50, lines 785–838)

They fought fiercely with weapons against the heathen *here*, which assailed them strongly, seeking to destroy them and drive them from the land which God had given them, and suppress the praise of God. Then Machabeus the great thegn of God with his five sons fought with the *here* much more frequently than you will believe, and they won the victory through the true God, in whom they believed according to Moses' law. They did not want to fight just with fair words, speaking well but changing it afterwards, lest they should be struck by the heavy words which the prophet spoke about a nation thus: 'And the Lord was enraged with anger against his people and rejected his inheritance, and gave them into the hands of the heathens, and their enemies truly had power over them, and the cruel enemies oppressed them sorely and they were humbled under their hands.' Machabeus that great champion of God did not want this judgement upon him, through God's anger, but preferred to call earnestly with faith to God, saying: 'Give us, dear Lord, your true help in our troubles and make us strong, because man's help is weak and in vain. But let us show strength through the almighty god and he will bring to nothing our cruel enemies.' Machabeus then fulfilled those words with mighty deeds, and overcame his enemies, and therefore his victorious actions are set down in two books in the Bible, to the honour of God, and I turned them into English; read them if you wish as counsel for yourselves.

The concept of divine wrath with the English is here, but what Ælfric now envisages is anger not for failing to support the monasteries, but for failing to honour promises to fight. His reference to promising much and performing little brings us very close to the tones of the anonymous Londoner or East Anglian who wrote the *Chronicle* account of the period, and indeed to Offa's remark in *Maldon* that many who spoke bravely in the meadhall would not fight when battle came. Old Testament story here provides a model for fusing national and religious interests in a resolute and military defence against the Danes.

When Ælfric wrote this he was probably in close contact with ealdorman Æthelmær, who seems at this time to have been out of favour with the court and taking shelter in Ælfric's monastery at Eynsham. Perhaps this plea for firm resistance reflects his influence. If so, even Æthelmær had eventually to change his mind: it was he who led the south-western thegns in submission to Sweyn in 1013, while Ethelred and London fought on.[21] If, as is generally assumed, Ælfric died before that crisis, he never had to face the failure of his paradigm and the difficulties which his view of the Vikings as the forces of the devil would have posed.

---

[21] Yorke, 'Æthelmær', 20.

[The last twenty pages of Godden's article address Wulfstan's response to the same tumultuous circumstances as affected Ælfric, with the difference that Wulfstan (d. 1023) lived on for perhaps another dozen years, being 'driven by circumstance to develop new perspectives', in Godden's words (p. 143).]

11

Translating, Editing, and Making it New

A topic of lively interest among recent critics of Old English literature has been the process of mediation by which works dating from the Anglo-Saxon period have been presented to modern readers through the work of translators and editors. Of comparable interest is the use that modern authors, poets in particular, have made of Old English literature in their creative work. Both these topics, in turn, intersect with research into the processes – often inflected by ideology – by which the discipline of Anglo-Saxon studies has been shaped and formed, stage by stage, since the sixteenth century.[1] Self-reflexivity about the methods and assumptions of literary criticism, as well as about the place of Old English studies within a larger world of letters and belief, is thus far more characteristic of recent criticism than of that of earlier decades, when positivistic modes of thought were more generally in vogue and the tenets of good philology were rarely problematized.

Translating

The question of how best to translate Old English verse into the idiom of a modern language has been a matter of lively interest ever since the 'discovery' of that verse in the early decades of the nineteenth century. Not until then were the formal principles governing the

---

[1] Since this topic is the subject of my book *The Idea of Anglo-Saxon England 1066–1901: Remembering, Forgetting, Deciphering, and Renewing the Past* (Oxford: Wiley Blackwell, 2015), there is no need to treat it here. Two previous publications in this area, each one expressive of a different perspective, are *Anglo-Saxon Scholarship: The First Three Centuries*, ed. Carl T. Berkhout and Milton McC. Gatch (Boston: Hall, 1982), and Allen J. Frantzen's *Desire for Origins: New Language, Old English, and Teaching the Tradition* (New Brunswick: Rutgers University Press, 1990). While the anthology edited by Berkhout and Gatch is generally celebratory in tone, Frantzen offers a wide-ranging critique of Old English scholarship as always invested in the ideologies of its historical era.

Old English Literature: A Guide to Criticism with Selected Readings, First Edition. John D. Niles.
© 2016 John D. Niles. Published 2016 by John Wiley & Sons, Ltd.

composition of Old Germanic alliterative verse understood with much clarity. Illustrative translations of Old English poetry soon came to be produced in some numbers, whether on their own or embedded in the surveys of that earlier literature that were produced by such scholars as Sharon Turner and John Josias Conybeare.[2] As the nineteenth century progressed, a good deal of interest centred on the question of how best to translate *Beowulf*, a poem that was widely regarded as a stylistic tour de force and the supreme surviving example of Old English narrative verse.

In his 2011 book *Translating Beowulf: Modern Versions in English Verse*, Hugh Magennis offers a full and insightful analysis of modern efforts to translate *Beowulf* – despite that poem's stylistic alterity – into an idiom that modern readers can appreciate and enjoy in its own right, regardless of their level of competence in Old English.[3] The book's first two chapters review the theory of translation and the special stylistic features of the old alliterative verse form. Magennis then turns to the modern reception of Old English literature, paying close attention to translations of *Beowulf* into the medium of verse and tracing this story chronologically from the late eighteenth century to the early twenty-first. Four additional chapters of the book offer sustained discussion of four landmark translations: these are the ones by the Scottish poet Edwin Morgan (1952), the American translator and academic Burton Raffel (1963), the English translator and academic Michael J. Alexander (1973), and the Irish Nobel-Prize-winning poet Seamus Heaney (1999). A final chapter deals with additional post-1950 verse translations. In accord with leading theorists, Magennis distinguishes between 'domesticating' translations, which try to erase the fact of translation by suppressing linguistic and cultural differences, and 'foreignizing' translations, which seek to call attention to the 'otherness' of the source-text through such devices as archaisms, non-standard syntax, and imitative metre. William Morris's translation *The Tale of Beowulf, Sometime King of the Weder Geats* – issued initially in 1895 by the Kelmscott Press in a deluxe limited edition – is an extreme example of the 'foreignizing' type, for with its unrelenting archaisms based largely on Old English and Old Norse lexical roots, it presents readers with a healthy dose of what Chris Jones has termed 'the shock of the old'.[4]

Magennis is far from being the first distinguished scholar and critic of Old English literature to deal with the topic of translation, though his is the most systematic survey of translations of *Beowulf* that has yet seen print.[5] He was preceded by J.R.R. Tolkien, in particular. In his 1940 study 'On Translating *Beowulf*', which served as the preface to J.R. Clark Hall's prose translation of *Beowulf* dating originally from 1911, Tolkien analysed the

---

[2]   Note chap. 6, 'The Romantics and the Discovery of Old English Verse', of my study *The Idea of Anglo-Saxon England 1066–1901*, as well as other parts of that book that discuss Longfellow, Tennyson, William Morris, and other nineteenth-century translators of Old English.

[3]   Hugh Magennis, *Translating Beowulf: Modern Versions in English Verse* (Cambridge: D.S. Brewer, 2011).

[4]   Chris Jones, *Strange Likeness: The Use of Old English in Twentieth-Century Poetry* (Oxford: Oxford University Press, 2006), 6.

[5]   Note also Marijane Osborn, 'Translations, Versions, Illustrations', chap. 18 (pp. 341–72) of the *Beowulf Handbook*, a survey that extends to the early 1990s, and R.M. Liuzza, 'Lost in Translation: Some Versions of *Beowulf* in the Nineteenth Century', *ES* 83 (2002): 281–95.

special challenges faced by translators of that poem.[6] Chiefly intended for those studying the poem in the original language, Tolkien's essay offers keen insights into the question of how best to translate Old English poetic diction, with its striking metaphors and its occasional kennings. What could not be inferred from this essay is that Tolkien himself, not fully satisfied with existing versions of *Beowulf*, would eventually complete his own translation of that poem. Although this never saw print during his lifetime, Tolkien laboured over it with care, and it has recently been brought to light.[7] It is written in prose of a transparent and yet muscular character. It is scrupulously accurate, in a manner that reflects Tolkien's superb competence as a textual scholar. Its style owes something to William Morris's artful prose translations from Old Norse, though not to Morris's unreadable verse translation of *Beowulf*. There are archaisms ('vouchsafed', 'spake' and the like); there are word-order inversions ('good was that mansion', 'glad was the heart'); there are rhetorical interjections ('Lo!' 'Nay', and the like). Altogether it is a splendid read for those who have a taste for neo-medievalism and who mistrust the liberties so often taken by translators who use verse as their medium.

Other critical essays that address the art of translating Old English verse include Alain Renoir's stylish 1978 essay 'The Ugly and the Unfaithful: *Beowulf* through the Translator's Eye';[8] Stanley B. Greenfield's 1979 article 'Esthetics and Meaning and the Translation of Old English Poetry', best read perhaps in conjunction with his own 1992 translation of the poem;[9] and my own 1993 essay 'Rewriting *Beowulf*: The Task of Translation'.[10] In this study I argue that the ire that is often directed at a literary translator for infidelity to a source text can be misdirected, for what all translations represent, even the most literal ones, is one or another act of transmutation. The art of literary translation can thus be likened to alchemy: what is wanted is for a gifted poet-scholar to turn the good metal of an original text into the gold of a new version of it, one that people will be eager to read in its own right. Unfortunately, as we all know, the reverse of that process can happen all too easily, as the gold of a masterpiece is turned into lead in the hands of a writer of mediocre talent.

6   J.R.R. Tolkien, 'On Translating *Beowulf* ', first published as the preface to the 1940 edn of *Beowulf and the Finnsburg Fragment*, trans. John R. Clark Hall (London: Allen & Unwin, 1940), repr. in *J.R.R. Tolkien: The Monsters and the Critics and Other Essays*, ed. Christopher Tolkien (London: Allen & Unwin, 1983), 49–79.

7   J.R.R. Tolkien, *Beowulf: A Translation and Commentary, Together with Sellic Spell*, ed. Christopher Tolkien (Boston: Houghton Mifflin, 2014).

8   Alain Renoir, 'The Ugly and the Unfaithful: *Beowulf* through the Translator's Eye', *Allegorica* 3 (1978): 161–71.

9   Stanley B. Greenfield, 'Esthetics and Meaning and the Translation of Old English Poetry', in *Old English Poetry: Essays on Style*, ed. Daniel G. Calder (Berkeley: University of California Press, 1979), 91–110. Greenfield wrote this essay while working on his own translation, published subsequently as *A Readable Beowulf: The Old English Epic Newly Translated* (Carbondale: Southern Illinois University Press, 1982). Even while observing the somewhat arbitrary constraints of a seven-count syllabic form, this translation is both graceful and philologically exact. In its effort to be readable, it tends towards the domesticating end of the spectrum.

10   'Rewriting *Beowulf*: The Task of Translation', *College English* 55 (1993): 858–78.

Among recent translations of *Beowulf*, Seamus Heaney's brilliant 1999 version of that poem has naturally attracted much critical attention.[11] Indeed, one can hardly think of another recent publication pertaining to the literature of medieval Europe that has had as wide an impact as this one, thanks not just to its multiple editions and printed formats but also to its widespread dissemination via BBC radio broadcasts, boxed cassette tapes, and a boxed CD-ROM. Like any strong translation of a literary work, Heaney's remaking of *Beowulf* is at the same time an act of criticism. Heaney takes issue with the timeworn misconception that, in order to reflect its source, a translation of an Old English poem should be simple in syntax and monosyllabic in diction. Instead, while remaining faithful to the sentence-by-sentence content of the original poem (though not its phrase-by-phrase syntax), Heaney makes vigorous use of the vast resources of the current English lexicon. This includes liberal use of cosmopolitan polysyllabic diction, in addition to an occasional northern English dialect word and, controversially, a scattering of Irish locutions. By this means he communicates a sense of the actual sophistication and flair of the *Beowulf* poet's style, which is anything but primitive or merely 'Germanic'.

Among critics who have discussed Heaney's translation in warmly commendatory terms, Hugh Magennis has emphasized that 'there are telling literary correspondences [...] between the *Beowulf* of Seamus Heaney and the original poem.' These include 'dignity and solemnity of utterance', a 'masterful use of rhythm and sound', and a vocabulary that stretches 'from the apparently banal to the thrillingly unexpected'.[12] Other critics have discovered a seamless continuity between Heaney's translation of *Beowulf* and his work as a distinguished poet in his own right; for indeed, Heaney's research into the Anglo-Saxon, Celtic, and early Germanic past is often cited as one of the wellsprings of his poetic imagination. Among the specialists who have written on Heaney's *Beowulf*, often tracing strong continuities with his original poetry, are Inge Milfull and Hans Sauer,[13] Daniel Donoghue,[14] Conor McCarthy,[15] Heather O'Donoghue,[16] and myself,[17] to cite just a partial list.

---

[11]　Seamus Heaney, *Beowulf* (London: Faber, 1999; New York: Norton, 2000), repr. in Donoghue, 3–78 (though without Heaney's prose Introduction, which is a carefully wrought work of art in its own right). The American edition published by W.W. Norton is a dual-language one with facing-page Old English text. Heaney's translation is featured in his and my co-authored book *Beowulf: An Illustrated Edition* (New York: Norton, 2008), where it is accompanied by facing-page images, chiefly drawn from the Iron Age archaeological record, that provide a counterpoint to the text.

[12]　Magennis, *Translating Beowulf*, chap. 7 (pp. 161–90): 'Seamus Heaney: A Living Speech Raised to the Power of Verse', at 188.

[13]　Inge B. Milfull and Hans Sauer, 'Seamus Heaney: Ulster, Old English, and *Beowulf*', in *Bookmarks From the Past: Studies in Early English Language and Literature in Honour of Helmut Gneuss*, ed. Lucia Kornexl and Ursula Lenker (Frankfurt: Peter Lang, 2003), 81–141.

[14]　Daniel Donoghue, 'The Philologer Poet: Seamus Heaney and the Translation of *Beowulf*', *Harvard Review* 19 (2000): 12–21, repr. in Donoghue, 237–47.

[15]　Conor McCarthy, '*Beowulf*', chap. 3 (pp. 86–126) of his *Seamus Heaney and Medieval Poetry* (Cambridge: D.S. Brewer, 2008).

[16]　Heather O'Donoghue, 'Heaney, *Beowulf*, and the Medieval Literature of the North', in *The Cambridge Companion to Seamus Heaney*, ed. Bernard O'Donoghue (Cambridge: Cambridge University Press, 2009), 192–205.

[17]　'Heaney's *Beowulf* Six Years Later', chap. 9 (pp. 325–53) of my *Old English Heroic Poems and the Social Life of Texts* (Turnhout: Brepols, 2007).

Still there are persons who may prefer a translation of *Beowulf* that is 'somewhat quieter than most others', whether for personal reading or for use in the classroom. That is a phrase used by Roy M. Liuzza with reference to his own lucid verse translation, which happened to come out in the same year, 2000, that Heaney's translation was published in North America.[18] Liuzza's appealing classroom edition includes many pedagogical aids, including a stellar Introduction that surveys the state of the art in *Beowulf* criticism and an appendix with excerpts from no fewer than twenty prior translations of the poem.

Equally deserving of praise is Dick Ringler's *Beowulf: A New Translation for Oral Delivery*, published in 2007 with a substantial scholarly Introduction.[19] This translation represents no slight achievement, for it is a faithful reworking of the poem into a metre that, while maintaining remarkable fluency, also maintains structural alliteration and observes the rules of the Sievers/Bliss system of scansion of Old English verse. Like the original poem, Ringler's translation is meant to be heard by the ear rather than read silently from the printed page. An audiobook – one done in the style of a radio drama, with multiple voices and sound effects – is available in the form of a CD-ROM package, and Ringler's reading of the text is available to listeners via the Digital Collections of the University of Wisconsin Library.[20]

Other poems of the Old English corpus present individual challenges for the translator. Arguably the single most influential translation of an Old English shorter poem that has been made, with the possible exception of Tennyson's 1880 version of *The Battle of Brunanburh*, is Ezra Pound's brilliantly hyperliteral translation of *The Seafarer*. First published in Pound's 1912 collection *Ripostes*, this poem was later included in Pound's book *Cathay* and, thereafter, in his book of collected poems *Personae*, in addition to reprints published elsewhere. In his 1982 article 'The Might of the North', Fred C. Robinson has drawn on the resources of the Pound Archive at the Beinecke Rare Book and Manuscript Library of Yale University to trace the sources on which Pound relied when fashioning this work, with its arresting diction and syntax and its abruptly truncated ending.[21] Controversially, Pound's manner of ending the poem converts it from a work of Christian devotion into one that celebrates the secular ideal of courage in the face of adversity. Robinson disputes the common misapprehension that Pound's performance 'is to a considerable extent the result of schoolboy howlers and naive butchering of the original text by a man who had dabbled only superficially in Anglo-Saxon' (p. 199). On the contrary, he demonstrates that Pound made a

---

[18] R.M. Liuzza, *Beowulf: A New Verse Translation* (Peterborough, Ontario: Broadview Press, 2000); quotation from p. 47. Liuzza's translation has elicited the praise of Hans Sauer in his 2004 essay 'Heaneywulf, Liuzzawulf: Two Recent Translations of *Beowulf*', in *Of Remembrance the Keye: Medieval Literature and its Impact through the Ages*, ed. Uwe Böker (Frankfurt am Main: Peter Lang, 2004), 331–48.

[19] Dick Ringler, *Beowulf: A New Translation for Oral Delivery* (Indianapolis: Hackett, 2007).

[20] Dick Ringler, *Beowulf: The Complete Story, A Drama*, a boxed CD-ROM set (Madison, WI: Nemo Productions, 2006). The text and the streamed sound file can be accessed at: http://digital.library. wisc.edu/1711.dl/Literature.RinglBeowulf.

[21] Fred C. Robinson, '"The Might of the North": Pound's Anglo-Saxon Studies and *The Seafarer*', *The Yale Review* 71 (1982): 199–224, repr. in Robinson, 239–58. Pound's translation stops at line 99 of the original poem, which numbers 124 lines in current editions; he did not regard the poem's last lines as forming part of its original design.

serious study of Old English verse and produced his translation in accord with 'the philological techniques which he had learned from the books and teachers at his disposal' (p. 224): Pound valued his translation highly as an element in his broad aim 'to gather from the past a live tradition'. This last point has been developed by Chris Jones in the first chapter of his 2006 book *Strange Likeness: The Use of Old English in Twentieth-Century Poetry*.[22] Jones shows that Pound's reading of Old English poetry had a powerful effect on his great work the *Cantos*, the first canto of which starts off with a paraphrase from Homer's *Odyssey* in an alliterative measure reminiscent of that of *The Seafarer*.

Editing

While the challenge of translating Old English poetry is well known and is often discussed in the critical literature, this is much less true of the challenge of scholarly editing. Indeed, the editing of Old English texts is not normally thought of as falling into the category of literary criticism at all, even though one could argue that no other activity is so insistent in its demands on the scholar's critical intelligence and powers of judgement. The influence of a good – or poor – scholarly edition, as well, may be such as to establish the lines within which that work is generally understood for many years to come. Although these matters may seem self-evident, they have only come to the forefront of scholarly consciousness during the past thirty years or so.

The history of editing Old English texts is addressed by J.R. Hall in a chapter written for the 1995 book *Scholarly Editing: A Guide to Research*.[23] Hall offers a discriminating review of editions that date from as early as the 1560s. At the start of his essay, he draws a sharp contrast between the untidy manuscript culture of the Anglo-Saxons and the 'machine-finished' books of our own day:[24]

> The typical Old English work in manuscript is written in Anglo-Saxon minuscule, a hand last used in the twelfth century; is not always clearly distinguished (or distinguishable) from works preceding or following; and often displays unsystematic accentuation, punctuation, capitalization, spelling, and morpheme division. In poetic texts there is the added complication that the verses are virtually always written across the page, like prose. Literate Anglo-Saxons, to the manner born, took manuscript texts in stride, finding in their predictable variety and ambiguity the quiet comfort of the familiar. Literate modern readers find the texts irregular, untame, alien, lacking [...] the 'machine-finish' of our own productions. To edit the texts is to make them accessible, in more than one sense, to contemporary readers.

---

22   Chris Jones, '"Ear for the Sea-Surge": Pound's Use of Old English', chap. 1 (pp. 17–67) of his book *Strange Likeness* (cited in n. 4 above).

23   J.R. Hall, 'Old English Literature', in *Scholarly Editing: A Guide to Research*, ed. D.C. Greetham (New York: Modern Language Association, 1995), 149–83. Of related interest is Roberta J. Dewa's more specialized study 'Of Editors and the Old English Poetry of the Exeter Book: A Brief History of Progress', in *'Lastworda Betst': Essays in Memory of Christine E. Fell*, ed. Carole Hough and Kathryn A. Lowe (Donington: Shaun Tyas, 2002), 18–40.

24   Quotation from p. 150, omitting an allusion that Hall makes to the medievalist Geoffrey Shepherd, who uses the 'machine-finish' figure of speech in a slightly different context.

In the main part of this essay Hall shows how, century by century, individual editors have resolved the question of how to make works of Old English literature accessible to people of our machine age without transmuting them beyond recognition.

The diversity of opinions held by experts as to the best principles of editing Old English texts will be evident to anyone consulting three separate anthologies of critical essays on that topic that have been published in recent years.[25] These are Fred C. Robinson's 1994 essay collection *The Editing of Old English*, which brings together one scholar's solutions to a number of individual editorial problems; the 1994 anthology of critical essays *The Editing of Old English*, edited by D.G. Scragg and Paul E. Szarmach, which offers a number of different theoretical and practical perspectives; and the 1998 anthology *New Approaches to Editing Old English Verse*, edited by Sarah Larratt Keefer and Katherine O'Brien O'Keeffe, which offers yet additional perspectives pertaining to different sets of source-texts. If any generalization can be made on the basis of these three books, it is that there is little point in trying to define a single set of methods to apply to editing across the board. Rather, apt methods for each editorial project have to be devised depending on both the nature of the text – or, in some instances, each set of texts to be grouped together in a series – and the edition's purpose. This last factor entails thought about the readership for which the book is aimed, whether this is to be a circle of specialists or a more broadly representative sector of the educated public. Indeed, the question faced by translators as to whether to 'domesticate' or 'foreignize' a text has relevance to scholarly editing as well. Here too there is a danger that one editor may 'domesticate' a text to the point that it loses all tooth and nail, while another editor may 'foreignize' a text to the point that only the most dedicated specialists will want to use this edition, or will be competent to do so. Earlier in the present book, I have gone on record as personally favouring scholarly editions, or sets of editions, that are as inclusive as possible as regards their potential readership as long as all accepted standards of philological precision are observed; but within that paradigm, there is still room for sharp differences from one project to the next.

The intellectual issues attendant upon the task of editing Old English texts have not been more lucidly or interestingly discussed than by Roy M. Liuzza in his 2006 essay 'Scribes of the Mind'.[26] Here, from an editorial perspective, Liuzza comes to grips with the problems of authorship, anonymity, and 'the flux of texts' that are touched on in an earlier chapter of the present book. As Liuzza states, 'Most evidence for the transmission of vernacular texts in Anglo-Saxon England suggests that scribal participation in the recomposition of their copy-texts was often extensive; scribes acted, in other words, like modern editors, mediating between an earlier version of a text and its later readers, tailoring the text for its new context' (p. 271). Such a state of affairs, he argues, requires that the editor be

---

[25]   Fred C. Robinson, *The Editing of Old English* (Oxford: Blackwell, 1994); *The Editing of Old English: Papers from the 1990 Manchester Conference*, ed. D.G. Scragg and Paul E. Szarmach (Woodbridge: D.S. Brewer, 1994); and *New Approaches to Editing Old English Verse*, ed. Sarah Larratt Keefer and Katherine O'Brien O'Keeffe (Cambridge: D.S. Brewer, 1998).

[26]   R.M. Liuzza, 'Scribes of the Mind: Editing Old English, in Theory and in Practice', in *The Power of Words: Anglo-Saxon Studies Presented to Donald G. Scragg on his Seventieth Birthday*, ed. Hugh Magennis and Jonathan Wilcox (Morgantown: West Virginia University Press, 2006), 243–77.

keenly alert to the 'material text' to which O'Brien O'Keefe refers in her 1994 essay 'Editing and the Material Text'.[27] As Liuzza goes on to suggest: 'Each surviving copy' of what we think of as a given work 'is a unique version' (p. 271). While modern critical theory may persuade us of the need to respect each and every scribal copy of a work as representing a unique voice, 'it is however the fragmentary, mediated, and unknowable nature of Old English manuscript texts themselves, more than any contemporary theory of the nature of textuality and meaning', he argues, 'that requires us to adopt an editorial practice that respects and preserves as much evidence as possible of the material and social contexts in which these texts were made and used' (p. 272).

Making it New

In addition to the making of translations and critical editions, one common form of homage to an earlier author or body of literature is through literary imitation or adaptation. A point of entry to that creative realm, as regards the Old English literary records, is provided by Chris Jones in his chapter 'Old English after 1066'. This forms a valuable addition to the second (2013) edition of the *Cambridge Companion to Old English Literature*.[28] Jones surveys key moments in the use or adaptation of elements of Old English literature from a time soon after the Norman Conquest, through the early modern period, to the time of Walter Scott, William Morris, Gerard Manley Hopkins, and the twentieth-century authors Ezra Pound, W.H. Auden, and Seamus Heaney, among others. Jones's chapter complements his book *Strange Likeness*, which deals with the twentieth-century authors Pound, Auden, Edwin Morgan, and Heaney in considerable depth. A briefer study along similar lines is Nicholas Howe's 1998 essay 'The Afterlife of Old English Poetry'.[29] This deals with the influence of Old English literature on the poetry of Auden, the English poet Christopher Hill, and the poet Thom Gunn, a native of the UK who attended Cambridge University and subsequently taught for many years on the faculty of the University of California, Berkeley. Jones and Howe make clear that even though the Old English literary tradition went into eclipse after the Norman Conquest, its subsequent recovery has had a distinct impact on English literary history, especially among twentieth-century poets whose first encounter with the brilliant language-effects of Anglo-Saxon verse was in the university classroom.

The addition of Jones's essay 'Old English after 1066' to the revised 2013 edition of the *Cambridge Companion* signposts the increasing attention being devoted to literary adaptation in recent Old English criticism. This interest is manifest also in the chapter 'Anglo-Saxon Afterlives' that concludes Magennis's 2001 book *The Cambridge Introduction to*

---

[27]   Katherine O'Brien O'Keeffe, 'Editing and the Material Text', in Scragg and Szarmach, *The Editing of Old English*, 147–54.

[28]   Chris Jones, 'Old English after 1066', in Godden & Lapidge, 313–30, with tips for further reading at 344–47.

[29]   Nicholas Howe, 'Praise and Lament: The Afterlife of Old English Poetry in Auden, Hill, and Gunn', in *Words and Works: Studies in Medieval English Language and Literature in Honour of Fred C. Robinson*, ed. Peter S. Baker and Nicholas Howe (Toronto: University of Toronto Press, 1998), 293–310.

Anglo-Saxon Literature,[30] and it is likewise evident in the 2000 volume *Literary Appropriations of the Anglo-Saxons*, edited by Donald Scragg and Carole Weinberg.[31] This collection of critical essays touches on eight centuries of literary activity from Laȝamon's *Brut* and the *South English Legendary* to the age of Tennyson and Tolkien. Likewise, the 2010 book *Anglo-Saxon Culture and the Modern Imagination*, edited by David Clark and Nicholas Perkins,[32] traces the influence of concepts of Anglo-Saxon England in the thought and arts of the late nineteenth and twentieth centuries. The range of this volume spans poetry, film, pedagogy, book design, opera, comics, and the mystery novel, among other genres or modes, as the contributors trace the appeal of Old English themes both in the marketplace and among a literary elite.

Given J.R.R. Tolkien's prominence as a poet and novelist in addition to his having been an Oxford professor of Old English language and literature, a matter of special interest is Tolkien's creative use of Old English names, themes, situations, and stylistic traits in his own work. Tolkien's 1953 study 'The Homecoming of Beorhtnoth Beorhthelm's Son' stands out in this regard.[33] As has been mentioned in Chapter 5 above, this one-of-a-kind publication consists of two parts: first, an initial 'one-act drama' set on the field of battle at Maldon during the night after the battle is imagined to have been fought, and second, an essay titled '*Ofermod*' on the theme of 'overweening pride' in *The Battle of Maldon* and *Beowulf*. Like '*Beowulf*: The Monsters and the Critics', this study in its entirety merits recognition as one of the most artful of twentieth-century writings on Old English literature. Its first part, the 'Homecoming' verse drama, has been discussed by Marie Nelson in an article published in 2008 in which she calls attention to its 'strong performance possibilities',[34] though only three occasions were then known when in fact the play had been performed. As Nelson points out, the text contains echoes of certain passages not just of *The Battle of Maldon* but also of *Beowulf*. A noteworthy example is when one of the actors in Tolkien's drama, Torhthelm by name, spontaneously begins to chant a eulogy of his dead leader, the ealdorman Beorhtnoth (d. 991), in terms that atavistically recall the funeral lament for King Beowulf with which that poem set in a much earlier age comes to an end:[35]

> Build high the barrow his bones to keep!
> For here shall be hid both helm and sword;
> and to the ground be given golden corslet,

---

[30]   Hugh Magennis, 'Anglo-Saxon Afterlives, Medieval to Modern: Later Uses and Appropriations of Anglo-Saxon Writings', chap. 5 (pp. 165–89) of his *Cambridge Introduction to Anglo-Saxon Literature* (Cambridge: Cambridge University Press, 2011).

[31]   *Literary Appropriations of the Anglo-Saxons from the Thirteenth to the Twentieth Century*, ed. Donald Scragg and Carole Weinberg (Cambridge: Cambridge University Press, 2000).

[32]   *Anglo-Saxon Culture and the Modern Imagination*, ed. David Clark and Nicholas Perkins (Cambridge: D.S. Brewer, 2010).

[33]   J.R.R. Tolkien, 'The Homecoming of Beorhtnoth Beorhthelm's Son', *Essays and Studies* 6 (1953): 1–18.

[34]   Marie Nelson, '"The Homecoming of Beorhtnoth Beorhthelm's Son": J.R.R. Tolkien's Sequel to *The Battle of Maldon*', *Mythlore* 26 (2008): 65–87, at 65. Cf. Thomas Honegger, 'The Homecoming of Beorhtnoth: Philology and the Literary Muse', *Tolkien Studies* 4 (2007): 189–99.

[35]   Nelson, 'The Homecoming', 71; Tolkien, 'The Homecoming', 7.

and rich raiment and rings gleaming,
wealth unbegrudged for the well-beloved:
of the friends of men first and noblest,
to his hearth-comrades help unfailing,
to his folk the fairest father of peoples.

The neo-medieval aesthetic that permeated Tolkien's literary imagination is seen here to good advantage.

At the time when he wrote 'The Homecoming of Beorhtnoth Beorhthelm's Son', Tolkien must also have been at work on his greater work *The Lord of the Rings*, a trilogy whose three parts were published in the years 1954–55. In this major work of fantasy literature, Tolkien celebrates the victory of an unlikely anti-hero, the hobbit *Frodo* – or, better, a pair of unlikely anti-heroes, the two hobbits *Frodo* and *Samwise* – in a struggle of cosmic proportions waged against the dark, evil, and seemingly all-powerful kingdom of *Mordor*. Anyone familiar with the Old English language will immediately recognize the influence of that ancestral tongue here, for these three proper names echo respectively the Old English adjective *frod* 'wise'; the compound adjective *sam-wis*, glossed by Bosworth and Toller as 'dull, foolish' but probably meaning something closer to 'only half-wise'; and the noun *morðor*, a word with meanings that extend from 'murder' to 'mortal sin' to 'horrible torment' of the sort that devils and damned souls suffer in hell.

Such etymological connections as these are discussed by Clive Tolley in his 2007 study 'Old English Influence on *The Lord of the Rings*'.[36] Tolley calls attention to manifold ways in which Tolkien draws on his familiarity with the literature of the Anglo-Saxons, *Beowulf* in particular, to lend his narrative a quasi-mythological dimension. This aspect of *The Lord of the Rings* comes into the foreground, for example, when the four travellers Gandalf, Aragorn, Gimli, and Legolas arrive at Meduseld (OE *meduseld* 'mead-hall'), which is the hall of King Théoden (OE *þeoden* 'lord', 'prince'), in the settlement of Edoras (OE *eodoras* 'dwellings'). Clearly the four comrades-in-arms are now entering an Anglo-Saxon-style settlement, whatever its surplus character may be. Though some of Tolkien's etymological wordplay could be said to represent no more than ornament, at times it can help a well-informed reader construe the true nature of characters whose aims or motives are hidden. It is worth knowing, for example, that the wizard Saruman, the counterpart to Frodo's ally the wizard Gandalf, bears a name derived from the Old English common noun *searu*. Portentiously, the meaning of that word ranges from neutral 'contrivance' to negative 'artifice, wile, deceit, treachery', with the negative end of the spectrum being by far the dominant one.

A Selection from the Criticism

Among the major authors of the modern period whose creative work, like that of Pound, Tolkien, and Heaney, was deeply affected by their knowledge of Old English language and literature, one of the most eminent is the Argentine essayist, short story writer, translator,

---

[36] Clive Tolley, 'Old English Influence on *The Lord of the Rings*', in *Beowulf and Other Stories: A New Introduction to Old English, Old Icelandic and Anglo-Norman Literatures*, ed. Richard North and Joe Allard (Harlow: Pearson Longman, 2007), 38–62.

and poet Jorge Luis Borges (1899–1986). In the essay that follows (and that concludes this book), Joshua Byron Smith analyses this aspect of Borges's career within the context of Borges's lifelong interest in the art of translation, which he sometimes spoke of as a master metaphor for the processes by which cultures themselves exist and are renewed.

A native of Buenos Aires, Borges grew up as a bilingual speaker of Spanish and English. While his mother was of Uruguayan background, his father was part Spanish, part Portuguese, and half English. Between 1914 and 1921 Borges lived with his family in Europe, chiefly in Switzerland, where he studied for a time at the Collège de Genève. For many years after his return to Argentina he made his living chiefly by his pen, producing a wide range of highly innovative writings, whether classifiable as fiction or non-fiction (for he made audacious attempts to efface the difference between those two categories). In 1955, in recognition of his international stature as a man of letters, he was appointed Director of the National Public Library and at the same time Professor of English Literature at the University of Buenos Aires. At about this same time he became completely blind, although this fact did not deter him from continuing to create, teach, and publish. Regarded by many as a writer of Nobel-Prize-winning stature though he never received that award, he has been called the most important Spanish-language author since Cervantes. While Old English literature was just one of his passions, it was by no means the least significant of them. The major medieval electronic resource 'The Labyrinth', which is cited in the Select Bibliography at the end of this book, uses as its epigraph a sentence by Borges drawn from his 1941 short story 'The Garden of Forking Paths'. This reads, 'I thought of a labyrinth of labyrinths, of one sinuous spreading labyrinth that would encompass the past and the future and in some way involve the stars.'

Joshua Byron Smith completed the PhD in English at Northwestern University in 2011. He currently holds the position of Assistant Professor in the Department of English at the University of Arkansas, where he has also served as Associate Director of the programme in Medieval and Renaissance Studies. He wrote a preliminary version of the present essay while enrolled as a first-year graduate student in a seminar on 'The Discovery and Invention of Old English Literature' that I had the pleasure of teaching at the Newberry Library, Chicago, in 2005. His specialties include multilingualism in medieval Britain, Anglo-Welsh literary exchange in particular. Smith's essay can profitably be read alongside M.J. Toswell's 2014 book *Borges the Unacknowledged Medievalist*, which reviews Borges's fascination with Old English and Old Norse language and literature in the context of Borges's medievalism considered as a whole.[37]

For Further Reading

Borges, Jorge Luis. 2014. *Ancient Germanic Literatures.* Trans. M.J. Toswell. Old English Publications: Studies and Criticism, 1. Tempe, AZ: ACMRS. The original study dates from 1951.
Chance, Jane, ed. 2003. *Tolkien the Medievalist.* London: Routledge.

---

[37]   M.J. Toswell, *Borges the Unacknowledged Medievalist: Old English and Old Norse in his Life and Work* (New York: Palgrave Macmillan, 2014).

Delanty, Greg, and Michael Matto. 2010. *The Word Exchange: Anglo-Saxon Poems in Translation*. New York: Norton.

Gillespie, Vincent, and Anne Hudson, eds. 2013. *Probable Truth: Editing Medieval Texts from Britain in the Twenty-First Century*. Turnhout: Brepols.

Glassgold, Peter, trans. and ed. 1985. *Hwæt! A Little Old English Anthology of American Modernist Poetry*. Washington, DC: Sun & Moon Press.

Milosh, Joseph. 1978. 'John Gardner's *Grendel*: Sources and Analogues', *Contemporary Literature* 19: 48–57.

Mitchell, Bruce. 1996. 'J.R.R. Tolkien and Old English Studies: An Appreciation'. *Mythlore* 21: 206–12.

Niles, John D. 1996. 'Appropriations: A Concept of Culture'. In *Anglo-Saxonism and the Construction of Social Identity*, ed. Allen J. Frantzen and John D. Niles, 202–28. Gainesville: University Press of Florida.

Niles, John D. 2008. 'Old English Verse and Twentieth-Century Poets'. *Contemporary Literature* 49: 293–99. [A review essay taking Chris Jones's book *Strange Likeness* as its focal point.]

O'Donoghue, Bernard. 2010. 'Old English Poetry'. In *The Cambridge History of English Poetry*, ed. Michael O'Neill, 7–25. Cambridge: Cambridge University Press.

Robinson, Fred C. 1993. 'Ezra Pound and Old English Translational Tradition'. In Robinson, 259–74.

Toswell, M.J. 1998. 'How Pedantry Meets Intertextuality: Editing the Old English Metrical Psalter'. In *New Approaches to Editing Old English Verse*, ed. Sarah Larratt Keefer and Katherine O'Brien O'Keeffe, 79–93. Cambridge: D.S. Brewer.

Joshua Byron Smith, 'Borges and Old English'

In the Cimetière des Rois in Geneva, Switzerland, close to John Calvin's final resting place, lies a tombstone decorated with inscriptions of Old English and Old Norse verse and adorned with an image of armed Anglo-Saxon warriors.[1] Here Jorge Luis Borges (1899–1986), one of the twentieth century's most famous and accomplished writers, is buried. Although Borges's fascination with Old English consumed a large part of his later years, his critics have tended to treat his passion for the language as passing tourists in Geneva treat his unconventional tombstone: they politely acknowledge it, count it as one of this Argentinian author's many quirks, and move on. Anglo-Saxon studies, however, had a profound influence on Borges. After he learned Old English late in life, his enthusiasm and love for that language and its literature never flagged, and he spent a

---

[1]   The Old English inscription reads 'and ne forhtedon na'. This is verse 21b of *The Battle of Maldon*, one of Borges's favorite texts. It occurs as part of a passage of indirect discourse in which the English leader Byrhtnoth admonishes his troops that they should stand firm 'and they should be not afraid'. Taken in isolation, however, the verse could equally well be translated 'and they never felt fear', while if converted to the grammar of direct discourse, it would mean 'and be not afraid'.

good deal of his later life reading, studying, and promoting this example of what he called 'language at its dawn'.[2]

That Borges should learn a new language in his fifties is not particularly surprising: from a young age his intellectual life had been the product of a well-cultivated multilingualism. Borges had been raised in Buenos Aires as a bilingual speaker of English and Spanish. Fanny Haslam, his paternal grandmother, was an Englishwoman who lived most of her life with the youngest of her two sons, Jorge Guillermo Borges, who was Jorge Luis's father. Although Jorge Guillermo spoke English fluently, it was Fanny who taught Jorge Luis English. Together they would work through English readers and recite the King James Bible. Soon he had the run of his father's library, which contained a large number of English and American works. Borges would later claim that growing up within this multilingual library was 'the chief event of my life'.[3]

In 1914, Jorge Guillermo decided to relocate his family to Geneva, where Borges attended secondary school and studied French, German, and Latin. The language barrier caused Borges some difficulty in school. Latin was the only subject in which he initially excelled, but within a few years he could boast proficiency in French as well. During the long nights of World War I, Borges occupied himself by improving his German. Growing up a polyglot fostered a vibrant interest in foreign languages that persisted through his life. As an adult, Borges taught himself enough Italian to read Dante, studied Old Norse, and took avidly to Anglo-Saxon. Even after studying all of these tongues, at the age of eighty-three, he still felt a lure for more languages.[4]

Borges did not collect languages willy-nilly, however, but had strong reasons for pursuing the ones he learned. Why, then, did Old English make such a strong and lasting impression on him? A quick overview of Borges's sentiments regarding foreign languages will help explain how and why he came to be so enamored of the Anglo-Saxon tongue.

Borges's multilingualism gave his work a cosmopolitan tilt, but it also led him to appreciate languages not for their utility but for their intellectual heritage and for the literary themes particular to that heritage. German, for example, appealed to him not as a means of talking to Berliners, but rather as a vehicle for encountering Schopenhauer and Heine. Each language brought with it a different set of authors and a unique *Weltanschauung*. Borges would claim that 'every language is a way of perceiving the

---

[2]   A phrase from his poem 'Al iniciar el estudio de la gramática anglosajona' (Upon Embarking on the Study of Anglo-Saxon), from Jorge Luis Borges, *Obra poética 1923–1985*, ed. Carlos V. Frías (Buenos Aires: Emecé, 1994), 155. All of Borges's poems referred to in the present paper are cited from this edition. Translations are from *Selected Poems: Jorge Luis Borges*, ed. Alexander Coleman (New York: Penguin, 1999). Translations of prose, unless noted otherwise, are my own.

[3]   Jorge Luis Borges, 'An Autobiographical Essay', in *The Aleph and Other Stories, 1933–1969*, ed. Norman Thomas di Giovanni (New York: Dutton, 1970), 209.

[4]   'Jorge Luis Borges Discusses Hispanic Literature (Interview)', in *Borges the Poet*, ed. Carlos Cortínez (Fayetteville: University of Arkansas Press, 1986), 47.

world',[5] and he loved how the language and literature of Anglo-Saxon England opened up a new vista. The stern heroes of Old English literature fascinated Borges in a way that matched his interest in figures from the fringes of Argentinean culture.[6] *Gauchos* and *compadritos*, Argentinean wild-west cowboys and urban dandified knife fighters, pepper Borges's short stories. These daring, lone men long captivated the imagination of Borges, whose upbringing in relative isolation from the harsher social realities of Buenos Aires provided enough distance to make these characters enticing. Much of his early career as an author was devoted to romanticizing and mythologizing such heroes. Old English literature, peopled with boastful and valiant warriors, appealed to the same sensibility: both Anglo-Saxon poetry and the popular stories that Borges heard in the barrios of Buenos Aires mythologized battle and violent confrontation.

Old English literature thus allowed Borges to continue his pursuit of themes that he had first encountered in the popular culture of Buenos Aires, and he occasionally made this connection explicit. During a university lecture Borges once compared Beowulf's verbal dueling with Unferth (at lines 530 ff. of *Beowulf*) to the popular ballads that celebrated the local *compadritos* of Buenos Aires.[7] In a way, Anglo-Saxon literary culture did what Borges had once sought to do in his own art – it aestheticized courageous, combative figures, who also were possessed of a deep sense of loyalty.[8] For Borges, so intimate was the link between a language and its literary themes that he veered toward linguistic determinism. Old English was 'predestined for epic, which is to say, for the celebration of courage and of loyalty'.[9] When Borges found elements in Old English literature that dealt with topics other than heroic prowess – the bulk of the elegies, for example – he believed them to be of Celtic provenance.[10]

---

[5]   'Cada idioma es un modo de sentir el universo': from *El otro Borges: Entrevistas (1960–1986)*, ed. Fernando Mateo (Buenos Aires: Equis, 1997), 179.

[6]   See Edwin Williamson, *Borges: A Life* (New York: Viking, 2004), 42–49.

[7]   *Borges Profesor: Curso de literatura inglesa dictado en la Universidad de Buenos Aires*, ed. Martín Arias and Martín Hadis (Buenos Aires: Emecé, 2000), 54–55.

[8]   Speaking of Borges's decision to study Old English, Edwin Williamson sees a connection between these two interests. He writes: 'Borges's interest in epic and myth reawakened in a curiously attenuated form in this period. In his youth he had read epic poems because he aspired to mythologize the criollos in a verse history of Argentina, but at this stage in his life, his interest revived as an exercise in amateur scholarship': Williamson, *Borges: A Life*, 342–43.

[9]   ' ... predestinado a la épica, es decir a la celebración del coraje y de la lealtad'. Arias and Hadis, *Borges Profesor*, 94.

[10] 'Yo he conjeturado – ésta es una conjetura personal mía, no se encuentra en ningún libro, que yo sepa – que esta poesía melancólica y personal puede deberse a la procedencia celta, puede ser de origin celta' (94) (I have surmised – this is a personal guess of mine, it is not to be found in any book of which I know – that this sorrowful, personal poetry might be due to a Celtic source, it might be of Celtic origin). Borges likely could not have consulted P.L. Henry's book *The Early English and Celtic Lyric* (London: Allen & Unwin, 1966), where possible connections of this kind are discussed; this book was published when Borges was sixty-seven.

At its core, Old English was for Borges a language of heroes and epic. While German provided him with Heine and Schopenhauer, the literature of the Anglo-Saxons touched upon themes that had excited Borges since his youth and that he would long continue to pursue.

Borges was fascinated by the aesthetic qualities of different languages. For him each language, each word even, contained an innate aesthetic experience. Citing his agreement with the Italian philosopher Benedetto Croce, Borges believed that 'a language is an aesthetic deed.'[11] During interviews or lectures Borges would often single out certain words, especially English or Anglo-Saxon words, for their innate beauty ('moon' and 'dim' were two of his favorites).[12] He admired languages as works of art, picking out this peculiarity of grammar or that aspect of phonology as praiseworthy, and he delivered critical judgments that sound as if he were reviewing foreign languages for *The New York Review of Books*. For example, he judged that German had a music and rhythm that could make it 'the most perfect of all [languages]', and he approvingly remarked that German 'still has the possibilities of English and has not lost its declensions'.[13] His critical opinion of Old English was succinct yet revealing; he called it a 'chosen language'.[14] In speaking of its aesthetics, Borges remarked that 'Old English, which was a language of hard consonants and open vowels, was richer and harsher than modern English.'[15] The fact that Old English poetry was highly attuned to orality gave him immense pleasure. With his prodigious memory, Borges would recite Old English verse to all who would listen – and even to those who would not. (In a lecture he once joked that if anyone had the patience or courage to come to another talk, they may have more Old English 'inflicted' upon them.[16]) Above all, Borges relished the alliterative play of Anglo-Saxon verse and took pleasure in the sound and rhythm of Old English.

The study of Old English offered Borges more, however, than a literature containing heroic characters and a language that met his aesthetic needs. It also served Borges as a tool with which he could explore two of his favorite and most enduring themes: origins and originality.

---

[11] 'Un idioma es un hecho estético': Alejandro Vaccaro, *Borges: Vida y literatura* (Buenos Aires: Edhasa, 2006), 710.

[12] E.g. 'Borges Discusses North American Literature (Interview)', in *Borges the Poet*, ed. Cortínez, 76–77.

[13] 'Para mí sería la más perfecta de todas, ya que tiene las posibilidades del inglés, y no ha perdido las declinaciones': Antonio Carrizo, *Borges el memorioso: Conversaciones de Jorge Luis Borges con Antonio Carrizo*, 2nd edn (Mexico City: Fondo de Cultura Economica, 1983), 257. Cf. 'Al idioma alemán' (*Obra poética 1923–1985*, 393).

[14] 'Un idioma elegido': Mateo, *El otro Borges*, 156.

[15] 'El inglés antiguo, idioma de duras consonantes y vocales abiertas, era más sonoro y más áspero que el moderno': Jorge Luis Borges and María Esther Vázquez, *Literaturas germánicas medievales* (Buenos Aires: Emecé, 1966), 14.

[16] Jorge Luis Borges, *This Craft of Verse*, ed. Calin-Andrei Mihailescu (Cambridge, MA: Harvard University Press, 2000), 16.

Whereas the earliest proponents of Old English studies – sixteenth-century Protestants, for the most part – sought a solid historical foundation for their work of religious reform,[17] Borges used Old English to plumb both his own family history and the literary history of the West. Throughout Borges's life, his family's genealogy would both haunt and inspire him. His father, Jorge Guillermo Borges, was a philosophical anarchist and a mildly successful writer who struggled all his life to complete a masterpiece.[18] Borges's mother, a lifelong conservative Catholic, insisted on maintaining the lifestyle of her staunchly upper-class background, even when the family suffered monetary woes. Borges's ancestors also included famous Argentinean military figures, a fact that pressed heavily upon him. Borges would obsess over his family's origins.[19] The weight of these ancestral archetypes drove Borges to *Ultraísmo*, an artistic movement that considered itself the vanguard of modernist literature and respected originality as one of its most precious ideals.[20] For a time, Borges was one of the leading figures of *Ultraísmo*, but he soon broke from that movement when Macedonio Fernández, an older writer and café philosopher whom Borges briefly idolized, introduced him to two key ideas that would come to dominate much of his writing: the unreality of the material world and the nonexistence of the individual subject. From these ideas, coupled with similar concepts he gleaned from Schopenhauer, Borges began to distrust any notion of originality. Instead, he suggested that humankind experienced a continuous circularity in which each individual possessed the infinite possibilities of being someone else.

One of Borges's best-known short stories illustrates his suspicion of originality. In *El Inmortal* (The Immortal) the protagonist discovers the lost city of the immortals and, after drinking some water, he too manages to shed his mortality. The immortals are not represented as being single self-contained individuals; rather, thanks to their longevity, over the years they have realized many different selves. Readers meet the man who was once Homer, but has long ceased to be Homer. The identities of the immortals shift throughout time, and their past lives can even be forgotten: 'Among the Immortals … every act (every thought) is the echo of others that preceded it in the past, with no visible beginning, and the faithful presage of others that will repeat it

---

[17] See for example Michael Murphy, 'Antiquary to Academic: The Progress of Anglo-Saxon Scholarship', in *Anglo-Saxon Scholarship: The First Three Centuries*, ed. Carl T. Berkhout and Milton McC. Gatch (Boston: Hall, 1982), 1–17.

[18] Borges, 'An Autobiographical Essay', 204 ff.

[19] While many critics have noted that Borges struggled with these identities, Edwin Williamson, in his recent biography *Borges: A Life*, has made Borges's relationship with the identities of his avant-garde father and his nationalist mother the key narrative strand.

[20] For more information about Borges and the Ultraist movement, see Thorpe Running, *Borges's Ultraist Movement and Its Poets* (Lathrup Village, MI: International Books, 1981).

in the future, *ad vertiginem*.'[21] There is then nothing new under the sun, only iterations and echoes. Critic Gene Bell-Villada explains: 'Everything, moreover, will happen again sometime; thus, in the worldview of the Immortals, nothing is unique and nothing has value in itself, because any event inevitably echoes the past and foreshadows the future.'[22] Borges enjoyed entertaining the idea that, though the soul itself is immortal, it could be embodied in many different selves, as with the immortals in the short story. Thus, the individual soul could contain the past and the future, fracturing any notions of originality and origins into myriad patterns of ceaseless repetition. Revealingly, much of Borges's rhetoric about Old English fits into this pattern.

Regarding his own origins and his own identity, Old English offered Borges another venue in which he could examine his family history, which intrigued him his whole life. Through his father's English descent, Borges claimed kinship with Saxons and (he wistfully hoped) Vikings. He admitted his family's connection with Anglo-Saxon England may have been more romantic than historical:

> Another factor that impelled me [towards the study of Anglo-Saxon] was my ancestry. It may be no more than a romantic superstition of mine, but the fact that the Haslams lived in Northumbria and Mercia – or, as they are today called, Northumberland and the Midlands – links me with a Saxon and perhaps a Danish past.[23]

The possibility of Danish ancestors was of particular interest to him because Norah Lange, the romantic interest of much of his early life, was of Scandinavian descent. Edmund Williamson, in his biography of Borges, maintains that through that relationship, Borges mythologized his own Saxon heritage: 'That fact that his blood was predominantly "Saxon" while Norah's was Scandinavian no doubt suggested an analogy between Norah's conquest of his affection and the Viking raids on Northumbria, with the resultant mingling of blood that produced the English race.'[24] This type of analogy is a familiar one. Since Borges believed that his present self was no more than a temporary gathering of past and future Borgeses, of past and future events, viewing his relationship with Norah in the light of Viking and English interactions is typical of his cultivation of a deeply personal relationship with Anglo-Saxon history. Old English allowed him to delve deeper into this personal mythology.

---

[21] 'Entre los Inmortales … cada acto (y cada pensamiento) es el eco de otros que en el pasado lo antecedieron, sin principio visible, o el fiel presagio de otros que en el futuro lo repetirán hasta el vértigo': Jorge Luis Borges, *Obras completas*, ed. Carlos V. Frías, 3 vols (Barcelona: Emecé, 1989–96), vol. 1: 542. Translation from Jorge Luis Borges, *Collected Fictions*, trans. Andrew Hurley (London: Penguin 1999), 192.

[22] Gene H. Bell-Vilada, *Borges and His Fiction: A Guide to His Mind and Art*, Texas Pan American Series (Austin: University of Texas Press, 2000), 238.

[23] Borges, 'An Autobiographical Essay', 251–52. Cf. Borges's poem 'Un Lector', in his *Obra poética 1923–1985*, 359–60.

[24] Williamson, *Borges: A Life*, 145.

Through the ancient literature of his ancestors, he could perhaps glimpse a past itera-
tion of his current life. Anglo-Saxon, then, could help him make sense of the current
Borges.

Learning Old English thus linked the current Borges with a past one. In 'Al iniciar
el estudio de la gramática anglosajona' (Upon Embarking on the Study of Anglo-
Saxon), a poem he wrote a few years after beginning to study the language, Borges
stands on the banks of a 'great river' – naturally taken to be the Río de la Plata, which
provides Buenos Aires with its port – that is implicitly compared to the waterways of
the North Sea. Here Borges returns to the 'harsh and painstaking words' that he
himself had spoken in the days of Northumbria and Mercia. To have been both an
Anglo-Saxon and a modern Argentinean alludes to Borges's belief that the individual
soul is a composite of past identities and possibilities:

> After some fifty generations
> (such gulfs are opened to us all by time)
> I come back on the far shore of a vast river
> never reached by the Norsemen's long ships
> to the harsh and work-wrought words
> which, with a tongue now dust,
> I used in the days of Northumbria and Mercia
> before becoming Haslam or Borges.[25]

Later in the poem, these harsh words are called 'symbols of other symbols' and 'variations of future English'. Old English, therefore, conforms to Borges's views about
the composition of the individual: the language, like the soul, is a site of endless
repetition and variation. While Old English did not provide Borges with any definitive knowledge about himself, it did provide a potent locus for contemplating the past
possibilities of his soul. This allowance was one of the deepest pleasures that Borges
found in Anglo-Saxon studies. He eloquently describes this process in 'Composición
escrita en un ejemplar de la gesta de *Beowulf*' (A Poem Written in a Copy of *Beowulf*):

> At various times I have asked myself what reasons
> moved me to study while my night came down,
> without particular hope of satisfaction,
> the language of the blunt-tongued Anglo-Saxons.

---

[25] Translated by Alastair Reid in Coleman, *Selected Poems: Jorge Luis Borges*, 129. This poem
is similar to 'Sudden Light' by Dante Gabriel Rossetti, a poem which Borges knew and
which he associated with immortality: see María Esther Vázquez, *Borges, sus días y su
tiempo* (Barcelona: J. Vergara, 1984), 58. The Spanish text reads as follows: 'Al cabo de
cincuenta generaciones / (Tales abismos nos depara a todos el tiempo) / Vuelvo en la mar-
gen ulterior de un gran río / Que no alcanzaron los dragones del viking, / A las ásperas y
laboriosas palabras / Que, con una boca hecha polvo, / Usé en los días de Nortumbria y de
Mercia, / Antes de ser Haslam o Borges' (*Obra poética 1923–1985*, 154).

> Used up by the years my memory
> loses its grip on words that I have vainly
> repeated and repeated. My life in the same way
> weaves and unweaves its weary history.
> Then I tell myself: it must be that the soul
> has some secret sufficient way of knowing
> that it is immortal, that its vast encompassing
> circle can take in all, accomplish all.
> Beyond my anxiety and beyond this writing
> the universe waits, inexhaustible, inviting.[26]

Again, we see the link between Old English and the immortal soul. Repetitions of ancient words are compared to the speaker's own life and its 'weary history', as both have been used up throughout the years. Memory finally reaches a point of exhaustion and begins to fail, which understandably causes 'anxiety' as it connotes the loss of individuality. In the end, the speaker draws solace from the immortality of the soul, which can 'take in all, accomplish all'. Studying Old English becomes analogous with the 'inexhaustible' universe. It is an exercise in dying, in finding comfort in the past iterations of the soul and in the hope of ones to come. This concept helps explain Borges's deeply personal relationship with Anglo-Saxon; in it he could explore his life-long pursuit for knowledge of his own identity. Indeed, in a recorded conversation about this same poem, Borges states that he has been studying Old English 'precisely because he knows his nature to be immortal'.[27] He then asks, refusing to say if he is speaking in earnest or jest, 'Why couldn't my soul have spoken in an earlier body, in the tenth century, that language which would afterwards be transformed into English?'[28] Because Borges believed that his immortal soul had once spoken the language of the Anglo-Saxons, learning that tongue was a reclamation of a forgotten self. This is why Borges could say that learning Old English was 'as intimate an experience … as looking at a sunset or falling in love'.[29]

---

[26] Translated by Alastair Reid in Coleman, *Selected Poems: Jorge Luis Borges*, 207. The Spanish text reads as follows: 'A veces me pregunto qué razones / Me mueven a estudiar sin esperanza / De precisión, mientras mi noche avanza, / La lengua de los ásperos sajones. / Gastada por los años la memoria / Deja caer la en vano repetida / Palabra y es así como mi vida / Teje y desteje su cansada historia, / Será (me digo entonces) que de un modo / Secreto y suficiente el alma sabe / Que es inmortal y que su vasto y grave / Círculo abarca todo y puede todo. / Más allá de este afán y de este verso / Me aguarda inagotable el universo' (*Obra poética 1923–1985*, 226).

[27] María Esther Vázquez, *Borges: Esplendor y derrota* (Barcelona: Tusquets, 1996), 218, reporting a conversation that took place in New Mexico in 1961.

[28] Vázquez, *Borges: Esplendor y derrota*, 218.

[29] Borges, 'An Autobiographical Essay', 253.

While Borges gladly described his personal relationship to Old English in interviews and poetry, his lectures and books on the subject reveal yet another reason the
language piqued his interest. Borges did not miss the symbolism in claiming that Old
English was a 'chosen language' – it was chosen, Borges believed, to grow into the full
stature of modern English, whose literature Borges cherished above all others. Borges
claimed that 'English [ancestry] is more important [to me than Spanish] because I
have read almost everything in English.'[30] That is not to say that Borges had read all
that had been written in English – he typically claimed ignorance of anything published after 1950 – but rather that almost everything he read, he read in English.
Indeed, he first encountered *Don Quixote*, the most famous work in all of Spanish
literature, in English, and when he later read it in the original, it 'sounded like a bad
translation'.[31] Borges rarely spoke English, especially in his earlier years, reserving its
use for his grandmother and a few of his closest friends. Furthermore, he never spent
more than two weeks in an English-speaking country until he had reached his sixties.
English became an intellectual medium, one he associated with literature and philosophy – not vernacular speech. When Borges arrived on the campus of the
University of Texas at Austin in 1961, where he had been invited as a visiting professor, he overheard some laborers speaking, naturally, English. He later remarked, 'I
heard ditch diggers who worked on campus speaking in English, a language I had
until then always thought of as being denied that class of people.'[32] Apart from displaying the tin ear that Borges occasionally had when discussing class issues, this
anecdote illustrates the degree to which Borges considered English a bookish, treas-
ured language.

Old English offered Borges an opportunity to trace the genealogy of this intellectual medium. Just as Borges believed that the soul was a composite of echoes of the
past and future, he also believed that literature exhibited these same qualities. Borges
understood Old English to be part of the *longue durée* of English literature. Tracing
Anglo-Saxon themes, sounds, and culture throughout the entirety of English literature delighted him immensely. Importantly, Borges was not interested in finding Old
English borrowings or allusions in the works of Auden, Hopkins, or Tolkien (to
whose work, incidentally, he was indifferent).[33] Instead, certain Anglo-Saxon poems,
even specific lines, were said to prefigure later authors. For example, Borges would
repeatedly insist that the first few lines of *The Seafarer* prefigured Walt Whitman's

---

[30] 'Creo que lo inglés es más importante porque yo he leído casi todo en inglés': Carrizo,
Borges el memorioso, 57.

[31] Borges, 'An Autobiographical Essay', 209.

[32] Borges, 'An Autobiographical Essay', 254.

[33] When asked his opinion on Tolkien's works, Borges replied, 'I was certainly defeated by
them. I attempted them, several times over, and in the end he was the victor. I was defeated,
and I left off reading him. I never understood them. To me, they were pointless, but perhaps
not to more astute readers.' 'Borges Discusses North American Literature (Interview)', in
Borges the Poet, ed. Cortínez, 78.

Song of Myself.[34] Although the speaker's lament in *The Seafarer* could not differ more in tone from Whitman's celebratory poem, Borges sees in *The Seafarer* an intense focus on the speaker's story, much as we see in Whitman's poem, especially its first line: 'I celebrate myself, and sing myself.' Compare that to the opening of *The Seafarer* and you see what Borges means: 'I can tell the true riddle of my own self, and speak of my experiences.'[35] This type of bold, fanciful connection is how Borges would speak of the relationship between Old English and later literary history. Just as he could find a piece of the current Borges in Old English literature, he could find a bit of Whitman – or any of his favorite authors – there as well.

The English language, Borges believed, was forged by millennia of poets. He borrowed this idea from Emerson, who termed this phenomenon 'fossil poetry'.[36] Borges explains,

> If you use a language, you are indebted to those unknown poets who made the language. But when I am speaking in English, I am receiving the gifts of many dead men, the gifts of many ghosts, and in the case of Spanish the same thing, of course. In the case of all languages. All those dead men are still giving me their gifts. And I'm duly thankful for them, though I don't know their names.[37]

It should come as no surprise, then, that Borges wanted to excavate his favorite literature. Through his Anglo-Saxon studies, Borges could observe these earlier poets at work. He adored interesting etymologies, often quizzing his friends about the roots of this or that word. And finding remnants of Old English alliteration, such as 'kith and kin' or 'friend or foe', was yet another way in which Borges could assert continuity between Anglo-Saxon literature and later literary traditions.[38]

Most nineteenth- and twentieth-century writers who had an affinity for Old English studied it formally at university, as Auden, Heaney, Hopkins, and others did.[39] Borges, though, taught himself in a rather idiosyncratic manner. In 1955, after teaching a four-month survey course in English literature at the University of Buenos Aires, a small group of students came to him at the Biblioteca Nacional, where Borges held an official post. He asked them if they would like to explore the older form of the language, to which they replied 'yes'.[40] Armed with Sweet's *Anglo-Saxon Reader*,

---

[34] See Arias and Hadis, *Borges Profesor*, 91; Jorge Luis Borges and María Kodama, *Breve antología anglosajona* in *Obras completas en colaboración* (Santiago de Chile: La Ciudad, 1978), 796; Borges and Vázquez, *Literaturas germánicas medievales*, 24–25.

[35] *Anglo-Saxon Poetry*, ed. S.A.J. Bradley (London: Dent, 1982), 332.

[36] Ralph Waldo Emerson, 'The Poet', in his *Complete Works*, vol. 3 (Boston: Houghton Mifflin, 1903), 22.

[37] Cortínez, *Borges the Poet*, 87–88.

[38] Borges and Vázquez, *Literaturas germánicas medievales*, 15.

[39] See Chris Jones, *Strange Likeness: The Use of Old English in Twentieth-Century Poetry* (Oxford: Oxford University Press, 2006).

[40] Vázquez, *Borges: Esplendor y derrota*, 217.

a dictionary, and his knowledge of German, Borges began to lead a small class in deciphering the intricacies of 'a language at its dawn'. In 'An Autobiographical Essay', Borges strikingly describes his first reaction to the language:

> We skipped the grammar as much as we could and pronounced the words like German. All at once, we fell in love with a sentence in which Rome (*Romeburh*) was mentioned. We got drunk on these words and rushed down Peru Street shouting them at the top of our voices … I had always thought of English literature as the richest in the world; the discovery now of a secret chamber at the very threshold of that literature came to me as an additional gift. Personally, I knew that the adventure would be an endless one, and that I could go on studying Old English for the rest of my days.[41]

Since the word *Romeburh* appears only once in Sweet's grammar and reader, one can pinpoint the sentence that spurred Borges and his students into such excitement: 'On þām ylcan tīman cōm ēac sum bisceop fram Rōmebyrig.'[42] To most students of Old English, this sentence, which is from Ælfric's *Life of King Oswald*, will seem unremarkable, but not so for Borges. Similarly, Borges was delighted to find that the Mediterranean Sea had been called 'the Sea of the Vandals' (*Vendelsæ*).[43] Another passage that helped to cement his decision to pursue the language came from a reference in the *Anglo-Saxon Chronicle* to a date 'four hundred summers after Troy, the city of the Greeks, was destroyed'. Musing on that passage five years later, Borges suggested that perhaps its allure was 'the act of finding the old story of fallen Troy on the shores of the North Sea'. However, it is also worth noting that all three of the passages that initially left Borges rapt contain earlier versions of place names; these would seem to fit in with Borges's affinity for finding earlier iterations of present entities, be it the soul or literary tradition. Regardless, Borges quickly took to the language that had always fascinated him.[44]

Borges continued his Old English reading group for many years, first meeting in the Biblioteca Nacional on Saturday mornings and later, after his fame had grown great, at his apartment. Of course, Borges's blindness severely hampered his literary activity.[45] Frustrated at his inability to picture the letters *thorn* (þ) and *eth* (ð) in his

---

[41] Borges, 'An Autobiographical Essay', 252.

[42] Henry Sweet, *An Anglo-Saxon Reader*, 7th ed. (Oxford: Clarendon, 1904), 83. The same passage is included in later editions.

[43] Vázquez, *Borges: Esplendor y derrota*, 217. The rest of the present paragraph relies on this same passage.

[44] Vázquez (218–19) remarks that three Anglo-Saxon works that impelled Borges to further study were *The Dream of the Rood*, *The Grave*, and the works of the Venerable Bede. The second of these (which will be discussed below) is normally classified as early Middle English.

[45] In addition to the factors mentioned above, Martín Hadis suggests that Borges's blindness also compelled him toward the study of Old English: see his study 'Borges y el anglosajón', in *El Lenguaraz: Revista académica del Colegio de Traductores Públicos de la Ciudad de Buenos Aires* (April 2003), 59–74.

mind, he made his students sketch two very large pictures of them on a chalkboard. Happily, he was then able to imagine fully those pages that he could not see.[46] Once he had become one of the most famous literary figures in Europe and South America, he could draw from an inexhaustible line of devotees to read to him. It was, however, María Kodama, the last great love of his life, who would become his constant companion, amanuensis, and finally his wife. María had attended the Old English reading group and eventually earned a doctorate in English literature. She co-wrote several of Borges's later treatises and was herself a fine scholar. María made it possible for Borges to continue his pursuit of Old English (and later Old Norse).

In Willis Barnstone's memoirs of Borges lies a fascinating glimpse of Borges's Old English reading group in 1975. The aging poet sat on a couch and had developed the curious habit of having one of his students hold up a book to 'show' Borges what the group was reading aloud, 'as if Borges [could] see and decipher the words'.[47] Borges always possessed a preternatural ability for memorization, and during this session Barnstone notes that 'he [knew] most of the works by heart.' Barnstone, having been asked to read aloud in a language foreign to him, became the victim of the poet's humor. Borges 'clearly [enjoyed] his ignorance'. What becomes increasingly clear through this memoir is the sheer pleasure that Borges, who had long since mastered the Anglo-Saxon tongue, derived from teaching and hearing Old English literature. Indeed, these sessions are remembered as ebullient affairs: 'The acts of plunder, cowardice, the enumeration of flights across the sea, the stabbings, the counting of jewels, gold, and black horses, somehow gave rise to constant laughter and Borges laughed the loudest.'[48]

Borges eventually graduated from amateur enthusiast to respectable scholar of Old English. Since he had taught himself, however, his pronunciation was idiosyncratic. According to María Esther Vázquez, a close friend who collaborated with Borges on several projects, Borges's Old English class 'very imaginatively invented a harsh and solemn pronunciation that sounded to the unlearned like a bugle in the battlefield'.[49] Vázquez also recalls that when Borges visited the University of St Andrews in 1964, he had an audience with Anglo-Saxon specialists, whereupon it became clear that their pronunciation of Old English was very different from Borges's invented one.[50] That Borges sought out advice from specialists in the field, I think, shows that his interest in Old English quickly developed another facet. While he certainly utilized

[46] 'Borges habla de Borges: Entrevista con Rita Guibert', in *Jorge Luis Borges*, ed. Jaime Alazraki (Madrid: Taurus, 1976), 321.

[47] Willis Barnstone, *With Borges on an Ordinary Evening in Buenos Aires* (Urbana: University of Illinois Press, 1993), 49. The following quotations are from that same source, at 49 and 51.

[48] Barnstone, 'With Borges in Buenos Aires (1975)', in *Jorge Luis Borges: Conversations*, ed. Richard Burgin (Jackson: University Press of Mississippi, 1998), 139.

[49] 'Con mucha fantasía inventaron una pronunciación dura y solemne que al profano le sonaría como un clarín en el campo de batalla': Vázquez, *Borges: Esplendor y derrota*, 218.

[50] Vázquez, *Borges: Esplendor y derrota*, 219.

the language for his own artistic purposes, he also developed a genuine interest in its academic scholarship. In September 1961, Borges spent a semester as a visiting professor at the University of Texas at Austin. In addition to teaching a class on Argentinean literature, he attended Dr Rudolph Williard's seminars on Old English.[51] He would later incorporate some of Williard's advice into his own writings on the topic. Aside from discussing Old English with specialists, he also sought out and read Anglo-Saxon scholarship. Borges often stated that after his blindness, the only new literature that he had read to him concerned Old English and Old Norse – everything else was rereading.[52] Borges's dogged pursuit of scholarship is evident in his lectures and writing. For example, in *Literaturas germánicas medievales*, Borges mentions Otto Jespersen, Grímur Thorkelin, N.F.S. Grundtvig, J.R. Clark Hall, John Earle, William Morris, W.P. Ker, Martin Lehnert, and a host of other scholars. His taste in Anglo-Saxon critics seems to have mirrored his general reading practices: older works outnumber more recent ones, and eccentric choices make their way into his discussions. Looking again at *Literaturas germánicas medievales*, for example, George Saintsbury and Maurice de Wulf inform his excursus – two turn-of-the-century scholars of English rhetoric and medieval philosophy, respectively.[53] Furthermore, owing to his multilingualism, Borges was familiar with translations and scholarship in German and French.[54] He clearly cared about Anglo-Saxon scholarship, and his desire to obtain it is nicely illustrated in an anecdote recounted by an admiring visitor, William Goldhurst. Though the two had never met before, Borges almost immediately asked Goldhurst if he knew anything about Old English poetry. After a brief chat about *The Battle of Maldon*, the visitor asked Borges if he had heard about a recent theory that specific lines of *Beowulf,* which seemed to lack the proper number of metrical stresses, were meant as placeholders for musical fillers. Having not heard this theory before, Borges was 'extremely interested' and 'a bit chagrined, as though he should have been aware all along of such footnote-knowledge'.[55] Anything, it appears, having to do with Anglo-Saxon or Old Norse literature Borges avidly consumed.

Indeed, Borges seems to have read the whole of the Old English poetical corpus. (The only prose that seems to have seriously held his attention was the *Anglo-Saxon Chronicle*.) Borges's lectures to his English literature course at the University of Buenos Aires display the fruits of his learning, his love of Old English, and the importance that he felt the Anglo-Saxon period commanded in literary history. Indeed, he devoted

---

51 Emir Rodriguez Monegal, *Jorge Luis Borges: A Literary Biography* (New York: Dutton, 1978), 445.

52 See e.g. Donald Yates, 'Borges: Philosopher? Poet? Revolutionary? (Interview),' in *Jorge Luis Borges: Conversations*, ed. Burgin, 196, and Barnstone, 'With Borges in Buenos Aires (1975)'.

53 Borges and Vázquez, *Literaturas germánicas medievales*, 21, 31.

54 See for example the end matter of *Literaturas germánicas medievales*, 136–38.

55 William Goldhurst, 'Appointment with Borges', *Humanities in the South: Newsletter of the Southern Humanities Council* 47 (1978): 1–2 (at p. 2).

almost one third of the whole course to Old English. These lectures are a fascinating mix of points familiar to introductory students of Old English literature – the importance of *ofermod* in *The Battle of Maldon*, for example – and Borges's own idiosyncratic understanding of English literature.[56] Of course, one of these idiosyncrasies was Borges's insistence that Old English anticipated much later literary moments. For example, he noted that the period's elegiac verse foreshadowed, almost a millennium beforehand, the Romantic movement, one of many instances where Borges betrays his belief in the *longue durée* of English literary culture.[57] And authors who rarely grace any discussion of Anglo-Saxon literature – Kipling, Chesterton, Tennyson, and T.S. Eliot, to name a few – lend these lectures an eclectic quality. His lectures are not, however, dominated by these eccentricities, and an attentive student would have gained much that is still considered essential introductory material.

As most university lecturers do, Borges would often speak generically of 'scholars' and 'books', instead of citing exact names. And undoubtedly much of his knowledge of scholarship – such as the supposed musical breaks in *Beowulf* – would have been passed to him in conversations. His blindness, too, hampered his ability to search out scholarship on his own, and surely his residence in Buenos Aires, far from the main resources for British medieval studies, did little to improve the situation. Thus, discovering what scholarship made its way to Borges remains a difficult task. He clearly accepted the theory, popular among turn-of-the-century scholars, that *Beowulf* was in some sense a vernacular version of Vergil's *Aeneid*, for he almost always mentions this relationship when discussing the Old English poem.[58] In addition, he adds his own twist to this argument. With a good deal of imaginative scope, he explains that vernacular epics like *Beowulf* appeared earlier among the Germanic peoples for the same reason that Biblical translations did so. Citing the nineteenth-century scholar Francis Palgrave as his authority, Borges reports that Romance speakers would have found Biblical translations to be parodic because they would have recognized that their Romance vernacular was closely related to the Latin of the Vulgate. Thus, any romance translation would run the risk of looking like a poorly adapted parody of the Vulgate's exalted Latin. Applying Palgrave's thesis to the epic, Borges suggests that for the same reason, Romance speakers did not produce epic poetry like *Beowulf*, as it would have seemed a shoddy parody of Vergil. Thus Germanic speakers could compose *Beowulf* because their 'vernacular language so drastically differed from Latin, that upon reading *Beowulf* nobody would think that they were reading a parody of the *Aeneid*'.[59] Elegantly simple, this rationale for the existence of the poem at a relatively early date demonstrates Borges's active engagement with academic scholarship.

---

[56] Arias and Hadis, *Borges Profesor*, 82–83.
[57] Arias and Hadis, *Borges Profesor*, 94.
[58] E.g. Arias and Hadis, *Borges Profesor*, 62–63; Borges and Kodama, *Breve antología anglosajona*, 789; Borges and Vázquez, *Literaturas germánicas medievales*, 20–21.
[59] 'Porque esa lengua vernácula difería tan profundamente del latín, que nadie al leer el *Beowulf* podía pensar que estaba leyendo una parodia de la *Eneida*': Arias and Hadis, *Borges Profesor*, 63.

Borges did not confine his enthusiasm for Old English to his small group, to interviewers, or even to the students in his literature courses. Indeed, he took a leading role in popularizing Old English literature throughout the Spanish-speaking world. He wrote a handful of scholarly works to popularize the language that had so consumed him.[60] In 1932, long before he had any first-hand knowledge of Old English or Old Norse, Borges published a short treatise on Old Norse kennings in the literary journal *Sur*, titled 'Noticia de los kenningar'.[61] The article is quite informative, seeing that Borges's main source was a translation of the *Edda*, and it includes a fairly large list of kennings. Surprisingly, in 1951 Borges and Delia Igenieros published *Antiguas literaturas germánicas* (*Ancient Germanic Literatures*) without having actually learned a medieval Germanic language. Despite that fact, the volume proved to be one of his more successful works of that period.[62] After Borges had studied Old English and Old Norse he issued a corrected and more detailed version of this book in 1966, under the title *Literaturas germánicas medievales*. This volume, thanks partly to the assistance of Dr Rudolph Willard,[63] remains a valuable introduction to the subject. Its tripartite structure harkens back to the earliest editions of medieval Germanic languages: Gothic is dealt with first and its entry is understandably the briefest. The sections on Old English and Old Norse include a general discussion of metrics and a succinct historical summary. Borges then discusses several of his favorite poems and passages, offering translations or general summary. *Literaturas germánicas medievales* is an accurate and professional publication that usually expresses the current scholarly consensus regarding dates, genre, and provenance. A useful bibliography is provided for those interested in pursuing further study. In the work's prologue one again sees the impetus that drew Borges into the study of medieval Germanic languages: 'Those who read the sagas will see in them the prefiguration of the modern novel. Those who study Anglo-Saxon poetry and, beyond that, the poetry of the skalds will discover strange and baroque examples of metaphor.'[64] Again, we find Borges promoting his notion that modern English literature contains distant Anglo-Saxon reflexes.

Aside from the 1965 *Introducción a la literatura inglesa* (Introduction to English Literature) in which Borges discusses the Anglo-Saxon epic,[65] the last major work

---

[60] Technically he co-wrote them, though much of the writing is undeniably his.

[61] 'Noticia de los kennigar' was later republished in the volume *Historia de la eternidad* as simply 'Las Kenningar'. See Borges, *Obras Completas*, vol. 1: 368–81.

[62] Monegal, *Jorge Luis Borges: A Literary Biography*, 419.

[63] Willard was the co-author, with Roger Sherman Loomis, of *Medieval English Verse and Prose in Modernized Versions* (New York: Appleton-Century-Crofts, 1948). He also edited *The Blickling Homilies*, EEMF 10 (Copenhagen: Rosenkilde and Bagger, 1960).

[64] 'Quienes lean las sagas verán prefigurada en ellas la novela moderna: quienes estudien las poesía sajona y, más aún, la escáldica, descubrirán extraños y barrocos ejemplos de la metáfora': Borges and Vázquez, *Literaturas germánicas medievales*, 8.

[65] Jorge Luis Borges and María Esther Vázquez, *Introduccíon a la literatura inglesa* (Buenos Aires: Columba, 1965).

that he published on Old English literature was the 1978 *Breve antología anglosajona*, which was co-authored by María Kodama. Although the opinions expressed in this volume, as well as its prose style, are undeniably Borgesian, it was surely María who did much of the work. Her doctoral studies in English literature focused on the Anglo-Saxon period. Borges probably received current scholarly opinions through María who, after reading articles and books, would relate the interesting bits to the aging blind poet. The volume's short prologue repeats many of his familiar observations on Old English. Borges provides a concise history of the Angles, Saxons, and Jutes and then lays out the barest basics of Old English versification. He calls this treatise a 'fragmentary volume' and expresses the hope that it will induce others to more serious study.

The *Breve antología anglosajona* consists of prose translations of *Beowulf* (Scyld's ship funeral), *The Fight at Finnsburg*, *Deor*, *The Seafarer*, 'The Voyages of Ohthere', and *Solomon and Saturn*. His only translation in the medium of verse is of *The Grave*, a poem that is usually classified as early Middle English. The Old English seems to effortlessly lend itself to Borges's famous prose style. Borges renders the oblique, euphemistic construction of Anglo-Saxon verse into Spanish without destroying its allusive quality. For example, 'Him ðā Scyld gewāt tō gescæphwīle / felahrōr fēran on Frēan wære' (*Beowulf* 26–27) is translated as 'En la hora de su destino, Scyld, fuerte aún, buscó el amparo de su Señor' (At his destined time, Scyld, still strong, found the shelter of his Lord).[66] The celebrated refrain of *Deor*, 'Þæs oferēode; þisses swā mæg', becomes the equally elegant 'Esas cosas pasaron; también pasarán éstas.'[67] After each translation, Borges supplies a note, which usually reiterates his notion of the reverberation of Old English poets among other authors, such as asserting that *Beowulf* contains echoes of Homeric poetry. The most striking piece of this small volume is Borges's translation of *The Grave*. Longfellow, one of Borges's favorite authors, had produced a fairly literal translation of this poem and undoubtedly this translation helped to pique Borges's interest in this seldom studied work.[68] Borges had previously published a prose translation in his *Literaturas germánicas medievales*, and in an article he states that the only place where he could find an edition of the original text was Martin Lehnert's *Poetry and Prose of the Anglo-Saxons*.[69] Borges's translation is in the style that he uses when imitating or translating Whitman, as the final lines of the poem show:[70]

---

[66] Borges and Kodama, *Breve antología anglosajona*, 789.

[67] Borges and Kodama, *Breve antología anglosajona*, 793.

[68] Henry Wadsworth Longfellow, *Poems and Other Writings* (New York: Library of America, 2000), 697–98.

[69] Martin Lehnert, *Poetry and Prose of the Anglo-Saxons*, 2 vols. (Halle: Niemeyer, 1955–56), vol. 1: 36. This anthology was published in a second revised edition in 1960. Lehnert includes Longfellow's translation at vol. 1: 97–89.

[70] Cf. Walt Whitman, *Hojas de hierba*, trans. Jorge Luis Borges (Buenos Aires: Juárez, 1969).

Ningún amigo irá visitarte y a preguntarte si esa casa te gusta.
Nadie abrirá la puerta.
Nadie bajará a ese lugar porque muy pronto serás aborrecible a los ojos.
Tu cabeza será despojada de su cabello y la hermosura de tu pelo se apagará.[71]

No friend will visit you and ask if this house pleases you.
No one will open the door.
No one will descend to this place, for very soon you will be loathsome to look upon.
Your head will be shorn of its hair, and the beauty of your skin will fade.

The alternation of long and short lines and the initial alliteration and repetition all create a Spanish approximation of Whitman's characteristic free verse, which Borges deeply admired. *La Sepultura*, as Borges entitles it, obviously appealed to his imagination; he liked to romantically cite it as the last poem the Anglo-Saxons produced.

Perhaps one reason that so little attention has been given to Borges and his use of Anglo-Saxon literature is that this influence is most strongly felt in his later poetry, which is decidedly less popular than his short stories, the most famous of which he wrote before he began to study Old English.[72] Accordingly, Borges's general interest in the Middle Ages is often mentioned, but seldom pursued. Yet Borges read deeply in medieval literature: He knew Augustine, Gildas, Bede, *The Song of Roland*, *The Nibelungenlied*, and Aquinas, to name only a few authors and works. His passion for Old Norse literature, which I have only mentioned in passing, was as boundless as that for Old English, but is even less understood. Borges himself believed that medieval literature, with its allegorical playfulness and its occasionally recondite content, was somewhat underappreciated. Speaking of the ability of medieval readers to be at ease with different allegorical interpretations, an ability that Borges thought was almost lost to modern readers, he told his students, 'It must not be assumed that we are necessarily more complex than the people of the Middle Ages, people who were versed in theology and in theological subtleties. Surely we have gained much, but it is possible that we have lost something.'[73] Without appreciating Borges's own enduring relationship with the literature and thought of the Middle Ages, we too are at risk of losing something.

---

[71] *Breve antología anglosajona*, 797.

[72] For more poems that have explicitly Anglo-Saxon themes see: 'Un sajón' (*Obra poética 1923–1985*, 204); 'Hengest Cyning' (*Obra poética 1923–1985*, 227); 'Fragmento' (*Obra poética 1923–1985*, 229); 'A una espada en York Minster' (*Obra poética 1923–1985*, 231); 'A un poeta sajón' (*Obra poética 1923–1985*, 278); 'Hengist quiere hombres' (*Obra poética 1923–1985*, 408); 'Brunanburh, 937 A.D.' (*Obra poética 1923–1985*, 452).

[73] 'No hay que suponer que nosotros somos necesariamente más complejos que los hombres de la Edad Media, hombres versados en teología y en las sutilezas teológicas. Sin duda hemos ganado mucho, pero es possible que hayamos perdido algo': Arias and Hadis, *Borges Profesor*, 98.

For Borges, what Anglo-Saxon studies offered was a source of constant and inexhaustible pleasure. Echoing the Venerable Bede's passion for knowledge, Borges claimed that in his pursuit of Old English 'the pleasure of studying, not the vanity of mastering, has been my chief aim.'[74] Speaking modestly about his passion, Borges remarked, 'I know I won't ever possess [Old English and Old Icelandic], but I also know that this sort of slow journey toward the impossible somehow is a pleasure.'[75] A particular incident is worth mentioning in this connection. Visiting Germany in 1964, Borges was asked if he wished to go anywhere special; he chose Schleswig, on the Baltic coast. Having arrived at the beach, Borges, deeply moved, knelt on the sand and wet his hands in the Baltic, all the while reciting Old English verse about the sea.[76] Indeed, this degree of reverence for the Anglo-Saxon past might well be felt by one who finds in it personal understanding, haunting beauty, and boisterous laughter.

---

[74] Borges, 'An Autobiographical Essay', 252.

[75] *Siete Conversaciones con Jorge Luis Borges*, ed. Fernando Sorrentino (Buenos Aires: Casa Pardo, 1973), 87.

[76] Vázquez, *Borges: Esplendor y derrota*, 238.

Afterword

A person taking a retrospective view of the modern criticism of Old English literature might well be reminded of the refrain uttered by the fictive poet Deor, in the Exeter Book poem that now bears his name: *þæs ofereode; þisses swa mæg*. Whether one thinks of the philological zeal of early twentieth-century scholars; the turn towards New Critical models during the mid-twentieth century; the illusions that were once cherished by oral-formulaicists and by exegetically minded critics alike that a single master-key might be found to unlock the mysteries of Old English literature; the turn towards Theory during the 1980s and 1990s, sometimes demonized and sometimes enthroned like a bold new god; or the 'back to the manuscripts' movement of the early twenty-first century, which is still so much with us as to be almost impervious to critique, one can survey this scholarly expanse with a certain tranquillity, secure in the knowledge that 'this too shall pass', even though the influence of each approach may be lasting. Importantly, the mantra that the melancholic-sounding Deor utters to this effect is expressive of hope. No state of affairs is eternal, he affirms, whether blissful or bleak. New adventures of an unforeseen kind await us around the next bend of the road, or may await at least our successors, who will be in a position to profit from our achievements and missteps.

This book has sought to give a balanced account of certain main currents in the criticism of Old English literature since the beginning of the twentieth century, with an emphasis on the last forty years or so. Since, like anyone else working in this field, I have views about some matters, the book cannot be called free from personal values and judgements. If it were so, then it would be a plodding thing indeed. Still, I have tried not to let my own views stand in the way of a fair and dispassionate account of what others have had to say. Rather than promoting any one critical school or method, I have preferred to point to the enduring values of sound philology, a well-informed sense of the historical context within which texts are produced, and an open mind. My chief aim has been to give readers a sense of the dynamic character of the critical work that has been done in this field and that is still being done today. The selections from the critical literature that are reproduced here, from Joyce Hill's analysis of Anglo-Saxon pedagogy to Joshua Byron Smith's study of Borges's lasting

Old English Literature: A Guide to Criticism with Selected Readings, First Edition. John D. Niles.
© 2016 John D. Niles. Published 2016 by John Wiley & Sons, Ltd.

love affair with Old English, ought to be sufficient to fulfil the book's chief aim regardless of the rest of its contents. If the book has an agenda, it is to encourage appreciation of what stands to be gained when a variety of critical aims, methods, and perspectives are adopted in conjunction with one another.

I am aware of how selective the book's contents have had to be. Many topics of interest have been slighted. Countless scholars and publications have gone unmentioned, whether because of constraints of space, the need to exclude whole scholarly domains or subdomains, or the limits of the author's knowledge. For practical reasons, the number of items cited in the lists headed 'For Further Reading' that conclude each chapter has been capped at about ten, despite a strong temptation to exceed that number. I am confident that those readers who wish to pursue any topic in greater depth than is attempted here will be able to do so either by consulting the scholarly resources cited in the present book or by recourse to standard bibliographies. Among these, the most comprehensive and accessible one as regards studies published since 1972 is the searchable online bibliographical database maintained on the *Old English Newsletter* website. This can be consulted at: http://www.oenewsletter.org/OENDB/index.php.

One impressive aspect of the field of Old English literary studies is its collective learning, which is capacious indeed at the present time (though knowledge, one must remember, only exists when renewed in the minds and hearts of persons of succeeding generations). Another impressive aspect of the field is its collegiality. While this quality may not leap to the eye in scholarly books and articles (which can be adversarial, as befits the search for truth), those who make use of the resources of the *Old English Newsletter* will be struck by the warmly collegial nature of that enterprise. Such persons will recognize why I wish to dedicate this book, now that it is done, to the five scholars who have served successively as editors of that newsletter since its modest origins in 1967 — namely Stanley J. Kahrl (1931–89), Paul E. Szarmach, Jonathan Wilcox, Roy M. Liuzza, and Stephen J. Harris. Their achievements would have been impossible without the assistance of colleagues who have served over the years as that journal's associate editors, including Alan K. Brown, Carl T. Berkhout, Rowland L. Collins, Joseph B. Trahern, Peter S. Baker, Robert D. Fulk, Thomas N. Hall, Robert Hasenfratz, and Daniel Donoghue. The efforts of those persons have depended in turn on all those colleagues, probably numbering in the hundreds by now, who have served as reviewers for the journal's annual annotated bibliography of work done in the field. Comparable to these labours are the ones that since 1972 have gone into the annual compilation of bibliographies for the multidisciplinary journal *Anglo-Saxon England*. The present book would have been almost impossible to write were it not for these generous acts of service to the profession.

Select Bibliography

The following list is meant to be of use to persons either setting out in the field of Old English literary studies or conducting more advanced research. Its emphasis is on relatively recent publications. It is best used in conjunction with the preceding chapters, where notice is taken of particular editions, critical studies, and other scholarly resources. The organization of the list is as follows:

1. Literature
   General
   Noteworthy editions
   Anthologies of reprinted critical essays
   Books of translations
   Beowulf
      Editions and other scholarly resources
      Bibliographies
      Anthologies of reprinted critical essays
2. Language
   Lexical resources
   Grammar, metre
   Classroom texts
3. Additional resources
   Encyclopedias
   Specialized journals
   Bibliographies
   Electronic resources
      Manuscripts and script
      Facsimiles

Old English Literature: A Guide to Criticism with Selected Readings, First Edition. John D. Niles.
© 2016 John D. Niles. Published 2016 by John Wiley & Sons, Ltd.

1. Literature

General

Aertsen, Henk, and Rolf H. Bremmer, Jr. 1994. *Companion to Old English Poetry*. Amsterdam: VU University Press. With short chapters of an introductory nature written by specialists in the field.

Amodio, Mark C. 2014. *The Anglo-Saxon Literature Handbook*. Oxford: Wiley-Blackwell. An overview of the major works, genres, and themes of Old English literature with attention to historical backgrounds and critical approaches.

Discenza, Nicole Guenther, and Paul E. Szarmach, eds. 2014. *A Companion to Alfred the Great*. Leiden: Brill. With eleven contributions representing the perspectives of history, literature, and art history.

Donoghue, Daniel. 2004. *Old English Literature: A Short Introduction*. Oxford: Blackwell. A cosmopolitan guide to the literature organized around five themes: the vow, the hall, the miracle, the pulpit, and the scholar.

Fulk, R.D., and Christopher Cain. 2003. *A History of Old English Literature*. Oxford: Blackwell. An authoritative survey of Old English poetry and prose, with an initial chapter on 'The Chronology and Varieties of Old English Literature'.

Godden, Malcolm, and Michael Lapidge, eds. 2013. *The Cambridge Companion to Old English Literature*, 2nd edn. Cambridge: Cambridge University Press. With seventeen chapters written by specialists.

Greenfield, Stanley G., and Daniel G. Calder. 1986. *A New Critical History of Old English Literature*. New York: New York University Press. A judicious review of Old English literature and its modern critical reception; includes an introductory chapter by Michael Lapidge on Anglo-Latin literature.

Johnson, David F., and Elaine Treharne, eds. 2005. *Readings in Medieval Texts: Interpreting Old and Middle English Literature*. Oxford: Oxford University Press. The first twelve chapters, written by specialists in Old English literature, address particular poems, types, or genres.

Magennis, Hugh. 2011. *The Cambridge Introduction to Anglo-Saxon Literature*. Cambridge: Cambridge University Press. Noteworthy for its integrated discussion of prose and verse, Old English and Anglo-Latin, and devotional and worldly literature.

Magennis, Hugh, and Mary Swan, eds. 2009. *A Companion to Ælfric*. Leiden: Brill. With fifteen chapters by specialists; an indispensable resource for study of this major author.

O'Brien O'Keeffe, Katherine, ed. 1997. *Reading Old English Texts*. Cambridge: Cambridge University Press. Includes nine chapters, each written by a specialist, on such topics as source study, historicist approaches, oral tradition, and feminist criticism.

Pulsiano, Phillip, and Elaine Treharne, eds. 2001. *A Companion to Anglo-Saxon Literature*. Oxford: Blackwell. With many short chapters by specialists on topics ancillary to the literature, including authorship, audience, genres, sources, and the history of the field.

Stodnick, Jacqueline, and Renée R. Trilling, eds. 2012. *A Handbook of Anglo-Saxon Studies*. Oxford: Wiley-Blackwell. With eighteen chapters that explore topics of current interest, including the relationship between Anglo-Saxon studies and contemporary critical theory.

Noteworthy editions

Clemoes, Peter, and Malcolm Godden, eds. 1979–2000. *Ælfric's Catholic Homilies*. 3 vols. Oxford: Oxford University Press. The three volumes are as follows:

- *First Series: Text*, ed. Clemoes (1997).
- *The Second Series: Text*, ed. Godden (1979).
- *Introduction, Commentary, and Glossary*, by Godden (2000).

Colgrave, Bertram, and R.A.B. Mynors. 1969. *Bede's Ecclesiastical History of the English People.* Oxford: Clarendon Press, 1969. A dual-language edition with Latin text and English translation on facing pages.

Klinck, Anne L. 1992. *The Old English Elegies: A Critical Edition and Genre Study.* Montreal: McGill–Queen's University Press. Reissued with a supplementary bibliography, 2001.

Krapp, George Philip, and Elliott Van Kirk Dobbie, eds. 1931–53. The Anglo-Saxon Poetic Records. 6 vols. New York: Columbia University Press. The standard collective edition of Old English verse. Its constituent volumes are as follows:

1. *The Junius Manuscript*, ed. Krapp (1931)
2. *The Vercelli Book*, ed. Krapp (1932)
3. *The Exeter Book*, ed. Krapp and Dobbie (1936)
4. *Beowulf and Judith*, ed. Dobbie (1953)
5. *The Paris Psalter and The Meters of Boethius*, ed. Krapp (1932)
6. *The Anglo-Saxon Minor Poems*, ed. Dobbie (1942)

Muir, Bernard J., ed. 2000. *The Exeter Anthology of Old English Poetry: An Edition of Exeter Dean and Chapter MS 3501*, 2nd edn. Exeter: University of Exeter Press. Published under the same title in 2006 was an electronic facsimile of the Exeter Book, produced by Muir and Nick Kennedy as a DVD.

Ziolkowski, Jan M., gen. ed. 2010–. Dumbarton Oaks Medieval Library. A number of Old English titles are included in this handsome series. Each volume includes a facing-page modern English translation of the original texts. As of the end of 2015, the following volumes pertaining to Old English literature are available:

- *The Beowulf Manuscript*, ed. R.D. Fulk (2010)
- *Old Testament Narratives*, ed. Daniel Anlezark (2011)
- *Old English Shorter Poems*, vol. 1: *Religious and Didactic*, ed. Christopher A. Jones (2012)
- *The Old English Boethius*, ed. Susan Irvine and Malcolm R. Godden (2012)
- *The Old English Poems of Cynewulf*, ed. Robert E. Bjork (2013)
- *Old English Poems of Christ and His Saints*, ed. Mary Clayton (2013)
- *Old English Shorter Poems*, vol. 2: *Wisdom and Lyric*, ed. Robert E. Bjork (2014)
- *Old English Psalms*, ed. Patrick P. O'Neill (2016)

Anthologies of reprinted critical essays

Bessinger, Jess B., and Stanley J. Kahrl, eds. 1968. *Essential Articles for the Study of Old English Poetry.* Hamden, CT: Archon Books.

Bjork, Robert E., ed. 1996. *Cynewulf: Basic Readings.* New York: Garland.

Liuzza, R.M., ed. 2002. *Old English Literature: Critical Essays.* New Haven: Yale University Press.

Liuzza, R.M., ed. 2002. *The Poems of MS Junius 11: Basic Readings.* New York: Routledge.

O'Brien O'Keeffe, Katherine, ed. 1993. *Old English Shorter Poems: Basic Readings.* New York: Garland.

Richards, Mary P., ed. 1994. *Anglo-Saxon Manuscripts: Basic Readings.* New York: Garland.

Stevens, Martin, and Jerome Mandel, eds. 1968. *Old English Literature: Twenty-Two Analytical Essays.* Lincoln: University of Nebraska Press.

Szarmach, Paul E, ed. 2000. *Old English Prose: Basic Readings.* New York: Garland.

Books of translations

Bradley, S.A.J., trans. 1982. *Anglo-Saxon Poetry*. London: Dent. Reliable prose translations of almost the whole extant body of Old English verse, with an informed commentary; the translations are faithful enough to be usable for scholarly purposes.

Crossley-Holland, Kevin, trans. 1984. *The Anglo-Saxon World: An Anthology*. Oxford: Oxford University Press. A selection of both prose and poetry, including *Beowulf*; the translations of verse are readable but sometimes less than exact.

Raffel, Burton, trans. 1998. *Poems and Prose from the Old English*, ed. Alexandra H. Olsen and Burton Raffel, with introductions by Olsen. New Haven: Yale University Press. The translations of verse, done with style, do not strive to be literal.

Swanton, Michael, trans. 1993. *Anglo-Saxon Prose*, 2nd edn. London: Dent. First published 1975. Straightforward translations of a miscellany of Old English prose texts.

Williamson, Craig, ed. and trans. 2011. *Beowulf and Other Old English Poems*. Philadelphia: University of Pennsylvania Press. Artful translations of a number of poems.

Beowulf

Editions and other scholarly resources

Bjork, Robert E., and John D. Niles, eds. 1997. *A Beowulf Handbook*. Lincoln: University of Nebraska Press. Eighteen chapters by specialists, each one headed by a capsule chronology of relevant scholarship. A comprehensive guide to modern scholarship on the poem up to the 1990s.

Chickering, Howell D., Jr, ed. 2006. *Beowulf: A Dual-Language Edition*, 3rd edn. New York: Random House. Includes text and translation on facing pages, with an introduction, commentary, and other study aids. First published 1977.

Clark, George. 1990. *Beowulf*. Boston: Twayne. A concise study of the poem and its meaning, with remarks on its critical reception.

Fulk, R.D., Robert E. Bjork, and John D. Niles, eds. 2008. *Klaeber's Beowulf and The Fight at Finnsburg*, 4th edn. Toronto: University of Toronto Press. The chief scholarly edition of *Beowulf*, based on Klaeber's earlier edition but thoroughly revised.

Mitchell, Bruce, and Fred C. Robinson, eds. 1998. *Beowulf: An Edition*. Oxford: Blackwell. A classroom edition with expert introduction, glossary, and notes.

Orchard, Andy. 2003. *A Critical Companion to Beowulf*. Cambridge: D.S. Brewer. Covers virtually all aspects of the poem, with extensive references to the critical literature.

Shippey, T.A., and Andreas Haarder, eds. 1998. *Beowulf: The Critical Heritage*. London: Routledge. Includes extensive quotations, expertly translated from foreign languages where necessary, from nineteenth- and twentieth-century *Beowulf* criticism, along with a substantial Introduction.

Bibliographies

Hasenfratz, Robert J. 1993. *Beowulf Scholarship: An Annotated Bibliography, 1979–1990*. New York: Garland. Updates Short's 1980 bibliography, with excellent annotations.

Short, Douglas D. 1980. *Beowulf Scholarship: An Annotated Bibliography*. New York: Garland. Selective; concentrates on the more recent criticism through the year 1978, with brief annotations. Note also Short's complementary essay '*Beowulf* and Modern Critical Tradition', in *A Fair Day in the Affections: Literary Essays in Honor of Robert B. White Jr*, ed. Jack D. Durant and M. Thomas Hester (Raleigh: Winston Press, 1980), 1–23.

Anthologies of reprinted critical essays

Baker, Peter S., ed. 1995. *Beowulf: Basic Readings*. New York: Garland. Eleven reprinted essays and two new ones. Reissued in 2000 with the title *The Beowulf Reader*.

Donoghue, Daniel, ed. 2002. *Beowulf: A Verse Translation: Authoritative Text, Contexts, Criticism*. New York: Norton. A Norton Critical Edition. Includes Seamus Heaney's verse translation of the poem and some ancillary items, including eight reprinted critical essays.

Fulk, R.D., ed. 1991. *Interpretations of Beowulf: A Critical Anthology*. Bloomington: Indiana University Press. Seventeen reprinted studies.

Howe, Nicholas, ed. 2002. *Beowulf: A Prose Translation*. New York: Norton. An alternative Norton Critical Edition. Includes a hyperliteral prose translation by E. Talbot Donaldson plus a number of ancillary items, including seven reprinted critical essays.

2. Language

Lexical resources

Barney, Stephen A. 1985. *Word-Hoard: An Introduction to Old English Vocabulary*, 2nd edn. Yale University Press. A grouped frequency word-list; includes a brief etymological essay on each lexical cluster.

Bessinger, Jess B., ed. 1969. *A Concordance to Beowulf*. Ithaca: Cornell University Press. More complete than the preceding item for this one poem; each simplex of compound words is cited.

Bessinger, Jess, ed. 1978. *A Concordance to the Anglo-Saxon Poetic Records*. Ithaca: Cornell University Press. Includes an index of poetic compounds.

Bosworth, Joseph, and T. Northcote Toller. 1898–1972. *An Anglo-Saxon Dictionary*. Oxford: Oxford University Press. In three parts: main volume 1898; supplement by Toller, 1921; enlarged addenda and corrigenda by A. Campbell, 1972. The best available dictionary for that part of the Old English lexicon not yet published by the *DOE*; provides many illustrative quotations.

Cameron, Angus. 1983. *Old English Word Studies: A Preliminary Author and Word Index*. Toronto: University of Toronto Press. Includes, on microfiche, a bibliography of Old English lexical studies published up to the early 1980s.

Healey, Antoinette diPaolo et al. 1986–. *Dictionary of Old English*. Toronto: University of Toronto Press. As of the end of 2015, entries for the letters A, Æ, B, C, D, E, F, and G are available by online subscription, as well as on CD-ROM.

Roberts, Jane, and Christian Kay. 1995. *A Thesaurus of Old English*. 2 vols. London: King's College. Groups Old English vocabulary topically, sorting out its relations to all areas of experience.

Grammar, metre

Brunner, Karl. 1965. *Altenglische Grammatik*. Tübingen: Niemeyer. Based on Eduard Sievers's *Angelsächsische grammatik* (1898).

Campbell, A. 1959. *Old English Grammar*. Oxford: Clarendon Press. A standard reference book for speakers of English.

Fulk, R.D. 1992. *A History of Old English Meter*. Philadelphia: University of Pennsylvania Press. More than a metrical history, for it attempts to develop a system of dating Old English poetry on metrical grounds.

Mitchell, Bruce. 1985. *Old English Syntax*. 2 vols. Oxford: Clarendon Press. A definitive study of the subject, with many illustrative examples.

Sievers, Eduard. 1903. *An Old English Grammar*, ed. and trans. Albert S. Cook, 3rd edn. Boston: Ginn & Co. Based on Sievers's *Angelsächsische grammatik* (1898).

Classroom texts

Baker, Peter S. 2000. *Introduction to Old English*. Oxford: Blackwell. An introductory grammar and reader that is responsive to the needs of students who have little background in language studies. Also available online: see the Medieval Institute web site listed below under 'Electronic resources'.

Cassidy, Frederic G., and Richard N. Ringler. 1971. *Bright's Old English Grammar and Reader*, 3rd edn. New York: Holt. Step-by-step lessons in the phonology and grammar of Old English plus an ample selection of expertly annotated readings in both prose and poetry.

Marsden, Richard. 2004. *The Cambridge Old English Reader*. Cambridge: Cambridge University Press. Includes fifty-six individual texts and a short reference grammar of Old English.

Mitchell, Bruce, and Fred C. Robinson. 2012. *A Guide to Old English*, 8th edn. Oxford: Blackwell. Offers initial lessons in phonology and grammar and a variety of readings in both verse and prose.

Pope, John C. 2001. *Eight Old English Poems*, 3rd edn, revised by R.D. Fulk. New York: Norton. An exemplary student and scholarly edition of certain widely admired Old English poems.

Whitelock, Dorothy, ed. 1967. *Sweet's Anglo-Saxon Reader in Prose and Verse*, 15th edn. Oxford: Oxford University Press. Used for many years as a standard teaching text, especially in the UK, and still a valuable resource.

3. Additional resources

Encyclopedias

Lapidge, Michael, gen. ed. 1999. *The Blackwell Encyclopaedia of Anglo-Saxon England*. Oxford: Blackwell. An indispensable adjunct to Anglo-Saxon studies.

Szarmach, Paul E., gen. ed. 1998. *Medieval England: An Encyclopedia*. New York: Garland. With many articles on Anglo-Saxon topics.

Specialized journals

Anglo-Saxon England. An interdisciplinary journal published annually since 1972 by Cambridge University Press.

Old English Newsletter. Published since 1967 for the Old English Division of the Modern Language Association of America; currently based at the Department of English at The University of Massachusetts, Amherst. Features news, conference reports, abstracts of papers, short articles, and a basic annual bibliography as well as a substantial annual annotated bibliography titled *The Year's Work in Old English Studies*.

Bibliographies

Greenfield, Stanley B., and Fred C. Robinson. 1980. *A Bibliography of Publications on Old English Literature to the End of 1972*. Toronto: University of Toronto Press. Comprehensive listings up to 1972; interprets 'literature' broadly. Supplemented since 1972 by the annual bibliographies published by the *Old English Newsletter* and *Anglo-Saxon England*.

Pulsiano, Phillip. 1988. *An Annotated Bibliography of North American Doctoral Dissertations on Old English Language and Literature*. Cambridge: Boydell and Brewer.

Electronic resources

Since these tend to be subject to flux, only a select few are listed here.

- Dictionary of Old English. The Dictionary's web site offers information about access to The Old English Corpus, an electronic database of all surviving texts containing Old English, and to the Dictionary itself, whether through individual purchase or institutional subscription: http://www.doe.utoronto.ca
- The International Society of Anglo-Saxonists. The web site serves as a gateway for resources in the field and provides information about the biennial conference sponsored by this organization: http://www.isasweb.net
- The Labyrinth: Resources for Medieval Studies, Georgetown University. A gateway providing links to scholarly resources for Medieval Studies in general and Old English studies in particular: https://blogs.commons.georgetown.edu/labyrinth/
- The Medieval Institute, Western Michigan University. Provides access to the Rawlinson Center homepage and other useful resources, including Peter S. Baker's *Electronic Introduction to Old English* (3rd edn, 2012): https://wmich.edu/medieval/
- *Old English Newsletter* (*OEN*). A source for news, announcements, and information on the changing world of Anglo-Saxon studies. Its annual bibliographies are used by thousands of scholars worldwide: http://www.oenewsletter.org

Manuscripts and script

Gneuss, Helmut, and Michael Lapidge. 2014. *Anglo-Saxon Manuscripts: A Bibliographical Handlist of Manuscripts and Manuscript Fragments Written or Owned in England up to 1100*. Toronto: University of Toronto Press. Supplants Gneuss's 2001 *Handlist of Anglo-Saxon Manuscripts* and provides an invaluable complement to the next item.

Ker, Neil R. 1957. *Catalogue of Manuscripts Containing Anglo-Saxon*. Oxford: Oxford University Press. Ker's Introduction includes a capsule account of Old English palaeography. Note also Ker, 'A Supplement to "Catalogue of Manuscripts Containing Anglo-Saxon"', *ASE* 5 (1976): 121–31 (incorporated into the reissue of Ker's book that came out in 1990) and Mary Blockley, 'Further Addenda and Corrigenda to N.R. Ker's *Catalogue*', *Notes and Queries* n.s. 29 (1982): 1–3 (repr. in *Readings: MSS*, 79–85).

Roberts, Jane. 2005. *Guide to Scripts Used in English Writings up to 1500*. London: British Library. Includes facsimiles and transcriptions of manuscript pages written in Latin or Old English, along with an informed commentary.

Facsimiles

New facsimiles of manuscripts from the Anglo-Saxon age appear with some frequency, and some older ones remain of great value. Up-to-date information about electronic facsimiles of medieval manuscripts or manuscript pages can be obtained by consulting the web sites of individual libraries or archives, for example the British Library, London; the Bodleian Library, Oxford; and the Parker Library of Corpus Christi College, Cambridge. Neither older printed volumes nor electronic facsimiles are included in the following select list.

Brown, Michelle P. 2007. *Manuscripts from the Anglo-Saxon Age*. Toronto: University of Toronto Press. With numerous colour plates.

Clemoes, Peter, gen. ed. Early English Manuscripts in Facsimile. Copenhagen, 1951–. Twenty-nine volumes published through 2001. Printed facsimiles of manuscripts deemed to be essential records of Anglo-Saxon literary culture.

1. *The Thorkelin Transcripts of Beowulf*, ed. Kemp Malone (1951)
2. *The Leningrad Bede*, ed. O. Arngart (1952)
3. *The Tollemache Orosius*, ed. Alistair Campbell (1953)
4. *The Peterborough Chronicle*, ed. D. Whitelock (1954)
5. *Bald's Leechbook*, ed. C.E. Wright (1955)
6. *The Pastoral Care* (3 MSS), ed. N.R. Ker (1956)
7. *Textus Roffensis, Part 1*, ed. C.E. Wright (1955)
8. *The Paris Psalter*, ed. B. Colgrave (1958)
9. *The Moore Bede*, ed. Peter Hunter Blair (1962)
10. *Blickling Homilies*, ed. R. Willard (1960)
11. *Textus Roffensis, Part 2*, ed. Peter Sawyer (1962)
12. *The Nowell Codex*, ed. Kemp Malone (1963)
13. *Ælfric's First Series of Catholic Homilies*, ed. Norman Eliason and Peter Clemoes (1966)
14. *The Vespasian Psalter*, ed. David H. Wright (1967)
15. *The Rule of St. Benedict*, ed. D.H. Farmer (1968)
16. *The Durham Ritual*, ed. T.J. Brown (1969)
17. *A Wulfstan Manuscript Containing Institutes, Laws, and Homilies*, ed. H.R. Loyn (1971)
18. *The Old English Illustrated Hexateuch*, ed. C.R. Dodwell (1974)
19. *The Vercelli Book*, ed. Celia Sisam (1976)
20. *The Durham Gospels*, ed. Christopher D. Verey et al. (1980)
21. *An Eleventh-Century Anglo-Saxon Illustrated Miscellany*, ed. P. McGurk (1983)
22. *The Epinal, Erfurt, Werden, and Corpus Glossaries*, ed. Geoffrey Harlow (1988)
23. *Old English Verse Texts from Many Sources*, ed. Fred C. Robinson and E.G. Stanley (1991)
24. *The Tanner Bede*, ed. D.H. Farmer (1992)
25. *The Copenhagen Wulfstan Collection*, ed. James E. Cross and Jennifer Morrish Turberg (1993)
26. *The Liber Vitae of the New Minster and Hyde Abbey, Winchester*, ed. Simon Keynes (1996)
27. *The Old English Illustrated Pharmacopoeia*, ed. M.A. D'Aronco and M.L. Cameron (1998)
28 & 29 *The Codex Aureus: An Eighth-Century Gospel Book, Part 1*, 2 vols, ed. Richard Gameson (2001)

• Doane, A.N., and Matthew Hussey, ed. *Anglo-Saxon Manuscripts in Microfiche Facsimile*. Binghamton: State University of New York Press and Tempe AZ: ACMRS. Approximately two dozen volumes published (or pending publication) through 2015 out of a projected forty or so, with many individual contributors. The series will eventually include facsimiles of all manuscripts containing Old English. An expert description of each manuscript is offered by the editor or co-editors of each volume. A list of published and forthcoming titles is available at the ASMMF web site: http://www.sfu.ca/english/asmmf.html

Index of Modern Authors Cited

Included in the following select index are twentieth- and twenty-first-century medievalists whose specific contributions to Old English or Anglo-Saxon studies are highlighted in the main body of this book or in its notes, or who are cited in the lists headed 'For Further Reading'. The index does not extend to the reading selections featured at the end of chapters 2–11.

Old English Literature: A Guide to Criticism with Selected Readings, First Edition. John D. Niles.
© 2016 John D. Niles. Published 2016 by John Wiley & Sons, Ltd.

General Index

The selections from the criticism that are appended to chapters 2–11 are only lightly indexed.

Old English Literature: A Guide to Criticism with Selected Readings, First Edition. John D. Niles.
© 2016 John D. Niles. Published 2016 by John Wiley & Sons, Ltd.